8 38.50

MULTI-LEVEL PLANNING: CASE STUDIES IN MEXICO

MULTI-LEVEL PLANNING: CASE STUDIES IN MEXICO

Edited by

LOUIS M. GOREUX

and

ALAN S. MANNE

Foreword by Hollis B. Chenery

Contributors:

Luciano Barraza
Luz María Bassoco
John H. Duloy
Guillermo Fernández de la Garza
Yves Franchet
Richard A. Inman
Donald B. Keesing
János Kornai

Gary P. Kutcher
Roger D. Norton
Teresa Rendón
Leopoldo Solís
Saúl Trejo Reyes
José Alberto Valencia
Donald L. Winkelmann

1973

NORTH-HOLLAND PUBLISHING COMPANY – AMSTERDAM · LONDON
AMERICAN ELSEVIER PUBLISHING COMPANY, INC. – NEW YORK

Library of Congress Catalog Card Number: 72 93090

North-Holland ISBN: 0 7204 30704

Publishers:
NORTH-HOLLAND PUBLISHING COMPANY – AMSTERDAM
NORTH-HOLLAND PUBLISHING COMPANY, LTD. – LONDON

Sole distributors for the U.S.A. and Canada:
AMERICAN ELSEVIER PUBLISHING COMPANY, INC.
52 VANDERBILT AVENUE, NEW YORK, N.Y. 10017

PRINTED IN THE NETHERLANDS

FOREWORD

This monograph is the first in a series now under preparation at the World Bank's Development Research Center. The series is intended as a channel for the publication of policy-oriented studies that also command wide professional interest. Some of the studies will be focused on a single country, while others will have a multi-country orientation.

This first monograph deals with the problem of interdependence within a single country. It is intended to point the way towards a better understanding of the theory and practice of multi-level planning. By studying one country in depth, it is hoped that simplified analytical methods may be evolved, and that these short-cut methods may be applied in other nations where the data base is weaker than in Mexico.

This book is the product of a collaborative effort between a number of institutions. The names of 17 contributors appear on the title page, but an even larger number have participated with advice, data and editorial suggestions. We are grateful to all these individuals for their contributions to the success of this study.

Hollis B. Chenery

TABLE OF CONTENTS

vii

PART I. AN OVERVIEW

I.1. INTRODUCTION

Louis M. GOREUX and Alan S. MANNE

... It seems, therefore, as if, for a complete and rigorous solution of the problems relative to some parts of the economic system, it were indispensable to take the entire system into consideration. But this would surpass the powers of mathematical analysis and of our practical methods of calculation, even if the values of all the constants could be assigned to them numerically. The object of this chapter and of the following one is to show how far it is possible to avoid this difficulty, while maintaining a certain kind of approximation, and to carry on, by the aid of mathematical symbols, a useful analysis of the most general questions which this subject brings up.

A. Cournot (1838, p. 108)

1. Objectives and scope

Interdependence in planning is the central concern of this monograph. This problem is analyzed through a system of optimizing models corresponding to three different levels of aggregation. As shown in figure 1, at the highest level of aggregation, there is a multi-sector model of the Mexican economy. At the intermediate level, there are two sectoral models, one for agriculture and the other for energy. At the lowest level of aggregation, there is one model for an agricultural district and another for electric power plants and transmission lines.

This system is used to analyze policy decisions at three levels. At the central level, the decisions may refer to the rate of domestic savings and to the level of borrowing from abroad. At the sectoral level, they may relate to subsidies on fertilizer use or the pricing policy for industrial fuels. At the regional level, they may relate to specific investment projects, such as an irrigation scheme or a transmission line for electric power.

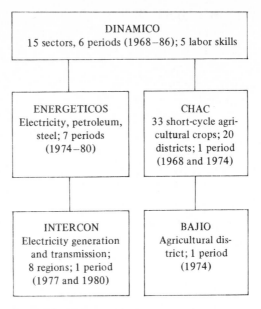

Fig. 1. System of interrelated models.

If this system of models were to provide a perfect representation of the true world, how might it be used for decision making? To apply the general equilibrium approach, the entire system of models should be solved simultaneously. A decision based on this solution would then be 'optimal' in the sense that it would take account of all possible interactions within the system. This optimal decision could be interpreted as the outcome which would prevail in a perfectly competitive market — making the usual assumptions on the absence of externalities, economies-of-scale, etc. Alternatively, it could be interpreted as centralized decision-making, if the center had perfect knowledge of the entire economy. [1]

[1] Cf. Boulding (1966, p. 8): 'There is a great deal of evidence that almost all organizational structures tend to produce false images in the decision-maker, and that the larger and more authoritarian the organization, the better the chance that its top decision-makers will be operating in purely imaginary worlds. This perhaps is the most fundamental reason for supposing that there are ultimately diminishing returns to scale.'

Applying the partial equilibrium approach, only one component of the system would be solved. For example, if an investment decision is to be made in an agricultural district, only the model of that particular district need be solved. However, to follow this approach, some information is needed on the rest of the system. With perfect competition, the market provides the signals. With indicative planning, the signals may be expressed in the form of shadow prices. The latter should reflect the opportunity costs to the rest of the economy of the factors used by the district and the commodities produced by it. If the decisions made in one part of the system (the district in this example) cannot affect economic scarcities in the rest of the system, decentralized decision-making is easy. But, if these decisions can affect the prices of some of the goods or factors used in the rest of the system, an iterative procedure may be required to reach optimality.

Iterations have been described by Walras as the 'tâtonnements' through which the market finds its equilibrium. As argued by J. Kornai (below, chapter V.3), it is preferable to interpret them literally, as the steps required to solve a decomposable problem within a computer. The intermediate steps do not affect the real world. The final step is the only one that matters. In a computer, a very large number of iterations can be made; but in the actual planning process, only very few iterations can take place between the central and the sectoral agencies. In project decisions, the team assessing the project is supposed to receive instructions from the higher level bodies on the values of the shadow prices to be used. Normally, these instructions are not revised on the basis of the project assessment.

Decentralized decision-making without iterations is a simplified procedure. It may result in some loss of social welfare. However, this loss may be sufficiently small to be more than offset by the gain resulting from a simpler and faster decision process. In this case, the simplified procedure is all that we want. This procedure is called 'suboptimization' and the corresponding solution 'nearly optimal', in order to differentiate it from the 'optimal' solution obtained by solving the entire system simultaneously.

The problem of suboptimization may be illustrated with a specific investment project, for example, lining an irrigation canal. Does the social return on this investment exceed the opportunity cost of capital in the rest of the economy? We could define the project narrowly and measure its output in terms of the cubic meters of water saved. It might be acceptable to take as given the shadow prices of the project's inputs (e.g., cement, labor and transportation services). It would be much more questionable, however, whether the shadow price of the water saved could be taken as given. There is no competitive market for this item. The shadow price of water in the area is likely to depend on the number of cubic meters of water saved and on the changes in the cropping pattern induced by the increased availability of water. With such a narrowly defined project, its social benefits could not be measured unequivocally; the price of the output could well depend on the investment decision to be made. To avoid this difficulty, the boundaries of the analysis could be enlarged by measuring the benefits of the project in terms of the additional crop production. It might now be acceptable to take as given the shadow prices of the crops, but probably not the cropping pattern.

By enlarging the boundaries, we have simultaneously enlarged the options and the volume of the information to be gathered. Canal lining now becomes only one among many investment activities which can be applied to increase the value added within the watershed. Both the mix of investment activities and the cropping pattern have become choice variables. In our system of models, this enlarged suboptimization problem is represented by the model of a district.

2. The problem of linkage

One of our concerns is to investigate the conditions under which suboptimization is possible at the level of a project, a region, or a sector. What signals are needed from the rest of the economy in the form of shadow prices, quantitative allocations or a combination of both? How sensitive are these signals and the resulting decisions to a modification of the social objectives or constraints?

It is not sufficient, however, to transmit instructions downwards. It is also necessary to send summary information on the production possibilities and the market prospects from the lower to the higher levels. In this way, a sectoral model could be built up from detailed studies conducted at the project level. Similarly, an aggregated multi-sector model (or part of it) could be built up from detailed sectoral studies. Should we then build a system of interconnected specialized models or a single multipurpose master model?

Clearly, this study does not answer all these questions, but our failures may be as instructive as our successes. In order to measure the welfare loss from simplified procedures, the system as a whole should have been solved. This was not possible because the methodology and the statistical data base were not uniform throughout the study. Figure 1 actually consists of three subsystems dealing respectively with the economy as a whole, energy and agriculture. Each was constructed by a different research team.

The agricultural subsystem is internally consistent. It is solved as a single model, and the linkages between the districts and the sector are analyzed formally. But the data base of the agricultural model is not consistent with that of the agricultural sector in the economy-wide model. The former, which is limited to short-cycle crops, covers only half the value added by the latter. The statistical definitions of the agricultural labor force and the concepts of labor employment are not the same in the two cases. By making crude adjustments, a formal link was established between the agricultural and the economy-wide models.

Similarly, the energy subsystem is internally consistent. It consists of three subsectors: steel, power and petroleum. It is solved as a single model, and the linkages among subsectors are formally analyzed. The energy model has not been linked directly to the economy-wide model because the subsectors of the energy model cover only part of the corresponding sectors in the economy-wide model. Thus, the steel subsector, which extends only through the ingot stage, covers just a small part of the sector called 'basic metals' in the economy-wide model.

In a study of interdependence, the choice of agriculture and energy may appear to be an odd combination. The selection of two more closely related sectors would have led to a more interesting study of the interdependence within the system as a whole. Agriculture could have been combined with machinery, because these two sectors provide the greatest scope for earning (or saving) foreign exchange. Alternatively, agriculture could have been combined with services, since these are the two sectors providing the greatest scope for labor employment. The ready availability of basic data, together with the interest and cooperation of the Mexican public agencies, provided strong reasons for selecting energy rather than manufacturing or services. Moreover, within the research budget available, it was impossible to undertake a large data-gathering effort in addition to that required for agriculture. At any rate, although linkages are weak between energy and the rest of the economy, they are important within the energy sector itself.

One research strategy would have been to select two closely connected sectors and to enforce uniformity in methodological and statistical concepts throughout. The other strategy was to consider the collaboration of the Mexican agencies as an essential factor and to pay particular attention to the specific problems with which they were concerned. The first strategy would have led to a more interesting analysis of the system as a whole and to a more academic type of study. The second strategy, the one we followed, has probably led to a more realistic and useful study of the individual sectors.

3. The three subsystems

3.1. Economy-wide model

DINAMICO, a 15-sector and 6-period model, can be evaluated in two ways. First, it can be considered in isolation. At the aggregative level, it provides a tool for analyzing broad economic alternatives. Second, it can be considered as a component of a system. From its primal solution, it provides orders of magnitude for the

main economic aggregates. From its dual solution, it provides shadow prices for the resources common to different sectors. Thus, in
a two-level planning process, it could be used to generate internally consistent projections of the demand for the output of each
sector and the shadow prices of capital, foreign exchange and
labor.

Perhaps the most interesting feature of the model is the introduction of labor constraints. Since unskilled labor is plentiful
while skilled labor is scarce, a distinction among five skills has
been made. Once labor demands are defined in terms of skill categories, endogenous training activities must be introduced to provide sufficient flexibility on the supply side to upgrade skills. The
treatment of labor in DINAMICO is quite controversial, for the
model is largely based upon the assumption of full employment.
The labor norms were estimated without making any allowance
for unemployment, open or disguised, in the base period.

The impact of the labor constraints on the marginal productivity of capital is quite typical. With labor a free good, as in many
development planning models, the marginal productivity of capital
equals the economy-wide output-capital ratio. Thus, when all
labor constraints are eliminated from DINAMICO, the shadow
price of capital is of the order of 30% per year. When labor constraints are introduced, the shadow price of capital drops to between 15 and 20%. This range is broadly consistent with the gross
annual return on capital estimated from other data sources.

Borrowing from abroad is an endogenous activity in DINAMI-
CO. In practice, this activity is limited by the country's debt re-
payment capacity and/or by the desire to maintain national ownership. Due to these constraints, the marginal domestic productivity of capital may exceed the marginal cost of importing capital.
Thus in the basic case, the marginal domestic productivity is equal
to 20%, which exceeds the 15% annual cost of private foreign
capital.

The shadow price of foreign exchange reflects partly the limitations on capital imports but mainly the limited scope for expanding exports. In DINAMICO, the marginal source of export earnings
is, in most cases, an activity called 'high-cost manufacturing ex-

ports'. This activity would have to be subsidized during the infant industry stage. It is assumed that new manufactured exports are produced at 30% above world prices when they are first introduced on the market, and that as a result of 'learning by doing', they are competitive with world prices 18 years later. Because no bounds are imposed upon these high-cost exports, the value assumed for the initial cost differential is critical for the determination of the foreign exchange premium. When the cost differential is changed from 30% to 50%, the premium rises from 15% to 35%.

The shadow prices derived from DINAMICO are reasonably credible and stable. With a five-skill and six-period model, this is not a trivial achievement. However, complex optimizing models are not constructed just to generate shadow prices which, taken one by one, appear consistent with prior intuition. They are constructed to provide consistent sets of signals, as well as a framework for analyzing how the entire set is modified when assumptions are changed.

For example, consider the various implications of relaxing limitations on capital imports. The shadow price of capital then falls from its 20% value in the basic case towards the lower bound of 15%. [2] Due to the larger capital inflow, total investments and GDP rise. This increases the demand for labor. The total wage bill rises, partly on account of higher shadow wages for given skills and partly on account of skill upgrading. The shadow price of foreign exchange falls at the time of additional capital inflows, but it rises when the additional profits are remitted abroad.

Assume now that we have to suboptimize within a sector, but without the benefit of an economy-wide model. Using shortcut methods, we could guess high and low values for the growth rate of GDP and for the shadow prices of capital, foreign exchange and labor. Not knowing the interrelations among these four variables, we would be faced with $4^2 = 16$ combinations, all equally likely. If it were not assumed that relative prices remain constant throughout the projection period, the number of parametric variations in a dynamic sectoral model would become hopelessly high.

---

[2] It becomes optimal to import large amounts of capital during the early time periods.

3.2. Energy

Since the energy models are more disaggregated than DINAMICO, they are more operational. DINAMICO is based on an input-output framework. For each sector, there is a single product-mix which can be produced according to a single technology. The energy models, which are based on process analysis, are not subject to this limitation. The single aggregate called 'petroleum products' in DINAMICO is replaced in ENERGETICOS by a variety of petroleum products. Each of these can be produced according to different technologies.

Optimizing models are appropriate for analyzing investment choices in the petroleum and electric power industries. In Mexico, each of these industries is managed by a single publicly owned enterprise. The main linkage between the two enterprises is the industrial fuel used to produce electric power. The choice between nuclear and fossil electric power plants makes a substantial difference in the domestic demand for petroleum products. Since Mexico is nearly self-sufficient in petroleum products, the country could become a marginal importer or a marginal exporter depending on the choice made. Because of the difference between import and export prices, the opportunity cost of this fuel is not independent of the choice between fossil and nuclear plants.

The steel sector was also included in ENERGETICOS, because it was thought that the choice among steel processes could conceivably make enough difference in the demand for fuel and power to affect the shadow price of fuel. This was not the case. As things turned out, a single steel process dominated the others throughout the range in which the cost sensitivity analysis was conducted.

ENERGETICOS takes account of the interdependence between the production of power and petroleum, but it ignores the problem of location. This problem is studied in INTERCON, a regionally disaggregated model dealing only with power plants and transmission lines. At the level of aggregation used in DINAMICO (the economy-wide model), investments in the electricity sector can be treated as a single divisible activity. In INTERCON, investment activities become a series of integer variables. Consider a transmission line linking points A and B. Only two options are available: a new line of 400 KV or none at all. Indivisibilities also affect the installation of nuclear power plants at point A. The choice is between no plant or one of 600 or two units totalling 1 200 MW.

INTERCON indicates that it is optimal to install two nuclear plants in San Luis and to link the north and south through transmission lines from that point. This was not obvious *a priori*. (Before allowing for indivisibilities, the optimal solution was not to invest in any power plant in San Luis (below, chapter III.1, table 8). As this volume goes to press, it seems that the site selected will not be the first best solution of INTERCON, but rather the third best. However, between the first and the third best solutions, the cost differential is only 0.2% (below, chapter III.1, table 10). This is well below any realistic margin of error in cost estimation. A programming model, such as INTERCON, is useful to identify several project combinations which are almost equally good from an economic viewpoint. To arrive at a final decision, detailed site appraisals must be conducted. Moreover, even though they cannot easily be included in a mathematical model, non-economic factors may enter into the final decision.

3.3. Agriculture

The agricultural sector required the greatest data collection effort and absorbed the largest share of the research budget for this monograph. It is probably the most innovative part of the study, and it is the part which was considered the most relevant to policy decisions in Mexico.

The agricultural model, CHAC, is the largest of all. [3] It is decomposable into 20 district submodels, and it combines detailed process analysis of production alternatives, along with two types of behavioral relationships. One characterizes the quantity-price demand curves for 33 individual crops. The other characterizes the supply of agricultural labor. The latter reflects not only the differ-

---

[3] CHAC has 1500 rows and 3400 columns, while DINAMICO has 316 rows and 421 columns.

ence in the labor reservation prices among various categories of workers in different regions but also the scope for migration.

On the production side, a wide range of technologies is available for each crop. In total, the model includes more than 2000 cropping activities. On the demand side, it allows for substitution among crops on the domestic market and also for imports and exports. The model has a wide margin of choices regarding both the technology-mix and the product-mix. Because of this flexibility, CHAC is well suited for the analysis of factor substitution and for the study of comparative advantage among crops and among districts.

By maximizing the sum of producers' and consumers' surplus, the model simulates a competitive equilibrium. This equilibrium may be modified by various policy instruments: production controls, export subsidies, fertilizer subsidies, the interest rate, charges on irrigation water and wage legislation.

Because of the complexities of the substitution effects in a model where product prices are determined endogenously, the incidence of a given policy measure is not obvious *a priori*. Consider the impact of an increase in the interest rate. As could be expected, labor employment rises and the demand for capital falls. At the same time, production declines, agricultural prices rise and the consumers' surplus falls. The ultimate impact on producers is a sharp increase in farmers' monetary income and a lesser gain in real agricultural income (below, chapter IV.3, tables 5 and 6).

The impact of a simultaneous change in several policy measures cannot be approximated just by adding up the impact of each measure taken in isolation. Due to the interaction effects, a piecemeal analysis of agricultural policies can be quite misleading. All items in the full policy package (interest rate, export subsidies, water rates, etc.) must be analyzed simultaneously.

Some of the conclusions of this study may be noted here. First, due to the worsening of the agricultural terms of trade, the gap is widening between the growth rates of physical production and of sectoral income. This reflects the low value of the price and income elasticities and the limited scope for import substitution. In other words, Mexican agriculture is now facing the second generation problems of the Green Revolution. The question is 'no longer simply how to increase production, ... but how to bring about structural changes which will lead to an expansion of domestic demand'. Second, if production controls were feasible, farmers' incomes could be substantially increased. This would result mainly in an income transfer from consumers to producers, at the cost of a very small loss in aggregate welfare. Third, Mexico's comparative advantage would be to increase agricultural exports. Present policies lead to a non-optimal export mix. Fourth, there is a considerable fraction of the agricultural labor force unemployed both seasonally and throughout the year. With conventional policy instruments, there appears to be only a limited scope for improving this situation through short-cycle crops.

After this overview of the sector, let us consider the microanalysis of a district. BAJIO is only one among 20 district submodels included in CHAC. What differentiates it from the other nineteen is a greater level of disaggregation. In BAJIO, a distinction is made between small and large farms. Management constraints are introduced for certain crops, and a greater choice of technologies is available. Taking advantage of the more disaggregated data, the model is used to rank investment projects according to their rates of return. It is also used to measure the price elasticities of demand for physical capital and for unskilled labor by types of farms. The model shows that the optimal level of mechanization depends upon farm size.

4. A reader's guide

This volume is organized into three main parts, each self-contained. Parts II, III and IV deal respectively with the economy as a whole, energy and agriculture.

The second part is divided into six chapters. Chapter II.1 deals with labor and employment in DINAMICO. Chapter II.2 describes the data sources and the extrapolation of the input-output and capital matrices. Through an imputation of distributive shares to labor and to physical capital, this chapter provides an independent cross-check between the national accounts, the input-output matrices, and the data on human and physical capital. Chapter II.3 provides the algebraic formulation of DINAMICO and presents the results for the basic case. Readers who are familiar with programming techniques may wish to start with this chapter. Chapter II.4, devoted to sensitivity analyses, illustrates a number of trade-offs such as present versus future consumption, and the growth of total consumption versus labor's share. Chapter II.5 contains a critique of DINAMICO, and Chapter II.6 presents EXPORTA, another type of economy-wide model — one that is disaggregated into 45 sectors and corrected for tariff distortions. EXPORTA leads to more pessimistic results than DINAMICO with respect to the employment problem.

The third part deals with the energy sector, and is divided into three chapters. Chapter III.1 describes INTERCON, a multi-region mixed integer programming model for investments in electricity generating plants and transmission lines. Chapter III.2 analyzes the interdependencies between the petroleum, electricity and the steel sectors in a more aggregated model. Chapter III.3 presents the results of linkage experiments between ENERGETICOS and DINAMICO.

The fourth part concerns the agricultural sector. It begins with a comprehensive description of the sectoral model (chapter IV.1). This is followed by a presentation of the basic data (chapter IV.2). The results of CHAC are summarized in seasonal estimates of the extent of agricultural unemployment, rankings of crops by comparative advantage in international trade, and the tradeoffs confronting policy makers. Chapters IV.4 and IV.5 describe BAJIO, a submodel for one producing district. It analyzes factor substitution and the impact of sectoral information on decisions in the district. Chapter IV.6 describes a linkage experiment between CHAC and DINAMICO. The concluding chapter IV.7 presents the views of two policy makers on the utility of such models.

The fifth part reviews decomposition procedures together with their organizational implications. Chapter V.1 and V.2 are rather technical. The first describes a Benders-type mixed integer programming algorithm specifically adapted for project selection. The second is an experiment in matrix partitioning applied to the Dantzig-Wolfe decomposition algorithm. It investigates devices for speeding up convergence, using a regional model composed of five agricultural districts (PACIFICO). The last chapter (V.3) deals with the philosophy of multi-level planning. It recognizes the need to compromise between the theoretical simplicity of decomposition and the complexities of the real world. It also stresses that the design of interconnected models cannot be left to each individual research team.

To help the reader in obtaining an overview, two additional chapters are included in Part I. Chapter I.2 provides a comparative analysis of the seven models in this monograph. Chapter I.3 summarizes our findings on the problem of interdependence.

In a study addressed to various audiences and written by 17 different authors, a certain degree of repetition is unavoidable. For readers with specialized interests, the following suggestions may be helpful. Those mainly interested in economic policy issues might start with chapters II.4, IV.3, and IV.7. Those interested in programming techniques might start with chapters I.2, II.3, III.1, III.2, and IV.1. Finally, those interested in linkages and multi-level planning might prefer to start with chapters I.3, III.3, IV.6, and Part V.

References

Boulding, K.E., 'The economics of knowledge and the knowledge of economics', *American Economic Review*, May 1966.

Cournot, A., *Researches into the mathematical principles of the theory of wealth*, 1838, translated by N.T. Bacon. Homewood, Ill., Richard D. Irwin, 1963.

I.2. COMPARATIVE ANALYSIS OF
THE PROGRAMMING MODELS

Louis M. GOREUX

In the introductory chapter, five models belonging to a loosely connected system were briefly described. As will be recalled, DI-NAMICO covers the entire economy. ENERGETICOS covers steel, power and petroleum. INTERCON is a multi-region model for power plants and transmission lines. CHAC covers the agricultural sector. Finally, BAJIO is a component of CHAC; it differs from the other 19 districts models embedded in CHAC by its greater level of disaggregation. Two new models are now introduced to the collection. One, EXPORTA, is an economy-wide model comparable in scope to DINAMICO. Its primary purpose is to investigate the most efficient way to improve the Mexican trade balance. The other, PACIFICO, is a regional agricultural model designed to experiment with decomposition procedures.

The main characteristics of the seven models are summarized in four tables. A comparative analysis of these characteristics is presented in this chapter by reviewing successively the objective function, the supply-demand balances and the treatment of physical and human capital.

1. Dimension, scope and objective function (table 1)

Information on size and scope may best be read from table 1. Here we shall concentrate upon the objective function.

Only DINAMICO and ENERGETICOS are optimized dynamically — that is, over time. For INTERCON, recursive optimization is used. For the other four models, the optimization refers to a single target year.

Table 1
Characteristics of the seven programming models:

	Economy as a whole		Energy
Model name	DINAMICO	EXPORTA	ENERGETICOS
Chapter number	II.1−5	II.6	III.2−3
Dimensions			
Number of rows	316	322	213
Number of columns	421	273	350
Scope			
Sectoral coverage	————— Economy-wide —————		Electricity generation, petroleum production and refining, steel ingots
	15 input-output sectors	45 input-output sectors	
Spatial disaggregation	———————————————— None ———		
Time coverage	1968−71−74−77− 80−83−86	1970−76	1974−75−76−77−78− 79−80 plus 1985−90− 95 for electricity only
Objective function	Dynamic maximiza- tion of consumption, subject to gradualist path, and target growth rate of 7%	Static maximization of either GNP or net exports	Dynamic maximization of discounted costs (net of export earnings), to satisfy fixed demands

In DINAMICO, the objective is to maximize the flow of consumption subject to a 'gradualist' consumption path. This path requires that consumption increments rise by a constant percentage each year throughout the planning horizon. With this formulation, there is a smooth transition from the near-term to the long-term target growth rate of total consumption. The long-term target, the initial level and the initial increment together determine the entire consumption path. The maximand is therefore expressed as the initial increment of consumption.

The target growth rate, which may also be called the asymptotic growth rate, is equal to 7% in the basic case. The tradeoff between

dimensions, scope and objective function

| INTERCON III.1 | Agriculture | | |
	CHAC IV.1−3	BAJIO IV.4−5	PACIFICO V.2
1977 1980			
517 557	1500	380	187
603 642	3400	800	382
Electricity generation and transmission	Short-cycle agricultural crops		
	Nation-wide	One district	Pacific Northwest
8 regions, 12 transmission links	20 districts (11 irrigated, 6 dry, 3 tropical)	4 farm types (irrigated/dry; large/small)	5 irrigated districts
1974−77−80	─────────── 1968−74 ───────────		1968
Recursive cost minimization, to satisfy fixed demands in 1977 and 1980	Static maximization of the sum of producers' and consumers' surplus in 1968 and in 1974	Static maximization of producers' surplus in 1968 and in 1974	Static maximization of the sum of producers' surplus in 1968

consuming more today or tomorrow can be analyzed by lowering this rate to 6% or raising it to 8%. Today's consumption level must be consistent with the level of savings. In turn, the level of savings must be consistent with the degree of fiscal austerity politically acceptable today.

The discounted flow of consumption and the value of terminal consumption were used as two alternative formulations of DI-NAMICO's maximand. These alternative formulations have a comparatively small effect upon consumption during the near future period, through 1980. This lack of sensitivity is due to the 30% upper bound on the marginal propensity to save. The savings constraint, which was never binding in the basic case, becomes critical when terminal consumption (or the discounted flow of consumption) is used as the maximand.

In ENERGETICOS, the minimand is always the discounted value of costs. The dynamic tradeoffs are between installing 600 MW nuclear plants in the latter half of the 1970's, or waiting till the 1980's for the availability of 1000 MW nuclear plants, or waiting until 1990 for breeder reactors.

A similar type of dynamic tradeoff arises with INTERCON. Over time, the cost of fossil fuel is expected to rise, and the cost of nuclear fuel is expected to fall. Recursive optimization is used in INTERCON as a shortcut for simultaneous dynamic optimization. Sensitivity tests suggest that this approximation, which reduces the computation time to less than one-sixth, provides a nearly optimal solution.

In EXPORTA, which is a one-period model, the objective is to maximize terminal GDP — either with or without an employment constraint. In the neighborhood of the unconstrained maximum, the cost of creating a few additional jobs is small. This cost increases rapidly, however, as one gets further from the optimal solution without an employment constraint. Maximizing net export earnings is used as an alternative objective. However, maximizing export earnings without any income constraint is not a very meaningful economic concept. As it turns out, capital, modern labor and traditional labor become simultaneously unemployed. (See below, chapter II.6, table 3.)

In the agricultural models CHAC and PACIFICO, the maximand is the sum of producers' and consumers' surplus at a given point in time. This may be considered as a device to reach a competitive market solution. It could also be interpreted as a social welfare function; it would then be necessary to assume that the utilities derived from different commodities are cardinal and separable. In addition, a number of accounting rows are introduced. These refer to the farmers' income, consumers' surplus, the government budget, capital requirements, net export earnings, the level of employment and the wage bill of landless workers by district, region and for Mexico as a whole. These rows can be used as constraints to measure tradeoffs.

2. Supply-demand balances (table 2)

2.1. Production

The two economy-wide models (DINAMICO and EXPORTA) are based on an input-output framework and do not allow for technological choices within sectors. [1] The other five models, based on process analysis, provide wide scope for substitution. The use of process analysis for agriculture and energy is relatively easy, as the outputs of these sectors can be expressed in terms of a limited number of homogeneous products. For machinery, this would have been much more difficult.

2.2. Domestic demand

In the two economy-wide models, the final demands for the output in each sector are constrained to vary in fixed proportions. In DINAMICO, these proportions could have been calculated, for every decision year, on the basis of Engel coefficients, taking as given the rates of population and income growth. Since the rate of GDP growth generated by DINAMICO varies within fairly narrow limits (below, chapter II.4), the propensities to consume could have been adjusted to the GDP growth rate found for the basic case. This would have led to a satisfactory approximation of the income effect. As described in chapter II.2, section 3 below, a simpler procedure was actually followed. The treatment of the income effect may, nevertheless, be considered as adequate. The principal shortcoming of DINAMICO, as of any other input-output model, lies in its inability to deal with substitution effects. The composition of the consumption-mix is not allowed to vary in response to changes in product prices.

The sectoral models ignore the income effects which could result from a modification in the sectoral strategy. But in the agricultural model, the price effects are taken into account. One of the most interesting features of CHAC is its inclusion of quantity-

---

[1] Except for agriculture in DINAMICO.

Table 2
Supply-demand

	Economy as a whole		Energy
Model name Chapter number	DINAMICO II.1–3	EXPORTA II.6	ENERGETICOS III.2–3
Supply-demand balances			
Production	One single technology for each sector except agriculture where capital-labor substitution is allowed	lower and upper bounds on output for each sector	Several types
Domestic demand	Final demand of out- put in each sector proportional to aggre- gate consumption	Final demand of out- put in each sector a linear function of aggregate income	——————— Exogen-
	Investments and interindustry demands gen- erated endogenously		Interindustry demands generated endogenously
Export demand	Upper and lower bounds on 10 mer- chandise exports plus tourism. No bounds on high-cost manu- factured exports	Indirect bounds through upper and lower limits on out- put. Domestic prices converted into inter- national prices through nominal implicit protection rates	Unlimited exports of petroleum products at fixed prices
Imports	Non-competitive; fixed import propensities for final demand, intermediate inputs and investment demands		Unlimited imports of petroleum products at fixed prices

price demand curves. Demand substitutability is allowed among products belonging to a given commodity group, (e.g., between wheat and maize, within the cereals group), but not among groups (e.g., between the cereals and fruits groups).

2.3. Imports and exports

DINAMICO and EXPORTA do not allow for a choice between

balances

	Agriculture		
INTERCON III.1	CHAC IV.1−8	BAJIO IV.4−5	PACIFICO V.2
of process	Several technologies available for each crop		
	2345 cropping activities for 33 crops for 20 districts	40 cropping activities for 4 crops on dry land; 544 for 14 crops on irrigated land	162 cropping activities for 16 crops
ous	———	Price-quantity demand curves given exogenously; 33 commodity prices endogenous	Infinitely elastic demand at exogenously given prices	Price-quantity demand curves given exogenously; 16 crop prices endogenous
None	Upper bounds on exports; fixed export prices	Not applicable	Unlimited exports of 3 crops; fixed export prices
None	21 importable commodities; fixed import prices	Not applicable	None

domestic production and imports. All imports are viewed as non-competitive. The two models do allow for a choice in the export-mix. Since EXPORTA is corrected for effective protection, one can assess the comparative advantage among sectors in earning foreign exchange. The original DINAMICO was based on the price structure prevailing in 1960, and its results were biased against agriculture in favor of manufacturing. (Manufacturing was protected by 20–30% in 1960. [2])

In DINAMICO, the choice in the export-mix is limited by lower and upper bounds on sectoral exports and tourism. In practice, the model has only a limited margin of choice in the export-mix. Exports are always at their upper bound, except for agriculture, tourism and high-cost manufactures. This leads to a very rigid structure of the commodity balances. Recall that in DINAMICO, domestic consumption of sectoral outputs are in fixed proportions, that all imports are non-substitutable, and that, except for agriculture, there are no technological choices within sectors.

The energy and agricultural sector models allow for a choice in the export-mix and the import-mix. When a given product can be both imported and exported, the export price cannot exceed the import price. The difference reflects transportation costs and, in some cases, a preference for self-sufficiency. The knife-edge effect observed for aggregate agricultural exports in DINAMICO disappears in CHAC, where exports and imports are defined in terms of individual commodities.

2.4. A simplified interpretation of the objective function

For the energy and agricultural models, figure 1 provides a simplified one-product representation of the objective function. In all cases, the supply curve (S) is upward sloping and measures the marginal cost of domestic production. [3] But the five cases differ in their assumptions regarding the domestic and the international demand for the product.

Case 1 corresponds to the treatment of electricity in INTERCON and in ENERGETICOS. The item can neither be imported

---

[2] In response to the EXPORTA results, DINAMICO was revised (see editor's note at the end of chapter II.5). Interestingly enough, when DINAMICO's original coefficients were adjusted both for 'nominal implicit protection' (using EXPORTA's estimates) and for the capital-labor substitution rate (using CHAC's estimates), the balance shifted in favor of agricultural exports. After these informal information flows, DINAMICO's direction of comparative advantage became consistent with that of EXPORTA.

[3] The curve S refers only to the cost of resources which are not specific to the sector (or the district). If the sector produces several commodities simultaneously, the curve S cannot be computed for one commodity in isolation.

Case	Domestic demand	Exports, imports	Objective function	Diagrammatic representation
1. INTERCON and ENERGE-TICOS (part III)	$\eta_D = 0$	None	Minimize cost	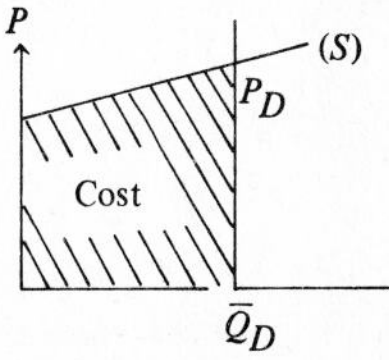
2. Little and Mirrlees (1968)		Fixed inter-national prices; $\bar{P}_m = \bar{P}_x$; $\eta_m = \eta_x = \infty$	Maximize pro-ducers' surplus at fixed inter-national (or domestic) prices	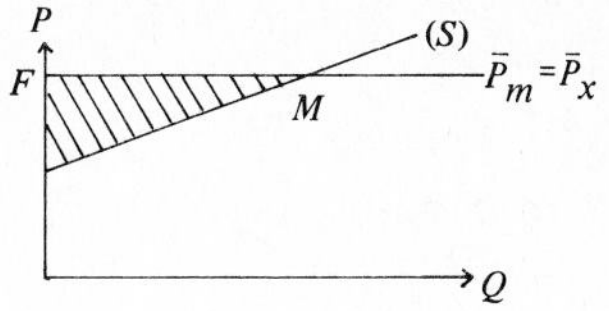
BAJIO, chapters IV.4–5	Fixed domes-tic prices; $\eta_D = \infty$			
3. CHAC (part IV) non-tradable commodi-ties	$-\infty < \eta_D < 0$	None	Maximize sum of consumers' and producers' surplus	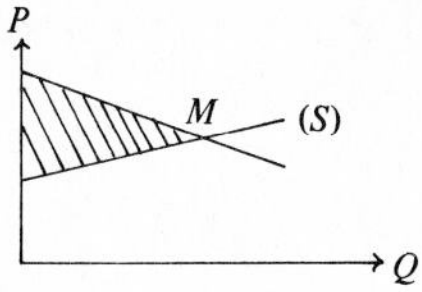
4. CHAC (part IV) tradable commodi-ties	$-\infty < \eta_D < 0$	$\bar{P}_m < \bar{P}_x$	Maximize sum of consumers' and producers' surplus	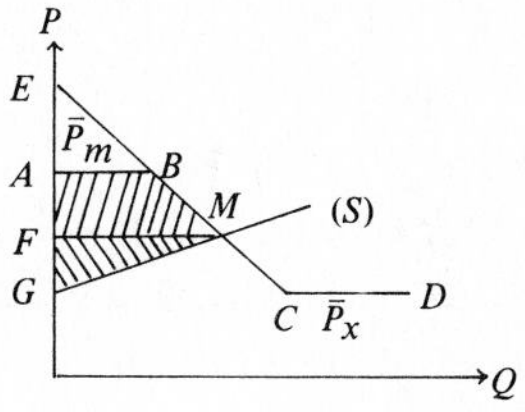
5. Optimal export tax	None	$-\infty < \eta_x < 0$	Maximize national returns	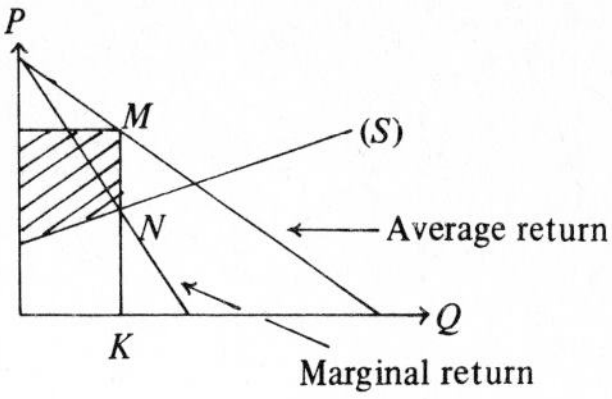

Fig. 1. Comparison of assumptions on domestic demand, exports and imports.

nor exported. Domestic demand is perfectly price-inelastic, and the level of domestic requirements $\bar{Q}_D$ is given exogenously. The hatched area measures the minimum cost of fulfilling these requirements. The efficiency price is determined endogenously at P_D.

Case 2 corresponds to the 'small country' approach taken by Little and Mirrlees (1968). The item's international price is an exogenous datum. It is assumed that the country will always import at a unit cost of $\bar{P}_m$, or will always export with earnings of $\bar{P}_x$. Alternatively, with a zero cost of transport to world markets, $\bar{P}_m = \bar{P}_x$. With these assumptions, the domestic demand curve becomes irrelevant, and the optimal quantity supplied is *FM*. The maximand, shown by the hatched area, measures the producers' surplus, that is, the value added by the resources specific to the sector (or the district). The producers' surplus and the shadow prices of the domestic resources are expressed in terms of international prices. The approach followed in the direct solution of BAJIO (below, chapter IV.5), is similar in the sense that product prices are fixed exogenously for the district.

Case 3 corresponds to the classical partial equilibrium analysis of producers' and consumers' surplus. The market is viewed as a mechanism for maximizing the sum of producers' and consumers' (see, e.g., Harberger 1971).

Case 4 differs from the third by the introduction of import and export possibilities. In the agricultural sector model, $\bar{P}_m$ and $\bar{P}_x$ may be measured in terms of Mexican pesos by multiplying the world import and export prices by the shadow price of foreign exchange. If the country can always import at a cost of $\bar{P}_m$, it is never optimal to produce at a marginal domestic cost higher than $\bar{P}_m$. The utility added by the sector is measured by the hatched area between the supply curve (*S*) and the residual demand curve *ABCD*. The area *ABE* remains invariant, and may be omitted from the suboptimization. Cases 3 and 4 can be visualized as simplified representations of CHAC. These apply respectively to the non-tradable and the internationally tradable commodities.

In the third and fourth cases, the contribution of the sector is expressed in terms of social utility added. This concept, which depends upon cardinal interpersonal utility comparison, 'incorporates a greater degree of subtlety of economic analysis than does national income methodology' (Harberger 1971). However, unlike Harberger, who claims that utilities 'should normally be added without regard to the individuals to whom they accrue', the authors of Part IV have measured how total benefits are distributed between consumers (ABMF) and producers (FMG). In particular, they have evaluated the impact of controls restricting domestic supply.

Case 5 illustrates a similar distributional problem in an international context. For a given product, Mexico exports its entire output and faces a downward-sloping demand curve for its exports. If a zero weight is given to the gains of foreign consumers, the product should be valued at its marginal return to Mexico (KN). Even if a project accounts for a small share of the country's production, the social benefits should be valued on the basis of the marginal return to Mexico (KN) — not at the price (KM) at which the output of the project could be sold abroad. The difference (MN) between average and marginal returns measures the optimum level of an export tax. Within a country, if the distribution weight given to consumers were positive but smaller than the one given to producers, the shadow price would be lower than KM but higher than KN. This example illustrates how the allocation of distribution weights, within or between countries, affects the shadow prices to be used for project appraisal.

3. Physical capital (table 3)

In DINAMICO and EXPORTA, it is assumed that there is no reserve of unemployed capacity in the base period. Sectoral production in year t is limited by the output in year 0 plus the capacity installed between year 0 and year t. Both models have constant gestation lags for capacity creation — three years in the case of DINAMICO and one year for EXPORTA.

With a finite planning horizon, there is an element of arbitrari-

Table 3
Characteristics of the seven

	DINAMICO	EXPORTA	ENERGETICOS
Physical capital			
Initial resource endowment	Capacity in 15 sectors	Capacity in 45 sectors	Capacity by type of process
Investment choices	Additional capacity in 15 sectors. Replacement of agricultural workers at constant marginal rate of capital-labor substitutions	Additional capacity in 45 sectors	Additional capacity transmission lines) Choice among mutu-tions of projects trea 648 combinations
Capital constraints	Endogenous domestic savings (limited by grad-ualist consumption path and 30% upper bound on marginal propensity to save) + Exogenous concessional capital imports + Endogenous private capital imports	Exogenous aggregate investment	Unbounded amounts Yearly service charge
Terminal conditions	3-year gestation lag. Physical capital forma-tion in 1986 related to 1986-89 output growth	1-year gestation lag. 1976 investment re-lated to cumulated 1970−75 investment through stock-flow conversion factor	————————

ness [4] in the terminal conditions. In the case of DINAMICO, sec-toral investments in 1986 must satisfy a capacity growth rate during the post-terminal period (1986–89). In EXPORTA, mini-mum sectoral investments in 1976 are defined as a fraction of the cumulated investment between 1970 and 1975.

For EXPORTA, since there is a predetermined upper bound on aggregate investment during the five-year planning horizon, the choices are limited to investment allocations among sectors. In DINAMICO, aggregate investment is endogenous. It is bounded by a combination of three constraints: the gradualist consumption

---

[4] To reduce horizon effects, a model may be extended beyond the near future planning period. Thus, in DINAMICO, the results generally refer to the near future period ending in 1980, even though the computations extend through 1986.

programming models: physical capital

INTERCON	CHAC	BAJIO	PACIFICO
Capacity by type of plants and transmission lines	———————— Land and water by month and ———————— by district by farm type		by district
by types of plants (or ally exclusive combina- ed as integer variables: 252 combinations	Canal lining, small dams, tubewells, land leveling, and machinery by district by farm type		None
of capital available at exogenously given discount rates on new investments covering amortization and return on capital			None
————————————	Not applicable ————————————————————		

path with a target annual growth rate of 7%; a 30% upper bound on the marginal propensity to save; and limits on capital imports.

In the five other models, initial capacities are expressed in terms of process capacities or in terms of the availabilities of land and water in specific areas. Capacity can be increased [5] by installing new plants, digging wells, lining canals, etc. Since the sector (or subsector) can borrow unlimited amounts of capital at a given discount rate, the annualized direct cost of an investment activity is exogenous. [6] Therefore, it can be treated like any other cost item whose price is exogenous. Thus, in CHAC (or BAJIO), it is

---

[5] Except in PACIFICO, where capacities are given.
[6] The capital recovery factor includes amortization as well as interest charges.

Table 4
Human

	DINAMICO	EXPORTA	ENERGETICOS
Human capital			
Initial endowment	Exogenous supply of 5 labor skills	Exogenous supply of modern and traditional labor	Not ap-
Human capital formation	Endogenous educational activities	None	Not ap-
Migration	Endogenous from rural to urban, at cost of urban services	———————	— Not applicable —
Labor requirement	Annual: fixed labor coefficients for each sector		Labor costs aggregatstic cost items
Efficiency wage	Positive efficiency wages in agriculture, based on full employment. Positive wage differential between skills, based on positive levels of skill upgrading or training activities	Positive efficiency wages for modern labor, based on full employment. Zero wages for traditional labor, based on unemployment.	Exogenously

optimal to invest as long as the annual cost of the investment activity is lower than the increment in the payoff added by the capacity increment. A demand curve for capital can then be constructed by solving the model for different values of the discount rate.

4. Human capital (table 4)

In EXPORTA, the labor force is divided into two categories (modern and traditional labor). In DINAMICO, it is divided into five labor skills (from engineers and scientists down to unskilled agricultural workers). In both models, the production of a unit of sectoral output requires fixed input quantities of labor of specified

apital

NTERCON	CHAC	BAJIO	PACIFICO
licable	——————— Farm family labor ———————		
	by district, plus landless labor pool for each of 4 regions	by farm type	by district plus landless labor pool
licable	None	——————— None ———————	
———————	Endogenous among regions	Not applicable	
d with other dome-	Monthly: fixed labor coefficients for each cropping activity		
iven market wages	Not lower than exogenously given reservation wages differentiated by farm family labor and landless workers, by regions		

skills. In both models, the efficiency wage of a given labor skill is positive only if all members of this category are utilized. The efficiency wage falls to zero if part of the labor force remains unemployed. If the model is to provide a level of employment higher than in the unconstrained optimal solution, the value of the maximand is reduced, and the marginal productivity of that labor type becomes negative. This case is illustrated in the top diagram of figure 1, which refers to traditional labor in EXPORTA. (See also below, chapter II.6, table 4.)

When the supply of the various labor skills is taken as exogenous, it may turn out that, for some skills, the supply exceeds demand. The efficiency wage of this one type is then zero, while for other types the shadow price may be extremely high. This is precisely what occurs with EXPORTA, where modern and traditional labor have to be used in fixed proportions within each sector. In the income maximizing solutions, traditional labor is always redundant, and modern labor is a binding constraint. This occurs because there is no way of transforming traditional into modern labor.

To avoid this problem, which would have been particularly serious in a dynamic model, human capital formation is introduced as an endogenous variable in DINAMICO. Postprimary education is treated strictly as an investment activity, ignoring the direct consumption benefits of education. For a 16% rate of return on human capital (which corresponds approximately to the return on physical capital), the long-term equilibrium (von Neumann) wage ratio between engineers and unskilled urban workers is equal to 12. This is close to the base-year ratio and therefore provides a cross-check on the educational norms used.

Direct substitution between primary factors (capital and unskilled labor) is included only in the agricultural sector of DINAMICO. There, workers can be replaced by capital at a fixed marginal rate of substitution. The agricultural workers thus replaced can then be transformed into urban unskilled workers at an annual cost, an intermediate input of urban services. This transformation cost operates in much the same way as a reservation wage. It leads to a positive differential between the efficiency wages of unskilled urban and agricultural workers.

The middle diagram of figure 2 refers to unskilled agricultural labor in DINAMICO. The demand curves (D_1, D_2, and D_3) characterize three alternative schedules of the total demand for this labor skill in year t. The demand includes not only those needed in agriculture, but also the additional workers needed in the urban areas. The direct supply of unskilled agricultural workers available in year t would be OA if the capital-labor substitution activity were operated at zero level in that year. If additional workers are needed, an unlimited number can be replaced by capital at a constant marginal rate of capital-labor substitution, and at an annual cost equal to AB per worker. In effect, the supply of agricultural

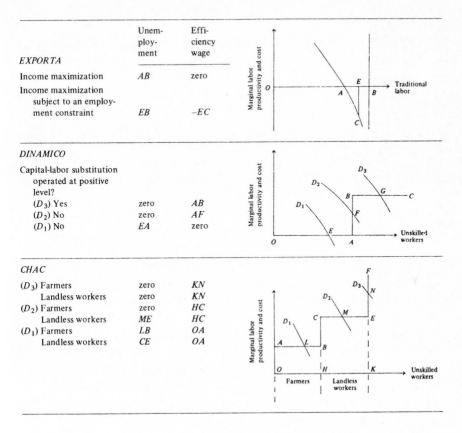

	Unem-ploy-ment	Effi-ciency wage	
EXPORTA			
Income maximization	*AB*	zero	
Income maximization subject to an employment constraint	*EB*	*−EC*	
DINAMICO			
Capital-labor substitution operated at positive level?			
(D_3) Yes	zero	*AB*	
(D_2) No	zero	*AF*	
(D_1) No	*EA*	zero	
CHAC			
(D_3) Farmers	zero	*KN*	
Landless workers	zero	*KN*	
(D_2) Farmers	zero	*HC*	
Landless workers	*ME*	*HC*	
(D_1) Farmers	*LB*	*OA*	
Landless workers	*CE*	*OA*	

Fig. 2. Unemployment and efficiency wages.

labor and its substitute is represented by the step function *OABC*. Again, as in EXPORTA, unemployment implies that the efficiency wage is zero.

In CHAC, labor requirements are specified monthly for each cropping activity. The sector is treated as a price-taker for skilled workers, but as a supply curve taker for those who are unskilled. On the supply side, a distinction is made between farm family labor and landless workers. Both have a reservation price for their labor, i.e., the price below which they will not accept work. The labor reservation price is lower for farmers than for landless workers. Since the productivity of farmers and landless workers is assumed to be same, the farmers are employed first. The monthly supply curve of agricultural labor in a district is represented, therefore, on the bottom diagram of figure 1, by the step function *ABCEF*. Under demand schedule D_1, part of the farmers (*LB*) remain unemployed in a given month; the marginal productivity of those who are working is equal to the farmers' reservation wage (*OA*). Under demand schedule D_2, some but not all of the landless workers are employed. The marginal productivity of both farmers and landless workers is then equal to the reservation price of landless workers (*HC*). The level of *HC* approximately reflects market wages. [7]

As it turns out, in the agricultural model, the demand schedule is generally in the position D_1 or D_2, but very rarely in the position D_3. When the labor reservation prices are increased, the staircase *ABCEF* of figure 1 is lifted upward, and the level of employment is reduced. Vice versa, when labor reservation prices are reduced, the level of employment rises. Even so, a large fraction of the labor force remains unemployed.

On the contrary, in DINAMICO, the demand schedule is generally in the position D_3, sometimes in the position D_2, but very seldom in the position D_1. Consequently, full employment prevails and additional capital has to be invested in agriculture to release the workers needed in the rest of the economy.

Let us consider how these conflicting results come about. In the agricultural model, unemployment is computed as the residual $A-B-C$, where A, B and C are defined as follows:

A: Total agricultural labor force, including farm family labor expressed in terms of male adult equivalents.

B: Agricultural labor required for the activities excluded from the model: livestock and tree crop activities plus activities linked with general farm management, marketing of the farm products and various ancillary services.

C: Labor requirements for short-term cycle crops computed in the model from labor norms based on agronomical studies.

---

[7] The treatment of labor in CHAC is actually more complex than it appears on figure 1. This diagram ignores regional migration, as well as the distinction between quarterly labor contracts for farmers and monthly contracts for landless workers.

Anyone familiar with agricultural statistics in developing countries will recognize that it is not an easy matter to measure accurately the residual $A-B-C$. Also, labor requirements under B are likely to be sensitive to the reservation price for labor.

The authors of DINAMICO state that they are unable to find reliable data on urban or rural unemployment in Mexico. They adopt the extreme solution that the labor force is fully employed in the statistical base-year of 1968. They distribute the total 1968 labor force by skill and by sector. The 1968 labor norms are then computed by dividing the number of workers by the observed output in each sector for that year. These norms, therefore, incorporate whatever disguised unemployment might have prevailed in 1968. (If the rate of unemployment had been equal to 10%, the 1968 labor norms would be overestimated by 10%.) The 1968 norms are then extrapolated on the basis of exogenous rates of labor productivity gains, differentiated by sector and by skill. Thus, for construction, commerce and services − three sectors which together employed over 55% of the unskilled urban labor force in 1968 − labor productivity is assumed to increase by 1.5% a year (below, chapter II.1, table 4). These rates, which are derived from international comparisons, cannot be estimated accurately, and they affect the shadow prices for labor obtained in the dual solution. Given the present structure of DINAMICO, the shadow prices do not behave plausibly unless there is full employment.

In practice, DINAMICO and CHAC operate roughly as follows: In DINAMICO, the full employment assumption is given, and the shadow price of labor is the unknown determined by solving the model. In CHAC, the labor shadow prices are predetermined, to a very large extent, by the selection made for the labor reservation wage rates; the level of unemployment is the unknown.

References

Harberger, A.C., 'Three basic postulates for applied welfare economics: an interpretive essay', *Journal of Economic Literature*, September 1971.
Little, I.M.D., and J.A. Mirrlees, *Manual of industrial project analysis in developing countries*, Vol. II: *Social cost benefit analysis*. Paris, Development Centre of the Organization for Economic Cooperation and Development, 1968.

I.3. THE PROBLEM OF INTERDEPENDENCE

Louis M. GOREUX

In this volume, the interdependence of economic decisions is studied in two ways. The first consists of progressively enlarging the scope of the model. This approach is rigorous, but it is very expensive in terms of data collection. Moreover, the scope for enlargement is limited by the size of the models that computers can solve and economists (or policy-makers) comprehend. The second approach is to build several models, each self-contained, and to establish some linkages between them.

1. The single model approach

1.1. Agricultural models

In discussing the suboptimization problem in chapter I.1 above, we started with the example of canal lining. It was argued that the output of the project should not be defined in terms of cubic meters of water saved, but in terms of additional crop production. This led us to use the model of the agricultural district as the basic unit.

At the level of the district, suboptimization is possible provided two conditions are met. First, the district can be treated as a price-taker for the commodities it produces and for the resources it shares with the rest of the economy. Second, the correct prices of these commodities and these resources can be obtained from outside sources.

Consider the first condition. For most of the common resources it uses (petroleum, machinery, capital, ...), the district may generally be treated as a price-taker. However, for some of the commodities it produces, this assumption may not be acceptable. In the case of high regional specialization, a relatively small area may account for a substantial part of the total domestic supply of a particular commodity. Moreover, even if each single district taken in isolation may be treated as a price-taker, a group of districts may not.

Consider now the second condition — the correctness of the exogenous prices. For those commodities which will always be imported at fixed prices, no problem arises. For those which will always be exported and can be exported at fixed prices in unlimited quantities, no problem arises either. But, for all other commodities, some device is needed to provide the district with the appropriate prices. [1]

A solution, the one followed in this study, is to enlarge the scope of the model from the boundaries of the district to those of the country. Crop prices, which were treated as exogenous data for the district model, become endogenous variables in the sectoral model. In this process, BAJIO (the first district model constructed) is embedded in CHAC. Consequently, solving BAJIO alone with the shadow prices of CHAC is equivalent to solving BAJIO embedded in CHAC. But, each time the value of a parameter is modified in CHAC, the signals sent to BAJIO in the form of a shadow price vector have to be adjusted. Thus, a modification in the rate of interest leads to a new optimal solution of CHAC and therefore to a new shadow price for each crop.

The impact of such a change is measured by the authors of chapter IV.5 below. In one case, they compute BAJIO's investment response to a variation in the interest rate by following a partial equilibrium analysis at the level of the district. They solve BAJIO directly with two different values of the interest rate, retaining the same set of product prices. In the other case, they solve

---

[1] The problem also arises for the price of common sectoral resources other than commodities (for example, unskilled labor moving between regions). However, the impact of variations in crop prices is by far the most important in CHAC. For simplicity of exposition, the discussion is therefore limited to these prices.

BAJIO embedded in CHAC. The investment response thus computed differs from the previous one, since it takes into account the reactions of the other districts as well as those of the consumers. The most dramatic change in the signals sent from the sector to the district is probably associated with a modification in the relative weights given to producers' and consumers' gains. This is illustrated by introducing sectoral income as a binding constraint. In the case of commodities with a low demand price elasticity on the domestic market, there is a severe reduction in the shadow prices applied for evaluating production decisions.

CHAC is a two-level planning model which can be solved both directly and iteratively. It can therefore be used to illustrate the decentralized decision-making process discussed by Kornai in chapter V.3 below. This process was simulated with PACIFICO, a simplified version of CHAC. Since this decomposition experiment sheds light on the problem of linkage between models, it deserves some attention.

PACIFICO is a regional model composed of five districts. Each district has an endowment of resources specific to the district, such as water and land. It can buy other resources (e.g. fertilizers and tractor fuel) at fixed prices in unlimited quantities. It has a choice among 162 cropping activities to produce 16 commodities. But the prices of these commodities depend on the total output of the five districts. For this reason, the district models cannot be solved independently. It is necessary to solve a system composed of five district submodels linked by a regional submodel. The latter translates the quantity-price demand curves for the commodities originating from the region in terms of constraints common to the five districts.

The direct solution of PACIFICO, a model of 187 rows, presents no problem. In the indirect solution, using a decomposition algorithm, on each cycle the region announces tentative prices, and the districts reply with production proposals. Two different iterative procedures are followed, as shown in table 1.

In the first variant, the region initially selects one single combination for the prices of the 16 commodities and sends it to the districts. On the basis of this particular price combination, each

Table 1
Iterative procedures used in PACIFICO

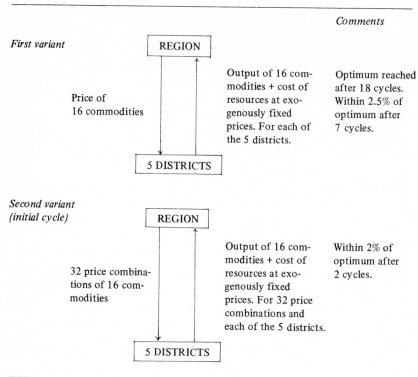

First variant

REGION

Price of
16 commodities

5 DISTRICTS

*Second variant
(initial cycle)*

REGION

32 price combina-
tions of 16 com-
modities

5 DISTRICTS

Comments

Output of 16 com-
modities + cost of
resources at exo-
genously fixed
prices. For each of
the 5 districts.

Optimum reached
after 18 cycles.
Within 2.5% of
optimum after
7 cycles.

Output of 16 com-
modities + cost of
resources at exo-
genously fixed
prices. For 32 price
combinations and
each of the 5 districts.

Within 2% of
optimum after
2 cycles.

district optimizes the levels of its production activities, and transmits its corresponding production proposal to the region. This proposal is expressed in an aggregate form, specifying only the total cost incurred and the amounts produced of each of the 16 commodities. The region adds up all district proposals, computes the corresponding commodity prices and sends the adjusted price vector to the districts. The districts solve a second optimizing problem and send a second production proposal back to the region.

The iterative procedure converges because, at each cycle, the new district proposal is adjoined to those sent by that particular district in the earlier cycles. To maximize its objective function, the region can use any convex combination [2] of the proposals accumulated for each district. The set of shadow prices generated by this optimization at the regional level is sent to the districts in the following cycle. As shown in table 8 of chapter V.2 below, the value of the objective function increases slowly during the first three cycles. It rises rapidly during the following four, and then slowly again till cycle 18, when optimality is reached. The shadow price vector varies from one cycle to the next. During the early cycles, some of the prices fluctuate violently.

In the second variant, convergence is accelerated by sending more information during the first cycle. Some economic insight is required to choose the initial price combinations. Although there are 16 commodities, price variations are likely to occur for only 5 commodities (or commodity groups). For these five, two extreme prices are selected. This leads to $2^5 = 32$ different price combinations. During the first cycle, each district optimizes its production activities on the basis of these 32 price combinations and transmits 32 different production proposals back to the region. In turn, the region selects for each district that convex combination of the 32 production proposals which maximizes its objective function. The shadow price vector thus obtained is sent to the districts at the second cycle. As it turns out, by the end of the second cycle, the maximand is only 2% short of optimality.

This experiment suggests that a satisfactory solution may be reached rapidly, if the decisions made at the lower level affect the shadow prices of only a few common resources. In this example, if the regional objective function had been sufficiently close to optimality after the first cycle, the regional problem could have been solved by adding 160 (5×32) columns, but only 5 rows to the regional submodel. This device can be useful for linking large-scale models, since the number of rows is the major computational constraint. As will be seen later, this property is used to link the

---

[2] If the production proposals were not accumulated, the procedure could diverge, as in an explosive cobweb. Since proposals are cumulated, a constraint has to be introduced to insure that the combination selected by the region is feasible for the district. That is, the combination satisfies the constraints on resources specific to the district, e.g., land and water.

agricultural and the economy-wide models. However, if the direct solution can be handled within the high speed memory of the computer, this requires less time than the indirect solution. Efficient decomposition programs were not available during the early 1970's. For these reasons, CHAC (a .model of 1,500 rows) was solved directly.

1.2. Energy models

Let us start again with a typical project decision. Should Mexico build a nuclear power plant? If the demand for electrical power were the same during each of the 24 hours of the day, the requirements for electrical power could be expressed in terms of a single product called 'energy'. It would then be fairly simple to compare the cost of a nuclear plant with other types of plants. But, as shown in figure 1, the demand for power is much higher during the four peak-hours (*OA*) than during the twenty off-peak hours (*ED*), sometimes termed the 'base load'. The problem of the sup-

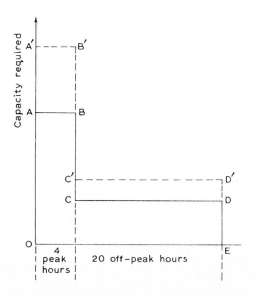

Fig. 1. Power requirements during peak and off-peak hours.

plier is to meet the given power requirements at the lowest cost. The requirements can be represented, for two different years, by the load curves $OABCDE$ and $OA'B'C'D'E$.

It may not be optimal to meet the full increment required ($AA'B'B$ and $CC'D'D$) with a nuclear plant. Since the increment required during the 20 off-peak hours (CC') is much smaller than the increment required during the four peak hours (AA'), such a plant would remain grossly underutilized for 20 hours a day. Also, it may not be optimal to install a nuclear plant which would just meet the increment in the off-peak hours (CC'). It might be less expensive to install a larger nuclear plant and to meet the peak demand with some of the existing plants previously used for the base load. The introduction of a nuclear unit in the system may therefore require a modification in the rates of utilization of many other plants. For this reason, it is not possible to compare directly the cost of operating a nuclear and a fossil plant. It is necessary to minimize the cost of satisfying the power requirements for the system as a whole.

In ENERGETICOS, the power requirements (load curves) are given exogenously for ten different years. The endogenous variables are the mix of the power plants to be installed and the hours at which the old and the new plants are to be operated. All these variables are determined simultaneously by minimizing the present value of discounted costs over the planning horizon.

The choice between nuclear and fossil plants may have implications not only for the existing power plants but also for the petroleum sector. The problem of interdependence between the power and the petroleum sectors can be illustrated, in a highly simplified [3] form, from the diagram shown in figure 2.

If Mexico were a net importer of fuel, the opportunity cost of fuel to the Mexican economy would correspond to the c.i.f. price $\bar{P}_m$. But, if Mexico were a net exporter, the opportunity cost of

---

[3] To simplify, it is assumed that the petroleum sector produces only fuel. In fact, the sector produces and can export or import several petroleum products. If the sector imports, it is generally optimal to import crude oil. If the sector exports, it is generally optimal to export gasoline. Moreover, the dynamic optimization problem of ENERGETICOS is analyzed here in a static context.

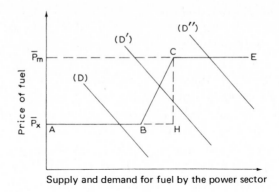

Supply and demand for fuel by the power sector

Fig. 2. Supply curve of fuel to the power sector (*ABCD*) and demand curve for fuel by the power sector (*D*).

fuel would be reduced to $\bar{P}_x$, based on f.o.b. prices. On the one hand, since there are rising marginal costs in the petroleum sector, the supply curve of fuel to the power sector is represented by *ABCE*. On the other, the fuel demand of the power sector is represented by the curves *D*, *D'* or *D''*. For some values of the discount rate and the foreign exchange premium, the demand of the power sector is quite sensitive to the price of fuel. This occurs when it is optimal to install nuclear plants at the price $\bar{P}_m$, but fossil plants at the price $\bar{P}_x$. If it were certain that the fuel demand curve of the power sector would always be in the position *D* or would always be in the position *D''*, the petroleum and the power problems could be solved independently. But, if this demand curve is in the position *D'*, the two problems ought to be solved simultaneously. As it turns out, the demand curve is, in some cases, in position *D'*. It is therefore useful to embed the power and the petroleum submodels into a single model. In this enlarged model ENERGETICOS, the shadow price of fuel becomes an endogenous variable.

The most complex interdependence problem in the energy sector is that investments are bulky, and that there are often increasing returns to scale. For this reason, alternative investment packages are defined as sets of plants of given sizes installed in given years. Six such alternative investment packages are considered for steel, 9 for petroleum, and 12 for electricity. Since one, and only one, package can be selected in each subsector, there are a total of $6 \times 9 \times 12 = 648$ mutually exclusive investment strategies for the sector.

At one extreme, if the choice of an investment strategy had no impact on the shadow prices of the sectoral resources, the best strategy could be selected by solving only a single optimization problem. At the other extreme, if the shadow prices computed for a given strategy had no relevance for assessing the cost of other strategies, the sector would have to solve 648 optimization problems. In practice, because the shadow prices computed for a given strategy can be used to eliminate other strategies, the global optimum was reached by solving no more than 26 out of the 648 individual optimization problems.

Figure 3 provides an intuitive explanation of this property. Consider two strategies n and m. Through the simplex method, it is possible to compute the minimum cost z^n (or z^m) of meeting the sectoral requirements. The associated shadow price vector is π^n (or π^m). For this optimizing problem, strategy n (or m) is treated as given; all the remaining unknowns are continuous variables.

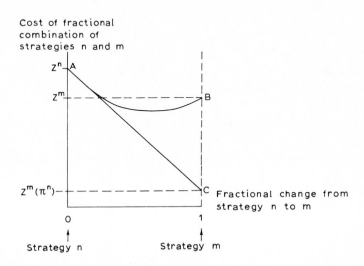

Fig. 3. Lower bound on costs for project combination m.

Now imagine that strategies n and m are perfectly divisible, so that it is possible to move continuously from one to the other. When the integer constraints are removed, the cost of the mix between strategies n and m cannot be higher than the linear combination of the costs z^n and z^m, which were computed with integer constraints. Consequently, the cost of the mix is represented by the convex curve AB. The slope of AC (the tangent at point A) may be interpreted as the reduced costs vector corresponding to shadow prices π^n. The ordinate of point C is z^m (π^n). This ordinate may be interpreted as the cost of strategy m measured at shadow prices π^n. Since point B is above point C, $z^m(\pi^n)$ provides a lower bound on the true cost of following strategy m.

Solving the optimization problem for strategy n immediately provides an upper bound z^n for the cost. This also provides a

Table 2

Iterative procedure for selecting the lowest cost among 648 mutually exclusive investment strategies: ENERGETICOS

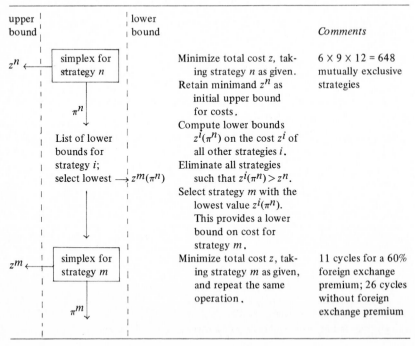

upper bound		lower bound	Comments
$z^n \leftarrow$	simplex for strategy n		Minimize total cost z, taking strategy n as given. Retain minimand z^n as initial upper bound for costs.	6 × 9 × 12 = 648 mutually exclusive strategies
	π^n		Compute lower bounds $z^i(\pi^n)$ on the cost z^i of all other strategies i.	
	List of lower bounds for strategy i; select lowest $\rightarrow z^m(\pi^n)$		Eliminate all strategies such that $z^i(\pi^n) > z^n$. Select strategy m with the lowest value $z^i(\pi^n)$. This provides a lower bound on cost for strategy m.	
$z^m \leftarrow$	simplex for strategy m		Minimize total cost z, taking strategy m as given, and repeat the same operation.	11 cycles for a 60% foreign exchange premium; 26 cycles without foreign exchange premium
	π^m			

shadow price vector π^n, which can be used to eliminate all strategies i for which $z^i (\pi^n)$ is greater than z^n. This would occur if point C lay above point A. A number of strategies can therefore be eliminated without solving any new optimization problem. The strategy m, with the lowest cost bound $z^m (\pi^n)$, is then used as a starting-point for the second cycle, as outlined in table 2. The number of cycles required for optimality depends on the margin between the upper and lower bounds and on the sensitivity of the shadow prices to alternative strategies. The number of cycles is therefore indicative of the degree of interdependence in the system. [4]

In ENERGETICOS, the optimum investment strategy was identified after 11 cycles in the case of a 60% foreign exchange premium and 26 cycles in the absence of a premium. With a high premium, the strategies which include nuclear electricity plants are eliminated during the early cycles. This stabilizes the shadow price of industrial fuel (which is sensitive to the choice between the nuclear and the fossil plants), and consequently accelerates the convergence.

2. On linking self-contained models

There is a fundamental difference between the higher level submodel of an integrated system such as PACIFICO and the higher level model (DINAMICO) of the loosely connected system outlined in figure 4.

In PACIFICO, the regional submodel does not include any production activities; these enter only in the district submodels. Consequently, the regional submodel cannot be solved independently from the district submodels.

In the system outlined in figure 4, DINAMICO contains production activities for all the sectors and can be solved independently from the lower-level models. ENERGETICOS and CHAC also con-

---

[4] The number of cycles is not a perfect index because it is also affected by the choice of the starting-point. Nevertheless, the results reported in table 5 of chapter V.1 below, suggest that this index is not too sensitive to the choice of the starting-point.

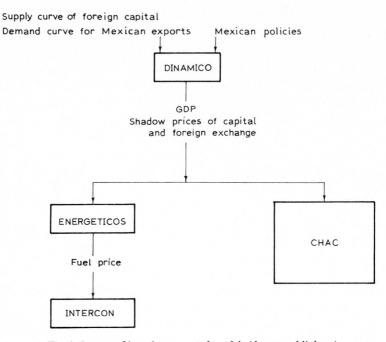

Fig. 4. System of loosely connected models (downward linkage).

tain production activities. On the one hand, the production activities of the sectoral models are based on detailed engineering and agricultural data. On the other, the production activities of DINA-MICO are derived from an aggregate input-output table of the Mexican economy, a completely different source of data. The system therefore contains redundancies and inconsistencies. Because of these redundancies, each of the four models belonging to the system can be solved independently. The problem is to investigate whether the independent solution of one of these models can be significantly improved by linking this particular model to others in the system.

2.1. Downward linkages

As shown in figure 4, DINAMICO can send the sectoral models three types of signals: the shadow prices of capital and foreign exchange and the level of GDP. The latter is used to compute the energy requirements in ENERGETICOS and the levels of the quantity-price demand schedules in CHAC. Similarly, ENERGETICOS can send the fuel price to INTERCON. What is the difference between the solutions with and without downward linkages?

To solve the sectoral models without linkages, some values for GDP and for the shadow prices of capital and foreign exchange have to be selected. For the most uncertain parameters (the shadow prices in this case), higher and lower bounds may be selected. The sectoral models can then be solved with parametric variations within these bounds. This is, as a matter of fact, the procedure which was followed with ENERGETICOS, because this model was finalized before DINAMICO.

The independent solution of ENERGETICOS shows that the choice of investment in the steel subsector is not influenced by variations of the shadow prices. To make an investment choice in the steel subsector, nothing can be learned from downward linkages. For petroleum and power, however, the choice of the optimal investment pattern is sensitive to the levels of the shadow prices. For these two subsectors, downward linkages are therefore useful. This narrows the margin of uncertainty, but does not lead to an unequivocal answer because the solution of DINAMICO depends on a series of assumptions relating to external factors and internal policies.

To correctly interpret the results of the sectoral models corresponding to different values of the exogenous parameters, the downward linkage is important. In a partial equilibrium framework, the difficulty of interpreting the impact of a change in the rate of interest has been illustrated earlier by a comparison between the direct solution of BAJIO and the solution of BAJIO embedded into CHAC. The same problem arises between the sectoral and the economy-wide models. If there is a change in the opportunity cost of capital to the Mexican economy, the premium on foreign exchange and the rate of GDP growth are likely to change simultaneously. To know how these various changes are related, their primary cause has to be identified. The changes could reflect a modification in the international commodity and capital markets. They could also reflect a tightening of the fiscal policy or a shift of emphasis in the national objectives, say away from increasing aggregate GDP and toward improving the distribution of income.

The first step is therefore to identify a number of different situations, each reflecting given assumptions on the environment of the Mexican economy and on the national policies and objectives. The second is to solve the economy-wide model for each of these situations. The third is to solve the sectoral models for the particular set of signals (GDP and shadow prices) corresponding to each particular situation.

2.2. Upward linkages

The extent to which the solution of the lower-level model can be improved from downward linkages depends on the quality of the signals received from the higher-level model. Obviously, it is desirable to improve the quality of these signals. One way to do this is to replace the production vectors of DINAMICO by vectors derived from the sectoral models. Since the latter are based on more detailed technological information, presumably they are more accurate. In addition, this substitution would have the advantage of eliminating redundancies and inconsistencies from the system. Upward linkages are, unfortunately, considerably more difficult than downward linkages.

One extreme solution is to embed the lower level model into the higher level one. In the case of our self-contained models, this would have required a good deal of work. The data base, the statistical coverage and the objective functions were by no means uniform. For this reason, only partial linkages have been attempted in this study. Their rationale may be illustrated in relation to the decomposition experiment conducted with PACIFICO.

As will be recalled, in the second variant, the district initially sends the region 32 production proposals corresponding to 32 different price combinations received from the region. If the same principle were to be applied in the linkage between a sectoral model and DINAMICO, the vector characterizing the activities of the sector in DINAMICO would be replaced by a series of vectors generated by the sectoral model. These vectors would summarize, in terms of all the aggregates of DINAMICO, the strategies optimal for the sector under particular combinations of the shadow prices of the central resources and of the level of disposable income.

To link CHAC with DINAMICO (below, chapter IV.6), a number of simplifications are made. It is assumed that a distinction can be made among three types of central resources used in agriculture. For the *first* type (unskilled labor, capital and export earnings), it is recognized that the choices made within the sector can substantially affect the shadow prices of the central resources. Consequently, to speed up convergence, the same device is followed as on the initial cycle of PACIFICO. Three different values are selected for agricultural wages, the discount rate and the foreign exchange premium. Out of the 27 (= 3^3) possible combinations of these shadow prices, 3 were eliminated. Each of the 24 remaining combinations defines a different state of the environment, and leads to a different optimal agricultural strategy. For the *second* type of central resources (semi-skilled labor, chemicals, petroleum products and machinery), it is recognized that the quantities used depend on the strategy selected. But, it is assumed that their prices are not substantially affected because the sector is a small user of these items. Consequently, a single price is selected in the first iteration. For the *third* type (all other central resources), it is assumed that the strategy selected in the sector has a negligible effect upon the prices and the quantities used. Consequently, the DINAMICO coefficients are kept unchanged.

For a given strategy, the information derived from the optimal solution of CHAC is summarized for DINAMICHAC in the form of 8 growth rates — one for the total agricultural output and one for each of the 7 central resources listed above under types one and two. The agricultural vectors of DINAMICO are replaced in DINAMICHAC by 24 vectors [5] characterizing each of the 24 alter-

[5] Due to differences in statistical coverages and concepts, the agricultural vectors of DINAMICHAC are not completely new vectors generated directly from CHAC. They are modifications of the original DINAMICO vectors, but they reflect the substitutability among factors and the sectoral constraints, as measured from the 24 solutions of CHAC.

native strategies of the sector. The unknowns in DINAMICHAC are the levels at which each of the 24 strategies are operated. These levels are subject to a convexity constraint, which ensures that the sector-specific constraints (such as availability of land and water) are satisfied.

The shadow price vector obtained by solving DINAMICHAC is not returned to CHAC. The interchange between CHAC and DI-NAMICO is therefore limited to a single cycle. The solution thus obtained could nevertheless be satisfactory if the three assumptions made earlier were approximately fulfilled and if the variation in the level of disposable income remained sufficiently small not to warrant adjusting the level of CHAC's demand curves.

Imagine that these assumptions can be further simplified. Suppose that the choice of agricultural strategies can have a substantial impact only on the prices and quantities of labor and capital. Selecting three alternative shadow prices for capital and another three for labor would define $3 \times 3 = 9$ different price combinations. The 9 optimal strategies associated with these combinations would then be represented by 9 vectors. Each of these 9 vectors would have a particular entry in the capital, labor and output rows, but a common entry in the other DINAMICO rows. In other words, CHAC would send DINAMICO a capital-labor substitution curve approximated by 8 linear segments, for each point in time. This curve would replace the original capital-labor substitution activity of DINAMICO, for which a constant rate of substitution had been assumed. Treating this curve as an exogenous datum in DINAMICO is equivalent to terminating the interchange of information between DINAMICO and CHAC after one cycle.

We started with one extreme solution. It was to embed CHAC and DINAMICO together. We end with another extreme solution. It is to send from CHAC to DINAMICO only one curve which characterizes the possibilities of substituting capital for labor in agriculture. In between these two extremes, there is a wide spectrum of alternatives. The solution selected by the authors of DINAMICHAC was to transmit a hypersurface in a 7-dimensional space.

The treatment of demand raised a problem in the DINAMI-

CHAC linkage. As will be recalled, the income effect is endogenous in DINAMICO but exogenous in CHAC, while the price effect is endogenous in CHAC but neglected in DINAMICO. It is awkward to allow for endogenous income and price effects simultaneously in a linear programming model. The device used was to compute the growth of agricultural output, after having solved CHAC, on the basis of CHAC shadow prices. A Fisher index was used for this purpose. If this device provided a satisfactory approximation, account could be taken of the price effect in the lower level model and of the income effect in the higher level one.

Compared with the basic solution of DINAMICO, the linkage brings two substantial changes. First, more foreign exchange can be earned by agriculture. Second, without raising the sectoral capital-output ratio, more labor can be released from agriculture. Unfortunately, the effects of introducing CHAC's technology into DINAMICO are overshadowed by inconsistencies in the treatment of unskilled labor. From the base year, CHAC starts with a much higher estimate of the labor force than DINAMICO does. Furthermore, there is no satisfactory way to deal with a large pool of unemployed workers in DINAMICO. [6]

In the case of ENERGETICOS, the upward linkage with DINAMICO does not raise conceptual problems. But it raises data gathering problems. The three subsectors of ENERGETICOS cover only parts of the three corresponding sectors of DINAMICO. Since ENERGETICOS accounts for only 4−5% of total investment, imports and GDP, the results of a formal linkage are, *a priori*, unlikely to differ much from those obtained by solving the two models sequentially. In chapter III.3 below, this hypothesis is tested by calculating the upper bounds on the possible impact of a linkage.

In one experiment, six different combinations are selected for the rate of interest and the foreign exchange premium. The optimal energy strategies corresponding to these six combinations are quite different. But the difference between the most and the least costly strategies (valued at conventional market prices) does not

---

[6] To overcome these difficulties, some adjustments would be required in DINAMICO. It was not possible to include these adjustments in this volume, because the agricultural model was the last part to be completed.

exceed 4%. It is then assumed that a better choice of technologies could save as much as 20% of the resources used in the energy sector. Even then, the resulting increase in GDP and in the demand for electricity would be less than 1%.

In another experiment, it is assumed that DINAMICO could replace the capital and foreign exchange requirements of the most costly of the six energy strategies by those of the least costly strategy. This provides an upper bound on the savings which could be derived from the substitutability between capital and foreign exchange. It again turns out that the gain in GDP and the change in the shadow prices of capital and foreign exchange would be insignificant.

These experiments suggest that, for capital and foreign exchange, the energy sector can be treated as a price-taker and that, for GDP, it can be treated as a quantity-taker. Under those conditions, to make decisions in the energy sector, nothing would be learned from an upward linkage with DINAMICO.

It does not seem either that ENERGETICOS would gain very much from a formal linkage with INTERCON. This can be illustrated by the problem of the peak power capacity required for Mexico. If all regions were interconnected and if no electricity was lost in transmission, the peak capacity required for the country as a whole would be equal to the sum of the peak capacities in each region. There is a tradeoff, however, between building a new transmission line and installing additional capacity. This tradeoff is analyzed in INTERCON, an 8-region model. As it turns out in the optimal solution, the peak capacity required for the country as a whole exceeds by only 0.7% the lower bound which could have been computed by ignoring the regional problem altogether, as was done in ENERGETICOS.

3. Conclusion

In practice, we are always solving suboptimization problems. Even a multi-sector and multi-period model of a single economy could be considered a partial equilibrium analysis of the world economy. The practical problem is, therefore, to define what should be the proper boundaries of a partial equilibrium analysis, given the questions we want to answer.

For project decisions, the boundaries of the project should be such that the instructions to be given to the project analysts can be established independently of the options to be selected by them. These instruction need not be expressed solely in the form of shadow prices or quantitative allocations. They can also be expressed in terms of price-quantity demand (or supply) curves, provided the level of the curve cannot be substantially affected by the options to be made. For bulky investments, the choice among mutually exclusive investment packages may affect the shadow prices of sectoral resources. This was found to be the case for nuclear power plants. Then the project decision must be embedded within a model of the sector.

The instructions given to the project analysts need be no more than intuitive judgments coming from higher up in the organization. In this volume, the instructions come from the solutions of higher level models. Some signals (e.g., the values of the interest rate and the foreign exchange premium) come from the solution of the economy-wide model (DINAMICO); others (e.g., the commodity prices) from the solution of the sectoral model.

In the agricultural sector, the scope of a project analysis is defined by the boundaries of the district. The model of the district is itself embedded into the model of the sector. Consequently, solving the district model alone with the shadow prices of the sectoral model is practically equivalent to solving the district model embedded in the sectoral model. The option is only between solving the sectoral model directly through the simplex method or solving it iteratively by decomposition.

In the indirect solution, the model is decomposed into one higher level submodel and a series of district submodels. The function of the higher level submodel is to clear the market and to announce tentative prices. The function of the district submodels is to submit production proposals. The decomposition experiments provided useful insights into the problem of linkages, but the decomposition technique proved to be considerably more expensive than direct solution.

By enlarging the scope of the analysis from the boundaries of the district to those of the sector, the constant product price assumption can be relaxed. This is particularly important when the country imports few products and when the price elasticity on the domestic market is low. The effect of taking interdependence into account is best illustrated by tables 4–6 in chapter IV.3 below. The impacts of alternative policy packages on various parties (farmers, landless workers, consumers, ...) are quite different from those which would have been estimated by assuming constant product prices.

Broadening the boundaries of the models often proved quite instructive, but attempting to link four independently constructed models was more frustrating. Establishing downward linkages is easy enough. It consists in transmitting from the economy-wide to the sectoral models consistent sets of signals (the shadow price of capital and foreign exchange, and the level of aggregate demand). With such downward linkages, the number of parametric variations worth considering at the sectoral level is considerably reduced. Moreover, the interpretation of the parametric variation selected is greatly improved.

Our failure was in establishing significant upward linkages. In the case of energy, a series of tests suggested that little could be learned from upward linkages (from INTERCON to ENERGETI-COS and to DINAMICO). Consequently, no formal linkage was established in the energy sector. In the case of agriculture, something was learned from an upward linkage to DINAMICO. But the significance of the formal linkage was largely obscured by incompatibilities in the treatment of labor. This experiment is nevertheless interesting from a methodological point of view. It shows how the detailed technological information available in a sectoral model can be transmitted in the condensed form of a curve or a hypersurface to a more aggregated economy-wide model. It also shows how important is the uniform treatment of the data base common to the two models.

PART II. MULTI-SECTOR MODELS

II.1. MANPOWER PROJECTIONS *

Donald B. KEESING and Alan S. MANNE **

1. Introduction

This chapter describes the projection of human resources within DINAMICO, and contains an introduction to the formal model structure given in chapter II.3 below. DINAMICO includes not only input-output, capital investment and foreign trade constraints, but also supply and demand constraints for five skill classes of manpower. This analysis is not designed primarily for manpower planning. Rather, it is intended to yield macroeconomic projections together with efficiency prices for key factors of production. The model incorporates certain aspects of Mexico's potential in human resources: labor input coefficients, human capital formation through education, and skill substitution. Aspects less subject to measurement and purposeful control – for example, changes in behavioral patterns, attitudes and class structure – have necessarily been omitted.

* This is a revised version of a paper presented at the Second World Congress of the Econometric Society, Cambridge, September, 1970. The earlier version was translated into Spanish, and appeared in *Demografía y Economía*, El Colegio de México, 5, no. 2 (1971).

** Having received help in various phases of this study from many individuals, we would like to thank all those who have contributed their advice and assistance. Special thanks are due to Lic. Leopoldo Solís, Dr. Luciano Barraza, Ing. Víctor Ramírez Izquierdo, Lic. Antonio Suárez McAuliffe, Lic. Saúl Trejo, and Lic. Alfredo Santos Arenas (Banco de México); Dr. Gustavo Cabrera Acevedo, Lic. José B. Morelos, Ing. Luis Unikel and Sra. Clara J. de Bialostozky (El Colegio de México); Lic. Gerardo Bueno (Nacional Financiera); Professor János Kornai (Hungarian Academy of Sciences); Dr. Louis Goreux (IBRD); Professors Mordecai Kurz and Clark W. Reynolds and Mr. Richard Inman (Stanford University).

The quality of the underlying data is uneven, and the model is inevitably simplified compared to the realities of the Mexican economy. In consequence, much caution must be exercised in using the results. More confidence is to be attached to the aggregate projections and long-term trends than to the year-to-year or sectoral details.

The results are consistent with the growth of gross domestic product at an average annual rate of 7% from 1968 to 1980. It turns out that skilled and unskilled labor, investment capital and foreign exchange are all scarce factors that jointly limit this growth rate.

Perhaps the most controversial of our results are those that relate to unskilled labor. According to DINAMICO, with continuing economic growth during the 1970's, it will be optimal to substitute other factors of production in place of unskilled agricultural labor. As a result, the absolute numbers engaged in agriculture are likely to remain approximately constant. This finding hinges upon a number of optimistic assumptions:

(1) There is perfect foresight – hence no interruptions or disturbances in the growth process. No market imperfections prevent efficient utilization of resources.

(2) Rapid growth is projected in the supply of complementary factors of production: physical capital and skilled manpower, among others. This is a necessary condition for the expansion of demand for unskilled workers outside traditional agriculture.

(3) It is assumed that labor productivity will grow steadily, but not dramatically: 3.5% per year in manufacturing and 1.5% in services.

(4) Perhaps the most controversial of these assumptions is that no allowance has been made for a large initial pool of disguised unemployment. This pool exists, but we know of no reliable measurements of its size. In Mexico, we suspect that poverty is related to low productivity and to seasonal unemployment in traditional agriculture.

These labor demand projections stand in contrast to the trend toward rising unemployment observed in other developing countries. [1] The results suggest that a turning-point can be reached, and that continuing structural changes begin to create shortages of unskilled labor. There is reason to believe that this might occur because Mexico has already gone through a long-sustained process of economic development. By comparison, up to the 1930's modernization seems clearly to have thrown people out of traditional occupations faster than it created new jobs. [2]

2. The analysis of human resources in DINAMICO

DINAMICO is a linear programming model with 316 rows. Scarce resources are to be allocated among sectors and activities in each time period so as to maximize the growth of consumption, subject to the condition that *increments* of consumption must grow at 7% per year after 1971. (This implies that the growth rate of consumption will increase over time, gradually approaching 7%.) Economic growth is also subject to an array of other constraints and consistency requirements, e.g., input-output relationships, investment requirements for capacity expansion, and constraints that affect the balance of payments. Following the aggregation employed in Banco de México (1970b), the production activities of the economy are classified into 15 sectors.

This research work began in 1969 and extended into 1971. Accordingly, the model focusses on seven representative points of time – each three years apart – with 1968 as the statistical base year. For items such as labor skills, an eighth period (1989) is included to reduce 'horizon effects'. Successive periods are identified by the index t, with $t = 0$ for 1968, $t = 1$ for 1971, etc.

The main scarce resources are defined to be the output and the capacity of each sector in each time period, the availability of labor of five skill classes, capital investment, and foreign exchange.

---

[1] See Frank (1968), Oshima (1968), and Thorbecke (1970), to cite only three references from a large and alarming literature.

[2] See Keesing (1969).

After the statistical base year, increments of physical capital and skilled labor are produced endogenously at a cost in scarce resources. Additional activities (exports of high-cost manufactures) are also included for expanding the supply of foreign exchange at a high marginal cost — beyond the limits permitted by specific upper bounds on export growth in each sector. Total labor supplies are projected exogenously, and unskilled labor is regarded as a primary factor. The skill-mix, however, may be upgraded through activities for human capital formation and for replacing unskilled agricultural labor with physical capital.

The demand for labor is determined on the basis of rigid labor input coefficients for each production sector and each skill class. To describe the process of increases in labor productivity, it is assumed that technical progress is *disembodied*. [3] Each production sector is characterized by labor input coefficients that diminish over time.

For the initial transition (from 1968 to 1971), the growth of skilled as well as unskilled labor is estimated exogenously on the basis of educational and demographic trends. The resulting supply rigidity extends to 1974 in the case of scientists and engineers, due to the six-year lead time for their training. Subsequent increments in the labor supply are taken as partly exogenous and partly endogenous through educational activities. The labor of students and teachers is regarded as the only input to the endogenous human capital formation activities.

To help offset supply rigidities, the model includes possibilities for skill substitution. These help avoid short-term bottlenecks in the three highest classes of skills (those based on formal education). In each case, labor from the next highest skill category may be substituted for the missing skill. Costs take the form of diminished labor productivity in the associated labor force. It is assumed

---

[3] An earlier version had been based upon the assumption of embodied technical progress. Labor input requirements then depend only upon the date at which new physical and human capital are created — not upon the date at which they are utilized. The embodiment hypothesis has a number of advantages — both theoretical and empirical. In the context of DINAMICO, however, this proved to be rather cumbersome. Data processing, revisions, and explanations are all facilitated by the simpler hypothesis of disembodied change.

that these upgrading activities are available only during the two initial periods.

Two other substitution possibilities are included in every period. First, labor can be upgraded from class 5 (unskilled agricultural labor) to class 4 (unskilled labor outside agriculture) at a cost in terms of urban services. Thus, either directly or through education, labor can be raised from lower to higher skill categories, but always at a cost. Second, labor can be downgraded freely to lower skill classes. Typically, it is optimal to employ the upgrading, but not the downgrading activities.

Unlike the terminal conditions for physical capital formation, there is no provision for training additional skilled labor in 1989 for use in subsequent years. During the terminal year, the economically active labor force is allocated only among the sectors producing goods and services. Further research is needed in order to arrive at a model specification that will reduce horizon effects in the case of human resources.

3. Definitions of skill classes

The labor force is divided into five skill classes, referred to as $s = 1$, 2, 3, 4 and 5. These are defined as:
   1. Engineers and scientists.
   2. Other professional and technical workers.
   3. Administrative and clerical workers.
   4. Manual and sales workers outside agriculture.
   5. Unskilled agricultural workers.

The 1960 supply has been estimated mainly on the basis of occupational data from the population census. For 1968, the growth of classes 1, 2, and 3 is based on a demand projection for the same occupations.

   1. *Scientists and engineers* are defined as engineers, chemists, other natural scientists, agronomists and veterinarians, with or without titles, but with full university training or the equivalent.

   2. *Other professional and technical workers* comprise all types of workers listed as professional or technical in the Mexican popu-

lation censuses of 1950 and 1960, except scientists and engineers as defined above. In practice, this is a heterogeneous category with a wide range in educational backgrounds — from unlettered entertainers through highly-trained doctors and university professors.

3. *Administrative and clerical workers* are defined for 1960 through a set of census occupational categories, including all clerical workers, one-tenth of all sales workers, and the managerial and administrative personnel in larger enterprises. [4]

The remaining workers are unskilled. They have been divided between the fourth and fifth categories, depending only on whether they are engaged in agriculture. In choosing skill categories, it has been impossible to distinguish between skilled and semi-skilled workers. It has also been impossible to take explicit account of the upgrading of workers into higher skill categories through on-the-job training rather than formal education. These omissions are caused by an almost total lack of data.

This five-way skill classification oversimplifies reality. It is a compromise that keeps DINAMICO within manageable size, and permits us to take advantage of the manpower data available, not only for Mexico but also for other countries. For other purposes, it may be essential to define labor categories in greater detail than is done here.

4. Exogenously projected manpower supplies

Table 1 summarizes the exogenous projection of manpower supplies available in each period, prior to the effects of endogenous activities for education and for skill substitution. The projections of population and the total labor force are based on demographic estimates, and allow for changes in the age and sex structure of the

---

[4] Managerial and administrative personnel include those defined by the census as *personal directivo* outside agriculture; agricultural owners and large-scale entrepreneurs in the category *patrón–empresario–empleador;* and an allowance for operator-owners in transport and construction.

Table 1

Projections of population and of manpower skills (*before* effects of endogenous activities for human capital formation and skill substitution)

(unit: thousands of persons)

	Year Period t	1950	1960	1968 0	1971 1	1974 2	1977 3	1980 4	1983 5	1986 6	1989 7
	Population	25,792	36,004	47,599	52,949	58,832	65,162	71,942	79,300	87,159	95,241
Active labor force	Skill class 1	19	37	77	97	117	137	157	177	197	217
	Skill class 2	188	373	646	791	936	1,081	1,226	1,371	1,516	1,661
	Skill class 3	545	915	1,382	1,623	1,864	2,105	2,346	2,587	2,828	3,069
	Skill class 4	2,711	3,916	5,451	6,125	6,906	7,827	8,966	10,291	11,746	13,416
	Subtotal, classes 1–4	3,463	5,241	7,556	8,636	9,823	11,150	12,695	14,426	16,287	18,363
	Skill class 5	4,809	6,091	7,024	7,389	7,841	8,321	8,830	9,370	9,943	10,552
	Total, classes 1–5	8,272	11,332	14,580	16,025	17,664	19,471	21,525	23,796	26,230	28,915
% annual growth rates	Population		3.4	3.6	3.6	3.6	3.5	3.4	3.3	3.2	3.0
	Skill class 1		6.9	9.6	8.0	6.5	5.4	4.6	4.1	3.6	3.3
	Skill class 2		7.1	7.1	7.0	5.8	4.9	4.3	3.8	3.4	3.1
	Skill class 3		5.3	5.3	5.5	4.7	4.1	3.7	3.3	3.0	2.8
	Skill class 4		3.7	4.2	4.0	4.1	4.3	4.6	4.7	4.5	4.5
	Total, classes 1–4		4.2	4.7	4.5	4.4	4.3	4.4	4.4	4.2	4.1
	Skill class 5		2.4	1.8	1.7	2.0	2.0	2.0	2.0	2.0	2.0
	Total, classes 1–5		3.2	3.2	3.2	3.3	3.3	3.4	3.4	3.3	3.3

For skill categories, see section 3 above.

population. [5]

After 1971, class 5 labor is taken to grow at just 2% a year in the absence of any differential between unskilled urban and rural wages. Since the rate of natural increase of population is at least as high on farms as off, class 5 labor would grow by at least 3.3% if there were no rural-urban migration. Table 1 implies that some 40% of the annual increment in the rural labor force will transfer automatically out of agriculture even in the absence of any wage differential. On this basis, the non-agriculture work force would grow at 4.4% per year during the 1970's.

Between 1968 and 1971, the rates of expansion in the supplies of skill classes 1−3 are projected as a continuation of the trends from 1960 to 1968. Subsequently, in the absence of the endogenous skill formation activities, the educational system would continue to produce these three skills at the 1968−71 rate. This means that the increments would continue at a constant arithmetic rate. (E.g., the supply of manpower skill 3 is increased by 241,000 persons during each three-year period following 1968). The supply of skill 4 is computed as the balance of the non-agricultural work force.

Other than that which is implicit in these growth projections, no specific allowance is made for the supply of students in the educational pipeline. Admittedly, this is a shortcut device. In a more complete model of manpower planning, it would be preferable − although more tedious−to make an explicit calculation of the initial inventory of students and teachers and of the subsequent increases in that inventory.

How might these manpower projections be affected by unemployment? The 1960 census is quite unrevealing, for it classified only 183,000 people as unemployed. This recorded unemploy-

---

[5] Heavy reliance has been placed on projection II of Benítez and Cabrera (1966), but attention has also been paid to their other figures and to projections in CELADE (1966), Tabah (1968), and unpublished projections of the 1985 labor force by José B. Morelos. These other projections are compatible with our labor force estimates except that Tabah foresees a sharper decline in the rate of population and labor force growth. Preliminary results of the 1970 population census suggest that the rate of population growth may have been below the estimates used here.

ment represented just 1.6% of the labor force, and much of this may have been frictional. [6]

5. Sectoral distribution of the labor force by skill class in 1960 and 1968

For these projections, it is essential to estimate the sectoral distribution of the labor force by skill class in 1960 (the latest year for

Table 2

Labor force distribution by sector and skill class, 1960

(unit: thousands of man-years of skill s)

Sector j	Skill class s					
	1	2	3	4	5	Total
1. Agriculture, livestock, forestry, and fishing	1.73	15.53	35.24	–	6,091.04	6,143.54
2. Mining and quarrying	3.58	3.58	6.95	88.13	–	102.24
3. Petroleum and coal	3.26	4.57	13.05	44.38	–	65.26
4. Food, beverages, tobacco	1.62	3.24	29.73	235.67	–	270.26
5. Textiles, apparel, leather	1.46	4.86	20.41	459.41	–	486.14
6. Wood, furniture, paper, printing	0.82	6.09	14.28	188.88	–	210.07
7. Chemicals, rubber, plastics	3.76	4.54	23.34	45.15	–	76.78
8. Non-metallic mineral products	0.46	0.91	4.56	70.03	–	75.96
9. Basic metals	0.87	1.06	3.91	42.51	–	48.35
10. Machinery	3.72	10.37	41.33	307.14	–	362.56
11. Construction	5.47	12.77	42.62	347.42	–	408.28
12. Electricity	2.14	1.42	13.79	24.09	–	41.44
13. Commerce	1.16	22.13	196.00	839.37	–	1,058.66
14. Transport and communications	1.30	5.22	79.94	270.48	–	356.94
15. Services (including government)	5.65	276.83	389.32	953.73	–	1,625.53
Total	37.00	373.11	914.67	3,916.19	6,091.04	11,332.01

[6] The number of unemployed can be put into further perspective by noting that, of the 11,332,000 people recorded in the labor force by the 1960 census, 562,000 were youths under fifteen, and 456,000 were age seventy or over.

Table 3
Labor force distribution by sector and skill class, 1968
(unit: thousands of man-years of skill s)

Sector j	Skill class s					
	1	2	3	4	5	Total
1. Agriculture	5.41	27.05	62.22	–	7,024.00	7,118.68
2. Mining	3.76	3.76	7.30	92.49	–	107.31
3. Petroleum	4.37	6.11	17.46	59.37	–	87.31
4. Food	2.38	5.10	37.42	295.28	–	340.18
5. Textiles	1.89	6.31	26.50	596.32	–	631.02
6. Wood	1.43	10.61	21.22	253.44	–	286.70
7. Chemicals	5.85	7.04	36.29	70.20	–	119.38
8. Non-metallic	1.05	2.10	8.76	104.84	–	116.75
9. Basic metals	1.52	2.28	7.18	73.47	–	84.45
10. Machinery	18.57	28.37	78.31	491.40	–	616.65
11. Construction	9.16	21.85	73.32	600.63	–	704.96
12. Electricity	3.94	2.58	25.32	44.02	–	75.77
13. Commerce	2.20	30.02	297.30	1,135.01	–	1,464.53
14. Transport	1.82	6.84	102.12	345.11	–	455.89
15. Services	13.65	485.98	581.37	1,289.42	–	2,370.42
Total	77.00	646.00	1,382.00	5,451.00	7,024.00	14,580.00

which census data were available) and in 1968. By combining the 1968 table with output levels for that year and with subsequent rates of change in productivity, we then extrapolate for the labor input coefficients during the following years.

The estimates of the total labor force in each sector in 1960 (table 2) are based on the revised data from the population census together with a hitherto unused source, a systematic expansion of an unpublished 1.225% sample of the census made by El Colegio de México. In almost all cases, these estimates accord well with the disaggregated published findings of the 1950 population census and the 1950–60 trends in output. We believe these to be more accurate than previous sectoral labor force estimates for Mexico.

The allocation of the 1960 labor force among skill classes (table 2) has been accomplished with the help of occupational mix data from the census and census samples supplemented by labor skill mix coefficients for other countries. Sources and methods for these calculations, including the operational definitions of the five skill classes, are available in a separate document. This document also includes an account of the steps by which we moved from the 1960 picture (table 2) to the comparable estimates for 1968 (table 3). [7]

6. Time trends in labor input norms

Tables 2 and 3 together indicate the rate of growth in labor inputs for each sector between 1960 and 1968. By combining these rates with the growth of output, we arrive at the implied changes in average labor productivity shown in table 4. The 1968 labor force was estimated through an indirect process. [8] Rather than suppose that the pre-1968 rates of productivity gain will continue during the following years, it seemed preferable to adopt somewhat subjective estimates. For the three highest skill classes ($s = 1, 2, 3$), the annual gains in productivity σ_{sj} are 1.0, 1.0 and 1.5%, respec-

---

[7] See Donald B. Keesing, 'Derivation of DINAMICO's labor force skill distribution, 1960 and 1968', Appendix A, Memorandum 70–7, July 1970, available upon request to Development Research Center, International Bank for Reconstruction and Development, 1818 H. Street, N.W., Washington, D.C. 20433. – Table 3 (for 1968) was extrapolated from table 2 (for 1960), taking account of analogous coefficients for the U.S.A. and other industrialized countries. Many of the changes in skill-mix reflect intrasectoral shifts in the product mixes caused by declines in the proportion of output originating in subsectors requiring low proportions of skilled labor, as compared to more skill-intensive subsectors. Thus, for example, in sector 6 the output of paper products and publishing has been growing faster than that of wood products and furniture. In section 10, the production of automobiles and machinery has grown faster than garage, repair or blacksmith services. In sector 15, education and medical services have been expanding faster than domestic or laundry services. – In a majority of sectors, by 1960, Mexican skill mixes were comparable to those in more advanced industrial countries. It must be acknowledged that some of the similarities, especially in 1968, are the result of our use of industrial countries' skill mixes as a guide to skill coefficients in Mexico. Regarding similarities among skill coefficients in different countries, see Horowitz et al. (1966) and Keesing (1971).

[8] Computed productivity gains from 1960 to 1968 reflect changes in vintages of capital, the subsector mix and the skill composition of the labor force in each sector. By contrast, our projected rates of disembodied productivity growth (σ_{sj}) are based upon the assumption of no further changes in the skill and subsector composition for individual sectors.

Table 4
Time trends in labor productivity (unit: annual percentage growth rates)

Sector j	Gross output, 1950– 68 [a]	Labor input, 1950– 68 [b]	Implied labor productivity gains			σ_{sj}, projected labor productivity gains after 1968 [b] (skill classes $s = 4, 5$)
			1950– 68	1950– 60	1960– 68	
1. Agriculture	4.7	2.2	2.5	2.6	2.3	2.0 [c]
2. Mining	2.1	1.8	0.3	−0.6	1.4	1.5
3. Petroleum	7.7	6.7	1.0	−1.2	3.7	3.5
4. Food	5.9	3.9	2.0	0.8	3.6	3.5
5. Textiles	5.2	2.7	2.5	1.4	3.9	3.5
6. Wood	5.7	4.2	1.5	0.1	3.3	3.5
7. Chemicals	10.2	7.3	2.9	2.4	3.6	3.5
8. Non-metallic	8.8	4.7	4.1	3.9	4.3	3.5
9. Basic metals	11.5	7.5	4.0	4.3	3.7	3.5
10. Machinery	11.3	8.9	2.4	−0.4	5.8	3.5
11. Construction	7.9	6.6	1.3	1.2	1.4	1.5
12. Electricity	12.0	6.4	5.6	6.6	4.7	3.5
13. Commerce	6.3	3.6	2.7	2.8	2.6	3.5
14. Transportation	5.1	4.4	0.7	−0.8	2.7	1.5
15. Services	6.2	4.8	1.4	0.4	2.7	1.5

[a] Source of gross output, 1950 and 1960: Banco de México (1969, Table 124). Source of gross output, 1968: below, chapter II.2, table 3. Source of labor input, 1950: Secretaría de Economía (1955). 'Insufficiently specified workers' in 1950 have been assigned one-third to commerce and one-third to services. The others were omitted from the computation. Source of labor input, 1960 and 1968: this chapter, tables 2 and 3.
[b] For skill classes 1–3, $\sigma_{1j} = \sigma_{2j} = 1.0\%$, and $\sigma_{3j} = 1.5\%$ for all sectors j.
[c] Within agriculture, additional labor productivity gains are determined endogenously.

tively, in all sectors. For unskilled labor ($s = 4, 5$) — that is, for 85% of the 1968 labor force — the annual productivity gains σ_{sj} range from 1.5% (in mining, construction, transportation and services) up to 3.5% (in manufacturing, electricity and commerce). In most sectors, the projected gains are higher than those experienced over the period 1950–68. In this way, we have attempted to avoid overestimating the employment opportunities for unskilled labor outside agriculture.

Within agriculture, exogenous unskilled labor productivity gains are taken at 2.0% per year. In addition, endogenous productivity gains are available through capital-labor substitution activities in that sector.

Formally, the labor input coefficients l_{sj}^t are calculated as follows. Recall that 1968 corresponds to year 0, and that three years lie between each of the representative points of time t:

$$
\begin{bmatrix}
\text{input} \\
\text{coefficient} \\
\text{for labor} \\
\text{skill } s, \\
\text{sector } j, \\
\text{year } t
\end{bmatrix}
=
\begin{bmatrix}
\text{time trend} \\
\text{factor for} \\
\text{reduction of} \\
\text{labor input } s, \\
\text{sector } j; \\
\text{from table 4}
\end{bmatrix}
\cdot
\begin{bmatrix}
\text{total number} \\
\text{with skill } s \\
\text{employed in} \\
\text{sector } j \\
\text{during 1968} \\
(\text{year } t = 0); \\
\text{from table 3}
\end{bmatrix}
\div
\begin{bmatrix}
\text{gross output,} \\
\text{sector } j, \\
\text{1968; from} \\
\text{table 3,} \\
\text{ch.II.2 below}
\end{bmatrix}
$$

$$
l_{sj}^t = \left[\ \left(\frac{1}{1+\sigma_{sj}}\right)^{3t}\ \right] \cdot \left[\ L_{sj}^0\ \right] \div \left[\ X_j^0\ \right]
$$

$(s = 1, ..., 5; j = 1, ..., 15; t = 1, ..., 7)$

Since these labor demand coefficients are derived from the identical table used for estimating the supply of skills, any biases are likely to be offsetting. If for example, the expansion of class 3 labor supply has been overstated between 1960 and 1968, then the input requirements for class 3 labor in subsequent years has been similarly overstated. This feature reduces the sensitivity to errors in extrapolation during the years since the census of 1960.

7. Capital-labor substitution in agriculture

DINAMICO includes a non-negative activity labelled KA^t. This denotes the amount of capital added to agriculture during year t in substitution for unskilled labor. The marginal rate of substitution between capital and labor has been estimated through the following line of reasoning: First, make the neoclassical assumption that the 1960 wage of 2,400 pesos *was* equal to the marginal productivity of an unskilled agricultural laborer. Next, suppose that capital has an annual marginal product $r = 16\%$ per year in agriculture.

Then, for 1960 it may be computed that the marginal rate of substitution = (2,400 pesos per man-year) ÷ (r per year) = 2,400 ÷ 0.16 = 15,000 pesos of capital per man.

For the years subsequent to 1960, it is supposed that the marginal productivity of capital remains constant, and that agricultural labor's productivity rises at 2.0% per year. (From table 4, recall that σ_{51} = 2.0%.) At a point y years after 1960, therefore, the amount of capital required to release one man is 15 $(1.02)^y$ thousands of pesos.

Clearly, this method overstates the elasticity of substitution between capital and labor. This is to be viewed as a first-order Taylor's series approximation to the production function. Once a detailed model becomes available for the agricultural sector [9], it should be possible to quantify the distortions introduced into DINAMICO through assuming a constant marginal rate of substitution. Here is an instance in which there can be a two-way flow of information between separately constructed models, despite the absence of a formal computational link.

8. Education activities; von Neumann equilibrium wage structure

To expand labor supplies beyond the numbers already specified exogenously in table 1, there are endogenous activities for human capital formation. ED_s^t denotes the education (human capital formation) activity for producing labor of skill s that *first* becomes available in period t. There is one such activity for each of the three highest labor skills (s = 1, 2, 3).

In estimating the coefficients for these activities, classroom space and other physical inputs have been neglected. It is supposed that the principal input is the opportunity cost of labor time in the form of student's earnings foregone plus the time of teachers and auxiliary educational personnel. No explicit budgetary constraint is placed upon educational expenditures. The three activi-

---

[9] Editor's note: These lines were written before the DINAMICO–CHAC linkage experiments described below, in chapter IV.6.

ties represent a greatly simplified version of Mexico's processes for human capital formation:

Higher technical education (ED_1^t) requires six years (two periods). This activity produces class 1 labor, plus a byproduct of class 2 labor, through inputs of class 1 and 2 labor (as teachers) and class 3 labor (as students). Because of the two-period lag, the activity is available only for $t = 3, 4, ..., 7$.

Other professional education (ED_2^t) produces class 2 labor in three years (one time period) with inputs of class 1 and 2 labor (as teachers) and class 3 labor (as students).

Secondary education (ED_3^t) produces class 3 labor in three years with inputs of class 2 and 3 labor (as teachers and auxiliary

Table 5
Coefficients for human capital formation activities

Constraint [a]	Unknown [b]		
	ED_1^t ($t = 3, 4, ..., 7$)	ED_2^t ($t = 2, 3, ..., 7$)	ED_3^t ($t = 2, 3, ..., 7$)
D1, $t-2$	−0.17		
D2, $t-2$	−0.09		
D3, $t-2$	−2.00		
D4, $t-2$			
D1, $t-1$	−0.14	−0.02	
D2, $t-1$		−0.18	−0.16
D3, $t-1$	−1.40	−1.90	−0.04
D4, $t-1$			−2.00
D1, t	1.00		
D2, t	0.30	1.00	
D3, t	−1.30	−1.00	1.00
D4, t			−1.00
D1, $t+1$	1.00		
D2, $t+1$	0.30	1.00	
D3, $t+1$	−1.30	−1.00	1.00
D4, $t+1$			−1.00
	⋮	⋮	⋮

[a] Constraint Ds, t refers to the total supply of labor of class s at time period t.

[b] Activity ED_s^t refers to the inputs and outputs required to produce one person with skill s, *first* available as a member of the labor force in period t.

personnel) and class 4 labor (as students). Given the growing numbers of those who have completed primary education, it is reasonable to suppose that there will be no difficulty in finding qualified candidates for secondary education from within the class 4 (unskilled urban) work force.

The coefficients of the education activities are given in table 5. Consider, for example, column ED_3^t. These coefficients refer to the education of one person in skill category 3. During period $t-1$, because of attrition, this educational process requires inputs of two students of skill 4. Also required during that period are teachers and auxiliary personnel: 0.16 persons of skill 2 and 0.04 of skill 3. During periods t, $t+1$ and thereafter, this process makes available one additional person of skill 3, and it reduces the availability of unskilled labor (category 4) by one person. Faculty-student ratios and attrition ratios have been estimated through Mexican educational statistics for the years 1964 through 1968. The three-year post-secondary training cycle for 'other professional and technical personnel' is a rough approximation to a weighted average for this labor class as a whole.

Once a person has entered skill category s in period t, he remains in that category during all future time periods ($t+1$, $t+2$, ...). These activities include no allowance for labor force attrition through death and other natural causes. Conversely, no allowance is made for learning by doing, a factor which more than offsets the natural attrition of the labor force during the years immediately following formal education.

As an independent check upon the education norms shown in table 5, we have calculated the von Neumann prices — assuming that the rate of return on human capital is a datum, and that the relative wage rates for the different skills are to remain constant over the indefinite future. Denote the present value price of skill s at time t by p_s^t, and take skill 4 at time 0 as the numéraire. Then $p_4^0 = 1.0$. The unknowns are p_1^0, p_2^0 and p_3^0. All other labor prices may be calculated as follows: $p_s^t = \beta^t\, p_s^0$, where β is the three-year present value factor for the rate of return on human capital. To solve for the three unknowns p_s^0, there are three simultaneous equations to ensure that the discounted cost of producing each skill will just be matched by the discounted benefits. E.g., for skill 3, recalling that $p_4^0 = 1.0$:

discounted benefits   discounted costs

$$\underbrace{\sum_{t=0}^{\infty} \beta^t p_3^0}_{} = \underbrace{\beta^{-1}[0.16p_2^0 + 0.04p_3^0 + 2.00] + \sum_{t=0}^{\infty} \beta^t}_{}.$$

In order to solve the three simultaneous equations, a value must be specified for the annual rate of return on human capital. Then, because β denotes a three-year present value factor, $\beta = (1/1 + r)^3$. For $r = 8$, 12, ..., 28% per year, the resulting structure of efficiency prices is shown in table 6. [10] The higher the rate of return on human capital, the greater is the inequality of wage income. When $r = 16\%$ per year (which would mean that the rates of return on human and physical capital are similar), the skill differentials are of the same order of magnitude as prevailed in Mexico during the 1960's.

Table 6

Equilibrium relative wages for skill classes 1–4 (von Neumann model of human capital formation with skill class 4 as numéraire)

Exogenously specified rate of return on human capital, r (% per year)	8	12	16	20	24	28	Rough estimate of 1960 annual wages (relative to skill class.4)
Three-year present value factor for human capital, $\beta = [1/(1+r)]^3$	0.7938	0.7117	0.6406	0.5787	0.5244	0.4768	
Wages for skill class 1, p_1^0	3.42	6.28	11.88	24.17	58.14	238.67	10.00
Wages for skill class 2, p_2^0	2.59	4.08	6.51	10.94	21.08	65.83	4.17
Wages for skill class 3, p_3^0	1.64	2.11	2.77	3.84	6.09	15.43	3.00
Wages for skill class 4, p_4^0	1.00	1.00	1.00	1.00	1.00	1.00	1.00

[10] For $r \geqslant 30\%$, there is no nonnegative set of labor prices that will satisfy the three conditions ensuring equality between discounted costs and benefits.

72   D.B. Keesing, A.S. Manne, Manpower projections

9. Substitution among skill classes

Direct substitution between skills is incorporated through labor upgrading and downgrading activities. It is supposed that upgrading of labor from class 5 to class 4, and downgrading of labor to the next lowest skill class (i.e., from class 1 to 2, 2 to 3, etc.) can take place in every time period. The use of upgrading activities to augment class 1, 2 and 3 labor is included only in the first two time periods (1971 and 1974). Subsequently, further skill requirements are to be met through education.

Table 7 summarizes the coefficients assigned to these activities. Downward substitution is represented by nonnegative linear programming unknowns LD_s^t ($s = 1, 2, 3, 4$), defined as the amount of labor downgraded from skill category s to $s + 1$ during period t. Thus, class 1 labor is qualified to do the job of class 2 labor, class 2 of class 3, etc.

Table 7
Coefficients for skill substitution activities ($t = 1, 2, ..., 7$)

Con-straint	Unit of measurement	Labor downgrading activities				Labor upgrading activities			
		LD_1^t	LD_2^t	LD_3^t	LD_4^t	UL_1^t [a]	UL_2^t [a]	UL_3^t [a]	UL_4^t
D 1t	millions of man-years	−1.0				1.0			
D 2t	millions of man-years	1.0	−1.0			−1.0	1.0		
D 3t	millions of man-years		1.0	−1.0		−0.5	−1.0	1.0	
D 4t	millions of man-years			1.0	−1.0	−4.0	−2.0	−3.0	1.0
D 5t	millions of man-years				1.0				−1.0
A15t [b]	billions of 1960 pesos								−2.4

Skill categories:	Rough estimate of 1960 annual wage (thousands of pesos per man-year)
s = 1. Engineers and scientists	72.0
s = 2. Other professional and technical workers	30.0
s = 3. Administrative and clerical workers	21.6
s = 4. Manual and sales workers outside agriculture	7.2
s = 5. Unskilled agricultural workers	2.4

[a] Activities UL_s^t ($s = 1, 2, 3$) are intended to represent short-term substitution options for the three top skill classes, hence are restricted to the early time periods ($t = 1, 2$).
[b] Definition of sector 15: services, including government.

In the reverse direction, the transfer of labor from class 5 to class 4 would correspond to migration out of agriculture. Some migration would occur even with a zero differential between urban and rural wages. To transfer more labor out of agriculture (beyond what would occur with a zero wage differential), and to qualify this labor for work in the non-agricultural sectors of the economy, we have postulated the labor upgrading activity UL_4^t. Through this activity, one agricultural worker may be converted into an unskilled nonagricultural worker in any time period at a recurring annual cost of 2,400 pesos' worth of urban services (housing, health, education, banking, cinema, etc.). [11] Here the 2,400 pesos' worth of services is regarded as an interindustry input associated with the conversion of one type of labor into another. No direct utility is ascribed to this transformation cost. By excluding these services from our definition of aggregate consumption, we depart from national income accounting conventions.

In the activities that provide short-run substitution for the three highest skill categories (UL_s^t, where $s = 1, 2, 3$ and $t = 1, 2$), all inputs consist of lower-valued labor skills. The coefficients can be interpreted to mean that personnel from the next lower skill class may be substituted for properly trained personnel, but that the consequence will be a fall in the productivity of the rest of the labor force. For example, the coefficients of activity UL_1^t imply that if an engineer must be temporarily replaced with a technician, there will be serious inefficiencies in the rest of the production process, and that these inefficiencies will generate a demand for an additional half a clerical worker together with four manual workers. The coefficients of activity UL_2^t mean that if a professional such as a teacher or doctor is replaced by an improperly trained class 3 substitute, the economy will lose the service of two class 4 workers as a direct or indirect result.

Together, the activities summarized in table 7 help to set upper and lower limits on the ratios between the efficiency prices of

[11] The figure of 2,400 pesos was estimated as half of the differential between urban and rural wages in 1960. Rather than suppose that this entire differential is spent on services, it would have been somewhat more accurate to distribute this amount among other sectors as well.

each class of labor. For example, the activities LD_3^t and UL_3^t together imply that in the first two periods, the efficiency wage of clerical workers must lie somewhere in the range of one and three times that of manual workers. After the first two periods, no upgrading activities are available for class 3 labor, but the downgrading activities ensure that the efficiency wage of skill 3 cannot fall below that of skill 4.

10. Results

Tables 8 and 9 contain estimates of the sources and uses of skilled manpower through 1980. These projections are interdependent, and have been derived through DINAMICO's general equilibrium

Table 8
Labor force distribution by sector and skill class, 1980
(unit: thousands of persons)

Sector j	Skill class s					
	1	2	3	4	5	Total
1. Agriculture	8	40	87	–	6,765 [a]	6,900
2. Mining	6	6	10	131	–	153
3. Petroleum	9	12	33	90	–	144
4. Food	4	10	72	452	–	538
5. Textiles	4	14	54	953	–	1,025
6. Wood	3	22	41	385	–	451
7. Chemicals	16	19	93	142	–	270
8. Non-metallic	3	5	20	194	–	222
9. Basic metals	5	7	21	167	–	200
10. Machinery	61	92	241	1,195	–	1,589
11. Construction	18	43	135	1,108	–	1,304
12. Electricity	12	8	74	102	–	196
13. Commerce	4	59	545	1,645	–	2,253
14. Transportation	3	12	164	553	–	732
15. Services	27	961	1,083	2,404	–	4,475
Total	183	1,310	2,673	9,521	6,765	20,452

[a] Employment requirements *after* allowing for capital-labor substitution activities, KA^t. Their net effect is to release 2,464,000 unskilled agricultural workers.

structure. The manpower requirements by sector of use in 1980 (table 8) have been determined simultaneously with the growth of output. High growth rates are projected in sectors such as machinery, chemicals, basic metals, and electricity. These fast-growing industries require a higher proportion of scientists and engineers than do the slow-growing ones. As a result, the total requirements

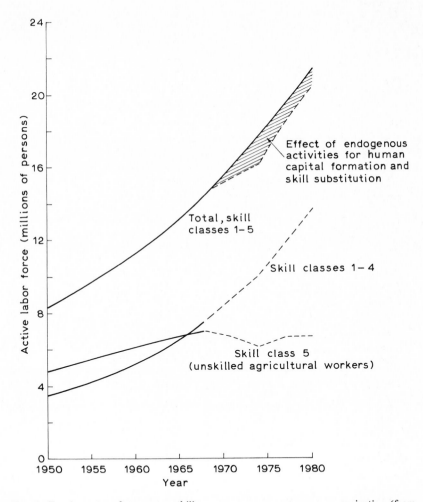

Fig. 1. Employment of manpower skills. ———: exogenous manpower projection (from table 1); - - - - -: endogenous labour requirements (from table 9).

Table 9
Labor availability and requirements

Con-straints Dst	Exogenous manpower projection (from table 1)	Human capital formation										
		ED_1^3	ED_1^4	ED_1^5	ED_1^6	ED_2^3	ED_2^4	ED_2^5	ED_3^2	ED_3^3	ED_3^4	ED_3^5
D11	97	−3										
D12	117	−2	−3			−2						
D13	137	16	−2	−4			−1					
D14	157	16	19	−3	−4			−2				
D21	791	−1							−26			
D22	936		−2			−14				−51		
D23	1081	5		−2		80	−12				−52	
D24	1226	5	6		−2	80	69	−17				−57
D31	1623	−33							−6			
D32	1864	−23	−37			−153			160	−13		
D33	2105	−21	−26	−42		−80	−132		160	316	−13	
D34	2346	−21	−25	−29	−50	−80	−69	−186	160	316	325	−14
D41	6125								−319			
D42	6906								−160	−633		
D43	7827								−160	−316	−649	
D44	8966								−160	−316	−325	−709
D51	7389											
D52	7841											
D53	8321											
D54	8830											
Totals												
$t = 1$	16025	−37							−351			
$t = 2$	17664	−25	−42			−169				−697		
$t = 3$	19471		−28	−48			−145				−714	
$t = 4$	21525			−32	−56			−205				−780

for scientists and engineers increase at an average annual rate of 7.5% between 1968 and 1980.

Figure 1 summarizes the employment requirements at selected

unit: thousands of persons)

	UL_1^1	UL_1^2	UL_2^1	UL_2^2	UL_3^1	UL_3^2	UL_4^1	UL_4^2	UL_4^3	UL_4^4	Subtotal	Labor requirements RQL_s^t
	1										−2	95
		7									0	117
											9	146
											26	183
	−1		11								−17	774
		−7		64							−10	926
											19	1100
											84	1310
	−1		−11		61						10	1633
		−3		−64		186					53	1917
											162	2267
											327	2673
	−5		−22		−182		680				152	6277
		−27		−127		−558		1750			245	7151
									1588		463	8290
										2065	555	9521
							−680				−680	6709
								−1750			−1750	6091
									−1588		−1588	6733
										−2065	−2065	6765
	−6		−22		−121						−537	15488
		−30		−127		−372					−1462	16202
											−935	18536
											−1073	20452

Labor upgrading *(spanning the UL columns)*

points of time. According to this figure, the requirements for classes 1–4 will continue to grow more rapidly than for unskilled agricultural labor. Through capital-labor substitution, enough unskilled workers will be released so that the absolute numbers engaged in agriculture will remain close to the 1968 level. [12] With this shift in the skill-mix, there should be increased opportunities for individuals to move away from low-paying employment in traditional agriculture.

According to table 9, the requirements for labor class 3 will grow at the rate of 5.6% per year. This result checks roughly with the growth of the gross domestic product (6.9% per year), less the assumed rate of productivity growth for these workers (1.5%). A 5.6% growth rate would also be consistent with the 1950–68 trend for skill class 3.

Table 9 traces the alternative sources of skilled manpower at four representative points in time from 1971 through 1980. The leftmost column denotes the labor skills available if there were *no* increase in the rate of skill formation above that estimated for the years 1968–71. The middle columns indicate how the skill-mix may be upgraded beyond this level through endogenous activities for human capital formation and for skill substitution. (These results were calculated by multiplying the optimal activity levels against the skill formation and substitution coefficients of tables 5 and 7.) Labor inputs are indicated by negative quantities and outputs by positive quantities. The next to last column shows the net change resulting from these endogenous activities. Finally, the rightmost column matches with the manpower requirements already given in table 8.

At the bottom of Table 9, there appear four rows labeled 'Totals' – one for each of four representative points of time from 1971 onward. These rows explain the shaded area that appears in figure 1. Each row indicates the number of workers whose services

---

[12] Caution: There is a systematic error of specification in DINAMICO – the absence of capital-labor substitution activities outside agriculture. By supposing that there are rigid capital-labor ratios in the non-agricultural sector, any errors in estimating the manpower requirements elsewhere will lead to offsetting errors in agriculture's requirements for capital-labor substitution. With 14 million people employed outside agriculture in 1980, even a 1% error in estimating these requirements would lead to an error of 140,000 workers in the activity levels for rural-urban transfer and for capital-labor substitution in agriculture. The direction of this error could be either positive or negative.

are absorbed through the endogenous activities ED_s^t and UL_s^t. After period $t = 2$ (1974), all of these losses are associated with the addition of students and teachers to the educational pipeline. [13] In this way, teachers' salaries and students' foregone earnings are counted among the costs of human capital formation. This procedure may have led us to exaggerate the demand for labor within the Mexican economy. Suppose that the manpower requirements of the educational system could be met through the school-age population alone, with no reduction in the manpower available for employment elsewhere. On this extreme assumption — in effect, a zero opportunity cost for students' earnings foregone — the bottommost row shows that DINAMICO would have underestimated the total labor force available by 1,073,000 persons in 1980. In turn, this would lead to an overestimate of the requirements for capital-labor substitution in agriculture (activities KA^t) and an overestimate of the rural-urban labor transfer (activities UL_4^t).

Positive intensities are associated with each of the rural-urban transfer activities. These magnitudes are substantially larger than any possible errors in the numbers absorbed through increases in the educational pipeline. For example, $UL_4^4 = 2,065$. By 1980, therefore, the cumulative number who had transferred from rural to urban employment would be 2,065,000 persons. This number would be in addition to those whom we assume would have migrated to the cities even in the absence of wage differentials.

According to table 9, it is optimal to operate virtually every one of the human capital formation activities ED_s^t at a positive intensity. This means upgrading the skill-mix by amounts exceeding the 1968–71 increment, and implies further increases in the capacity

[13] It is evident that some distortions are occurring during period $t = 2$ (1974). In that year, because of the skill substitution activities UL_s^2, we may have overstated the requirements for rural-urban transfer by $30 + 127 + 372 = 529,000$ workers. — *Additional note*: After these lines had been written, DINAMICO was rerun to allow both for the educational pipeline and also for a 10% rate of unrecorded unemployment in skill classes 1–4. This modification eliminated most of the distortions shown at the bottom of table 9 and in the shaded area of figure 1. It reduced but did not eliminate the need for capital-labor substitution in agriculture. For 1980, the unskilled agricultural work force became 7.5 in place of the 6.765 million persons shown in table 8.

and output of middle and higher education. Consider, for example, skill class 3. The 1968–71 increment is estimated at 241,000 persons. An equal increment is projected exogenously between 1971 and 1974. Since activity $ED_3^2 = 160$, the total 1971–74 increase would be 241 + 160 = 401,000 persons.

Viewed as projections of the economically justified demand for middle and higher education, the ED_s^t activities suffer from a serious bias. Quite apart from errors in projecting requirements for skilled occupations, this model disregards the benefits of upgrading the training of the labor force *within* each skill class. As a result, the economically justified demand for education is probably underestimated.

During the 1960–68 period, Mexico upgraded the education of its population so rapidly that the labor force became significantly more educated within each skill class. Side calculations suggest that the mean educational attainments of increments to the labor force during these years must have been about two grades higher than the average schooling within the identical skill class in 1960. Upgrading probably contributes to 'disembodied' productivity growth – here taken to be exogenous. This specification error cannot easily be rectified. Mechanisms that link schooling and productivity growth are notoriously difficult to prove, let alone measure. Our calculation therefore excludes all demands for middle and higher education beyond that necessary to supply manpower trained to the same standards as in the 1960's.

Taking into account these probable biases, DINAMICO's results are broadly consistent with the planned rates of expansion of middle and higher education. On this basis, Mexico does not face serious quantitative bottlenecks involving major classes of skilled manpower. If postprimary education continues to expand at annual rates exceeding 7%, this need not lead to a surplus of skilled labor, but rather to a continuing increase in the educational standards for each job category.

References

Adelman, I., 'A linear programming model of educational planning: a case study of Argentina', in: *The theory and design of economic development,* edited by I. Adelman and E. Thorbecke. Baltimore, Johns Hopkins Press, 1966.

Banco de México, *Cuadro de insumo producto de México, 1960.* December 1966.

Banco de México, *Encuesta soble ingresos y gastos familiares en México – 1963.* 1966.

Banco de México, Departamento de Estudios Económicos, *Cuentas nacionales y acervos de capital, consolidadas y por tipo de actividad económica, 1950–1967.* June 1969.

Banco de México, Departamento de Estudios Económicos, *La dualidad de la agricultura Mexicana.* Study directed by Saúl Trejo. 1970(a).

Banco de México, Departamento de Estudios Económicos, *Proyecciones de la económia Mexicana para 1976.* 1970(b).

Banco de México, Departamento de Investigaciones Industriales, *El empleo de personal técnico en la industria de transformación.* 1959.

Banco de México, Oficina de Recursos Humanos, y Secretaria Técnica de la Comisión Nacional de Planeamiento Integral de Educación, *Información estadística.* March 1968.

Barraza, L., 'La dualidad en la agricultura Mexicana', *Revista del Colegio de Economistas de México,* 1969.

Benítez Zenteno, R., *Análisis demográfico de México.* Universidad Nacional de México, Instituto de Investigaciones Sociales, 1961.

Benítez Zenteno, R., and G. Cabrera Acevedo, *Proyecciones de la población de México, 1960–80.* Banco de México, Depto. de Investigaciones Industriales, Oficina de Recursos Humanos, 1966.

Bowles, S., *Planning educational systems for economic growth.* Cambridge, Mass., Harvard University Press, 1969.

Bruno, M., 'A programming model for Israel', in: *The theory and design of economic development,* edited by I. Adelman and E. Thorbecke. Baltimore, Johns Hopkins Press 1966.

Carnoy, M., 'Earnings and schooling in Mexico', *Economic Development and Cultural Change.* 15, no. 4 (July 1967) 408–419.

Carnoy, M., 'Rates of return to schooling in Latin America', *Journal of Human Resources* 2, no. 3, (Summer 1967) 359–374.

Centro Latinoamericano de Demografía (CELADE), *Boletín demográfico,* año 2, vol. III, January 1969. (Includes projections of Mexico's population and its age structure through 1985.)

Davis, R.G., *Scientific, engineering and technical education in Mexico.* Education and World Affairs Occasional Report No. 3. New York, April 1967.

Eckstein, S., *El marco macroeconomico del problema agrario Mexicano.* Centro de Investigaciones Agrarias, 1970.

El Colegio de México, Centro de Estudios Económicos y Demográficos, *Estudios de problación y fuerza de trabajo, con base en una muestra del censo de población en 1960.* México, D.F., June 1966. See also portion extracted as 'Informe' in *Demografía y Economía* 2, no. 2 (1968).

Frank, C.R., Jr., 'Urban unemployment and economic growth in Africa', *Oxford Economic Papers.* 20, no. 2 (July 1968).

Horowitz, M., M. Zymelman and I.L. Herrnstadt, *Manpower requirements for planning: an international comparison approach,* 2 vols. Boston, Northeastern University, December, 1966.

Isbister, J., *The growth of employment in Mexico.* Unpublished dissertation, Princeton University, 1969.

Isbister, J., 'Urban employment and wages in a developing economy: the case of Mexico'. Unpublished draft, University of California at Santa Cruz, December 1969.

Keesing, D.B., 'Different countries' labor skill coefficients and the skill intensity of international trade flows', *Journal of International Economics,* November 1971.

Keesing, D.B., 'Structural change early in development: Mexico's changing industrial and occupational structure from 1895 to 1950', *Journal of Economic History* 29, no. 4 (December 1969) 716–738.

Lajous Vargas, A., *Aspectos de la educación superior y el empleo de profesionistas en México, 1959–1967.* Thesis presented to Escuela Nacional de Economía, Universidad Nacional Autónoma de México, 1967.

Lajous Vargas, A., 'Aspectos regionales de la expansión de la educación superior en México, 1959–1967', *Demografía y Economía* 2, no. 3 (1968) 404–427.

Lamartine Yates, P., *El desarrollo regional de México.* Banco de México, Depto. de Investigaciones Industriales, 1961.

Myers, C.N., *Education and national development in Mexico.* Industrial Relations Section, Department of Economics, Princeton University, Princeton, N.J., 1965.

Navarrete, I.M. de, *La distribución del ingreso y el desarrollo económico de México.* Instituto de Investigaciones Económicas, Escuela Nacional de Economía, Universidad Nacional Autónoma de México, 1960.

Oshima, H.T., 'Growth and unemployment in post war Asia', in: *Structure and development in Asian economies.* Tokyo, Japan Economic Research Center, December 1968.

Reynolds, C.W., *The Mexican economy: twentieth century structure and growth.* New Haven, Yale University Press, 1970.

Secretaría de Educación Pública, Dirección General de Enseñanza Superior y Investigación Cientifica, *Concentración estadistica del sistema educativo, México 1968.* September 1960.

Secretaría de Economía, Dirección General de Estadística, *Séptimo censo general de población, 6 de Junio de 1950, Resumen General.* 1953.

Secretaría de Economía, Dirección General de Estadística, *Séptimo censo general de población 1950.* Parte Especial 1955.

Secretaría de Industria y Comercio, Dirección General de Estadística, *Anuario estadístico de los Estados Unidos Mexicanos.* various editions through 1966–67.

Secretaría de Industria y Comercio, Dirección General de Estadística, *IV censos agrícola-ganadero y ejidal 1960, resumen general.* 1965.

Secretaría de Industria y Comercio, Dirección General de Estadística, *VIII censo general de población, 1960. Población económicamente activa (rectificación a los cuadros 25, 26 y 27 del resumen general ya publicado).* 1964.

Secretaría de Industria y Comercio, Dirección General de Estadística, *VIII censo general de población, 1960, resumen general.* 1962.

Secretaría de Industria y Comercio, Dirección General de Estadística, *VIII censo industrial 1966, datos de 1965, resumen general.* 1967.

Secretaría de Industria y Comercio, Dirección General de Muestreo, *La población económicamente activa de México en Junio de 1964,* 3 vols. 1964.

Solís, L., *La realidad económica Mexicana: retrovisión y perspectivas.* México, Siglo XXI Editores, 1970.

Strassman, W.P., *Technological change and economic development, the manufacturing experience of Mexico and Puerto Rico.* Ithaca, N.Y., Cornell University Press, 1968.

Tabah, L., 'Proyecciones de población activa a través de representaciones matriciales', *Demografía y Economía* 2, no. 2 (1968). 205–240.

Thorbecke, E., 'Unemployment and underemployment in the developing world'. Paper presented to Columbia University Conference on International Economic Development, Williamsburg, Virginia and New York, February 15–21, 1970.

Todaro, M.P., 'An analysis of industrialization, employment and unemployment in less developed countries', *Yale Economic Essays,* Fall 1968.

Unikel, L., 'El proceso de urbanización en México: distribución y crecimiento de la población urbana', *Demografía y Economia* 2, no. 2 (1968) 139–182.

United Nations, 'Income distribution in Latin America', *Economic Bulletin for Latin America,* 12 (October 1967) 38–60.

U.S. Department of Commerce, *Census of population 1960.* Special Reports on *Occupation by industry*, and *Residence overseas.*

Universidad Nacional Autónoma de México (UNAM), *Anuario estadístico 1959.* 1960.

Urquidi, V.L., and A. Lajous Vargas, *Educación superior, ciencia y tecnología en el desarrollo económico de México.* México, D.F., El Colegio de México, 1967.

Wilkie, J.W., *The Mexican revolution: federal expenditures and social change since 1910.* Berkeley and Los Angeles, University of California Press, 1967.

II.2. NUMERICAL DATA FOR MULTI-SECTOR PLANNING

Yves FRANCHET, Richard A. INMAN and Alan S. MANNE *

1. Data sources

This describes the basic data that have been employed in DINAMI-CO. These data have been derived from internal working papers and from five documents produced by Banco de México, Departamento de Estudios Económicos. For convenience, the five source documents will be abbreviated hereafter as follows:

IP = *Cuadro de Insumo Producto de México, 1960,* December 1966

AJ = *Ajuste del Modelo Sectorial,* by J. Sandee, September 1967

CN = *Cuentas Nacionales y Acervos de Capital, 1950–1967,* June 1969

PRO = *Proyecciones de la Economía Mexicana par 1976,* 1969

IA = *Informe Anual, 1969,* 1970.

In constructing coefficients for DINAMICO, we have followed the official estimates of the national accounts – as these estimates stood during 1971. During that year, the official time series was

* The authors are indebted to Lic. Leopoldo Solís for having provided access to the resources of the Departamento de Estudios Económicos, Banco de México. Lic. Antonio Suárez McAuliffe supplied data that have been utilized in this report. For participating in various phases of this work, thanks also go to Lic. Alfredo Santos Arenas, Lic. Javier Cortés, Lic. Benjamín Gallegos, and Lic. Juan Manuel Galarza (Banco de México), to Ings. Guillermo Fernández de la Garza and José Alberto Valencia (Comisión Federal de Electricidad), Mr. Hans Bergendorff (International Bank for Reconstruction and Development), and to Ing. Enrique Novelo Berrón (Stanford University).

once more undergoing a revision. Hopefully, during the course of this revision, an improved data base will be developed. Meanwhile – despite known inconsistencies and biases – we have had to work with the existing material. The reader is urged to recall that the quality of these data is uneven, and that much caution must be exercised in interpreting long-term projections based upon them.

It is not easy to distinguish between those aberrations of DI-NAMICO that stem from defects in the economic formulation and those that stem from the basic data themselves. Below, for example, it will be seen that for the census year of 1960, plausible values are obtained for the aggregate returns imputed to capital and labor. Among individual sectors, however, there are wide variations in the rates of return imputed to capital. These variations could stem from wage differences between sectors, from errors in the historical estimates of the value added by the 'service' sector, or from errors in estimating the commerce and transport margins between producers' and market prices.

Table 1 identifies the 15-sector classification scheme adopted here. This table also provides a key for aggregating the 45-sector

Table 1
Identification of sectors

Sectors 1–15	Key to aggregation from 45-order matrix
1. Agriculture, livestock, forestry, and fishing	1–4
2. Mining and quarrying	5, 6
3. Production and refining of petroleum and coal products	7
4. Food, beverages and tobacco	8–12
5. Textiles, apparel and leather products	13–15, 19
6. Wood, furniture, paper and printing	16–18
7. Chemicals, rubber and plastic products	20–27
8. Non-metallic mineral products	28
9. Basic metals	29
10. Machinery	30–35
11. Construction	36
12. Electricity	37
13. Commerce	41
14. Transport and communications	39, 40
15. Services (including government)	38, 42–45

classification that is also employed in Mexican national accounts and input-output matrices. For six major sectors, including those three that appear explicitly within the process analysis model of the energy sector, it will be noted that there is no difference between the 15- and the 45-sector classification. Regardless of which of these two levels of aggregation is adopted, it is doubtful that one could employ the resulting model for determining the details of comparative advantage. Given the aggregation and the inconsistencies in the national accounts, one cannot expect to be safe in concluding, for example, that it is preferable to expand the exports of tourism rather than 'basic metals'. From DINAMICO, one can hope for little more than consistency checks upon demand targets and for shadow prices to be applied within more detailed models for sectoral and project decisions. This is the rationale for multi-level planning.

2. Current account transactions

A 45-sector interindustry transactions matrix is available for the census year, 1960. Also available is a 15-sector aggregation of this matrix. (See documents IP and AJ, respectively.) For consistency with the most recently revised estimates of the national accounts (documents CN and IA), we have made a number of adjustments to the matrix shown in document AJ, table NM4. The adjusted transactions table is reproduced here as table 2. This is the statistical base for all subsequent projections of input-output coefficients in 1960 *producers'* prices.

Note that table 2 contains 15 columns and 15 rows for domestic interindustry transactions. The next three rows are: (16) imports [1], (17) errors and omissions, and (18) value added. Columns 16–21 refer to the various components of final demand. The

---

[1] In constructing Mexican input-output matrices, it has been customary to regard all imports as 'non-competitive', and to attribute them to their sector of destination rather than sector of origin. This practice – although a satisfactory shortcut for balance-of-payments projections – makes it quite difficult to trace out the domestic implications of alternative rates of import substitution.

Table 2
Interindustry transactions, 1960

(A) Intermediate demands

Sector of origin	Sector of destination					
	Agri-culture	Mining	Petrol-eum	Food	Textiles	Wood
	1	2	3	4	5	6
1. Agriculture	2.028	0.014	0.001	8.049	1.091	0.521
2. Mining	0.001	1.007	0.128	0.025	0.004	0.008
3. Petroleum	0.621	0.154	2.944	0.445	0.185	0.097
4. Food	1.660	0.012	0.011	4.697	0.054	0.033
5. Textiles	0.522	0.012	0.015	0.094	2.565	0.038
6. Wood	0.123	0.035	0.074	0.438	0.100	1.038
7. Chemicals	0.741	0.099	0.054	0.134	0.661	0.134
8. Non-metallic	0.003	0.012	0.007	0.252	0.008	0.013
9. Basic metals	0.048	0.068	0.025	0.144	0.058	0.039
10. Machinery	0.224	0.050	0.048	0.317	0.114	0.051
11. Construction	0.140	0.024	0.026	0.045	0.038	0.016
12. Electricity	0.073	0.106	0.003	0.165	0.122	0.062
13. Commerce	1.199	0.165	0.197	2.632	1.527	0.483
14. Transportation	0.001	0.009	0.012	0.057	0.032	0.021
15. Services	0.159	0.152	0.227	0.681	0.337	0.241
1–15. Sum	7.543	1.919	3.772	18.175	6.896	2.795
16. Imports	0.548	0.061	0.704	0.567	0.599	0.440
17. Errors and omissions	0.105	0.025	0.023	0.093	0.028	0.021
1–17. Sum	8.196	2.005	4.499	18.835	7.523	3.256
18. Value added, gross	23.970	2.306	5.128	10.620	5.434	2.347
1–18. Sum, gross value of production	32.166	4.311	9.627	29.455	12.957	5.603

column totals for 1960 are denoted by X_j^{60}. It is to be understood, therefore, that X_j^{60} refers to gross production in sector j for columns 1–15, and to the aggregate of final demand component j for columns 16–21.

For 1968, estimates were available on value added and gross

billions of 1960 pesos)

hem-cals	Non-metallic	Basic metals	Machin-ery	Con-struc-tion	Elec-tricity	Com-merce	Trans-porta-tion	Ser-vices	Sum
	8	9	10	11	12	13	14	15	1–15
.550	0.001	0.002	0.028	0.003	0.0	0.004	0.0	0.018	12.310
.093	0.109	0.455	0.143	0.216	0.005	0.010	0.007	0.006	2.217
.126	0.218	0.275	0.173	0.124	0.216	0.163	1.022	0.094	6.857
.130	0.005	0.021	0.026	0.041	0.002	0.056	0.028	0.109	6.885
.094	0.012	0.025	0.081	0.038	0.005	0.090	0.012	0.084	3.687
.246	0.092	0.043	0.182	0.613	0.013	0.428	0.048	0.357	3.830
.018	0.049	0.034	0.430	0.191	0.011	0.078	0.304	0.318	4.256
.056	0.180	0.063	0.051	1.428	0.001	0.020	0.002	0.017	2.113
.066	0.033	0.873	1.249	1.166	0.013	0.132	0.027	0.149	4.090
.095	0.043	0.057	0.904	0.867	0.052	0.206	0.097	0.463	3.588
.020	0.025	0.022	0.011	0.060	0.043	0.083	0.072	0.367	0.992
.075	0.075	0.062	0.063	0.049	0.080	0.250	0.030	0.156	1.371
.869	0.249	0.314	0.544	1.660	0.093	0.351	0.619	1.280	12.182
.030	0.008	0.007	0.046	0.020	0.012	2.943	0.024	0.130	3.352
.347	0.078	0.239	0.312	0.348	0.043	1.610	0.243	5.439	10.456
.815	1.177	2.492	4.243	6.824	0.589	6.424	2.535	8.987	78.186
.664	0.156	0.366	1.934	0.921	0.107	0.119	0.482	0.429	9.097
.057	0.013	0.046	0.047	0.088	0.007	0.116	0.027	0.344	1.040
.536	1.346	2.904	6.224	7.833	0.703	6.659	3.044	9.760	88.323
.245	1.182	1.786	4.278	6.105	1.502	46.880	4.996	30.732	150.511
.781	2.528	4.690	10.502	13.938	2.205	53.539	8.040	40.492	238.834

value of production [2] in each of the 15 producing sectors, but not on the interindustry transactions by sectors of origin and destination.

[2] Source IA indicates the value added in each of the 15 sectors during each of the years 1960 through 1968. Pooling this with the information on value added and gross production for 1967 (source CN), we have extrapolated by one year to the gross production levels for 1968.

Table 2 (continued)

(B) Final demands

Sector of origin	Household consumption	Government consumption	Tourists' consumption	Exports	Investment, fixed	Investment, inventories	Sum	Sum gross value production
	16	17	18	19	20	21	16−21	1−2
1. Agriculture	14.846	0.013	0.073	2.880	0.943	1.101	19.856	32.1
2. Mining	0.002	0.001	0.0	2.007	0.024	0.060	2.094	4.3
3. Petroleum	2.257	0.116	0.0	0.173	0.002	0.222	2.770	9.6
4. Food	19.711	0.042	0.083	2.300	0.040	0.394	22.570	29.4
5. Textiles	7.835	0.023	0.190	0.651	0.027	0.544	9.270	12.9
6. Wood	1.242	0.117	0.035	0.130	0.050	0.199	1.773	5.6
7. Chemicals	3.635	0.217	0.0	0.221	0.073	0.379	4.525	8.7
8. Non-metallic	0.099	0.117	0.0	0.072	0.026	0.101	0.415	2.5
9. Basic metals	0.0	0.024	0.0	0.092	0.222	0.262	0.600	4.6
10. Machinery	3.280	0.281	0.094	0.114	2.529	0.616	6.914	10.5
11. Construction	0.0	0.028	0.0	0.0	12.787	0.131	12.946	13.9
12. Electricity	0.540	0.179	0.0	0.0	0.115	0.0	0.834	2.2
13. Commerce	35.835	0.222	0.336	1.125	3.625	0.214	41.357	53.5
14. Transportation	4.309	0.180	0.111	0.001	0.087	0.0	4.688	8.0
15. Services	20.580	7.501	1.166	0.217	0.572	0.0	30.036	40.4
1−15. Sum	114.171	9.061	2.088	9.983	21.122	4.223	160.648	238.8
16. Imports	1.313	0.231	0.0	0.055	3.840	0.479	5.918	15.0
17. Errors and omissions	−0.036	−1.009	0.0	0.010	0.0	0.0	−1.035	0.0
1−17. Sum	115.448	8.283	2.088	10.048	24.962	4.702	165.531	253.8
18. Value added, gross	0.000	0.000	0.000	0.000	0.000	0.000	0.000	150.5
1−18. Sum, gross value of production	115.448	8.283	2.088	10.048	24.962	4.702	165.531	404.3

Similarly, for the final demand sectors, the aggregates were available, but not the detailed vectors by sectors of origin. To update the 1960 matrix to 1968, the RAS row and column correction technique could have been applied. (See Bacharach 1970.) Instead, we found that a simpler technique — uniform row correction factors – produced satisfactory results with this particular body of data. The implied annual rates of technological change in the coefficients for row i are denoted by ρ_i, and are indicated in the rightmost column of table 3.

Formally, the row correction procedure may be described as follows: Let A_{ij}^{60} denote the input from sector i per unit of gross output or final demand component j during 1960. The product $A_{ij}^{60} X_j^{60}$ is the entry in row i and column j of the transactions matrix for that year (table 2). For 1968, there are independently available estimates of the following quantities: X_j^{68} (column totals), Y_i^{68} (row totals) and $A_{i,19}^{68} X_{19}^{68}$ (the export vector). Except for the export vector (column 19), the 1968 input-output coefficients A_{ij}^{68} are not available. Suppose, however, that the coefficients are changing during these eight years at an annual geometric rate, ρ_i. Then $A_{ij}^{68} = (1 + \rho_i)^8 A_{ij}^{60}$. With this hypothesis of *disem*-bodied (and unexplained) technological change, we may apply the known data (A_{ij}^{60}, X_j^{68}, Y_j^{68} and $A_{i,19}^{68} X_{19}^{68}$), performing a separate calculation for each row i to determine a value for ρ_i so that:

$$\sum_{\substack{j=1; \\ j \neq 19}}^{21} A_{ij}^{68} X_j^{68} = \sum_{\substack{j=1; \\ j \neq 19}}^{21} (1+\rho_i)^8 A_{ij}^{60} X_j^{68} = Y_i^{68} - A_{i,19}^{68} X_{19}^{68}$$

$$(i = 1, ..., 16)$$

If this row correction procedure were an exact representation of the 1960–68 process of technological change – and if there were no errors and omissions for the 1960 matrix – there would be no errors and omissions for the 1968 matrix. (See line 17 of both matrices.) Clearly, this is too much to expect from a procedure as crude as that of uniform row correction. Fortunately, although there are individual columns in which this prediction error is sizeable, the algebraic total for line 17 is virtually zero.

On this basis – by no means a solid foundation – table 3 was adopted for forecasting interindustry flows over a planning horizon that begins in 1968. The more distant the date t for which these flows are forecast, the less reliable will be the estimate of A_{ij}^t.

Table 3

(A) Intermediate demands

Sector of origin [a]	Sector of destination					
	Agri-culture	Mining	Petrol-eum	Food	Tex-tiles	Wood
	1	2	3	4	5	6
1. Agriculture	2.400	0.014	0.002	11.312	1.623	0.777
2. Mining	0.001	0.825	0.157	0.029	0.005	0.010
3. Petroleum	0.875	0.183	5.261	0.744	0.328	0.172
4. Food	2.379	0.015	0.020	7.994	0.097	0.060
5. Textiles	0.785	0.015	0.029	0.168	4.846	0.072
6. Wood	0.168	0.041	0.128	0.712	0.172	1.790
7. Chemicals	1.197	0.135	0.111	0.257	1.342	0.273
8. Non-metallic	0.005	0.016	0.014	0.468	0.016	0.026
9. Basic metals	0.073	0.087	0.048	0.260	0.111	0.075
10. Machinery	0.435	0.082	0.118	0.731	0.278	0.125
11. Construction	0.191	0.028	0.045	0.073	0.065	0.028
12. Electricity	0.144	0.177	0.008	0.387	0.303	0.154
13. Commerce	1.643	0.191	0.342	4.282	2.630	0.834
14. Transportation	0.001	0.010	0.020	0.087	0.052	0.034
15. Services	0.220	0.178	0.399	1.120	0.587	0.420
1–15. Sum	10.517	1.997	6.701	28.625	12.454	4.848
16. Imports	0.552	0.052	0.900	0.678	0.758	0.558
17. Errors and omissions	1.148	0.374	−1.403	2.006	−0.196	0.080
1–17. Sum	12.217	2.423	6.198	31.309	13.016	5.487
18. Value added, gross	32.558	2.651	10.803	17.380	9.655	4.340
1–18. Sum, gross value of production	44.775	5.074	17.001	48.689	22.671	9.827

For forecasting the coefficients for years subsequent to 1968, the uniform row correction procedure was again followed. For most rows, the forecast values of ρ_i are identical to those appearing in table 3. The exceptions are rows 2, 10, 12 and 16 (mining, machinery, electricity and imports) — those in which the 1960–68 annual rate of change exceeded + 3% or fell below −3%. Rather than suppose that these rapid rates will continue into the indefi-

billions of 1960 pesos)

Chem- icals	Non- metal- lic	Basic metals	Machin- ery	Con- struc- tion	Elec- tricity	Com- merce	Trans- por- tation	Serv- ices	Sum
7	8	9	10	11	12	13	14	15	1–15
0.954	0.002	0.004	0.062	0.005	0.0	0.006	0.0	0.027	17.187
0.132	0.161	0.727	0.258	0.289	0.009	0.012	0.008	0.007	2.628
0.260	0.467	0.639	0.454	0.241	0.562	0.277	1.620	0.170	12.253
0.273	0.011	0.050	0.069	0.081	0.005	0.097	0.045	0.200	11.396
0.207	0.027	0.062	0.227	0.079	0.014	0.163	0.020	0.162	6.875
0.493	0.191	0.097	0.464	1.158	0.033	0.706	0.074	0.626	6.854
2.410	0.120	0.091	1.294	0.426	0.033	0.152	0.553	0.658	9.051
0.128	0.428	0.163	0.149	3.084	0.003	0.038	0.004	0.034	4.575
0.147	0.076	2.189	3.538	2.447	0.037	0.242	0.046	0.290	9.666
0.271	0.127	0.183	3.272	2.325	0.187	0.483	0.212	1.153	9.982
0.040	0.052	0.050	0.028	0.113	0.108	0.137	0.111	0.642	1.709
0.217	0.225	0.202	0.232	0.134	0.292	0.596	0.067	0.395	3.533
1.745	0.519	0.710	1.388	3.138	0.235	0.580	0.955	2.248	21.439
0.057	0.016	0.015	0.110	0.036	0.029	4.566	0.035	0.214	5.280
0.704	0.164	0.546	0.805	0.665	0.110	2.687	0.379	9.653	18.637
8.038	2.587	5.726	12.349	14.219	1.656	10.739	4.128	16.481	141.065
2.456	0.239	0.608	3.629	1.280	0.199	0.144	0.547	0.554	13.155
0.018	−0.025	0.479	−1.107	−0.570	−0.414	−3.966	−0.189	5.065	1.300
0.512	2.801	6.813	14.871	14.930	1.441	6.918	4.485	22.099	155.520
7.401	2.550	3.955	12.360	11.844	4.228	82.920	8.113	50.143	260.901
7.913	5.351	10.768	27.231	26.774	5.669	89.838	12.598	72.242	416.421

nite future, we have set $\rho_{10} = \rho_{12} = +3\%$, and $\rho_2 = \rho_{16} = -3\%$. Note that the row corrections for imports and for domestically produced machinery tend to offset each other. In effect, this allows for a reduction in the growth of import substitution.

To illustrate the process of extrapolating from the 1968 transactions matrix, table 4 contains the coefficients inserted into DINAMICO for the year 1980 (time index $t = 4$). Consider the

Table 3 (continued)

(B) Final demands

Sector of origin [a]	Sector of destination							
	House-hold con-sump-tion	Govern-ment con-sump-tion	Tour-ists' con-sump-tion	Ex-ports	Invest-ment, fixed	Invest-ment, invent-ories	Sum	Sum gross value prod-tion
	16	17	18	19	20	21	16−21	1−2
1. Agriculture	20.894	0.024	0.125	3.860	1.590	1.095	27.588	44.7
2. Mining	0.002	0.001	0.0	2.360	0.033	0.049	2.446	5.6
3. Petroleum	3.780	0.251	0.0	0.450	0.004	0.263	4.748	17.0
4. Food	33.592	0.092	0.173	2.880	0.082	0.474	37.293	48.6
5. Textiles	14.003	0.053	0.415	0.580	0.058	0.687	15.796	22.6
6. Wood	2.021	0.246	0.070	0.310	0.097	0.229	2.973	9.8
7. Chemicals	6.982	0.538	0.0	0.660	0.168	0.514	8.862	17.9
8. Non-metallic	0.184	0.281	0.0	0.120	0.058	0.133	0.776	5.3
9. Basic metals	0.0	0.056	0.0	0.230	0.481	0.335	1.102	10.1
10. Machinery	7.579	0.838	0.265	0.560	7.001	1.006	17.249	27.2
11. Construction	0.0	0.059	0.0	0.0	24.856	0.150	25.065	26.7
12. Electricity	1.269	0.543	0.0	0.0	0.324	0.0	2.136	5.6
13. Commerce	58.382	0.467	0.668	1.560	7.075	0.246	68.399	89.8
14. Transportation	6.595	0.356	0.207	0.0	0.160	0.0	7.318	12.5
15. Services	33.888	15.945	2.344	0.300	1.128	0.0	53.605	72.2
1−15. Sum	189.172	19.750	4.268	13.870	43.114	5.181	275.355	416.4
16. Imports	1.573	0.357	0.0	0.0	5.510	0.405	7.845	21.0
17. Errors and omissions	0.355	−2.407	−0.048	0.000	0.876	−0.087	−1.311	−0.6
1−17. Sum	191.100	17.700	4.220	13.870	49.500	5.500	281.890	437.4
18. Value added, gross	0.0	0.0	0.0	0.0	0.0	0.0	0.0	260.9
1−18. Sum, gross value of production	191.100	17.700	4.220	13.870	49.500	5.500	281.890	698.3

[a] Row correction factors ρ_j, annual rates of technological change, %: Row 1, −2.0; 2, −4.4; 3, 0.1; 4, 0.4; 5, 1.0; 6, −0.2; 7, 1.9; 8, 1.5; 9, 1.1; 10, 4.3; 11, −0.2; 12, 4.5; 13, −0.2; 14, −1.0; 15, −0.1; 16, −4.0.

agriculture sector ($j = 1$). The column vector of inputs and outputs for this sector are calculated as follows:

sector of origin i	input per unit of gross output, sector 1, 1980	coefficients $a^4_{i,1}$ appearing in DINAMICO; 1980 time index $t = 4$; sign convention: inputs positive, outputs negative
1. agri-culture	$[(1+\rho_1)^{12}][A^{68}_{1,1}X^{68}_1] \div [X^{68}_1]$ $= [(1-0.020)^{12}][2.400] \div [44.775]$ $= 0.042$	$a^4_{1,1} = 0.042 - 1.000$ $= -0.958$
4. food	$[(1+\rho_4)^{12}][A^{68}_{4,1}X^{68}_1] \div [X^{68}_1]$ $= [(1+0.004)^{12}][2.379] \div [44.775]$ $= 0.056$	$a^4_{4,1} = 0.056$
16. im-ports	$[(1+\rho_{16})^{12}][A^{68}_{16,1}X^{68}_1] \div [X^{68}_1]$ $= [(1-0.030)^{12}][0.552] \div [44.775]$ $= 0.009$	$a^4_{16,1} = 0.009$

For assessing changes in the Mexican economy over the period 1960–68, it is of some interest to decompose the sources of production growth into three components of demand: a time trend factor for the coefficients of row i (ρ_i), an economy-wide production growth rate (7.2% per year), and a residual to be attributed to shifts in the interindustry composition of output. (See table 5.) In general, the residual is positive for those sectors that supply inputs to rapidly growing sectors (e.g., basic metals and imports), and is negative for those that supply slowly growing sectors (e.g., agriculture and food). If the residuals were all zero, there would be no need for an interindustry table to forecast future levels of output. It would then be sufficient to add together an economy-wide ag-

Table 4

Coefficients a_{ij}^4 appearing in DINAMICO; 1980 time index $t = 4$

Sector of origin j	Sector of destination j					
	Agri-culture	Mining	Petrol-eum	Food	Tex-tiles	Wood
	1	2	3	4	5	6
1. Agriculture	−0.958	0.002	0.000	0.182	0.056	0.062
2. Mining	0.000	−0.887	0.006	0.000	0.000	0.001
3. Petroleum	0.020	0.037	−0.828	0.016	0.015	0.018
4. Food	0.056	0.003	0.001	−0.828	0.004	0.006
5. Textiles	0.020	0.003	0.002	0.004	−0.760	0.008
6. Wood	0.004	0.008	0.007	0.014	0.007	−0.822
7. Chemicals	0.033	0.033	0.008	0.007	0.074	0.035
8. Non-metallic	0.000	0.004	0.001	0.011	0.001	0.003
9. Basic metals	0.002	0.020	0.003	0.006	0.006	0.009
10. Machinery	0.014	0.023	0.010	0.021	0.018	0.018
11. Construction	0.004	0.005	0.003	0.001	0.003	0.003
12. Electricity	0.005	0.050	0.001	0.011	0.019	0.022
13. Commerce	0.036	0.037	0.020	0.086	0.113	0.083
14. Transportation	0.000	0.002	0.001	0.002	0.002	0.003
15. Services	0.005	0.035	0.023	0.023	0.026	0.042
16. Imports	0.009	0.007	0.037	0.010	0.023	0.039
1−16. Sum = value added per unit of gross output	−0.752	−0.619	−0.562	−0.434	−0.393	−0.470

gregate growth rate and an industry-specific row correction rate. The larger the residual in table 5 (see p. 98), the less satisfactory would be this approximation.

3. Consumption and tourist expenditures

Table 6 (p. 99) illustrates the computation of two of the final demand vectors entering into DINAMICO. Household and government consumption expenditures have been combined into the vector apc_i^t, the average propensity to consume item i in year t. Similarly,

Sign convention: inputs positive, outputs negative

Chemicals	Non-metallic	Basic metals	Machinery	Construction	Electricity	Commerce	Transportation	Services
7	8	9	10	11	12	13	14	15
0.042	0.000	0.000	0.002	0.000	0.0	0.000	0.0	0.000
0.005	0.021	0.047	0.007	0.007	0.001	0.000	0.000	0.000
0.015	0.089	0.060	0.017	0.009	0.101	0.003	0.131	0.002
0.016	0.002	0.005	0.003	0.003	0.001	0.001	0.004	0.003
0.013	0.006	0.006	0.009	0.003	0.003	0.002	0.002	0.003
0.027	0.035	0.009	0.017	0.042	0.006	0.008	0.006	0.008
0.832	0.028	0.011	0.059	0.020	0.007	0.002	0.055	0.011
0.009	−0.905	0.018	0.007	0.137	0.001	0.001	0.000	0.001
0.009	0.016	−0.768	0.148	0.104	0.007	0.003	0.004	0.005
0.022	0.034	0.024	−0.829	0.124	0.047	0.008	0.024	0.023
0.002	0.009	0.004	0.001	−0.996	0.019	0.001	0.009	0.009
0.017	0.060	0.027	0.012	0.007	−0.927	0.009	0.008	0.008
0.095	0.095	0.064	0.050	0.114	0.041	−0.994	0.074	0.030
0.003	0.003	0.001	0.004	0.001	0.004	0.045	−0.998	0.003
0.039	0.030	0.050	0.029	0.025	0.019	0.030	0.030	−0.867
0.095	0.031	0.039	0.092	0.033	0.024	0.001	0.030	0.005
0.423	−0.445	−0.401	−0.372	−0.365	−0.646	−0.879	−0.622	−0.757

the vector apz_i^t denotes the sector-of-origin ratios of foreign tourist expenditures in Mexico during time period t. These are shown for two representative points of time: 1968 ($t = 0$) and 1980 ($t = 4$).

Note that apc_i^t and apz_i^t are based upon the final demand vector appearing in the 1968 transactions matrix (table 3). The annual technological change factors ρ_i have been applied to obtain the sector-of-origin ratios for subsequent years. Column correction factors are then applied to ensure that the fractions spent on individual items will add up to 100% of total consumption expenditures. Generally, the consumption structure changes over time in a direction that is consistent with Engel curve estimates.

Table 5
Sources of demand growth, 1960−68 (annual percentage growth rates)

	Gross production, sector i, [a] γ_i	Row correction factors, ρ_i [b]	+	Sum of gross production, sectors 1−15 [a]	+	Residual attributed to shift in inter-industry composition of output
1. Agriculture	4.2	−2.0		7.2		−1.0
2. Mining	2.0	−4.4		7.2		−0.8
3. Petroleum	7.4	0.1		7.2		0.1
4. Food	6.5	0.4		7.2		−1.1
5. Textiles	7.2	1.0		7.2		−1.0
6. Wood	7.3	−0.2		7.2		0.3
7. Chemicals	9.3	1.9		7.2		0.2
8. Non-metallic	9.8	1.5		7.2		1.1
9. Basic metals	10.9	1.1		7.2		2.6
10. Machinery	12.7	4.3		7.2		1.2
11. Construction	8.5	−0.2		7.2		1.5
12. Electricity	12.5	4.5		7.2		0.8
13. Commerce	6.7	−0.2		7.2		−0.3
14. Transportation	5.8	−0.1		7.2		−0.4
15. Services	7.5	−0.1		7.2		0.4
16. Imports	4.3	−4.0		7.2		1.1

[a] Source: Row totals, tables 2 and 3.
[b] Source: table 3.

E.g., the fraction spent on agricultural products (apc_1^t) moves down from 0.100 in 1968 to 0.077 in 1980. Similarly, the fraction spent on machinery (apc_{10}^t) moves up from 0.040 to 0.057.

If one were engaged only in the econometric estimation of consumption patterns, this technique of projection could easily be improved upon. One would then allow explicitly for the population size, the income distribution, and the urban-rural composition. In DINAMICO, however, our aim is not necessarily to arrive at the most accurate pattern of consumption expenditures. This would conflict with another objective − formulating the model so as to simplify the basic data processing steps. The simpler these steps, the easier it becomes to revise the model when new data become available. Indeed, it is not clear that there would be major

Table 6
Sector-of-origin ratios, consumption and tourist expenditures

Sector of origin	Household and government consumption propensities, apc_i^t		Tourist expenditure propensities, apz_i^t	
	1968 [a] ($t = 0$)	1980 [b] ($t = 4$)	1968 [c] ($t = 0$)	1980 [d] ($t = 4$)
1. Agriculture	0.100	0.077	0.030	0.023
2. Mining	0	0	0	0
3. Petroleum	0.019	0.019	0	0
4. Food	0.161	0.166	0.041	0.041
5. Textiles	0.067	0.074	0.098	0.107
6. Wood	0.011	0.010	0.017	0.016
7. Chemicals	0.036	0.044	0	0
8. Non-metallic	0.002	0.003	0	0
9. Basic metals	0	0	0	0
10. Machinery	0.040	0.057	0.063	0.087
11. Construction	0	0	0	0
12. Electricity	0.009	0.012	0	0
13. Commerce	0.283	0.270	0.158	0.150
14. Transportation	0.033	0.029	0.049	0.042
15. Services	0.240	0.233	0.555	0.534
16. Imports	0.009	0.006	0	0
17. Errors and omissions	−0.010	0	−0.011	0
Total	1.000	1.000	1.000	1.000
Column correction factors	−	$\mu_c^4 = 0.981$		$\mu_z^2 = 0.970$

[a] Source: table 3, columns 16 and 17.
[b] $apc_i^4 = apc_i^0(1+\rho_i)^{12}\mu_c^4$, where μ_c^4 is determined so that $\sum_{i=1}^{16} apc_i^4 = 1.000$.
[c] Source: table 3, column 18.
[d] $apz_i^4 = apz_i^0(1+\rho_i)^{12}\mu_z^4$, where μ_z^4 is determined so that $\sum_{i=1}^{16} apz_i^4 = 1.000$.

gains in accuracy by allowing explicitly for the population size, income distribution or urban-rural composition. These variables change slowly over time, and time trends are in any event included in the technological change rates ρ_i.

4. Capital coefficients

Capital coefficients are not used directly in the construction of national accounts − hence have received less research effort than matrices of current account transactions. The most reliable data available to us were those that appear in document CN, table 168. This source provides year-by-year estimates (from 1949 to 1967) of the *total* capital stocks held by the government and by each of 45 producing sectors. (These stocks are stated in terms of 1960 pesos.) By aggregating the 1967 capital and output data into the 15-sector classification, the ratios of capital per unit of gross output may be obtained for each sector. [3] These coefficients k_j are employed as control totals for the capital coefficients matrix.

Let b_{ij} denote the ratio of capital originating in sector i per unit of gross output in sector j ($i = 1, ..., 16; j = 1, ..., 15$). For estimating the matrix of capital coefficients b_{ij}, there was no alternative but to rely upon an inadequately documented source (AJ, table NM8). This source provides sector-of-origin ratios b_{ij}/k_j. Multiplying by the control totals k_j, it is then straightforward to obtain the coefficients b_{ij}. Upon checking this matrix, we became convinced that it overstated the diagonal elements b_{ii} and understated the investment requirements to be supplied by the construction sector. To remedy these defects, the following steps were taken:

(1) An allowance was made for differences in the sector-of-origin ratios between privately and publicly held capital stocks in sectors 1 and 14 (agriculture and transport, respectively).

---

[3] In estimating the capital coefficients k_j, we found it important to allocate the government's capital stocks to their sector of actual use rather than to sector 15. (Sector 15 includes government as well as privately-supplied services.) E.g., the capital value of the nation's highways was allocated to sector 14, transport. Similarly, the capital value of publicly-owned irrigation facilities was allocated to sector 1, agriculture. Prior to these corrections, it was observed that there were a number of anomalous cases of 'mixing of flows'. E.g., unless public irrigation investments are allocated to sector 1, DINAMICO will overstate Mexico's comparative advantage in agriculture and understate its advantage in tourism (which originates largely in sector 15).

(2) For those sectors that are major suppliers [4] of capital goods ($i = 10, 11, 13, 15$ and 16), a row correction factor was determined, λ_i. This factor was calculated so as to equate the actual 1968 investment originating in sector i (according to table 3 above) with the 1968 investment requirements predicted by the capital coefficients b_{ij} through the acceleration principle formula: $\sum_{j=1}^{15} b_{ij}\gamma_j X_j^{68}$. In this prediction formula, γ_j denotes the 1960—68 average annual growth rate (table 5). The product $\gamma_j X_j^{68}$ provides a smoothed estimate of the one-year increase in gross output — hence the requirements for capacity to be added in 1968.

(3) Column correction factors μ_j were determined so that $\mu_j \sum_{i=1}^{16} \lambda_i b_{ij} = k_j$. This last step ensured that the revised capital coefficients would sum up to the originally stipulated control totals k_j.

Table 7 contains the matrix that results from this series of steps. It also contains the row and column correction factors λ_i and μ_j. To the extent that these factors depart from unity, there is evidence of inconsistency between the various sources of information concerning investment requirements.

Denote the capital coefficients that emerge from this series of revisions by $\hat{b}_{ij} = \lambda_i \mu_j b_{ij}$. In order to employ these revised coefficients within DINAMICO, one further step is needed — applying the row correction factor ρ_i to allow for the annual rates of change in the input coefficients. Recall that the time index $t = 0$ in 1968, and that three years elapse between each of the seven points of time represented in DINAMICO. Then, for year t, the trend-corrected capital coefficients b_{ij}^t and k_j^t are predicted through the following expressions:

$$b_{ij}^t = \hat{b}_{ij}(1+\rho_i)^{3t} \quad \text{and} \quad k_j^t = \sum_{i=1}^{16} b_{ij}^t \qquad (t = 0, 1, ..., 6)$$

[4] Note that the commerce sector (13) is a major 'supplier' of capital goods. This occurs because of the accounting conventions with respect to producers' prices and commerce margins.

Table 7
Capital-gross output

Sector of origin, i		Sector of destination j					
		Agri-culture	Mining	Petrol-eum	Food	Tex-tiles	Wood
		1	2	3	4	5	6
$\hat{b}_{ij} =$ $\lambda_i \mu_i b_{ij}$	1. Agriculture	0.934					
	2. Mining		0.124				
	3. Petroleum			0.004			
	4. Food				0.048		
	5. Textiles					0.047	
	6. Wood						0.154
	7. Chemicals						
	8. Non-metallic						
	9. Basic metals						
	10. Machinery	0.207	0.261	0.395	0.197	0.155	0.300
	11. Construction	0.588	0.331	0.615	0.299	0.145	0.296
	12. Electricity						
	13. Commerce	0.224	0.204	0.378	0.193	0.194	0.307
	14. Transportation						
	15. Services	0.039					
	16. Imports	0.262	0.100	0.339	0.183	0.264	0.316
k_j	1–16. Sum [a]	2.242	1.020	1.731	0.920	0.805	1.373
	Column correction factors, μ_j	1.004	1.030	1.028	1.030	1.066	1.066

[a] Due to rounding, totals do not add.

5. Imputed returns to labor and capital

In Mexican statistics, it has been the practice to distinguish between two categories of income: (1) wages and salaries (*sueldos y salarios*) received by paid employees, and (2) interest, profits and mixed incomes (*ingresos de capital y mixtos*). Given the share of family-operated business (peasant proprietorships and small com-

atios, b_{ij} and k_j

hem- als	Non- metal- lic	Basic metals	Machin- ery	Con- struc- tion	Elec- tricity	Com- merce	Trans- porta- tion	Serv- ices	Row correc- tion factors, λ_i
	8	9	10	11	12	13	14	15	
									1.000
									1.000
									1.000
									1.000
									1.000
									1.000
.102									1.000
	0.088								1.000
		0.352							1.000
.203	0.319	0.263	0.176	0.085	0.886	0.189	1.634	0.273	0.868
.232	0.447	0.275	0.235	0.015	2.109	0.169	5.173	2.328	1.230
					0.462				1.000
.294	0.279	0.348	0.234	0.070	0.707	0.126	1.363	0.199	0.804
							0.159		1.000
							0.196	0.154	0.609
.455	0.202	0.497	0.336	0.042	0.369	0.011	0.835	0.055	0.967
.286	1.334	1.736	0.980	0.212	4.534	0.494	9.360	3.010	
.058	1.030	1.052	1.052	1.136	0.984	1.057	0.975	0.919	

mercial enterprises) in the national income, it is not easy to separate category (2) into distributive shares – the returns to labor and
to capital.

Table 8 contains our estimates of these shares. The leftmost
column (value added) is taken directly from source document IA.
The imputed returns to labor are estimated from the wage and
labor force data that appear in chapter II.1 above. The gross return

Table 8
Imputed returns to labor and capital, 1960
(unit: billions of pesos)

Sector *j*	Value added [a]	Imputed returns to labor [b]	Imputed gross return to capital	Capital stock [c]	Gross return on capital stock (% per year)
1. Agriculture	23.970	15.970	8.000	73.417	11%
2. Mining	2.306	1.150	1.156	4.946	23
3. Petroleum	5.128	0.973 [d]	4.155	17.334	24
4. Food	10.620	2.553	8.067	22.920	35
5. Textiles	5.434	4.000	1.434	13.832	10
6. Wood	2.347	1.910	0.437	8.212	5
7. Chemicals	3.245	1.236	2.009	9.826	20
8. Non-metallic	1.182	0.663	0.519	3.941	13
9. Basic metals	1.786	0.485 [d]	1.301	9.822	13
10. Machinery	4.278	3.683	0.595	15.045	4
11. Construction	6.105	4.199	1.906	3.698	52
12. Electricity	1.502	0.668 [d]	0.834	10.060	8
13. Commerce	46.880	11.024	35.856	24.120	149
14. Transportation	4.996	3.924	1.072	78.836	1
15. Services	30.732	23.988	6.744	132.184	5
Total	150.511	76.426	74.085	428.193	17

[a] Source: IA.

[b] Estimated by multiplying the labor force distribution that appears above, chapter II.1, table 2, together with the rough estimates of annual wage rates shown in table 7 of that chapter. That is, this column is based upon neglecting intersectoral differences in the wages and salaries paid to labor of a given skill. This does not provide an accurate estimate of the labor costs actually paid by each sector, but rather is intended for consistency with the internal logic of DINAMICO. There, the identical shadow price is imputed to each labor skill – regardless of the sector in which the skill is employed.

[c] Source: CN, table 168.

[d] This figure lies below that reported as wages and salaries in source IP. These sectors pay higher-than-average wages for labor of a given skill. For these sectors, therefore, our procedure understates the wage costs and overstates the rate of return on capital.

on capital is then obtained as a residual after subtracting labor costs from value added.

The fourth column in table 8 indicates the sectoral distribution of Mexico's capital stock. These figures were taken from the same source, and publicly-owned capital was allocated in the same way as for estimating the sectoral capital coefficients k_j. On this basis, the economy-wide ratio of gross returns to capital stock is $74/428 = 17\%$ per year. [5] This is an average return on capital which appears high to a foreigner, but is by no means out of line with the anticipations of investors in Mexico.

A somewhat unsatisfactory feature of table 8 is the fact that this procedure leads to wide variations in the estimates of the rate of return on capital invested in individual sectors. Taken literally, the table implies that one can earn 149% per year by investing in commerce and yet only 1% by investing in transportation services. One does not need to belong to the Chicago school of economics to be suspicious of such wide differences in the productivity of capital. It is quite likely that these variations stem not only from wage differences between sectors, but also from faulty imputations of commerce and transport margins.

There is little that can be done to correct defects in the statistical material for the 1960 census year. Table 8 provides an immediate explanation, however, of the shadow price structure that emerges from DINAMICO. Because of the optimization framework of that model, the shadow prices of inputs and outputs are determined simultaneously so that the rate of return on each capital good and on each class of labor skill is identical in each sector using these factors of production. The resulting shadow prices may be anticipated directly from table 8 – a low price for the services produced by the commerce sector and a high price for transport services. Until these inconsistences have been removed from the base-year transactions matrix, we may expect to continue finding spuriously wide differences in the base-year rates of return on capital – hence wide differences in the shadow prices of the items produced by individual sectors.

From tables 2 and 8, one final cross-check is available on the data that have entered into DINAMICO. The 1960 aggregate ratio

---

[5] The returns to capital are gross of two cost items: depreciation and indirect taxes less subsidies. According to IP, these items amounted to a total of 14.590 billion pesos. Subtracting this entire amount from the imputed gross return on capital, the net return drops to 14% per year.

of capital stock to gross domestic product is (428/150.5) = 2.84. This value does not differ in magnitude from 2.66, the 1960–68 *incremental* capital-output ratio shown below, chapter II.3, table 6. These cross-checks lend credibility to the aggregate results of DINAMICO – although not to the sectoral details on comparative advantage.

Reference

Bacharach, M., *Biproportional matrices and input-output change.* Cambridge, Cambridge University Press, 1970.

II.3. DINAMICO, A DYNAMIC MULTI-SECTOR, MULTI-SKILL MODEL

Alan S. MANNE *

Lubin. But surely any change would be so extremely gradual that —

Conrad. Don't deceive yourself. It's only the politicians who improve the world so gradually that nobody can see the improvement. The notion that Nature does not proceed by jumps is only one of the budget of plausible lies that we call classical education. Nature always proceeds by jumps. She may spend twenty thousand years making up her mind to jump; but when she makes it up at last, the jump is big enough to take us into a new age.

G.B. Shaw, *Back to Methuselah*

1. Introduction

This work is intended as a step toward multi-level planning — identifying the information flows necessary for consistency between project, sectoral and macroeconomic decisions. To build a macroeconomic model that will yield shadow prices relevant to specific project decisions, it appears essential to allow for labor inputs. Otherwise, it is implied that the marginal productivity of

* The author is indebted to Leopoldo Solís for having provided access to the resources of the Departamento de Estudios Económicos, Banco de Mexico. Helpful comments on successive drafts were received from: Bela Balassa, Charles Blitzer, Gerardo Bueno, Yves Franchet, Louis Goreux, Donald Keesing, János Kornai, Mordecai Kurz, Lance Taylor and Thomas Vietorisz. All computational aspects — including programs for matrix generation — were handled by Richard Inman. The specific facts, methods of analysis and conclusions are the sole responsibility of the individual author. The present version of both this and the following chapter were written during a year in which the author held a Ford Foundation fellowhip at the Center for Advanced Study in the Behavioral Sciences.

labor is zero. With a constant returns technology, this in turn implies that the marginal productivity of capital will coincide with the economy-wide average output-capital ratio. As noted by Harberger (1967, p. 142), a zero shadow price for labor (hence a high shadow price for capital) is 'virtually a kiss of death for projects with long gestation periods or long economic lives'.

For a macroeconomic model to generate meaningful criteria for project decisions, it is not sufficient that 'labor' have a positive shadow price. Since the skill-mix differs substantially among alternative investment projects and since wage differentials between skill groups appear quite wide in Mexico, it is essential to separate labor by skill categories. Skill disaggregation is easier said than done.

In the initial experiments, we adopted a manpower requirements formulation − hoping to avoid the data difficulties inherent in a human capital formation approach. The manpower availability in each skill category was projected exogenously − as though the supply of labor skills was completely inelastic. Employing this formulation, plus an activity analysis technology that turned out to be virtually as rigid as a Leontief system, there were major difficulties with respect to the shadow price of labor. The efficiency price differentials between skills were either zero − or with a minor perturbation in labor availability, these differentials became unbelievably large. [1] Under the influence of Marshall's dictum (*natura non facit saltum*), we have therefore searched for additional elements of substitution, and have turned away from regarding labor skills as a demographically given primary factor of production. Much like Correa and Tinbergen (1962), Spiegelman et al. (1965), Adelman (1966) and Bowles (1967), the current version of DINAMICO includes endogenous time-phased activities for upgrading unskilled into skilled manpower. Also included are activities for capital-labor substitution in agriculture and for short-run substitution between skills.

---

[1] Much the same experience is reported in Bruno (1966, pp. 343−345). Apparently, in both these numerical models, there was insufficient indirect substitution via international trade to avoid knife-edge behavior of the shadow price with respect to the exogenously specified availability of labor skills.

This is a model for indicative — not for imperative planning. The model does not include the complexities of collective choice, of multi-person organizations, and of incentives for implementation. The structure is a deterministic one — linear programming. With the exception of labor, this dynamic multi-sector model (for short, DINAMICO) follows along familiar lines. Among the standard ingredients are: a current account interindustry matrix, a labor skill matrix, capital coefficients linking investment demands to capacity expansion in future time periods, and alternative activities for trade-balance improvement. [2] In part, foreign exchange is viewed as an exogenously given primary resource — and in part as an item for which there exist substitution possibilities. In addition to foreign exchange earnings through traditional exports and tourism, the model allows for the possibility of exporting manufactures from high-cost 'infant' industries. It is supposed that foreign exchange is also available through capital inflows — one portion on concessional terms and another portion through direct private foreign investment.

Among the policy issues which can be examined through DI-NAMICO are: near-future versus distant future increases in aggregate consumption; alternative time paths of dependence upon foreign capital inflows; and the income distribution effects of increasing labor's productivity within the agriculture sector. These alternatives are examined in the next chapter. Here, we have focused on the effects of labor constraints within a multi-sector model. These calculations suggest that Mexico is approaching the end of the labor surplus phase of her development, and that capital-labor substitution in agriculture could become increasingly significant.

---

[2] It is assumed that the reader is already familiar with standard references on dynamic numerical planning models, e.g., Adelman (1966), Chenery and MacEwan (1966), Bruno (1967), Eckaus and Parikh (1968), Bruno et al. (1970), Murakami et al. (1970), and Westphal (1971).

2. Key simplifications — time, foreign exchange and domestic savings

In this 18-year planning model, horizon effects are handled through terminal conditions for physical capital formation so that a 'gradualist' consumption path will remain feasible over an infinite post-terminal period. It is postulated that there is an average lag of three years between the input of investment resources and the full capacity available from that input, ignoring the differences in gestation lags between sectors. To simplify still further, the workings of the economy are examined at three-year intervals between representative points of time beginning with the statistical base year, 1968. The notation for the time index t is as follows:

Representative year, t	Calendar year
0	1968 (1968 employed only in setting initial conditions)
1	1971
2	1974
3	1977
4	1980
5	1983
6	1986
7	1989 (1989 employed only in setting terminal conditions)

Re initial conditions: For the base year ($t = 0$), it is assumed that all quantities are known except for the distribution of aggregate investment by sector of destination. The increase in output between year 0 and 1 is limited to three times the annual output capacity created by the input of aggregate investment resources during year 0. By imposing a constraint upon aggregate investment — but not on the availabilities of individual capital goods — we attempt to offset the short-run rigidities of the acceleration principle, and compensate for errors in estimates of the initial conditions.

In this type of planning model, it appears essential to avoid 'tightness' with respect to primary factors of production (see Kurz 1969). Labor skill substitution and international trade [3] constitute the sources of primary factor substitution that are quantified here. Had more reliable data been available, DINAMICO would have included an explicitly nonlinear relationship between the inputs and outputs of these items. Despite the existence of studies on the average costs of import substitution in Mexico, we did not succeed in finding reliable estimates of a *curve* for the supply of import substitutes. For this reason, imports are viewed as 'non-competitive' inputs to each domestic component of demand — the import coefficients being subject to downward trends over time.

On the export side also, the lack of data prevented any explicit estimates of diminishing returns. (See the incorrect signs and the low significance of the price elasticities reported in such econometric studies as those of Houthakker and Magee (1969).) Here, just as in Bruno (1967), the earnings from tourism and the exports of each of ten merchandise trade items are regarded as endogenous variables — limited both by upper and lower bounds predetermined on the basis of individual commodity projections. This formulation is intended to suggest the direction, although not the magnitude of comparative advantage. [4] By following national income accounting conventions, this version of DINAMICO fails to allow properly for differences between domestic producers' prices and international prices. (See below, chapter II.5 and the editor's note at the end of that chapter.)

[3] From 1954 to this date (1971), Mexico has maintained its foreign exchange rate stable at 12.5 pesos per U.S. $. Throughout this period, there have been no restrictions on convertibility, nor have there been large subsidies on exports. Mexico has encouraged import substitution in the manufacturing sector through high tariffs and quantitative restrictions. For reviews of the country's trade policies and overall development, see Bueno (1971), Ibarra (1970), King (1970) and Solís (1970).

[4] In estimating the direction of comparative advantage from DINAMICO, perhaps the most serious drawback is the extent of aggregation and the reliance upon national accounts rather than process analysis data. E.g., all categories of machinery — farm implements, autos and electrical transformers — are combined within a single sector. Extreme caution must therefore be applied before concluding that Mexico's comparative advantage does or does not lie in producing 'machinery'. At this level of aggregation, one can hope for little more than consistency checks on the demand targets and for shadow prices to be applied within sectoral calculations.

As a *marginal* trade balance improvement activity, we have included the possibility of exporting 'infant' high-cost manufactures. It is supposed that the domestic cost of these products (at 1960 producers' prices) will exceed the foreign exchange earnings by 30% at the time the item is first exported, and that this cost differential will drop to zero through the experience acquired during an 18-year period. [5] The 30% figure is based partly upon estimates of the average differential between the domestic and international prices of manufactured goods. (See the estimates of 'nominal implicit protection' in Bueno (1971), tables 8.7 and 8.8.) In part also, a differential of this magnitude might be needed in order to allow for increased marketing costs and for promotional pricing in the international market. Since the high-cost exports turn out to be marginal sources of foreign exchange, the assumed cost differential is likely to exert a significant influence upon the shadow price of foreign exchange within DINAMICO. (See appendix to this chapter.) Accordingly, the sensitivity analyses include a test for the implications of a 50% differential rather than 30%.

To complete the specification of foreign exchange flows, it is necessary to allow for the possibility of importing capital. Among developing nations, Mexico enjoys a high reputation for creditworthiness. By 1968, however, the net inflows of foreign capital had already reached 45% of the nation's foreign exchange earnings. Given the difficulties of generating foreign exchange to cover debt service and profit remittances, it appears unsafe to reply upon an ever-increasing volume of external financing. It is therefore supposed that the net inflow on concessional terms will diminish gradually over time. Moreover, to avoid an increase in the fraction of Mexico's capital stock that is foreign owned, it is supposed that – although there may be year-to-year variations – the average inflows of direct private foreign investment are not to increase above the 1971 rate. The cost of interest and profit remittances on foreign private capital is taken to be 15% per year.

---

[5] In effect, this differential represents an investment cost incurred during the learning phase. Like human capital formation, this is an investment cost that is not covered by conventional accounting measures.

Even during 1968, when foreign capital inflows had reached a new peak, domestic savings financed the bulk of Mexico's investment outlays. Domestic savings are limited by political constraints upon the ability to raise tax revenues and upon the ability of public sector enterprises to be self-financing. To reflect this feature, DINAMICO contains an explicit constraint of 30% upon the marginal domestic propensity to save. (This value is well above the marginal propensity of 23.2% for the period 1960—68.) More important, a savings constraint arises through the maximand — choosing the highest among those 'gradualist' consumption paths that approach the target annual growth rate of 7%. Given this formulation, the optimal marginal domestic savings propensity does not necessarily remain constant at 30% over time.

3. Labor skills

In order to build a macroeconomic structure that is capable of being linked to specific project decisions, a more detailed classification scheme for labor was adopted than is customary for dynamic input-output models. (See table 1.) Following a suggestion by Donald Keesing, labor has been subdivided into five skill categories — each skill being required in fixed proportions per unit of domestic production. The level of aggregation here is intended as a compromise, one that is sufficiently aggregative so as to make use of

Table 1
Identification of labor skill categories

Skill category s		Rough estimate of 1960 annual wage (thousands of pesos)
1	Engineers and scientists	72.0
2	Other professional and technical workers	30.0
3	Administrative and clerical workers	21.6
4	Manual and sales workers outside agriculture	7.2
5	Unskilled agricultural workers	2.4

existing Mexican manpower statistics together with international comparisons, and sufficiently disaggregated so as to distinguish between labor categories with wage differentials of two or three-to-one. [6]

With the five-way classification of table 1, it is plausible to postulate downward substitution. E.g., 'engineers and scientists' can replace 'other professional and technical workers' on a one-for-one basis. Similarly, if an unskilled urban worker cannot be employed otherwise, he can always return to the agricultural sector. Note one immediate implication. The shadow price of labor in a high-skill category can never drop below that in a low-skill category — which in turn must be positive as long as labor and capital remain substitutes. This specific formulation stems from our view that Mexico's poverty is related to low productivity and to seasonal unemployment in traditional agriculture.

Typically, it is non-optimal for labor to be downgraded from any of the skill categories. This result has suggested the importance of including activities for labor upgrading and for substituting physical capital in place of agricultural workers. It is supposed that in 1960, the marginal rate of substitution was 15,000 pesos' worth of investment costs per man released from agriculture and that subsequently the substitution rate has been rising at 2% per year. [7]

Following the tradition of Lewis (1954), it is assumed that unskilled workers may be transferred from rural into urban occupations through a continuing input of urban services: 2,400 pesos' worth per man-year. (This annual transformation cost of 2,400 pesos equals 50% of the urban-rural wage differential estimated for 1960.) Here the 2,400 pesos' worth of services are viewed as an

---

[6] An unsolved problem remains the fact that within a given category, there are inefficiencies, market imperfections and/or geographical differentials such that the identical skill commands a wage 50% higher in one enterprise than in another.

[7] Ideally, there ought to have been activities specified for capital-labor substitution outside agriculture, e.g., for replacing neighborhood *tiendas* with supermarkets. For this, the data problems would have been even more severe than with agriculture. Moreover, it should be recalled that almost 50% of Mexico's 1968 labor force was engaged in agriculture; and that output per man is lowest in this sector. Agriculture is therefore likely to remain the major source for releasing unskilled manpower throughout the 1970's and 1980's.

interindustry input associated with the conversion of one type of labor into another. No direct utility is ascribed to the transformation cost. By excluding this flow of services from the definition of aggregate consumption, we depart from national income accounting conventions.

For producing skill classes 1–3, there are educational activities which absorb labor inputs (students and teachers) during early time periods, and which operate with an appropriate time delay — a lag of six years for engineers and scientists and three years for other skills. To avoid unrealistic short-run bottlenecks, there are activities for skill substitution during time periods 1 and 2. These imply, e.g., that an engineer may be replaced temporarily with a technical worker, but that there will then be serious inefficiencies in the rest of the production process, and that these inefficiencies will generate demands for additional low-skilled workers. For further details on the manpower aspects of DINAMICO, and for a calculation of the von Neumann equilibrium prices of human capital, see above, chapter II.1.

4. Algebraic formulation

In the algebraic formulation that follows, the symbols i and j are employed as row and column indices, respectively, for the 15 domestic producing sectors. For non-competitive imports, the row index $i = 16$. The symbol s identifies the five labor skill categories. For the basic numerical data and sources, see the two preceding chapters. Unless specified otherwise, all items are valued in terms of 1960 domestic producers' prices.

Altogether, the programming matrix contains 316 constraint rows, 421 activity columns and some 4,000 non-zero coefficients. At this size, numerical optimization did not prove to be a bottleneck. The model evolved during a two-year period of experimentation. With a continuing series of improvements in the basic data, there were six successive versions of the 'basic case'. Eventually, a special-purpose program was written to generate the matrix and to facilitate data revisions.

Table 2
Summary of constraint rows [a]
(unit: billions of 1960 pesos unless otherwise specified)

Constraint group		Number of rows
(Ait)	Material balances	90
(Bjt)	Capacity	90
(Ci)	Terminal investment	15
(Dst) and (DRQLst)	Labor demands and supplies (unit: millions of man-years)	70
(Et)	Exports	6
(Ft), (FGAPt) and (FFDP)	Foreign exchange, resource gap and direct private capital inflow	13
(GINVt), (GSAVt) and (GGDPt)	Macroeconomic definitions	19
(Ht)	Gradualist consumption path	6
(Jt)	Domestic savings constraint	6
(MXR)	Maximand row	1
	TOTAL	316

[a] The linear programming code MPS 360 makes it inexpensive to impose upper bounds on individual activities. Hence these 138 bounds are excluded from this row count.

DINAMICO's rows and activities are summarized in tables 2–4. For defining the activities, all unbarred upper-case symbols denote linear programming unknowns, and all other symbols denote parameters. A raised index denotes a time superscript, except for those expressions bracketed by parentheses. In the case of such parenthetical expressions, a raised index denotes an exponent.

(Ait) *Material balances*: For each item i and year t, these ensure that the requirements for consumption, investment, merchandise exports and tourism not exceed the domestic output less current account interindustry inputs. For the input-output coefficients a_{ij}^t, note the convention that positive values denote current account inputs, and that negative values denote the output of sector j net

Table 3
Summary of activity columns
(unit: billions of 1960 pesos unless otherwise specified)

			Number of activity columns
output; capacity increases	X_j^t	gross output of sector , year t	90
	V_j^t	one-year increase in capacity of sector j, investment resources expended in year t	105
labor skills	LD_s^t	labor downgraded from labor category s, year t (unit: millions of man-years)	28
	UL_s^t	labor upgraded into labor category s, year t (unit: millions of man-years)	13
	KA^t	capital added to agriculture in substitution for unskilled labor	7
	ED_s^t	education activities for human capital formation, skill s, first available in year t (unit: millions of man-years)	17
	RQL_s^t	requirements for labor skill s, year t (unit: millions of man-years)	35
exports	Z_i^t	exports of item i, year t	60
	ZM^τ	exports of high-cost manufactures, *first* exported in year τ	6
	ZA^t	aggregate merchandise exports, year t	6
	ZT^t	tourism earnings, year t	6
capital inflows, remittances	$RGAP^t$	resource gap, year t	6
	$\overline{FC}^t$	concessional foreign capital inflows, net of amortization, exogenous, year t	6
	FDP^t	foreign direct private capital inflows, net of amortization, year t	6
	$\overline{INFDP}$	interest and profit remittances on foreign direct private capital inflows prior to year 1, exogenous	1
macro-economic variables	INV^t	gross domestic investment, year t	7
	SAV^t	gross domestic savings, year t	7
	CON^t	consumption expenditures, household and government, year t	8
	GDP^t	gross domestic product, year t	7
		Total	421

Table 4
Detached coefficients tableau – period t ($t = 1, ..., 6$ unless noted otherwise)

Rows	X_j^t ($t=0,...,6$)	V_j^t	V_j^τ ($\tau=0,...,t-1$)	LD_s^t ($t=1,...,7$)	UL_s^t ($t=1,...,7$)	KA^t ($t=0,...,6$)	KA^τ ($\tau=0,...,t-1$)	ED_s^t ($t=2,...,7$)	ED_s^τ ($\tau\neq t$)	RQL_s^t ($t=0,...,7$)	Z_i^t ($i=1,...,10$)	ZM^t	ZM^τ ($\tau=1,...,t-1$)	ZA^t	ZT_i^t
	Output; capacity increase			Labor skills							Exports				
Ait ($i=1,...,15$)	a_{ij}^t	b_{ij}^t		*		*					I	*	*	*	apz_i^t
Bjt ($j=1,...,15$)	I		$-3I$												
DRQLst ($s=1,...,5$)	l_{sj}^t				*	*		*		$-I$					
Dst ($s=1,...,5; t=1,...,7$)				*	*			*	*	I					
Et	$a_{16,j}^t$	$b_{16,j}^t$									$-1.$	$-1.$	$-1.$	0.8658	
Ft				*										$-1.$	$-1.$
FGAPt															
FFDP (no time index)															
GINVT ($t=0,...,6$)	k_j^t					1.									
GSAVt															
GGDPt															
Ht															
Jt															
bounds on individual unknowns											UP / LO				UP / LO

bounds on individual unknowns: UP = upper bound;   LO = lower bound;   FX = fixed value;   FR = unrestricted in sign

Notes:

* = non-zero element; I = element belonging to appropriate row and column of identity matrix.

Missing rows: (C_i^t), (DRQLs7). These relate only to terminal conditions. In order to include these rows, the physical size of this tableau would have to be increased still further.

Table 4 (continued)

Rows \ Columns	Capital inflows, remittances					Macroeconomic variables								Right-hand side constants
						(period t)				(period $t+1$ and $t-1$)				
	$RGAP^t$	$\overline{FC}^t$	FDP^t	FDP^t ($\tau=1,...,t-1$)	$\overline{INFDP}$	INV^t ($t=0,...,6$)	SAV^t ($t=0,...,6$)	CON^t ($t=0,...,7$)	GDP^t ($t=0,...,6$)	CON^{t-1}	CON^{t+1}	SAV^{t-1}	GDP^{t-1}	
Ait ($i=1,...,15$)								apc_i^t						$\leqslant 0$
Bit ($j=1,...,15$)														$\leqslant \overline{X}_j^0$
DRQLst ($s=1,...,15$)														$= 0$
Dst ($s=1,...,5$; $t=1,...,7$)														$\leqslant *$
Et	$-1.$													$= 0$
Ft	$1.$	$-1.$	$-1.$	$*$	$1.$			apc_{16}^t						$= 0$
FGAPt	$1.$													$= -\overline{INFC}^t$
FFDP (no time index)				$1.$										$\leqslant *$
GINVT ($t=0,...,6$)	$-1.$					$-1.$								$= 0$
GSAVt						$1.$	$-1.$							$= 0$
GGDPt									$1.$					$= 0$
Ht								$-[1+(1+g)^3]$	$-1.$	$1.$	$(1+g)^3$			$= 0$
Jt							$1.$		$- mps$			$-1.$	mps	$\leqslant 0$
	FR	FX	UP		FX									

of inputs to itself. The coefficients carry a time superscript to allow for technological change, e.g., an increase in the inputs of chemicals, machinery and electricity per unit of output and a decrease in the inputs of agricultural products.

The household and government consumption of item i is taken to be proportional to total expenditures on all items combined (the variable CON^t), with the coefficient apc_i^t representing the average propensity to consume item i. Since the coefficients carry a time superscript, the resulting predictions of demand do not differ greatly from those that would have been obtained through a nonlinear Engel curve formulation. It is predicted that a diminishing fraction will be spent on agricultural products and an increasing fraction on machinery in the form of consumers' durables. Similarly, the pattern of tourist expenditures is predicted through the average propensity coefficients apz_i^t — with total tourist expenditures an endogenous unknown, ZT^t.

Investment requirements are generated through the acceleration principle. That is, for all 15 sectors of destination j, the coefficients b_{ij}^t (capital originating in sector i per unit of capacity added in sector j) are multiplied by the one-year capacity increases V_j^t. For capital-labor substitution in agriculture, the unknowns KA^t are normalized in terms of the capital investment. Hence these unknowns are multiplied by the sector-of-origin ratios for investment in agriculture, $b_{i_1}^t / k_1^t$.

The material balances include terms related to the merchandise export activities Z_i^t, the exports of high-cost manufactures (activities ZM^t), and the commerce and service margins on merchandise exports. Also included is another source of demand: the 2,400 pesos' worth of urban services consumed per man-year converted from rural to urban employment through the labor upgrading activity UL_4^t.

A(it) *Material balances* (continued)

$$
\begin{bmatrix} \text{average} \\ \text{propensity} \\ \text{to consume} \\ \text{item } i \end{bmatrix}
\begin{bmatrix} \text{aggregate} \\ \text{consumption} \end{bmatrix}
+
\begin{bmatrix} \text{capital} \\ \text{originating} \\ \text{in sector } i \\ \text{per unit of} \\ \text{capacity} \\ \text{added in} \\ \text{sector } j \end{bmatrix}
\begin{bmatrix} \text{one-year} \\ \text{increase in} \\ \text{capacity of} \\ \text{sector } j \end{bmatrix}
$$

$$
[\ apc_i^t\ ]\ [\ CON^t\ ] + [\ \sum_{j=1}^{15} b_{ij}^t\ ]\ [\ V_j^t\ ]
$$

$$
+
\begin{bmatrix} \text{capital} \\ \text{originating} \\ \text{in sector } i \\ \text{per unit of} \\ \text{investment in} \\ \text{sector 1,} \\ \text{agriculture} \end{bmatrix}
\begin{bmatrix} \text{capital added} \\ \text{to agriculture} \\ \text{in substitution} \\ \text{for unskilled} \\ \text{labor} \end{bmatrix}
+
\begin{bmatrix} \text{merchandise} \\ \text{exports} \\ (i = 1, ..., 10) \end{bmatrix}
$$

$$
+ [\ b_{i1}^t / k_1^t\ ]\ [\ KA^t\ ] + [\ Z_i^t\ ]
$$

$$
+
\begin{bmatrix} \text{tourists'} \\ \text{average} \\ \text{propensity} \\ \text{to consume} \\ \text{item } i \end{bmatrix}
\begin{bmatrix} \text{tourism} \\ \text{earnings} \end{bmatrix}
+
\begin{bmatrix} \text{terms related} \\ \text{to commerce and} \\ \text{service\_margins} \\ (i = 13, 15) \text{ and} \\ \text{to high-cost exports;} \\ \text{see constraints} \\ \text{(Et) and appendix} \end{bmatrix}
$$

$$
+ [\ apz_i^t\ ]\ [\ ZT^t\ ] +
$$

$$
+
\begin{bmatrix} \text{requirements from} \\ \text{service sector} \\ \text{for converting} \\ \text{rural to urban} \\ \text{labor } (i = 15) \end{bmatrix}
+
\begin{bmatrix} \text{net output } (-) \\ \text{or input } (+) \\ \text{from sector } i \\ \text{per unit of} \\ \text{gross output,} \\ \text{sector } j \end{bmatrix}
\begin{bmatrix} \text{gross output,} \\ \text{sector } j \end{bmatrix}
$$

$$
+ [\ 2.4\ UL_4^t\ ] + [\ \sum_{j=1}^{15} a_{ij}^t\ ]\ [\ X_j^t\ ] \leqslant 0
$$

$$
(i = 1, ..., 15;\ t = 1, ..., 6)
$$

(Bjt) *Capacity constraints:* For each sector j and year t, these ensure that the increase over the base-year output will not exceed the capacity added during the prior periods. In other words, whatever may have been the level of excess capacity during the base year, it is supposed that the absolute amount of such excess capacity will remain unchanged in the future. This simplification was adopted – not because excess capacity was zero during the base year – but rather because we know of no successful attempts to measure it.

Constraints (Bjt) are written as though there is an average lag of 3 years between the input of investment resources and the full capacity available from that input. Since there are 3 years between representative points of time, and since the unknown V_j^τ refers to a one-year capacity increment in year τ, these unknowns are multiplied by a time factor of 3 years:

$$X_j^t \leqslant \bar{X}_j^0 + \sum_{\tau=0}^{t-1} 3V_j^\tau \qquad (j = 1, ..., 15; t = 1, ..., 6) .$$

(Ci) *Terminal investment constraints:* These are intended to avoid horizon effects – dependence of the initial investment allocations upon the arbitrary 18 year horizon length. For simpler dynamic input-output models (see Hopkins 1969 and Manne 1970), it is possible to state sufficient conditions under which these constraints ensure that *increments* in investment and consumption will grow optimally at the annual rate of g in all sectors during the post-terminal period. Unlike the simpler models, the following expression does not ensure that foreign exchange inflows and outflows will remain balanced during the post-terminal period. A still more serious error arises from the fact that DINAMICO includes primary factors of production that cannot themselves be produced within the economy – unskilled labor, export bounds and foreign capital inflows. Hence, further empirical testing is required before being able to assert that constraints (Ci) permit DINAMICO to avoid horizon effects with respect to physical capital formation:

(Ci) *Terminal investment constraints* (continued)

$$\begin{bmatrix} \text{consumption increment} \\ \text{between 1986 and 1989} \end{bmatrix}$$

$$\begin{bmatrix} \text{average} \\ \text{propensity} \\ \text{to consume} \\ \text{item } i \end{bmatrix} \begin{bmatrix} \text{increment in} \\ \text{aggregate} \\ \text{consumption} \\ \text{between 1986} \\ \text{and 1989} \end{bmatrix} + \begin{bmatrix} \text{capital} \\ \text{originating} \\ \text{in sector } i \\ \text{per unit of} \\ \text{capacity} \\ \text{added in} \\ \text{sector } j \end{bmatrix} \begin{bmatrix} \text{three-year} \\ \text{growth} \\ \text{rate} \end{bmatrix} \begin{bmatrix} \text{one-year} \\ \text{increase} \\ \text{in capacity} \\ \text{of sector } j \end{bmatrix}$$

$$[\quad apc_i^6 \quad] [CON^7 - CON^6] + [\quad \sum_{j=1}^{15} b_{ij}^6 \quad] [(1+g)^3 - 1] [\quad V_j^6 \quad]$$

$$+ \begin{bmatrix} \text{exogenous increment} \\ \text{in requirements for} \\ \text{exports and tourism} \\ \text{between 1986 and 1989} \end{bmatrix} \leqslant \begin{bmatrix} \text{output increment between 1986} \\ \text{and 1989, net of interindustry} \\ \text{requirements} \end{bmatrix}$$

$$\sum_{j=1}^{15} - a_{ij}^6 \, 3V_j^6$$

$(i = 1, ..., 15)$

(DRQLst) *Definition of labor requirements*: These equations define the demand for labor skill s in period t. Requirements (the unknowns RQL_s^t) are intended to coincide with the census definition of *económicamente activos*, i.e., those workers gainfully employed in skill s, period t. The labor input coefficients l_{sj}^t are predicted as though each skill were required in fixed proportions per unit of output in sector j — and as though these inputs were diminishing over time through a process of disembodied technical change.

Since the capital-labor substitution activities for the agricultural sector (KA^t) have been normalized in terms of the amount of capital added, the marginal rates of substitution appear directly within the labor requirement constraints DRQLst. Unlike investments in other sectors, it is supposed that these substitution activities have a negligible gestation lag. It does not take long to replace men with a tractor. Accordingly, these constraints are written as though the capital-labor substitution activity during period t will have an immediate effect upon the labor requirements in that period:

$$
\begin{bmatrix} \text{requirement} \\ \text{for skill } s \end{bmatrix} = \begin{bmatrix} \text{input of} \\ \text{skill } s \\ \text{per unit of} \\ \text{gross output,} \\ \text{sector } j \end{bmatrix} \begin{bmatrix} \text{gross} \\ \text{output,} \\ \text{sector } j \end{bmatrix}
$$

$$
RQL_s^t = \sum_{j=1}^{15} [l_{sj}^t] \quad [\ X_j^t\ ]
$$

$$
- \begin{bmatrix} \text{unskilled agricultural} \\ \text{labor released per unit} \\ \text{of cumulative capital;} \\ \text{marginal rate of} \\ \text{substitution, changing} \\ \text{at 2\% per year from} \\ \text{1960 rate } (s = 5) \end{bmatrix} \begin{bmatrix} \text{cumulative} \\ \text{capital} \\ \text{added in} \\ \text{substitution} \\ \text{for unskilled} \\ \text{labor} \end{bmatrix}
$$

$$
- [\ \frac{1}{15(1.02)^{8+3t}}\ ]\ [KA^t + 3\sum_{\tau=0}^{t-1} KA^\tau]
$$

$$
(s = 1, ..., 5; t = 1, ..., 6)
$$

Similarly, for the terminal period:

$$
RQL_s^7 = \sum_{j=1}^{15} l_{sj}^7 (X_j^6 + 3V_j^6) - \begin{bmatrix} (s = 5) \\ \dfrac{3}{15(1.02)^{29}} \sum_{\tau=0}^{6} KA^\tau \end{bmatrix}
$$

$$
(s = 1, ..., 5)
$$

(Dst) *Labor demands and supplies*: on the left-hand side of these constraints, there appear the unknowns RQL_s^t, the demand for labor skill s in period t. The right-hand side contains the exogenous manpower availability estimates. Also on the right-hand side, there appear the terms related to the endogenous inputs and outputs from the human capital formation and the skill substitution activities described in chapter II.1 above.

$$
\begin{bmatrix}
\text{requirement for} \\
\text{skill } s,\ \text{period } t \\
\\
RQL_s^t
\end{bmatrix}
\leq
\begin{bmatrix}
\text{exogenously} \\
\text{projected} \\
\text{availability}
\end{bmatrix}
+
\begin{bmatrix}
\text{net availability produced} \\
\text{endogenously by human} \\
\text{capital formation and skill} \\
\text{substitution activities} \\
\\
ED_s^t,\ LD_s^t\ \text{and}\ UL_s^t
\end{bmatrix}
$$

$(s = 1, ..., 5; t = 1, ..., 7)$

Even though constraints Dst extend through period 7, note that this formulation does *not* eliminate horizon effects with respect to human capital formation. [8] During the terminal period, no endogenous provision is made for post-terminal increases in the stock of human capital. For an alternative approach that provides

---

[8] There is a logical inconsistency between the terminal conditions postulated for physical and for human capital formation. To see this, let the symbol y_i^t denote the *excess* of supply over demand for item i in period t. Then rows Ait, Bjt and Ci imply that for physical capital formation and for the material balances:

$$y_i^6 \geqslant 0 \quad\text{and}\quad y_i^7 - y_i^6 \geqslant 0 .$$

These conditions look similar, but are in fact more restrictive than those for human capital formation (rows Dst and DRQLst), which together imply:

$$y_i^6 \geqslant 0 \quad\text{and}\quad y_i^7 \geqslant 0 .$$

For a given item i, the first pair of inequalities would imply the second. The converse does not hold.

for these post-terminal increases, see Blitzer (1971, pp. 43–45). [9]

(Et) *Export earnings*: The six rows that appear explicitly are those that define ZA^t, the total foreign exchange earned through merchandise exports. With commerce and service margins totaling 13.42%, the producers' price [10] value is 86.58% of this total:

$$
\begin{bmatrix}
\text{foreign exchange earnings} \\
\text{from merchandise exports,} \\
\text{items } 1-10; \text{valued at} \\
\text{producers' prices}
\end{bmatrix}
+
\begin{bmatrix}
\text{foreign exchange earnings from} \\
\text{high-cost manufactures } \textit{first} \\
\text{exported in year } \tau = 1, ..., t; \\
\text{valued at producers' prices}
\end{bmatrix}
$$

$$
\sum_{i=1}^{10} Z_i^t \qquad + \qquad \sum_{\tau=1}^{t} ZM^\tau
$$

$$
= 0.8658 \, ZA^t
$$

$$(t = 1, ..., 6)$$

---

[9] Charles Blitzer and Richard Inman have experimented with an alternative to DINAMICO's terminal investment conditions. They converted the human capital formation constraints (rows Ds 7) into incremental form, analogous to the terminal constraints on physical capital formation (rows Ci). They then applied exponential smoothing to extrapolate the terminal activity levels for human capital formation. In addition, they modified rows Ci to allow for hitherto neglected changes in certain components, e.g., the effect of differences between the input-output coefficients a_{ij}^6 and a_{ij}^7.

With this reformulation, there was a reduction in the horizon effects for human capital formation, and there was a smoothing of the time series for activities ED_s^t, UL_s^t and KA^t. Fortunately, during time periods 1–4, there were only minor changes in the macroeconomic variables, the production and employment levels, and the efficiency prices. Because of the insensitivity during the initial decade of the planning horizon – and because the reformulation would have made the exposition of DINAMICO more cumbersome than the present version – these suggested changes have not been incorporated in the terminal conditions.

[10] In accordance with national income accounting conventions, exports are valued here at domestic producers' prices. For estimating the direction of comparative advantage, it would have been more logical to value exports at international prices. See below, chapter II.5, and the note at the end of that chapter.

For material balance constraints (A13t) and (A15t), the quantity ZA^t helps to calculate the value of exports originating in the commerce and service sectors. These margins are regarded as interindustry input requirements proportional to the aggregate value of merchandise exports.

commerce margins: $0.1125\ ZA^t$ (rows (A13t))
service margins: $0.0217\ ZA^t$ (rows (A15t))

In equations (Et), now refer back to the terms other than ZA^t. The export earnings from merchandise item i are denoted by Z_i^t ($i = 1, ..., 10$). On the basis of commodity projections − taking account of world income changes and income elasticities − specific upper and lower bounds are imposed upon the growth rate of these items. (See table 5 for the numerical values of the growth limits upon exports − and also the limits upon earnings from tourism.) With the lower and upper bounds (ϵ_i and e_i, respective-

Table 5
Upper and lower bounds on export growth rates

	Lower bound on annual growth rate, ϵ_i (%)	Upper bound on annual growth rate, e_i (%)
1. Agriculture, livestock, forestry and fishing	2.0	6.0
2. Mining and quarrying	0	4.0
3. Production and refining of petroleum and coal products	0	1.5
4. Food, beverages and tobacco	0	6.0
5. Textiles, apparel and leather products	0	4.5
6. Wood, furniture, paper and printing	0	6.0
7. Chemicals, rubber and plastic products	0	10.0
8. Non-metallic mineral products	0	7.5
9. Basic metals	0	10.0
10. Machinery	0	12.0
T. Tourism in the interior of Mexico	8.0	13.0

ly) expressed as annual rates, it follows that:

$$\bar{Z}_i^0(1+\epsilon_i)^{3t} \leqslant Z_i^t \leqslant \bar{\bar{Z}}_i^0(1+e_i)^{3t} \qquad (i = 1, ..., 10; t = 1, ..., 6)$$

$$\overline{ZT}^0(1+\epsilon_T)^{3t} \leqslant ZT^t \leqslant \overline{\overline{ZT}}^0(1+e_T)^{3t} \quad (t = 1, ..., 6) .$$

Since the 132 preceding bounds are imposed upon individual unknowns, these need not appear explicitly within the detached coefficients tableau. (See the rows labeled 'bounds' in table 4.) No upper bounds have been placed upon the activities ZM^τ, high-cost manufactured exports. For details on this marginal source of export earnings, see the appendix below.

(Ft) *Foreign exchange*: For each period t, there is a row that measures the inputs and outputs of foreign exchange from the import and export activities. [11] The 'resource gap' between foreign exchange earnings and import requirements is to be financed through foreign capital inflows:

$$\begin{bmatrix} \text{average propensity} \\ \text{to import} \\ \text{consumption goods} \\ \text{and services;} \\ \text{non-competitive} \end{bmatrix} \begin{bmatrix} \text{aggregate} \\ \text{consump-} \\ \text{tion} \end{bmatrix} + \begin{bmatrix} \text{imports of} \\ \text{intermediate} \\ \text{goods per} \\ \text{unit of out-} \\ \text{put, sector} \\ j; \text{non-} \\ \text{competitive} \end{bmatrix} \begin{bmatrix} \text{gross} \\ \text{output,} \\ \text{sector } j \end{bmatrix}$$

$$[\quad apc_{16}^t \quad] [\ CON^t \ ] + \sum_{j=1}^{15} [a_{16,j}^t] \quad [\ X_j^t \ ]$$

---

[11] These rows include no specific projections for 'frontier transactions' or for the expenditures of Mexican tourists abroad. It is supposed that these items cancel out, and that their net effect upon foreign exchange flows is zero.

$$+ \begin{bmatrix} \text{imports of} \\ \text{capital goods} \\ \text{per unit of} \\ \text{capacity added,} \\ \text{sector } j; \\ \text{non-competitive} \end{bmatrix} \begin{bmatrix} \text{one-year} \\ \text{increase in} \\ \text{capacity of} \\ \text{sector } j \end{bmatrix} + \begin{bmatrix} \text{imports of} \\ \text{capital goods} \\ \text{per unit of} \\ \text{investment} \\ \text{in sector 1,} \\ \text{agriculture;} \\ \text{non-competitive} \end{bmatrix} \begin{bmatrix} \text{capital} \\ \text{added to} \\ \text{agriculture} \\ \text{in substitu-} \\ \text{tion for} \\ \text{unskilled} \\ \text{labor} \end{bmatrix}$$

$$+ \sum_{j=1}^{15} [b^t_{16,j}] \quad [\quad V^t_j \quad] + [\quad b^t_{16,1}/k^t_1 \quad] [\quad KA^t \quad]$$

$$= \begin{array}{c} \text{aggregate} \\ \text{export} \\ \text{earnings} \end{array} + \begin{array}{c} \text{tourism} \\ \text{earnings} \end{array} + \begin{array}{c} \text{resource} \\ \text{gap} \end{array}$$

$$ZA^t \quad + \quad ZT^t \quad + RGAP^t$$

$(t = 1, ..., 6)$

In the foreign exchange rows (Ft), note the rigidity of the import requirements implicit in the non-competitive import coefficients [12] for consumption goods, intermediate goods and capital goods. These rigidities are at least partially offset by the trade-balance improving activities in the terms related to exports and tourism earnings.

(FGAPt) *Resource gap – financial flows*: These rows define the financial components of the 'resource gap': capital inflows less amortization, interest and profit remittances. Since there are negative as well as positive components of this gap, the variable $RGAP^t$ may take on either negative or positive values:

---

[12] Imports are defined as originating in sector 16. Non-competitive import coefficients are therefore identified by the sector-of-origin subscript $i = 16$.

$$RGAP^t =$$

$$
\begin{bmatrix}
\text{capital} \\
\text{inflows,} \\
\text{concessional} \\
\text{terms,} \\
\text{exogenous}
\end{bmatrix}
+
\begin{bmatrix}
\text{direct} \\
\text{private} \\
\text{capital} \\
\text{inflows,} \\
\text{endogenous}
\end{bmatrix}
-
\begin{bmatrix}
\text{interest on} \\
\text{concessional} \\
\text{capital inflows} \\
\text{of prior years,} \\
\text{exogenous}
\end{bmatrix}
$$

$$\overline{FC}^t \quad + \quad FDP^t \quad - \quad \overline{INFC}^t$$

$$
-
\begin{bmatrix}
\text{interest and} \\
\text{profit remittances} \\
\text{on direct private} \\
\text{capital inflows} \\
\text{of prior years,} \\
\text{exogenous}
\end{bmatrix}
-
\begin{bmatrix}
\text{payments for} \\
\text{capital inflows} \\
\text{received in} \\
\text{year 1 and in} \\
\text{each third sub-} \\
\text{sequent year}
\end{bmatrix}
$$

$$
- \quad \overline{INFDP} \quad - \begin{bmatrix} (1.15)^3 - 1 \\ = 0.521 \end{bmatrix} \begin{bmatrix} \sum_{\tau=1}^{t-1} FDP^\tau \end{bmatrix}
$$

Capital inflows have been grouped under two headings: $\overline{FC}^t$ and FDP^t. The high-cost alternative (FDP^t) is taken as an endogenous flow, and the low-cost alternative ($\overline{FC}^t$) as exogenous. Given the time path of inflows on concessional terms — and given the term structure of interest rates — there is an exogenously determined time path of interest payments due on the loans.[13] The annual payments are identified by the symbol $\overline{INFC}^t$.

For calculating the interest and profit remittances due on private capital inflows of prior years, two terms appear in equations (FGAPt). The first of these ($\overline{INFDP}$) measures the annual amounts due to foreigners in payment for capital invested in Mexico prior to year 1. This is an exogenously specified initial condition, and could be reduced only through modifying the status quo of for-

[13] These exogenously specified quantities have been adapted by Hans Bergendorff and Yves Franchet from an internal document of the International Bank for Reconstruction and Development. The specific numerical values are shown along with the foreign exchange projections in table 7 below.

eign property holders – e.g., through increased taxes or through expropriation.

Equations (FGAPt) also contain an endogenous component to measure the annual amounts due to foreign private investors. These are income payments for capital inflows received *within* the planning horizon of DINAMICO. Because of the three-year interval between successive points of time, it is supposed that the interest and profit remittances are also paid at three-year intervals – accumulating these amounts at a 15% annual cost of capital. Consider, for example, activity FDP^1. For each billion pesos of capital inflows received during period 1, this activity generates 0.521 billion pesos' worth of interest and profit remittance outflows during each third subsequent year. Even aside from ideological considerations related to foreign ownership, this is an expensive source of capital. Depending on its marginal productivity, private foreign capital may or may not be worth the cost.

(FFDP) *Direct private capital inflows, increase over planning horizon*: This constraint provides a bound on the cumulative increase of foreign ownership of Mexico's capital stock. For year 1 (1971), net private capital inflows are projected to be in the neighborhood of 5 billion pesos. If the *average* inflows are not to exceed this level during each of the six representative years of our planning horizon, the following constraint must be imposed:

$$\sum_{t=1}^{6} FDP^t \leqslant (6)(5) = 30 \text{ billion pesos at 1960 prices.}$$

To allow for some flexibility in timing, but to avoid sharp year-to-year fluctuations, the following are also stipulated as upper bounds on flows in individual years:

$FDP^1 \leqslant 5.0$ billion pesos at 1960 prices

$FDP^t \leqslant 5.5$ billion pesos at 1960 prices ($t = 2, ..., 5$)

$FDP^6 \leqslant 5.0$ billion pesos at 1960 prices

(G) *Macroeconomic definitions*: The 19 macroeconomic identities follow conventional lines. The only constraint referring to the 1968 base-year investment allocation is (GINVO). It is this constraint through which we attempt to offset the short-run rigidity of the acceleration principle, and to compensate for errors in our estimates of the initial capacities in each sector. The definitions of aggregate investment, domestic savings and gross domestic product are, respectively:

$$\begin{bmatrix} \text{sectoral} \\ \text{gross} \\ \text{capital-} \\ \text{output} \\ \text{ratio} \end{bmatrix} \begin{bmatrix} \text{one-year} \\ \text{capacity} \\ \text{increase} \end{bmatrix} + \begin{bmatrix} \text{capital added} \\ \text{to agriculture} \\ \text{in substitution} \\ \text{for unskilled} \\ \text{labor} \end{bmatrix} = \begin{bmatrix} \text{aggregate} \\ \text{gross} \\ \text{investment} \end{bmatrix}$$

(GINVt) $$\sum_{j=1}^{15} [k_j^t] \ [\ V_j^t \ ] + [\ \ KA^t \ \ ] = [\ \ INV^t \ \ ]$$

where $INV^0 = 55.0$ billion pesos at 1960 prices

$$(t = 0, ..., 6)$$

$$\begin{bmatrix} \text{gross} \\ \text{domestic} \\ \text{savings} \end{bmatrix} + \begin{bmatrix} \text{resource} \\ \text{gap} \end{bmatrix}$$

(GSAVt) $INV^t = \quad SAV^t \quad + \quad RGAP^t$ $(t = 1, ..., 6)$

$$\begin{bmatrix} \text{gross} \\ \text{domestic} \\ \text{product} \end{bmatrix} = \begin{bmatrix} \text{aggregate} \\ \text{consumption} \end{bmatrix} + \begin{bmatrix} \text{gross} \\ \text{domestic} \\ \text{savings} \end{bmatrix}$$

(GGDPt) $GDP^t \quad = \quad CON^t \quad + \quad SAV^t$ $(t = 1, ..., 6)$

(Ht) *Gradualist consumption path*: Following the Ramsey (1928) tradition on the optimal savings problem, it would have been possible to define the maximand in terms of a separable, piecewise linear utility function, and to test for sensitivity of the optimal program with respect to an elasticity of utility and to a utility discount factor. As an alternative – in the interest of simplification — here the time path of consumption is restricted to follow a gradualist form. That is, *increments* in aggregate consumption are required to grow at the annual rate g. (The nominal value of $g = 7\%$ per year.) By raising or lowering this subjective policy parameter, it is possible to examine the tradeoff between near-future versus distant future increases in consumption. The gradualist restriction is expressed as follows:

$$CON^{t+1} - CON^t = (1+g)^3 [CON^t - CON^{t-1}] \qquad (t = 1, ..., 6)$$

where $CON^0 = 208.8$ billion pesos at 1960 prices.

Note that constraints (Ht) imply that total consumption will *eventually* grow at the rate g, but that this target is not necessarily reached during the first few years. Note also that these constraints are consistent with those for terminal investment, (Ci).

(Jt) *Domestic savings constraint*: For assigning a numerical value to the marginal propensity to save, it is instructive to recall the Fel'dman-Domar-Mahalanobis results. Suppose that the net inflow of foreign capital remains approximately constant (not necessarily zero), and that the incremental capital-output ratio also remains approximately constant at some value k. (For Mexico, the value of k would lie in the neighborhood of 3.0.) Then the target growth rate g must be proportional to the marginal propensity to save, *mps*. With $g = 7\%$, we would have: $mps = g \cdot k = (0.07)(3.0) = 0.21$. If the *mps* were restricted to 0.21, this would not permit investment to grow during years in which there was a substantial drop in the inflows of foreign capital. Accordingly, constraints (Jt) are formulated so that the *mps* might be as high as 0.30. These savings constraints are not necessarily binding at any point of time:

$$\begin{bmatrix} \text{savings} \\ \text{increase} \end{bmatrix} \leqslant \begin{bmatrix} \text{marginal} \\ \text{propensity} \\ \text{to save} \end{bmatrix} \begin{bmatrix} GDP \\ \text{increase} \end{bmatrix}$$

$$[SAV^t - SAV^{t-1}] \leqslant [mps = 0.30] [GDP^t - GDP^{t-1}]$$

$$(t = 1, ..., 6)$$

where $SAV^0 = 52.1$ billion pesos at 1960 prices.

(MXR) *Maximand row*: Given the gradualist restrictions (Ht), we may — without loss of generality — state the maximand as any one of the unknowns CON^t. Here the maximand is taken as CON^1. This then defines the unit in terms of which all dual variables are measured.

5. Results — primal variables

The following chapter contains sensitivity analyses with respect to policy parameters such as g, the target growth rate. Here we concentrate upon the effect of the labor skill constraints. Unless specified otherwise, all of the following tables refer to the basic case in which the skill constraints Dst are included.

With these limits included, the 1968–80 optimal growth rate of GDP is projected at 6.9% — virtually identical to the 1960–68

Table 6
Macroeconomic results

| | Year | 1960 | 1968 | 1971 | 1974 | 1977 | 1980 | 1983 | 1986 | |
	Period t		0	1	2	3	4	5	6	
Unit: billions of 1960 pesos	GDP	150.5	260.9	319.7	385.5	476.7	582.6	710.3	852.6	
	CON	123.7	208.8	251.4	303.6	367.5	445.8	541.8	659.3	
	SAV	26.8	52.1	68.3	81.9	109.2	136.8	168.5	193.3	
	RGAP	2.9	2.9	2.5	0	−4.0	−8.6	−15.5	−17.6	
	INV	29.7	55.0	70.8	81.9	105.2	128.2	153.0	175.7	
										1968-80
Unit: annual growth rates (%)	GDP		7.1	7.0	6.4	7.3	6.9	6.8	6.3	6.9
	CON		6.8	6.4	6.5	6.6	6.7	6.7	6.8	6.5
	SAV		8.7	9.4	6.2	10.1	7.8	7.2	4.7	8.4
	INV		8.0	8.8	5.0	8.7	6.8	6.1	4.7	7.3
incremental capital-output ratio			2.66	2.81	3.23	2.69	2.98	3.01	3.23	
marginal propensity to save (%)			23.2	27.5	20.7	29.9	26.1	24.8	17.4	
average propensity to save (%)			17.8	20.0	21.4	21.2	22.9	23.5	23.7	22.7

Macroeconomic definitions: $GDP = CON + SAV$; $INV = SAV + RGAP$.

historically observed rate. (See table 6.) Like a Fel'dman-Domar-Mahalanobis (FDM) model, it will be observed that the growth rate of aggregate consumption keeps rising gradually from 6.4% toward the target annual rate of 7.0%. Unlike an FDM model, neither the growth rate of investment nor the marginal propensity to save nor the incremental capital-output ratio remains constant over time.

As a check upon the plausibility of the macroeconomic results, it can be seen that the incremental capital-output ratio – although not constant over time – would be of the same order of magnitude as that observed during the years 1960–68. Typically, the marginal savings propensity is higher than that observed in the past, but lies below 30%. The average savings propensity keeps rising throughout the 1970's, and follows a less erratic time path than does the *mps*.

The foreign exchange projections are summarized in table 7. For the years 1968–80, note that imports are projected to rise at 5.8% per year – more rapidly than during the period 1960–68. This result depends heavily upon our assumptions concerning the non-competitive import coefficients ($a^t_{16,j}$, $b^t_{16,j}$ and apc^t_{16}). In projecting the time trends for these coefficients, it has been assumed that there would be a slowdown in the rate of high-cost import substitution from that experienced during the 1960–68 period.

In order to pay for imports – and offset the substantial rise in interest and profit remittances – foreign exchange earnings would have to increase at an annual rate of 8.8% during 1968–80. This would be much higher than the 5.2% rate of increase experienced during the earlier period. To accelerate exports and tourism to this extent, it is clear that major changes in export policies would be needed. For a range of suggestions on such alternatives, see Bueno (1971). Still another possibility would be to reduce the incentives for the inflow of direct foreign private capital. This policy could lead to balance-of-payments difficulties during the early 1970's, but would help prevent a steep rise in interest and profit remittances during the latter half of the decade.

In table 7, we have shown the total foreign exchange earnings,

Table 7
Foreign exchange projection
(unit: billions of 1960 pesos)

Year Period t	1960	1968 0	1971 1	1974 2	1977 3	1980 4	1983 5	1986 6	Corresponding symbols in rows (Ft) and (FGAPt) [a]	Unit: annual growth rates (%) 1960–68	1968–80
Imports	15.0	21.0	25.8	29.9	35.4	41.2	47.0	51.4	$apc_{16}CON + \sum_{j=1}^{15} a_{16,j}X_j$ $+ \sum_{j=1}^{15} b_{16,j}V_j$ $+ (b_{16,1}/k_1)KA$	4.3	5.8
Less: export earnings + tourism	−12.1	−18.1	−23.3	−29.9	−39.4	−49.8	−62.5	−69.0	$ZA + ZT$	5.2	8.8
Resource gap	2.9	2.9	2.5	0	−4.0	−8.6	−15.5	−17.6	$RGAP$	0.0	–
Foreign capital inflows, concessional	2.0	2.1	4.3	4.7	4.3	3.1	1.5	−0.5	$\overline{FC}$	0.6	3.3
Foreign capital inflows, direct private	3.4	6.0	5.0	5.5	5.5	5.5	3.5	5.0	$\overline{FDP}$	7.3	−0.7
Less: interest on concessional capital inflows of prior years	−0.7	−1.4	−1.9	−2.7	−3.4	−4.0	−4.4	−4.2	$\overline{INFC}$	9.1	9.1
Less: interest and profit remittances on direct private capital inflows of prior years	−1.8	−3.8	−4.9	−7.5	−10.4	−13.2	−16.1	−17.9	$INFDP + 0.521 \sum_{\tau=1}^{t-1} FDP^\tau$	9.8	10.9
Resource gap	2.9	2.9	2.5	0	−4.0	−8.6	−15.5	−17.6	$RGAP$	–	–

[a] Superscript t omitted except where necessary to avoid ambiguity.

but not the sectoral mix that underlies this total. If taken literally, the primal solution of DINAMICO indicates that it is optimal to increase export earnings through manufactured products (activities ZM^t), even if these should require an initial subsidy of 30%. Given the opportunity cost of labor skills and of other items, apparently this is preferable to obtaining foreign exchange through tourism or through primary agricultural products.

To avoid bang-bang solutions of this character, it would be desirable to disaggregate each sector more finely and to introduce downward-sloping demand curves for each item. These features have been introduced into CHAC, the process analysis model of the agricultural sector. There, for example, maize and tomatoes are analyzed as separate items rather than added together. Now suppose that the dual solution to DINAMICO were introduced among the parameters of the sectoral planning model. The latter might then indicate that it is optimal to export an individual agricultural product such as tomatoes − although non-optimal to export maize. For comparative advantage calculations of this type, it seems preferable to employ multi-level planning, rather than attempt to apply literally the primal solution to a model that is as heavily aggregated as DINAMICO.

Tables 8 and 9 summarize the gross production levels and the percentage composition of investment. In most sectors, output and investment rise at a smooth rate during the years 1968–80. These time series are closely consistent with the 1960–68 trends. (The most erratic time series is that of KA^t, investment in capital-labor substitution within the agricultural sector.) The reader is warned against too literal an interpretation of these tables. In particular, the year-by-year growth rates are likely to be less reliable than the 1968–80 average. Because of the absence of census data for the base year 1968, that year's transactions matrix has not been estimated accurately. Still less reliable is the exogenously specified allowance for the supply of manpower initially within the educational pipeline. This leads to a number of anomalies in the 1968 and 1971 sectoral composition of investment. The more accurate the estimate that can be made of the initial conditions, the fewer of these anomalies are likely to remain.

Table 8
Gross production levels (unit: billions of 1960 pesos)

Year	1960	1968	1971	1974	1977	1980	1983	1986	Unit: annual growth rates (%)	
Period t		0	1	2	3	4	5	6	1960–68	1968–80
Sector j										
1. Agriculture	32.166	44.775	51.946	56.313	65.809	74.615	86.305	95.359	4.2%	4.3%
2. Mining	4.311	5.074	5.716	6.472	7.492	8.593	9.811	11.096	2.0	4.5
3. Petroleum	9.627	17.001	20.362	24.967	31.284	38.964	48.497	59.640	7.4	7.2
4. Food	29.455	48.689	59.341	73.305	91.445	112.799	138.873	166.857	6.5	7.3
5. Textiles	12.957	22.671	27.266	34.266	43.410	54.759	69.088	86.203	7.2	7.6
6. Wood	5.603	9.827	11.887	14.560	18.277	22.568	27.672	33.260	7.3	7.2
7. Chemicals	8.781	17.913	23.093	30.629	41.278	54.767	72.332	92.775	9.3	9.8
8. Non-metallic	2.528	5.351	6.977	8.682	11.611	14.935	49.251	63.326	9.8	8.9
9. Basic metals	4.690	10.768	14.554	19.623	27.237	37.010	49.251	63.326	10.9	10.8
10. Machinery	10.502	27.231	38.861	52.998	73.606	100.074	133.944	172.985	12.7	11.5
11. Construction	13.938	26.774	34.462	38.982	49.253	59.055	69.089	81.571	8.5	6.8
12. Electricity	2.205	5.669	7.672	10.467	14.453	19.818	26.920	35.459	12.5	11.0
13. Commerce	53.539	89.838	109.380	132.380	161.899	196.719	237.903	284.281	6.7	6.7
14. Transportation	8.040	12.598	14.702	17.300	20.463	24.152	28.452	33.415	5.8	5.6
15. Services	40.492	72.242	88.676	109.622	132.137	160.993	195.590	235.581	7.5	6.9

Table 9

Percentage composition of net investment by sector of destination

Sector j	Net capital stock [a] 1967	Annual net investment						
		1968	1971	1974	1977	1980	1983	1986
1a. Agriculture, capital-labor substitution (KA^t)		5.9%	11.7%	0.0%	5.1%	3.3%	7.5%	0.0%
1b. Agriculture, other		9.7	4.5	8.2	5.8	6.2	3.9	7.9
1. Agriculture, total	15.1%	15.6	16.2	8.2	10.9	9.5	11.4	7.9
2. Mining	0.8	0.4	0.4	0.4	0.4	0.3	0.3	0.4
3. Petroleum	4.1	3.5	3.8	4.5	4.3	4.4	4.4	4.4
4. Food	6.5	5.9	6.0	6.8	6.3	6.4	5.8	6.2
5. Textiles	2.6	2.2	2.6	2.9	2.8	2.9	3.0	2.8
6. Wood	2.0	1.7	1.7	2.1	1.9	1.8	1.7	1.9
7. Chemicals	3.2	4.0	4.5	5.4	5.3	5.7	5.6	4.7
8. Non-metallic	1.0	1.3	1.1	1.6	1.5	1.5	1.5	1.4
9. Basic metals	2.6	4.0	4.1	5.4	5.3	5.5	5.3	4.7
10. Machinery	3.6	6.9	6.4	8.0	7.9	8.3	8.0	6.9
11. Construction	0.8	1.0	0.5	0.9	0.7	0.6	0.7	0.9
12. Electricity	3.3	5.5	6.1	7.6	8.2	9.1	9.4	7.6
13. Commerce	6.4	5.9	5.5	6.3	6.0	6.0	5.9	7.2
14. Transportation	16.5	11.9	11.5	12.2	11.1	10.7	10.5	13.7
15. Services	31.5	30.2	29.6	27.7	27.4	27.3	26.5	29.3
Total	100.0	100.0	100.0	100.0	100.0	100.0	100.0	100.0

[a] Source: Banco de México, Departamento de Estudios Económicos, *Cuentas Nacionales* (1969), Table 168.

6. Results — dual variables for foreign exchange and labor

If a macroeconomic model is to be linked to sectoral and project investment decisions, the efficiency prices (also called shadow prices or dual variables) play a key role. Past experience with project evaluation through numerical multi-sector models has led to skeptical comments such as: 'Since drastic simplification is an unavoidable necessity in using linear programming models for an entire economy, there is no way of avoiding serious uncertainty as to the validity of the resulting "shadow prices".' (Harberger 1968, p. 243).

In the case of DINAMICO, it has turned out that the shadow prices are not altogether unbelievable, and we are tempted to point to the converse of Harberger's proposition: 'Since drastic simplification is an unavoidable necessity in analysing single projects (e.g., the assumption that most relative prices will remain constant over time), there is no way of avoiding serious uncertainty as to the validity of the resulting project decisions.'

In interpreting DINAMICO, recall that the dual variable for row i refers to the change in the maximand CON^1 per unit change in the right-hand-side constant of row i. These values would be increased in absolute magnitude — but remain unchanged in relative magnitude — if the maximand were changed to CON^2 or CON^3 ... or CON^7. The numéraire is arbitrary — even though measured in terms of 1960 pesos.

The dual variables refer to the *present values* of each item in terms of the maximand. Hence, for a given commodity such as foreign exchange or skill class 1 labor, these prices typically declined over time. [14] Since the relative prices of foreign exchange, labor, etc., do not necessarily remain constant from one period to the next, it is possible for there to be a different 'own' rate of interest for each commodity. Unlike aggregate growth models, there need not be one rate of return on capital. Similarly, there need not be one number that defines the shadow price of foreign exchange.

Consider, for example, foreign exchange. There is one dual vari-

---

[14] Typically, the efficiency price in the terminal period *exceeds* that in the pre-terminal period. (Compare periods 5 and 6 in table 10.) In simpler dynamic input-output models — with similar terminal conditions but without exogenously given primary factors of production — these high values may be explained by the 'terminal capacity valuation lemma'. (See Manne 1970.) That is, the terminal value of physical capacity may be interpreted as the sum of the one-period capacity rentals over the balance of an infinite planning horizon. It is conjectured that a similar interpretation is valid for DINAMICO — despite the presence of primary factors of production such as labor.

Table 10
Efficiency prices of foreign exchange and of tradable manufactures

Item	Year	1971	1974	1977	1980	1983	1986	'Own' rate of interest, 1974–80, annual rate (%)
	Period t	1	2	3	4	5	6	
Foreign exchange [a,b]		121.87	72.40	41.62	24.72	15.84	23.66	19.6
Tradable manufactures [a,c]		105.68	62.82	36.14	21.50	12.76	20.35	19.6
Efficiency price of foreign exchange relative to price of tradable manufactures		1.15	1.15	1.15	1.15	1.24	1.16	

[a] Unit: 1960 pesos' worth of maximand CON^1 per thousand 1960 pesos' worth of item.

[b] Dual variable, rows Ft.

[c] Let π_i^t denote the dual variable of tradable manufactured item i in period t. As in defining the export activities ZM^t (see appendix below), let z_i denote the fraction of item i in the composite of tradable manufactured items. Then the efficiency price of tradable manufactures is defined as the weighted average price of these items: $\Sigma_i z_i \pi_i^t$

able for each of the foreign exchange rows (Ft). The top line of table 10 contains the values of these dual variables for each of the six representative years. These numerical values are given directly in terms of the maximand, CON^1. Suppose, for example, that Mexico were to receive a grant of 1000 pesos of foreign exchange during the initial time period ($t = 1$). The dual variable for row F1 shows that this would permit an immediate consumption increase of 121.87 pesos, or 12% of the foreign grant. In subsequent years, following the gradualist path constraints (Ht), the consumption increase would grow at the annual rate of $g = 7\%$.

In the literature on project evaluation, it is common to refer to *the* shadow price of foreign exchange. A similar convention is followed when discussing policy instruments such as tariff rates, export subsidies or foreign exchange parities. In a static aggregate model, with only a single item in the domestic economy, it is quite unambiguous what is meant by the shadow price of foreign exchange. With a multi-sector model, however, there is ambiguity.

The price will depend upon whether the domestic numéraire is taken to be agricultural products or manufactures or services.

In table 10, for comparing the shadow price of foreign exchange with that of domestic items, we have taken the numéraire to be tradable manufactures. This convention is consistent with the fact that Mexico's imports consist almost entirely of manufactures, and that her exports will increasingly consist of such items. With this numéraire, it turns out that the shadow price of foreign exchange is approximately 15% higher than its conventional price. It will also be seen that the relative prices of foreign exchange and of tradable manufactures remain constant during the 1970's, and that the 'own' rate of interest on both these items is 19.6% per year between 1974 and 1980. [15]

We now turn from one primary resource (foreign exchange) to another (labor). Dual variables for the labor constraints are presented in three forms. (See table 11.) In the leftmost group of three columns, the numerical value is given directly in terms of the maximand CON^1. The rightmost column presents the 'own' rate of interest for each skill that is implied by these dual variables.

The middle group of three columns contains a more conventional normalization, relating the efficiency price of labor to that of consumption goods during the same period of time. By referring back to table 1, it can be seen that these values are of the same orders of magnitudes as those that prevailed in 1960. [16] According to table 11, the efficiency price differentials between

---

[15] Suppose that an item has a positive price at all points of time. For that item, the 'own' rate of interest between, say, 1974 and 1980 ($t = 2$ and $t = 4$) is defined as the annual rate r such that:

$$\frac{\text{dual variable for item in 1974}}{\text{dual variable for item in 1980}} = (1+r)^6 .$$

The own rate of interest helps to summarize any changes in relative prices. Over time, two items will have constant relative prices if and only if they have identical own rates of interest.

[16] Caveat: In table 11, the fact that the own rate is higher for skill class 3 than for class 2 does *not* mean that an improvement could be made in the maximand by increasing the availability of the one skill class and reducing that of the other by an equal number of man-years. All that is implied is a change in the relative price of the two labor skills.

Table 11
Efficiency wages, dual variables for labor constraints Dst

Skill s	(Unit: thousands of 1960 pesos' worth of maximand CON^1 per man-year of skill s)					(Unit: thousands of 1960 pesos per man-year of skill s, normalized by dual variable for consumption goods in year t)					'Own' rate of interest, 1974–80, annual rate (%)
Year Period t	1971 1	1974 2	1977 3	1980 4	1983 5	1971 1	1974 2	1977 3	1980 4	1983 5	
1. Engineers and scientists	8.954	5.314	4.367	2.524	1.676	79.3	78.3	110.1	106.9	119.2	13
2. Other professional and technical workers	4.264	2.530	2.207	1.371	0.652	37.8	37.3	55.7	58.1	46.4	11
3. Administrative and clerical workers	2.558	1.518	0.839	0.456	0.401	22.6	22.4	21.2	19.3	28.5	22
4. Manual and sales workers outside agriculture	0.853	0.506	0.252	0.198	0.111	7.6	7.5	6.4	8.4	7.9	17
4. Unskilled agricultural workers	0.464	0.274	0.107	0.112	0.061	4.1	4.0	2.7	4.7	4.3	16

high and low skills will not diminish over time. [17] For the 1970's, it remains doubtful whether any reduction in skill differentials will prove to be a significant factor in relieving the glaring inequalities of income distribution that have been characteristic of Mexico's past pattern of development. Relief *can* be anticipated from the upward shift in the skill-mix of the labor force, and the corresponding increase in wages relative to property income.

7. Effects of eliminating the labor constraints

When the labor constraints Dst are omitted, the GDP growth rate rises from 6.9 to 7.6% per year during 1968–80. In this case, the 1980 total work force requirements for skill classes 1–5 are 20% higher than when the labor constraints are imposed. Most of this increase would consist of demand for unskilled agricultural workers.

Table 12 compares the effect of the labor constraints upon the dual variables for the material balance rows, foreign exchange and consumption goods. When the labor constraints are eliminated – with initial capacities and foreign exchange then the only primary factors of production – one billion 1960 pesos' worth of transport services (sector 14) has a shadow price 8–9 times that of one billion 1960 pesos' worth of commerce services (sector 13). With the introduction of labor constraints, the differentials in relative prices tend to narrow between sectors, and are not dominated by the capital coefficients. Moreover – as anticipated by the argument in Harberger (1967, p. 142) – with the introduction of labor

---

[17] Despite one-for-one substitution possibilities between unskilled urban and rural labor, there is at all times a positive differential in the shadow prices between skill classes 4 and 5. This is implied by the fact that it is optimal to assign positive intensities to the labor upgrading variables UL_4^t during all time periods, and by the fact that this simultaneously generates a requirement for urban service inputs (2,400 pesos per man-year). To this extent, DINAMICO resembles such models as those of Sen (1962) and Marglin (1967) for choice of techniques in a labor-surplus economy with an institutionally fixed real wage rate and fixed savings propensities. Unlike the Sen-Marglin formulation, here the choice of techniques also depends upon the skill-mix – hence upon the human capital formation activities for producing the more highly valued skill classes.

Table 12
Effect of labor constraints upon dual variables
(unit: 1960 pesos' worth of maximand CON^1 per thousand 1960 pesos' worth of item)

		Labor constraints eliminated			Basic case – labor constraints included		
Year Period t		1974 2	1980 4	'Own' rates of interest, 1974–80, annual rate (%)	1974 2	1980 4	'Own' rates of interest, 1974–80, annual rate (%)
Constraint row							
A1t	Agriculture	122.81	22.71	32	91.74	31.67	19
A2t	Mining	85.19	16.54	31	54.39	19.60	19
A3t	Petroleum	120.85	22.62	32	53.69	18.39	20
A4t	Food	99.60	18.31	33	56.61	18.70	20
A5t	Textiles	94.62	17.98	32	61.66	21.09	20
A6t	Wood	121.17	22.58	32	73.87	25.11	20
A7t	Chemicals	122.42	22.62	33	62.64	21.34	20
A8t	Non-metallic	117.73	23.39	31	63.97	22.64	19
A9t	Basic metals	153.98	30.40	31	67.05	23.67	19
A10t	Machinery	117.60	22.71	32	71.55	25.57	19
A11t	Construction	77.21	15.80	30	58.18	21.47	18
A12t	Electricity	238.76	49.88	30	98.29	35.99	18
A13t	Commerce	48.31	9.34	32	31.25	10.55	20
A14t	Transportation	417.49	78.50	32	176.51	60.17	20
A15t	Services	139.85	26.45	32	96.71	35.48	18
Ft	Foreign exchange	130.91	24.61	32	72.40	24.72	20
	Consumption goods [a]	110.60	20.85	32	67.84	23.61	19

[a] Let π_i^t denote the dual variable of item i in period t. As in the material balance rows (Ait), let apc_i^t denote the fraction of item i in the composite of consumption goods, period t. Then the efficiency price of consumption goods is defined as the weighted average price of these items: $\Sigma_i apc_i^t \pi_i^t$.

constraints, the 'own' rates of interest decline sharply. They are no longer of the order of magnitude of the aggregate output-capital ratio (30–33% per year), but decline to the range of 19–20%. This range would be consistent with the independent estimate for

1960 that 17% was the *gross* rate of return on capital, before depreciation and indirect taxes. (See above, chapter II.2, table 8.) This would also be consistent with a 15% *net* rate of return as the reservation price of foreign private investors.

In table 12, it can be seen that despite the technological time trends operating on each of the input-output coefficients, the relative prices of individual items do not change significantly over time. Under these circumstances, it becomes meaningful to refer to one economy-wide rate of return on physical capital – just as in a single-good aggregative model. So ... if the 4,000 coefficients of DINAMICO were error-free ... and if Mexico were to pursue an optimal plan ... and if resources were not in fact compartmentalized between sectors because of imperfect financial intermediation ... then for purposes of decentralized project evaluation during the 1970's, DINAMICO suggests that the appropriate efficiency price of capital would be in the neighborhood of a 15% annual net rate of return.

8. Appendix: High-cost export activities

8.1. Algebraic formulation

The unknowns ZM^τ are defined so that these refer to the foreign exchange earnings *first* produced by high-cost manufactures in year τ. In equation (Et) for year t, therefore, the foreign exchange earnings are written as the sum of the amounts added in each of the three-year periods from 1 through t inclusive:

$$\sum_{\tau=1}^{t} ZM^\tau$$

With this definition of the unknowns ZM^τ, we now calculate the implications for domestic production through the coefficients that appear in the material balances, rows (Ait). Let the fraction of high-cost manufactures originating in sector i be an exogenous quantity [18], z_i. At the time such an item is first exported, its domestic production cost (i.e., the producers' price) lies 30% above the foreign exchange earnings from the item. During the following 18 years, with increasing experience, this cost differential (the nominal implicit protection rate) drops linearly to zero. With the initial cost differential at 30%, this means a drop of 5 percentage points during each three-year interval between successive points of time. For material balance row (Ait) — that is, for item i, period t — the following term then measures the export requirement (in producers' prices) associated with the activity ZM^τ:

$$z_i[1.30-0.05(t-\tau)]ZM^\tau \qquad \text{(material balance rows (Ait);}$$
$$i = 4, ..., 10; t = 1, ..., 6; \tau = 1, ..., t)$$

Consider an example. For high-cost exports originating in the machinery sector ($i = 10$), the sector-of-origin ratio $z_{10} = 21.4\%$. Learn-by-doing therefore affects the material balance rows (A10t) and the total export earnings rows (Et) as follows:

---

[18] Here, because of the level of aggregation, no attempt has been made to arrive at optimal ratios z_i through comparative advantage calculations. Instead, these ratios have been set proportional to the 1986 export-mix, assuming that each manufactured item will grow at its maximum rate e_i between 1968 and 1986. With this export-mix, the rapidly growing items (chemicals and machinery) are weighted more heavily than in the statistical base year 1968:

Sector i	Proportion of 1968 export-mix of manufactures	z_i, proportion of 1986 export-mix of manufactures (assuming maximum growth rates, e_i)
4. Food, beverages and tobacco	53.9%	40.9%
5. Textiles, apparel and leather products	10.9	6.4
6. Wood, furniture, paper and printing	5.8	4.4
7. Chemicals, rubber and plastic products	12.4	18.3
8. Non-metallic mineral products	2.2	2.2
9. Basic metals	4.3	6.4
10. Machinery	10.5	21.4
Total	100.0	100.0

$(0.214) (1.30 \, ZM^1)$	row (A10,1)
$(0.214) (1.25 \, ZM^1 + 1.30 \, ZM^2)$	row (A10,2)
$\vdots \qquad \vdots \qquad \vdots$	$\vdots$
$(0.214) (1.05 \, ZM^1 + 1.10 \, ZM^2 + ... + 1.30 \, ZM^6)$	row (A10,6)
(ZM^1)	row (E1)
$(ZM^1 + \quad ZM^2)$	row (E2)
$\vdots \qquad \vdots$	$\vdots$
$(ZM^1 + \quad ZM^2 + ... + \quad ZM^6)$	row (E6)

8.2. Effect upon shadow prices

To what extent is the shadow price of foreign exchange predetermined by having taken 30% as the estimate of the initial cost differential between producers' prices and export earnings? What is the effect of learning rates upon this shadow price? Now suppose that: (1) it is optimal to assign a positive intensity to the activity ZM^t at all future points of time t; (2) it is optimal for the shadow price of foreign exchange to remain constant in terms of the export-mix of tradable manufactures; and (3) there is a constant 'own' rate of interest on both foreign exchange and tradable manufactures. Corresponding to this 'own' rate, there is a one-period present value factor β, where $0 < \beta < 1$. Suppose for example, that the 'own' rate of interest is 20% per year. Since there are three years between time periods, $\beta = (1/1.20)^3$.

Let p denote the ratio of the shadow price of foreign exchange to that of tradable manufactures. Then this ratio may be calculated through the complementary slackness (zero profit) condition associated with the activities ZM^t:

$$\begin{bmatrix} \text{value of} \\ \text{export earnings} \\ \text{produced per} \\ \text{unit of} \\ \text{activity } ZM^t \end{bmatrix} = \begin{bmatrix} \text{domestic producers' cost of} \\ \text{tradable manufactures required} \\ \text{per unit of activity } ZM^t \end{bmatrix}$$

Or:

$$\sum_{\tau=t}^{\infty} p\beta^{\tau} = 1.30\beta^t + 1.25\beta^{t+1} + \dots + 1.05\beta^{t+5} + \sum_{\tau=t+6}^{\infty} \beta^{\tau}$$

$$\therefore p = (1.30 + 1.25\beta + \dots + 1.05\beta^5)(1-\beta) + \beta^6$$

For both optimal solutions reported within this chapter, it turns out that conditions (1)–(3) are satisfied approximately. In the basic case, for example, the 'own' rate of interest on foreign exchange is close to 20% per year, and therefore $\beta = (1/1.20)^3 = 0.579$. The complementary slackness relation enables us to calculate that $p = 1.23$. This checks closely with the dual variables for export earnings (rows (Et)) – when these are measured relative to the domestic producers' cost of tradable manufactures.

This value of $p(= 1.23)$ is somewhat higher than the shadow price of foreign exchange reported in table 10 above. The discrepancy may be explained, however, by the commerce and service margins associated with the aggregate export earnings activity ZA^t. Because of these margins, there is a difference between the shadow price of export earnings at producers' prices (rows (Et)) and the shadow price of foreign exchange at market prices (rows (Ft)).

References

Adelman, I., 'A linear programming model of educational planning: a case study of Argentina', in: *The theory and design of economic development*, edited by I. Adelman and E. Thorbecke. Baltimore, Johns Hopkins Press, 1966, chapter 14.

Blitzer, C., 'A perspective planning model for Turkey, 1969–84'. Ph.D. dissertation submitted to Department of Economics, Stanford University, August 1971.

Bowles, S., 'Efficient allocation of resources in education', *Quarterly Journal of Economics*, May 1967.

Bruno, M., 'A programming model for Israel', in: *The theory and design of economic development*, edited by I. Adelman and E. Thorbecke. Baltimore, Johns Hopkins Press, 1966, chapter 12.

Bruno, M., 'Optimal patterns of trade and development', *Review of Economics and Statistics*, November 1967.

Bruno, M., C. Dougherty and M. Fraenkel, 'Dynamic input-output, trade and development', in: *Applications of input-output analysis*, edited by A. Carter and A. Bródy. Amsterdam, North-Holland Publ. Co., 1970, chapter 3.

Bueno, G., 'The structure of protection in Mexico', in: B. Balassa, *The structure of protection in developing countries.* Baltimore, Johns Hopkins Press, 1971, chapter 8.

Chenery, H.B., and A. MacEwan, 'Optimal patterns of growth and aid: the case of Pakistan', in: *The theory and design of economic development,* edited by I. Adelman and E. Thorbecke. Baltimore, Johns Hopkins Press, 1966, chapter 6.

Correa, H., and J. Tinbergen, 'Quantitative adaptation of education to accelerated growth', *Kyklos,* 1962, fasc. 4.

Eckaus, R.S. and K.S. Parikh, *Planning for growth.* Cambridge, Mass., M.I.T. Press, 1968.

Harberger, A., 'Techniques of project appraisal', in: *National economic planning,* edited by M. Millikan. New York, National Bureau of Economic Research, Columbia University Press, 1967.

Harberger, A., Survey of literature on cost-benefit analysis for industrial project evaluation', in: *Evaluation of industrial projects.* New York, United Nations Industrial Development Organization, Sales No.: E.67.II.B.23, 1968, chapter 18.

Hopkins, D.S.P., 'Sufficient conditions for optimality in infinite horizon linear economic models'. Technical Report No. 69–3, Operations Research House, Stanford University, March 1969.

Houthakker, H.S. and S.P. Magee, 'Income and price elasticities in world trade', *Review of Economics and Statistics,* May 1969.

Ibarra, D., 'Mercados, desarrollo y política económica: perspectivas de la economía de México', *El Perfil de México en 1980,* Vol. I. México, Siglo XXI Editores, 1970.

King, T., *Mexico, industrialization and trade policies since 1940.* London, Oxford University Press, 1970.

Kurz, M., 'Tightness and substitution in the theory of capital', *Journal of Economic Theory,* October 1969.

Lewis, A., 'Economic development with unlimited supplies of labour', *The Manchester School,* May 1954.

Manne, A.S., 'Sufficient conditions for optimality in an infinite horizon development plan', *Econometrica,* January 1970.

Marglin, S.A., 'The rate of interest and the value of capital with unlimited supplies of labor', in: *Essays on the theory of optimal economic growth,* edited by K. Shell. Cambridge, Mass., M.I.T. Press, 1967, essay 8.

Murakami, Y., K. Tokoyama and J. Tsukui, 'Efficient paths of accumulation and the turnpike of the Japanese economy', in: *Applications of input-output analysis,* edited by A. Carter and A. Bródy. Amsterdam, North-Holland Publ. Co., 1970, chapter 2.

Ramsey, F.P., 'A mathematical theory of saving', *Economic Journal,* December 1928.

Sen, A.K., *Choice of techniques.* Oxford, Basil Blackwell, 1962.

Solís, L., *La realidad económica mexicana: retrovisión y perspectivas.* México, Siglo XXI Editores, 1970.

Spiegelman, R.G., E.L. Baum and L.E. Talbert, *Application of activity analysis to regional development planning.* Technical Bulletin 1339, U.S. Department of Agriculture, Washington, D.C., March 1965.

Westphal, L., *Planning investments with economies of scale.* Amsterdam, North-Holland Publ. Co., 1971.

II.4. ECONOMIC ALTERNATIVES FOR MEXICO:
A QUANTITATIVE ANALYSIS *

Alan S. MANNE *

1. Introduction

For a numerical optimizing model to be useful, it is not sufficient
to stop with a single plausible solution, and to affirm that this is
an impeccably optimal answer to the problem stated. Within five
minutes after reading a description of DINAMICO, any trained
economist should be able to draw up a list of half a dozen alternatives to the problem stated. Many (although not all) of these variants would be logically consistent. Each would lead to another
optimal solution. This chapter deals with the quantitative analysis
of several such alternatives. These are among those that have been
mentioned most frequently by reviewers of previous reports on
DINAMICO.

Before entering into details, it is worth reminding the reader of
one assumption that underlies any sensitivity analysis. Not all alternatives can be considered simultaneously. This is intended to be
a controlled experiment in which only a few variants are com-

* This is a revised version of a paper presented at the Conference on the Role of the
Computer in Economic and Social Research in Latin America, Cuernavaca, Mexico,
October 25–29, 1971.

** The author is indebted to Leopoldo Solís for having provided access to the resources of the Departamento de Estudios Económicos, Banco de México. Helpful comments on successive drafts were received from: Bela Balassa, Charles Blitzer, Gerardo
Bueno, Yves Franchet, Louis Goreux, Donald Keesing, János Kornai, Mordecai Kurz,
Lance Taylor, and Thomas Vietorisz. All computational aspects – including programs
for matrix generation – were handled by Richard Inman. The specific facts, methods of
analysis, and conclusions are the sole responsibility of the individual author.

pared. The remainder of the model is tagged ceteris paribus − that is, provisionally acceptable. *With* the ceteris paribus assumption, the controlled experiment helps us to measure which economic interdependences are strong, and which are negligible. Without ceteris paribus, the controlled experiment becomes an exercise in futility.

2. Alternatives to the basic case

For ease in future reference, we define the 'basic case' to be the one described in the three preceding chapters. Table 1 contains a

Table 1
Alternatives to the basic case

Assumptions underlying the basic case	Alternative assumptions	Identification number of alternative case
Maximand: aggregate consumption, subject to gradualist restriction and annual growth target $g = 7\%$	Maximand: same except growth target $g = 6\%$	1
	Maximand: same except growth target $g = 8\%$	2
	Maximand: discounted consumption	3
	Maximand: terminal consumption	4
Initial differential of 30% between domestic costs and foreign exchange earnings from high-cost manufactured exports	Initial export cost differential = 50%	5
Direct private capital inflows (FDPt) restricted to an average of 5.0 and a maximum of 5.5 billion pesos in any one year	Same average rate, but − except for the initial and terminal years − no limit on inflows (FDPt) in any one year	6
Includes constraints on the supply and demand for labor skills	Labor constraints eliminated	7
Allows for capital-labor substitution in agriculture through activities KA^t	Doubled marginal productivity of labor in agriculture, thereby doubling cost of activities KA^t	8

Table 2

Macroeconomic results (unit: billions of 1960 pesos unless stated otherwise)

Period t	CON^t		SAV^t		INV^t		GDP^t		mps, 1968–80 $= \dfrac{SAV^4 - SAV^0}{GDP^4 - GDP^0}$ (%)	Annual GDP growth, 1968–80 (%)
Year	1974 2	1980 4	1974 2	1980 4	1974 2	1980 4	1974 2	1980 4		
Case identification										
0. basic case	303.6	445.8	81.9	136.8	81.9	128.2	385.5	582.6	26.3	6.9
1. $g = 6\%$	308.1	448.8	78.3	123.9	78.3	115.2	386.4	572.7	23.0	6.8
2. $g = 8\%$	298.9	441.9	89.0	150.2	89.0	142.6	387.8	592.1	29.6	7.1
3. discounted consumption	298.9	442.6	90.7	152.3	91.8	144.7	389.7	594.9	30.0	7.1
4. terminal consumption	295.8	434.4	89.4	148.8	86.5	145.4	385.2	583.2	30.0	6.9
5. 50% export cost differential	303.1	444.6	81.3	136.3	81.3	127.6	384.4	580.8	26.3	6.9
6. no annual limits on FDPt	303.7	446.0	83.2	143.2	87.6	125.5	386.8	589.2	27.7	7.0
7. labor constraints eliminated	316.6	478.4	89.5	146.6	89.5	137.9	406.1	624.9	26.0	7.6
8. doubled capital-labor substitution rate	300.2	437.3	86.1	132.3	86.1	123.6	386.3	569.6	26.0	6.7

Table
Resource gap – financial flow

	Foreign direct private capital inflows, FDPt						Less: interest and profit remittances on direct priv capital inflows of prior ye			
Year	1971	1974	1977	1980	1983	1986	1971	1974	1977	198
Period t	1	2	3	4	5	6	1	2	3	4
Case identification										
0. basic case	5.0	5.5	5.5	5.5	3.5	5.0	−4.9	−7.5	−10.4	−1.
1. $g = 6\%$	5.0	5.5	5.5	5.5	3.5	5.0	−4.9	−7.5	−10.4	−1:
2. $g = 8\%$	5.0	5.5	3.5	5.5	5.5	5.0	−4.9	−7.5	−10.4	−1:
3. discounted consumption	3.0	5.5	5.5	5.5	5.5	5.0	−4.9	−6.5	− 9.3	−1:
4. terminal consumption	0	0	0	2.4	5.5	5.0	−4.9	−4.9	− 4.9	− 4
5. 50% export cost differential	5.0	5.5	5.5	5.5	3.5	5.0	−4.9	−7.5	−10.4	−1:
6. no annual limits on FDPt	5.0	9.9	9.3	0.8	0	5.0	−4.9	−7.5	−12.7	−1:
7. labor constraints eliminated	5.0	5.5	5.5	5.5	3.5	5.0	−4.9	−7.5	−10.4	−1.
8. doubled capital-labor substitution rate	5.0	5.5	1.3	3.2	5.5	5.0	−4.9	−7.5	−10.4	−1)

list of the eight alternatives to be evaluated here. These eight cases refer to alternative formulations of DINAMICO's constraints on the primary factors of production: foreign exchange and labor. Also considered are alternatives to the maximand adopted for the basic case: aggregate consumption, subject to a 'gradualist' constraint on the time path and a target annual growth rate $g = 7\%$. The eight alternatives are examined one at a time − neglecting interactions between them.

The individual alternatives stem not only from different value judgements as to what is desirable, but also from different practical judgements as to what is politically or technically feasible. E.g., one policy-maker will say that the basic case is altogether too pessimistic in projecting the subsidy required for promoting manufactured exports. Another will say that we have been too optimistic on this score. Case 5 permits us to check for the indirect

nit: billions of 1960 pesos)

1983	1986	Concessional capital inflows less interest $FC^t - INFC^t$						= Resource gap, $RGAP^t$					
		1971	1974	1977	1980	1983	1986	1971	1974	1977	1980	1983	1986
5	6	1	2	3	4	5	6	1	2	3	4	5	6
16.1	−17.9	2.4	2.0	0.9	−0.9	−2.9	−4.7	2.5	0	−4.0	−8.6	−15.5	−17.6
16.1	−17.9	2.4	2.0	0.9	−0.9	−2.9	−4.7	2.5	0	−4.0	−8.6	−15.5	−17.6
15.1	−17.9	2.4	2.0	0.9	−0.9	−2.9	−4.7	2.5	0	−6.0	−7.6	−12.5	−17.6
15.1	−17.9	2.4	2.0	0.9	−0.9	−2.9	−4.7	0.5	1.0	−2.9	−7.6	−12.5	−17.6
6.1	− 9.0	2.4	2.0	0.9	−0.9	−2.9	−4.7	−2.5	−2.9	−4.0	−3.4	− 3.5	− 8.7
16.1	−17.9	2.4	2.0	0.9	−0.9	−2.9	−4.7	2.5	0	−4.0	−8.6	−15.5	−17.6
17.9	−17.9	2.4	2.0	0.9	−0.9	−2.9	−4.7	2.5	4.4	−2.5	−17.7	−20.8	−17.6
16.1	−17.9	2.4	2.0	0.9	−0.9	−2.9	−4.7	2.5	0	−4.0	−8.6	−15.5	−17.6
12.7	−15.6	2.4	2.0	0.9	−0.9	−2.9	−4.7	2.5	0	−8.2	−8.7	−10.1	−15.3

implications of these alternative views. Similarly, through case 6 another aspect of the foreign exchange constraints may be examined — the year-by-year limits on the inflows of foreign private capital.

A priori, it might be supposed that alternatives 5 and 6 would have a significant effect upon the GDP growth rate. Similarly, one might have anticipated sizable macroeconomic effects from such alternatives as: (1) and (2) changing the annual growth target to 6 or 8%; or (3) changing the maximand to discounted consumption; or (4) changing the maximand to terminal consumption.

Under each of these alternatives — when taken one at a time — it turns out that the 1968–80 optimal annual GDP growth rate varies only between 6.8 and 7.1%. The output growth rates for individual sectors also tend to be insensitive to the variations considered under cases (1)–(6). The effects are concentrated upon a comparatively small number of primal variables: the amount of capital-labor substitution within agriculture, the inflows of foreign capital, and the marginal export activities for trade-balance improvement.

It is not until we turn to cases 7 and 8 — those involving the labor constraints — that the alternatives become radically different. Case 7 is calculated as though the marginal productivity of labor in Mexican agriculture were zero, as though there were no social costs of rural-urban labor transfer, and as though the social product foregone by creating human capital were also zero. With the labor surplus hypothesis carried to this extreme, all labor constraints may be neglected. The marginal productivity of physical capital would rise to 30–33% per year — virtually identical to the incremental ratio of aggregate output to physical capital. This also means that the 1968–80 optimal annual GDP growth rate would be 7.6%, and that each sector's output requirements would be increased correspondingly.

From the viewpoint of income distribution, perhaps the most significant alternative is case 8. Here the labor constraints are re-introduced. It is supposed that long-term credit is made available to the agricultural sector on more favorable terms than heretofore, and that this policy is pushed far enough so as to double the marginal rate of substitution of capital for unskilled agricultural workers. The macroeconomic and foreign trade effects are not sizeable, but the income distribution then shifts significantly in favor of unskilled labor.

For a quantitative comparison of alternatives, the results are summarized in tables 2–7. (Further details are to be found in the computer listings. These are available for inspection in the author's office.) Tables 2–7 are arranged as follows:

Table 2. Macroeconomic results

Table 3. Resource gap — financial flows

Table 4. Foreign exchange projections, 1980

Table 5. Efficiency prices of foreign exchange and foreign aid

Table 6. Gross production levels, 1980

Table 7. Employment, efficiency wages and labor income, 1980

Table 4

Foreign exchange projections, 1980 (unit: billions of 1960 pesos)

Case identification	Imports	Merchandise exports, at producers' prices, Z_i^4										Exports of high-cost manufactures, at producers' prices, $\sum_{\tau=1}^4 ZM^\tau$	Foreign exchange earnings, at market prices		Resource gap, $RGAP^4$ = imports $-ZA^4-ZT^4$
		$i=1$	2	3	4	5	6	7	8	9	10		Merchandise exports [a] ZA^4	Tourism ZT^4	
0. basic case	41.13	4.90	3.78	0.54	5.80	0.98	0.62	2.07	0.29	0.72	2.18	12.01	39.14	10.63	− 8.64
1. $g = 6\%$	38.95	4.90	3.78	0.54	5.80	0.98	0.62	2.07	0.29	0.72	2.18	10.13	36.96	10.63	− 8.64
2. $g = 8\%$	43.27	4.90	3.78	0.54	5.80	0.98	0.62	2.07	0.29	0.72	1.80	13.34	40.23	10.63	− 7.59
3. discounted consumption	43.87	4.90	3.78	0.54	5.80	0.98	0.62	2.07	0.29	0.72	2.18	13.48	40.83	10.63	− 7.59
4. terminal consumption	43.11	4.90	3.78	0.54	5.80	0.98	0.62	2.07	0.29	0.72	2.18	9.21	35.90	10.63	− 3.42
5. 50% export cost differential	40.37	7.77	3.78	0.54	5.80	0.98	0.62	2.07	0.29	0.72	2.18	8.26	38.12	10.89	− 8.64
6. no annual limits on FDPt	41.15	4.90	3.78	0.54	5.80	0.98	0.62	2.07	0.29	0.72	2.18	19.84	48.19	10.63	−17.67
7. labor constraints eliminated	43.25	7.77	3.78	0.54	5.80	0.98	0.62	2.07	0.29	0.23	2.18	4.84	33.60	18.29	− 8.64
8. doubled capital-labor substitution rate	39.71	4.90	3.78	0.54	5.80	0.98	0.62	2.07	0.29	0.72	2.18	10.84	37.78	10.63	− 8.70
Exogenously specified upper bound, $Z_i^0(1+\epsilon_i)^{12}$ [12]		7.77	3.78	0.54	5.80	0.98	0.62	2.07	0.29	0.72	2.18	—	—	18.29	
Exogenously specified lower bound, $Z_i^0(1+\epsilon_i)^{12}$ [12]		4.90	2.36	0.45	2.88	0.58	0.31	0.66	0.12	0.23	0.56	0	—	10.63	

[a] ZA^4 = merchandise exports, at market prices
$0.8658\, ZA^4$ = merchandise exports, at producers' prices = $\sum_{i=1}^{10} Z_i^4 + \sum_{\tau=1}^4 ZM^\tau$.
$0.1125\, ZA^4$ = commerce margins on merchandise exports
$0.0217\, ZA^4$ = service margins on merchandise exports

Table 5

Efficiency prices of foreign exchange and foreign aid

	Unit: 1960 pesos' worth of maximand [a] per thousand 1960 pesos' worth of item				Efficiency price of foreign exchange relative to price of tradable manufactures		'Own' rate of interest on foreign exchange, 1974–80, annual rate (%)
	Foreign exchange (rows (Ft))		Foreign aid (rows FGAPt))				
Year	1974	1980	1974	1980	1974	1980	
Period t	2	4	2	4	2	4	
Case identification							
0. basic case	72.40	24.72	72.40	24.72	1.15	1.15	20
1. $g = 6\%$	77.07	26.17	77.07	26.17	1.15	1.15	20
2. $g = 8\%$	74.41	20.55	61.85	25.98	1.16	1.13	24
3. discounted consumption	547.92	238.20	759.36	333.96	1.13	1.13	15
4. terminal consumption	373.61	290.17	1,284.79	892.91	1.02	1.20	4
5. 50% export cost differential	82.08	29.92	78.49	29.92	1.28	1.35	18
6. no annual limits on FDPt	71.31	27.22	62.97	27.22	1.05	1.21	17
7. labor constraints eliminated	130.91	24.61	130.91	24.61	1.17	1.17	32
8. doubled capital-labor substitution rate	53.59	22.96	53.59	22.96	1.13	1.17	15

[a] Except for cases 3 and 4, the maximand is CON^1, and the units of measurement of efficiency prices are therefore identical. In case 3, the unit of measurement refers to discounted consumption; in case 4, to terminal consumption.

Table 6

Gross production levels, 1980 (unit: billions of 1960 pesos)

Sector j Case identification	Agriculture 1	Mining 2	Petroleum 3	Food 4	Textiles 5	Wood 6	Chemicals 7	Non-metallic 8	Basic metals 9	Machinery 10	Construction 11	Electricity 12	Commerce 13	Transportation 14	Services 15
0. basic case	74.6	8.6	39.0	112.8	54.8	22.6	54.8	14.9	37.0	100.1	59.1	19.8	196.7	24.2	161.0
1. g = 6%	73.3	8.4	38.3	112.0	54.6	21.9	53.7	14.0[a]	34.9	95.2	53.9[a]	19.4	193.9	24.1	159.1
2. g = 8%	76.3	8.8	39.5	112.9	54.7	23.1	55.6	16.0[a]	39.1[a]	104.4	64.9[a]	20.2	199.1	24.2	162.1
3. discounted consumption	76.2	8.9	39.7	113.3	54.8	23.3	55.9	16.1[a]	39.6[a]	106.1[a]	65.4[a]	20.3	200.2	24.3	163.5
4. terminal consumption	74.4	8.8	38.9	108.5	53.4	22.6	53.6	15.9[a]	38.6	103.8	65.9[a]	19.9	196.3	23.8	161.3
5. 50% export cost differential	77.4	8.5	38.8	110.9	54.4	22.3	53.8	14.9	36.3	98.4	59.9	19.7	195.5	24.1	160.4
6. no annual limits on FDPt	76.5	8.7	39.5	118.1	55.8	23.3	57.4	15.2	38.1	101.8	58.5	20.0	198.2	24.3	161.5
7. labor constraints eliminated	80.0[a]	8.8	41.3[a]	115.7	58.7[a]	23.6	56.1	15.9[a]	37.9	105.5[a]	65.4[a]	21.1[a]	210.2[a]	26.2[a]	170.3[a]
8. doubled capital-labor substitution rate	74.0	8.4	38.0	110.1	53.6	21.9	53.2	14.4	35.7	96.7	56.8	19.3	192.0	23.6	156.6

[a] Differs by more than 5% from level shown for basic case.

Case identif- ication	Labor skill s [a]	Employment, RQL_s^4 (unit: millions of persons)						
		1	2	3	4	5	Sub total, 1–4	Total, 1–5
0. basic case		0.183	1.310	2.673	9.521	6.765	13.687	20.452
1. $g = 6\%$		0.176	1.286	2.619	9.265	7.350	13.346	20.696
2. $g = 8\%$		0.189	1.328	2.720	9.759	6.359	13.996	20.355
3. discounted consumption		0.191	1.339	2.741	9.836	5.996	14.107	20.103
4. terminal consumption		0.187	1.319	2.693	9.667	5.734	13.886	19.600
5. 50% export cost differential		0.182	1.305	2.661	9.467	6.884	13.615	20.499
6. no annual limits on FDPt		0.186	1.318	2.698	9.623	6.901	13.825	20.726
7. labor constraints eliminated		0.193	1.387	2.839	10.134	9.895	14.553	24.448
8. doubled capital-labor substitution rate		0.178	1.274	2.602	9.254	7.239	13.308	20.547

[a] Skill category: $s = 1$, Engineers and scientists; $s = 2$, Other professional and technical workers; $s = 3$, Administrative and clerical workers; $s = 4$, Manual and sales workers outside agriculture; $s = 5$, Unskilled agricultural workers.

3. Alternative objective functions

Cases 1–4 all deal with the problem of welfare distribution between successive generations – near future versus distant future increases in aggregate consumption. Somewhat surprisingly, these different objective functions do not lead to great differences in the absolute levels of consumption during the early time periods. (See figure 1 and table 8.)

For *cases 1 and 2*, the tradeoffs are examined through variations in the asymptotic target growth rate – still retaining the restriction that the time path be of the gradualist form with *increments* of consumption growing geometrically at the annual rate of g. In

d labor income, 1980

fficiency wages, annual aver-e centered on 1980, [b] (unit: ousands of 1960 pesos per an-year of skill s)					Labor income = (employment)(efficiency wages) (unit: billions of 1960 pesos)						Aggregate consumption (billions of 1960 pesos) CON^4	Labor income, fraction of aggregate consumption
1	2	3	4	5	1	2	3	4	5	Total, 1–5		
2.1	53.4	23.0	7.5	3.9	20.5	70.0	61.5	71.4	26.4	249.8	445.8	56%
6.8	53.7	23.4	7.5	3.9	18.8	69.1	61.3	69.5	28.7	247.4	448.8	55
29.4	59.9	24.1	7.9	4.2	24.5	79.5	65.6	77.1	26.7	273.4	441.9	62
75.9	41.8	17.7	8.2	4.8	14.5	56.0	48.5	80.7	28.8	228.5	442.6	52
1.8	21.1	12.7	8.7	5.5	7.8	27.8	34.2	84.1	31.5	185.4	434.4	43
1.6	52.0	22.9	7.6	4.0	20.3	67.0	60.9	71.9	27.5	248.5	444.6	56
7.9	53.8	24.2	7.9	4.2	21.9	70.9	65.3	76.0	29.0	263.1	446.0	59
–	–	–	–	–	–	–	–	–	–	–	478.4	–
0.2	52.8	24.2	11.3	7.9	16.1	67.3	63.0	104.6	57.2	308.2	437.3	70

[b] Average of efficiency wages for 1977, 1980 and 1983, normalized by dual variable for consumption ods.

case 1, for example, the target rate is reduced from 7% to 6%. This policy would make it possible to increase CON^1 from 251.4 to 254.1 billion pesos. Higher consumption levels would also be achieved during periods $t = 2,3$, and 4, but lower levels during all subsequent time periods. Symmetrical effects are obtained when the target growth rate is raised to 8%. That is, case 2 provides lower consumption levels than the basic case during periods 1–4, but higher levels thereafter.

Although these alternatives differ from each other by less than 1% in the absolute levels of near-term consumption, they do have different implications for near-term fiscal policiy. By lowering the annual growth target from 7% to 6%, the 1968–80 marginal savings propensity is reduced from 26.3 to 23.0% (table 2). This

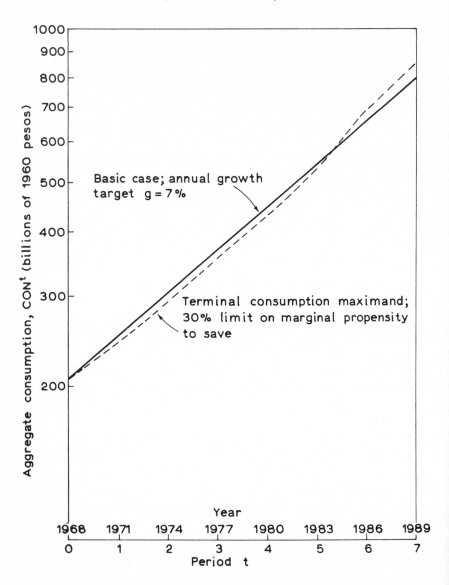

Fig. 1. Alternative time paths of aggregate consumption.

Table 8
Aggregate consumption, CON^t; effect of alternative objectives
(unit: billions of 1960 pesos)

Year	1968	1971	1974	1977	1980	1983	1986	1989
Period t	0	1	2	3	4	5	6	7
Case identification								
0. basic case		208.8	251.4	303.6	367.5	445.8	541.8	659.3	803.3
1. $g = 6\%$		208.8	254.1	308.1	372.3	448.8	540.0	648.6	777.9
2. $g = 8\%$		208.8	248.7	298.9	362.2	441.9	542.2	668.7	828.0
3. discounted consumption		208.8	245.3	298.9	363.5	442.6	542.5	692.7	848.6
4. terminal consumption		208.8	245.9	295.8	359.5	434.4	535.9	700.1	857.6

means lower taxes and lower prices on the products of public sector enterprises. Over the long term, of course, this 'soft' option leads to a lower aggregate growth rate and lower employment opportunities. Conversely, if the growth target is raised to 8%, the required 1968–80 marginal savings propensity is 29.6%. The fiscal policy tasks would become correspondingly more onerous, but the 1980 employment opportunities would then increase from 13.7 to 14.0 million jobs within the four highest-paying skill categories. (See table 7.)

In all cases, we have supposed that there are political constraints upon Mexico's fiscal policies, and that it would be infeasible to push the marginal savings propensity above 30%. [1] With the gradualist objective function (cases 0, 1 and 2), typically it turns out that the 30% savings limit is a redundant constraint. [2] When the gradualist objective function is replaced by that of maximizing discounted consumption (*case 3*) or terminal consumption (*case 4*), the savings constraints become critically important. Without

[1] For the statistical base period 1960–68, the marginal savings propensity was 23.2%.

[2] In case 2, the 30% limit on the domestic savings propensity is binding only during periods 2, 3, 4. Even during these periods, the shadow prices are quite low for the savings constraints, rows (GSAVt).

them, the time path of aggregate consumption is exceedingly erratic from one period to the next. *With* a 30% upper bound upon the marginal propensity to save, then − even under a growth-maximizing criterion such as terminal consumption − there are no sharp discontinuities in the optimal consumption level between two successive periods. When the savings constraint is operative, the specific form of the objective function has little effect upon the optimal values of the primal variables. [3]

We now examine more closely the logical relationship between the maximand of discounted consumption and that of terminal consumption. Let CON^t denote the aggregate consumption obtained in time period t. For $t = 1, ..., 6$, CON^t is an endogenously determined unknown. In setting terminal conditions for cases 3 and 4, it is supposed that the absolute level of consumption grows geometrically at the annual rate g during the infinite horizon following period 6. With three years between representative points of time, it is convenient to define a three-year growth factor $\gamma = (1 + g)^3$. Then $CON^7 = [(1 + g)^3] \; CON^6 = [\gamma] \; CON^6$. And in general $CON^t = [(\gamma)^{t-7}] \; CON^7$ (for $t = 7, 8, ..., \infty$).

Let future consumption be discounted at the one-year rate r, and let the corresponding present-value factor for each three-year interval be $\beta = (1/1 + r)^3$. In order to ensure convergence over the infinite planning horizon, it is supposed that the consumption discount rate exceeds the target growth rate. [4] That is, $r > g > 0$. Then, for an infinite planning horizon, the maximand may be calculated as the following linear function of $CON^1 ... CON^7$:

---

[3] The optimal *dual* solution is sensitive to differences in the objective functions. For example, it turns out that the 1974−80 own rate of interest on foreign exchange is 15% per year in case 3 and 4% in case 4. (See table 5.)

These numerical results are roughly consistent with those that may be obtained analytically for an aggregative model of a labor surplus economy with a single capital good. Through such a model, it may also be shown that the growth target employed in a gradualist model does *not* affect the own rate of interest. See Manne (1972).

[4] If $r \leqslant g$ and it is feasible to set $CON^7 > 0$, the discounted consumption criterion leads to a paradoxical result. The objective function will be unbounded − regardless of how small a positive value is assigned to CON^7.

$$\text{discounted consumption maximand} = \sum_{t=1}^{\infty} \beta^t \, CON^t$$

$$= \sum_{t=1}^{6} \beta^t \, CON^t + \sum_{t=7}^{\infty} [(\beta)^t (\gamma)^{t-7}] CON^7$$

$$= \sum_{t=1}^{6} \beta^t \, CON^t + [\beta^7/(1-\beta\gamma)] CON^7$$

To evaluate this maximand numerically, we have retained 7% as the annual target for post-terminal growth, and have taken 15% as the annual discount rate on future consumption. [5] That is, case 3 is defined by setting $\beta = (1/1.15)^3 = 0.658$, and $\gamma = (1.07)^3 = 1.225$. The coefficients in the discounted consumption maximand are therefore:

$$\beta^1 = 0.658$$
$$\beta^2 = 0.432$$
$$\vdots \qquad \vdots$$
$$\beta^6 = 0.081$$
$$\beta^7/(1-\beta\gamma) = 0.273.$$

Case 4 has the identical constraints to case 3, but a different objective function. Like a 'turnpike' growth model, the maximand is CON^7, the level of aggregate consumption reached during the terminal year. Despite the difference in appearance, it can be shown that there is a close relationship between the objective functions considered in cases 3 and 4. The latter may be viewed as a special case of the former — a limiting case obtained by lowering

---

[5] In principle, the consumption discount rate is a subjectively determined parameter — one that expresses the social rate of time preference. It is sheer coincidence that the same numerical value has been employed as for the cost of foreign private capital.

the discount rate sufficiently. [6] With this interpretation, the objective functions of cases 3 and 4 have the identical structure – that of discounted consumption. The only difference is that the consumption discount rate is 15% in case 3, and that it approaches 7% in case 4. The numerical results (table 8) imply that the optimal solution is insensitive to variations in the discount rate within a rather wide range – from 7 to 15% per year. With this form of model, apparently the upper bound on the marginal savings rate has far more influence upon the optimal consumption path than does the subjectively-determined time discount rate.

4. Foreign exchange

In the basic case, it turns out that the efficiency price of foreign exchange is 1.15 – taking the domestic producers' price of tradable manufactures as the numéraire. Before advocating that 15% is therefore an appropriate tariff rate or export subsidy or adjustment in foreign exchange parity, it is essential to check through the reasoning that led to this numerical result. In DINAMICO, one of the least reliable econometric components is the marginal cost of export earnings. The basic case was set up as though there were no limits upon the export of 'infant' high-cost manufactures. It is supposed that the domestic cost of these products will exceed the foreign exchange earnings by 30% at the time the manufactured item is first exported, and that this cost differential will drop to

---

[6] This proposition may be stated as follows: The lower the discount rate, the more nearly will the objective functions coincide for the maximand of discounted consumption and that of terminal consumption – assuming always that $r > g$.

Proof: First, multiply all terms in the discounted consumption maximand by the positive quantity $(1-\beta\gamma)/\beta^7$. With this change of units, 1.0 is the coefficient of CON^7 – just as with the terminal consumption maximand. For $t = 1, ..., 6$, the discounted consumption maximand coefficients of CON^t are then $[(\beta)^{t-7}][1-\beta\gamma]$. Now hold the post-terminal growth rate fixed, and reduce the discount rate r. As r approaches g from above, the product $\beta\gamma = [(1+g)/(1+r)]^3 < 1$, but approaches 1. For $t = 1, ..., 6$, the discounted consumption maximand coefficients of CON^t therefore approach zero – just as with the terminal consumption maximand. This completes the proof.

zero through the experience acquired during an 18-year period. [7] As an alternative, *case 5* is calculated as though these marginal export items will have an initial cost disadvantage of 50 rather than 30%. We continue to suppose that it will require 18 years of experience before the cost differential can be eliminated.

Case 5 makes little or no difference in the macroeconomic results (table 2), the pattern of foreign capital inflows (table 3), the aggregate requirements for imports (table 4), the gross production levels (table 6), or the employment levels (table 7). From the viewpoint of overall reliability of DINAMICO, it is fortunate that the principal effects of this parameter change are concentrated upon a small number of variables: the commodity composition of exports (table 4) and the shadow price of foreign exchange (table 5). It becomes optimal to reduce the 1980 exports of high-cost manufactures from 12.01 to 8.26 billion pesos, and to offset this loss of foreign exchange through an increase in agricultural exports. Associated with this shift in the direction of comparative advantage, there is a shift in the shadow price of foreign exchange. It no longer remains 1.15, but increases to 1.35 in 1980 — still taking the price of tradable manufactures as the numéraire. Case 5 also means that foreign aid would have a higher marginal productivity than in the basic case. [8]

[7] Presumably, in order to provide a financial incentive for the export of high-cost manufactures from individual enterprises, it would be necessary to provide export subsidies. Such subsidies might take a number of forms — either outright or in the form of permission to import raw materials and equipment duty-free. (Mexico is not a member country of the GATT.) With any of these measures, there are administrative difficulties — but no more so than in the case of existing import restrictions. The principal difference between an import tariff and an export subsidy is that the one provides an inflow of pesos to the treasury, and that the other generates an outflow.

[8] Except for cases 3 and 4, the 30% limit upon the marginal savings propensity is not a critical constraint. Except for these cases, therefore, it makes little or no difference whether the impact of additional foreign aid is measured through the shadow price of the foreign exchange rows (Ft) or through the resource gap rows (FGAPt). Cases 3 and 4 are typical of the 'two-gap' phenomenon. There, foreign aid has considerably more leverage than foreign exchange earnings alone. For further discussion of the two-gap model, see the interchange between Chenery and Strout (1968) and Fei and Ranis (1968). The shadow price of the domestic savings rows (GSAVt) may be read off from table 5 here. In all cases, this equals the difference between the shadow price of rows (Ft) and (FGAPt). To prove this proposition, refer back to the coefficients of the resource gap activity $RGAP^t$ and of the concessional foreign aid activity FC^t in table 4, chapter II [3] above.

Case 6 provides an instance of interdependence between the optimal time path of capital inflows, the shadow price of foreign exchange and the composition of exports. This case eliminates the year-by-year limits on the private capital inflows FDP^t ($t = 2, ...,$ 5), but retains the overall constraint that the average inflows are not to increase above the 1971 rate. Case 6 has little effect upon the macroeconomic results or the gross production or the employment levels. The effects are concentrated upon the sources and uses of foreign exchange. It now becomes optimal to allow exports to lag and to incur a sizeable foreign exchange deficit during periods 2 and 3, then to push up the level of high-cost manufactured exports to 19.84 billion pesos in period 4 (1980), and to run a sizeable foreign exchange surplus (17.67 billion pesos) in that year. Associated with this shift in the time pattern of exports, the shadow price of foreign exchange would rise over time — from 1.05 to 1.21 between periods 2 and 4 (1974 and 1980, respectively). This also means that the marginal productivity of foreign aid would be lower during period 2 and higher during period 4 than in the basic case (see table 5).

From case 6, it cannot be concluded that year-by-year constraints on foreign capital inflows are essential in a model of this type. Other devices may also be employed to avoid sharp discontinuities in the time pattern of exports. Among such devices are: an upward-sloping supply curve of foreign capital, a downward-sloping demand curve for exports, or a recursive programming constraint on the rate of growth of exports. [9] Among these alternative devices, the simplest to estimate is the year-by-year limit on private capital inflows. For the basic case, this has the disadvantage that the upper bound is an effective constraint during the early time periods, and that the unknowns FDP^t appear to be predetermined. It does not happen, however, that the upper

---

[9] Let Z_i^t denote the exports of item i during period t, and let e_i denote the maximum feasible rate of growth of this item between periods $t-1$ and t. Then a recursive programming constraint on exports would be written: $Z_i^t \leq (1 + e_i)Z_i^{t-1}$. See Day (1963) and Bruno et al. (1970). — Note that a recursive programming constraint refers to *pairs* of unknowns, but that the export bounds in DINAMICO are imposed upon individual unknowns.

bound is always an effective constraint during the initial time periods. For examples, see cases 2, 4, and 8 in table 3.

5. Employment and income distribution

For *case 7*, the labor constraints have been eliminated. This makes it possible to achieve a significantly higher aggregate growth rate, higher output rates in individual sectors, and greater employment opportunities outside traditional agriculture. It has already been noted that a zero shadow price for labor implies a high shadow price for capital. Almost equally dramatic are the implications for comparative advantage in foreign trade. With a zero shadow price for labor, it becomes optimal to set agricultural exports and tourism earnings at their upper rather than their lower bounds, and to place less dependence upon high-cost manufactured exports (see table 5). [10] Case 7 is included here for the sake of completeness — not because we believe that it provides a realistic basis for projections.

Increasingly, Mexican policy-makers are directing research toward the sources of inequities in income distribution. There is strong evidence that, along with the increase in average incomes, the extent of inequality worsened between 1950 and 1963. (During those years, the Gini coefficient of inequality increased from 0.50 to 0.55.) In part, this problem arises from interregional differences in development — and from imperfect labor mobility between regions. In 1965, for example, the 8 highest-income regions accounted for 30.3% of the total population, and produced 11,075 pesos per capita. The 17 lowest-income regions, with 43.8% of the population, produced only 2,417 pesos per capita. (Source: Navarrete (1970, p. 41 and table 8).)

[10] Rather than suppose that the marginal productivity of labor is zero in all skill classes (case 7), it might have been worth exploring a less extreme version of the labor surplus hypothesis. Suppose, for example, that the only change in the basic case had been to assume that unskilled agricultural labor has a zero or a low marginal product. It would then be optimal to shift the composition of foreign exchange earnings — setting agricultural exports at their upper bounds and reducing the exports of high-cost manufactures. The comparative advantage results of DINAMICO would then resemble those of EXPORTA.

Not only regional but also occupational differences are a significant source of inequalities. During each of the years between 1950 and 1967, in industry and services the per capita output exceeded that in agriculture by a factor of approximately 5 : 1. Even within agriculture — despite the post-Revolution policies of agrarian reform and land redistribution — the pattern of development has been 'dualistic'. In the irrigated districts of the north, farming is commercialized and produces high economic returns. Elsewhere — in the central plateau and the south — subsistence agriculture is hard-pressed to keep up with the demographic pressures. (See Solís 1970, pp. 148 and 291.)

DINAMICO is too highly aggregated to be helpful in analyzing the detailed regional aspects of income inequalities and labor mobility. *Case 8* is focussed on only one dimension of the tradeoff between aggregate growth versus equity in income distribution. As proxy measures for these concepts, we have taken aggregate consumption and labor's income share [11], both as of 1980 ($t = 4$). By measuring labor's income at efficiency wages, this implies that money transfer payments could not be large enough to achieve a significant redistribution of real income between social classes. (If money transfers could be made sufficiently large — and transfers entailed no loss in productive efficiency — the question of a growth-equity tradeoff would not arise.)

Case 8 has been constructed as follows: Suppose that public infrastructure investments are made available for the benefit of the smallholders in the densely-populated central and southern centers of Mexican agriculture. These investments might take the form of extension services, roads, tractors, irrigation and land levelling. To the extent that the aggregate demand for agricultural products is inelastic, these investments might have to be made at the expense of northern agriculture. It is possible that this would lead to a loss

---

[11] From the viewpoint of economic theory, these measures are unsatisfactory proxies. A *cardinal* social welfare function would be a more appropriate device for analyzing the tradeoff between aggregate growth and equity. This follows from the 'impersonality' criterion of Harsanyi (1955) — which in turn is related to risk aversion and individual decisions under uncertainty. See also Atkinson (1970) and Sen (1970, ch. 9).

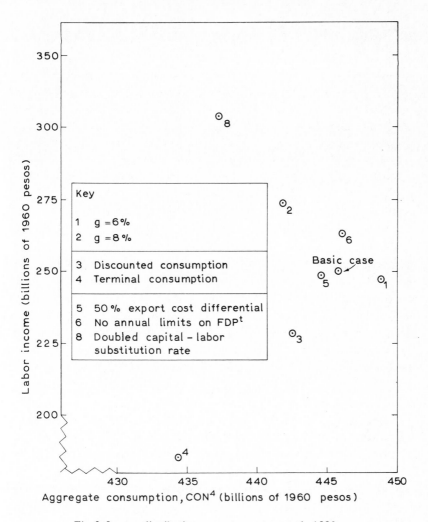

Fig. 2. Income distribution versus aggregate growth, 1980.

in economic efficiency, but that nonetheless — from the viewpoint of income distribution — this would prove to be a desirable shift in investment policy.

For case 8, it is supposed that this reorientation of agricultural policy is pushed far enough so as to double the marginal rate of substitution of capital for unskilled agricultural workers. [12] It turns out that this would have a significant effect not only upon the efficiency wage of agricultural workers, but also upon that of unskilled urban workers. (See table 7 and figure 2.) Other policy measures would also affect labor's share, e.g., case 2, where the target annual growth rate is raised to 8%. None of the alternatives, however, would exert as pronounced an effect upon income distribution as this shift in the direction of agricultural investments. In 1980, this would make it possible to double the income of unskilled agricultural workers – from 26.4 to 57.2 billion pesos at 1960 prices. Total labor income would increase from 249.8 to 308.2. The loss in aggregate consumption (from 445.8 to 437.3 billion pesos) might well be worth the gain in equity from such a policy.

References

Atkinson, A.B., 'On the measurement of inequality', *Journal of Economic Theory*, September 1970.

Bruno, M., C. Dougherty and M. Fraenkel, 'Dynamic input-output, trade and development', in: *Applications of input-output analysis*, A.P. Carter and A. Bródy. Amsterdam, North-Holland Publ. Co., 1970, chapter 3.

Chenery, H.B., and A.M. Strout, '"Reply" to a Comment by Fei and Ranis', *American Economic Review*, September 1968.

Day, R., *Recursive programming and production response*. Amsterdam, North-Holland Publ. Co., 1963.

Fei, J.C.H., and G. Ranis, 'Foreign assistance and economic development: comment', *American Economic Review*, September 1968.

Harsanyi, J.C., 'Cardinal welfare, individualistic ethics, and interpersonal comparisons of utility', *Journal of Political Economy*, August 1955.

Manne, A.S., 'On the efficiency price of capital in a dual economy'. Working Paper No. 9, Economics Series, IMSSS, Stanford University, April 1972.

Navarrete, I.M. de, 'La distribucion del ingreso en México: tendencias y perspectivas', *El Perfil de México en 1980*, México, Siglo XXI Editores, 1970.

Sen, A.K., *Collective choice and social welfare*. San Francisco, Holden-Day, 1970.

Solís, L., *La realidad económica mexicana: retrovisión y perspectivas*. México, Siglo XXI Editores, 1970.

[12] For the basic case, at a point of time y years after 1960, the labor substitution coefficients are calculated as though it would require $15(1.02)^y$ thousand pesos of capital to replace one unskilled agricultural worker. For case 8, this marginal rate of substitution is instead taken to be $30(1.02)^y$.

II.5. COMMENTS ON DINAMICO *

Saúl TREJO REYES

1. Introduction

DINAMICO is an example of what can be achieved with numerical models if enough time and effort are spent on such work. At the same time, it gives us a clear idea of the many statistical and theoretical difficulties still remaining in model construction, especially with regard to developing countries where the statistical base is weak.

The linear programming model itself covers six periods, each three years long. Each period is linked to the others through activities for the accumulation of physical and human capital. This is straightforward enough, and presents no theoretical difficulties. I shall concentrate most of these remarks on the interpretation and usefulness of the model as a tool for policy decisions.

2. Domestic versus international prices

A gradualist consumption path is employed as the objective function. This means that the optimal pattern of output also implies a certain pattern of dynamic comparative advantage for the economy, given the nature of the optimizing decision in each period and given that the model must generate most of its foreign exchange requirements through merchandise and service exports. In this re-

* This is a revised version of a paper presented at the Conference on the Role of the Computer in Economic and Social Research in Latin America, Cuernavaca, Mexico, October 25–29, 1971.

gard, one crucial element which will affect the results are the input-output matrices for each period, projected for the future at three-year intervals beginning in 1968. A difficulty exists in using such matrices, expressed at domestic prices, for determining an optimal growth pattern. Domestic prices are seriously distorted by protection. When a sector's inputs are evaluated at domestic prices, those sectors where effective protection is lowest come out worst-off. They appear to be high-cost activities and thus not the ones whose output should be expanded rapidly. With interindustry matrices valued at base-year domestic prices, there are difficulties in using the dual solution for project evaluation. See Bacha and Taylor (1971). Thus, I do not believe that DINAMICO's shadow prices accurately reflect the opportunity costs for individual sectors. The results must be used carefully, if at all, for determining the direction of comparative advantage. The valuation of input-output matrices at domestic prices, in effect, biases the results towards a relatively autarchic pattern of development.

The use of domestic prices may account for the somewhat puzzling results of the 'basic case', according to which it is optimal for Mexico to export manufactures rather than agricultural products. Note, however, that when the initial export differential for high-cost manufactures is raised from 30% (in the basic case) to the more plausible level of 50% (in alternative case 5), the direction of comparative advantage shifts back to agricultural products. In EXPORTA, we have avoided this difficulty by converting domestic prices into international prices through nominal implicit tariff rates, and then reestimating the entire interindustry transactions matrix at international prices.

3. Employment projections

A second source of data difficulty relates to the employment projections. Fixed sectoral coefficients, when estimated without taking into consideration the dualistic nature of the economy and the process of diffusion of technology, are apt to give highly misleading results. For one thing, labor is implicitly assumed to be fully employed in each sector; thus, the labor force in each activity is taken to be the labor *required* for producing that sector's output. This biases the results not only in agriculture, where there exists a large amount of underemployment, but also in industry, where the nature of the diffusion of technological progress does not seem to be adequately reflected in the labor coefficients used in the model.

The choice of data affects DINAMICO's results substantially. The comparative advantage pattern is of particular importance. A multi-sector model could provide guidelines as to which sectors of the economy should be given highest priority from the point of view of export promotion and future growth policies. However, it is in this regard that the data used would seem to affect the results. Since labor requirements for industry are lowest and since industrial products in general have the highest rates of effective protection, this biases the comparative advantage results of the model toward industrial products. This conclusion is reinforced by alternative solution 7 (above, chapter II.4). There, when the labor constraints are eliminated, it is optimal for agriculture to expand its exports significantly in relation to the other sectors.

The formulation of DINAMICO represents an advance in the field, and yet this is still more of an exercise in model building than a tool for immediate application by Mexico's policy makers. By way of comparison, I should like to point to EXPORTA. This is a 45-sector linear programming model for the Mexican economy. Since this is a single-period model, capital formation is analyzed in a simpler way than in DINAMICO. In terms of sectoral coverage, however, EXPORTA is more highly disaggregated. It takes into consideration both the structure of tariff protection and the technological dualism aspects of the economy. It shows, for instance, that Mexico's comparative advantage is at present in primary rather than manufactured products. At the same time, EXPORTA indicates a serious unemployment problem during the 1970's, especially for unskilled labor. This is supported by other studies on the relationship between industrialization and employment growth in Mexico. These point to a diminishing labor absorption on the part of the industrial sector, as a result of the nature of the process of diffusion of technology. (See Trejo 1971.) This differs quite radically from DINAMICO's much more optimistic results with regard to labor absorption.

4. Concluding comments

The fact that there is room for improving the reliability of DI-NAMICO should not in any way detract from its merits. Quite the contrary. Ultimately, these efforts in model building are likely to prove highly useful for policy-making in Mexico. Even in its present form, the aggregate shadow prices of DINAMICO (for labor, capital and foreign exchange) could be applied in the evaluation of public sector investment projects. Also of great importance, the attempt to look into Mexico's long-term growth prospects provides at least a rough idea of the tradeoffs which should form one of the key elements in any policy decision.

Editor's note

Following the suggestions made in this chapter, the DINAMICO matrix was revised to allow for 'nominal implicit protection' — that is, for sectoral differences in the ratio of domestic to world prices of exportable commodities. By itself, this change was not strong enough to shift Mexico's comparative advantage away from exports of manufactures and toward unprocessed agricultural products. When combined, however, with a lowering of the opportunity cost of unskilled agricultural labor, the direction of comparative advantage is shifted toward agricultural products. This shift takes place when the cost of capital-labor substitution is lowered from 15,000 to 10,000 pesos per man in 1960. The efficiency wage for unskilled labor then drops in virtually the same proportion as the marginal rate of capital-labor substitution.

One side effect of allowing for nominal implicit protection: The shadow price premium on foreign exchange rises from 15% to 28% or more in terms of manufactured exports. The other macroeconomic variables do not change significantly.

References

Bacha, E., and L. Taylor, 'Foreign exchange shadow prices: a critical review of current theories', *Quarterly Journal of Economics*, May 1971.

Trejo, S., *Industrialization and employment growth: Mexico 1950–1965*. Dissertation presented to Yale University, April 1971.

II.6. EXPORTA, A MULTI-SECTOR MODEL FOR OPTIMAL GROWTH AND EXPORT POLICIES *

Saúl TREJO REYES **

1. Introduction

This paper presents the results of EXPORTA, a multi-sector model for analyzing optimal export promotion and sectoral growth policies in Mexico. It is hoped that a model which operates at the 45-sector level of disaggregation will provide, as one of its main results, shadow prices for both the primary factors of production (capital, labor, foreign exchange) and also for intermediate inputs. Eventually, such shadow prices may prove useful in the evaluation of investment projects from the viewpoint of social profitability. At the same time, by tracing out efficiency frontiers for the economy (through variations in the availability of exogenous factors of production and through experimentation with different objective functions), we obtain insights into the pattern of comparative advantage of the economy and into the implications of alternative economic policies.

* This is a revised version of a paper which was published in *El Trimestre Económico*, No. 152 (1971). The present version incorporates substantial changes in the model and presents the results of a series of new experiments. The opinions expressed in this paper are the exclusive responsibility of the author, and should not in any way be interpreted to represent the view of the institutions with which the author is associated.

** The author would like to thank those who at various stages commented on the work, including Antonio Aspra, Gerardo Bueno, Alan S. Manne and Leopoldo Solís. He would also like to acknowledge the capable programming and research assistance of Jose Alberto Valencia, César Peralta and Fernando Sánchez Ugarte.

Of course, the results must not be pressed beyond certain limits which are set by the reliability of the data and by the theoretical shortcomings of the model itself. This type of model can be useful as a source of, and testing ground for, general policy guidelines. To be really helpful in policy decisions, multi-level planning is needed. These calculations must be cross-checked against more detailed sectoral models. An aggregate model serves as a consistency check for alternative policies and a long-term forecast of the economy's capacity to achieve different policy objectives.

This is a one-period model. The linear programming objective function for the terminal year is defined as either the maximization of national income (see Bruno 1966), or else as the maximization of the balance of trade when exports are valued at world prices. [1] Despite the fact that this is a one-period model, it is felt that the disaggregation into 45 sectors (roughly comparable to the two-digit SITC classification) has some advantages over DINAMICO with its 15-sector level of aggregation. Thus, it is thought that the two approaches are complementary. A comparison of the results can be a useful way of testing out the assumption of each.

2. The problem of protection

In using input-output and national income data of developing countries, one of the main problems is the fact that domestic prices are distorted by the protectionist policies generally followed by such countries. Similarly, when a linear programming model is expressed in terms of domestic prices, the optimal solution may not reflect the real scarcities in the economy, and the shadow prices so obtained would not be an accurate guide to the real opportunity costs. (See Corden 1966 and Bacha and Taylor 1971.)

The impact of protection on the cost structure of the economy may be seen through the framework of the theory of effective

[1] Due to lack of satisfactory econometric estimates, it has not been possible to incorporate demand functions for Mexico's exports within EXPORTA. If this can be done in the future, we will obtain a more reliable measure of the direction of comparative advantage for individual items – and also for the aggregate balance of trade.

protection. This, together with the input-output assumption of fixed coefficients of production, may be used to estimate an input-output matrix at world prices.

The starting-point for our analysis was the 1960 input-output table (Banco de México 1966), and the work of Bueno (1971) on the structure of protection in Mexico. Under the simplifying assumption of fixed physical coefficients, it was first necessary to convert the 1960 flow matrix into world prices. Let X_{ij} denote the domestically-valued flow from sector i to j. Each of these quantities was divided by $(1 + t_i)$, where t_i is the nominal implicit tariff rate for the output of sector i. This assumes that for all of that sector's output, domestic prices are $(1 + t_i)$ times the world price. With regard to value added in sector j, since this is expressed in domestic prices in the input-output table and in the national income accounts, it must be divided by $(1 + z_j)$, where z_j is the rate of effective protection to the value added in sector j. This gives us an estimate of value added at world prices for each sector. Once the flow matrix is converted to world prices, it is then possible to estimate the coefficients matrix under such conditions.

This procedure requires a number of simplifying assumptions such as fixed physical input-output coefficients and fixed domestic price ratios between the primary inputs of capital and labor. The weighted effective and nominal protection rates must be accurate estimates of the differentials between domestic and world prices. It is supposed that these differentials are not affected by the quantities imported or exported.

3. Alternative objective functions

Taking advantage of the fact that the input-output matrix used in EXPORTA is expressed at world prices, it was decided to experiment with two alternative objective functions. This permits us to identify those sectors in which Mexico might have a comparative advantage for exporting, and to see how the direction of comparative advantage might shift under alternative assumptions. No specific limits have been placed upon the export of any one item.

The first objective function is to maximize national income $Y = GDP$, where exports are valued at internal prices, that is:

$$Y = \sum_{i=1}^{45} (E_i - M_i + D_i) , \qquad (1)$$

where E_i represents the exports of sector i, M_i its imports, and D_i the sector's deliveries to domestic final uses, consumption and investment.

The maximand refers to the terminal year of a six-year planning period. Thus, the problem is to allocate resources during the first five years of the period so as to maximize national income in the sixth year, subject to a set of constraints on terminal year investment. It was assumed that there is a one-year lag between the time an investment is made and the time it becomes productive. Hence, investments during the sixth year do not contribute to productive capacity in that year.

With this first objective function, exports are valued at internal prices. This means that we are really determining which sectors are able to produce one pesos' worth of output at least cost, assuming that output is valued at internal prices. Of course, this leads to biases in the case of export items. These solutions therefore provide only a measure of comparative efficiency for production at domestic prices.

The second objective function does take into account the fact that exports are sold at world prices. In general, these are lower than domestic prices at the 1960 exchange rate. Thus, the balance of trade maximand is:

$$\sum_{i=1}^{45} \left[\left(\frac{1}{1+t_i} \right) E_i - M_i \right] , \qquad (2)$$

where t_i is the nominal rate of protection for sector i's goods. It is assumed that this reflects the price differential between internal and world prices. The solutions obtained with this objective function thus provide a more stringent test of a sector's ability to produce exportable goods profitably, since such output is valued at export prices.

With different objective functions, a comparison of the results provides useful information about the production possibility frontier of the economy and about the tradeoffs between different policy objectives − the balance of payments, national income, and employment. The use of alternative functions is also of interest with regard to the dual solutions, since the shadow prices vary according to the objective functions. Such variations reflect the changes in the opportunity cost of primary resources depending on the policy objectives. Thus, through their use for project evaluation, the shadow prices could constitute a useful link to the project level decisions in the public sector.

4. Formulation of the model

The problem was formulated as the maximization, over a six-year planning horizon ending in 1976, of each of the objective functions discussed in the previous section, subject to a series of restrictions, both sectoral and global. For an algebraic summary of the model, see tables 1 and 2.

Rows 1−45 consist of material balances for each sector. These ensure that the supplies of each good (gross output plus imports) will cover the intermediate uses plus the final demands for consumption, investment and exports.

Rows 46−90 refer to non-competitive imports − those linked to the levels of production and of gross investment in sector i. In these restrictions, we also include those imports which are linked to the level of income rather than to the level of output of any one sector.

Rows 91−135 constitute a series of sectoral demand functions, relating the level of national income linearly to the final demand deliveries (consumption and investment). The constants d_i define the marginal propensity to consume and invest item i.

Rows 136−180 link the final year investment in each sector to the investment that has taken place in that sector during the previous five years. This ensures that the structure of investment in the final year will correspond roughly with that during the intermediate period. To estimate the stock-flow conversion factors β_i,

Table 1

Identification of variables, constants and parameters

Variables (annual rates in terminal year unless specified otherwise)

X_i	Gross output of sector i
E_i	Exports of sector i
D_i	Deliveries by sector i to final demand uses
I_i	Investment by sector i
M_i	Total imports, sector i
Y	Gross national product
$\sum_{t=1}^{5}(1+g_i)^t$	Index in which g_i denotes annual growth rate of investment, sector i
S_t	Domestic savings
F_t	Balance of trade deficit

Constants and parameters

a_{ij}	Input coefficients from sector i per unit of gross output in sector j
m_i	Average propensity to import inputs, sector i
m_i^*	Intermediate plus final imports of sector i as a proportion of X_i
n_i	Import content of sector i investment
d_i	Marginal propensity to consume item i with respect to Y_t
k_i	Marginal and average capital-output ratios, sector i
β_i	Stock-flow conversion factor for terminal year investment, sector i
k_i	Sectoral capital-output ratio
l_{ij}	Labor-output ratio, sector i (separate coefficients j for modern and traditional types of labor)
I_{i0}	Investment, sector i, base year
K_{i0}	Capital stock, sector i, base year
Y_0	GNP, base year
D_{i0}	Final demand, sector i, base year
s	Marginal propensity to save
S_0	Domestic savings, base year
L_j	Labor available, modern or traditional sector j, terminal year

it is necessary to make a first-round estimate of the sectoral growth rates g_i. In principle, it would have been possible to use the results of one solution to recalculate these factors for a second-round estimate. For the present purpose, however, the iterative process did not appear worthwhile.

Summary of restrictions

Row identification number	Description of row				
1–45	Sectoral material balances	$(1+m_i)X_i - \sum_{j=1}^{45} a_{ij}X_j - E_i$		$-D_i$	$= 0$
46–90	Non-competitive imports	$m_i^* X_i$		$+ n_i I_i - M_i$	$= 0$
91–135	Final demand			D_i	$-d_i Y_t \geqslant D_{i0} - d_i Y_0$
136–180	Terminal year investment		$-\beta_i I_{i0} \sum_{t=1}^{5} (1+g_i)^t$	$+ I_i$	$\geqslant 0$
181–225	Capacity	$k_i X_i$	$- I_{i0} \sum_{t=1}^{5} (1+g_i)^t$		$\leqslant K_{i0}$
226	Investment, intermediate years		$\sum_i [I_{i0} \sum_{t=1}^{5} (1+g_i)^t]$		$\leqslant \sum_{t=1}^{5} [(S_t + F_t)]$
227–228	Labor constraints	$\sum_{i=1}^{45} l_{ij} X_i$			$\leqslant L_j$
229	Terminal year investment			$-\sum_i I_i \qquad + sY_t \geqslant sY_0 - S_0 - F_t$	
230	Terminal year savings			$S_t - sY_t \geqslant S_0 - sY_0$	
231	Gross national product	$\sum_i [1/(1+t_i)]E_i$	$+ \sum_i D_i$	$-\sum_i M_i - Y_t = 0$	
232	Balance of trade	$\sum_i [1/(1+t_i)]E_i$		$-\sum_i M_i \qquad \geqslant -F_t$	
233–322	Gross output bounds	X_i X_i			$\geqslant X_i \min$ $\leqslant X_i \max$

Rows 181–225 refer to the capital stock required by each sector within the terminal year. A one-year lag was assumed between the time an investment takes place and the moment it comes into use. Hence, investment during years 1–5 (but not during year 6) contributes to the capital stock available during year 6. For the 45-sector level of aggregation, there did not exist a capital coefficients matrix by origin and destination. We were therefore constrained to measure the use of capital through a single aggregate capital-output ratio k_i for each producing sector i.

Following the sectoral restrictions 1–225, there are a number of aggregate balances to be satisfied: investment during the intermediate years, labor constraints, investment, savings, gross national product and the balance of trade during the terminal year. These aggregate balances are identified as rows 226–232. In addition, to allow for inelasticities of supply, there are lower and upper bounds specified for the output of each sector during the terminal year – respectively $X_{i\,\min}$ and $X_{i\,\max}$.

5. The labor force in EXPORTA

In models of this type, it is of great importance to include all primary factors. Since the labor force statistics are not very reliable, the construction of labor coefficients is particularly difficult. Basically, we start from the premise that the Mexican economy is of a dualistic nature (with a 'modern' and 'traditional' sector co-existing in each economic activity). Also, we postulate that the diffusion of technological progress: (a) raises average labor productivity faster in the modern than in the traditional sector, and (b) displaces the share of traditional-type firms, so that over time the modern sector of the economy accounts for an ever larger share of both aggregate output and employment.

This dualistic process has rather important dynamic implications for employment – both with regard to its aggregate level and to its sectoral composition. It means that in any given industry, the elasticity of employment with respect to output growth will be falling at a rate greater than would be expected by simply considering the rates of average labor productivity increase in the modern sector firms. That is, in any given industry, firms which are more capital- and less labor-intensive will be expanding their output more rapidly than traditional firms. This will change the skill mix of the industry over time. In particular, it will affect the requirements of modern sector labor and traditional sector labor per unit of output.

Although these two types of labor might be considered analogous to two different skill grades, there is the additional fact that they are used by different types of firms. Given the imperfections of the labor markets in developing countries, the share of output and labor in each of the two types of activities will substantially affect the resulting income distribution patterns over time. See Trejo (1971).

EXPORTA has been constructed so that for each of the sectors in the model there are two types of labor: that employed by the modern and by the traditional sector. Aggregate labor supplies of each of the two types j are projected exogenously, and the two labor coefficients l_{ij} (modern sector labor and traditional labor) for each economic activity i are determined separately. [2]

It is important to note that, even though both types of labor are assumed to be required in fixed proportions per unit of output, the fixed coefficients themselves are the result of a process of technological diffusion. The key variables are the rate of increase of average labor productivity in the modern and the traditional activities, and the speed with which modern activities are displacing the traditional ones.

Although it is felt that this approach captures the essential features of the dualistic nature of the economy with regard to labor,

---

[2] Based on several sources, an initial division of the economy into traditional and modern activities was made for 1950, 1960, and 1965. The labor force in each activity was then assigned to either the modern or traditional sector. We also estimated the speed of the process of diffusion, that is, the rate of displacement of traditional by modern activities. The definitional basis for the dualistic separation varies from one sector to another. In manufacturing, it is based primarily on firm size. In agriculture, it is based on capital-labor and output-land ratios. In services, it depends both on productivity and on type of activity criteria. In other sectors, independent analyses were made. For further details, see the author's papers cited below.

it is still somewhat rigid in that it does not provide for an explicit choice between alternative traditional and modern activities for producing a given good. In principle also, the rate of displacement of the traditional sector depends on the rate of growth of the sector's total output — which is in turn, an endogenous variable within EXPORTA. Despite these shortcomings, this approach has been found useful in analyzing the employment implications of alternative growth strategies. Given the magnitude of the employment problem in Mexico at present and in the foreseeable future, this is of great importance.

The dualistic diffusion model was employed directly for estimating all labor coefficients with the exception of the agricultural sector. There it was believed that the observed labor inputs did not accurately reflect the existence of underemployment. We therefore modified these input coefficients, reducing them in both the modern and the traditional agricultural sectors to 40% below the level estimated through the diffusion model.

6. Tradeoffs between alternative objectives

To distinguish between alternative solutions, the symbol Y is used to identify those cases in which income is employed as the objective function. The symbol EI identifies those in which the balance of trade is the objective, with exports being valued at international prices. For each objective function, two different solutions may be obtained — with and without labor constraints. These are identified respectively through the symbols L and NL. Various cases correspond to differing levels of the exogenous inputs of capital and of the foreign exchange deficit. Up to four alternative levels of these exogenous inputs were considered. Thus, the case identified as YNL4 means that income is taken as the objective, that labor constraints are not included, and that the exogenous inputs of primary factors consisted of 390 billion pesos' worth of capital, and 9 billion pesos of foreign exchange deficit. See table 3.

When income is taken as the objective, the GNP level is much less sensitive to the availability of capital and foreign exchange

Table 3
Aggregate results from EXPORTA [a]

Solution identifi- cation	Capital available, intermediate years (billions of 1960 pesos)	Balance of trade deficit (billions of 1960 pesos)	GNP (billions of 1960 pesos) [b]	Employment (millions of workers)		
				Modern sectors	Tradi- tional sectors	Total
YL1	450.0	18.0	459.2 [e]	7.2	7.1	14.3
YL2	425.0	15.0	455.9 [e]	7.2	7.1	14.3
YL3	410.0	12.0	455.5 [e]	7.2	7.3	14.5
YL4	390.0	9.0	453.1 [e]	7.2	7.4	14.6
YNL1	450.0	18.0	485.7 [e]	8.0	8.5	16.5
YNL2	425.0	15.0	477.1 [e]	7.9	8.3	16.2
YNL4 [c]	390.0	9.0	460.7 [e]	7.6	8.1	15.7
EIL1	425.0 [d]	−45.2 [e]	416.5	6,8	8.3	15.1
EIL2	400.0 [d]	−45.2 [e]	416.5	6.8	8.3	15.1
EINL1	425.0 [d]	−45.2 [e]	416.5	6.8	8.3	15.1
EINL2	400.0 [d]	−45.2 [e]	416.5	6.8	8.3	15.1
		Labor availability, L_j		7.2	11.2	18.4

[a] Results refer to terminal year (1976) unless specified otherwise.
[b] 1970 GDP: 304.0 billion pesos at 1960 prices.
[c] No solution YNL3 was computed.
[d] Capital utilized: 368 billion pesos at 1960 prices.
[e] Objective function.

when labor is taken as a constraint than when it is neglected. Between the extreme cases YL1 and YL4, the level of income differs in the terminal year by only 6.1 billion pesos. This is equivalent to a difference between 6.88% and 7.15% in the annual rate of GNP growth from 1970 to 1976. Along with this aggregate result, there is a substantial change in the optimal pattern of production. For example, it is optimal to increase the relative importance of agriculture when the availability of capital and foreign exchange falls.

In cases YL1−4 it turns out that the supply of labor to the modern sector of the economy is a binding constraint, but that there is a large surplus (4 out of 11 million workers) in the traditional sector of the economy. When capital and foreign exchange become scarce, the optimal pattern of production becomes more labor intensive. Despite the fall in national income, the employment of traditional sector labor rises from 7.1 to 7.4 million workers.

In general, the removal of the labor constraints (cases YNL 1–4) raises substantially the growth of national income. Since these cases impute a high productivity to physical capital formation, the GNP difference between cases YNL1 and YNL4 is consistent with an aggregate output-capital ratio of 40% per year = (485.7–460.7) ÷ (450.0–390.0)).

It is of great importance to observe the employment implications of *not* introducing a labor constraint. Modern sector employment increases substantially over the YL cases, but the increases in the use of traditional labor are even more striking. When modern sector labor is not a constraint, the sectors that expand rapidly are those that also absorb large amounts of traditional sector labor. Thus, there is complementarity in the use of both types of labor.

With foreign exchange as the maximand, only four alternative cases were computed – those corresponding to two different levels of capital inputs, with and without labor constraints. No explicit limit was placed upon the level of income. It then turned out that both the sectoral and the aggregate solutions were identical. Of the total capital available, only 368 billion pesos were utilized. Beyond this point, it appears that there are no investment opportunities for socially profitable exports. This occurred despite the conversion of the cost structure of inputs into world prices.

By comparing the various cases, we may obtain some idea of the tradeoffs between conflicting objectives – national income, employment, and the balance of payments. Note that the 1976 GNP is about 9% lower when the balance of trade is the objective function and labor is a constraint (EIL solutions) than when gross national product is the objective (YL solutions). Over a six-year period, this implies a difference of 1.3% per annum in the GNP growth rate. The difference is quite substantial when compared to the average annual growth rates of 6.5–7.0% which Mexico achieved during the 1960's.

With labor taken to be a constraint, the last column of table 3 indicates that for the export-oriented cases, the total labor use is 0.5–0.8 million workers greater than in the GNP-oriented solutions. Traditional labor use increases by nearly one million, but modern sector labor is not fully utilized. Thus, it would seem that the best output pattern from the export viewpoint is also a rather labor intensive pattern – more so than the GNP maximizing output combination. When labor is not a constraint, the GNP maximizing solutions, (YNL 1–4) imply a substantially higher use of labor than do the export maximizing solutions. Most of this difference in employment (about 90% of it) appears in the use of modern sector labor. For income maximizing purposes, the optimal activities are those where the share of the modern sector is high. For maximizing foreign exchange earnings, the optimal activities are those where the traditional sector predominates, and which are therefore more labor intensive.

7. Employment as a policy objective

Even under the most optimistic solutions (cases YL1 and YL2 in table 3), there would be 4.1 million unemployed (or underemployed) workers in 1976. Since employment is a major policy objective in Mexico, a series of sensitivity analyses were used to trace out the tradeoffs between employment and income growth.

The base for these sensitivity analyses was case YL2. All conditions were held the same, except that the employment of labor in the traditional sectors was increased parametrically above the level that is optimal for this case. Figure 1 shows the cost (in terms of 1976 GNP foregone) of stipulating these additional amounts of employment. Table 4 provides this same information in tabular form.

According to this analysis, a substantial fall in unemployment (1.3 million additional jobs) can be obtained at less than 5,000 pesos (in 1960 prices, U.S. $400) per man at the margin. This does not seem to be an unreasonable price to pay for creating additional employment and redistributing income. If, however, we attempt

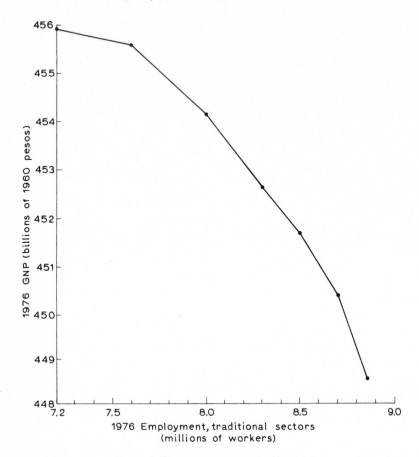

Fig. 1. GNP – employment tradeoffs.

to increase the level of traditional employment above 8.6 millions (leaving 2.6 millions still unemployed), the costs rise sharply. Thus, EXPORTA provides useful insights into the resource reallocation needed in order to generate additional employment. This is of particular importance, given the low employment creation prospects in manufacturing during the 1970's. See Trejo (1971).

In general, when EXPORTA is required to use larger amounts of traditional labor, it is optimal for the primary producing sectors to grow at the maximum rates allowed. This is to be expected, since these are the most labor intensive activities in the economy. Under

Table 4
Costs of employment creation

Employment, traditional sectors (millions of workers)	1976 GNP (millions of 1960 pesos)	Shadow price of labor, modern sectors (1960 pesos per worker)	Shadow price of labor, traditional sectors (1960 pesos per worker)	Average cost of employment creation, traditional sectors (1960 pesos per worker)
7.200 [a]	455,914 [a]	41,021 [a]	0 [a]	
7.600	455,590	43,652	− 1,690	810
8.000	454,139	48,346	− 4,846	3,660
8.300	452,682	48,492	− 4,953	4,850
8.500	451,691	48,492	− 4,953	4,950
8.700	450,447	54,465	− 7,167	6,230
8.850	448,695	64,800	−50,839	11,700

[a] Solution YL2.

the restriction that more labor is to be used, the income maximizing product-mix thus comes to resemble the export oriented EIL solutions.

8. Results − dual variables

In general, when no labor constraints are included, the shadow prices obtained for capital are rather high − roughly 40% per year as the marginal rate of return in solutions YNL2 and YNL3. However, when the capital availability is increased (in YNL1), this shadow price decreases to about 10%, a rather drastic fall. A 40% return is close to the average productivity of capital. The sharp drop occurs when the capital availability rises above the most plausible levels projected for the 1971−75 period.

When labor constraints are introduced, the marginal productivity of capital falls to a level below 10% per year. At that point, the modern sector labor constraint becomes the most binding bottleneck, and the shadow price of modern labor rises to 40,000 pesos (= U.S. $3,200 man-year). It seems that the marginal productivity of capital is highly sensitive to the modern sector labor constraint.

If this constraint were to be relaxed, the marginal productivity of capital would rise. In all cases, traditional sector labor is redundant, and therefore has a zero opportunity cost.

It turns out that the shadow price of foreign exchange is about 1.33 times the official exchange rate in all four cases YL1−4, being lowest when capital is most abundant. This shadow price does not seem to be too far out of line with the price differentials observed by Bueno (1971) for some manufactured goods. These results are also similar to DINAMICO's alternative case 5 above, (chapter II.4). Of course, the eventual use of these shadow prices for project evaluation would require further refinements of the labor force projections, as well as a better understanding of the technological diffusion aspects of labor productivity. The shadow prices are sensitive to the specification of the labor restrictions. This may be seen from table 4 and from the experiments in generating a 'marginal cost of employment creation' function. There, when the economy was required to employ an additional 1.6 million units of traditional labor, the marginal productivity of modern labor rose steeply − from 41,000 to 65,000 pesos. This clearly demonstrates the importance of the modern sector labor restriction in determining the labor absorption capacity of the economy.

9. Policy implications

There are three major aspects to the policy implications from EXPORTA: (1) the pattern of comparative advantage and the variations in this pattern according to the policy objectives expressed in the maximand; (2) the shadow prices and their possible use in project evaluation for public investment decisions; and (3) the function indicating the marginal cost of employment creation.

One of the main limitations in the present model is the lack of export demand and supply functions. This difficulty might have been overcome through setting upper bounds on the growth of individual types of exports. In the absence of reliable data, this use of a priori restrictions was regarded as undesirable. Instead, in view of the inelasticity of domestic supplies, it seemed preferable to place upper and lower bounds on the growth of total output in each sector. Further improvements of EXPORTA will depend upon increases in the reliability of the data on the marginal cost of export earnings.

References

Bacha, E. and L. Taylor, 'Foreign exchange shadow prices: a critical review of current theories', *Quarterly Journal of Economics*, May, 1971.

Balassa, B., 'Tariff protection in industrial countries: an evaluation', *Journal of Political Economy*, December 1965.

Banco de México, S.A., *Cuadro de insumo producto para 1960*. Departamento de Estudios Económicos, 1966.

Banco de México, S.A., 'Los servicios modernos y tradicionales en México'. Study directed by Saúl Trejo. 1969. (Mimeographed.)

Banco de México, S.A., 'La dualidad económica en la agricultura Mexicana'. Study directed by Saúl Trejo. 1969. (Mimeographed.)

Banco de México, S.A., 'La dualidad en el sector manufacturero en México'. Study directed by Saúl Trejo. 1969. (Mimeographed.)

Bruno, M., 'A programming model for Israel', in: *The theory and design of economic development*, edited by I. Adelman and E. Thorbecke. Baltimore, Johns Hopkins, 1966.

Bueno, Gerardo M., 'The structure of protection in Mexico', in: B. Balassa, *The structure of protection in developing countries*. Baltimore, Johns Hopkins, 1971.

Corden, W.M., 'The structure of a tariff system and the effective protective rate', *Journal of Political Economy*, June 1966.

Nelson, R.R., 'A diffusion model of international productivity differences in manufacturing industry', *American Economic Review,* December 1968.

Solís, L., *La realidad económica Mexicana: retrovisión y perspectivas*. México, Siglo XXI Editores, 1970.

Trejo, S., *Industrialization and employment growth: Mexico 1950–1965*. Dissertation submitted to Yale University, April 1971.

PART III. THE ENERGY SECTOR

III.1. MULTI-LEVEL PLANNING FOR ELECTRIC POWER PROJECTS *

Guillermo FERNÁNDEZ de la GARZA, Alan S. MANNE
and José Alberto VALENCIA

1. Introduction

Until converted into investment decisions on specific projects, a macroeconomic development plan remains non-operational. [1] In principle, to be sure, an individual project cannot be evaluated without a clear view of the entire system within which it is to operate. In practice, this ideal is approached through identifying one-way linkages – parameters that influence the project decision, but that are not significantly influenced by it.

Following the suggestive terminology of Simon (1962, pp. 468 and 474), a project is the 'lowest level of elementary subsystem' in a hierarchically organized complex system. One-at-a-time decisions on individual projects are likely to be near-optimal if the projects belong to *'nearly decomposable* systems, in which the interactions among the subsystems are weak, but not negligible. ... In the long run, the behavior of any one of the components depends in only an aggregate way on the behavior of the other components.'

We begin by examining a typical case – the evaluation of a nuclear versus a fossil fuel electricity plant in Mexico during the

* For help in various phases, the authors are much indebted to: Ings. Juan Eibenschutz and Roberto Fabre and Lic. Bosco Muro (Comisión Federal de Electricidad) and to Mr. Richard Inman (Stanford University). The specific facts, methods of analysis, and conclusions are the sole responsibility of the individual authors.

[1] On the relations between the macro and the micro stages of development planning, see Tinbergen (1967), chapter 9.

late 1970's. In this and the following chapters, the fossil-nuclear choice is reexamined within systems of increasing complexity: IN-TERCON, a multi-region model that introduces tradeoffs between electricity generation and transmission; ENERGETICOS, a process analysis that introduces tradeoffs between investments in electric power versus those in the petroleum sector; and DINAMICO, a multi-sector macroeconomic model.

If the identical system of aggregation were maintained in moving from the micro toward the macro stage, project evaluation would become increasingly more realistic — but increasingly less manageable from the viewpoint of data-gathering, computation and timeliness of results. Clearly, the identical system of aggregation is inappropriate at the project, sectoral and multi-sector stages of planning. This chapter concludes with some speculations on what are likely to be the gains from evaluating electricity projects within models of ever-increasing complexity, what are likely to be the distortions associated with ever-increasing aggregation of information, and what purposes are served by multi-level planning. [2]

2. A single-plant comparison of nuclear versus fossil fuel projects

Traditionally, project analysis has taken some such form as that shown in figure 1. A project (a nuclear power plant in a specific region [3]) is evaluated against an alternative (a fossil fuel plant) converting all investment, operating and fuel costs into equivalent annual flows. [4] Typically, it is supposed that the project choice

---

[2] On multi-level planning, see Kornai (1967), esp. ch. 25.

[3] At no point does this paper attempt to quantify the environmental and pollution hazards associated with the two alternative sources of electricity. The problem varies significantly from one site to another. To offset thermal pollution in the case of nuclear power plants, there is an allowance for differences in investment costs between individual regions.

[4] For the detailed numerical data that underlie figure 1, see table 6 below. The nuclear and fossil plant types are those identified as N1 and F2, respectively. — Of the 8 regions into which the Mexican electricity system has been divided, the OR (Eastern) region is the one in which fossil fuel costs are lowest. This then is the region least favorable to the introduction of nuclear power plants.

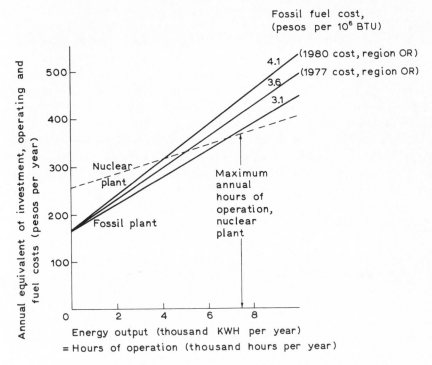

Fig. 1. Single plant cost comparison (per KW of installed power capacity).

will exert no influence over such evaluation parameters as the cost of capital or of foreign exchange. Typically also, the project decision will be tested for sensitivity to a number of parameters. The single-plant comparison shows immediately that the optimal process decision is sensitive to the cost of fossil fuel (expected to rise during the 1970's) and to the number of hours of operation of the plant. [5]

[5] An electricity plant produces joint products: power and energy. Power refers to the output at an instant of time. Energy refers to the integral of power output over time.

One kilowatt (KW) of *power* capacity operated for 1,000 hours will produce 1,000 kilowatt-hours (KWH) of electrical *energy*. The following units of measurement are also employed:

$$10^6 \text{ KW} = 1 \text{ GW}, \qquad 10^9 \text{ KWH} = 1 \text{ TWH}.$$

The number of hours of operation of an individual power plant is a parameter that is *not* independent of the mix of other units within the system. For example, the Mexican grid contains a substantial number of hydroelectric units. These have a turbine/reservoir capacity ratio that permits the hydro plants to produce a large fraction of their energy output during the peak demand hours. This initially available plant-mix favors the introduction of nuclear units. Given the hydro plants in the system, nuclear units may be employed as 'base-load' plants — operated round-the-clock to take advantage of their low incremental costs per kilowatt-hour of energy. [6]

Ever since the pioneering study of Massé and Gibrat (1957) [7] at Electricité de France, it has been recognized that linear programming provides a tool for embedding individual project choices within a power systems framework — allowing, e.g., for complementarities between hydro and nuclear plants. Each plant is then viewed as a source of joint products: electricity available at different points of time during the daily, weekly and seasonal cycle of operations. INTERCON is a model in the Massé-Gibrat tradition — a model in which the number of hours of operation of each unit becomes an endogenous variable. This increase in generality is not costless. Data must now be collected on components of the system other than the individual project itself.

3. Algebraic formulation of static multi-region model

Unlike a single-project analysis, INTERCON is disaggregated in time and space. The demands at different points of time and space are to be met at minimum cost. The greater the interregional diversity in the quantities of energy demanded (or of hydroelectric energy supplied) at different points of time, the greater will be the cost savings from interconnection through transmission lines.

[6] For a more detailed exposition of this topic, see Berrie (1968), pp. 198–200.

[7] For two surveys of applications within the Massé-Gibrat framework, see Bessière (1969) and Anderson (1970). For a mixed integer programming application, see Gately (1970).

Table 1
Identification of indices

Class	Generic index for class	Specific values of index for members of class	
Plant type	i	I1	initially available gas turbine plants
		I2 and I3	initially available fossil plants
		HD	initially available hydroelectric plants
		F1	0.075 GW gas turbine plants
		F2	0.300 GW fossil plants
		F3	0.600 GW fossil plants
		N1	0.600 GW nuclear plants
		N2	1.000 GW nuclear plants
Transmission line voltage	j	1	230 kv (kilovolt) transmission lines
		2	400 kv (kilovolt) transmission lines
Region	r	TC	Torreón-Chihuahua
		FM	Falcón-Monterrey
		TP	Tampico
		SL	San Luis
		OR	Eastern
		CL	Central
		OC	Western
		MS	Mazatlán-Sonora
Demand block	k	1	peak hours, March–June (486.7 hours) [a]
		2	off-peak hours, March–June (2,433.3 hours) [b]
		3	peak hours, July–October (486.7 hours) [a]
		4	off-peak hours, July–October (2,433.3 hours) [b]
		5	peak hours, November–March (486.7 hours) [a]
		6	off-peak hours, November–March (2.433.3 hours) [b]
Season	s	1	March–June
		2	July–October
		3	November–February
Representative year	t	1	March, 1977 – February, 1978
		2	March, 1980 – February, 1981

[a] For demand blocks $k = 1, 3, 5$, the time duration ηk is:

$$\eta k = 486.7 \; \frac{\text{peak hours}}{\text{season}} = \left(\frac{4 \text{ peak hours}}{\text{day}} \right) \left(\frac{365 \text{ days}}{\text{year}} \right) \left(\frac{\text{year}}{3 \text{ seasons}} \right)$$

[b] For demand blocks $k = 2, 4, 6$, the time duration ηk is:

$$\eta k = 2433.3 \; \frac{\text{peak hours}}{\text{season}} = \left(\frac{20 \text{ off-peak hours}}{\text{day}} \right) \left(\frac{365 \text{ days}}{\text{year}} \right) \left(\frac{\text{year}}{3 \text{ seasons}} \right)$$

The index t is employed to distinguish between two representative *years*: 1977 ($t = 1$), the first year in which a 0.600 GW nuclear plant might be in operation, and 1980 ($t = 2$), the first year for a 1.000 GW plant. Within each of these representative years, three four-month *seasons* are denoted by the subscript s. (Hydroelectric energy supplies differ markedly from one to another of these seasons.) The 4 daily peak hours are distinguished from the 20 off-peak hours by the *energy demand block* subscript k. (See table 1.) The annual peak power demand occurs either in season 2 or 3 — depending upon the region.

The index r identifies the eight *regions* that might be interconnected by transmission lines. Each region is simplified as though it formed a single representative point. The distances for 12 possible transmission links — and the fossil fuel costs within each region — are shown on figure 2. Isolated systems (e.g., those in Baja California) have been excluded from INTERCON.

Transmission costs and line losses depend upon the line voltage. To distinguish between 230 kv and 400 kv lines, we employ the *transmission line voltage* subscript j. Electric power generating

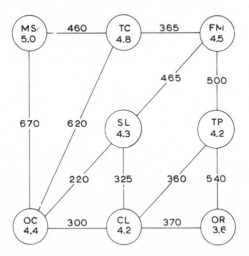

Fig. 2. Schematic diagram of distances (km) and 1977 fossil fuel prices (pesos per million BTU). Note: Between 1977 and 1980, it is supposed that fossil fuel prices will increase by 0.5 pesos per million BTU in each region.

Table 2
Number of constraint rows, single-period models

Row description	Unit of measurement (annual flow)	Row identifying letter(s)	Row indices	Year t = 1 Region r = TC	FM	TP	SL	OR	CL	OC	MS	rr'	Total number of rows	Year t = 2 Region r = TC	FM	TP	SL	OR	CL	OC	MS	rr'	Total number of rows
Peak power demand	GW	GW	rst	2	2	2	2	2	2	2	2		16	2	2	2	2	2	2	2	2		16
Energy demand	TWH	TWH	rkt	6	6	6	6	6	6	6	6		48	6	6	6	6	6	6	6	6		48
Peak power generation capacity	GW	G	irt	4	4	3	0	4	4	4	4		27	4	4	3	0	4	4	4	4		27
Energy generating capacity	TWH	E	$irkt$	24	30	24	15	30	30	30	30		213	24	30	36	21	42	42	42	30		267
Fossil fuel requirements	10^{12} BTU	CF	rt	1	1	1	1	1	1	1	1		8	1	1	1	1	1	1	1	1		8
Hydro turbine limits	TWH	EHD	rkt	6	6	6	0	6	6	6	6		42	6	6	6	0	6	6	6	6		42
Hydro reservoir limits	TWH	HD	rst	3	3	3	0	3	3	3	3		21	3	3	3	0	3	3	3	3		21
Peak power transmission	GW	U	$jrr'st$									32	32									32	32
Energy transmission	TWH	V	$jrr'kt$									96	96									96	96
Project capacity, nuclear	GW	CPN	rt		1		1		1	1			4										0
Project capacity, transmission	GW	CPT	$rr't$									6	6										0
Mutual exclusivity	–	MUEX	–										4										0
Total number of rows				46	53	45	25	52	53	53	52	134	517	46	52	57	30	64	64	64	52	128	557

Table 3
Number of activity columns, single-period models

Column description	Unit of measurement	Column identifying letter(s)	Column indices	Year t = 1 Region r = TC	FM	TP	SL	OR	CL	OC	MS	rr'	Total number of columns	Year t = 2 Region r = TC	FM	TP	SL	OR	CL	OC	MS	rr'	Total number of columns
Peak power capacity utilized	GW	G	irt	6	7	6	3	7	7	7	7		50	6	7	7	4	8	9	9	7		57
Energy generation, above minimum	TWH	E	$irkt$	30	36	30	15	36	36	36	36		255	30	36	42	21	48	48	48	36		309
Fossil fuel requirements	10^{12} BTU	CF	rt	1	1	1	1	1	1	1	1		8	1	1	1	1	1	1	1	1		8
Peak power transmitted	GW	U	$jrr'st$									64	64									64	64
Energy transmitted	TWH	V	$jrr'kt$									192	192.									192	192
Transmission capacity installed	GW	T	$jrr't$									12	12									12	12
Zero-one variables for transmission and nuclear generating projects	–	Y	–									22	22										0
Total number of columns				37	44	37	19	44	44	44	44	268	22	603	37	44	50	26	57	58	58	44	268	642

plants are distinguished from one another by the *plant type* subscript i. (Again see table 1.)

When formulated as a mixed integer programming model for the single representative year 1977 ($t = 1$), INTERCON contains 517 rows and 603 non-slack columns. Since additional types of generating units will be available in 1980 ($t = 2$), there are more rows and columns in the programming model for the later year — 557 rows and 642 columns. See tables 2 and 3 for a row and column summary. The unknowns refer to the installation and utilization of either generating or transmission capacity.

To simplify typesetting and to avoid subscripts, the various indices (i, j, k, r, s and t) appear on the identical line as the remainder of the name of a row or a column. For example, the row (GW rst) refers to peak power in region r, season s, year t. The column Girt refers to peak power capacity of generating plant type i, utilized in region r, year t. *Coefficients* are identified by a lowercase Greek letter and then by the various indices. For example, the line loss coefficient $\alpha jr'r$ refers to the peak power received in region r per unit transmitted from region r', employing the line voltage j.

With these notational conventions, the peak power and the energy demand constraints (GWrst and TWHrkt) are written, respectively:

$$
\begin{array}{ll}
\text{(GW}rst) & \left(\begin{array}{c}\text{peak power}\\\text{capacity}\\\text{utilized}\\\text{in region } r\end{array}\right) + \left(\begin{array}{c}\text{peak power received}\\\text{in region } r \text{ per}\\\text{unit transmitted}\\\text{from region } r\end{array}\right)\left(\begin{array}{c}\text{peak power}\\\text{transmitted to}\\\text{region } r \text{ from}\\\text{region } r'\end{array}\right)
\end{array}
$$

$$
\sum_i \text{G}irt \;+\; \sum_j \sum_{r' \neq r} (\alpha jr'\, r) \qquad (\text{U}jr'rst)
$$

$$
- \left(\begin{array}{c}\text{peak power}\\\text{transmitted to}\\\text{region } r' \text{ from}\\\text{region } r\end{array}\right) \geqslant \left(\begin{array}{c}\text{peak power}\\\text{demand, region } r,\\\text{season } s, \text{ year } t\end{array}\right)
$$

$$
- \sum_j \sum_{r' \neq r} \text{U}jrr'st
$$

(TWHrkt)

$$\begin{pmatrix} \text{minimum hours} \\ \text{for energy} \\ \text{generation,} \\ \text{plant type } i, \\ \text{block } k \end{pmatrix} \begin{pmatrix} \text{peak power} \\ \text{capacity} \\ \text{utilized,} \\ \text{plant type } i \end{pmatrix} + \begin{array}{c} \text{energy generation,} \\ \text{above minimum,} \\ \text{plant type } i \end{array}$$

$$\sum_i (\beta i k) \qquad\qquad (Girt) \qquad + \qquad \sum_i Eirkt$$

$$- \begin{pmatrix} \text{energy received} \\ \text{in region } r \\ \text{per unit} \\ \text{transmitted} \\ \text{from region } r' \end{pmatrix} \begin{pmatrix} \text{energy} \\ \text{transmitted} \\ \text{to region } r \\ \text{from region } r' \end{pmatrix} - \begin{array}{c} \text{energy} \\ \text{transmitted} \\ \text{to region } r' \\ \text{from region } r \end{array}$$

$$\sum_j \sum_{r' \neq r} (\alpha jr'r) \qquad (Vjr'rkt) \qquad -\sum_j \sum_{r' \neq r} Vjrr'kt$$

$$\geqslant \begin{pmatrix} \text{energy demand,} \\ \text{region } r, \\ \text{block } k, \\ \text{year } t \end{pmatrix}$$

For the initially available plant types, the peak power capacity is a datum. Upper bounds on the individual unknowns are therefore:

$$(Girt) \quad \begin{pmatrix} \text{peak power} \\ \text{capacity} \\ \text{utilized,} \\ \text{plant type } i \\ Girt \end{pmatrix} \leqslant \begin{pmatrix} \text{peak power} \\ \text{capacity} \\ \text{available,} \\ \text{plant type } i \end{pmatrix} \quad (i = \text{I1, I2, I3, HD}).$$

In order for the boilers of fossil and nuclear plants to remain fired up so as to meet the daily demand peaks, these units cannot be operated at power levels below 25% of their capacity. This minimum limit has already been introduced through the coefficients $\beta i k$ in rows (TWHrkt). The operating time available *above* these minimum levels is given by the coefficient γik. This leads to the following upper bounds on above-minimum energy production for each plant type, region, block and time period:

(E$irkt$)

$$\begin{pmatrix} \text{energy} \\ \text{generation,} \\ \text{above} \\ \text{minimum} \end{pmatrix} \leqslant \begin{pmatrix} \text{hours for energy} \\ \text{generation above} \\ \text{minimum, plant} \\ \text{type } i, \text{block } k \end{pmatrix} \begin{pmatrix} \text{peak power} \\ \text{capacity} \\ \text{utilized,} \\ \text{plant type } i \end{pmatrix}$$

$$\text{E}irkt \quad \leqslant \quad \gamma ik \quad\quad\quad \text{G}irt \quad (i \neq \text{HD})$$

The fossil fuel requirements (i.e., the fuel inputs for plants other than hydro and nuclear) are calculated through equations (CFrt):

(CFrt)

$$\begin{pmatrix} \text{fossil fuel} \\ \text{requirements} \end{pmatrix} = \begin{pmatrix} \text{fossil fuel} \\ \text{requirement per} \\ \text{GW for minimum} \\ \text{annual energy} \\ \text{generation} \end{pmatrix} \begin{pmatrix} \text{GW of peak} \\ \text{power capacity} \\ \text{utilized, fossil} \\ \text{plant type } i \end{pmatrix}$$

$$\text{CF}rt \quad = \quad \sum_i (\delta ir) \quad\quad\quad (\text{G}irt)$$

$$+ \begin{pmatrix} \text{fossil fuel} \\ \text{requirement per} \\ \text{TWH of energy} \\ \text{generation above} \\ \text{minimum} \end{pmatrix} \begin{pmatrix} \text{TWH of energy} \\ \text{generation,} \\ \text{above minimum} \\ \text{fossil plant type } i \end{pmatrix}$$

$$+ \quad \sum_i \sum_k (\epsilon ir) \quad\quad\quad (\text{E}irkt) \quad (i \neq \text{HD}, \text{N1}, \text{N2})$$

Turbine limits imply the following upper bounds on hydro operations:

(EHDrkt)

$$\begin{array}{cc} \text{hydroelectric energy} & \begin{pmatrix} \text{hydroelectric energy} \\ \text{generation} \\ \text{limit, block } k \end{pmatrix} \\ \text{generated, block } k & \\ \text{EHD}krt \quad \leqslant & \end{array}$$

$$(k = 1, 2, ..., 6)$$

The following constraints are derived from reservoir limits governing hydro energy output during season s. No attempt has been made to allow for the stochastic character of hydro energy flows:

(HDrst)   hydroelectric energy $\begin{pmatrix} \text{hydroelectric energy available} \\ \text{during season } s \text{ containing} \\ \text{blocks } k \text{ and } k+1 \end{pmatrix}$
generated, blocks k
and $k+1$

$$\text{EHD}krt + \text{EHD}(k+1)rt \leqslant \qquad\qquad (s = 1, 2, 3)$$

For each of the 12 possible pairs of points r and r', there are capacity constraints on the peak power and on the energy transmitted. These constraints are identified as: (U$jrr'st$) and (V$jrr'kt$) respectively:

(U$jrr'st$)

peak power transmitted
between regions r
and r', season s $\begin{pmatrix} \text{initially} \\ \text{available} \\ \text{capacity} \end{pmatrix} + \begin{pmatrix} \text{capacity installed} \\ \text{between initial} \\ \text{date and year } t \end{pmatrix}$

$$\text{U}jrr'kt + \text{U}jr'rkt \quad \leqslant \qquad\qquad\qquad\qquad + \quad \text{T}jrr't$$

(V$jrr'kt$)

energy transmitted $\begin{pmatrix} \text{hours per} \\ \text{year,} \\ \text{block } k \end{pmatrix}\begin{pmatrix} \text{power transmission} \\ \text{capacity available} \\ \text{between region } r \\ \text{and } r', \text{year } t \end{pmatrix}$
between regions r
and r', block k

$$\text{V}jrr'kt + \text{V}jr'rkt \quad \leqslant \qquad (\eta k) \qquad \begin{pmatrix} \text{initially} \\ \text{available} + \text{T}jrr't \\ \text{capacity} \end{pmatrix}$$

For the time duration coefficients ηk, refer back to table 1.

4. Numerical data

Tables 4–7 contain most of the numerical data for INTERCON. [8] At the time the model was constructed (1970), these data represented the most plausible estimates available within the Comisión Federal de Electricidad. Inevitably, they are subject to revision as newer information becomes available. These are approximately – but not altogether – consistent with the data employed within the energy sector model ENERGETICOS and the macroeconomic model DINAMICO.

The INTERCON programming problem is stated as one of supplying the electricity demands at minimum cost to the electricity producing enterprise. [9] This criterion does not necessarily coincide

Table 4
Peak power demands (unit: GW)

Year	1977			1980			
t	1			2			
Season s	2	3	Regional seasonal peak	2	3	Regional seasonal peak	Per year increase, 1977–80 (%)
Region r							
TC	0.563	0.506	0.563	0.690	0.620	0.690	7.0%
FM	1.297	1.228	1.297	1.931	1.829	1.931	14.2
TP	0.175	0.181	0.181	0.277	0.285	0.285	16.4
SL	0	0	0	0	0	0	–
OR	2.687	2.769	2.769	4.097	4.223	4.223	15.1
CL	4.174	4.450	4.450	5.617	5.987	5.987	10.6
OC	1.581	1.698	1.698	2.240	2.403	2.403	12.3
MS	0.810	0.586	0.810	1.190	0.862	1.190	13.7
Total	11.287	11.418	11.768	16.042	16.209	16.709	12.4

[8] On the assumption that these were of limited general interest, we have not reproduced the region-by-region distribution of either the energy demands for each time block or the hydro supplies for each season. A sample of these data (for the OR region) appears in table 13 below. For the complete details, worksheets are available for inspection in the authors' offices.

[9] We have reproduced only the basic data from which the cost coefficients were derived. These basic data are more directly understandable than the list of coefficients associated with more than 600 individual activities.

Table 5

Characteristics of initially available generating plants [a]

Plant identification index i / Region r	Fossil fuel requirements, e_{ir} (10^{12} BTU per TWH of energy)				Combined capacity of all units initially available (GW)					Regional demands and capacity deficits (GW), year $t = 1$	
	I1	I2	I3	HD	I1	I2	I3	HD	Total capacity	Regional seasonal peak demand	Capacity deficit
TC	15.9252	14.5446	11.3772	0	0.158	0.063	0.216	0.038	0.475	0.563	0.088
FM	15.9931	11.2834	9.6236	0	0.056	0.610	0.150	0.071	0.887	1.297	0.410
TP	15.9931	9.6236	–	0	0.014	0.300	0	0.018	0.332	0.181	0
SL	–	–	–	–	0	0	0	0	0	0	0
OR	16.542	12.9469	10.7149	0	0.062	0.066	0.117	1.428	1.673	2.769	1.096
CL	15.6641	11.0920	9.4377	0	0.152	0.226	1.050	2.060	3.488	4.450	0.962
OC	16.1381	13.0048	9.6236	0	0.064	0.040	0.750	0.572	1.426	1.698	0.272
MS	15.9408	13.3228	10.8342	0	0.095	0.098	0.232	0.192	0.617	0.810	0.193
Total					0.601	1.403	2.515	4.379	8.898	11.768	3.021

[a] Since the historical investment cost of these facilities is a datum, these costs are omitted from the minimand. Future operating and maintenance costs are not bygones, and these are therefore included.

with minimizing the costs to the Mexican economy as a whole. Here the evaluation of investments is based upon a 10% annual rate of return on capital, converting domestic currency costs into foreign exchange at the conventional rate of 12.5 pesos per U.S. dollar. (For a sensitivity analysis of the fossil-nuclear choice with respect to the discount rate and the foreign exchange scarcity premium, see below, chapter III.2, tables 12 and 13.) In order to arrive at a static approximation to a dynamic investment planning problem, the initial investment costs have been converted to annual flows through 'capital recovery factors'.

Some features of the solution may be anticipated directly from the basic data. According to table 4, the country-wide peak power demand occurs during season 3 (November–February). The only regions that constitute an exception to the countrywide pattern are the three northern ones (TC, FM and MS). There, the irrigation and air conditioning loads shift the annual peak into season 2 (July–October). Once that transmission links are established between the north and the south, the July–October peak power demand constraints are non-binding in any region, and can be satisfied at zero incremental cost.

The lack of diversity between regional demands may be quantified through a calculation for year $t = 1$ (1977). With no transmission between regions, the regional seasonal peak demands would lead to requirements totalling 11.768 GW of installed generating capacity. If all regions were interconnected and there were no transmission losses, the countrywide peak would occur during season 3, and these demands would lead to a total of 11.418 GW of capacity. (See table 4.) In other words, interconnection would reduce the capacity requirements by at most 0.350 GW = 11.768 − 11.418 GW. This saving (3% of installed generating capacity) could be a significant gain to the electricity producing enterprise. From the viewpoint of constructing a model of the energy sector or of the economy as a whole, however, this immediately suggests that it would be an acceptable simplification to allow for an annual peak, and to neglect the peak that occurs during each individual season. If seasonal disaggregation of the peak were to enter into macroeconomic planning, this would also imply the need for

Table 6
Characteristics of generating plants available by 1980

Plant type			Fossil			Nuclear	
Identification index i			F1 [a]	F2	F3	N1	N2
Capacity of single unit (GW)			0.075	0.300	0.600	0.600	1.000
Thousands of hours per year available for energy generation [b]	minimum, β_{ik}	$k = 1, 3, 5$	0	0.1095	0.1095	0.1034	0.1034
		$k = 2, 4, 6$	0	0.5475	0.5475	0.5171	0.5171
	above minimum, γ_{ik}	$k = 1, 3, 5$	0.3942	0.3285	0.3285	0.3102	0.3102
		$k = 2, 4, 6$	0	1.6425	1.6425	1.5512	1.5512
Fossil fuel requirements [c] $(10^{12}$ BTU)	per GW for minimum annual energy, δ_{ir}		0	18.7048	17.7390	0	0
	per TWH of energy generation above minimum, ϵ_{ir}		15.000	9.490	9.000	0	0
Operating and investment costs $(10^6$ pesos)	nuclear fuel cost per TWH [c]		0	0	0	15.66	15.20
	fixed annual operating and maintenance costs of single units [c]		1.5	9.4	13.0	20.5	25.5
	initial investment cost for single unit [d]		75.0	428.0	780.0	1380.0 [e,f]	2160.0 [e]
Year t in which plant type may first be installed in region r, 1977 $(t = 1)$, or 1980 $(t = 2)$	$r =$	TC	1	1	n.a. [g]	n.a.	n.a.
		FM	1	1	n.a.	1	n.a.
		TP	1	1	2	n.a.	2
		SL	1	1	n.a.	1	2
		OR	1	1	2	n.a.	2
		CL	1	1	2	1	2
		OC	1	1	2	1	2
		MS	1	1	n.a.	2	n.a.

[a] F1 index refers to gas turbines. It is non-optimal to employ these as 'base-load' units, i.e., during the off-peak time blocks 2, 4 and 6. It may, however, be optimal to employ these for peak hours and/or reserve power capacity.

[b] Calculated through the following coefficients:

plant type	gas turbine	other fossil	nuclear
identification index i	F1	F2, F3	N1, N2
operating hours available, fraction of year (time other than that required for scheduled maintenance and for unscheduled repairs)	0.81	0.90	0.85
minimum time for energy production, fraction of operating hours (time required for boilers to remain fired up so as to meet daily peak)	0	0.25	0.25

Footnotes to table 6 (continued)

E.g., since there are 0.4867 thousand hours per year in time blocks, 1, 3 and 5, the βik factor for these blocks and for i = F2 is:

β F2 k = (0.90)(0.25)(0.4867) = 0.1095 thousand hours.

Similarly, since there are 2.4333 thousand hours per year in time blocks 2, 4 and 6, the γik factor for these blocks and for i = F2 is:

γ F2 k = (0.90)(0.75)(2.433) = 1.6425 thousand hours.

c For fuel and operating costs, the present value factor is $(1/1.10)^{0.5}$, as though these costs were paid at the middle of year t.

d The initial investment costs have been converted into equivalent constant annual flows through 'capital recovery factors'. For INTERCON, these factors are based upon a 10% annual cost of capital. The service life is taken to be 20 years for gas turbines (plant type F1) and 30 years for all other generating and transmission facilities. Assuming that the first annual payment is made on January 1 of year t, the capital recovery factor is therefore 10.68% per year for gas turbines and 9.64% for all other facilities.

e The nuclear plant cost estimates refer to all regions other than CL and OC. For these two regions, the following is assumed:

region r	investment cost for single nuclear unit (million pesos)		reason for additional investment costs in region r
	0.600 GW unit	1.000 GW unit	
CL	1460	2240	additional transmission line, 200 km
OC	1440	2260	additional cooling tower

f For constructing two nuclear plants (each 0.600 GW) at a single location for use in 1977 (t = 1), it is supposed that there would be a saving of 20% (276 million pesos) in the investment cost for the second unit.

g n.a. = not available.

geographical disaggregation of power demands — e.g., a distinction between the demand in the north and that in the south.

From the basic data, one may observe not only the lack of demand diversity between regions but also the size of the regional capacity deficits. For table 5, we have erred on the side of overestimating these deficits. That is, transmission is neglected, and it is supposed that each region would require sufficient capacity to meet its own seasonal peak demand. On that basis, between 1975 and 1977 (year t = 1), it would be necessary to add 3.021 GW to the installed capacity. This magnitude is equivalent to five nuclear

Table 7
Characteristics of transmission lines (zero compensation)

Line number	Region r'	Region r	Distance (km)	Line voltage: 230 kv (j = 1)		Line voltage: 400 kv (j = 2)				
				Initially available capacity (GW)	Power received in region r per unit transmitted from region r', $\alpha 1 r' r$	Initially available capacity (GW)	Power transmission capacity for new line (GW)	Capital investment cost for new line (million pesos)	Power received in region r per unit transmitted from region r', $\alpha 2 r' r$
1	SL	OC	220	0	–	0	0.846	79.2	0.9794
2	CL	OC	300	0.300	0.9519	0.687	0.687	108.0	0.9619
3	SL	CL	325	0	–	0	0.650	117.0	0.9696
4	TP	CL	360	0	–	0	0.613	129.6	0.9660
5	TC	FM	365	0.300	0.9458	0	0.605	131.4	0.9658
6	OR	CL	370	0.300	0.9453	0.602	0.602	133.2	0.9653
7	TC	MS	460	0	–	0	0.513	165.6	0.9570
8	FM	SL	465	0	–	0	0.512	167.4	0.9560
9	FM	TP	500	0	–	0	0.471	180.0	0.9532
10	TP	OR	540	0.300	0.9295	0	0.443	194.4	0.9495
11	TC	OC	620	0	–	0	0.403	223.2	0.9420
12	OC	MS	670	0	–	0	0.380	241.2	0.9373

plants, each unit 0.600 GW in size. [10] If the five construction projects were all completed on schedule, there could be substantial amounts of temporary excess capacity. More likely — with five hastily constructed nuclear plants — there would occur delays which could easily wipe out any cost savings to be obtained from a nuclear program. Because of the likelihood of these construction difficulties, it has therefore been supposed that at most two nuclear units (each 0.600 GW in capacity) could be available by 1977. For capacity added in subsequent years, this construction scheduling limit has been removed.

Among the process options listed in table 6, note that no new hydroelectric generating projects are listed. This simplification was adopted — partly because Mexico is close to exhausting her supply of low-cost hydro sites, and partly because hydro project costs have been consistently underestimated in the past.

5. Mixed integer programming formulation

Divisibility is one of the axioms that underlies the theory of linear programming. This assumption creates no special difficulties with fossil fuel plants installed prior to 1977. Moreover, for all types of capacity added subsequent to 1977, the economies-of-scale are not large in relation to the annual increases in power demand. For transmission links and nuclear generating plants installed prior to 1977, there *are* difficulties with divisibility. When INTERCON is solved as a linear program for this year, it turns out that the optimal capacity additions consist, for the most part, of fractional nuclear plants and fractional transmission lines (table 8).

To avoid solutions that call for fractional units, a mixed integer programming model was employed. So as to apply the IPE algorithm (described below, in chapter V.1), all zero-one variables have been defined as 'projects' and grouped into 'mutual exclusivity

---

[10] After allowing for transmission and for the gains from regional diversity, it turns out that the required capacity increment would be equivalent to four rather than five units. See the INTERCON results reported in table 11 below.

Table 8
Optimal [a] linear programming solution to single-period model for $t = 1$ (1977)

Region r	Nuclear generating capacity added in region r; level of linear programming variables G N1r1	Fraction of one 0.600 GW plant
FM	0.629 GW	1.05
SL	0.004 GW	0.01
CL	0.104 GW	0.17
OC	0.252 GW	0.42
MS	0.211 GW	0.35
Total	1.200 GW	2.00

Regions r and r'	400 kv transmission capacity added between regions r and r'; linear programming variables T 2rr'1	400 kv transmission capacity for one line added between regions r and r'	Fraction of one 400 kv line between regions r and r'
SL-OC	0.096 GW	0.846 GW	0.11
TP-CL	0.003 GW	0.613 GW	0.01
FM-SL	0.097 GW	0.512 GW	0.19
FM-TP	0.159 GW	0.471 GW	0.34
OC-MS	0.144 GW	0.380 GW	0.38

[a] Total annual costs: 1976 million pesos.

sets'. Table 9 describes the relations between these project variables (which may take on the value of either zero or one) and the continuous linear programming unknowns.

In order to reduce the computer time spent on mixed integer programming, the original formulation was simplified in several ways. One such simplification consisted of dropping four regions as possible locations for nuclear power plants. These four appeared to be unpromising locations — either because of low capacity deficits (regions TC and TP), or because of low fossil fuel prices (region OR), or because of an isolated position in the transmission network (region MS).

For each of the four regions that remain as candidates for the installation of nuclear capacity (that is, for r = FM, SL, CL and OC), table 9 contains an equation identified as (CPNr). These four equations link the zero-one project variables to the continuous linear programming unknowns GN1r1, which define the nuclear capacity additions in the four regions. (For the four noncandidate regions, the continuous unknowns GN1r1 are removed from the matrix at this point.)

Fourteen mutually exclusive 'projects' for nuclear generating capacity have been defined. (Mutual exclusivity is ensured through the constraint MUEX1.) If the first of the 14 projects is adopted (i.e., if $Y1,1 = 1.0$), no nuclear capacity is added. If project 2 is adopted (i.e., if $Y2,1 = 1.0$), one plant of 0.600 GW will be added, and this unit will be located in region FM. Similarly, if $Y14,1 = 1.0$, two units totalling 1.200 GW will be located in region OC. Note that the 14 alternatives have been defined so that no matter which of them is adopted, no more than 1.200 GW of nuclear capacity will be added to the system prior to year $t = 1$.

As another step in economizing upon the mixed integer computations, we reduced the number of transmission links from 12 to 6 possibilities during the initial time period. For each of these 6 possibilities, there is a continuous linear programming unknown T2rr'1 which defines the transmission capacity to be added between regions r and r' — employing a 400 kv line and installing this capacity prior to year 1. Table 9 shows that these 6 continuous variables are linked to the zero-one 'projects' through the 6 equations (CPTrr').

The transmission links have been grouped into three mutual exclusivity sets. Mutual exclusivity is ensured through the three constraints MUEX2,3,4. Two of the three sets are based upon geographical complementarity between transmission links. Within a set, individual projects are distinguished by the index p. For the three projects identified as $Yp,2$ ($p = 1, 2, 3$), SL is employed as the junction point between the north and the south. For projects $Yp,3$ ($p = 1, 2, 3$), TP is the junction point. Projects $Yp,4$ ($p = 1, 2$) refer to an either-or choice on a single transmission link, OC-MS.

Within the columns defining the transmission projects, the coefficients refer to the capacity of a 400 kv line. E.g., from table 9, it can be seen that if project $Y2,2$ is operated at unit intensity, this

Table
Tableau for linking continuous variable

	Continuous variables, nuclear generating capacity				Mutually
Column identification	GN1FM1	GN1SL1	GN1CL1	GN1OC1	Y1,1 Y
Row identification					
nuclear	CPNFM	−1.0				0
generating	CPNSL		−1.0			
capacity (GW)	CPNCL			−1.0		
	CPNOC				−1.0	
	MUEX1					1.0 1.

Continuous variables, transmission capacity

	T2SLOC1	T2SLCL1	T2TPCL1	T2FMSL1	T2FMTP1	T2OCM
Column identification						
Row identification						
	CPTSLOC	−1.0					
	CPTSLCL		−1.0				
	CPTTPCL			−1.0			
transmission	CPTFMSL				−1.0		
capacity	CPTFMTP					−1.0	
(GW)	CPTOCMS						−1.0
	MUEX2						
	MUEX3						
	MUEX4						

would imply the construction of two links joining at SL. The longer of these (FM-SL) would have a transmission capacity of 0.512 GW, and the shorter (SL-OC) would have 0.846 GW.

To summarize the definitions presented in table 9: There are 14 mutually exclusive nuclear generating projects, 3 mutually exclusive transmission projects with SL as the junction point, 3 projects with TP as the junction point, and 2 projects for the OC-MS link. This leads to 14 × 3 × 3 × 2 = 252 logically possible alternative combinations. Hereafter, these 252 combinations will be identified through a four-number sequence identifying which of the projects

:o indivisible 'projects'

exclusive projects, nuclear generating capacity, set 1

Y3,1	Y4,1	Y5,1	Y6,1	Y7,1	Y8,1	Y9,1	Y10,1	Y11,1	Y12,1	Y13,1	Y14,1	
			0.6	0.6	0.6							= 0
0.6			0.6			0.6	0.6		1.2			= 0
	0.6			0.6		0.6		0.6		1.2		= 0
		0.6			0.6		0.6	0.6			1.2	= 0
1.0	1.0	1.0	1.0	1.0	1.0	1.0	1.0	1.0	1.0	1.0	1.0	= 1.0

Mutually exclusive transmission projects

Set 2			Set 3			Set 4		
Y1,2	Y2,2	Y3,2	Y1,3	Y2,3	Y3,3	Y1,4	Y2,4	
	0.846	0.846						= 0
		0.650						= 0
					0.613			= 0
	0.512	0.512						= 0
				0.471	0.471			= 0
							0.380	= 0
1.0	1.0	1.0						= 1.0
			1.0	1.0	1.0			= 1.0
						1.0	1.0	= 1.0

has been selected within each set. E.g., combination (12, 2, 1, 2) refers to adopting project number 12 in the first mutual exclusivity set, number 2 in the second, 1 in the third, and 2 in the fourth.

6. Recursive dynamic optimization

INTERCON could have been handled directly as a dynamic investment planning problem. In addition to the multi-region static model already described in sections 3 and 5 above, the following *irreversibility* constraints would be imposed — both for generating and for transmission capacity other than the initially available units. These multi-period linkage rows are the only ones in which variables with the time index t would appear simultaneously with others having the time index $t + 1$:

$$Gir \quad t+1 \geqslant Gir \quad t$$
$$Tjrr' \quad t+1 \geqslant Tjrr' \quad t$$

If the regional and seasonal disaggregation of INTERCON were retained, a dynamic problem would require upwards of 500 rows for each year distinguished over the planning horizon. As an alternative to this, we have attempted to economize on computer time through a recursive optimization procedure. [11] First the static version for year $t = 1$ was solved as a mixed integer programming problem. Among other results, this indicated the capacity levels $Gir1$ and $Tjrr'1$. These values were then substituted as *constants* into the capacity irreversibility constraints and added to the static problem for year $t = 2$. Since these are lower bounds on individual unknowns, this adds a negligible amount to the time required for solving the static model.

Clearly, the recursive procedure produces a feasible solution to the multi-period problem. Equally clearly, since future-period data do not influence the capacity mix chosen in year 1, this may be a far from optimal solution. Because it fails to anticipate the upward trend in fossil fuel prices, the procedure would be biased in favor of adding fossil capacity during the initial year. On the other hand, to the extent that it eliminates any anticipation of the improved nuclear plants that will become available subsequently, the procedure is biased in favor of the initial nuclear process. (See the numerical data in figure 2 and table 6.) In order to overcome these objections — and simultaneously perform a sensitivity analysis — the identical recursive procedure has been applied to four alterna-

[11] Each static linear programming version of INTERCON required less than 10 minutes of execution time on the IBM 360/67 of Stanford University. A two-period dynamic version (solving simultaneously for the 1977 and 1980 capacity mix) required approximately two hours on this same machine.

Table 10
Summary of single-period, recursive optimizations

Project combination			(1,1,2,2)	(7,1,2,2)	(8,1,2,2)	(12,2,1,2)
Total annual costs	$t = 1$	(1977)	2,086.	2,006.	2,003.	2,002.
(unit: million pesos)	$t = 2$	(1980)	3,358.	3,266.	3,271.	3,260.
cumulative nuclear capacity installed [a] $t = 1$ (1977) (unit: GW)	region $r =$	FM	0	0.600	0.600	0
		SL	0	0	0	1.200
		CL	0	0.600	0	0
		OC	0	0	0.600	0
		Total	0	1.200	1.200	1.200
cumulative nuclear capacity installed [b] $t = 2$ (1980) (unit: GW)	region $r =$	TC	n.a.	n.a.	n.a.	n.a.
		FM	1.065	1.093	1.084	1.019
		TP	0.476	0.501	0.511	0.077
		SL	0	0	0	1.200
		OR	0.487	1.361	1.311	1.334
		CL	2.274	2.268	2.187	2.274
		OC	0.856	0.856	0.945	0.124
		MS	0.569	0.567	0.567	0.571
		Total	5.727	6.646	6.605	6.599
increment in 400 kv transmission capacity (1975–77) (unit: GW) [c]	regions rr'	SL-OC	0	0	0	0.846
		SL-CL	0	0	0	0
		TP-CL	0	0	0	0
		FM-SL	0	0	0	0.512
		FM-TP	0.471	0.471	0.471	0
		OC-MS	0.380	0.380	0.380	0.380
increment in 400 kv transmission capacity (1975–80) [d]	regions rr'	SL-OC	0	0	0	0.950
		CL-OC	0	0	0	0
		SL-CL	0	0	0	0
		TP-CL	0	0	0	0
		TC-FM	0.179	0.110	0.101	0.085
		OR-CL	0	0	0	0
		TC-MS	0.006	0	0.008	0.003
		FM-SL	0	0	0	0.512
		FM-TP	0.471	0.471	0.471	0
		TP-OP	0	0	0	0
		TC-OC	0	0	0	0
		OC-MS	0.380	0.380	0.380	0.380
annual fossil fuel requirements [e] (unit: 10^{12} BTU)	$t = 1$	(1977)	368.4	278.2	277.9	282.8
	$t = 2$	(1980)	172.8	108.4	101.2	112.7

[a] Equal to level of activity GN1r1.
[b] Equal to level of activities GN1r2 + GN2r2.
[c] Equal to level of activity T 2rr'1.
[d] Equal to level of activity T 2rr'2.
[e] Equal to level of activities $\sum_r$CFrt ($t = 1, 2$).

tive combinations of generating and transmission projects. (See table 10.)

For the static problem, project combination (12, 2, 1, 2) minimizes the total annual equivalent of investment plus operating costs during year $t = 1$. This solution — obtained through mixed integer programming — calls for the installation of two nuclear units at location SL, together with the following transmission lines: SL-OC, FM-SL and OC-MS.

Three alternatives to this solution were also calculated — arbitrarily [12] selecting one of the mutually exclusive *generating* projects and then applying mixed integer programming to select the least-cost combination of transmission projects. E.g., if no nuclear plant is to be built, the optimal transmission links would be: FM-TP and OC-MS. This combination is identified as (1, 1, 2, 2). If either nuclear project 7 or 8 were adopted, these transmission links would also be optimal. The two middle columns of table 10 are therefore identified as combinations (7, 1, 2, 2) and (8, 1, 2, 2).

Among the three combinations that call for the installation of two nuclear units with a capacity total of 1.200 GW, the total costs are virtually indistinguishable. These differ by less than any plausible margin for error in the basic data. Each is 4% less costly than combination (1, 1, 2, 2), the program in which no nuclear capacity is installed during the initial year. Of the four alternative solutions, note that (12, 2, 1, 2) is least costly during both planning periods. The empirical results suggest that this is a 'robust' combination, and that little would have been learned by formulating INTERCON as a two-period dynamic problem.

The bottommost lines of table 10 help to quantify the effects of nuclear power upon the oil and gas sector. If 1.200 GW of nuclear capacity were installed by 1977, the electricity industry's requirements for fossil fuel would be reduced from 368.4 to approximately 280 10^{12} BTU. Between 1977 and 1980, despite the increase in electricity output, the electricity sector's consumption

---

[12] These alternatives were not chosen in an altogether arbitrary way. Most of the preliminary site investigations for nuclear plants were based on an investment plan that resembled nuclear generating 'project' 7.

of fossil fuel would decline further. These reductions in demand are sizeable enough to affect the efficiency price of fossil fuel. For an explicit examination of this price-quantity interdependence, see ENERGETICOS.

7. Operation of the grid; marginal cost of electricity

Figures 3, 4 and tables 11−13 contain numerical results on project combination (12, 2, 1, 2), the least-cost solution obtained through

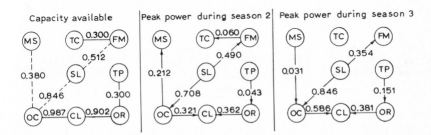

Fig. 3. Schematic diagram of power transmission (unit: GW) − year $t = 1$ (1977); project combination (12, 2, 1, 2). Note: Peak power is equal to level of activities $\sum_{j=1}^{2} Uj\,rr's1$ for season s.

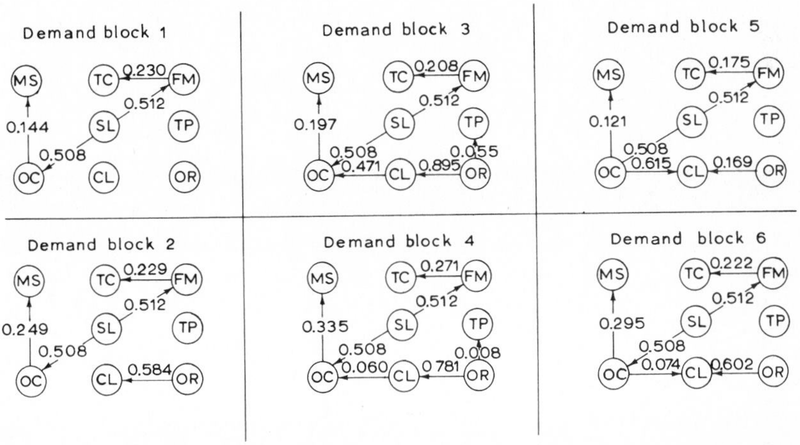

Fig. 4. Schematic diagram of energy transmission, year $t = 1$ (1977); project combination (12, 2, 1, 2); TWH converted into GW equivalents by time factors ηk. Note: Equal to level of activities $\sum_{j=1}^{2} Vj\,rr'k1$ for block k.

the recursive optimization procedure. These are typical of the results obtained for the other project combinations. The details should not be taken too literally, but they help to illustrate how the grid's operations are simulated by INTERCON.

Table 11 summarizes the mix of generating capacities available for operation during year $t = 1$. The bulk of the 1975−77 capacity increase is concentrated at two locations: SL (1.200 GW of nuclear capacity) and OR (1.336 GW of fossil capacity). For each of the static multi-region cases that have been run, the OR region has proved to be the most preferable location for installing fossil capacity. The result is immediately understandable as soon as one recalls that this is the region where fossil fuel costs are lowest.

The country-wide total of installed generating capacity lies between the country-wide peak and the regional seasonal peak demands already shown in table 4 (11.418 and 11.768 GW respectively). Somewhat unexpected is the result that the optimal amount of installed capacity is 11.493 GW − almost as low as the countrywide peak. Apparently, the relative costs of transmission

Table 11
Cumulative capacity installed [a], $t = 1$ (1977),
project combination (12,2,1,2) (unit: GW)

Plant identification	Initially available fossil and hydro	Fossil		Nuclear	Total
Index i	I1 + I2 + I3 + HD	F1	F2	N1	
Region r					
TC	0.475	0	0.031	n.a. [b]	0.506
FM	0.887	0	0.003	0	0.890
TP	0.332	0	0	n.a.	0.332
SL	0	0	0	1.200	1.200
OR	1.673	0	1.336	n.a.	3.009
CL	3.488	0.025	0	0	3.513
OC	1.426	0	0	0	1.426
MS	0.617	0	0	n.a.	0.617
Total	8.898	0.025	1.370	1.200	11.493

[a] Equal to level of activity *Gir*1.
[b] n.a. = not available.

Table 12
Marginal cost of supplying electricity, $t = 1$ (1977),
project combination (12, 2, 1, 2)

Region r	Pesos per KW of peak power demand [a] season s =		Pesos per thousand KWH of energy demand [b] block k =					
	2	3	1	2	3	4	5	6
TC	0	106.32	51.18	51.18	51.18	51.18	51.18	51.18
FM	0	106.79	48.41	48.41	48.41	48.41	48.41	48.41
TP	0	112.92	38.54	38.54	38.43	38.43	38.54	38.54
SL	0	102.09	39.54	39.54	38.08	38.08	39.54	39.54
OR	0	121.48	39.39	39.39	35.72	35.72	40.10	40.10
CL	0	125.85	40.80	40.80	37.79	37.79	41.54	41.54
OC	0	122.31	40.37	40.37	38.88	38.88	40.37	40.37
MS	0	114.64	43.07	43.07	41.18	41.18	43.07	43.07

[a] Equal to dual variable, constraint row GWrs1.
[b] Equal to dual variable, constraint row TWHrk1.

and of generating capacity are such that it is optimal [13] to interconnect each region to at least one other. Transmission then permits the northern and the southern regions to interchange power during their respective peak periods, seasons 2 and 3 respectively.

The transmission linkages also help in understanding the set of optimal marginal costs. In table 12, it can be seen that there is a zero marginal cost of meeting power demands during season 2. For season 3 (the countrywide peak demand period), the marginal annual costs vary from one region to another, but lie within the range of 102.09 to 125.85 pesos per kilowatt.

[13] As a byproduct of the IPE mixed integer programming computations, there is readily available a numerical example of the tradeoffs between transmission and generating costs. If no nuclear plants are to be added to the system, the optimal project combination is (1, 1, 2, 2). For year $t = 1$, this combination has an annual cost of 2086 million pesos for generation and transmission. If the FM-TP and OC-MS transmission lines are eliminated, but no nuclear plants are to be added to the system, this combination of projects would be identified as (1, 1, 1, 1,). For this combination, total costs would increase to 2,123 million pesos. There would be a saving of 41 million pesos on the FM-TP and OC-MS transmission lines, but an increase of 78 in the generating costs.

Table 13

Generation and transmission of energy, OR region, $t = 1$ (1977), project combination (12, 2, 1, 2)

		Block k (unit: TWH)						Fossil fuel energy cost, plant type i (pesos per thousand KWH) [a]
		1	2	3	4	5	6	
Generation, minimum	$\sum_i \beta_{ik}$ GiOR1	0.167	0.832	0.167	0.832	0.167	0.832	0
Generation, above minimum EiORk1 activities $i =$	HD	0.086	1.639	0.634	2.291	0.219	1.931	0
	F2	0.439	2.195	0.439	2.195	0.439	2.195	32.57
	I3	0.038	0.192	0	0	0.038	0.192	36.78
	I2	0	0	0	0	0	0	44.44
	I1	0	0	0	0	0	0	56.78
Transmission from region OR	V2ORCLk1	0	−1.421	−0.293	−1.465	−0.082	−1.465	
	V1ORCLk1	0	0	−0.146	−0.179	0	0	
	V1ORTPk1	0	0	−0.027	−0.019	0	0	
Energy demand, region OR, block k, year 1		0.730	3.436	0.774	3.655	0.781	3.685	
Marginal cost of supplying energy (pesos per thousand KWH)		39.39	39.39	35.72	35.72	40.10	40.10	

[a] Fossil fuel energy cost $= \left(\dfrac{10^6\ \text{BTU}}{10^3\ \text{KWH}}\right)\left(\dfrac{\text{pesos}}{10^6\ \text{BTU}}\right)\left(\begin{array}{l}\text{present value factor} - \text{as though}\\ \text{fuel costs were paid at midyear}\end{array}\right)$

(region OR, year 1) $= (\varepsilon_i \text{OR})(3.6)\left(\dfrac{1}{1.10}\right)^{0.5}$

These marginal costs for power and for energy lie somewhat below the values suggested by the single-plant analysis for a fossil generating unit. According to figure 1, the annual costs of such a plant would be 167.40 pesos per kilowatt of peak power. [14] For energy produced by this unit — even when fossil fuel is priced as low as 3.6 pesos per million BTU — the costs are estimated at 49.31 pesos per thousand kilowatt-hours.

The formulation of INTERCON is such that the marginal costs of supplying energy will vary from one region r and one demand block k to another. (The marginal costs for energy in year 1 are equal to the dual variables associated with the 48 constraint rows TWH $rk1$.) According to table 12, there are interregional differences of up to 30% in the marginal cost of energy. E.g., during time blocks 1 and 2, the cost per thousand KWH ranges from 39.39 pesos in region OR (where fossil fuel costs are low) up to 51.18 pesos in region TC (where fossil fuel costs are high). Within each of the regions, the marginal cost of energy does not vary widely from one demand block to another. The largest differences occur in region OR. We now take a closer look at the annual cycle in the operation of each type of plant within this one region.

For table 13, the plants of the OR region have been ranked in ascending order of their marginal fuel cost. These costs are zero not only for the energy produced by hydroelectric units, but also for the minimum quantities of energy produced in fossil units so that the boilers will remain fired up to meet the daily demand peaks. Within the OR region, the low-cost plant type (F2) is operated at its maximum level throughout the year, and the high-cost types (I2 and I1) are operated at their minimum levels. The marginal plants are those identified as I3. These units would be oper-

---

[14] These numbers are not directly comparable with the marginal costs for peak power that emerge from the sectoral model ENERGETICOS (below, chapter III.2, next to rightmost column of table 3). The sectoral model has no regional dimension — hence contains no tradeoffs between generating and transmission costs. Instead, the investment and operating costs for transmission lines are taken to be directly proportional to the demand for peak power. With this definition of 'peak power', it is to be expected that the marginal costs of meeting the demand will appear considerably higher in ENERGETICOS than in INTERCON.

ated at their minimum rate during time blocks 3 and 4, and at their maximum rate during the other four blocks. Note that the cost of operating these marginal units is 36.78 pesos per thousand KWH. According to table 12, this lies above the marginal cost of supplying energy in the OR region during blocks 3 and 4 (35.72 pesos) and below the marginal costs during the other four time blocks (39.39 or 40.10 pesos).

One detail of the annual operating cycle is not recorded explicitly in these tables — the fact that the hydroelectric turbine capacity constraints are non-binding. Indeed, these constraints (EDH krt) are non-binding in any of the regions during year $t = 1$. This means that hydroelectric energy can be shifted freely from the off-peak to the peak time blocks within each season, subject only to the reservoir constraints (HDrst). It is for this reason that table 12 indicated the marginal cost of energy to be identical during each of the two time blocks that form a season. Even during year $t = 2$ (1980), when substantial amounts of nuclear capacity have been added to the system and are operated as base-load units, the hydroelectric turbine capacity constraints remain non-binding in virtually all of the regions. [15]

8. Effects of aggregation — the implications for multi-level planning

From this case study, what lessons have been learned about aggregation? Are kilowatt-hours interchangeable between different points of time and space? Regrettably, INTERCON provides no all-purpose answer to these questions. This will depend upon the policy decision to which the model is addressed, how quickly an answer is needed, and what are the data-gathering and computa-

---

[15] TP is the only region in which the turbine constraints are operative during 1980. This might therefore be the first location in Mexico at which it would be optimal to install pumped storage facilities. These facilities consume energy during the off-peak hours of the daily cycle, and produce it during the peak hours. In order for such investments to be worthwhile, there must be a sizeable differential between the marginal cost of energy during the two blocks of time.

tional costs. E.g., if an investment decision entails significant tradeoffs between generating versus transmission facilities, it is clear that spatial disaggregation must be introduced into the evaluation of the project. Moreover, since one of the purposes of transmission is to take advantage of regional diversities in the timing of electricity supplies and demands, it follows that seasonal disaggregation is needed – say, six demand blocks within an annual cycle of operations.

Alternatively, if a model is addressed to the problems of linkage between the electricity sector and the balance of the economy, it is much less clear that seasonal and spatial disaggregation will prove to be worth the costs of data-gathering and computation. [16] Consider the ENERGETICOS model. There, instead of taking the fossil fuel price as an exogenously given parameter, the electricity sector's decisions are embedded within a broader framework, and are linked to decisions in the oil and gas sector. For ENERGETICOS, no regionally disaggregated investment planning model of the petroleum sector was readily available. Even for the drilling department of the petroleum enterprise itself, it would be no easy task to estimate the regional distribution of future oil and gas wells!

All would be lost if each level in a problem-solving hierarchy insisted upon halting its work until some other level had produced a completely satisfactory set of disaggregated data. Typically, this is the point where aggregation enters into multi-level planning – as a substitute for missing pieces of information. Here aggregation is employed because too few data are available. This is a more difficult problem to formalize than the aggregation problem typically described in the econometric literature – the case where too many data are available, and the aim is then to reduce the volume of numerical computations. Cf. Fisher (1969).

INTERCON, which contains both a spatial and a seasonal di-

---

[16] For understanding a system, the extent of disaggregation need not be as detailed as for understanding the components of that system. Here is a dictum in search of a theory! Would the theory depend upon the finiteness of the information processing capability of a single human mind? Cf. Miller (1956).

mension, helps to place bounds on the possible errors created by aggregation. It suggests that: (1) There will be virtually no error if we neglect the regional diversity of power demands and characterize the annual peak in terms of the countrywide total. (2) Within a region, there will be negligible daily and seasonal variations in the marginal cost of electrical *energy*. (3) From one region to another, the marginal cost of electrical energy will not differ by more than 30%.

Aggregation rules – together with error bounds – are not readily transferable from one nation or decade to another. They are, however, among the vital information flows which enable one level to assist the next in a hierarchy for solving complex problems. Each of the simplifications that emerges from INTERCON can be useful in constructing ENERGETICOS, a planning model with a broader scope. In turn, the aggregated results of ENERGETICOS may be embedded within the macroeconomic model DINAMICO to check whether the energy sector's investment decisions are likely to alter the economy-wide efficiency prices of, say, foreign exchange, capital and skilled labor. As things turn out (below, chapter III.3), the energy sector exerts a negligible influence upon these macroeconomic efficiency prices. This series of multi-level planning studies suggests that there are diminishing returns from systems analysis. Beyond a certain point, the analyst can neglect the feedback effects upon the system within which the individual project decision is embedded.

References

Anderson, D., 'Investment analysis in electricity supply using computer models'. Economics Department Working Paper. Washington, D.C., International Bank for Reconstruction and Development, 1970.

Berrie, T.W., 'The economics of system planning in bulk electricity supply', in: *Public enterprise*, edited by R. Turvey. Middlesex, Penguin Books, 1968, chapter 5.

Bessière, F., 'Methods of choosing production equipment at Electricité de France', *European Economic Review*, Winter 1969.

Fisher, W.D., *Clustering and aggregation in economics*. Baltimore, Johns Hopkins Press, 1969.

Gately, D., 'Investment planning for the electric power industry: an integer programming approach'. Research Report 7035, Department of Economics, University of Western Ontario, London, Canada, November 1970.

Kornai, J., *Mathematical planning of structural decisions*. Budapest, Publishing House of the Hungarian Academy of Sciences, 1967.

Massé, P., and R. Gibrat, 'Applications of linear programming to investments in the electric power industry', *Management Science*, April 1957.

Miller, G.A., 'The magical number seven, plus or minus two: some limits on our capacity for processing information', *Psychological Review*, March 1956.

Simon, H., 'The architecture of complexity', *Proceeding of the American Philosophical Society,* December 1962.

Tinbergen, J., *Development planning*. New York, McGraw-Hill, 1967.

III.2. ENERGETICOS, A PROCESS ANALYSIS
OF THE ENERGY SECTORS *

Guillermo FERNÁNDEZ de la GARZA and Alan S. MANNE

1. Introduction

ENERGETICOS is one in a series of multi-level planning models. In its level of aggregation, it forms an intermediate stage between INTERCON (which is geographically disaggregated within the electric power industry) and DINAMICO (a dynamic input-output model of the entire Mexican economy). Together, this series is intended to define the information flows necessary for consistency between project, sectoral and macroeconomic decisions.

The sectoral model ENERGETICOS allows explicitly for substitution between alternative processes within Mexico's energy-producing industries: petroleum, gas, and electricity. [1] Also included are alternative energy-using activities for iron and steel manufacturing. Except for process substitution within the steel industry, we have not attempted to quantify the elasticity of demand with respect to the price of energy products. It is supposed

* For help in various phases, the authors are much indebted to: Ing. Raúl Meyer (Petróleos Mexicanos), Ings. Victor L. Games and Carlos Velasco (Instituto Mexicano del Petróleo), Lic. Gerardo Bueno and Ing. Fernando González Vargas (Nacional Financiera, S.A.); Ings. Juan Eibenschutz, Roberto Fabre, and José Alberto Valencia, and Lic. Bosco Muro (Comisión Federal de Electricidad); Mr. Richard Inman (Stanford University). The specific facts, methods of analysis, and conclusions are the sole responsibility of the individual authors.
[1] The scope of ENERGETICOS is similar to that of an energy sector model developed by the Ministry of Power, United Kingdon. See Forster and Whitting (1968).

that the energy sectors are price-takers with respect to their inputs (e.g., foreign exchange, labor, capital equipment and nuclear fuel), but that they are output-takers with respect to deliveries elsewhere within the Mexican economy.

Here, in projecting the exogenous final demands for each item, trend extrapolation methods were used. These projections were intended to be consistent with a 6.5 − 7.0% annual future growth rate of Mexico's gross domestic product. The demand projections have been compared against the results of DINAMICO. Because of the input-output categories employed in the more aggregative model (e.g., 'basic metals', not 'steel ingots'), it was not possible to arrive at a fully satisfactory cross-check between the two levels of planning.

For ENERGETICOS, the optimization is phrased as one of choosing investments in alternative processes so as to meet the output targets at minimum discounted costs, taking account of intersectoral flows. Each solution generates a set of incremental costs for supplying each product. Except for petroleum products, export levels are specified exogenously.

With this formulation, the principal source of interdependence arises from the intersectoral flows of industrial fuel. ('Industrial fuel' means natural gas and residual fuel oil converted into their calorific equivalents.) Both gas and residual fuel oil are supplied under conditions of increasing marginal cost within the petroleum industry. There are tradeoff possibilities between these fossil fuels and the introduction of nuclear plants within the electric power industry. The rate of nuclear power development could make a significant difference in the efficiency price of fuel. Similarly, within the steel industry, there are process alternatives which could have a sizeable impact upon the energy sector.

Several institutional features are to be noted at this point: Both the fossil fuel producer (Petróleos Mexicanos) and the electric utility consumer (Comisión Federal de Electricidad) are publicly-owned enterprises. The transfer price of industrial fuel is determined administratively at a high political level, and is *not* closely linked to the international fuel price prevailing in the Caribbean area. During the period since the petroleum expropriation of

1938, Mexico's policy has been to remain largely self-sufficient with respect to imports and exports of petroleum products, and to stimulate industrialization through low prices for energy products.

For investment planning within Mexico's energy sector, the major uncertainty appears to be the future of exploration and producing costs for domestic crude oil and natural gas. Now that domestic sources of petroleum are becoming increasingly costly, one of the key policy issues is a reexamination of the country's tradition of self-sufficiency. This in turn has macroeconomic implications with respect to the balance-of-payments, and could affect the efficiency price of foreign exchange. Raising the price of energy products could slow down the growth of those demands that are here regarded as predetermined.

2. Simplifications – time and space

Principally because of uncertainties in predicting the location of future domestic oil and gas production, ENERGETICOS does not contain a regional dimension. Each process is idealized as though it were located at a single representative point in space. This simplification has the advantage that it reduces the size of computations, and it eliminates those detailed investigations that would be needed to correct the transport costs for anomalies within the existing structure of pipeline and railway rates. The simplification means, however, that the present model cannot be employed directly for the choice of optimal plant locations, and that there is a need for multi-level planning.

Consider, for example, the choice between a coke-intensive process versus an electricity-intensive process in the steel industry. At a specific project location, the analyst can readily allow for the fact that the relative advantage of these two alternative processes will depend upon the transport costs from the coke producing areas of northeast Mexico. This is an obvious case in which geographical disaggregation can be more readily handled at the level of project selection than at a macroeconomic level. For a static model in which there *is* a simultaneous evaluation of site and process alternatives within the steel sector and an attempt to correct for rail rate anomalies, see Quintana et al. (1968). Similarly, for a geographically disaggregated analysis of the electric power sector – one in which transmission projects are evaluated simultaneously with generating plants – see INTERCON.

The dimension of time plays a key role in any investment model. Here the initial year is chosen as 1974, the earliest date for which the installed capacities are not already (as of 1970) predetermined by past investment decisions and time lags. For the period 1974–80, material balances are computed year-by-year. In the electric power sector, three additional five-year time intervals are considered – the first extending over 1981–85, the second 1986–90, and the third 1991–95. This time horizon is sufficiently long to allow for the eventual success of breeder reactor technology, and hence a sharp future decrease in the worth of the initially installed nuclear plants. For the entire 15 year period 1981–95, it is supposed that the price of fossil fuel is a datum to the electric power sector. For the near future period 1974–80, the marginal cost of fossil fuel is one of the elements to be determined simultaneously with the other unknowns of the programming problem.

Annual disaggregation proves to be particularly useful for analyzing the temporary imports and exports which need to be synchronized with the installation of major indivisible units of capacity. See the Appendix, where indivisibilities are introduced through mixed integer programming. Elsewhere, with linear programming as the solution technique, indivisibilities have been neglected.

Because of the programming framework, a further difficulty arises. Throughout, 'certainty equivalents' have been employed. E.g., instead of regarding water inflows to the hydroelectric system as a probabilistic phenomenon, these are taken at their mean values. Similarly, instead of allowing for the influence of plant size upon the electricity generating system's reliability with respect to unscheduled downtime, an arbitrary downtime factor of 12% has been taken for reserve capacity. For studies of the Mexican electric power sector which handle one or another of these stochastic phenomena explicitly, see Stanford Research Institute (1968), and

Rogers (1970). The computational techniques employed in these references cannot be readily extended to multi-sector optimal investment planning — hence the use of deterministic programming methods here.

3. Structure of the programming model

From figure 1, it will be seen that the coefficients of ENERGETICOS may be arranged in block-angular form — one block corresponding to each of the three industries: petroleum and gas (PE), electricity (EL), and iron and steel (ST). The only intersectoral flows consist of three items: industrial fuel, peak power and electrical energy. From the signs within the topmost block, note that the sectors may be arranged in triangular order so that the common items flow in only one direction. The interindustry flows

Block	Number of rows in block	Prefix employed for row identification	Description of row			
Common items	27	CM BTU	industrial fuel	+	−	−
		CM GW	peak power	0	+	−
		CM TWH	electrical energy	0	+	−
Petroleum and gas	67	PE				
Electricity	48	EL				
Iron and steel	71	ST				
Total	213					

Fig. 1. Block-angular form of coefficients matrix for ENERGETICOS.

Table 1
Row identification

Sector	Number of rows in sector	Prefix of sector employed for row identification	Suffix of row identification (omitting time index t)
Common items	$27 = \dfrac{1 \times 7}{+ 2 \times 10}$	CM	BTU
		CM	GW
		CM	TWH
Petroleum and gas	$67^{a} = \dfrac{7 \times 7}{+ 3 \times 6}$	PE	GSD
		PE	CRD
		PE	GSR
		PE	LPG
		PE	GSL
		PE	KD
		PE	FO
		PE	CPj
Electricity	$48^{b} = \dfrac{4 \times 10}{+ 1 \times 8}$	EL	TRA
		EL	RQF
		EL	CNV
		EL	LMF
		EL	LMN
Iron and steel	$71 = \dfrac{5 \times 7}{+ 6 \times 6}$	ST	RQF
		ST	ORE
		ST	SCRAP
		ST	COK
		ST	ING
		ST	CPj

time index t:	0	1	2	3	4	5	6	11	16	21
year:	1974	1975	1976	1977	1978	1979	1980	1985	1990	1995

[a] Excludes upper bounds on individual unknowns referring to domestic availability of dry gas and crude oil at three progressively higher levels of marginal cost.

[b] Excludes lower bounds on individual unknowns referring to installation of fossil units in geographically isolated system.

have been simplified so that, for example, the petroleum industry is taken to be a producer of industrial fuel, but not a significant consumer of electricity. The electricity sector consumes industrial fuel. The steel sector consumes both industrial fuel and electricity. In the numerical computations, no advantage was taken of this triangular structure.

Once the interfaces were defined through the common items (prefix CM), it proved possible to construct and to test the sub-for ENERGETICOS

Description of row	Unit of measurement (annual flow)	Exponent of 10 for unit of measurement
industrial fuel [c]	BTU	12
peak power [c]	GW	0
electrical energy [c]	TWH	0
dry gas (fuel oil equivalent)	barrel	6
crude oil	barrel	6
refinery gas (fuel oil equivalent)	barrel	6
liquefied petroleum gas [c]	barrel	6
gasoline [c]	barrel	6
kerosine and diesel oil [c]	barrel	6
residual fuel oil	barrel	6
capacity irreversibility − process j (j = C, V, H)	barrel	6
requirements for additional transmission capacity	GW	0
industrial fuel requirements − electricity sector	BTU	12
convex curve − initial fossil	−	−
energy limit − new fossil	TWH	0
energy limit − early nuclear	TWH	0
industrial fuel requirements − steel	BTU	12
iron ore	ton	6
ferrous scrap	ton	6
coke	ton	6
steel ingots [c]	ton	6
capacity irreversibility − process j (j = 1, ..., 6)	ton	6

[c] Demand projected exogenously − either in part or in total.

models independently. [2] The following sections describe the submodels in increasing order of their complexity − first steel, then electricity and finally petroleum. For each sector, the formulation and the results are described together.

Table 1 identifies the 213 rows that appear within ENERGETI-

[2] Since the energy sector was viewed as a price-taker for capital, foreign exchange, etc., the cost of these items entered into the objective function, but not into the common (CM) rows.

Table 2

Cost definitions – central submatrix (at 1970 prices and conventional exchange rate of 12.5 pesos per U.S. dollar)

Row description	Unit of measurement	Row identification	Current costs incurred in year t	Present value of import costs	Import component of current costs incurred in year t
			CSt	CS MPV	CS MCURt
cost minimand, present value	10^6 pesos discounted to year 0 (1974) at 10% per year	CS PV	$(0.909)^t$	0.15	
current costs incurred in year t	10^6 pesos, year t	CS CURt	1.000		
present value of import costs	10^6 pesos discounted to year 0 (1974) at 10% per year	CS MPV		−1.000	$(0.909)^t$
import component of current costs incurred in year t	10^6 pesos, year t	CS MCURt			1.000

COS. [3] In addition, there are 15 rows that have been employed for convenience in converting future costs into their present value, and for converting foreign exchange costs into their domestic value. Table 2 gives the *central* submatrix of cost definitions, and indicates the numerical values adopted for the macroeconomic cost parameters: a 10% annual discount rate [4] and a 15% level of protection against imports, converting foreign exchange into domestic currency at the conventional rate of 12.5 pesos per U.S. dollar. These cost parameters are similar to those currently employed for project evaluation by public sector enterprises. Section 7 of this chapter contains a sensitivity analysis with respect to the discount rate and the shadow price of foreign exchange.

To avoid 'horizon effects', initial investment costs have been converted into annual flows through a capital recovery factor determined by the service life of the capital equipment and the 10% opportunity cost of capital. Beginning with the year in which capacity is first available, the discounted annual flows are then summed over the balance of the planning horizon.

4. Iron and steel industry

Within the iron and steel industry, the principal opportunities for substitution between energy sources occur prior to the rolling stage. It is for this reason that the rolling processes have been omitted from the optimization here, and that steel ingots are viewed as the end product. Following Bueno and González Vargas (1969), it is estimated that the demand for ingots will increase at

---

[3] A detailed computer listing is available for inspection at the office of either of the authors and also at the IBRD Development Research Center. A simplex solution required 2 minutes on the IBM 360/67 at Stanford University.

[4] If capital were allocated throughout the Mexican economy so that the rate of return was identical in all sectors, the macroeconomic model DINAMICO suggests that 15% would probably be more appropriate than a 10% discount rate. Given the present structure of Mexico's financial institutions, however, the cost of capital to public sector enterprises in the petroleum, electricity and steel industries is lower than that to private enterprises in such sectors as commercial agriculture, tourism, and motor vehicle manufacturing.

Tabl

Detached coefficients mat

Row (for identification and units of measurement, see tables 1 and 2)	Definition of fossil fuel and raw material inputs for new ingot capacity				Inputs and outputs from six alternative integrated processes for 1.0 million tons/year of ingots	
	ST RQFt	ST OREt	ST SCRAPt	ST CORt	ST 1t	ST 2t
cost item [b] CS CURt		−80	−500	−300	− 595	− 459
CS MCURt			−500		− 51	− 50
common items, CM BTUt	−1.0					
CM GWt					− 0.096	− 0.2
energy sector CM TWHt					− 0.718	− 2.0
material input, petroleum sector PE GSDt					− 2.710	
ST RQFt	1.0					
material ST OREt		1.0			− 1.155	− 1.3
inputs and ST SCRAPt			1.0		− 0.325	− 0.2
ingot outputs, ST COKt				1.0		− 0.3
steel sector ST INGt					1.000	1.0
energy inputs, % of ingot cost (based on conventional input prices for 1970) [d]					13%	30%
unit cost of ingots (based on shadow prices for 1977) − pesos per ton					1033	1063
unit cost of ingots (based on conventional input prices for 1970) − pesos per ton					972	1001

[a] Source: Ing. Fernando González Vargas, Nacional Financiera, S.A.

[b] The unit costs (CS CURt) include a gross return on initial investment of 19%/year (allowing for depreciation and opportunity cost of capital at 13%, plus 6% for maintenance, overhead and insurance), plus labor costs at 96,360 pesos per manyear of direct labor (allowing for overhead, supervision etc. at 1.2 times the 1970 direct labor costs) plus miscellaneous inputs (e.g., limestone). The import component (CS MCURt) of unit costs is taken as 5%/year on the initial investment costs. The six alternative integrated processes are defined as follows:

primary iron/scrap ratio

1. sponge iron (HYLSA) + electric steel furnace	70/30
2. electroreduction furnace + LD converter (CONOX)	75/25
3. prereduced pellets (SL-RN) + blast furnace + LD converter (CONOX)	75/25
4. prereduced pellets (SL-RN) + electric steel furnace	75/25
5. blast furnace + LD converter (CONOX)	75/25
6. nonintegrated electric steel furnace	0/100

iron and steel industry, year t (t = 0, 1, ..., 6) [a].

3t	ST 4t	ST 5t	ST 6t	Unit cost of inputs	
				1977 shadow prices associated with 10% annual discount rate, 15% preference to domestic inputs, and conventional exchange rate of 12.5 pesos per U.S. dollar	1970 conventional prices
536	−550	−418	− 416	1.00	1.00
61	− 37	− 55	− 27	0.15	0
				3.93	5.00
0.013	− 0.101	− 0.006	− 0.067	597.11	0 c
0.100	− 0.760	− 0.047	− 0.500	37.35	100.00 c
				24.87	18.40
4.589	− 2.950	− 1.640		3.93	5.00
1.237	− 1.237	− 1.320		80.00	80.00
0.275	− 0.275	− 0.275	− 1.050	575	500.00
0.400		− 0.650	− 0.050	300	300.00
1.000	1.000	1.000	1.000		
17%	10%	24%	6%		
952	913	897	1097		
925	877	869	1006		

[c] The conventional electricity price of 100 pesos/10^3 KWH is not directly comparable with the parately calculated marginal costs for energy and peak power. In order to compare the two for a und-the-clock major industrial consumer operating 7.5×10^3 hours per year, divide the peak power sts by 7.5, and add to the electrical energy costs shown above. Thus for 1977, the full costs would (597.11/7.5) + 37.35 = 116.96.

[d] Includes coke inputs.

the compound annual rate of 9.1% over the period 1974–80. [5]

To satisfy the demands for new ingot capacity, six alternative processes are considered – each corresponding to an integrated plant size of 1.0 million tons per year. (See table 3.) For each activity STjt, note that the cost coefficients in the row CSCURt include not only current account expenses such as labor, but also a capital recovery factor of 13% for depreciation plus opportunity cost of capital. With capital costs converted into annual costs, in order to ensure the irreversibility of investment, the process choices in successive time periods are linked by the following constraints:

(STCPjt)   STj, $t+1 \geqslant$ STj, t ($t = 0, ..., 5$).

To simplify presentation, the intermediate iron product (either pig iron or sponge iron) has been netted out from table 3, and the six alternative processes are each viewed as integrated from raw materials through the ingot state. It is supposed that the raw materials (iron ore, scrap and coke) will be available in unlimited quantities at a constant marginal cost. [6] E.g., the coefficient in the column STSCRAPt, and row CSCURt indicates the input price assumed for steel scrap, 500 pesos per ton. Since Mexico will continue to be an importer of scrap during the 1970's, this entire amount is also viewed as a current foreign exchange cost (row CSMCURt).

It is *not* assumed that industrial fuel will continue to be available to the steel industry at a constant marginal cost. The activities STRQFt define the steel industry's fossil fuel requirements (either in the form of residual fuel oil or natural gas), translating these requirements into their British thermal unit equivalents. These are

[5] In their demand estimates, Bueno and González Vargas made separate projections for flat and non-flat products and for seamless tubes, and then converted these into their ingot equivalents. – For 1974, the demand is taken at 6.237 million ingot tons. The existing plus planned production capacity in that year is taken at 5.180 million tons, excluding the project that is under consideration for Las Truchas.

[6] Since the cost of raw materials is exogenous, no explicit constraint rows need have been included for them. These rows have been included within the programming matrix so as to facilitate data processing and revisions.

the activities that link process choices within the steel and the petroleum industries. Note that energy inputs comprise between 6 and 30% of ingot costs, depending upon the process.

As things turn out, the optimal steel process choice is insensitive to the foreign exchange premium and the discount rate. In letting the discount rate range from 10% to 20% per year, and in letting the value of foreign exchange vary between the conventional exchange rate of 12.5 and the shadow price of 20.0 pesos per U.S. dollar, the optimal investment choice within the steel industry remains process 5: blast furnace + LD converter (CONOX).

For comparative purposes, table 3 indicates the unit cost of ingot production based both upon conventional 1970 input prices and also based upon the 1977 dual variables. Note that there is only a small difference between the costs of process 4 and 5, and that this difference is well within the range of likely errors in estimation. According to table 3, there is a 12–15% difference between the cost of ingots produced via the optimal process (#5) and the sponge iron process (#1). In order to reconcile this with the fact that a major new sponge iron project is under construction, one must recognize that the project has received investment inducements via low input prices for natural gas. One must also recognize that economies-of-scale are less pronounced with the sponge iron and with the electric steel furnace processes than with the others.

5. Electricity industry

ENERGETICOS is based upon results from earlier, more detailed models of Mexico's electric power industry. (See Stanford Research Institute 1968, Fernández and Manne 1969, and Rogers 1970.) For example, the demand for electricity is characterized here in terms of just two parameters of the annual load-duration curve: the annual peak power and the annual energy. This representation of demand is too aggregative to be altogether satisfactory for planning investments *within* the electric power sector. For example, in INTERCON, the decision problem entails tradeoffs between transmission and generating facilities. For evaluating these decisions, the annual load-duration curve was represented in terms of eight parameters: the peak power demand during each of two seasons plus the energy demand during six blocks of time. With interconnection between regions, it was then found that one of the two seasonal peaks dominated the other. Moreover, there was sufficient flexibility of hydroelectric operations so that — within a given region — the value of energy did not vary significantly between the six blocks of time.

On the basis of this prior information, no distinction is drawn here between time blocks within a year. Kilowatt-hours of electrical energy are aggregated into a single annual total. This simplifies the analysis of linkages between the electricity and the petroleum sector, but this also means that ENERGETICOS cannot solve those investment problems that relate to geographical tradeoffs between transmission and generating facilities. With the multi-level structure of INTERCON and ENERGETICOS, the facility location problem is handled as a separate suboptimization. [7]

The more detailed models of the electric power industry have suggested that no great error would be associated with several further simplifications: regarding the water inflows to the hydroelectric system as deterministic rather than probabilistic quantities, the omission of gas turbines for any purpose other than reserve capacity, a factor of 12% for reserve capacity, and the predetermined sizes selected for fossil and nuclear generating units. Although such simplifications would be unsatisfactory for investment planning within the electric power industry itself, they appear defensible for examining the linkage between electricity, petroleum and steel investment decisions.

ENERGETICOS is constructed as though the only process choice for new electrical generating capacity were nuclear power versus fossil fuel plants, and as though the only fossil fuels were residual oil and natural gas. Diesel units, coal burning plants and

---

[7] Suboptimization reduces the difficulties of data-gathering and of computations, but it is risky whenever there are significant interactions between the components of a system. Cf. Hitch (1953).

geothermal plants each have their place in Mexico's power grid, but are not expected to supply a major percentage of the new capacity. Investment choices have been omitted for new hydro-electric projects — partly because Mexico is close to exhausting her supply of low-cost hydroelectric sites and partly because hydro project costs have been consistently underestimated in the past.

The electricity sector's constraints are written out in table 4. [8] The first three sets of constraints (CMGWt), (CMTWHt) and (ELTRAt) refer to satisfying the peak, energy and transmission demands, after deducting the supplies available from the initial hydro and fossil installations. (See table 5 for the numerical values of the exogenously specified quantities.)

Not shown explicitly in table 4 are the lower bounds imposed on the individual unknowns FOSt. These lower bounds insure that fossil capacity will be installed in geographically isolated regions that are not interconnected with major grids.

Most of the details of table 4 are connected with the phenomenon of service shifting. That is, over time it can be anticipated that new thermal plants will be added to the system, and that these will have progressively lower energy costs. When a thermal unit enters into service, it is likely to operate as a base-load unit (i.e., at full capacity). The fluctuations in the daily load curve will be absorbed by older thermal plants or by hydro units. As time passes, it is typical that a thermal unit (whether a fossil or a nuclear plant) will be utilized at successively lower levels of capacity.

One formulation that provides for optimal service shifting may be illustrated in the case of new fossil fuel capacity. For this process choice, it is supposed that there are two types of un-knowns: $FOS\tau$ and XFt. The former denotes the peak capacity installed in period τ, and the latter denotes the above-minimum energy to be produced by new fossil plants in period t. Plants of this type cannot be operated at more than 90% of the 8,760 hours in the year. In order for the boilers to be fired up so as to meet the annual and daily peak, these units cannot be operated for less than

---

[8] This programming model resembles a number of those that have been constructed at Electricité de France. (See Massé and Gibrat 1957 and Bessière 1969.)

Table 4

Constraints for electric power industry ($t = 0, 1, ..., 6, 11, 16, 21$)

(CM GWt) cumulative new fossil capacity + cumulative nuclear capacity

$$\sum_{\tau=0}^{t} FOS\tau + \sum_{\tau=2}^{t} NUC\tau \geq \begin{matrix} \text{peak} \\ \text{final} \\ \text{demand} \end{matrix} - \begin{matrix} \text{initial} \\ \text{fossil} \\ \text{capacity} \end{matrix} - \begin{matrix} \text{hydro} \\ \text{capacity} \end{matrix}$$

(CM TWHt) generation from fossil $\left\{ \begin{matrix}\text{initial} & +\text{ new} \\ & \text{minimum}\end{matrix} + \begin{matrix}\text{new, above}\\ \text{minimum}\end{matrix}\right\}$ generation from nuclear $\left\{\begin{matrix}+\text{ early,} \\ \text{minimum}\end{matrix} \begin{matrix}+\text{ early,}\\ \text{above}\\ \text{minimum}\end{matrix} \begin{matrix}+\text{ late}\\ \text{at}\\ \text{maximum}\end{matrix}\right\}$

$$\sum_{k=1}^{5} (\alpha_k)\, INT kt + 1.971 \sum_{\tau=0}^{t} FOS\tau + XFt + 1.861 \sum_{\tau=2}^{\min(t,6)} NUC\tau + XNt + 7.446 \sum_{\tau=11}^{t} NUC\tau \geq \begin{matrix}\text{energy}\\\text{demand}\end{matrix} - \begin{matrix}\text{hydro}\\\text{energy}\end{matrix}$$

(EL TRAt) requirements for additional transmission capacity
$$= TRAt = FOSt + NUCt$$

(EL LMFt) energy generated in new fossil plants, above minimum
$$= XFt \leq 5.913 \sum_{\tau=0}^{t} FOS\tau$$

(EL LMNt) energy generated in early nuclear plants, above minimum $= XNt \leq 5.585 \sum_{\tau=2}^{\min(t,6)} NUC\tau$

(EL CNVt) convex curve − initial fossil
$$\sum_{k=1}^{5} INT kt = 1$$

(EL RQFt) industrial fuel requirements $= RQFt = \sum_{k=1}^{5} (\beta_k)\, INT kt + \begin{pmatrix}\text{heat}\\\text{rate,}\\\text{new}\\\text{fossil}\end{pmatrix}\left(1.971 \sum_{\tau=0}^{t} FOS\tau + XFt\right)$

Notes: Nuclear fuel inputs enter as cost coefficients for unknowns XNt, NUCt.
Prefix EL precedes identification of all unknowns shown above.

Table 5

Predetermined demands and capacities, electricity industry

period t	year	annual peak (GW)				annual energy (TWH)		
		peak final demand [a]	initial fossil capacity	hydro capacity	cumulative requirements for new peak capacity [b]	final demand [a]	hydro energy	demand for nonhydro
0	1974	7.74	4.04	3.88	0.67	39.00	14.25	24.75
1	1975	8.52	4.04	4.20	1.16	43.40	14.70	28.60
2	1976	9.48	4.04	4.35	1.99	47.50	16.40	31.10
3	1977	10.52	4.04	4.35	3.03	53.00	16.23	36.77
4	1978	11.65	4.04	5.27	3.31	59.50	20.96	38.54
5	1979	12.78	4.04	5.27	4.47	66.00	20.96	45.04
6	1980	14.17	4.04	5.27	5.86	74.00	20.96	53.04
11	1985	23.13	4.04	5.27	14.82	152.00	20.96	131.04
16	1990	36.52	4.04	5.27	28.21	208.00	20.96	187.04
21	1995	57.39	4.04	5.27	49.06	330.00	20.96	209.04
%/year growth of demand, 1974–80		10.6				11.3		

[a] Neglecting endogenous electricity demands from the steel industry.

[b] Requirements for new peak capacity = final demand − (1/1.12) (initial fossil + hydro capacity).

25% of the time. This accounts for the energy coefficient of FOSτ shown in the constraints CM TWHt. ((8.760) (0.90) (0.25) = 1.971 thousand hours per year.) During the remaining hours that these fossil units are available, one kilowatt of capacity cannot produce more than 5.913 thousand kilowatt-hours of energy – hence the coefficient of FOSτ in the energy limit ELLMFt.

For early nuclear power plants, a similar provision is made for service shifting. ('Early' means those nuclear plants installed between years 2 and 6, 1976–80.) The only difference between the coefficients for new fossil and early nuclear plants is that the latter

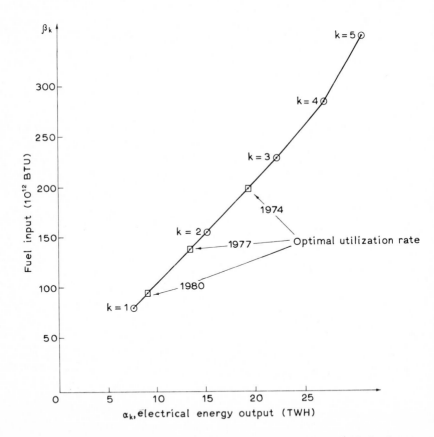

Fig. 2. Fuel input versus electrical energy generated by initially available fossil power stations.

are taken to have an annual availability factor of 85% rather than 90%. For the late nuclear plants (i.e., those installed between 1981 and 1995), it is supposed that these would be operated only for base-load purpose, and that service shifting may be neglected.

To describe the operations of the initially available fossil fuel plants, a preliminary suboptimization was employed to reduce the number of rows in ENERGETICOS. Because of differences between the thermal efficiency of these units, there is a technologically determined 'merit order' for their use. In order to minimize fossil fuel consumption — without increasing any other component of costs — kilowatt-hours would first be produced in the most efficient units up to their maximum capacity, then in the next most efficient units, and so on. Since the capacities of these units are already known, this leads to a predetermined relationship between the energy output and the fossil fuel input. (See figure 2.) To summarize this convex relationship, five levels of output are specified, and these are identified through the index $k = 1, 2, ..., 5$.

From figure 2, it can be seen that for each value of k there is a predetermined value of the total energy output (the coefficient α_k) and of the total fuel input (the coefficient β_k). The linear programming unknowns are not these inputs and outputs directly, but rather the 'interpolation weight' variables INTkt. Each unknown INTkt appear in three constraints: (CMTWHt), (ELRQFt), and (ELCNVt). The convex curve constraints (ELCNVt) ensure that the interpolation unknowns will add up to unity for each time period t. [9] During year 3 (1977), for example, it is optimal for the initial plants to produce 13.64 TWH. This is obtained by setting the unknowns INT 13 = 0.23 and INT 23 = 0.77. The corresponding energy output is interpolated through the coefficients α_1 and α_2 in the energy constraint (CMTWH3). Similarly, the fossil fuel input requirement is interpolated through the coefficients β_1 and β_2 in the fuel constraint (ELRQF3). On figure 2,

---

[9] The process of optimization, together with the convex shape of figure 2, ensures that it will never be optimal to assign positive intensities to two non-adjacent interpolation variables. E.g., it will not be optimal to set INT31>0 and simultaneously INT51>0. A reduction in fuel inputs could then be achieved by increasing the intensity of INT41, and reducing both INT31 and INT51.

Table 6
Costs in the electricity sector

		Generating plants				Transmission + gas turbines for reserve capacity + over-head costs per GW of transmission capacity
	Fossil	Fossil	Nuclear	Nuclear	Nuclear breeder	
Unit size	0.300 GW	1.000 GW	0.600 GW	1.000 GW	1.000 GW	
I						
I.1 Initial investment						
Total (M pesos)	426	1200	1374	2000	2000	1454
Annual change (%)	– 0.5 [a]	– 0.5 [a]	– 1.0 [b]	– 1.0 [b]	– 2.0 [c]	0.0
I.2 Unit cost (M pesos/GW)	1426	1200	2290	2000	2000	1454
I.3 Domestic cost component (%)	65.0	50.0	25.0	25.0	25.0	70.0
Annual change (%)	0.0	0.0	1.0 [b]	1.0 [b]	1.0 [c]	1.5 [a]
II Unit fuel cost (M pesos/TWH)	35.55 [d]	35.33 [d]	16.25	15.75	8.37	
Annual change (%)	0.0	0.0	– 1.0	– 1.0	– 2.0	
III Fixed operating costs (M pesos/year)	9.40	18.00	22.20	25.50	25.50	283.7
Domestic cost component (%)	100	100	100	100	100	100
IV First year available	1974	1981	1976	1981	1991	1974

[a] From 1974.
[b] From 1976.
[c] From 1986.
[d] Valuing fossil fuel at 3.95 pesos per MBTU from 1981.
Abbreviation: $M = 10^6$.

Table 7

Optimal program for installation of generating capacity (unit: GW installed per year)

Year	Fossil		Nuclear		Nuclear Breeder
	0.300 GW	1.000 GW	0.600 GW	1.000 GW	1.000 GW
1974	0.676	n.a. [b]	n.a.	n.a.	n.a.
1975	0.493	n.a.	n.a.	n.a.	n.a.
1976	0.050 [a]	n.a.	0.784	n.a.	n.a.
1977	0.026 [a]	n.a.	1.018	n.a.	n.a.
1978	0.043 [a]	n.a.	0.241	n.a.	n.a.
1979	0.058 [a]	n.a.	1.107	n.a.	n.a.
1980	0.064 [a]	n.a.	1.331	n.a.	n.a.
1981–85	n.a.	0	n.a.	1.786	n.a.
1986–90	n.a.	0	n.a.	2.678	n.a.
1991–95	n.a.	1.133	n.a.	n.a.	3.037

[a] Predetermined lower limit to ensure that fossil capacity will be installed in geographically isolated regions that are not interconnected with the major grids for the south, central and the northern systems.

[b] n.a. = not available.

note the decline in the optimal utilization rate for the older fossil units as lower-cost plants become available between 1974 and 1980.

In order to complete the input data for the electric power industry, cost coefficients must be calculated for each activity. These have been derived from the project characteristics given in table 6, interpolating linearly for investment and operating costs within each of the three successive five-year intervals 1980–85, 1985–90, and 1990–95.

With these numerical assumptions on costs, demands, utilization rates, etc., the optimal installation program for generating capacity is given in table 7. As is characteristic of linear programming, the solution tends to be of a bang-bang form: fossil units installed at their lower limit during 1976–80 and nuclear units for the balance of the capacity requirements between 1976 and 1990. During the period in which breeders first become available (1991–95), it is optimal to install a mix of fossil and breeder units. (If pumped-storage activities had been included explicitly within ENERGETI-

COS, it is likely that it would be optimal to install these rather than fossil units at the same time as breeders.) During 1976–80, the period of immediate interest, note that the annual capacity increments would be of the order of one or two nuclear units, each of 0.600 GW size.

6. Petroleum and gas industry

ENERGETICOS is stated as though the objective were to satisfy the domestic demands for petroleum products at minimum cost, exporting and importing whichever items are most advantageous. It is not stipulated that absolute priority be given to self-sufficiency, nor to employment within the petroleum and gas industry. Rather, the tradeoffs are explored between total costs and foreign exchange costs – allowing for a 15% rate of protection against imports.

In order to concentrate on the problem of intersectoral linkage, we have focussed on oil and gas production and on refining – excluding the transportation and marketing aspects. Within ENERGETICOS, the costs of domestic crude oil and gas production constitute the most problematical set of parameters. It is not at all clear what have been the past costs of domestic production – let alone what is appropriate in an extrapolation for a decade into the future.

Some clues on the future may be obtained from figure 3, a cumulative distribution of crude oil costs by fields in 1958, 1962 and 1966. The historical figures suggest: (a) that there was a significant increase in the domestic cost of crude oil between 1958 and 1962, but not between 1962 and 1966 (after deflation by the gross domestic product price index); (b) that there is a significant difference between the costs of production in individual fields; (c) that the average field has costs that are competitive with an import price of 27.5 pesos per barrel = U.S. $ 2.20 per barrel; and (d) that there has consistently been a small volume of production from marginal fields with costs that lie well above the import price.

The classical academic impulse is to conclude that the high-cost

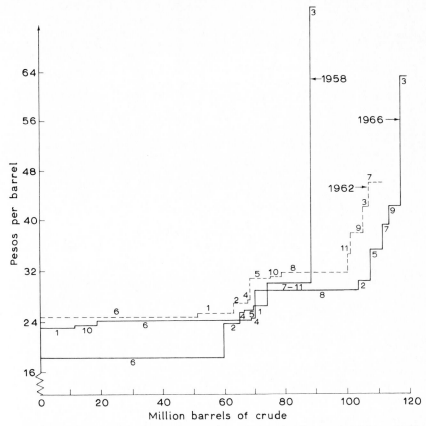

Fig. 3. Pemex Accounting Department estimates of crude oil costs by fields – 1958, 1962, 1966. Note: The numbers identify individual fields in successive years. The average cost of crude oil at 1966 prices (stated in pesos per barrel) was: in 1958, 22.4; in 1962, 28.0; in 1966, 27.2.

fields ought to be shut down, that imported crude replace the domestic output, and that the necessary foreign exchange be earned through shifting the displaced petroleum workers into producing, say, fruits and vegetables for export. A more pragmatic reaction would be to question whether the historical accounting estimates bear any relation to the economic theorist's definition of opportunity costs. Underlying figure 3 are arbitrary allocations between two joint products – crude oil and associated gas. There are quality differences between types of crude. There is the possi-

	Availability (unit: 10^6 barrels)				
	1974	1975	1976	1977	1978
Time period t	0	1	2	3	4
Crude oil	172.2	176.1	191.4	209.3	228.3
Condensates	31.9	34.5	37.2	39.6	42.2
Dry gas [b]	118.0	131.3	144.1	157.3	171.4

[a] Foreign exchange component (row CS MCURt) is taken at 10% of domestic costs and 100% of import price.

[b] Fuel oil equivalent of dry gas is 6.321 10^6 BTU per barrel of fuel oil.

bility that low-cost fields have not been exploited to their capacity in the past. There are arbitrary allocations of exploration and drilling costs, arbitrary estimates of proved reserves, and arbitrary allowances for the return on capital. Given this view of the data, it is hopeless to calculate an optimal make-or-buy choice for crude oil. For the decision maker who is subject to political pressure from petroleum workers, the line of least resistance is to adopt the criterion of self-sufficiency in raw materials – regardless of costs. (Considerations of this type are not unknown in the U.K. coal mines nor in the U.S. petroleum industry.)

Rather than abandon cost criteria completely, it seems preferable to make some assumptions on the supply curve for raw materials, and then to test how these assumptions influence the optimal choice of processes elsewhere within the system. For the decade of the 1970's, it can be supposed that the import price will remain constant at 27.5 pesos per barrel for crude oil and at 25.0 for the fuel oil equivalent of dry gas. (See table 8. [10]) Given the uncer-

---

[10] For many of the estimates that appear in tables 8–11, we are indebted to Ings. Raúl Meyer, Victor L. Games and Carlos Velasco.

nd cost of oil, condensates and dry gas

		Cost coefficients (row CS CURt) (unit: pesos per barrel) [a]				
1979 5	1980 6	1974–80 %/year growth rate	% of domestic supplies available at stated cost 85%	10%	5%	import price
234.5	255.0	6.8%	22.0	27.0	35.0	27.5
44.9	47.5	6.8	c	c	c	–
188.4	204.2	9.6	20.0	24.5	31.3	25.0 [d]

[c] Since the quantity of condensates is projected exogenously, no cost coefficients need to be estimated for this item.

[d] Import price of fuel oil.

tainties in cost extrapolations – and given the inevitable political pressures against imports – we have attempted to err in the direction of underestimating future domestic costs. For this reason, it is supposed that 85% of the future domestic supplies will be available at a cost substantially below that of imports, and that an additional 10% of the domestic supplies will be competitive if foreign exchange is valued at the conventional rate of 12.5 pesos per U.S. dollar. For the remaining 5% of potential oil and gas supplies, the cost parameters have been adjusted so that domestic material will cost more than imports even after allowance is made for a 15% rate of protection against imports. [11] Typically, unless there is a premium value assigned to foreign exchange, it then turns out to be optimal to exploit just 95% of the potentially available domestic supplies, and to import the balance of the raw material requirements for the petroleum refining industry.

[11] One barrel of fuel oil (or its dry gas equivalent) has a heat value of 6.321 million BTU. This factor may be employed for comparing these import prices and domestic costs (pesos per barrel) with the fossil fuel costs (pesos per million BTU) shown in chapter III.1 above.

Table

Matrix of coefficien

Row (for identification and units of measurement, see tables 1 and 2)	Activity	Initial (1973) refining capacity	New refining capacity [b]	
			conventional	visbreaking
		PECP73 [a]	PECt	PEVt
cost inputs	CSCURt		−6.2	−10.8
	CSMCURt		−0.62	− 1.08
physical	CMBTUt			
inputs (−)	PEGSDt			− 0.0181
and	PECRDt	−170.0	−1.0000	− 1.0000
outputs (+);	PEGSRt	5.9	0.0240	0.0090
unit:	PELPGt	12.5	0.0280	0.0602
10^6 barrels,	PEGSLt	71.5	0.2580	0.4876
except for	PEKDt	52.6	0.2770	0.2546
row CMBTUt	PEFOt	35.0	0.3870	0.2218

[a] Initial capacity activity is operated at level of 1.0 during all time periods.

[b] All three processing sequences are based upon an integrated new refinery with 115 TB/D of primary distillation capacity, 50 TB/D of vacuum distillation capacity, and a 10 TB/D gasolin reformer. Other capacities would be as follows (in TB/D = thousand barrels per stream day):

	conventional	visbreaking	maximum hydrogen processing
H oil	0	0	25
Isomax	0	30	30
Visbreaking	10	25	0
Catalytic cracking	27	0	0
Hydrogen (10^6 scf/day)	0	50	100

For alternative refining processes, it is straightforward to estimate physical inputs and outputs. (See table 9.) Each of the three
alternative activities for new refining capacity is viewed as though
it were vertically integrated from crude oil through refined products, after netting out intermediate materials such as vacuum gas

or petroleum refining

maximum hydrogen processing PEHt	Outputs per million barrels of domestic condensates [c] PEDCONt	Industrial fuel equivalents			
		PEQGSDt	PEQGSRt	PEQLPGt	PEQFOt
−16.4					
− 1.64					
		6.321	6.321	4.173	6.321
− 0.0328		−1.0			
− 1.0000					
0.0289			−1.0		
0.0836	0.5005				
0.5859	0.3900			−1.0	
0.2863	0.1095				
0.1282					−1.0

[c] Domestic condensates activity is operated at predetermined level during all time periods. See table 8 for this availability level.

oil. If crude oil were the only cost element and if the refining industry's objective were to maximize the output of gasoline (the highest-priced product), it would always be optimal to install process PEHt, maximum hydrogen processing. With a more complex objective function — satisfying demands at minimum costs — the optimal process choice is not maximum hydrogen processing. The process choice is sensitive to the refining cost coefficients shown in rows CSCURt and CSMCURt. [12]

Table 10 provides the marginal costs and optimal material balances for a representative year, 1977. For each year within the planning horizon of 1974–80, similar costs and material balances

[12] The numerical values adopted for these cost coefficients are based upon the rather shaky estimate that annual refinery costs — including capital charges, labor, overheads and refinery inputs other than oil and gas — will be 40% of the initial investment costs for an integrated plant.

Table 10

Marginal costs and optimal material balances, 1977 – petroleum industry (omitting inputs and output

Description of activity	Refining capacity			Domestic gas [a]		Domestic conden- sates	Domestic crude	
Activity identification	PECP73	PEC3	PEV3	PEDGSD3	PEDGSDA3	PEDCON3	PEDCRD3	PEDCRDA3
Item								
CM BTU3 [c]								
PE CSD3			− 0.4	133.7	9.9			
PE CRD3	−170.0	−7.7	−22.7				177.9	20.9
PE GSR3	5.9	0.2	0.2					
PE LPG3	12.5	0.2	1.4			19.8		
PE GSL3	71.5	2.0	11.1			15.4		
PE KD3	52.6	2.1	5.8			4.3		
PE FO3	35.0	3.0	5.0					

[a] Activity PE DGSD3 denotes domestic gas obtainable at cost of 20.0 pesos/barrel; PE DGSDA3 denotes domestic gas obtainable at 24.5 pesos/barrel.

[b] Activity PE DCRD3 denotes domestic crude obtainable at cost of 22.0 pesos/barrel; PE DCRDA3 denotes domestic crude obtainable at 27.0 pesos/barrel.

are available. Typically, as shown in table 11, the optimal solution entails small-scale imports of crude oil and liquefied petroleum gas, and virtual self-sufficiency in other items. With other numerical assumptions (e.g., a slower rate of introduction of nuclear power), the solution will change. In particular, note that the optimality of the solution depends upon the import and export prices assumed for the various raw materials and products. To the extent that table 11 overstates the transport and marketing cost differentials between the import and the export price of each

where optimal activity level is zero) (unit: millions of barrels/year − except for industrial fuel)

Fuel oil equivalents			Imports			Intersectoral flows		Final demand	Marginal cost of supplying item in 1977 (pesos/barrel except for industrial fuel)
P E Q G S D 3	P E Q G S R 3	P E Q F 0 3	P E M C R D 3	P E M L P G 3	P E M K D 3	E L R Q F 3	S T R Q F 3		
905.4	39.6	223.8				−231.7	−138.7	798.4	3.93
−143.2								0	24.87
			1.6					0	31.63
	− 6.3							0	24.87
				6.1				40.0	33.12
								100.0	44.06
					0.5			65.3	54.40
		− 35.4						7.6 d	24.87

c Unit: 10^{12} BTU/year.
d Includes asphalts only.

petroleum product, the results have been biased in favor of self-sufficiency.

7. Sensitivity analysis — discount rate and foreign exchange scarcity premium

Up to this point, all results have been based upon those project evaluation criteria that we believe to be typical within the energy

Table 11
Product demands; optimal imports and exports

Item	export/ import price (pesos/ barrel)		year period t	1974 0	1975 1	1976 2
industrial		final demand		616.5	672.0	732.5
fuel [a]		intersectoral flows, electricity		250.0	285.2	249.9
		intersectoral flows, steel [b]		117.2	124.2	130.9
liquefied petroleum	–	final demand		33.8	35.9	38.0
gas	28.8	imports		(5.3)	(6.0)	(6.0)
	–	final demand		80.0	86.3	93.0
gasoline	31.5	exports		3.9	0	0
	47.3	imports		0	0	0
kerosine and diesel oil	–	final demand		55.1	58.4	61.8
	31.5	exports		1.0	0	0
	47.3	imports		0	(0.6)	(0.4)
residual fuel oil	–	final demand [c]		5.9	6.5	7.0
	21.2	exports		0	0	0
	25.0	imports		(8.5)	(9.8)	0
crude oil	27.5	imports		(6.4)	(7.9)	(6.1)

[a] Unit: 10^{12} BTU/year.
[b] Total industrial fuel requirements for steel industry includes rolling stage. This excludes coke requirements, and refers only to fuel oil plus natural gas.

sector. It has been supposed that the public enterprises within this sector evaluate alternative projects as though capital were available at a 10% annual discount rate, as though foreign exchange were valued at the conventional rate of 12.5 pesos per U.S. dollar, and as though there were a 15% protection rate for domestic as against

nit: 10^6 barrels/year – except for industrial fuel)

977	1978	1979	1980	1974–80 year growth rate of final demand (%)	Identification of activity	Identification of item
3	4	5	6			
98.4	870.3	948.6	1034.0	9.0		
31.7	231.6	215.3	197.3		ELRQFt	CMBTUt
38.7	147.1	156.4	166.5		STRQFt	
40.0	42.0	44.0	45.8	5.2		PELPGt
(6.1)	(6.0)	(5.8)	(5.5)		PEMLPGt	
00.0	107.4	115.1	123.1	7.4		
0	0	0	0		PEXGSLt	PEGSLt
0	0	0	0		PEMGSLt	
65.3	68.9	73.4	76.7	5.7		
0	0	0	0		PEXKDt	PEKDt
(0.5)	0	(0.7)	(0.1)		PEMKDt	
7.6	8.2	8.9	9.6	8.5		
0	0	0	1.3		PEXFOt	PEFOt
0	0	0	0		PEMFOt	
(1.6)	0	(5.8)	(0.6)		PEMCRDt	PECRDt

[c] Includes asphalts only.

imported items. [13]

With respect to import substitution choices, a 15% protection

[13] Throughout the energy sector, domestic inputs are given preference over imported ones. For heavy electrical equipment financed by World Bank loans, the standard current practice for bid evaluation is a 15% preference rate. Outside the electrical sector, the protection criteria are seldom stated in explicit form.

Table 12
Effects of foreign exchange premium and of discount rate for petroleum, electricity and steel industries

annual discount rate = 10%

	Unit of measurement	p = foreign exchange scarcity premium (%)						
		0	10	20	30	40	50	60
Total discounted costs at conventional prices + 15% protection on imports	10^9 pesos discounted to 1974 (year 0) at 10% per year[a]	127.34	127.46	127.75	127.95	127.98	128.11	129.27
Total discounted import costs less export earnings, at conventional prices	10^9 pesos discounted to 1974 (year 0) at 10% per year[a]	23.67	21.91	20.06	19.29	19.22	10.90	16.70
1977 process choices Ingot output from 1974–77 capacity, steel process 5	10^6 ingot tons	2.9	2.9	2.9	2.9	2.9	2.9	2.9
Crude petroleum, domestic output, 1977	10^6 barrels	198.8	198.8	201.9	201.9	201.9	203.8	209.3
Crude petroleum, imports, 1977	10^6 barrels	1.6	3.0	0	0	0	0	0
Crude input to 1974–77 refining capacity (conventional)	10^6 barrels	7.7	10.7	10.9	10.9	10.9	14.9	23.4
Crude input to 1974–77 refining capacity (visbreaking)	10^6 barrels	22.7	21.1	21.0	21.0	21.0	18.9	15.9
Fossil electric generating capacity installed, 1974–77	MW = 10^3 KW	1,245	1,869	1,901	2,483	2,614	2,821	3,047
Nuclear electric generating capacity installed, 1976–77	MW = 10^3 KW	1,802	1,177	1,146	564	433	226	0

Table 12 (continued)

	Unit of measurement	p = foreign exchange scarcity premium (%) annual discount rate = 20%						
		0	10	20	30	40	50	60
Total discounted costs at conventional prices + 15% protection on imports	10^9 pesos discounted to 1974 (year 0) at 20% per year [a]	85.34	85.50	85.50	85.67	85.95	86.20	86.20
Total discounted import costs less export earnings, at conventional prices	10^9 pesos discounted to 1974 (year 0) at 20% per year [a]	18.35	13.35	13.35	12.60	11.89	11.30	11.30
1977 process choices — Ingot output from 1974–77 capacity, steel process 5	10^6 ingot tons	2.9	2.9	2.9	2.9	2.9	2.9	2.9
Crude petroleum, domestic output, 1977	10^6 barrels	177.9	198.8	198.8	198.8	198.8	201.9	201.9
Crude petroleum, imports, 1977	10^6 barrels	23.9	3.0	3.1	3.1	3.1	0	0
Crude input to 1974–1977 refining capacity (conventional)	10^6 barrels	10.7	10.7	10.9	10.9	10.9	10.9	10.9
Crude input to 1974–77 refining capacity (visbreaking)	10^6 barrels	21.1	21.1	21.0	21.0	21.0	21.0	21.0
Fossil electric generating capacity installed, 1974–77	MW = 10^3 KW	3,046	3,046	3,046	3,046	3,046	3,046	3,046
Nuclear electric generating capacity installed, 1974–77	MW = 10^3 KW	0	0	0	0	0	0	0

[a] Discounted over 1974–80 horizon for petroleum and steel industries; over 1974–75 horizon for electricity industry.

rate has effects that are identical to a 15% scarcity premium imputed to foreign exchange. With respect to export promotion, however, the two criteria differ. E.g., to stipulate a zero scarcity premium on foreign exchange and a 15% protection rate implies that the energy sector would prefer to save $ 1.00 of foreign exchange through import substitution rather than earn up to $ 1.15 of foreign exchange through exports. A domestic protection rate, then, is to be interpreted as a price that Mexico is willing to pay in order to insulate her economy from fluctuations transmitted through international trade.

An alternative interpretation of the 15% preference rate is the following: Even if absolute preference is to be given to domestic raw materials such as oil and gas, the consumers of these items should evaluate their own process alternatives as though fuel were not priced much above the international level. If marginal *domestic* cost pricing is applied in this 'second-best' situation, there will be an uneconomic stimulus to economize on oil and gas, e.g., to speed up the introduction of nuclear power into the electricity industry and of hydrogen processing into petroleum refineries.

Table 12 summarizes how the optimal solution would shift under alternative assumptions with respect to the foreign exchange premium and the discount rate – holding the protection rate constant at 15% of import costs. Let p denote the scarcity premium imputed to foreign exchange. Then, recalling the definitions given in table 2, the cost minimand represents the discounted sum of one-period costs. The costs incurred in period t would be evaluated as follows:

$$
\begin{array}{l}
\text{costs at} \\
\text{conventional} + 0.15\,(\text{import costs}) + p\,\begin{pmatrix}\text{import costs} -' \\ \text{export earnings}\end{pmatrix} \\
\text{prices}
\end{array}
$$

$$\text{CSCURt} \quad + 0.15\,(\text{CSMCURt}) \quad + p\,(\text{CSMCURt} - \text{CSXCURt}).$$

As p ranges between 0 and 60% (i.e., as the value of foreign exchange ranges between the conventional rate of 12.5 and the shadow price of 20.0 pesos per U.S. dollar [14]), note the decrease in the discounted import costs less export earnings. Total costs (evaluated at conventional prices) rise by a comparatively small amount.

Underlying the aggregative results, there are detailed import – export choices – which in turn depend upon the selection of production processes. For simplicity in presentation, table 12 summarizes the results for the single representative year, 1977. Within the steel industry, the optimal choice would remain process # 5 (blast furnace + LD converter) – regardless of whether the discount rate is 10% or 20% per year and regardless of whether $p = 0$ or $p = 60\%$.

Within the electric power and the petroleum sectors, the process choices are sensitive both to the discount rate and the foreign exchange premium. Some of these choices are self-evident, e.g., the shift to high-cost domestic crude as the foreign exchange scarcity premium increases. Not all the results are so clearcut. E.g., the higher the discount rate, the greater becomes the capital cost of the domestic fossil fuel supplied by the petroleum to the electricity industry. Nonetheless, in changing the annual discount rate from 10 to 20%, the lower becomes the optimal amount of nuclear electric generating capacity. The high capital cost component of nuclear capacity would more than offset the rise in fossil fuel costs.

Table 13 contains the six alternative time-phased vectors of investment and of foreign exchange expenditures that correspond to these process analysis results. In the next chapter, these vectors will be employed to show that the energy sector's process decisions are likely to have negligible feedback effects upon the final demands for its outputs or upon the efficiency prices of the sector's inputs. Under these conditions, a sectoral suboptimization need not diverge from a global optimization.

---

[14] Given the prevailing levels of effective tariffs on imports of consumers' durables, an efficiency price of 20.0 pesos is not altogether unrealistic. See Bueno (1971), table 8.7. DINAMICO suggests that p might lie between 15 and 35%. See above, chapter II.4, table 5.

Table 13

Macroeconomic implications of six alternative programs for petroleum, electricity and steel industri

(1970 prices)

Annual discount rate (%)		10			20		
Foreign exchange scarcity premium (%)		0	30	60	0	30	6
Investment expenditures	1974	3.39	3.94	4.08	3.09	3.39	3
	1975	2.83	2.99	2.87	2.03	2.83	2
for capacity	1976	5.25	4.56	4.54	4.18	4.59	4
	1977	6.01	5.62	5.61	5.25	5.39	5
first available	1978	3.36	3.20	3.09	3.25	3.33	3
	1979	6.28	6.13	5.95	5.45	5.63	5
in year (10^6 pesos)	1980	7.87	6.69	7.00	6.73	6.90	6
	Total	34.99	33.13	33.14	29.98	32.06	3
Import costs	1974	1.12	0.84	0.78	2.00	1.32	1
	1975	1.45	1.09	1.09	2.40	1.68	1
less export	1976	1.48	1.16	1.15	2.58	1.79	1
	1977	1.57	1.39	1.23	2.86	2.00	1
earnings	1978	1.43	1.34	1.29	2.86	1.97	1
	1979	1.92	1.58	1.63	3.57	2.58	2
(10^9 pesos)	1980	1.87	1.89	1.82	3.94	2.87	2
	Total	10.84	9.29	8.99	20.21	14.21	1
Export earnings	1974	0.16	0.16	0.19	0.16	0.16	0
	1975	0	0	0.02	0	0	0
(from petroleum	1976	0	0	0	0	0	0
	1977	0	0	0.09	0	0	0
products only)	1978	0	0.02	0.06	0	0	0
	1979	0	0	0.03	0	0	0
(10^9 pesos)	1980	0.03	0.02	0.11	0	0	0
	Total	0.19	0.20	0.50	0.16	0.16	0
Total discounted costs at conventional prices +15% protection on imports (10^9 pesos discounted to 1974 at 10% per year) [a]		127.34	127.95	129.27	128.62	132.43	13

[a] Discounted over 1974–80 horizon for petroleum and steel industries; over 1974–95 horizon 1 electricity industry.

8. Appendix: project indivisibilities

8.1. Model formulation

To allow for indivisible projects within ENERGETICOS, the IPE mixed integer programming algorithm was employed. Three mutual exclusivity sets were defined: one each for projects in the steel, petroleum and electric sector. Mutual exclusivity between 6 steel projects is ensured through the row MXST; between 9 petroleum projects through the row MXPE; and between 12 electricity projects through the row MXEL. (See tables 14–16.) Altogether, the number of logically possible project combinations is $N = 6 \times 9 \times 12 = 648$. Each of these alternative combinations is identified through a sequence of 3 numbers. E.g., (6, 4, 7) would identify the combination consisting of steel project 6, petroleum project 4, and electricity project 7.

For defining the individual projects, a number of simplifications were suggested by the original linear programming solutions. These helped to narrow down both the process alternatives and the dates at which new capacity might be installed. Linear programming indicated, for example, that 2.9 million tons of steel capacity and output were to be added cumulatively between years 0 and 3, and that it was optimal to install ingot process 5 (blast furnace + LD converter) regardless of whether the foreign exchange premium was 0 or 60%. For purposes of mixed integer programming with the IPE algorithm, we therefore focussed on steel process 5 – assuming that it could be installed only in indivisible plants of either 1.5 or 3.0 million tons. (These sizes are within the range of the alternatives that have been proposed for the Las Truchas mill.) Since processes 2–4 also require large mills, these were omitted from the IPE model. Processes 1 (sponge iron) and 6 (electric furnace) would not necessarily require large plants, and these activities were therefore retained as continuous variables.

With this background on the steel sector, six alternatives appeared to be worth investigation through the IPE algorithm. Table 14 provides the time-phasing and process definitions for these alternatives. It also indicates how the six zero-one project variables

Table 14
Tableau for linking continuous variables to indivisible projects in steel industry [a]

Row identification	Column identification	Continuous variables (cumulative ingot capacity added between 0 and t, and utilized in year t, process 5)					Mutually exclusive steel projects [b]						
		ST 50	ST 51	ST 52	ST 53	ST 54	Y1ST	Y2ST	Y3ST	Y4ST	Y5ST	Y6ST	
ingot capacity, process 5, year t (millions of tons) ⎧ STROW 0		-1					1.5	1.5	1.5			3.0	≥ 0
STROW 1							1.5	1.5	1.5		3.0	3.0	≥ 0
STROW 2				-1			1.5	1.5	3.0	3.0	3.0	3.0	≥ 0
STROW 3					-1		1.5	3.0	3.0	3.0	3.0	3.0	≥ 0
STROW 4						-1	1.5	3.0	3.0	3.0	3.0	3.0	≤ 0
MXST		1					1	1	1	1	1	1	$= 1$

[a] Cost coefficients in rows CS CURt and CS MCURt were extrapolated from those shown in table 3 for a 1.0 million ton plant, ingot process 5. The coefficient in row CS CURt (418 pesos per ton) covers the gross return on capital costs plus labor inputs. That in row CS MCURt (55 pesos per ton) covers the import component of capital costs. To estimate the economies of scale for a plant of 1.5 or 3.0 million ingot tons, a scaling exponent of 0.7 was then applied to these coefficients. That is

$$\frac{\text{cost for } x \text{ million tons}}{\text{cost for 1 million tons}} = x^{0.7}.$$

Note that $(1.5)^{0.7} = 1.33$, and that $(3.0)^{0.7} = 2.16$. This would mean that for a plant designed to produce 3.0 million ingot tons, the total annual equivalent of capital and labor costs would be only 2.16 times the amount required for a plant designed for 1.0 million tons.

[b] The six alternative projects may be interpreted as follows:

Y1ST. Add no integrated plants until after year 3; supply any capacity deficits from either process 1 (sponge iron) or process 6 (electric furnaces).

Y2ST. Add an integrated 1.5 million ton mill in year 0; supply any capacity deficits from processes 1 or 6.

Y3ST. Add an integrated 1.5 million ton mill in year 0; and add another in year 2.

Y4ST. Add an integrated 3.0 million ton mill in year 2.

Y5ST. Add an integrated 3.0 million ton mill in year 1.

Y6ST. Add an integrated 3.0 million ton mill in year 0.

are linked to the continuous variables ST5t through the rows STROWt and the direction of the inequality for that row. If, for example, project Y5ST = 1.0, this would mean that no additional large steel mill capacity was available during year 0, that up to 3.0 million tons could be utilized in years 1—3, and that at least 3.0 million tons were to be utilized in subsequent years. Following year 3, all steel sector process choices are viewed as continuous variables.

Table 15 shows a similar structure for the 9 mutually exclusive petroleum projects. Again, the definition of these projects was based partly upon the previous linear programming calculations. These indicated that it was non-optimal to adopt refining process PEHt (maximum hydrogen processing). The IPE computations were therefore confined to processes PECt (conventional processing) and PEVt (visbreaking). It was supposed that no more than one refinery would be added between years 2 and 5, and that this unit would have an annual crude intake identical to that being considered for the Tula plant: 50 million barrels of crude. The nine mutually exclusive refining alternatives are defined so that imports or exports of petroleum products will offset any temporary deficits or surpluses of installed capacity. If, for example, Y4PE = 1.0, this would mean that a 50 million barrel plant (visbreaking process) is to go onstream in year 3. At the import and export prices stipulated for ENERGETICOS (table 11), it then turns out to be optimal for gasoline to be imported in years 1 and 2, and to be exported in years 3 and 4 when refining capacity exceeds the domestic demands.

The structure of table 16 is similar to the two preceding ones — except that the continuous variables ELNUCt refer to the nuclear generating capacity added in year *t, not* to the cumulative amount added between year 0 and *t*. It is supposed that the size of each nuclear power unit would be 0.6 GW, and that either zero, one or two of these units would be added annually. Any deficits in nuclear capacity are offset through substituting the fossil process in its place. In the electricity sector — unlike petroleum refining — temporary imports and exports are neglected.

Table 1

Tableau for linking continuous variable

Row identification	Column identification	Continuous variables, refining processes (cumulative capacity added between year 0 and t, and utilized in year t)						
		visbreaking				conventional		
		PE V2	PE V3	PE V4	PE V5	PE C2	PE C3	PE C
visbreaking year t (millions of barrels)	PEVROW 2	-1						
	PEVROW 3		-1					
	PEVROW 4			-1				
	PEVROW 5				-1			
conventional processing year t (millions of barrels)	PECROW 2					-1		
	PECROW 3						-1	
	PECROW 4							-1
	PECROW 5							
	MXPE							

[a] Cost coefficients in rows CS CURt and CS MCURt were extrapolated from those shown in table 9, neglecting any economies of scale. Here, all refinery projects are taken to have the identical crude throughput capacity: 50 million barrels per year. This capacity is 37% larger than the unit on which table 9 was based.

[b] The nine alternative projects may be interpreted as follows:

Y1PE   Add no new refining capacity until after year 5; supply any deficits from imports of petroleum products.

Table 1

Tableau for linking continuous variable

Row identification	Column identification	Continuous variables (nuclear capacity added in year t)				
		ELNUC2	ELNUC3	ELNUC4	ELNUC5	ELNUC
nuclear generating capacity added in year t (GW)	ELROW 2	-1				
	ELROW 3		-1			
	ELROW 4			-1		
	ELROW 5				-1	
	ELROW 6					-1
	MXEL					

[a] The continuous variables ELNUCt refer to the nuclear capacity *added* in year t, and the cost coefficients for these variables are based upon a unit size of 0.6 GW. (See table 6.) No cost coefficients need therefore be added to rows CSCURt and CSMUCRt for the 12 project variables.

indivisible projects in petroleum industry [a]

C5	Mutually exclusive refinery projects [b]									
	visbreaking					conventional				
C5	Y1PE	Y2PE	Y3PE	Y4PE	Y5PE	Y6PE	Y7PE	Y8PE	Y9PE	
					50					≥ 0
				50	50					≥ 0
			50	50	50					≥ 0
		50	50	50	50					≥ 0
									50	≥ 0
								50	50	≥ 0
							50	50	50	≥ 0
1						50	50	50	50	≥ 0
	1	1	1	1	1	1	1	1	1	= 1

(Footnote b continued)

Y2PE	Add 50 million barrels of crude capacity (visbreaking process) in year 5; offset any temporary deficits or surpluses through imports or exports of petroleum products.
Y3PE	Same as Y2PE, except that the new refinery is to be brought onstream in year 4.
Y4PE	Same as Y2PE, except that the new refinery is to be brought onstream in year 3.
Y5PE	Same as Y2PE, except that the new refinery is to be brought onstream in year 2.
Y6PE–Y9PE	Same as Y2PE–Y5PE, except that the new refinery would employ conventional processing.

indivisible projects in electricity industry [a]

Mutually exclusive nuclear generating projects (size of each unit: 0.6 GW)

Y1EL	Y2EL	Y3EL	Y4EL	Y5EL	Y6EL	Y7EL	Y8EL	Y9EL	Y10EL	Y11EL	Y12EL	
					0.6	0.6	0.6	0.6	0.6	1.2	0.6	= 0
				0.6	0.6	0.6	0.6	0.6	1.2	0.6	0.6	= 0
			0.6	0.6	0.6	0.6	0.6	1.2	0.6	0.6	1.2	= 0
		0.6	0.6	0.6	0.6	0.6	1.2	0.6	0.6	0.6	1.2	= 0
	0.6	0.6	0.6	0.6	0.6	1.2	1.2	1.2	1.2	1.2	1.2	= 0
	1	1	1	1	1	1	1	1	1	1	1	= 1

8.2. Results

Results were computed for two alternative levels of the foreign exchange premium – holding the discount rate constant at 10% per year. The two IPE calculations may be summarized as follows:

Foreign exchange premium	60%	0
Optimal project combination	(6, 5, 1)	(6, 4, 7)
Total discounted costs + 15% protection on imports + foreign exchange premium (billions of pesos)	139.67	127.65
Number of steps required by IPE algorithm	11	26

In the steel sector, the optimal project choice is Y6SD – the installation of a 3.0 million ton mill in year 0. The cost of the initial excess capacity is more than offset by the economies-of-scale in subsequent years. Just as in the linear programming sensitivity analysis (table 13), it turns out that the choice of steel projects is insensitive to the foreign exchange premium.

In the petroleum sector also, the foreign exchange premium would have a minor effect. The optimal petroleum project is either Y5PE or Y4PE – which means only a one-year difference in the onstream date of a 50 million barrel plant (visbreaking process).

The choice of electricity projects *is* quite sensitive to the foreign exchange premium. If this were as high as 60%, the optimal project would be Y1EL. That is, it would be non-optimal to install nuclear generating units until some time well after year 6 (1980). With a zero foreign exchange premium, on the other hand, it would be optimal to install at least one nuclear unit each year.

What conclusions may be drawn about the extent of interdependence between project decisions in the steel, petroleum and electricity sectors? The number of steps required for convergence of the IPE algorithm may be an indicator of the strength or looseness of the coupling. Here the required number of steps is a small fraction of the logically possible maximum number ($N = 648$). If the project choices were highly interdependent, the efficiency prices would alter radically from one IPE step to the next, and many such steps would be required. [15] With perfect decomposability, on the other hand, the efficiency prices would not change at all, and a globally optimal combination could be located after just a single step. The IPE experiment suggests that ENERGETICOS provides an instance of *near*-decomposability.

References

Bessière, F., 'Methods of choosing production equipment at Electricité de France', *European Economic Review*, Winter 1969.

Bueno, G., 'The structure of protection in Mexico', in: B. Balassa, *The Structure of protection in developing countries*. Baltimore, John Hopkins Press, 1971, chapter 8.

Bueno, G., and F. González Vargas, 'La industria siderúrgica en México en los últimos años y sus perspectivas', *Hierro y Acero*, México, D.F., April 1969.

Fernández de la Garza, G., and A.S. Manne, 'A model for planning investments in generating facilities, Central-East-West systems of CFE, 1975–95'. Stanford, Calif., February 1969. (Mimeographed.)

Forster, C.I.K., and I.J. Whitting, 'An integrated mathematical model of the fuel economy', *Statistical News*, No. 3. London, Ministry of Power, November 1968.

Hitch, C., 'Sub-optimization in operations problems', *Operations Research*, May 1953.

Massé, P., and R. Gibrat, 'Applications of linear programming to investments in the electric power industry', *Management Science*, April 1957.

Quintana, C., G. Bueno and F. González Vargas, 'Process and site evaluation for the iron and steel industry in Mexico', in: *Evaluation of industrial projects*. United Nations ID/Ser. H/1, New York, 1968, chapter 21.

Rogers, S., 'A dynamic model for planning capacity expansion: an application to plant reliability and electric power systems'. Stanford, Calif., Department of Operations Research, Stanford University, May 1970.

Stanford Research Institute, *Decision analysis of nuclear power plants in electrical system expansion*. SRI Project 6496. Menlo Park, Calif., December 1968.

[15] For an example of closely complementary project decisons, see the steel-machinery example, below, chapter V.1.

III.3. ON LINKING ENERGETICOS TO DINAMICO *

Alan S. MANNE **

1. Introduction

Consider an investment decision for a single project. It is a counsel of perfection to declare that the project cannot be evaluated unless one has first constructed a model of the entire system within which the project is embedded. Such a system would be of infinite size and complexity. What we *can* attempt is to: (a) define the boundaries of a 'small world' within which the project is embedded; (b) construct a model of the project within the boundaries of that small world; and (c) check whether an extension of the boundaries is likely to make a significant difference in the policy recommendations that emerged from the model. This paper is concerned principally with step (c). It reports upon a simple test which permits us to conclude that although process substitution within the energy sector will produce indirect effects upon the remainder of the Mexican economy, these feedback effects will not in turn lead to significant changes in the demands for the outputs of the energy sector or the efficiency prices of its inputs. The test suggest that multi-level rather than simultaneous optimization techniques are appropriate for analyzing investment decisions within Mexico's energy sector.

This experiment was motivated by two numerical planning models – ENERGETICOS (a process analysis model of the energy

* This is a revised version of a paper presented at the Fifth International Conference on Input-Output Techniques, Geneva, January 1971.

** For their helpful comments on earlier drafts, the author is indebted to Louis Goreux and János Kornai. The numerical analysis was performed by Richard Inman.

sector) and DINAMICO (a dynamic multi-sector model of the Mexican economy). The latter was developed for macroeconomic purposes — calculating supply-demand balances and efficiency prices for foreign exchange, capital investment, and manpower skills. ENERGETICOS, on the other hand, was constructed for analyzing process alternatives — supply-demand balances and efficiency prices within the energy sector.

Both DINAMICO and ENERGETICOS had been formulated so as to be solvable via the identical algorithm — linear programming. Nonetheless, since the data base had been developed independently, it proved difficult to disaggregate the rows and columns so as to combine the two into a single model. E.g., in ENERGETICOS, electricity is disaggregated into 'peak power' and 'electrical energy'. Each of these items is measured in terms of physical units. In DINAMICO, there is a single input-output industry labelled 'electricity', and this is measured in terms of 1960 pesos. Product-mix disaggregation would have been even more difficult in the case of the two other input-output industries, parts of which are covered by ENERGETICOS: 'production and refining of petroleum and coal products' and 'basic metals'.

The *input*-mix to the energy sector is disaggregated further within the macroeconomic than in the sectoral model. In ENERGETICOS, manpower inputs are measured in terms of pesos and combined with all other current account costs. Within DINAMICO, manpower inputs into all sectors are disaggregated in terms of five skill categories, and are measured in terms of man-years.

Clearly, the disaggregation of the electric power product-mix is a step that improves the accuracy of project and process decisions within the energy sector. Similarly, the macroeconomic projections are improved by disaggregation of manpower skills. It remains an open question, however, whether accuracy would be still further improved by constructing a single model in which the energy sector's product-mix is disaggregated as finely as in ENERGETICOS and in which the manpower input-mix is disaggregated as finely as in DINAMICO. It is costly to gather the data needed to disaggregate rows so as to achieve consistency between the levels of aggregation adopted in two independently built models. Before making the data-gathering effort, it seems worthwhile to make an estimate of the outcome from the effort. This is the question to which the present chapter is addressed.

Why describe this question as one of 'elephant-rabbit stew'? Consider a stew obtained by cooking a single elephant, and suppose that *one* rabbit is added. The mixture is likely to taste a good deal like elephant stew. Similarly, if a sector constitutes a small fraction of an entire economy, then it is improbable that process substitution within the one sector will lead to significant feedback effects upon input costs or output quantities.

The elephant-rabbit situation is sketched on figure 1. This is an

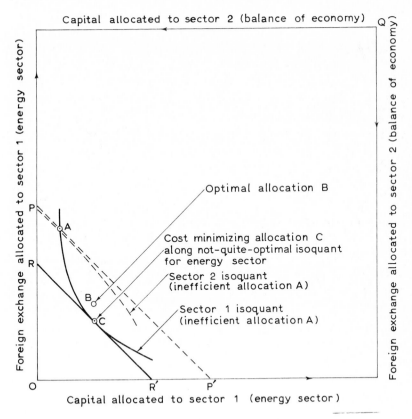

Fig. 1. Edgeworth-Bowley box diagram when energy sector is 'small'.

Edgeworth-Bowley box diagram for a two-sector, two-factor economy. Sector 1 produces energy products, and sector 2 produces all other items. There are two factors of production – capital and foreign exchange – and these are transferable between the two sectors. Denote the total capital and foreign exchange available by the vector Q. First, suppose that the factors have been allocated *in*efficiently: the vector A to the energy sector (sector 1) and the vector $Q-A$ to sector 2. Holding the product-mix constant in each sector, there will be a two-dimensional tradeoff curve between the inputs: the solid line isoquant for sector 1 and the dotted line isoquant for sector 2. Associated with this allocation, a different set of efficiency prices will prevail in the two sectors. Denote the efficiency prices *in sector 2* by the slope of the dotted price line *PAP'*.

Now in order to achieve global efficiency, it will be necessary to reallocate capital and foreign exchange so that the process choice and input-mix is shifted from A to some other point such as B. In general, the optimal allocation B will lie along a different isoquant than the inefficient allocation A, and will be supported by a different set of efficiency prices. We shall define the energy sector to be 'small', provided that: (1) the quantity of the energy sector's output at point B is close to the quantity at A, and (2) the slope of sector 2's isoquant through point B is close to the slope of *PAP'*. Thus, if the energy sector is 'small', it is sufficiently accurate for the sector to choose an input-mix such as C – one that minimizes its costs at the not-quite-optimal price line *RCR'* (parallel to *PAP'*), along the not-quite-optimal isoquant. [1] In this approximation, the energy sector is viewed as a price-taker with respect to its inputs and an output-taker with respect to its specialized product-mix. In order to optimize the process choice within the energy sector, it becomes unnecessary to construct a formal, disaggregated model for sectors 1 and 2 simultaneously. Rather, the input

---

[1] To guarantee that efficiency prices may be associated with each allocation of inputs, it is sufficient to impose a convexity condition upon the production set of sector 2. For this definition of a small sector, no convexity condition need be imposed upon sector 1. Thus, the energy sector may be 'small' and yet subject to economies-of-scale.

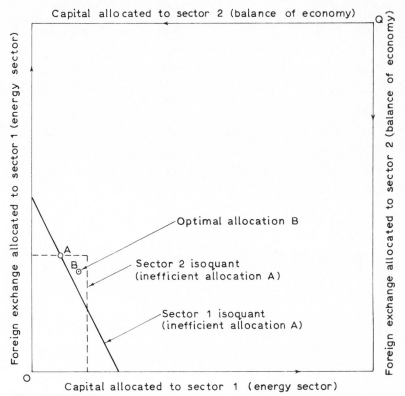

Fig. 2. Edgeworth-Bowley box diagram; low elasticity of factor substitution outside energy sector.

prices and the physical target for the product-mix are sufficient information to achieve efficient, decentralized planning within the energy sector. Perhaps it is because individual sectors are 'small' that price-quantity signals are combined in actual multi-level planning practice — unlike the Dantzig-Wolfe decomposition algorithm where only price signals are transmitted from the center to the periphery and only quantity signals from the periphery to the center. (See Malinvaud 1967 and Weitzman 1970.)

To check whether the energy sector satisfies the definition proposed here, it is *not* sufficient to verify that its input requirements are a small fraction of the totals available within the economy. Consider the Edgeworth-Bowley diagram in figure 2. In this example, there is such a low elasticity of substitution elsewhere that the energy sector's process choice itself determines the economy-wide marginal rates of substitution between capital and foreign exchange. The efficiency prices of these inputs are no longer exogenous data to the energy sector.

2. The linkage experiment − demands for the sector's product-mix

In order to conclude that the energy sector is 'small', two possible sources of feedback must be checked: (1) the effects upon the demands for the sector's product-mix, and (2) the effects upon the efficiency prices of its inputs. [2] In applying DINAMICO to measure feedback effects upon demands, we have begun with an extreme assumption − postulating that the choice of techniques would permit a 20% increase in the productivity of the capital, labor, and intermediate inputs required for output increments within the energy sector.

Modifying the input-output coefficients within the energy sectors to allow for a 20% productivity increase, and rerunning the basic case of DINAMICO, it turns out that the maximand (aggregate consumption) would increase from 242.4 to 243.4 billion pesos, and that there would be less than a 1% increase in the 1980 gross domestic product. The increase in demand for the energy sector's products would also be less than 1%. According to DINAMICO, then, there are negligible substitution effects upon the demand for energy products. This is an unreasonable implication − one that stems from non-substitutability within the Leontief structure of the multi-sector model. For simultaneous optimization of the energy sector with the balance of the Mexican economy, this experiment suggests that it would *not* be sufficient to disaggregate the rows of DINAMICO so as to be consistent with the product-

---

[2] Both linkage experiments were conducted with an earlier version of DINAMICO than the one described in this volume. The earlier version is reported in memorandum 70–12, available upon request to Development Research Center, International Bank for Reconstruction and Development, 1818 H. Street, N.W., Washington, D.C. 20433, U.S.A.

mix details of ENERGETICOS. In order to estimate the feedback effects of the process choice upon the demand for energy products, it would also be necessary to include alternative columns reflecting substitution possibilities for these energy products elsewhere within the economy.

Even after the data-gathering effort on row and column disaggregation, it is not clear that the feedback effects would be substantial. To check whether process substitution within the energy sector could affect demands or efficiency prices, six alternative solutions to ENERGETICOS were calculated. Like the isoquant for sector 1 in figure 1, each of these six represents an alternative process choice in which the deliveries of energy products to other sectors remain constant. Each is a summary of a cost-minimizing solution at a different price of capital and/or foreign exchange. The input prices have been predetermined within moderately realistic limits: a foreign exchange scarcity premium ranging from 0 to 60% and an annual discount rate of 10 and 20%. At the low discount rate and foreign exchange premium, it is optimal to install nuclear rather than fossil electric generating capacity. Conversely, when the discount rate and foreign exchange premium are at the high end of the predetermined range, the fossil process minimizes costs.

Table 1 contains most of the empirical evidence for the view that Mexico's energy sector is a price-taker for its inputs and an output-taker for its specialized product-mix. One piece of evidence is to be found in the bottommost line. This line compares the total discounted cost of the six alternative programs, evaluating all inputs at conventional prices: a 10% discount rate and a zero scarcity premium on foreign exchange. Given this cost structure, program 1 minimizes total discounted input costs. Note, however, that even with the most expensive alternative (program 6), the conventional costs would increase by only 4%. (A similar result holds true at each of the other input price combinations considered here.) Although the six programs are based upon different choices of technological process, none of these alternatives implies a radical difference in total costs. Hence, if the cost difference between the six process choices is 4% and if the long-run price

Table 1
Summary of six alternative cost-minimizing programs for energy sector
(unit: billions of 1960 pesos unless stated otherwise)

| | ENERGETICOS [a] program j | | | | | | Aggregative results from DINAMICO [b] | | |
	1	2	3	4	5	6	Aggregate investment	Aggregate import expenditures	Row identification item i
Investment expenditures for energy sector capacity first available in year									
1974	2.37	2.76	2.86	2.16	2.37	2.76	82.66		G1
1977	4.21	3.93	3.93	3.68	3.77	3.65	94.70		G2
1980	5.51	4.68	4.90	4.71	4.83	4.68	121.59		G3
Import costs less export earnings for energy sector in year									
1974	0.78	0.59	0.55	1.40	0.92	0.74		35.64	F2
1977	1.10	0.97	0.86	2.00	1.40	1.23		41.24	F3
1980	1.31	1.32	1.27	2.76	2.01	1.81		50.74	F4
Annual discount rate for which program j is optimal (%)	10	10	10	20	20	20			
Foreign exchange scarcity premium for which program j is optimal (%)	0	30	60	0	30	60			
Total discounted costs at conventional prices (billions of 1970 pesos discounted to 1974 at 10% per year)	127.34	127.95	129.27	128.62	132.43	132.68			

[a] Source: Tables 12 and 13, chapter III.2 above. In those tables, the energy sector's input requirements are stated in terms of 1970 prices. To convert 1970 into 1960 pesos, these were multiplied by a price correction factor of 0.70.

[b] Source: Memorandum 70-12, tables 2 and 3 (an early version of DINAMICO, not directly comparable with chapter II.3 of this volume).

elasticity of demand for energy products is as high as unity, this would mean that process substitution could not itself lead to a difference of more than 4% in the demand for these items. Such a difference would lie well within the range of probable forecasting errors.

3. The linkage experiment – efficiency prices for the sector's input-mix

Six alternative vectors of input requirements appear in table 1. Here, unlike the isoquants of figures 1 and 2, both foreign exchange and capital investment must be disaggregated in time: an input of each item for each of the three representative years 1974, 1977 and 1980. [3] To simplify the comparison of alternative programs, this neglects *differences* [4] in labor inputs and in current account interindustry inputs into the energy sector.

For comparison, the rightmost column of table 1 contains year-by-year projections of aggregate investment and aggregate import requirements from the macroeconomic model DINAMICO. It can be seen that there is no year in which the net import requirements for the energy sector exceed 5.4% of the total for all sectors. Moreover, there is no year in which the energy sector's investment requirements would exceed 4.5% of the economy-wide total. These percentages are suggestive, but not conclusive in themselves.

[3] The time-phasing of DINAMICO does not coincide with that of ENERGETICOS. The former is based on three-year intervals extending from 1968. The latter is based on year-by-year intervals from 1974 through 1980 and five-year intervals thereafter for the electricity sector through 1995. The difference in time-phasing is by no means arbitrary. Rather, it corresponds to differences in the policy decisions to which the two individual models are addressed.

[4] Provided that several components of the input vector remain identical between each of the six alternatives, it can be proved that these components may be neglected, and that this will not affect the test described below. Unfortunately, there is evidence that the neglected input components do differ from one to another of the six programs. In table 2 (which summarizes the experiments neglecting the inputs of labor and of current account interindustry flows), there is a 29% difference between the costs of programs 3 and 4. In itself, this does not invalidate the principal finding of the test – that there are no significant effects of the energy sector upon the efficiency prices of its inputs.

Recall figure 2, the Edgeworth-Bowley box diagram, where the elasticity of factor substitution is low outside the energy sector. It is because of this possibility that an explicit link might be needed between DINAMICO and ENERGETICOS.

To see why we adopted a particular test for feedback effects between the two models, it is important to realize that there is a wide gap between their statistical coverage. Such gaps are typical whenever the primary data for a process analysis model are gathered independently from those collected for national income accounting and input-output purposes. E.g., within DINAMICO, the electric power industry (input-output sector 12) includes facilities for hydroelectric power generation and for electricity distribution to small-scale commercial and residential consumers. Within ENERGETICOS, no process choice is considered for these facilities, and their input requirements are not included in table 1. Similarly, in ENERGETICOS the iron and steel process choices refer only to the primary ingot stage — omitting steel rolling and fabrication facilities and also omitting the non-ferrous metals plants that are included along with primary steel within the basic metals industry (input-output sector 9). For the petroleum, petrochemicals and coal products industry (input-output sector 3), there are similar difficulties in making comparisons of coverage between ENERGETICOS and DINAMICO. Worse yet, the accounting conventions for capital expenditures and for depletion are quite unclear in an industry where the returns are as uncertain as they are in the production of crude petroleum and natural gas.

In order to solve this coverage problem in a satisfactory way, more data-gathering work would be needed than went into ENERGETICOS itself. Our test represents a shortcut alternative to disaggregation — estimating an upper bound upon the intersectoral impact of process substitution. This bound is calculated as though the lowest-cost program were substituted in place of the highest-cost one, holding constant the product-mix within ENERGETICOS. That is, the DINAMICO optimization is repeated, allowing any convex combination of the six alternatives from ENERGETICOS to be increased — and simultaneously allowing any convex combination of the six programs to be decreased.

Table 2

Evaluation of six alternative programs for energy sector, employing dual variables from DINAMICO

DINAMICO row identification, item i	ENERGETICOS program j						Dual variables from DINAMICO (unit: pesos' worth of aggregate consumption maximand per thousand pesos' worth of item i)	
	Program summary coefficients α_{ij} (unit: billions of pesos, item i)						Before linkage, π_i^0	After linkage, π_i^1
	1	2	3	4	5	6		
G1	2.37	2.76	2.86	2.16	2.37	2.76	63.14	63.16
G2	4.21	3.93	3.93	3.68	3.77	3.65	51.70	51.58
G3	5.51	4.68	4.90	4.71	4.83	4.68	31.14	31.03
F2	0.78	0.59	0.55	1.40	0.92	0.74	93.17	91.61
F3	1.10	0.97	0.86	2.00	1.40	1.23	61.17	60.15
F4	1.31	1.32	1.27	2.76	2.01	1.81	87.22	86.99
Cost of program j evaluated at dual variables before linkage experiment (unit: millions of pesos' worth of maximand) = $\sum_i \alpha_{ij}\pi_i^0$	793	753	751	967	842	811		
Cost of program j evaluated at dual variables after linkage experiment (unit: millions of pesos' worth of maximand) = $\sum_i \alpha_{ij}\pi_i^1$	789	749	748	961	837	807		

To describe this linkage device algebraically, let the coefficient α_{ij} denote the aggregate requirement of DINAMICO item i by ENERGETICOS program j. (The matrix of these coefficients appears in the six leftmost columns and the six topmost rows of table 1, and is repeated in table 2.) Let the interpolation weight unknowns λ_j be nonnegative to allow for program increases, and let the interpolation weight unknowns μ_j be nonpositive to allow for program decreases. The activities operated at intensities λ_j and μ_j are adjoined to the original terms in DINAMICO as follows:

$$\sum_{j=1}^{6} \alpha_{ij}(\lambda_j + \mu_j) + \text{original terms in row } i \text{ of DINAMICO}$$

$$\sum_{j=1}^{6} \lambda_j = 1; \quad \lambda_j \geqslant 0$$

$$\sum_{j=1}^{6} \mu_j = -1; \quad \mu_j \leqslant 0.$$

When the interpolation weight variables λ_j and μ_j are added to DINAMICO, it is optimal to set $\lambda_3 = 1$ and $\mu_4 = -1$. This means altering the structure of input requirements as though the lowest-cost program ($j = 3$) could be substituted entirely in place of the highest-cost program ($j = 4$). This is exactly what might have been anticipated from a partial equilibrium analysis applying the efficiency prices prevailing in DINAMICO before the introduction of the energy sector's alternative programs into the general equilibrium system. From table 2, it can be seen that the efficiency prices of investment inputs and of foreign exchange are hardly affected by the substitution of the process alternatives. The value of the maximand (aggregate consumption) is increased in the fourth significant digit: from 242.359 to 242.572 billion pesos. [5] The ef-

---

[5] When energy sector process substitution is included within DINAMICO in this way, it is clear that the value of the maximand cannot be decreased. In order to cancel out the effect of the additional two rows and 12 columns, it would be sufficient to pick an arbitrary program j and set $\lambda_j = -\mu_j = 1$.

fects upon production levels are of similar orders-of-magnitude — close to the status of numerical roundoff errors.

4. Concluding comments

This experiment suggests no more than the following conclusions: Regardless of whether Mexico relies upon nuclear or fossil electric generating processes during the late 1970's, it is unlikely that the general economic environment will itself be affected by the process choice. The conclusion would hold even though between 1976 and 1980, there were nuclear capacity installed equivalent to six plants — each unit 0.6 GW in capacity and each costing over 100 million U.S. dollars in initial capital investment. Relative to the size and elasticity of substitution of the Mexican economy, this particular set of projects would introduce no more than second-order effects outside the energy sector. Clearly, the process choice affects the optimal quantity and the efficiency price of specific *intra*sectoral items such as industrial fossil fuel. This is the rationale for multi-level planning of investment decisions.

We do not assert that process substitution will generally lead to second-order effects. Here it is essential to avoid a logical snare, the fallacy of composition. When not one but 100 rabbits are added to an elephant stew, the taste of the mixture *does* change. Within DINAMICO, the results are significantly affected by the presence or absence of alternative processes for capital-labor substitution within the agricultural sector. (In 1968, half of Mexico's labor force was engaged in agriculture.) Effort in linking sectoral and macroeconomic models is more likely to be instructive in the case of agriculture than in the energy sector.

References

Malinvaud, E., 'Decentralized procedures for planning', in: *Activity Analysis in the Theory of Growth and Planning*, edited by E. Malinvaud and M.O.L. Bacharach. London, Macmillan, 1967, chapter 7.
Weitzman, M., 'Iterative multilevel planning with production targets', *Econometrica*, January 1970.

PART IV. THE AGRICULTURAL SECTOR

IV1. CHAC, A PROGRAMMING MODEL OF MEXICAN AGRICULTURE

John H. DULOY and Roger D. NORTON *

1. Introduction

Agriculture in Mexico, as in most developing economies, is a major source of employment and foreign exchange earnings. About half of the country's labor force is agricultural. Directly and indirectly through both raw and processed products, agriculture accounts for over half of export earnings. The crucial role played by agriculture in the economic development of Mexico is widely acknowledged. [1] It was partly because of this pivotal role that agriculture was singled out for detailed analysis in this multi-level planning study. It offers an opportunity to explore relationships between sector policies and economy-wide development strategies. Agriculture also provides an example of strong linkages between investment project decisions and sector-level policies. Agricultural trade

* The authors are grateful to Leopoldo Solís of the Secretaría de la Presidencia for his encouragement and continuous support and his patience during the long gestation period of this model. We also gratefully acknowledge the support of the Banco de México, which devoted considerable resources to this study. The agricultural study was conceived by Louis Goreux and Alan Manne, who have given us useful comments and criticism throughout, and it has drawn upon the earlier work of Luciano Barraza, now of the Secretaría de Agricultura y Ganadería. Dr. Barraza has provided helpful comments on several aspects of the study. The enormous burden of constructing most of the 80,000 coefficients in the model has been borne with unflagging energy and goodwill by Luz María Bassoco, of Presidencia, and Teresa Rendón, then of the Banco de México. Apostolos Condos and Donald Winkelmann provided helpful discussions of a number of aspects of the model's structure. Gary Kutcher became a (nearly prostrate) human link between the model and the computer, and gave useful comments on the model's design.

[1] See, for example, Solís (1970).

policies and policies on pricing inputs and products significantly
affect the rates of return estimated for individual projects.

Therefore the initial aim in constructing the agricultural model,
CHAC [2], was to formalize the major aspects of micro-level and
sectoral decision-making. In keeping with the orientation of this
volume, the broad theme of the agriculture study is linkages between different levels of decision-making, but as usual in model-
building, there is more than one underlying purpose.

Aside from the multi-level aspects, the sector study has also
been designed to serve both the Mexican Government's interest in
analytic tools for planning sectoral policies, and the World Bank's
interest in the methodology of project appraisal techniques and in
general policy planning models. As a tool for policy makers,
CHAC is designed to be addressed to questions of pricing policies,
trade policies, employment programs, and some categories of investment allocation. It is not particularly well suited for analyzing
agricultural research and extension programs, crop insurance policies, or credit policies. It is structured so that it is a simple matter
to change factor prices, including costs of labor, capital, water,
and agricultural chemicals, and to represent subsidies to production by crop and geographical area. The prices received by farmers
and paid by consumers for internationally tradeable commodities
also may be adjusted readily to reflect tariff, taxation, and exchange rate policies.

Commodity demand functions are included within the structure
of CHAC, and hence prices are determined by demand as well as
supply conditions. [3] Since relative product and factor prices are
the dominant policy instruments in agriculture, this feature of the
model gives scope for a wide variety of policy experiments.

The production side of the model is decomposable into submodels for each of twenty geographical areas (referred to as
'districts'). Under appropriate assumptions on prices, each submodel may be solved separately. (This permitted checking each

---

[2] CHAC takes its name from a rain god of the Maya.

[3] Some programming models yield marginal costs of production, or 'supply prices',
but in the absence of demand functions these do not yield market equilibrium prices.
See, e.g., Heady et al. (1966), and Piñeiro and McCalla (1971).

of the submodels prior to its inclusion in CHAC.) Three of the submodels, for the El Bajío districts, have been formulated with a wider array of farm types so that they may serve jointly as a 'project model'. The project model was first solved in isolation to estimate a rate of return schedule for potential fixed investments. It was then incorporated into the sector model to see how inter-regional comparative advantage affects the estimated benefits to investment in the area.

The version of CHAC reported here covers only short-cycle crops. [4] Tree crops, livestock, forestry, and fisheries have been excluded. There is significant interdependence between the short-cycle crops and livestock through forage production and pricing and through allocation of labor and capital. There is also competition with some long-cycle crops for land and other resources. Nevertheless, it was decided to limit the scope of this version in the interests of a more thorough treatment. Work is underway on companion models of tree crops and livestock. These may be solved independently, but also may be linked with CHAC for some purposes.

CHAC contains some 1,500 equations and 80,000 nonzero co-efficients. For the purposes of extensive experimentation and the linkage with DINAMICO, it appeared worthwhile to do some work with an aggregated version of CHAC. To date, only a few experiments have been conducted on aggregation effects.

2. Overview of the model

CHAC is a sector-wide model in the sense that it describes total national supply and use — production, imports, domestic demand, and exports — for the 33 principal short-cycle crops in Mexico. [5] It is a one-period model for the target year of 1974. The timing of investment decisions cannot be studied, but investment choices are

---

[4] Annual crops plus sugar cane and alfalfa.

[5] The 33 crops represent more than 99% of the value of production of short-cycle crops. See table 1 for a list of crops and production levels.

Table 1
Area harvested and value of production of the crops in CHAC (1966–67)

Crop [a]	Irrigated		Non-irrigated		Total	
	Area harvested (ha.)	Value (000 pesos)	Area harvested (ha.)	Value (000 pesos)	Area harvested (ha.)	Value (000 pesos)
Maize	441,939	826,407	7,844,996	7,681,953	8,286,935	8,508,360
Cotton fiber	415,997	2,521,700	279,382	887,876	695,379	3,409,576
Sugar cane	85,280	445,141	402,318	1,572,298	487,598	2,017,439
Beans	45,569	109,628	2,194,453	1,704,005	2,240,022	1,813,633
Wheat	421,685	1,113,180	304,910	304,050	726,595	1,417,230
Sorghum	268,037	487,479	307,823	414,040	575,860	901,519
Green alfalfa	24,784	151,465	83,347	602,982	108,131	754,447
Tomatoes	18,713	641,201	6,000	91,000	24,713	723,201
Rice (unhulled)	58,482	211,843	94,160	206,916	152,642	418,759
Sesame	36,349	71,281	215,760	278,877	252,109	350,158
Safflower	100,679	201,768	64,254	126,633	164,933	328,401
Strawberries	3,371	45,412	5,454	282,849	8,825	328,261
Tobacco	2,348	25,913	37,260	277,127	39,608	303,040
Watermelon	3,272	20,669	30,228	258,637	33,500	279,306
Potatoes	3,428	33,550	30,854	228,382	34,282	261,932
Green chile	5,975	57,337	36,527	150,417	42,502	207,754
Chickpeas	28,533	41,538	132,574	159,109	161,107	200,647
Barley	14,691	41,792	226,059	135,626	240,750	177,418
Pineapple	–	–	9,924	175,913	9,924	175,913
Dry chile	765	8,740	23,619	144,757	24,384	153,497
Dry alfalfa	31,989	137,819	–	–	31,989	137,819
Soybeans	42,601	122,771	11,642	12,635	54,243	135,406
Cantaloupe	7,167	68,689	8,567	65,272	15,734	133,961
Peanuts	5,452	16,473	57,229	103,982	62,681	120,455
Squash	–	–	16,150	110,279	16,150	110,279
Onions	1,725	12,306	15,281	72,014	17,006	84,320
Oats	963	1,993	74,457	54,131	75,420	56,124
Lima beans	1,307	2,283	46,393	51,422	47,700	53,705
Garlic	602	5,430	5,231	30,305	5,833	35,735
Flaxseed	4,369	10,917	14,133	22,755	18,502	33,672
Totals	2,076,072	7,434,725	12,578,985	16,206,242	14,655,057	23,640,967

[a] This list excludes cucumbers and cottonseed, and it shows only one of the two forms of barley (that which is harvested whole and grain barley). There are altogether 33 crops in the model.

Source: Secretaría de Recursos Hidráulicos, Dirección de Distritos de Riego; Secretaría de Agricultura y Ganadería, Dirección de Economía Agrícola.

included in the model. On the demand side, consumer behavior is regarded as price-dependent, and thus market-clearing commodity prices are endogenous to the model.

The crops included in CHAC represent about 49% of the value of production in DINAMICO's input-output sector 1. The other components of this input-ouput sector are fisheries, forestry, livestock, and long-cycle crops. The implications of this difference in coverage for the CHAC-DINAMICO link are discussed in chapter IV.6 below.

Basically, CHAC has been structured from the viewpoint of micro-economics rather than macro theory. One reflection of this is the level of disaggregation: individual farm products are distinguished and factor inputs are disaggregated seasonally. A less trivial reflection of the micro-economic orientation is the fact that the model describes a particular form of market equilibrium, in terms of prices and quantities, with corresponding representations of producer and consumer behavior. In most of the solutions reported here, the market form is taken to be competitive, but the same programming structure can be utilized to represent the sector as a monopolistic supplier of agricultural products. Purely as a descriptive matter, the competitive market mechanism is closer to the actual processes which determine production and prices in Mexican agriculture, and, therefore, has been adopted as the basis for the model. Government policies, such as price supports, import quotas, and input subsidies and their impacts on producers' incomes, employment, and other variables, are evaluated as interventions in a basically competitive market.

Factor markets are specified in less detail. All purchased inputs and services of machinery and draft animals are priced at observed market prices, except for those experiments in which input prices are explicitly subsidized or taxed. The supply of these inputs is assumed to be infinitely elastic. Water charges are included at the level of actual pumping costs for well water and administrative levies for the release of reservoir water. Since seasonal and annual limits to the availability of water are specified, the effective water price is augmented by a rental element. The rent is explicit in the dual solution. Cultivable land is specified in limited quantities. For land, the opportunity cost constitutes its entire valuation in the model. [6]

The labor supply functions are based on observed wages by region, and the labor market equilibrium is viewed as competitive. It is assumed that the services of hired labor are offered at observed market wages, and that farmers offer their services at a positive reservation price below the market wage. A low but positive value has been taken for the farmers' reservation wage. Despite the underemployment that is characteristic of Mexican agriculture, farmers' time always has an opportunity cost. This cost may reflect either the production foregone or the opportunity to engage in traditional social activities. (Through this device, CHAC allows for 'fence-mending' and other non-market production activities.)

This formulation means that the efficiency wage will be positive even during seasons in which there is underemployment. To this extent, the structure of CHAC follows the 'subsistence' wage tradition of Ricardo, Marx, and W. Arthur Lewis. It is, however, the money wage and not the real wage which is fixed. Since product prices may change, the real wage is variable. While the wage represents total earnings for hired labor, farmers in CHAC earn a rent in some seasons from land, water, and their labor. Thus total annual earnings for farmers are greater than the wage and are variable in the model.

In all solutions, the same maximand is used, the sum of producers' and consumers' surpluses. This ensures that the optimal solution will be a competitive market equilibrium. [7] The model is not solved under, say, an employment maximand. Employment should be viewed as a means to an end — an improved standard of living for the average citizen. Moreover, it is not clear which policy instruments, if any, could implement an employment-maximizing solution. Rather, the employment implications of specific policy changes are simulated. When policy changes are involved, the in-

---

[6] For a comparison of the actual land prices with those implied by the model's opportunity costs, see below, chapter IV.4.

[7] There may be departures from a competitive equilibrium when constraints are imposed to calculate the effects of government policy interventions.

struments are made explicit in the model, and thus the sectoral implications of a policy change can be estimated.

A brief mention of some major qualitative results of the model will help illuminate the essential points of its structure. When solved for different points in time, the model shows a higher social than private return to investments. Farmers' per capita incomes tend to grow rather slowly even though production may be increasing at the historical rate. This phenomenon is not inconsistent with the experience of many countries. The process of development has been accompanied by ever-increasing budgetary outlays on agricultural subsidies in order to counter adverse market pressures on incomes. This is a reflection of the assumption that the demand for most agricultural products is price-inelastic, and that the market structure is competitive. It will be optimal for an atomistic, price-taking producer to invest, although in the aggregate this may make producers worse off than otherwise.

In order to address these policy questions, a wide range of technological choices in production were included in the model, along with domestic demand and trade activities. There are more than 2,300 different production techniques for 33 crops in 20 districts, ranging from completely non-mechanized to completely mechanized, and including different degrees of efficacy in irrigation as well as in non-irrigated techniques. Throughout, this chapter describes the fully disaggregated structure. The aggregation to form CHAQUITO is discussed in section 11.

3. Basic structure of the model

Separation of sources of supply and demand, for both products and inputs, is the basic rule under which CHAC is specified. For each crop, there are production activities differentiated by location and technique, and, for 21 of the 33 crops, there are importing activities. There are corresponding activities for sales on the domestic and export markets. Effectively, the model contains multiple-step supply and demand functions for each crop, and these functions for different crops are interdependent. For most crops, the implicit sector-wide supply function contains dozens of steps, and in some cases there are more than one hundred steps. The demand formulation is flexible and permits an arbitrarily close approximation to a non-linear utility function.

The commodity balance equations require the clearing of markets, with simultaneous determination of equilibrium prices and quantities. Production for own-consumption is given an imputed price equal to the price for commercial production. For non-traded agricultural goods, the prices are completely endogenous. For internationally traded crops, however, they must lie between the import and export prices. The assumed import and export prices may be varied in alternative solutions to reflect different world market conditions and tariff policies. Some sets of prices may be fixed in order to investigate the effects of price support policies. Export quotas are incorporated for a number of crops to reflect the realities of international markets.

The incorporation of demand functions (instead of exogenous product prices) provides a more realistic description of the aggregate market conditions faced by farmers. Moreover, it reduces the tendency of programming models to seek solutions with extreme crop specialization. It also opens the door to investigation of the impacts of public interventions under different forms of market structure. With appropriate modifications in the objective function, the same model may simulate a sector which behaves either as a monopolistic supplier of products or as a collection of competitive producers. By casting one of the objective functions in the role of a constraint, it is possible to explore the tradeoffs and complementarities between producers' and consumers' welfare.

The cropping activities in the model also constitute factor demand activities. Factors are supplied by a separate set of activities, and there are balance equations to ensure equilibrium on the factor markets. Some factor supply functions are perfectly elastic (e.g., chemicals and capital), and others are perfectly inelastic (e.g., some categories of land). In the former category, factor prices are exogenous to the model, in the latter they are endogenous. In intermediate cases, they are endogenous within limits. Labor falls in the intermediate category. When factor prices are exogenous, the factor is regarded as a national resource, i.e., it has an opportunity cost in other sectors or in international trade. At the other extreme, there are factors in inelastic supply which have no economic use outside the sector in the short run. Agricultural land and water are placed in this category of sector-specific resources.

The demands for land, labor, and water are defined at seasonal intervals. [8] All other inputs are treated on an annual basis, including services of farm machinery and draft animals. Virtually all farm machinery is in the form of tractors and is used in the irrigated areas of the central plateau and the arid northern zones. Due to the nearly uniform year-round climate in these areas, there is not a very pronounced degree of seasonality in aggregate demand for machinery services. Hence, to simplify an already complex model, the seasonal specification has been dropped in the case of machinery.

Labor is divided into three classes: farm owners plus their family labor, hired (landless) agricultural labor, and machinery operators. Local and interregional migration activities are included for landless labor and for farmers on rainfed farms. [9] Machinery operators constitute less than five percent of the agricultural labor force, and their supply does not appear to be a bottleneck in Mexican agriculture. They are assumed to be supplied in fixed proportion to machinery services — with an infinite elasticity of supply. The wage for machinery operators is higher than the wage for hired labor. Both types of wages vary among regions, in accordance with observed behavior.

As noted, in any particular month, farmers are assumed to be willing to work for an own wage, or reservation price, which is lower than the hired labor wage. Thus, in ascending order of marginal cost, the sources of labor supply are the following: (1) using the labor of the farmer and his family, (2) hiring local landless labor, (3) hiring surplus landless labor from other regions, and (4)

---

[8] Monthly in CHAC and four-monthly in the aggregated version, CHAQUITO.

[9] Throughout this volume, the English words 'rainfed' and 'dryland' and the Spanish word 'temporal' are used interchangeably.

hiring landless labor away from lower-productivity employment in other regions. The model is structured in a form that permits ready adjustment of all wages, so that various experiments – such as measuring capital-labor substitution – may be conducted.

4. Spatial disaggregation

On the product supply side, each of the twenty submodels represents either irrigated, rainfed, or tropical cultivation, and each covers a particular set of counties or districts, which are not necessarily contiguous. [10] In the case of rainfed and tropical agriculture, the submodels are defined on the basis of annual rainfall and altitude, which determine climatic conditions. Cropping and investment activities are specified by submodel. The submodels are grouped into four geographical regions, and labor constraints are specified for each region, in order to capture the differential labor mobility and wage rates which exist in Mexico. The four regions are the Northwest, the North, the Central Plateau, and the South. In terms of the 'subsistence-modern' dichotomy, the irrigated submodels represent the modern, capital-intensive form of cultivation and the non-irrigated submodels tend to represent the subsistence regimes. This is an oversimplification, however. Within the irrigated submodels, there is considerable variation in degrees of mechanization, depending on the factor endowments and ecological conditions. Likewise, some parts of non-irrigated agriculture, especially tropical, cannot be properly called subsistence.

Although there are landless agricultural laborers who live in each region and gain a livelihood from part-time work on irrigated farms, the bulk of them reside in the Central Plateau region. In this region, there is closer access to the major urban centers for part-time work, and small rainfed plots may be cultivated. The dominant direction of seasonal labor migration is between the Central Plateau and the North and Northwest. There also is some movement from the South to the Central Plateau and the northern regions. Due to the distances involved, this is apt to be more

---

[10] The submodels and the data sources are described in chapter IV.2 below.

permanent than seasonal migration. To help limit the size of the model, seasonal and permanent migration activities have been specified only for the three directions of significant net interregional flow: (a) from Central Plateau to Northwest, (b) from Central Plateau to North, and (c) from South to Central Plateau. Observed wages for hired labor are lowest in the South and highest in the Northwest. This reflects, at least in part, the relative abundance of labor in the tropical areas and the Central Plateau. Migration is a gradual process, and regional wage differentials have persisted for decades.

The constraints for each district submodel — primarily the annual and monthly bounds on land, water, and farmers — form a block in the block-diagonal production tableau (see figure 1). Since the constraints in one block are independent of all other constraints, additional submodels may be added to the system, with appropriate modifications in the coverage of the existing submodels. In this way, the model may be focused on the detailed choices in one geographical area, while treating other areas in a more aggregate fashion.

Demand functions are specified nationally rather than for each geographical submodel. [11] The only exceptions are a few food crops for which separate regional markets are introduced in the South and in the Northwest. (There is a high cost of transportation between the tropics and the other parts of Mexico.) It is not assumed, however that each submodel can equally well supply the 'national' market. Spatial price differentials are used, and these reflect the differential transport costs faced by each submodel area, based on the historical patterns of transportation. Thus, the Northwest region farmers receive a lower farm-gate price for vegetables than do the Central Plateau farmers, for the latter are located closer to the major urban markets of Mexico City and Guadalajara. For export crops, proximity to major ports determines the spatial pattern of price differentials.

---

[11] This simplification was adopted because there was insufficient information on the spatial distribution of demand. Moreover, the introduction of local demand activities would enlarge the programming model still further.

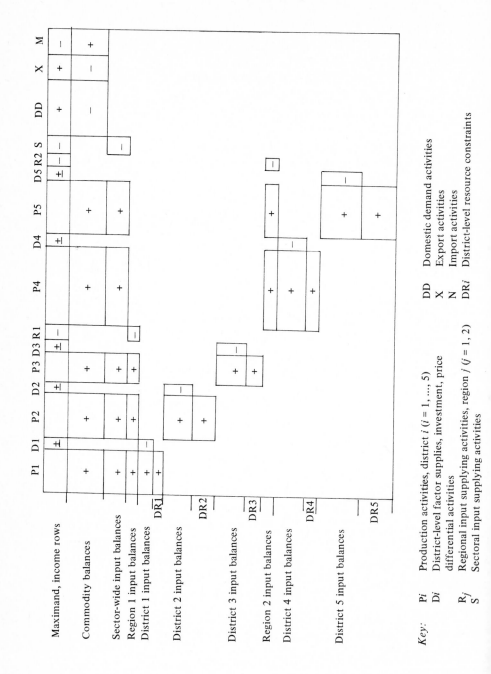

Key: Pi   Production activities, district i ($i = 1, ..., 5$)   DD   Domestic demand activities
      Di   District-level factor supplies, investment, price   X   Export activities
           differential activities   N   Import activities
      R_j Regional input supplying activities, region j ($j = 1, 2$)   DRi District-level resource constraints
      S   Sectoral input supplying activities

In the case of the South, the submodels there may sell corn, for example, against a downward sloping local demand schedule. By incurring a transportation charge, they may offer any additional corn on the national market. Similarly, the Central Plateau has the option of selling part of its output on the South's market, provided that it incurs the transportation cost differential.

5. The production technology set

CHAC contains 2,345 cropping activities to describe alternative techniques for producing the 33 crops. The range of variation in these activities is described fully in chapter IV.2 below. Each cropping activity defines a yield per hectare, together with fixed proportions of the following inputs: land (monthly), water (monthly and annual), labor (monthly), machinery services, draft animals, chemicals, purchased seeds, and short-term institutional credit. The relations between inputs and outputs are those which have been observed (and projected) in each locale, and not necessarily the biological or profit-maximizing optima. In principle, the possibilities for movement toward more efficient input-output mixes could be represented through activities for extension services. The existing data, however, do not provide a reliable basis for estimating the costs and benefits of extension.

The ratio of each input and output varies over the submodel for every crop. Some localities have shorter growing seasons than others, and so the number of months of land differs. Fertilization practices vary, especially between irrigated and non-irrigated areas. For irrigation, the amount of gross water release required at the dam depends on the length and condition of the canals. This too varies from area to area. In addition, there are systematic variations within many of the submodels in the input-output ratios — particularly in the amounts of water, machinery services, and labor per unit of output. [12]

---

[12] For a given crop, variations in water-output ratios occur within five of the ten irrigation submodels. The machinery and labor requirements per unit of output vary within all twenty submodels.

For some of the irrigation submodels, the land is grouped into four classes, based on efficiency of gross water use. [13] For all of the submodels, alternative degrees of mechanization have been specified in CHAC: totally non-mechanized (all power operations done with draft animals), partially mechanized, and fully mechanized (no draft animal use). Obviously there can be many degrees of partial mechanization, but in actuality the choices are discrete and few. E.g., plowing is done either with mules or with tractors, but not with both. To avoid overstating farmers' short-run flexibility, one-degree changes of technique are permitted between 1968 and 1974, but not two-degree changes. If the farmers in the area covered by one submodel were using totally non-mechanized techniques in the statistical base year, that submodel contains non-mechanized and partially mechanized techniques only. Similarly, it is assumed that fully mechanized farms may revert to partial mechanization but not to non-mechanization, even under drastic changes in relative prices.

The major advantage of mechanization, versus the use of draft animals, lies in land savings. One crop can be harvested, and the ground prepared for the next crop, significantly faster with tractors than with draft animals. [14] In some cases, this time saving makes it possible to plant a second crop during the year. This saving is shown in the model by requiring fewer months of land with the more mechanized techniques. If one hectare is required for ten instead of thirty days, the first month's land requirement is represented by a coefficient of 0.33 instead of 1.0.

Differential land (and labor) requirements also constitute the distinction between two forms of the same crop. For example, alfalfa may be sold green, at a lower price per ton, or left on the land longer and sold dry, at a higher price. In the case of barley, the farmer also faces a choice — of harvesting the entire plant and selling it as forage, or of using substantially less labor and harvest-

---

[13] This in turn is due to terrain conditions, distance from the water source, and state of repair of the canals.

[14] One might think that the same savings could be achieved by simply using more mule teams. As anyone who has worked with mules knows, however, there are limits to the number which one farmer can supervise.

ing only the grain. As in the case of alfalfa, there is a separate demand function for both types, so prices move in the model in response to these production choices. For grain barley, there is an additional component on the demand side, the demand for malt grain. There is a minor element of post-harvest on-farm processing for the grain which is destined for malt, but this is ignored here. There are then two domestic markets specified for grain barley: malt and non-malt.

For cotton also, CHAC contains two markets. This arises from the joint-product nature of cotton. Separate demand functions are specified for both cotton fiber and cotton seeds. In the case of seeds, the price depends partly on the volume of production of other oilseeds. Hence in the model, the profitability of growing cotton depends on (a) the demand schedule for cotton fiber, (b) the demand schedule for oilseeds, (c) the production surface for competing oilseeds crops, and (d) the production technology for cotton.

There is another dichotomy on the production side which is not explicit in CHAC, and that is the ejido-private classification of farms. The ejido, one of the products of the Mexican Revolution, is the institution of public ownership of farm land. An ejido farmer is granted life-long rights to work his land, but he may not sell it or lease it. [15] In some locales, the ejido is associated with collective farming. There has been considerable discussion of the relative efficiency of ejidos and their private counterparts, but the available evidence is ambiguous on this point. [16] The relevant consideration for CHAC is that production costs and yields are defined as averages over geographical areas. These averages include both ejidos and private farms. Since the numbers of farms in each category are stable, their contributions to the averages are stable. CHAC is not addressed to an evaluation of the ejido as an institution, but rather to sector-wide problems of supply, employment, trade, pricing, and resource allocation.

[15] The ejido has been the subject of innumerable treatises. Perhaps the definitive work is that of Eckstein (1966).

[16] See the analyses of agricultural census data for ejidal and non-ejidal tenures by Hertford (1971).

6. Factor supply activities

Three classes of factors may be distinguished in CHAC: those supplied at the level of each district submodel, those supplied at the regional level, and those supplied at the sector-wide level. At the submodel level, the fixed factors supplied are land, water, and the labor of farmers plus their families. Agricultural land is not priced, for it has no opportunity cost outside agriculture in the short run, but the dual solution of CHAC yields the value of rents which accrue to the land. Similarly, endowments of water are not priced, but the cost of tapping the water supply and providing it to farms is charged against the objective function. The reservation wage is charged for the labor of both farmers and their families; farmers may be fixed on the land in the short run, but their presence is due to a longer-run decision which is based in part on recognition of their opportunity cost. If it were assumed that farmers were willing to work for zero wages, cropping activities would enter the optimal basis which would not enter under more realistic assumptions, and hence all of the supply functions in the model would be biased toward overestimation of the supply offered at a given set of product prices. Also, unless extensive fiscal redistributional schemes are to be considered, policy-oriented models must, if they are to provide solutions amenable to implementation, be based on wage assumptions not altogether different from actual wages.

Factors supplied at the *regional* level include hired labor and chemical inputs, and services of draft animals. *Sector*-wide factor supply activities in CHAC include those for credit, improved seeds, and machinery services. A sector-wide water pricing activity has been included in order to perform sensitivity analyses on the effects of systematic sector-wide variations in water charges. Most of the factor supply activities are straightforward. Except for labor, all regional and sectoral inputs are assumed to be supplied with infinite elasticity.

A schematic tableau for the entire matrix of coefficients is presented in figure 1. For simplicity, this schematic rendering shows only two regions and five districts, instead of the four regions and twenty districts actually contained in CHAC. The empty areas of the matrix represent blocks of zero coefficients. For blocks containing nonzero coefficients, the sign is indicated. An algebraic statement of the model, along with a listing of rows and columns, is found in section 12 below.

7. Details on the treatment of labor in CHAC

Labor activities and constraints constitute the most complex part of the factor supply set. One of the major purposes of CHAC is to measure the impact of various policies on employment patterns, and the labor components of CHAC have been designed accordingly. Some of the elements of the labor structure have been mentioned. Monthly labor demands are generated within each submodel, and these demands are met either with local labor or through interregional migration. Through the labor supply activities, regional wage differentials are incorporated. These activities also provide for a reservation price for farmers' own labor which is different than the wage for landless, or day, labor.

The number of farmers is fixed for each district, and the number of landless laborers is given for each region. That is, either rural-urban migration is specified exogenously, or it is determined through links with DINAMICO. While farmers do migrate to cities, the number of farms in Mexico does not change very rapidly over time, so in the short run, it appears tenable to assume that the number of farmers in each locality is given. Farmers in non-irrigated areas in Mexico often work seasonally on irrigated farms, so this kind of labor transfer is allowed in the model. The reverse flow (farmers with irrigated land working on non-irrigated farms) virtually never occurs in Mexico, and so this is not included as an option. People leaving tropical areas are assumed to move permanently rather than temporarily, since the distances are so great.

The landless labor force is divided into four regional pools. If one region employs all the members of its pool in a particular month, it may draw redundant laborers from another region.

Regional wage differentials are incorporated in CHAC by multiplicative factors, so that the proportional differences remain constant when experiments are conducted with different base wage rates. Official 'minimum' wage rates exist, but generally they are not fully enforced. Accordingly, they have been used as the *maximum* wages in parametric variations on the price of labor and capital. In 1968, the regional averages of official minimum wages were (in 1968 pesos/day): 19.5, 20.5, 24.0, and 26.0 for the South, Central Plateau, North, and Northwest regions, respectively. In terms of the model structure, the South's wage rate (19.5 pesos) is the base wage. Solutions have also been conducted with base wages of 13.5 and 16.5 pesos [17], maintaining the same proportional regional differences.

The model is structured so that any ratio of the farmers' reservation wage to the day labor wage may be employed. In the solutions reported here, it is assumed that the ratio is 0.5. This gives a reservation wage for farmers ranging from 7.8 to 13.0 pesos per day, depending upon the region and the base wage assumption. Recall, however, that the efficiency wage may exceed these levels in many months, and that farmers receive income from their property as well as from their labor.

The district submodels essentially reflect one or more 'representative farms' in each district, since the production structures are taken from average data for the district or part-district. Hence, even within a fairly disaggregated model, there is a considerable degree of aggregation over farms. One consequence is an overstatement of resource mobility within the district. For example, since reservoir water is allocated centrally, it may be reasonable to assume that it can be reallocated in any manner, but in general this will not be possible for the water from private wells. In labor, too, there is an overstatement of mobility. Implicitly, the stock of farmers may be allocated in any manner among the farms in the district. In actuality, some farmers in a district may hire day labor during months when other farmers are idle. Farmers with irrigated

---

[17] At full employment (264 days per year), the daily wages of 13.5, 16.5 and 19.5 correspond to annual wages of 3,564, 4,356, and 5,148 pesos, respectively. In the 1960 prices of DINAMICO, these would be annual wages of 2,742, 3,351, and 3,960 pesos, respectively. According to Keesing and Manne (above, chapter II.1), the *1960* annual wage for unskilled agricultural labor was 2,400 pesos.

land rarely work as seasonal laborers for other farmers. That is, the low reservation wage applies only to work on their own farms.

To overcome CHAC's bias toward intra-district labor mobility, it has been specified so that farmers with irrigated land may not offer their labor services on a monthly basis, but only on a quarterly basis. Day labor is available monthly. [18] If both types of labor were supplied on a monthly basis, the lower reservation price of farmers would imply that day labor is hired only in the months when all farmers in the district were fully employed. With the quarterly contract device, this is not the case. For example, with a day labor wage of twenty pesos and a farmer reservation price of ten pesos, one-month peaks in labor demand would be met with hired labor, but two-months peaks would be met with farmers on quarterly contracts.

Figure 2 illustrates the impact of the quarterly contract assumption on labor hire patterns. Of course, the quantity of labor demanded depends in part on the crop supply specification, but if it is assumed for the moment that the seasonal demand for labor is fixed, the seasonal labor hiring pattern would look something like the solid line in the figure. If the reservation wage is half the day labor wage, and if quarterly contracts are used for farmers, then day labor will be hired to meet the peak demands represented by the dotted areas. Farmers will satisfy the remaining labor requirements. The shaded areas show the number of slack days for which a cost is incurred when in fact farmers are idle. [19]

If farmer availability were specified in the form of annual contracts, then farmer hire would correspond to the number of mandays which lie below both the solid line and the line AA'. Day labor hire would meet the remaining requirements. And if farmers were available monthly, then all labor requirements up to the line FF', representing the total number of farmers in the district, would be met with farmers.

To summarize, the amount of labor hired in the model depends

---

[18] In the aggregated version, CHAQUITO, the same effect is achieved with four-monthly hire periods for day labor and annual periods for farmers.

[19] These might be thought of as the 'fence-mending' periods.

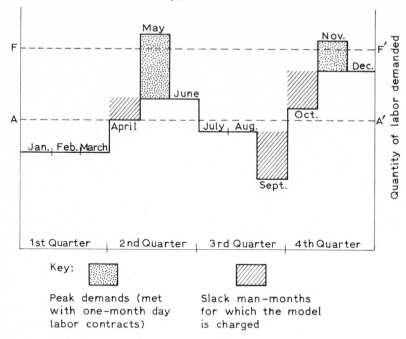

Fig. 2. Alternative labor hire patterns.

directly on four factors: (a) the wage rate for day labor, (b) the productivity of labor and other inputs to the various cropping activities, (c) the ratio of the farmer reservation wage to the day labor wage, and (d) the length of the farmer contract. The latter two factors are interrelated. Whatever set of assumptions is adopted, it should be designed to offset the implicit assumption of complete farmer mobility within a district. This complexity is the price we must pay in order to distinguish between the supply of labor from farmers and that from day laborers.

The reservation wage for farmers is clearly the most arbitrary element in the model. It should not be zero (the supply of labor would not then be positive), and yet it certainly is less than the day labor wage. Since the reservation wage is seasonal, it does not measure farmers' income, but rather the minimum return for which they would be willing to work in one season, mindful of the

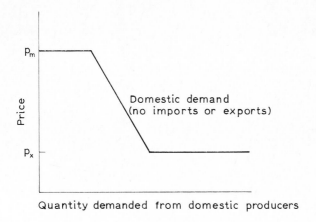

Fig. 3.

fact that the benefits will be reaped in another season. Hence its value is difficult to assess *a priori*. Because of its arbitrariness, some sensitivity tests have been run. The results (reported in chapter. IV.3 below) are reassuring. The changes in employment, exports, and other *primal* variables are relatively slight when major changes are made in the reservation wage.

8. The structure of demand

In its formulation of demand, CHAC differs from the conventional structure of sectoral planning models. In most sectoral planning models, the problem is stated as either that of minimizing the costs of producing a fixed product-mix [20], or of maximizing the sector's profits at exogenous input and output prices. In CHAC, demands and product prices are related endogenously through demand curves.

For a particular product, the demand function is illustrated in figure 3. It is assumed that all purchasers will pay the same price, and that all suppliers will receive this price. The import and export

---

[20] Cf. ENERGETICOS and INTERCON, part III.

prices are indicated by p_m and p_x respectively. Transportation costs account for part of the difference between p_m and p_x. This difference may be large for bulky agricultural products. Export and import prices are fixed exogenously. [21] Also, for convenience, all demand functions are assumed to be linear.

The purpose of this treatment of demand is threefold. Firstly, it means that a programming solution will correspond to a market equilibrium. The effects of various policies, e.g., subsidizing or taxing product prices or varying the exchange rate, etc., can then be investigated. Secondly, it allows the model greater flexibility. For instance, substitution between capital and labor (corresponding to different ratios of the wage rate to the rate of return on capital) can occur not only directly through the technology set or through changes in the commodity mix of exports, but also through substitution in domestic demand. Thirdly, it enables a more realistic appraisal of the benefits (and particularly of their distribution as between producers and consumers) accruing from an increase in agricultural output. Consider the not-unlikely situation of agricultural production for the domestic market at prices between p_m and p_x. If the domestic demand is price-inelastic, then the financial return to producers as a whole from an increase in output is negative. For consumers, the benefits are positive.

Two forms of market equilibrium are distinguished. The first, the competitive case, involves producers acting as price-takers and equating marginal costs to the prices of products. In the second, the monopolistic case, the sector maximizes its net income by equating marginal cost to the marginal revenue of products. As noted earlier, for agriculture the equilibrium prices and quantities of the competitive case correspond more closely to reality, but the monopolistic case proves to be useful for endogenous measurement of sector income.

The derivation of the objective function coefficients is as follows. For simplicity of exposition, it is first assumed that no exter-

---

[21] For non-traded commodities, the demand function is specified between arbitrarily wide bounds which reflect the relevant range of potential prices and quantities. For some crops, there are bounds on exports to represent quotas.

nal trade occurs. Import-export opportunities are introduced later. Assuming linearity and the absence of cross-price elasticities, the set of domestic demand functions may be written:

$$p = a + Bq, \tag{1}$$

where p is a $J \times 1$ vector of prices, a is a $J \times 1$ vector of constants, B is a $J \times J$ negative diagonal matrix, and q is a $J \times 1$ vector of quantities.

Defining $c(q)$ as a $J \times 1$ vector of total cost functions[22], the objective function for the competitive case is as follows:

$$Z = q[a + 0.5Bq] - c(q), \tag{2}$$

The maximization of (2) leads to the same results as a competitive market mechanism.

Proof: Setting $dZ/dq = 0$, this yields the equilibrium condition that price equals marginal cost:

$$p = a + Bq = c'(q). \tag{3}$$

The objective function, Z, can be decomposed into components which correspond to consumers' surplus and producers' surplus:

$$CS = 0.5q'[a - p] = -0.5q'Bq, \tag{4}$$

$$PS = q'p - c(q) = q'[a + Bq] - c(q). \tag{5}$$

The appropriate objective function for the monopolistic case is:

$$Y = q'[a + Bq] - c(q), \tag{6}$$

which yields the equilibrium condition:

---

[22] The supply functions of CHAC are in fact more complex than is implied by this simplified exposition of the supply function.

$$a + 2Bq = c'(q) , \tag{7}$$

where the left-hand term is a vector of marginal revenues.

In CHAC, the set of demand functions (1) is specified over commodity groups. It is assumed that demand substitution may occur within groups but not between groups. Hence, cross-elasticities are absent, and the matrix B is diagonal. If non-zero cross-elasticities are allowed between groups, the problem would become one of non-separable programming. [23] Within a group, there are column vectors to represent alternative product mixes.

To our knowledge, Samuelson (1952) was the first to mention the possibility of maximizing the sum of consumers' and producers' surpluses to compute a competitive equilibrium through an optimizing model. In models of spatial equilibrium with linear demand functions, the quadratic maximand (2) has been used directly by Takayama and Judge (1964, 1971). [24]

In writing the demand structure of CHAC, recall that producers' costs enter through the factor supply activities. The demand activities account only for the areas under the demand function (in the competitive case) or the area under the marginal revenue function (in the monopolistic case). In the competitive case, this area is [25]

$$W = q [a + 0.5 Bq] , \tag{8}$$

which is the function sketched in figure 4 together with the corresponding demand function, assuming that there is only one product and only three segments in the approximation. [26]

In (8), the maximand involves a quadratic form in q. For nonlinear demand functions, the maximand is nonquadratic. Hence

[23] For a treatment of the nonseparable case (still retaining linear programming computational techniques) see Candler et al. (1972). In constructing CHAC, it was felt that the quality of the available econometric information did not warrant the additional programming complexity implied by introducing explicit cross-elasticities of demand.

[24] For applications of this principle in linear programming models of agriculture, see Yaron et al. (1965) and Farhi and Vercueil (1969). Plessner (1971) treats the monopolistic maximand with quadratic programming.

[25] For the monopolistic case, it is $R = q' [a + Bq]$, where R is the total revenue function.

[26] For the computations in CHAC, ten segments were included for each product.

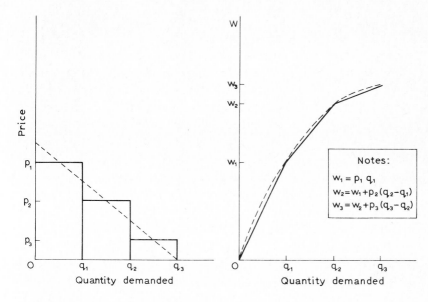

Fig. 4.

approximation procedures were devised in order to take advantage of the computational efficiencies of linear programming and yet permit the inclusion of demand functions. The technique used is similar to the grid linearization of separable programming. [27]

The linear programming tableau corresponding to the segmented approximation of the function W for one product is the following:

	Cropping activities	Selling activities					Right-hand side
Maximand	$-c_i$	w_1	w_2	w_3	...	w_n	
Commodity balance	y_i	$-q_1$	$-q_2$	$-q_3$	...	$-q_n$	$\geqslant$ 0
Demand constraint		1	1	1	...	1	$\leqslant$ 1,

where the c_i are costs associated with crop-producing activity i, the y_i are yields of the product in activity i, the w_j are values of W

---

[27] See Miller (1963).

corresponding to q_j, and the q_j are the total quantities sold at the limit of each segment of the function W.

Notice that by the concavity of W, no more than two of the n selling activities appear at positive intensities in an optimal solution. Through this formulation, the demand function can be transformed into a welfare function W, and this can be approximated as closely as desired without adding additional rows to the linear program.

The approach is readily extended to two or more products. For products in which the demand function is separable, there is one commodity balance and one convex combination constraint per product. For the case of product groups, there is one commodity balance per product and one convex combination constraint for the entire set of selling activities in the demand group.

The competitive and monopolistic cases can be combined by taking the total revenue function R as a constraint instead of as an objective function. It then becomes a constraint on producers' incomes at endogenous prices, and it corresponds to the policy instrument of supply controls. The price-quantity equilibrium in the model will move away from the competitive point and toward the monopolistic point to the extent necessary to satisfy this constraint. The market structure involves a non-linear constraint as well as a non-linear objective function, but again the technique of grid linearization is invoked. To our knowledge, CHAC is the first linear programming model to include an income constraint at endogenous prices. This is done through use of the programming structure appropriate for a description of the monopolistic market equilibrium.

In CHAC, it has been assumed that the off-diagonal elements of the matrix B are zero. The available information consisted of crude estimates of own-price elasticities for a number of individual commodities and commodity groups. (For the numerical values of the price and income elasticities, see table 2.) The demand group approximation procedure has the following properties [28]:

---

[28] Proofs of these properties are available from the authors upon request.

Table 2

Crops, types of cultivation, and price and income elasticities of demand in CHAC

Demand group	Crop [a]	Type of cultivation			Per capita income elasticity [b]	Own-price elasticity
		Irri-gated	Tem-poral	Trop-ical		
1	Wheat	*	*		0.315 }	−0.10
	Maize	*	*	*	−0.453	
2	Green chile	*	*		−0.119 }	−0.20
	Dry chile		*		−0.119	
3	Sugar cane	*		*	0.117	−0.25
4	Beans	*	*	*	0.330	
	Rice	*		*	0.250	−0.30
	Potatoes	*	*		0.330	
	Chickpeas	*	*		0.330	
5	Tomatoes	*	*		0.409	−0.40
6	Onions	*			0.598 }	−0.20
	Garlic	*			0.598	
7	Cucumber	*			0.598	−0.60
8	Squash		*		0.330	−0.40
9	Lima beans	*	*		0.245	−0.40
10	Forage maize	*	*	*	0.500	
	Oats		*		0.500	
	Grain sorghum	*	*	*	0.500	
	Forage barley	*			0.500	−0.30
	Grain barley	*	*		0.500	
	Green alfalfa	*			0.500	
	Chickpeas	*	*		0.500	
11	Malt barley	*	*		0.460	−0.10
12	Cotton fiber	*	*		0.639	−0.50
13	Cotton seed	*	*		0.614	
	Sesame	*	*	*	0.614	
	Flaxseed	*	*		0.614	−1.20
	Safflower	*	*		0.614	
	Soybeans	*		*	0.614	
	Peanuts	*	*		0.614	
14	Peanuts	*	*		0.330	−0.20

Table 2 (continued)

Demand group	Crop [a]	Type of cultivation			Per capita income elasticity [b]	Own-price elasticity
		Irri-gated	Tem-poral	Trop-ical		
15	Strawberries	*			0.330	
	Pineapple			*	0.330	
	Watermelon	*			0.330	−2.00
	Cantaloupe	*			0.330	
16	Tobacco			*	0.817	−0.10

[a] Some products appear in more than one demand group, and hence there are multiple domestic markets for these products (maize, peanuts, chickpeas, and barley). Malt barley and grain barley are the same product on the supply side.

[b] The demand functions are shifted so as to reflect the combined effects of the rate of population increase (3.5% per annum), per capita increase in gross domestic product (2.5% per annum), and the per capita income elasticity for the individual item. Taking these population and GDP shifts as exogenous data, the own-price elasticities are then applied for each demand group. In an optimal solution, a point is chosen endogenously along the price-quantity demand curve for the commodity group.

Sources:

Income elasticities: *Projections of agricultural supply and demand, 1965–1975.* Study for Mexico conducted jointly by the Banco de México, Secretaría de Agricultura y Ganadería, and the U.S. Department of Agriculture (1965).

Price elasticities: unpublished studies by L. Barraza and others.

(i) Because of the lack of information on the off-diagonal elements of B, the system does not reflect a complete range of price interdependence among commodities. [29] Some (but not all) commodities enter into demand groups. Each group is specified so that demand substitution may occur at marginal substitution rates equal to the price ratios in the base period. The system is structured so that substitution is constrained within preassigned bounds on the commodity mix within each group. For example, the various vegetable oils constitute one such demand group, in which substitution rates are determined by the *relative* prices of soybean oil, peanut oil, safflower oil, etc.

(ii) For any commodity group, both the consumers' surplus and

[29] This, of course, applies to the demand structure only. There is interdependence in product prices among all commodities arising from the interdependence of marginal costs on the supply side.

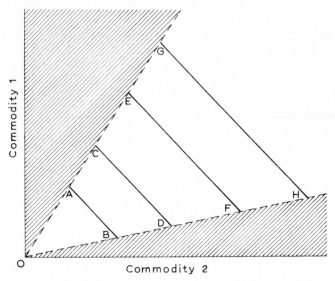

Fig. 5. A family of indifference curves for a two-commodity demand group.

producers' gross revenue are independent of the commodity mix in that group.

(iii) The system preserves the desirable property of the linearization of a concave functional, so that the area function, W can be approximated to any desired degree of accuracy by adding activities without adding additional rows.

(iv) The revenue function is approximated so that the demand activities have coefficients in rows defining producers' profits and incomes. These rows can be used as alternative objective functions, implying monopolistic behavior of the sector, or used as constraints upon the social welfare maximization encompassed by the competitive equilibrium objective function. Similarly, this last can be included as a constraint upon monopoly behavior.

(v) Export selling activities are included as additional demand activities for individual products, and import activities are added as alternatives to domestic producing activities. Import activities would never enter the optimal solution with a monopolistic objective unless the model also included a social welfare constraint.

For the indifference curves within a demand group, we have employed the piecewise linear approximation shown in figure 5.

There, in the case of a two-commodity group, the feasible area is the cone *GOH*. (The rays *OG* and *OH* define limits on the commodity mix within the group.) The indifference curves *AB*, *CD*, *EF* and *GH* are parallel to each other, and the marginal rate of substitution is equal to the ratio of the base-period relative prices.

9. Time and investment choices

Since CHAC's size makes it expensive to obtain simultaneous multi-period solutions, it has been formulated as a one-period static model. It is, however, solved for different points in time with appropriate projections of exogenous data. Investment activities are included. Even though the timing of investment projects cannot be treated, the alternative projects can be ranked with respect to social profitability.

The model is based on data for 1968. [30] Solutions are obtained both for 1968 and 1974. The base period solutions were used to check the model. Solutions for the later year constitute the policy experiments. Since the investment projects in the model are small-scale in nature, the time lapse between the experiments (1971) and the solution date was sufficient for the implementation of investment programs which might be formulated with the assistance of the model. The absorptive capacity limitations which constrain the amount of investment in any one locality in any year cannot be identified easily, so it was decided to solve for the final year of a single three-year period. This also conforms with DINAMICO, which treats 1971, 1974, etc., as 'representative' years.

Endowments of labor are projected from 1968 to 1974. No attempt is made to estimate rural-urban migration within CHAC. The labor force is projected at the natural increase rate, and rural-urban migration may be derived through linking the model to DINAMICO. Export demand limits (e.g., quotas) also are projected forward to the solution period. Disembodied technical progress is incorporated for purchased inputs and associated yield increases.

[30] Because of short-term fluctuations, the average of 1965–69 was used for yields and the average of 1967–69 for production and other variables.

The major difference, in terms of effects on the solutions, between the 1968 and 1974 versions is the rightward shift over time of the domestic demand functions. These shifts are calculated through income growth and income elasticities of demand for agriculture products.

Here, all investment choices have short gestation lags, e.g., well digging, canal lining, and land levelling. For these, it is assumed that the investment takes place instantaneously, and the resulting benefits commence immediately. The annualized costs and benefits are entered in the objective function and income constraints. Annualized investment costs are defined to be one year's straight-line depreciation plus one year's interest on the initial capital cost. [31] The current operating costs of a well are charged through current use activities. In the case of the three types of investment mentioned, the 'output' of the investment activity is an additional unit of irrigated land, an additional unit of net water availability, or an additional unit of higher-yield irrigated land.

Investment choices of longer gestation lags may also be represented through annualized costs and benefits. While this treatment does violence to some aspects of project analysis, it permits assessment of all major forms of investment in a locality for purposes of measuring the marginal efficiency of capital schedule. (See chapter IV.5 below, on the project model for the El Bajío region.)

10. Risk and dualism

Risk variables are the major omission on the production side of this version of CHAC. Perceived risk obviously plays an important role in farmers' decisions. Some attempts were made to incorporate it, but the data were insufficient to support the attempts. New lines of attack have been tentatively formulated, and it is likely that this element will eventually be included. In the meantime, it is instructive to discuss the reasons why earlier attempts

---

[31] Depreciation and interest charges are specified separately (rather than using a capital recovery factor) to facilitate solutions with parametric variations on the interest rate.

failed. First, it should be noted that district-level changes in crop-ping patterns implied by the solutions of CHAC generally are not more severe than the historical year-to-year changes observed in irrigated areas. Quite marked annual changes in planted acreage per crop — often 50% or more — are observed in these areas. Hence, even without allowing for risk variables to ensure greater crop diversification, the model's results appeared satisfactory. The principal difficulty arises in the more traditional, non-irrigated farms. There it is optimal to shift substantially away from maize and into sorghum when it is assumed that import barriers are weakened.

The first thought on handling risk was to utilize the crop insur-ance premiums of the national agricultural insurance company. One formulation of risk leads to a quadratic objective function, [32] but if it is assumed that the national crop insurance organization has made a linear approximation to the risk problem, insurance may be specified as a cost of production. The observed premiums may then be utilized as insurance input coefficients in the cropping activities. Unfortunately, this approach was vitiated by (a) incom-plete coverage of the sector in the insurance program, and (b) inconsistency among premiums in areas where there is coverage. If nothing else, this inquiry indicates that it might be fruitful to examine the premium-setting rules in the insurance program.

As a second approach, the method of year-to-year 'flexibility' constraints was examined. It was concluded that there is little objective basis for establishing appropriate parameters in such con-straints, especially in circumstances of highly flexible cropping patterns. It was decided to impose such constraints only after the initial solutions, if they appeared warranted by the results. As things turned out, it was not necessary to do so.

Consideration of risk emphasizes the relative inflexibility of non-irrigated agriculture. This is reflected by CHAC in fewer crop choices for non-irrigated, traditional agriculture. In the solutions, the difference made by irrigation showed up strongly in terms of

[32] See the classic work on mean-variance analysis in an optimizing model by Freund (1956).

responses to price subsidies. [33] When a subsidy of 5% was added to the wheat price, the long-run elasticity of response [34] was +5. However, when the maize price was subsidized a like amount, the elasticity of response was virtually zero. Effectively, farmers with irrigation face many alternatives of nearly equal profitability, and they will respond to minor perturbations of prices. On the other hand, farmers without irrigation who grow maize can grow little else easily. Stronger price changes are required to induce shifts in their traditional cropping patterns. These results indicate that, at least to a degree, CHAC has captured the dualistic aspects of Mexican agriculture.

11. The aggregated version, CHAQUITO

In order to reduce the computation costs for the experiments, an aggregated version (CHAQUITO) was constructed. The goal of the aggregation was a substantial reduction in the number of *rows*. To combine some crops into an aggregate product would not reduce the number of rows significantly, and it would do violence to the possibilities of substitution in demand. To aggregate districts [35] would reduce the row count considerably, but at the sacrifice of the richness in production alternatives which arises from varying proportions in factor endowments over districts. Hence these two alternatives were rejected in favor of aggregation over the monthly inputs of district-specific resources. The monthly rows for land, water, and labor were aggregated into four-monthly rows. This single step reduced the number of rows by 50%. The number of nonzero coefficients dropped by more than 25%.

Systematic tests of the consequences of aggregation have not yet been carried out. Nevertheless, some effects are apparent. First, there is a direct information loss regarding the seasonality of labor utilization. Second, as a consequence, the interregional mi-

---

[33] Not to be confused with a guaranteed price level.

[34] This is not quite the same as the elasticity of supply, for here the demand parameters enter into the determination of response.

[35] Even the disaggregated version implies considerable aggregation over actual agricultural districts.

gration results are severely distorted. Third, the sector-wide supply of products is altered only slightly. Fourth, the crop-by-crop comparative advantage in international trade changes only slightly.

Basically, the sector-wide supply functions for each crop do not appear to be affected significantly by this aggregation, but district-specific resource productivities are affected. Clearly, more work needs to be done on alternative aggregations.

Most of the results reported below, in chapter IV.3, are based on CHAQUITO. CHAC is used for estimates of the base-period income, employment, seasonality, and comparative advantage in trade. CHAQUITO is the basis for the linkage with DINAMICO reported in chapter IV.6 below.

12. Algebraic statement

In the case of large-scale programming models, matrix tableaus are often helpful in revealing the structure of the model. Nevertheless, the algebra is also useful (particularly for writing instructions for matrix generating computer routines), and so a statement is given here. A list of the types of rows and columns is given also. There exists a two-volume set of notebooks on CHAC, which contain more than 100 pages of tableaus, basic assumptions, and basic data. [36]

For the algebraic statement, special notation has been adopted. Capital Roman letters represent vector unknowns or right-hand side values, and small Roman letters both parameters and sub- and superscripts. Greek letters denote vector and scalar coefficients. In raw form, some of the vector symbols are burdened with several superscripts and subscripts, but in most equations only part of the vector is relevant, so an abbreviated notation is utilized. For example, the typical production activity is denoted X_{hij}^{dz}. That set which corresponds to all the vectors for producing crop j in district r is written X_j^r. The total production of crop j in district r is abbreviated, $y_j^r X_j^r$, where y_j^r signifies the row vector of yields for those activities producing crop j in region r. Given these conventions, the set of symbols in full form is set out in table 3.

---

[36] These may be consulted at the Development Research Center, International Bank for Reconstruction and Development.

Table 3
Notation for algebraic statement

Symbol	Description	Superscripts, subscripts
I. Variables:		
X_{hij}^{dz}	Crop production	d = district
		z = zone (subdistrict)
		h = degree of mechanization
		i = type of irrigation
I_n^d	Fixed investment	j = crop
		n = class of investment
T_j^d	Total crop production at the district level	
A^r	Regional supply of draft animal services	r = region
F^r	Regional supply of chemical inputs	
C	Sectoral supply of short-term credit	
K	Sectoral supply of machinery services (in tens of days)	
S	Sectoral supply of purchased seeds	
D_{ms}^g	Domestic demand	g = crop group
		m = commodity mix
		s = demand segment
E_j	Exports	
M_j	Imports	
P_j	Technical progress variable	
K'	Sectoral supply of machinery services (in 10,000 pesos)	
C^d	District-level counter for short-term credit	
CP	Private long-term capital used	
CT	Total long-term capital used	
W_g^d	Gravity water supply by district	
W_p^d	Well water supply by district	
W_g	Sector use of gravity water	
W_p	Sector use of pump water	
$SALS$	Sectoral wage charging activity	
$SALr$	Activities for charging regional wage differentials	
$LMAN$	Sector annual employment counter (man-years at full employment equivalent)	
$LMANt$	Sector monthly employment counter	
$dDLt$	Monthly day labor supply activities in each submodel	
$dFLq, dFLt$	Farm labor supply activities by submodel, quarterly in irrigation submodels, monthly otherwise (q = quarterly index; t = monthly index)	
$MDLrr't$	Migration activities for day labor from region r to region r' by months (rr' = 31, 32, 43)	
$MA33t$	Migration activities in region 3 for farmers to the pool of day laborers	
$MA44A$	Migration activities for region 4 farmers on annual basis	

Table 3 (continued)

Symbol	Description

II. Parameters:

Symbol	Description
α^g_{mj}	Quantity of crop j demanded in mix m of group g [a]
ω^g_s	Entry in maximand for demand group g and demand segment s (i.e., weighted average price for segment s of all crops in the group)
ρ^g_s	Entry in income rows for demand group g and demand segment s (i.e., weighted average marginal revenue for segment s of all crops in the group)
δ^g_m	Entry in the demand convex combination constraint for demand group g and mix m
κ	Ratio of farmer reservation wage to day labor wage
γ^{dz}_{ijt}	Water input coefficients ($i = i'$ for gravity-fed water; $i = i''$ for well water; t = month)
σ^d_j	Purchased seed input coefficients
ϕ^d_j	Chemical input coefficients
μ^d_{hj}	Machinery services input coefficients
β^d_{hjt}	Labor input requirements
θ^d_{hj}	Draft animal services input requirements
η^d_n	Capital costs per unit of investment project (n = class of investment project)
τ^d_{hj}	Credit input requirements
λ_r	Ratio of region r wage to region 4 wage

III. Prices:

Symbol	Description
p^e_j	Exports
p^m_j	Imports
p^l	Labor (region 4 hired labor wage)
p^k	Cost of machinery services, excluding interest cost and base wage component of machinery operators' wage
p^i	Long-term interest rate
p^c	Short-term interest rate
p^a_r	Regional unit cost of draft animal services
p^{wg}_d	Gravity water
p^{wp}_d	Well water

[a] The vector α_j is the union over g and m of all coefficients α^g_{mj}.

The equations of the system may be written as follows:

(i) *Commodity balances, sectoral and district*

33   (a) $y_j X_j + M_j - \alpha_j D^g - E_j + P_j \geq 0$

$$\left[\begin{array}{c}\text{Domestic} \\ \text{production}\end{array}\right] + \left[\text{Imports}\right] - \left[\begin{array}{c}\text{Domestic} \\ \text{sales}\end{array}\right] - \left[\text{Exports}\right]$$

$$+ \left[\begin{array}{c}\text{Adjustment for yield-enhancing} \\ \text{technical progress}\end{array}\right] \geq 0$$

176   (b) $y_j^d X_j^d - T_j^d = 0$, each d, j

$$\left[\begin{array}{c}\text{District-level} \\ \text{production in} \\ \text{various techniques}\end{array}\right] - \left[\begin{array}{c}\text{Definition of} \\ \text{district total crop} \\ \text{production}\end{array}\right] = 0$$

(ii) *Sectoral and regional labor balances*

(a) Sectoral wage accounting equation:

1     $-SALS + K + \sum_r \lambda_r SALr = 0$

$$- \left[\begin{array}{c}\text{Wage charging} \\ \text{activity}\end{array}\right] + \left[\begin{array}{c}\text{Accounting} \\ \text{activity for} \\ \text{employment of} \\ \text{machinery} \\ \text{operators}\end{array}\right] + \left[\begin{array}{c}\text{Regional wage} \\ \text{differentials} \times \\ \text{regional wage} \\ \text{accounting} \\ \text{activities}\end{array}\right] = 0.$$

4   (b) Regional wage accounting rows:

$$-SALr + \kappa RESr + \sum_{d \in r} \sum_t dDLt \leq 0, \quad \text{each } r$$

$$- \left[\begin{array}{c}\text{Regional wage} \\ \text{accounting} \\ \text{activities}\end{array}\right] + \left[\begin{array}{c}\text{Reservation wage ratio} \\ \times \text{ regional farmer} \\ \text{employment activity}\end{array}\right]$$

$$+ \left[\begin{array}{c}\text{Sum over districts and} \\ \text{months of regional day} \\ \text{labor employment}\end{array}\right] \leq 0$$

4   (c) Regional farmer employment accounting rows:

$$-RESr + 3 \sum_{d \in r} \sum_{q} dFLq + \sum_{d \in r} \sum_{t} dFLt = 0, \quad \text{each } r$$

$$- \begin{bmatrix} \text{Regional farmer} \\ \text{employment} \\ \text{activity} \end{bmatrix} + 3 \begin{bmatrix} \text{Sum over districts} \\ \text{and quarters of} \\ \text{quarterly farmer} \\ \text{employment} \end{bmatrix}^{37}$$

$$+ \begin{bmatrix} \text{Sum over districts} \\ \text{and months of} \\ \text{monthly farmer employment} \end{bmatrix}^{37} = 0$$

1   (d) Total employment accounting row in man-years:

$$-12LMAN + \sum_{t} LMANt = 0$$

$$-12 \begin{bmatrix} \text{Total employment} \\ \text{in man-years} \end{bmatrix} + \begin{bmatrix} \text{Sum over months of} \\ \text{total employment} \\ \text{in man-months} \end{bmatrix} = 0$$

12   (e) Total monthly employment accounting rows in man-months:

$$-2.2LMANt + \sum_{d} dDLt + \sum_{d} dFLq + \sum_{d} dFLt = 0,$$

each *t* and *q* such that $t \in q$

$$-2.2 \begin{bmatrix} \text{Total} \\ \text{employment} \\ \text{in month } t \end{bmatrix}^{38} + \begin{bmatrix} \text{Sum over districts of} \\ \text{day labor employment} \\ \text{in month } t \end{bmatrix}$$

$$+ \begin{bmatrix} \text{Sum over districts of} \\ \text{quarterly farmer} \\ \text{employment in the} \\ \text{quarter containing} \\ \text{month } t \end{bmatrix} + \begin{bmatrix} \text{Sum over districts} \\ \text{of monthly farmer} \\ \text{employment} \end{bmatrix} = 0$$

---

[37] In irrigation districts the quarterly contract device is used for farmers, but in non-irrigated districts farmers are assumed to be available on a monthly basis, so that seasonal migration to irrigated areas may occur.

[38] The activities for hiring farmers and day laborers are stated in units of tens of man-days per month (or quarter), and there are 22 working days per month; hence the conversion factor of 2.2 is required in the first term of this equation.

(f) Regional employment balances, by month:

24   (f.1) $\sum\limits_{d\in r} dDLt - MDL3rt \leqslant L_r,$ $r = 1, 2,$ each t

$$\begin{bmatrix} \text{Total employment} \\ \text{of day labor} \\ \text{in region } r \\ \text{in month } t \end{bmatrix} - \begin{bmatrix} \text{Migration of day} \\ \text{labor from Central} \\ \text{Plateau to region} \\ r \text{ in month } t \end{bmatrix} \leqslant \begin{bmatrix} \text{Pool of} \\ \text{landless labor} \\ \text{in region } r \end{bmatrix}$$

12   (f.2) $\sum\limits_{d\in r} dDLt + \sum\limits_{r=1}^{2} MDL3rt - MDL43A - MA33t \leqslant L_3,$

     $r = 3,$ each t

$$\begin{bmatrix} \text{Total employment} \\ \text{of day labor in} \\ \text{region } r = 3, \\ \text{month } t \end{bmatrix} + \begin{bmatrix} \text{Migration out} \\ \text{of region 3} \\ \text{in month } t \end{bmatrix} + \begin{bmatrix} \text{Migration from} \\ \text{region 4 to} \\ \text{region 3} \end{bmatrix}$$

$$+ \begin{bmatrix} \text{Movement of} \\ \text{dryland farmers} \\ \text{into day labor} \\ \text{pool in month } t \end{bmatrix} \leqslant \begin{bmatrix} \text{Pool of} \\ \text{landless labor} \\ \text{in region 3} \end{bmatrix}$$

12   (f.3) $\sum\limits_{d\in r} dDLt + MDL43A - MA44A \leqslant L_4,$ $r = 4,$ each t

$$\begin{bmatrix} \text{Total employment} \\ \text{of day labor} \\ \text{in region } r = 4, \\ \text{month } t \end{bmatrix} + \begin{bmatrix} \text{Migration from} \\ \text{region 4 to} \\ \text{region 3} \end{bmatrix} - \begin{bmatrix} \text{Transfer of} \\ \text{tropical farmers} \\ \text{to day labor pool} \end{bmatrix}$$

$$\leqslant \begin{bmatrix} \text{Pool of} \\ \text{landless labor} \\ \text{in region 4} \end{bmatrix}$$

(g) Migration constraints:

12   (g.1) $\sum\limits_{r=1}^{2} MDL3rt - MDL43A - MA33t \leqslant M_{3t},$ each t

[Bound on monthly migration out of region 3]

1   (g.2) $\displaystyle\sum_t \sum_{r=1}^{2} MDL3rt - 12MDL43A - \sum_t MA33t \leqslant M_3$

[Bound on annual migration out of region 3]

1   (g.3) $12MDL43A + 12MA44A \leqslant M_4$

[Bound on annual migration out of region 4]

(iii) *Sectoral and regional input balances (excluding labor)*

(a) Short-term credit balance [39]:

1        $\displaystyle\sum_d C^d - C \leqslant 0$

$\begin{bmatrix} \text{Sum of district credit} \\ \text{counting activities} \end{bmatrix} - \begin{bmatrix} \text{Sectoral interest-charging} \\ \text{activity for credit} \end{bmatrix} \leqslant 0$

1   (b) Machinery services balance:

$\displaystyle\sum_d \sum_h \sum_j \mu_{hj}^d X_{hj}^d - K \leqslant 0$

$\begin{bmatrix} \text{Sum of demands for} \\ \text{machinery services} \\ \text{in cropping activities} \end{bmatrix} - \begin{bmatrix} \text{Activity supplying} \\ \text{machinery services} \end{bmatrix} \leqslant 0$

1   (c) Balance for charging interest component of machinery services:

$K - 2.308 K' \leqslant 0$

$\begin{bmatrix} \text{Machinery services} \\ \text{in tens of work-days} \end{bmatrix} - 2.308 \begin{bmatrix} \text{Machinery services} \\ \text{in 10,000 pesos/year} \end{bmatrix}^{40} \leqslant 0$

---

[39] There are district-level credit balances which sum the demands for credit over cropping activities. There are also bounds on institutional credit allocations by crop which have been made non-operative in the solutions reported here. Since there is no bound on C, credit is provided in the model in infinitely elastic supply.

[40] The factor 2.308 converts from tens of days to 10,000 pesos per year, given the actual initial cost and lifetime of a typical piece of machinery in Mexico.

1 (d) Sectoral accounting row for use of gravity-fed water [41]:

$$\sum_d \sum_z \sum_j \gamma_{ij}^{dz} X_{ij}^{dz} - W_g = 0, \qquad i = i'$$

$$\left[\begin{matrix}\text{Total demands for} \\ \text{gravity water}\end{matrix}\right] - \left[\begin{matrix}\text{Gravity water} \\ \text{accounting activity}\end{matrix}\right] = 0$$

1 (e) Sectoral accounting row for use of well water:

$$\sum_d \sum_z \sum_j \gamma_{ij}^{dz} X_{ij}^{dz} - W_p = 0, \qquad i = i''$$

$$\left[\begin{matrix}\text{Total demands for} \\ \text{well water}\end{matrix}\right] - \left[\begin{matrix}\text{Well water} \\ \text{accounting activity}\end{matrix}\right] = 0$$

1 (f) Sectoral balance for purchased seeds [42]:

$$\sum_d \sum_j \sigma_j^d X_j^d - S \leqslant 0$$

$$\left[\begin{matrix}\text{Total demands for} \\ \text{purchased seeds}\end{matrix}\right] - \left[\begin{matrix}\text{Supply of} \\ \text{purchased seeds}\end{matrix}\right] \leqslant 0$$

4 (g) Regional balances for chemical inputs [43]:

$$\sum_{d \in r} \sum_j \phi_j^d X_j^d - F^r \leqslant 0, \qquad \text{each } r$$

$$\left[\begin{matrix}\text{Total regional demands} \\ \text{for fertilizers and} \\ \text{pesticides}\end{matrix}\right] - \left[\begin{matrix}\text{Regional supply} \\ \text{of fertilizers} \\ \text{and pesticides}\end{matrix}\right] \leqslant 0$$

[41] This row and the subsequent one permit experiments with uniform sector-wide changes in the price of water.

[42] Both terms in units of thousands of pesos.

[43] The indexes d and j on ϕ_j^d indicate that rates of fertilizer use vary over district and crop, but not over other dimensions such as zones or degrees of mechanization. Both terms in this expression are in units of thousands of pesos.

4   (h) Regional balances for draft animal services:

$$\sum_{d \in r} \sum_{h} \sum_{j} \theta_{hj}^d X_{hj}^d - A^r \leqslant 0, \qquad \text{each } r$$

$$\begin{bmatrix} \text{Total regional demands} \\ \text{for services of} \\ \text{draft animals} \end{bmatrix} - \begin{bmatrix} \text{Regional supply} \\ \text{of draft animal} \\ \text{services} \end{bmatrix} \leqslant 0$$

1   (j) Long-term private capital balances:

$$\sum_{d} \eta_n^d I_n^d - CP \leqslant 0,$$

$$\begin{bmatrix} \text{Costs of investment} \\ \text{activities financed} \\ \text{with private capital} \end{bmatrix} - \begin{bmatrix} \text{Supply of} \\ \text{private capital} \end{bmatrix} \leqslant 0$$

1   (k) Total long-term capital balance:

$$\sum_{d} \eta_n^d I_n^d + K' + CP - CT \leqslant 0, \text{ those } n \text{ not in equation (j)},$$

$$\begin{bmatrix} \text{Costs of investment} \\ \text{activities financed} \\ \text{with public capital} \end{bmatrix} + \begin{bmatrix} \text{Capital component} \\ \text{of machinery} \\ \text{services} \end{bmatrix} + \begin{bmatrix} \text{Private} \\ \text{capital} \\ \text{supplied} \end{bmatrix}$$

$$- \begin{bmatrix} \text{Total capital} \\ \text{supplied} \end{bmatrix} \leqslant 0$$

(iv) *District-level input balances*

204   (a) District labor balances:

$$\sum_{h} \sum_{j} \beta_{hjt}^d X_{hj}^d - dDLt - dFLt^{\,44} \leqslant 0, \qquad \text{each } d, t$$

---

[44] Or $dFLq$, depending on the district.

$$\begin{bmatrix} \text{Demands for labor,} \\ \text{district } d, \text{ month } t \end{bmatrix} - \begin{bmatrix} \text{Day labor hired, in} \\ \text{district } d, \text{ month } t \end{bmatrix}$$

$$- \begin{bmatrix} \text{Farmers employed in} \\ \text{district } d, \text{ month } t \end{bmatrix} \leqslant 0$$

18   (b) District credit balances [45]:

$$\sum_h \sum_h \tau_{hj}^d X_{hj}^d - C^d \leqslant 0, \quad \text{each } d$$

$$\begin{bmatrix} \text{Demands for credit,} \\ \text{district } d \end{bmatrix} - \begin{bmatrix} \text{Total district} \\ \text{credit required} \end{bmatrix} \leqslant 0$$

10   (c) District gravity water balances:

$$\sum_z \sum_j \gamma_{ij}^{dz} X_{ij}^{dz} - W_g^d \leqslant 0, \quad \text{each } d, \quad i = i'$$

$$\begin{bmatrix} \text{Demands for gravity} \\ \text{water, district } d \end{bmatrix} - \begin{bmatrix} \text{District } d \text{ activity} \\ \text{for charging costs} \\ \text{of gravity water} \end{bmatrix} \leqslant 0$$

4   (d) District well water balances :

$$\sum_z \sum_j \gamma_{ij}^{dz} X_{ij}^{dz} - W_p^d \leqslant 0, \quad \text{each } d, \quad i = i''$$

$$\begin{bmatrix} \text{Demands for well water,} \\ \text{district } d \end{bmatrix} - \begin{bmatrix} \text{District } d \text{ activity} \\ \text{for charging costs} \\ \text{of well water} \end{bmatrix} \leqslant 0$$

(v) *District resource constraints*

348   (a) Monthly land constraints:

$$X_t^{dz} \leqslant B_t^{dz}, \quad \text{each } d, z, t$$

$$\begin{bmatrix} \text{Land requirements for} \\ \text{cropping (units of} \\ X \text{ are hectares)} \end{bmatrix} \leqslant \begin{bmatrix} \text{Land availability} \\ \text{by district,} \\ \text{zone, month} \end{bmatrix}$$

[45] The three El Bajío submodels are grouped together in measuring credit requirements, so there are 18 balances instead of 20.

168   (b) Monthly gravity and pump water constraints:

$$\sum_z \sum_j \gamma_{ijt}^{dz} X_{ij}^{dz} \leqslant \overline{W}_{it}^d, \quad \text{each } d, t, i$$

$$\begin{bmatrix} \text{Total month } t \text{ water} \\ \text{demands, district } d, \\ \text{water type } i \end{bmatrix} \leqslant \begin{bmatrix} \text{Water delivery constraints} \\ \text{district } d, \text{ water type } i \end{bmatrix}$$

14   (c) Annual gravity and pump water constraints:

$$\sum_z \sum_j \gamma_{ij}^{dz} X_{ij}^{dz} \leqslant \overline{W}_i^d, \text{ each } d, i.$$

(d) District constraints on farmer and family labor:

44   (d.1) $dFLq \leqslant A_d$,   each q, each d with irrigation

36   (d.2) $dFLt - MA33t \leqslant A_d$
        each t, each d in region 3 without irrigation

12   (d.3) $dFLt - MA44A \leqslant A_d$
        each t, each d in region 4 without irrigation

(vi) *Technical progress balances* [46]

33      $\alpha_j^g D^g + E_j - M_j - P_j = 0$,   each j, g such that $j \in g$

$$\begin{bmatrix} \text{Total sales on} \\ \text{domestic markets} \end{bmatrix} + [\text{Exports}] - [\text{Imports}]$$

$$- \begin{bmatrix} \text{Technical} \\ \text{progress factor} \end{bmatrix} = 0$$

(vii) *Income constraints* [47]

1   (a) Farmers' profit:

$$\sum_g \sum_s \sum_m \rho_s^g D_{ms}^g + \sum_j p_j^e E_j - \sum_j p_j^m M_j - p^l SALS - p^k K$$

---

[46] These balances serve the purpose of adjusting total production to allow for exogenous changes over time in yields and associated inputs of seeds, chemicals, and credit.

[47] The seed and fertilizer supply activities are stated in terms of thousand pesos; while the objective function and income rows are in 10,000 pesos; hence the factor of 0.1 in these rows.

$$- p^i K' - p^c CP - 0.1 S - \sum_r 0.1 F^r - \sum_r p_r^a A$$

$$- \sum_d p_d^{wg} W_g^d - \sum_d p_d^{wp} W_p^d - (\Delta p^{wg}) W_g - (\Delta p^{wp}) W_p$$

$$+ \sum_d \sum_j (\Delta p)^d T_j^d \geqslant Y$$

where $(\Delta p)^{wg}$ and $(\Delta p)^{wp}$ indicate the uniform sector-wide changes in water prices, and $(\Delta p)^d$ indicates the district price differentials by crop.

$$\begin{bmatrix} \text{Gross revenue} \\ \text{from domestic sales} \end{bmatrix} + \begin{bmatrix} \text{Export} \\ \text{earnings} \end{bmatrix} - \begin{bmatrix} \text{Import} \\ \text{costs} \end{bmatrix} - \begin{bmatrix} \text{Total labor} \\ \text{costs} \end{bmatrix}$$

$$- \begin{bmatrix} \text{Interest on} \\ \text{long-term capital} \end{bmatrix} - \begin{bmatrix} \text{Interest on} \\ \text{short-term capital} \end{bmatrix} - \begin{bmatrix} \text{Seed} \\ \text{costs} \end{bmatrix}$$

$$- \begin{bmatrix} \text{Chemical} \\ \text{input costs} \end{bmatrix} - \begin{bmatrix} \text{Draft animal} \\ \text{service costs} \end{bmatrix} - \begin{bmatrix} \text{Gravity water} \\ \text{costs} \end{bmatrix}$$

$$- \begin{bmatrix} \text{Well water} \\ \text{costs} \end{bmatrix} - \begin{bmatrix} \text{Increments to} \\ \text{gravity water cost} \end{bmatrix} - \begin{bmatrix} \text{Increments to} \\ \text{well water cost} \end{bmatrix}$$

$$+ \begin{bmatrix} \text{District price} \\ \text{differences on crops} \end{bmatrix}$$

1 (b) Farmers' income:
This equation is the same as (vii.a) except that the term

$$+ \sum_r a_r RESr$$

is added, where a_r is the regional farmer reservation wage, to serve the purpose of adding farmers' wage income to profits in order to arrive at total farmers' income.

1 (c) Sector income:

This equation is the same as (vii.a) except that the following term is dropped:

$$-p^l SALS \, ,$$

and the price of machinery services, p^k, is reduced to take out labor costs. These adjustments result in an expression for total sector income which is defined as farmers' income plus wage income of day laborers.

1 (viii) *Objective function (maximand)*

$$\sum_g \sum_s \sum_m \omega_s^g D_{ms}^g + \sum_j p_j^e E_j - \sum_j p_j^m M_j - p^l SALS - p^k K - p^i CT - p^c CP$$

$$- 0.1 [S + \sum_r F^r] - \sum_r p_r^a A^r - \sum_j p_d^{wg} W_g^d - \sum_d p_d^{wp} W_p^d$$

$$- (\Delta p^{wg}) W_g - (\Delta p^{wp}) W_p + \sum_d \sum_j (\Delta p)^d T_j^d$$

There are differences between this and (vii.a) in the demand function term and in the role of long-term private and public capital. The first term of the objective function is the sum of consumers' and producers' surpluses rather than gross revenue. Total long-term capital is costed, via *CT*, instead of just private long-term capital.

For constraints (i)–(vii), the total number of rows is 1203. In addition, there are approximately 300 accounting rows.

References

Banco de México, Secretaría de Agricultura y Ganadería, and U.S. Department of Agriculture, *Projections of agricultural supply and demand, 1965–75*. 1965.

Candler, W., J.H. Duloy and R.D. Norton, 'Convex programming by implicit search'. February 1972. (Mimeographed.)

Eckstein, S., *El ejido colectivo en México*. México, Fondo de Cultura Ecónomica, 1966.

Farhi, L. and J. Vercueil, *Recherche pour une planification cohérente: le modèle de prévision du Ministère de L'Agriculture*. Paris, Éditions du Centre National de la Recherche Scientifique, 1969.

Freund, R., 'Introduction of risk into a programming model', *Econometrica*, 1956, 253–263.

Heady, E.O., N.S. Randhawa and M.D. Skold, 'Programming models for planning of the agricultural sector', in: *The theory and design of economic development*, edited by I. Adelman and E. Thorbecke. Baltimore, Johns Hopkins Press, 1966, chapter 13.

Hertford, R., 'Sources of change in Mexican agricultural production, 1940–65'. U.S. Department of Agriculture, Foreign Agricultural Economic Report No. 73, August 1971.

Miller, C., 'The simplex method for local separable programming', in: *Recent advances in mathematical programming*, edited by R.L. Graves and P. Wolfe. New York, Wiley 1963, chapter 12.

Piñeiro, M.E. and A.F. McCalla, 'Programming for agricultural price policy analysis', *The Review of Economics and Statistics* 53, No. 1 (February 1971) 59–66.

Plessner, Y., 'Computing equilibrium solutions for imperfectly competitive markets', *American Journal of Agricultural Economics* 53 (May 1971) 191–196.

Samuelson, P.A., 'Spatial price equilibrium and linear programming', *American Economic Review 42*, No. 3 (June 1952) 283–303.

Solís, L., *La realidad económica mexicana: retrovisión y perspectivas*. México, Siglo XXI Editores, 1970.

Takayama, T., and G.G. Judge, 'Equilibrium among spatially separated markets, a reformulation', *Econometrica*, October 1964.

Takayama, T., and G.G. Judge, *Spatial and temporal price and allocation models*. Amsterdam, North-Holland Publ. Co., 1971.

Yaron, D., Y. Plessner and E.O. Heady, 'Competitive equilibrium, an application of mathematical programming', *Canadian Journal of Agricultural Economics* 13, No. 2 (1965).

IV.2. THE TECHNOLOGY SET AND DATA BASE FOR CHAC

Luz María BASSOCO and Teresa RENDÓN *

1. Introduction

CHAC includes a set of agricultural supply functions. They are represented implicitly by a series of fixed-coefficient production activities which are differentiated by crop, by technique, and by location. In each location, the activity analysis model approximates a variable-coefficient production function at the district level. The same is true at the sector-wide level, for each crop and for the total value of agricultural output. An econometric specification of the production side would have confronted a number of deficiencies in the existing agricultural data series. For example, the sector-wide time series of production and prices are not very reliable. The spatial breakdown is less reliable, except for the irrigated areas. Beyond these problems, there is the fact that the time series do not include information on labor and other inputs. [1]

In these circumstances an activity analysis approach was adopted. It is based on estimates of discrete production alternatives, but the alternatives are sufficiently numerous so that aggregative behavior in CHAC is virtually continuous and nonlinear.

This chapter sets out the procedures used in constructing the spatial disaggregation scheme, the alternative input-output vectors, the resource availabilities, and other parameters for CHAC. Initial

---

* The authors wish to express their appreciation to Roger Norton for helpful comments on this chapter.

[1] The decennial agricultural censuses include information on a few basic inputs, but only for aggregate production and not by crop. For an econometric analysis of supply based on the census data, see Hertford (1971).

equilibrium conditions for product prices and quantities are also discussed, along with the prices of inputs which enter the productive process. In virtually all cases, the existing data could not be used directly, but rather were subjected to a series of transformations so that they conformed to the accounting concepts in the model.

A major aim was to develop procedures sufficiently general so that the production side of CHAC could be altered readily to incorporate more district-level detail or less, or to selectively aggregate some portions and disaggregate others in order to shift the focus of investigation. Another aim, regarding the technology set in particular, was to describe feasible technological alternatives other than the set of farming practices observed in the base period.

2. Definition of districts and regions

On the product supply side of CHAC, there are twenty submodels. Each represents either rainfed (temporal), irrigated, or tropical cultivation, and each covers a particular set of counties or districts, which are not necessarily contiguous. Cropping and investment activities are specified by submodel. The submodels are grouped into four major geographical regions, and labor constraints are specified for each region. This treatment reflects the different regional wage rates and the different degrees of interregional labor mobility.

For some submodels, the spatial building blocks are the administrative irrigation districts of the Secretaría de Recursos Hidráulicos. Some submodels represent individual irrigation districts, and others represent multiple districts. All but one of the single-district submodels are in the northwestern part of the country where most of the export crops are produced. However, the production matrices were designed so that it is a relatively simple matter to add submodels for individual districts in other areas.

In the case of temporal and tropical agriculture, the submodels are defined on the basis of altitude and annual rainfall rates, which together determine climatic conditions. In Mexico, crops are culti-

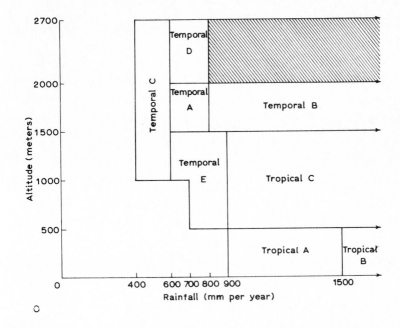

Fig. 1. Climatic definition of temporal and tropical submodels. ▧ Conditions not observed in Mexico; ☐ Pasture, forest, or barren land; Temporal A Conditions covered by Temporal submodel A in CHAC.

vated at altitudes ranging from sea level to 2700 m, and under rainfall conditions of 400 mm/year to more than 1500 mm/year. The kinds of crops cultivable, and their yields, vary considerably over climatic zones. Figure 1 shows the basis for defining the five temporal submodels (A to E) and the three tropical submodels (A to C).

The basic regions into which the submodels are grouped are as follows (see figure 2):

(I) The Northwest — an arid zone of large scale irrigation along a thousand-mile coastal strip between the Gulf of California and the Sierra Madre Occidental, plus Baja California. Agriculture is more extensively mechanized here than in any other region.

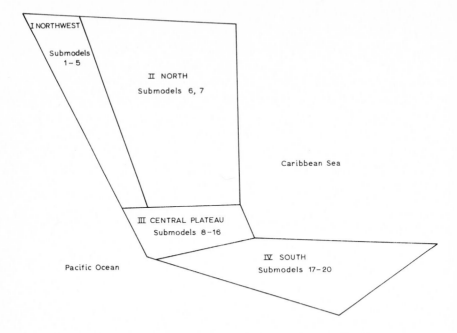

Fig. 2. Schematic map of regions and submodels in CHAC.

(II) The North — the rest of the northern part of the country; this region is also extremely arid and cultivable only with irrigation except for the eastern portions near the Gulf of Mexico.

(III) The Central Plateau — an area of mixed rainfed and irrigated farms, concentrated along the course of the Lerma River; the farms are generally smaller than in the North and Northwest; 20 years ago this was the most productive region in Mexican agriculture, but it has been surpassed by the northern regions.

(IV) The South — tropical agriculture with very few systems of water control; due to the mountainous terrain, this region is the most remote from the major urban markets.

Table 1 gives more exact descriptions of each submodel.

3. Production alternatives

For each of the twenty submodels, various production alternatives have been identified. Each alternative describes a production process which embodies a fixed combination of resource inputs for a given level of output. There are a total of 2345 column vectors representing such production alternatives in the model. (See table 2.) The production alternatives are functions of: (a) regional cropping patterns, (b) calendars of cultivation practices by crop, (c) classes of land by soil types, efficiency of water use, and climate, (d) modes of irrigation, and (e) degrees of mechanization.

3.1. Regional cropping patterns

In each of the submodels, crops were identified for production sets on the basis of the cropping patterns observed in the corresponding district during the 1960's. Since yields, fertilizer requirements, and other elements of the production vector are dependent on local soil and climate conditions, activities cannot be specified for crops which have not been grown previously in that district. This does not appear to be a serious omission in the Mexican context. Producers in irrigated areas already cultivate a wide variety of crops, and, on the other hand, there are only a limited number of crops which are well adapted to conditions of rainfed agriculture in Mexico.

The basis for crop selection in irrigation submodels is the time series of statistics published for irrigation districts by the Secretaría de Recursos Hidráulicos. [2] The information utilized for temporal and tropical submodels was provided by the Secretaría de Agricultura y Ganadería.

3.2. Calendars of cultivation practices

Several Mexican agencies compile cost of production estimates by crops and location, but these compilations are based on the se-

[2] See, for example, Secretaría de Recursos Hidráulicos (1969).

Table 1
Spatial components of CHAC

| Region | Location [a] | Submodels | | |
		Farm [b] type	Number	Name
Northwest	Río Yaqui	I	1	Río Yaqui
	Culiacán Río Humaya San Lorenzo }	I	2	Culmaya
	Río Colorado	I	3	Río Colorado
	Comisión del Fuerte	I	4	El Fuerte
	Remaining irrigation districts in the states of Baja California, Sonora, and Sinaloa	I	5	Residual Northwest
North	Irrigation districts in the states of Chihuahua, Coahuila and Durango	I	6	North Central
	Irrigation districts in the states of Nuevo León and Tamaulipas	I	7	Northeast
Central Plateau	Rainfed portions of the 17 municipios in Guanajuato which include the irrigation districts of Alto Río Lerma and La Begoña	{ LR SR	8 9	El Bajío A El Bajío B
	Alto Río Lerma La Begoña }	I	10	El Bajío Irrigated
	Mostly parts of the states of Puebla, Guanajuato, Hidalgo, and Querétaro	R	11	Temporal A
	Mostly the states of Jalisco, Michoacán and Morelos	R	12	Temporal B
(see figure 1)	Northern part of Central Plateau plus states further north	R	13	Temporal C
	Mostly the states of México, Tlaxcala	R	14	Temporal D
	Mostly portions of the states of Oaxaca, Guerrero, Colima, Michoacán, Tamaulipas	R	15	Temporal E
	The irrigation districts of 10 Central Plateau states	I	16	Central Irrigated

Table 1 (continued)

Region	Location [a]	Submodels		
		Farm [b] type	Number	Name
South	Mostly the states of Campeche, Yucatán, Quintana Roo, Nayarit	T	17	Tropical A
(see figure 1)	Mostly the states of Tabasco, Verácruz	T	18	Tropical B
	Mostly part of the states of Puebla, Chiapas, Verácruz, San Luis Potosi	T	19	Tropical C
	The irrigation districts in the tropical zones	I	20	South Irrigated

[a] For irrigation submodels, the location is defined in terms of the administrative irrigation districts of the Secretaría de Recursos Hidráulicos (S.R.H.). For rainfed and tropical areas, altitude and rainfall define the submodels, and each submodel's precise coverage is stated in terms of municipios (counties). Each municipio is assigned wholly to one submodel.

[b] The farm types are as follows: I – irrigated; LR – rainfed, large farms (ten has. or more); SR – rainfed, small farms (less than ten has.); R – rainfed; T – tropical. In many of the irrigation submodels there are additional distinctions among farms, based primarily on efficiency in water use.

quence of cultivation tasks and not on economic inputs. After identifying the crops to be included in the model, the next step was to establish the agricultural calendar for each of the 2,345 production activities. The calendar specifies the dates of planting, irrigating, fertilizing, crop tending, and harvesting.

The vector of production coefficients is derived from the agricultural calendar. For a given crop and location, the number of irrigation applications is not constant, but rather it varies with the month of planting. For a crop in a particular irrigation district, there are as many as four alternative planting dates in the model; two summer months and two winter months. For example, according to the activities for the Culmaya area, it is possible to cultivate corn either in summer or winter. Winter corn may be planted in December and harvested in June, or planted in January and harvested in July. Summer corn may occupy the land from May to November or from June to December. (See figure 3.)

Table 2
Production activities in CHAC by crop and by district

Crop	Geographic submodel																			Number of activities
	Río Yaqui	Culmaya	El Fuerte	North Central	Northeast	Río Colorado	Residual Northwest	El Bajío Temporal (2 submodels)	El Bajío Irrigated	Temporal A	Temporal B	Temporal C	Temporal D	Temporal E	Central Irrigated	Tropical A	Tropical B	Tropical C	South Irrigated	
Garlic						32	4		32						2					70
Dry alfalfa	16		24	12		32	6								2					92
Cotton	16		24	12		32	12							3	4					103
Green alfalfa		12	24	12			6		32						2					88
Rice		12	24				6								4		2		4	52
Oats												3	3							6
Sugar cane		12	24		6		6								4		2	2	4	60
Squash											3									3
Safflower	16	12	24	12		32	6							3						105
Peanuts				6					32		3				2					43
Onions									32						2					34
Forage barley	16			4		32	4								2					58
Grain barley	16			4		32	4		48				3		2					109
Dry chile											3									3
Green chile		12	24				12		32		3				2				2	87
Strawberries									32						2					34

Table 2 (continued)

Crop	Geographic submodel																			Number of activities
	Río Yaqui	Culmaya	El Fuerte	North Central	Northeast	Río Colorado	Residual Northwest	El Bajío Temporal (2 submodels)	El Bajío Irrigated	Temporal A	Temporal B	Temporal C	Temporal D	Temporal E	Central Irrigated	Tropical A	Tropical B	Tropical C	South Irrigated	
Beans		12	24				9	8	48	3	3	3	3	3	2	2	2	2		124
Chickpeas		12	24				6	8	48	3	3		3		2		2	2		106
Lima beans									32		3				2					37
Tomatoes		12	24	12			12		32						2					85
Sesame	16	12	24				12							3	4	2		2		75
Flaxseed	16	12	24				6		48					3						49
Corn	16	22	48	12	12	32	22	12	48	3	3	3	3	3	2	2	4	2	2	251
Cantaloupe		12	24				12								4					52
Potatoes			48				12						3							63
Cucumber		12					6								4					22
Pineapple											1									1
Watermelon		12	24				9								4					61
Sorghum	16	24	48	12	12	32	20	12	48	3	3			3	2		2	2	2	241
Soybeans	16	12	24				10									2				64
Tobacco					6											1				1
Wheat	16	12	24	12		32	8		48			3	3		2					166
Number of activities	176	214	528	110	36	288	210	40	544	12	27	12	21	21	60	9	13	10	14	2,345

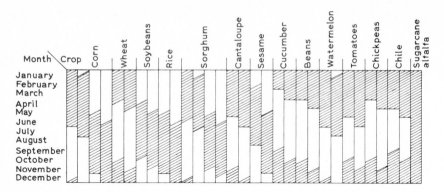

Fig. 3. Alternative calendars of cultivation in a sample submodel of CHAC (Culmaya.)
Note: Part shading ▨ indicates that one-third of a month is required under mechanized techniques; this becomes a full month with non-mechanized techniques.

For irrigation submodels, the alternative agricultural calendars were taken from information supplied by the Secretaría de Recursos Hidráulicos. For each temporal or tropical submodel, there exists only one planting date – and hence one calendar of cultivation activities – depending on the month in which the rains begin. Planting dates were taken from information supplied by the Secretaria de Agricultura y Ganadería.

3.3. Classes of land and water

The temporal and tropical submodels are defined on the basis of climatic conditions – hence are not necessarily contiguous. The irrigation submodels refer to the administrative irrigation districts of the Secretaría de Recursos Hidráulicos. [3] Within each district, there are as many as four zones demarcated by that ministry to represent varying degrees of efficiency in use of reservoir water. In each zone, a different amount of gross water release at the dam is required to achieve the same net amount of water on the field. The water losses depend upon the length of canals and their state of repair.

---

[3] In some cases, the area in these districts is augmented to provide coverage of lands irrigated by dispersed wells.

Irrigation water is specified in two forms: gravity and well water. The former includes water from reservoirs and river pumps, and its allocation is controlled by the Secretaría de Recursos Hidráulicos. The latter is supplied by private tubewells. In some of the irrigation submodels, both water sources are specified.

The water input norms differ for gravity and well water, due to larger transmission losses in the gravity-fed reticulation system. The prices also differ. For gravity water, the administrative levy is entered as a cost in the objective function. For well water, the pumping cost is entered. Since both types of water are available in limited quantities CHAC determines a shadow cost which normally exceeds these direct costs.

3.4. Degrees of mechanization

The irrigated—non-irrigated distinction is one of the ways in which CHAC distinguishes more capital-intensive and more labor-intensive agriculture. Individual crops also vary enormously in their unit labor requirements. [4] In addition alternative degrees of mechanization have been specified for each crop and location.

In CHAC in entirety there are three degrees of mechanization for each crop: mechanized, partially mechanized, and non-mechanized. In some locations, depending on the observed techniques in the base period, only two degrees are specified. To account for the time lapse inherent in adoption of new techniques, only one-degree changes of technique are permitted during the six-year period studied (1968—74). That is, for districts in which only nonmechanized techniques were observed in the base period, CHAC includes partially mechanized in addition to nonmechanized activities.

The alternative degrees of mechanization do not affect yields per hectare. The totally mechanized technique is defined so that operations requiring traction power are done with machinery rather than animals. These operations include land preparation, harvesting, and some intermediate cultivation steps. There are crop-specif-

---

[4] See tables 3 and 4 of this chapter, and also table 6 of chapter IV.4 below.

ic variations. For example, in Mexico cotton is always harvested manually, no matter how capital-intensive the other operations. In this case, the mechanized cotton production technique includes manual harvesting.

The partially mechanized technique refers to the practice of using mechanical power for land preparation and seeding, while using draft animals for all other operations. In the non-mechanized technique, draft animals are used for all traction operations. These discrete alternatives are the major ones observed in Mexico. When a farmer adopts only partial mechanization, he is very likely to use it at the beginning of the crop calendar in order to facilitate the process of getting the crop in the ground.

Machinery operators' time is one of the inputs for the mechanized techniques. When draft animals are used, a (much larger) input of unskilled agriculture labor is required. The input norms in CHAC reflect both kinds of labor. Since machinery operators do not appear to be a bottleneck in Mexico, the supply of their services is assumed to be perfectly elastic at a given price. Hence their services are not explicit inputs in CHAC, but they are reflected in the machinery cost entries in the objective function.

The input requirements for plowing, harvesting, and other power operations depend only on the degree of mechanization and, for harvesting, on the crop. They do not vary over districts. Plowing requirements per hectare are standard, and harvest requirements per ton are standard by crop. Through published data [5] and field surveys of one of the authors (Bassoco), it was possible to estimate these standard norms for each degree of mechanization. In this manner, activities were formed which represent degrees of mechanization other than those observed in a particular district.

---

[5] The basic published series on costs of production are those of the Secretaría de Recursos Hidráulicos, the Aseguradora Nacional Agrícola y Ganadera, the Instituto Nacional de Investigaciones Agrícolas, and the Banco Nacional de Crédito Ejidal.

4. Technical production coefficients

Information on agricultural production costs typically comes in the form of estimates of total expenses per 'operation', such as plowing, irrigation, and fertilizer applications. These estimates include costs of materials, labor, draft animals, and machinery services. There are also estimates of the number of distinct irrigation releases, fertilizer applications, weedings, etc., per crop and district. To form activities for CHAC, the problem was to convert this information into statements of required economic inputs, such as labor, fertilizer, and credit. To facilitate this conversion, the unit activity level in all cases was defined to be cultivation of one hectare, rather than one ton of output.

4.1. Labor, machinery, draft animals

For each crop and degree of mechanization, standard inputs of labor and services of machinery and draft animals have been defined for each operation in the agricultural calendar. These operations include both those which involve traction power and those which do not. They range from land preparation and seeding, through plant tending and application of water and chemical products, to the harvest. The standard inputs per operation are constant over districts. But the number of required operations varies over districts in some cases (plant tending, application of chemicals, water releases), and the yield per hectare also varies over districts. Hence the total labor requirement per hectare varies over districts for a given crop and a given degree of mechanization. The number of operations and yields per district are taken from data published by the four institutions mentioned above.

The assumption of standard inputs per operation, regardless of location, is not exactly true, but it is a close approximation to reality. The number of tractor hours required to plow a hectare varies somewhat, depending on the average soil conditions in a district, but it does not vary greatly. To carry out the standard operation concept, machinery use requirements have been normalized for a tractor of 60 horsepower. Inputs of labor, animal power,

Table 3

Sequence of standard operations for cotton cultivation (days of unskilled labor, machinery services, and draft animal services required per hectare by month)

Cultivation month and operation	Mechanized		Partially mechanized			Non-mechanized	
	Unskilled labor	Machinery	Unskilled labor	Machinery	Animals	Unskilled labor	Animals
1st Preparatory tasks							
Fallow		0.12		0.12		1.0	2.0
Cross-plowing		0.5		0.5		3.0	6.0
Harrowing		0.2		0.2		2.5	5.0
Land levelling		0.25		0.25		0.5	1.0
Canal cleaning	1.0		1.0			1.0	2.0
2nd Irrigation ditches							
Forming borders [a]	1.0	0.2	1.0	0.2		2.0	2.0
Linking borders [b]	1.0	0.2	1.0	0.2		2.0	
Water application	2.0		2.0			2.0	
Harrowing		0.2		0.2		2.0	4.0
Seeding and fertilization	0.2	0.2	0.2	0.2		4.0	
Maintenance of field works		0.2	0.2			2.0	
3rd Thinning plants	4.0		4.0			4.0	
Cultivation		0.2	2.0		4.0	2.0	4.0
Weeding	6.0		6.0			6.0	
Applications of insecticides (2) [c]							

Table 3 (continued)

Cultivation month and operation	Mechanized		Partially mechanized			Non-mechanized	
	Unskilled labor	Machinery	Unskilled labor	Machinery	Animals	Unskilled labor	Animals
4th Fertilization		0.2	2.0			2.0	
Cultivation		0.2	2.0		4.0	2.0	4.0
Weeding	6.0		6.0			6.0	
Water applications (2)	4.0		4.0			4.0	
Applications of insecticides (2)							
5th Cultivation		0.2	2.0		4.0	2.0	4.0
Weeding	12.0		6.0			12.0	
Water applications (2)	4.0		4.0			4.0	
Applications of insecticides (2)							
6th Weeding	6.0		6.0			6.0	
Water application	2.0		2.0			2.0	
Application of insecticides							
7th Harvest [d] (per ton)	11.0		11.0			11.0	
Transport to farm gate		0.12	2.0		4.0	2.0	4.0
8th Harvest [d] (per ton)	11.0		11.0			11.0	
Transport to farm gate		0.12	2.0		4.0	2.0	4.0
9th Harvest [d] (per ton)	11.0		11.0			11.0	
Transport to farm gate		0.12	2.0		4.0	2.0	4.0

[a] 'Bordeo'.
[b] 'Pegar bordos'.
[c] For cotton, insecticide applications are made by airplane.
[d] Normally the harvest covers three months, with 30%, 50%, and 20%, occurring in each successive month.

and machinery services are expressed in days of labor. This concept is the bridge between technical agronomic information and the cost estimates of CHAC. It also permits ready identification of those portions of input packages which vary over crops, districts, planting dates, and degrees of mechanization.

Apart from the differing degrees of mechanization, some crops are simply more labor-intensive than others. The *mechanized* form of cotton cultivation requires almost twice as much labor per hectare as the *non-mechanized* form of wheat cultivation. This may be seen from tables 3 and 4, which show the labor, machinery, and animal power inputs into the standard operations for two major crops (cotton and wheat).

The range of techniques in tables 3 and 4 imply certain elasticities of substitution of labor for capital. Calculated at the midpoints of the relevant range, they are as follows:

Cotton:	Mechanized to partially mechanized,	−0.178
	Partially mechanized to nonmechanized,	−0.231
Wheat:	Mechanized to partially mechanized,	−1.603
	Partially mechanized to nonmechanized,	−0.264

Grains offer more scope for factor substitution than cotton and many vegetables.

4.2. Land and water

The unit level of operation of the production activities is one hectare. Land inputs are specified monthly. Hence the normal land input coefficient is 1.0, signifying use of an entire hectare in a particular calendar month. An exception is made at the beginning of the cultivation cycle, when land preparation activities may require less than a full month. Plowing with draft animals, together with associated activities, usually requires a month's work. With mechanized techniques, however, the same operation requires about ten days. Hence in the mechanized technique, a coefficient of 0.33 is used instead of 1.0. These land savings can be important when double cropping is feasible. Another exception is made in the case of the harvest, also to differentiate techniques.

Table 4

Sequence of standard operations for wheat cultivation (days of unskilled labor, machinery services, and draft animal services required per hectare by month)

Cultivation month and operation	Mechanized		Partially mechanized			Non-mechanized		
	Unskilled labor	Machinery	Unskilled labor	Machinery	Animals	Unskilled labor	Machinery	Animals
1st Canal cleaning	1.0		1.0			1.0		
Fallow		0.5		0.5		3.0		6.0
Cross-plowing						2.5		5.0
Harrowing		0.2		0.2		0.5		1.0
Land levelling		0.25		0.25		1.0		2.0
2nd Irrigation ditches	1.0	0.2	1.0	0.2		2.0		2.0
Bordering or bench terracing		0.2		0.2		2.0		
Linking borders	1.0		1.0			4.0		
Seeding and fertilization	0.2	0.2	0.2	0.2		0.5		1.0
Harrowing								
Water application	2.0		2.0			2.0		
3rd Applications of herbicides		0.2	3.0			3.0		
Fertilization		0.2	2.0			2.0		
Water application	2.0		2.0			2.0		
4th Water application	2.0		2.0			2.0		
Application of insecticides		0.2	3.0			3.0		
Application of herbicides		0.2	3.0			3.0		
5th Water application	2.0		2.0			2.0		
Application of insecticides		0.2	3.0			3.0		
6th Water application	2.0		2.0			2.0		
7th Combine harvesting (per ton)		0.27		0.27				
Hand cutting						4.0		
Hand threshing							0.13	
Transport to farm gate	2.0	0.12	2.0		4.0	2.0		4.0

In some cases, land savings are related to the nature of the product. In the case of alfalfa and barley, the form of the crop harvested is reflected in the length of time for which the land is used. Green alfalfa occupies the land longer in the drying process.

From figure 3 above, it is possible to derive the monthly land coefficients for various cropping activities in the Culmaya sub-model. From the figure, it may be seen which double-cropping combinations are feasible and which are not. For example, a wheat-soybeans or wheat-sorghum rotation pattern is feasible, but wheat-sesame is not. In some cases, a particular rotation is prevented only because a mechanized harvest is not possible for one crop. This is most often true of fruits and vegetables. If it were possible to mechanize the harvest of cantaloupe, a soybean-cantaloupe rotation would be feasible. Tomatoes require a sufficiently long growing season so that they cannot be rotated with any other crop. Hence the cost of tomato cultivation includes the lost opportunity for double cropping.

The irrigation requirements are given by the irrigation schedules formulated by the Secretaría de Recursos Hidráulicos for each crop and district. The coefficients are measured in cubic feet of gross water release from the irrigation source. In some of the submodels, there are as many as four zones defined with respect to efficiency in gravity water use. Gross well water coefficients differ from those for gravity water, due to different rates of water loss in the reticulation systems.

4.3. Credit, fertilizer, improved seeds, yields

Short-term credit requirements are related to total production costs, and hence they vary over crop, district, and technique. The basis for estimation of credit requirements is the set of credit norms used by the Banco Nacional de Crédito Ejidal.

Inputs of fertilizers and pesticides are grouped together in a row defining chemical inputs. The coefficients are given in pesos rather than physical units. Inputs of improved seeds also are given in pesos. Both sets of coefficients reflect prevailing practices and yields in each submodel area.

Yields vary with the submodel (reflecting soil and climate conditions) and local practices regarding application of chemical inputs. For irrigation district submodels, these yields are five-year averages of yield statistics compiled by the Secretaría de Recursos Hidráulicos. For submodels representing non-irrigated agriculture, yields are compiled as appropriate weighted averages of state-level data in the national agricultural plan of the Secretaría de Agricultura y Ganadería. Table 5 shows the range of variation of yields in CHAC.

5. Sources of variation in the technical coefficients

In summary, variations in the technical coefficients in CHAC arise from two sources: (a) geographical differences which give rise to variations in cultivation calendars, fertilization and crop cultivation practices, irrigation requirements, and yields; and (b) alternative degrees of mechanization and efficiency in water use within the same submodel area.

Table 6 shows the effect of mechanization on the coefficients for labor, machinery services, and draft animal services. Coefficients for two sample submodels are shown. Table 7 summarizes the sources of variation in all types of coefficients, grouped by basic agricultural operations. In labor, for example, there are two kinds of coefficients: those which vary over submodel districts and those which do not. The latter include labor inputs for land preparation activities. For the harvest, labor inputs per ton are constant, but yields vary among districts. Coefficients which are district-specific are those related to cultural operations: weeding, fertilization, applications of insecticides, etc.

6. Restrictions on resource availability

6.1. Labor force

There are two sources for estimates of the agricultural labor force

Table
Yields by crops and submod|

Submodel/Crop	garlic	dry alfalfa	cotton fiber	cotton seed	green alfalfa	rice	oats
Culmaya					44.910	3.100	
Río Yaqui		12.154	0.828	1.421			
Río Colorado	7.000	7.962	0.972	1.667			
El Fuerte		8.679	0.828	1.421	43.897	2.600	
Residual Northwest	6.800	9.029	1.013	1.737	45.000	2.960	
North Central		16.270	0.833	1.428	72.000		
Northeast							
Central Irrigated	6.750	20.300	0.935	1.600	87.630	{5.667 / 3.300}	
South Irrigated						2.781	
Temporal							
A							
B							
C							0.50
D							0.80
E			{0.357 / 0.924}	{0.612 / 1.584}			
Tropical							
A_1							
A_2							
B_1						1.500	
B_2						2.500	
B_3							
B_4							
C_1							
C_2							
El Bajío Temporal							
1							
2							
3							
El Bajío Irrigated (nonlevel land)							
1							
2	5.500				80.000		
3	7.000				100.000		
El Bajío Irrigated (level land)							
1							
2	5.780				84.000		
3	7.350				105.000		

CHAC (metric tons/hectare)

cane	safflower	squash	peanuts	onions	forage barley	grain barley	dry chile	green chile	strawberries
4.320	0.750							5.130	
	1.646				13.471	2.400			
	1.493				10.986	2.234			
5.920	1.256							4.179	
5.944	1.674				13.044	2.600		8.265	
	1.360		2.300		13.000	1.870			
2.912									
5.840			2.200	9.200	10.370	3.101	1.700	10.393	11.701
4.778								6.945	
		8.333	1.277				1.250	2.775	
	0.750					0.709			
5.000									
8.000									
3.000									
8.000									
						2.500			
			3.000	10.000		3.300		5.000	12.500
			4.000	15.000		4.000		7.000	15.000
						2.620			
			3.150	10.500		3.460		5.250	13.100
			4.200	15.750		4.200		7.350	15.700

Table

Submodel/Crop	beans	chickpeas	lima beans	tomatoes	sesame	flaxseed	corn
Culmaya	0.970	0.840		20.320	0.760		1.7
Río Yaqui					0.750	1.646	3.6
Río Colorado							1.7
El Fuerte	1.322			30.483	0.790	1.998	2.3
Residual Northwest	1.760	1.470		10.830	0.720	1.364	2.3
North Central							1.8
Northeast							2.6
Central Irrigated	1.080	1.820	2.210	12.502	0.720		2.5
South Irrigated							1.5
Temporal							
A	0.378	0.606					0.6
B	0.380	0.800		6.600			1.6
C	0.439						0.5
D	0.353		0.722				0.8
E	0.550				0.684	0.700	0.7
Tropical							
A_1	0.500				0.450		0.8
A_2	0.800				0.650		1.8
B_1	0.800						1.6
B_2	1.200						3.0
B_3							1.6
B_4							3.0
C_1	0.800				0.450		1.6
C_2	1.200				0.650		3.0
El Bajío Temporal							
1	0.500						0.7
2	0.500	0.600					1.2
3	0.600	0.800					1.5
El Bajío Irrigated							
(nonlevel land)							
1	0.900	1.500					2.50
2	1.400	2.000	2.000	14.000			3.50
3	1.800	3.000	2.500	18.000			5.00
El Bajío Irrigated (level land)							
1	0.950	1.570					2.62
2	1.470	2.100	2.100	14.700			3.68
3	1.890	3.150	2.630	18.900			5.25

ontinued)

	potatoes	cucumber	pineapple	watermelon	sorghum	soybeans	tobacco	wheat
7.610		11.120		6.850	3.060	1.370		2.782
					4.957	1.879		3.862
					3.552			3.600
4.223	14.000			6.540	3.843	1.913		3.166
7.400	14.000	10.176		7.590	3.600	1.840		3.320
				15.000	3.400			2.270
					3.700			2.662
9.750	14.000	9.500		11.590	2.791			1.830
					1.661		1.856	
					1.946			
					2.687			
								0.500
	11.000							0.861
					1.200			
						1.000		
			25.000			1.500	1.430	
					2.000			
					3.500			
					2.000			
					3.500			
					1.200			
					2.000			
					2.500			
					3.500			2.500
					5.000			3.500
					7.000			4.500
					3.680			2.625
					5.250			3.675
					7.350			4.725

Table 6

Variation of cotton input coefficients with degrees of mechanization, in two sample districts [a] (unit: days)

Input	El Fuerte			Río Yaqui	
	Mechanized	Partly mechanized	Non-mechanized	Mechanized	Partly mechanized
Machinery services	3.63	2.07	0	3.23	2.07
Mule services	0	32.00	58.00	0	32.00
Labor:					
January	8.0	12.0	12.0		
February	8.0	10.0	10.0	1.0	1.0
March	8.0	10.0	10.0	4.2	4.2
April	8.0	10.0	10.0	12.0	14.0
May	10.2	12.2	12.2	8.0	12.0
June	13.7	15.7	15.7	12.0	14.0
July	5.5	7.5	7.5	8.0	8.0
August				8.2	10.2
September				13.7	15.7
October	1.0	1.0	9.0	5.5	7.5
November	4.2	4.2	14.0		
December	10.0	10.0	14.0		
Yield (tons/hectare):					
Cotton fiber	0.868	0.868	0.868	0.828	0.828
Cotton seed	1.488	1.488	1.488	1.421	1.421
(Total labor)	(76.6)	(92.6)	(108.4)	(72.6)	(86.6)

[a] With different planting dates, the months and, in some cases, the values of coefficients change.

in Mexico: the decennial population censuses and the agricultural censuses. More resources have been invested in the population censuses, and as a result they are widely considered to be more reliable. However, they are deficient in that they virtually ignore family labor. The agricultural census for 1960, on the other hand, lists 1.5 million unpaid family workers on ejidal farms alone (vs. 0.1 million family workers in the entire sector according to the population census for the same year). In spite of this problem, the population census of 1960 has been taken as the basis for the

Table 7
Sources of variation in the technical coefficients

Coefficient	Source of variation					
	Crop	Plant-ing date	Land class within a submodel	Type of irrigation (well or gravity)	Degree of mechan-ization	Sub-model
Unskilled labor						
Land preparation	X				X	
Harvest	X				X	X
Others	X				X	X
Machinery services						
Land preparation	X				X	
Harvest	X				X	X
Others	X				X	X
Draft animal services						
Land preparation	X				X	
Harvest	X					
Others	X				X	X
Land	X	X	X			X
Irrigation water	X		X	X		X
Chemical inputs	X	X				X
Improved seeds	X					X
Short-term credit	X			X		X
Yield	X	X				X

CHAC labor force, with suitable augmentation for family labor. The figures have been projected forward to 1968 in accordance with regional labor force growth rates calculated from the 1960 census and the preliminary tabulations of the 1970 census. These regional growth rates add up to about a 1.5% growth rate for the sector as a whole. [6] Total population has been increasing at about 3.5%, but annual rural-urban migration has amounted to about 2.0% of the rural population.

[6] Two percent is the growth rate assumed by Keesing and Manne for unskilled agricultural labor. See chapter II.1, section 4, above.

The population census itself contains two kinds of 'agricultural' labor force estimates. One is by occupational category and the other is by sector. For the sectors of agriculture (i.e., crops), livestock, forestry, hunting, and fishing, the total labor force is estimated at 6,143,530 in 1960. For the three occupational categories 'field workers', 'ejidal farmers', and 'non-ejidal farmers', the total is 4,642,453 persons. [7] This latter total is engaged in crop agriculture. Of this figure, 2,671,852 persons are listed as heads of farm households ('propietarios'), and 1,970,601 are essentially field workers.

To estimate the family labor component, recourse is made to the demographic figures on family composition. The average farm household has about 5.5 persons, and about half the population is under 15 years of age. Since a wife is occupied in the house most of the time, it is assumed that she contributes one-tenth the field work of her husband. These and other equivalence factors yield the following table:

Family member	(a) Number per household	(b) Labor equivalent factor	(c) = (a×b) Labor equivalent
Household head	1.00	1.00	1.00
Spouse	0.95	0.10	0.10
Children under 15	2.75	–	–
Children over 15	0.80	0.50	0.40
			1.50

On this basis, there are 1.5 male adult-equivalent laborers per family. This implies that the total family labor available in 1960 comprised 1,335,926 persons. This is less than the family labor estimated for ejidos alone in the agriculture census, but recall that the

[7] Table 27 of the 1960 population census.

reliability of the latter is doubtful. Also the CHAC estimate of the unskilled labor force is substantially higher than that used in DINAMICO, so it was deemed better to err on the conservative side than in the other direction.

Hence, the total labor force engaged in crop agriculture in 1960 is estimated as follows:

farm heads	2,671,852
family laborers	1,335,926
day laborers	1,970,601
total	5,978,379

Since CHAC excludes long-cycle crops, the labor force figure for the model is correspondingly reduced. The total labor force which appears in CHAC for 1968 is 5,181,945. This reflects both the 1960–68 labor force increase and an allowance for the labor engaged in long-cycle crops.

Farmers and family labor are specified by submodel in CHAC and day laborers by region. To obtain the figures for each spatial entity, county-level data from the 1960 census were aggregated. As noted, to arrive at 1968 estimates, the annual regional labor force growth rate during 1960–70 was utilized. [8]

6.2. Land and water

The monthly land restrictions in CHAC are based on cultivable land estimates by the Secretaría de Agricultura and the Secretaría de Recursos Hidráulicos. For non-irrigated submodels, the building blocks are counties. Each county is assigned to a submodel according to its altitude and rainfall (refer back to figure 1). For irrigation submodels, the building blocks are the administrative irrigation districts. In some submodels, additional land is included to represent scattered irrigation sites which lie outside the jurisdiction of the administrative districts.

[8] Based on preliminary 1970 population census data. Since the processing of the 1970 census was incomplete when the CHAC data were being compiled, the 1960 census was used as the base for the labor force estimates.

Table 8

Base-period domestic prices and production in CHAC (1968)

Crop	Farm-gate price [a] (pesos/ton)			Production (tons)			National average farm-gate price (pesos/ton)	National production (tons)
	Irrigated	Temporal	Tropical	Irrigated	Temporal	Tropical		
Garlic	2,213			31.0			2,213	31.0
Cotton fiber	2,459	2,381		1,270.8			2,447	1,504.1
Alfalfa (dry)	354						354	
Alfalfa (green)	126			10,932.0			126	10,932.0
Rice	1,134		1,358	368.6		131.8	1,219	500.4
Oats	653	805		22.0	87.2		774	109.2
Sugar cane	64		63	14,216.9		14,926.0	64	29,142.9
Safflower	1,544	1,552		173.4	75.3		1,546	248.7
Squash		576			108.1		576	108.1
Peanuts	1,593	1,298		24.5	50.7		1,391	75.2
Onions	637			122.7			637	122.7
Forage barley	86						86	
Grain barley	1,014	862		135.3	191.9		925	327.2
Dry chile	7,554	8,153		17.7	4.1		7,677	21.8
Green chile	1,413	1,651		121.5	50.9		1,496	171.5
Strawberries	1,977			109.3			1,977	109.3
Beans [e]	2,202	2,070	1,726	104.5	720.7	119.4	2,040	944.6
Chickpeas	1,153	967		24.4	159.2		992	183.6
Lima beans	855	865		14.2	31.9		862	45.4
Tomatoes [b]	1,998	1,255		586.2	78.8		1,906	665.0
Sesame	1,500	2,382	2,438	30.2	140.6	22.7	2,407	193.5

Table 8 (continued)

Crop	Farm-gate price [a] (pesos/ton)			Production (tons)			National average farm-gate price (pesos/ton)	National production (tons)
	Irrigated	Temporal	Tropical	Irrigated	Temporal	Tropical		
Flaxseed	1,701	1,661		8.8	10.1		1,680	18.9
Corn d,e	940	908	935	1,750.5	5,425.6	2,059.1	920	9,255.2
Cantaloupe	682			142.5			682	142.5
Potatoes	973	865		239.2	164.3		929	403.5
Cucumber c	1,301			20.5			1,301	20.5
Pineapple			513			297.6	513	297.6
Watermelon	777			187.6			777	187.6
Sorghum e	625	657	671	1,280.3	1,173.2	20.2	641	2,523.5
Soybeans	1,600		1,640	259.7		2.7	1,600	272.4
Tobacco			7,722			75.7	7,722	75.7
Wheat e	857	895		2,138.6	105.8		859	2,244.4

[a] For prices, a 1967–69 average is used.

[b] The average price of tomatoes is strongly influenced by the export prices. In CHAC, a base-period *domestic* price of 1150 pesos/ton is used.

[c] The average price of cucumbers is strongly influenced by the export price. In CHAC, a base-period *domestic* price of 586 pesos/ton is used.

[d] In the case of corn, it is assumed (on the basis of information contained in the National Agricultural Plan) that 63% of production goes to human consumption and 37% to forage uses.

[e] For corn, beans, sorghum, and wheat, the farm-gate prices in the table reflect the subsidies of CONASUPO. For CHAC, prices were adjusted to remove the influence of the subsidy. Thus the base-period prices used for these crops are as follows (in pesos/ton): corn 861, beans 1834, sorghum 633, wheat 800.

Water restrictions are specified annually and monthly in CHAC. For gravity water, the annual restrictions represent limitations on the annual rate of replenishment of reservoir water, while the monthly restrictions represent limitations on the capacity of the canal system for water delivery. [9] For pumped water from wells, the annual restrictions represent legal limits designed to maintain the water table level, and the monthly restrictions refer to pumping capacity.

7. Product prices

For the 1968 solutions of CHAC, the domestic demand curves are passed through a point representing actual base-period prices and quantities. For the 1974 solutions, this point is shifted to represent income and population growth and per capita income elasticities.

For prices, 1967–69 averages were used in order to minimize the effect of short-term fluctuations. Rather than using existing sector-wide price estimates, it was deemed better to construct new sector-wide estimates from micro-level data. Weighted averages of local prices were constructed. The Secretaría de Recursos Hidráulicos collects extensive information on local crop prices every year, so these were used as the basis for the sectoral estimates. It was assumed that neighboring irrigated and non-irrigated plots face the same price for a given crop. But, as reported in the statistics, prices vary substantially between regions and to a lesser extent between major areas within a region. This procedure permits the application of the S.R.H. price data to all producing areas, irrigated and non-irrigated. Prices were weighted with local production statistics for both kinds of agriculture.

Table 8 presents production estimates and computed average

---

[9] In two submodels, the monthly restrictions also represent water availability, with opportunities for intertemporal water transfer by holding it in the reservoir – at the cost of evaporation loss. For the Río Colorado submodel, which represents an area on the U.S. border, the monthly and annual restrictions are in accord with an international treaty on water use.

prices by crop for irrigated, temporal, and tropical areas and for the sector as a whole.

In the case of a few crops, the operations of the national price-support agency (CONASUPO) have resulted in a gap between the farm-gate price and the corresponding price to consumers, after accounting for processing and transportation costs. For these crops, CONASUPO incurs a budgetary deficit. For CHAC, it was necessary to reduce the farm-gate price of these crops by an amount which reflects the subsidy to consumers. This yields a market-clearing price and quantity, and the CHAC demand curves are passed through that point.

Export markets are specified independently of the domestic markets. For products which Mexico exports, it is assumed that the Mexican share of the world market is sufficiently small so that the country is a price-taker. In some cases, the quantity exported is limited by international agreement or by import quotas in other countries. [10] For imports also, the fixed-price assumption is made.

For exports, farm-gate prices are used. These are less than f.o.b. prices. For imports, prices appropriate to consumption in Mexico City are required; these are higher than c.i.f. prices. This puts imports on the same price basis as domestic sources of supply.

8. Factor prices

For sector-wide inputs, CHAC is based upon market prices. This includes hired labor, for which the wage varies over regions. [11] For land, a district-level resource, prices are completely endogenous. For water, the well pumping costs and administrative charges for release of reservoir water are registered in the objective function, but since quantities of available water are limited, the model also computes a shadow cost.

[10] In the case of sugar, two export markets have been introduced into CHAC: one reflecting the Mexican quota for U.S. imports and the other, at a lower price, reflecting the free international market.

[11] The pricing of labor, including imputation of farmers' reservation wages, is explained in chapter IV.1 above.

Table 9
Costs associated with the operation of one 60 h.p. tractor (1968 pesos) [a]

Acquisition costs:	
Tractor of 60 h.p.	75,364
Reversible plow with 3-furrow disc	14,200
18-disc harrow	9,250
Land-levelling blade	6,000
Broadcasting seeder	20,000
Cultivator	10,500
	135,314
Useful life:	10,000 hours

Gasoline and oil consumption:
diesel, 50 liters each 8 hours, at 0.4 pesos/liter
oil, 8 liters each 125 hours, at 8.0 pesos/liter
grease, 1 kg each 8 hours at 5.0 pesos/kilo

Maintenance:
transmission oil change, 30 liters each 1500 hours, at 6.5 pesos/liter
filter change each 250 hours, 30 pesos
tire change, one set each 3500 hours at 4,500 pesos/set
tune-up each 1000 hours, 300 pesos
cylinder change, 600 pesos

Summary of operating costs per hour:	
depreciation	13.50
gasoline, oil consumption	3.64
maintenance	2.38

[a] Apart from the operator's salary.

Table 9 shows the calculation of the market price of tractor services. Similar calculations were made for pumping costs of wells and services of draft animals.

References

Aseguradora Nacional Agrícola y Ganadera, *Programas de aseguramiento, ciclo prima- vera-verano 1968–69 y ciclo invierno 1968–69*. México.

Bassoco, Luz María and Donald L. Winkelmann, 'Programación de la producción agrícola de la parcela ejidal en tres obras de regadío en el estado de Quintana Roo'. Chapingo, México, Escuela Nacional de Agricultura, 1970.

Barrera Islas, Daniel, and Donald L. Winkelmann, 'Análisis económico del uso del agua y la mano de obra en el sector ejidal de la Comarca Lagunera'. Chapingo, Mexico, Centro de Economía Agrícola, 1969.

Conklin, Frank S., and Earl O. Heady, 'Uso optimo de los recursos agropecuarios en el distrito de Riego de la Begoña'. Chapingo, México, Centro de Economía Agrícola, 1968.

Gonzalez, Vicente and José Silos, *Economía de la produccion agrícola en el Bajío*. México, Instituto Nacional de Investigaciones Agrícolas, 1968.

Hertford, Reed, 'Sources of change in Mexican agricultural production, 1940–65'. U.S. Department of Agriculture, Foreign Agricultural Economic Report, No. 73. Washington, D.C., August 1971.

Secretaría de Agricultura y Ganadería, Plan Nacional Agrícola, 1968–69 and 1969–70. México, 1968 and 1969.

Secretaría de Industria y Comercio, *Anuarios de comercio exterior de 1955 a 1970*. México.

Secretaría de Industria y Comercio, Características de las personas ocupadas en el predio. *IV censo agrícola ganadero y ejidal, 1960,* México, 1965.

Secretaría de Industria y Comercio, *VIII censo de población, 1960*. México, 1964.

Secretaría de Recursos Hidráulicos, *Características en los distritos de riego*. México, 1969.

Secretaría de Recursos Hidráulicos, *Costos de produccíon de los principales cultivos en los distritos de riego*. México 1969 (and earlier years).

Secretaría de Recursos Hidráulicos, *Estadística agrícola para los ciclos 1966–67, 1967–68, 1968–69*. México.

IV.3. CHAC RESULTS: ECONOMIC ALTERNATIVES FOR MEXICAN AGRICULTURE *

John H. DULOY and Roger D. NORTON

1. General remarks

In general, three kinds of results have been derived from the CHAC study. First, a possible set of priorities for data improvement becomes apparent as the implications of the data are traced out. Proper data generation requires a dialogue between the users and the suppliers of information. Data of better quality are likely to be generated only after their usefulness has been demonstrated.

Second, by virtue of its comprehensiveness, the model accounts for all input requirements by season and locality. In the case of labor, this makes possible an estimate of the degree of underemployment — in total, seasonally, and locally. Although there are published figures on Mexico's agricultural labor force, to date there has been only one attempt to estimate the actual degree of employment or underemployment for the sector. [1] Third, the model permits a more precise definition of issues and tradeoffs. This is accomplished via the solutions which provide estimates of the consequences of specific policy changes.

* The authors are indebted to Luciano Barraza, Luz María Bassoco, Teresa Rendón, and Leopoldo Solís for extensive discussions of the results reported here. Louis Goreux, Bruce Johnston, Alan Manne and Guy Pfeffermann gave helpful comments on drafts of this chapter. Gary Kutcher carried the main burden of seeing the models through the computer.

[1] By the Centro de Investigaciones Agrarias (1970), using a small sample of farms.

On the data side, the model has already led to revisions of water input coefficients. Initial tests of the individual submodels showed inconsistencies between estimated water requirements per crop and the water availability in each irrigation district. Consequently, the Secretaría de Recursos Hidráulicos made extensive revisions of its water norms. For the longer run, there are two efforts under way in Mexico for agricultural data improvement. One is a continuous project for collection of both census-type information and production cost estimates by locality. [2] It is proceeding on a state-by-state basis, using stratified random sampling techniques and both aerial photography and directly-administered questionnaires. When these results become available, the quality of the information base will be vastly improved. There is also a less ambitious but more flexible attempt underway to devise more appropriate farm-level questionnaires, using a sample of districts in the Central Plateau. [3]

Rather than delay to take advantage of improved data, the CHAC study has proceeded via sensitivity analysis in areas of critical assumptions. The available data are, after all, the window through which policy makers view the world. They are the basis for decisions, and on those grounds alone are worth analyzing.

2. Policy instruments

A number of instruments have been considered. Among these are: the foreign exchange premium, changes in the interest rate, changes in the wage level, a subsidy on chemical inputs, a surcharge on irrigation water, and supply controls. Each of these instruments is viewed as an intervention in an otherwise competitive market.

A foreign exchange premium may be interpreted as a change in the exchange rate, but in the Mexican context it is more likely to

---

[2] This was initiated by Luciano Barraza in the Secretaría de Agricultura y Ganadería.

[3] This is under the direction of GASA, an interministerial group for agricultural policy analysis.

mean export subsidies and tariffs. Since these instruments have fiscal implications, the net budgetary outlays associated with a given premium level have been tabulated. Changes in the interest rate refer to long-term capital. The rate for short-term credit remains constant (at 12% per year) in the model. This of course assumes a separation between capital markets which is untenable [4], but the short-term rate is subsidized by public agencies. The objectionable nature of this assumption is lessened somewhat by the consideration that, for public investment project decisions, the long-term rate is more crucial than the short-term rate.

Of the instruments analyzed, changes in the wage rate are among the most difficult from the viewpoint of implementation at the sectoral level. Agricultural minimum wages have been legislated, but they are not particularly effective. This is to be expected in circumstances of substantial surplus labor. Thus, while the CHAC experiments with higher wages presumably refer to the possibility of altering the wage legislation, the realities of enforcement should be borne in mind. At best, wage legislation can affect directly only the incomes of day laborers, who constitute a small percentage of the employed labor. The chief significance of the CHAC wage experiments is for the linkage with DINAMICO (below, chapter IV.6). The CHAC wage experiments are designed mainly to show agriculture's response to wage changes which arise from reallocating labor to other sectors.

Subsidies on chemical inputs refer both to fertilizers and pesticides. Fertilizer distribution and pricing are controlled nationally. The newer fertilizer plants have lower costs than the old units, and there has been some discussion of a price reduction. Irrigation water from reservoirs is distributed to farmers at a price below its marginal productivity, and hence another experiment has been designed to evaluate the impact of raising that price. In that experiment, the price of well water (which reflects mainly the private pumping and maintenance costs) is left unchanged.

Supply controls refer specifically to reducing the quantity of products offered on the domestic market with the aim of raising

[4] There is an extensive literature on the relation between short-term and long-term interest rates. See, for example, Meiselman (1962).

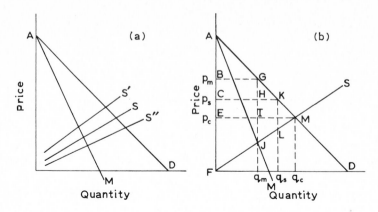

the average level of prices received for agricultural commodities. It does not necessarily refer to acreage controls, but these could be included within a supply control program. In the Mexican context, such a program could also be carried out by means of the crop-specific water and credit allocations which are utilized in some irrigation districts. A policy of supply controls would represent a partial movement toward a monopolistic market equilibrium, at the expense of consumers.

The alternative instruments are compared schematically in the one-crop diagram of figures 1a and 1b. The demand and marginal revenue curves are shown as AD and AM. The supply function (equal to marginal costs) will be S, in the absence of policy interventions.

In figure 1a, the new supply curve S' represents a possible form of the effect of policies which increase production costs, e.g., increases in the interest or wage rate or a water surcharge. It is apparent that the net effect on producers' incomes depends upon the elasticities of demand and supply. With the largely inelastic demand faced by agriculture, an increase in the interest rate paid by farmers may increase incomes through the price effects of a supply reduction. Of course, the income distribution within agriculture is also likely to be affected by a rise in the interest rate. The effects on the distribution and on the level of sector income cannot be predicted *a priori*.

Similarly, the supply curve S'' incorporates cost-reducing interventions such as reductions in the water or fertilizer price. Given the unfavorable effects upon the price of the crop, it is not at all obvious that these measures would improve the sector's income.

In figure 1b, the effects of supply controls are shown. The competitive price and quantity equilibrium points are denoted by p_c and q_c. The monopolistic solution is given by p_m and q_m. Supply controls for the domestic market lead to the point defined by p_s and q_s. Although supply control instruments are not introduced explicitly into the model, they are introduced implicitly through a lower bound on producers' surplus. In terms of figure 1b, this lower bound is represented by the area $CKLF$. This area is at least as large as the area EMF associated with the competitive equilibrium, and cannot exceed the area $BGJF$ associated with the monopolistic equilibrium. In CHAC, lower bounds on producers' surplus are imposed by a single constraint defined over all crops, while retaining the 'social welfare' maximand. It follows that this solution corresponds to a second-best optimum, selecting that set of supply controls which meets the producers' surplus constraint and which departs least from the welfare maximum defined at the competitive equilibrium.

Caution needs to be exercised in forecasting the effects of supply controls. These are notoriously difficult to enforce, even in countries with a well-developed administrative structure. Here the main reason for including these controls is to quantify the effects on other variables of substantial increases in producers' incomes.

3. Income and employment

Before going into the results of experiments with policy instruments, it is useful to examine the basic patterns in the absence of government interventions. CHAC has been solved under assumptions appropriate for both 1968 and 1974. The 1968 solutions help delineate the magnitude of the underemployment problem. The problem has both overall and seasonal dimensions. In overall terms, the model indicates that the short-cycle crops directly provide for about 2.4 million man-years of employment out of a labor force of 5.2 million persons. More precisely, this constitutes employment with a marginal productivity at least as great as the prevailing wage. A lower wage yields more employment, but the basic implication about actual conditions remains the same. There is substantial underemployment, as defined by persons working at tasks with zero or very low productivity.

Our definition of the labor force excludes those primarily engaged in long-cycle crops and livestock, but it includes some who undertake small-scale poultry, livestock, and tree crop operations as a sideline. Since these products are omitted from CHAC, the model slightly underestimates the level of employment.

The sector-wide annual average rates of employment are quite similar to those obtained by Thorbecke and Stoutjesdijk (1971) for Guatemala and Peru. They did not use an optimizing model, but they based their analysis on crop-specific input data similar to those incorporated in CHAC. They found that the actual agricultural output could have been produced with only 49% of the available man-days in Peru and 57% in Guatemala, given a work year of 250 days. CHAC gives a comparable figure of 46% for Mexico, assuming a work year of 264 days. With the 250-day assumption, the CHAC result is 49%. Implicitly, the Thorbecke-Stoutjesdijk results are based on the existing wage rate. These particular CHAC results are also based on the existing wage. Even if all wages could be reduced by 50%, the model indicates that employment would increase by 13.9%. [5] (This implies a price elasticity of only − 0.19 for the derived demand for labor at the midpoint of the arc. [6]) Clearly the amount of underemployment is extensive at any plausible wage.

The employment estimates are consistent with a 1970 study of the entire agriculture and livestock sector in Mexico. By extrapolating employment rates from a sample of farms, the study derives

---

[5] When wages are reduced by 50%, output increases by 2.5%. To maintain output constant, employment would therefore increase by only about 11%.

[6] This extremely inelastic estimate of the demand for labor is computed from the static version of the model for 1968. There are no investment options other than activities which supply machinery services.

an employment rate of about 59% for the entire sector, including day laborers. [7] This includes time spent on farm administration. Labor requirements for farm administration are estimated at about 13% of those for direct cropping activities. Adopting this figure for farm administration, the CHAC rate of employment becomes 51% or 54%, depending on the length of the work-year.

In CHAC, wages are not closely associated with incomes per farmer. Most of the farmers' income accrues from property income rather than from the assumed reservation wage. For 1968, the average income per man-year of employment was about 9,000 pesos, or 4,000 pesos per person in the labor force. For the agricultural population, this implies an income per capita from short-cycle crops of 1,100 pesos, averaged over all members of agricultural households. Even when allowances are made for side income, the picture is one of quite marginal income levels. By contrast, the 1967 per capita income was estimated at 6800 pesos for the nation as a whole. [8]

The CHAC income estimates are similar to those of the Centro de Investigaciones Agrarias. Putting together the CDIA estimates of income for farm families and day laborers, the average income per member of the labor force is estimated at 3,544 pesos in 1960. Allowing for inflation, this is about 4,600 pesos in 1968 prices. Extending this figure in accordance with national accounts estimates of growth in real sector income, it becomes 6,300 pesos in 1968 at 1968 prices, versus the CHAC figure of 4,000 pesos. The CDIA estimate includes income from livestock and tree crops, and CHAC does not. CHAC's coverage includes all of the lowest agricultural income class (day laborers and temporal farmers), and few members of the highest income class, and so the two figures appear roughly comparable.

[7] Centro de Investigaciones Agrarias (1970, Vol. I). The study gives the following figures: 276 man-days of employment per farm, and about 730,000 man-years of employment for day laborers in 1960. At one and one-half man-years of adult family labor per farm (including the farmer), and 264 work days per year, this is an employment rate of 70% for farmers and their families. Given the CHAC figure of 1.97 million day laborers in 1960, this is an employment rate of 37% for day laborers. The weighted average of these two employment rates is 59%.

[8] Derived from Solís (1970), table III.2.

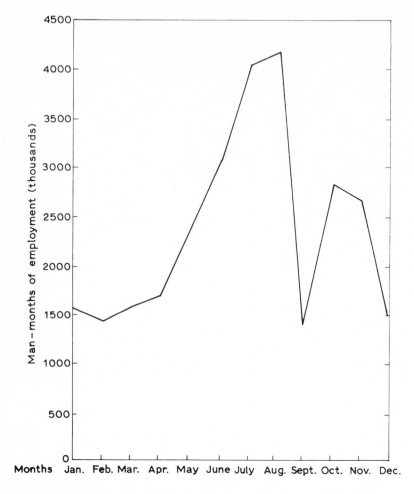

Fig. 2. CHAC estimate of seasonal employment in short-cycle crops (1968).
(Total labor available = 5,182 thousands.)

Within agriculture, there is considerable variation. For the subsistence farmer on non-irrigated land, the circumstances are even
bleaker than the averages suggest. These figures should not be
taken too literally, but they appear approximately indicative of
actual conditions. Here, the main interest is in the variation of the
figures under alternative government policies.

Seasonal fluctuations in agricultural employment are marked. The bulk of the variation occurs within non-irrigated agriculture. Figure 2 presents the seasonality in the CHAC results for 1968. The seasonality may be summarized by stating that 18% of the labor force cannot find even one month's employment at a marginal productivity equal to the current wage, 44% cannot find more than three months' employment at that productivity, and only 27% are so employed on a full-time basis. Given the inherent dependence of non-irrigated agriculture on seasonal cycles, it does not appear that the seasonality of employment can be reduced significantly through short-cycle crops. Enlarging the share of resources devoted to livestock is probably the most desirable way to reduce seasonal fluctuations within agriculture. Another alternative would be to expand irrigation and double cropping, but this could lead to reductions in crop prices and a worsening of the income distribution.

These results are not very sensitive to variations in the reservation wage assumption, which is the most arbitrary element of the model. Sensitivity tests were conducted for values of the reservation wage ranging from 40% to 70% of the market wage. Over that range, the elasticities [9] of response with respect to changes in the reservation wage were as follows:

total employment	−0.10
farmers' income	−0.05
day laborers' income	−0.34
sector income	−0.02
production	−0.03
exports	−0.09

For example, a 50% increase in the assumed reservation wage would lead to a 2.5% decrease in total farmers' income. (All of these elasticity estimates are based on the model for 1974, including investment choices.)

---

[9] Arc elasticities were calculated at the midpoint of the response function.

4. International trade

Another set of static results concerns comparative advantage in international trade. By utilizing the dual solutions, the crops can be ranked in terms of the gains to Mexico from additional units of exports or imports. A Bruno-style estimate of the peso cost of an additional dollar of foreign exchange earnings may be calculated from the dual values. [10] Table 1 shows the marginal gains (or losses) per ton in exports for selected crops. So that marginal changes from the actual situation could be evaluated, export bounds were set at or close to the actual export levels for 1967–69.

Column (5) in table 1 is the shadow price on the export bound, when positive, and the 'reduced cost' (in simplex terminology) for exporting, when negative. It may be visualized diagrammatically as in the single-good diagram, figure 3. The supply and demand curves are denoted S' and D', respectively. If the export price is p_1, then the shadow price on the export bound is the distance a. Suppose on the other hand, that the export price is p_2. Then there are no exports in the optimal solution, and the reduced cost for the export activity is the distance b. The marginal profits reported in column (5) of table 1, are the distance a (when positive) or b (when negative). In table 1, the crops are ranked in order of net profitability per ton. A horizontal line is drawn through the table at the point where the social profitability becomes negative, i.e., where the domestic and the export price coincide.

Table 2 ranks the crops according to degree of international comparative advantage, that is, in order of the marginal domestic cost of earning a dollar in exports. [11] A line is drawn through

[10] See Bruno (1967).

[11] The exchange costs for the most of the first seven crops in table 2 are somewhat too low, due to the omission of inputs of specialized management skills in most of the district submodels. In the submodel for the El Bajío district, where management inputs were explicitly analyzed, the shadow cost of this input is equivalent to 40 pesos per ton of tomatoes. This is 13% of the marginal cost of tomato production reported in table 1. Extrapolating from this example, the exchange cost of the first seven crops in table 2 should probably be increased by 10 to 15%. Even with this correction, these fruit and vegetable crops remain quite profitable to export. By 1969, Mexican tomato exports had captured two-thirds of the U.S. winter market. At that point, U.S. import quotas were imposed. During the 1960's, Mexican exports of short-cycle fruits and vegetables increased rapidly, and began to encounter protectionist restrictions in the U.S.

Table 1

Estimated profitability of selected Mexican agricultural products in international trade
(1967–69)

Crop (1)	Tons exported in base period [a] (2)	Tons exported in CHAC [b] (3)	Assumed export price [c] (pesos/ton) (4)	Marginal profits in CHAC (5)	Marginal cost of production in CHAC (pesos/ton) (6)
Strawberries	16,930	21,200	3,680	2,240	1,440
Sesame	8,300	16,600	3,981	2,200	1,781
Cantaloupe	45,051	45,051	2,003	1,420	583
Peanuts	4,150	8,300	2,500	1,170	1,130
Tomatoes	38,107	38,107	1,200	900	300
Watermelon	41,842	41,842	1,135	740	395
Potatoes	26	10,000	1,200	690	510
Cotton fiber	318,877	318,877	5,767	670	5,097
Cucumber	30,752	70,000	7,960	420	370
Pineapple	9,613	9,613	400	140	260
Green chile	16,700	25,100	748	130	618
Beans	66,400	99,600	1,846	100	1,746
Sugar cane [d]	7,967,628	7,967,628	68	20	48
Grain sorghum	2,140	–	566	–50	616
Cottonseed	–	–	416	–160	576
Oats	–	–	387	–290	677
Safflower	7,724	–	1,550	–380	1,930
Wheat	153,258	–	600	–460	1,060
Rice	137	–	750	–460	1,210
Corn	979,455	–	623	–480	1,103
Soybeans	–	–	800	–670	1,470

[a] Base period defined as 1967–69 average.

[b] Arbitrary export bounds imposed in CHAC for this solution in order to derive marginal valuations. For crops governed rigidly by international quotas, formal or informal, these bounds are set equal to the actual quantities exported.

[c] This is an average farm gate price (less than f.o.b. price). The export prices are notional in some cases, but there is sufficient information in the table to recalculate marginal profits on the basis of different prices.

[d] Sugar cane exports and prices are expressed in cane equivalents, although the export product is refined sugar.

table 2 at the official exchange rate of 12.5 pesos to the dollar. At that exchange rate, it is profitable to export the crops above the line but not those below the line. Following Bruno, the peso cost

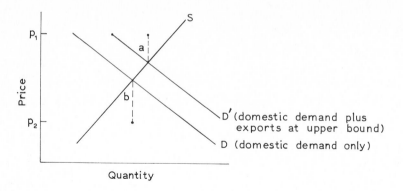

Fig. 3.

of earning a dollar may be called the 'exchange cost' for each crop. An average of the exchange costs, weighted by the proportion of the value of exports in 1967−69 for all exported crops, turns out to be 12.01 pesos per dollar, or 4% less than the official exchange rate.

In other words, crop exports could have been taxed up to 4% in 1967−69 without becoming unprofitable. [12] In contrast, there is widespread discussion of substantial subsidies to Mexican manu-factured exports to render them profitable in the international market place. (See above, chapter II.4.) This suggests an intersec-toral comparative advantage for agriculture vis-à-vis industry. The linkage experiment with DINAMICO also supports that suggestion (below, chapter IV.6).

Another notable fact about agricultural exports is the wide range of competitiveness. There is more than a ten-fold range in the exchange cost of different crops. Corn and wheat are two major crops in which the model shows negative profits in export-ing. In fact, the national price support agency incurs substantial budgetary losses to export the surplus production of these two crops. If corn and wheat exports were replaced by other crops

---

[12] Allowing for the cost of specialized management inputs into certain fruits and vegetables, the aggregate exchange cost for all exported crops is higher than 12, but still less than the exchange rate of 12.5.

Table 2

Ranking of crops by degree of comparative advantage in international trade, 1967–69

(1)	(2)	(3)	(4)	(5) [a]
Rank	Crop	Actual value exported in 1967–68 (millions of pesos)	Actual percentage of production exported in 1967–69	Exchange cost of crop
1	Onions	21.8	12	0.97
2	Garlic	25.2	14	2.36
3	Tomatoes	45.6	34	3.13
4	Cantaloupe	90.0	17	3.64
5	Tobacco	81.0	8	3.98
6	Watermelon	47.5	13	4.35
7	Strawberries	62.4	16	4.89
8	Potatoes	0.03	–	5.31
9	Sesame	33.0	4	5.59
10	Cucumbers	24.3	44	5.89
11	Chickpeas	3.9	1	6.09
12	Peanuts	10.4	5	6.14
13	Pineapple	3.8	3	8.13
14	Sugar cane	545.0	28	8.82
15	Squash	–	–	9.74
16	Dry chile	7.2	8	9.96
17	Green chile	12.5	9	10.33
18	Cotton·fiber	1840.0	64	11.05
19	Beans	122.5	6	11.82 [b]
20	Grain sorghum	1.2	–	13.60
21	Safflower	11.3	3	15.56
22	Oats	–	–	17.18
23	Cottonseed	–	–	17.31
24	Flaxseed	–	–	18.30
25	Rice	0.1	–	21.93
26	Wheat	92.0	7	22.08
27	Corn	610.0	10	22.13
28	Soybeans	–	–	22.97
29	Dry alfalfa	–	–	25.63
30	Grain barley	–	–	30.32
31	Lima beans	–	–	34.54

[a] Column (5) is the exchange cost, or the gross peso cost per dollar of export earnings. It is calculated as the ratio of the marginal production cost (in pesos) to the export price (in dollars). Production costs derived from CHAC are a composite of input costs which are exogenously priced and input costs which are endogenously valued by the model. Export prices are average farm-gate prices. The numbers in this column are derived from columns (4) and (6) in table 1, as 12.5 (6)/(4).

[b] A line is drawn through this table at the official exchange rate of 12.5 pesos to the dollar.

whose exchange cost averaged 12.5, the aggregate exchange cost for all crop exports would drop from 12.01 to 10.18. Even if sorghum alone were substituted for corn and wheat, the aggregate exchange cost would be 10.39. This substitution might be a useful policy on two other grounds: (a) recent studies have concluded that the world market demand for sorghum is likely to increase markedly during the 1970's, and (b) other aspects of the CHAC solutions indicate that sorghum is one of the few profitable alternatives to corn in non-irrigated areas. In any case, it appears that there could be substantial gains for Mexico in improving the commodity composition of agricultural exports.

5. Comparative statics results without policy intervention

To obtain comparative statics results, the model was solved for 1968 and 1974 separately. The assumptions for 1974 were identical with those of 1968, with the following exceptions:

(a) Domestic demand for agricultural products was assumed to grow in a manner consistent with the historical rate of GDP growth (6%) and estimated income elasticities. That is, price-quantity demand functions were shifted to the right by an appropriate amount.

(b) For products with limited export markets, the most reliable available recent estimates were adopted on the growth in export demands.

(c) Investment opportunities are included in the 1974 solution, to represent opportunities over the 1968–74 period. They are not included in the 1968 solution, for it is static.

(d) The labor force grows at 3.5% per annum, the historical rate of population increase. This increase is manifested only in the number of day laborers and farmers on non-irrigated land. The average farm size in irrigated areas appears to be more or less constant over time. Accordingly, in CHAC the number of farmers in the irrigated areas can be increased only by investments which expand the irrigated acreage. Rural-urban migration is beyond the scope of a sector model. It is treated in the course of the CHAC-

DINAMICO linkage. [13]

(e) Disembodied technical progress during 1968–74 was specified with respect to chemical inputs, purchased seeds, required short-term credit, and yield increments associated with these inputs. The rate of technical progress differs from crop to crop. Total chemical and seed input requirements are partly endogenous, via changing crop composition and the changing spatial allocation of each crop.

The consequences of these assumptions are shown in table 3, which presents the basic sector-wide results for the case of no policy interventions. The growth rate of production (4.65%) is comparable to the historical rate of 4.8% measured from 1930 to 1960. [14] However, sector income in the model expands at a rate much lower (3.2%) than the historical rate for total GDP, which was 5.2% during 1921–67. It is also lower than the observed growth rate for GDP originating in crop agriculture, which was 4.7% during 1921–67 and 3.8% during 1957–67.

Nevertheless, there is evidence that the model's results are consistent with recent trends which show a tendency for the paths of production and sector income to diverge. (That is, the intersectoral terms of trade are worsening from the viewpoint of agriculture, and more inputs are purchased from outside the sector per unit of output.) Although sectoral GDP was growing at 3.8% per year from 1957–67, a production index for the same period was expanding at a rate in excess of 5.0%, or somewhat more rapidly than the average for the post-Revolution period. This divergence is reflected by the changes in relative prices. The general rate of inflation during the 1957–67 period was 4.4%, but crop prices increased by only 2.9% per year. [15] CHAC's results suggest a con-

---

[13] See below, chapter IV.6. The historical natural increase rate of the population in Mexico has been about 3.5% per year. Rural-urban migration in the 1960's was sufficient to reduce the agricultural labor force growth rate to 2.0%. In the results of CHAC, labor is sufficiently redundant so that it would have made no difference for the 1974 solutions if the agricultural labor force had increased at 2.0% per year instead of 3.5%.

[14] Historical growth rates quoted in this paragraph are from Solís (1970), chapters III and IV.

[15] Computed from time series data from the Secretaría de Agricultura y Ganadería.

Table 3
1968–74 growth rates from basic solutions [a]
(unit: billion 1968 pesos, unless stated otherwise)

Variable	1968	1974 base case	Growth rate
Maximand [b]	69.95	88.29	4.0%
Consumers' surplus	61.08	77.99	4.2%
Producers' surplus	8.87	10.30	2.5%
Sector income	13.99	16.88	3.2%
Farmers' income	13.21	15.37	2.6%
Day laborers' income	0.79	1.03	4.5%
Production [c]	100.00	131.73	4.65%
Net exports	3.43	5.09	6.8%
Employment [d]	2088	2460	2.8%
Chemical inputs	4.34	5.59	4.3%
Machinery use	7.48	8.87	2.9%
Draft animal use [e]	146.1	174.3	3.0%
Short-term credit	18.45	24.26	4.7%

[a] Based on interest rate of 12%, base wage of 13.5 pesos/day, and no foreign exchange premium.

[b] Maximand is the sum of consumers' and producers' surplus.

[c] Fisher quantum index based on endogenous prices.

[d] Unit: thousand man-years.

[e] Unit: thousands of work-days.

tinuation of this trend in the absence of significant policy intervention: According to the model, net sector income is growing less rapidly than production by a margin of 1.4–1.5% per year, which is identical to the margin experienced over 1957–67. Consequently, assuming a 6.0% rate of overall growth for 1968–74 (down from the 7.0% rate of the preceding decade), CHAC projects a further slippage in the agricultutal GDP growth rate, from 3.8% to 3.2%. [16] Assuming a continued overall economic growth rate of 7.0%, the sector GDP growth rate would be closer to the 3.8% figure.

[16] CHAC's results in actuality led to the discovery of the emerging gap between sectoral income and production growth rates. Although the statistics on this point have been available, they had not been remarked upon. Apparently the fact that a new trend has emerged had not been grasped prior to the CHAC analysis.

It should be noted that subsidies to agriculture, effected primarily through the national agency for price supports (CONASUPO), have not been extensive enough to alter basic trends. In 1968, the net operating deficit of CONASUPO was equal to about 6.0% of net sector income as measured in CHAC.

During the 1960's, imports formed a lower percentage of total supply than at any time since 1910–21. For the 1970's, therefore, the possibilities for import substitution are virtually exhausted. If exports are not expanded sufficiently, the domestic price elasticities of demand, taken together with low income elasticities of demand, will almost surely hold down the growth of producers' incomes to the low rates experienced in the 1960's.

There are a number of grounds on which the basic comparative static results of CHAC may be questioned. Aside from general questions of validating a programming model, the major reservations regarding the results of table 3 are as follows:

(a) the income elasticities and the aggregate income growth rate may be too low;

(b) the price elasticities may be underestimated;

(c) the investment activities may be misspecified in a manner such that investment is overstated;

(d) the export market potential may be underestimated;

(e) the yield-enhancing effects of disembodied technical change may be overstated.

In addition, in comparing the results with historical evidence, it should be borne in mind that there are no direct estimates of income originating in agriculture. National income accountants are usually forced to rely on crude methods of estimation. In these circumstances, one asks only for approximate cross-checks with the historical estimates.

Without attempting a proper answer to the validation question, a few remarks are made regarding these major possible sources of error.

(a) *Income elasticities and income growth.* Limitations of time have precluded sensitivity tests on this point, but the elasticities used in the model are comparable with those estimated elsewhere. [17] Even with a 7.0% economy-wide rate of GDP growth, there would still be a gap of 1.5% between the annual growth rates of sector production and sector income.

(b) *Price elasticities*. A test with a 50% increase in all the absolute values of the price elasticities changed the results only slightly.

(c) *Investment*. There are no readily available data on the categories of investment encompassed in CHAC. Sketchy information indicates that CHAC understates — rather than overstates — investment in the sector. No doubt, this is due to our admittedly crude specification of investment activities. Given the inelastic demands, this error would tend to cause an overestimate of the growth of sector income.

(d) *Exports*. If anything, the possibilities of export expansion have been overestimated. The basic 1968 and 1974 solutions show an annual rate of expansion of 6.8% (for short-cycle crops). Total crop exports expanded at annual rates of 8.9% and 1.2% during the decades 1950–60 and 1960–70, respectively. The CDIA projects a growth rate of 1.7% for crop exports during 1970–75. [18]

(e) *Technical change*. The disembodied component of technical change is simply an extrapolation of past trends for the yields of each crop. It is difficult to evaluate the correctness of this extrapolation.

The major intertemporal findings, a further relative decline in agricultural terms of trade and incomes, and a slowdown in the absolute rate of expansion of sector income, clearly need further testing before being accepted. Nevertheless, they appear plausible *a priori*, given the export and domestic demand situations. This process is likely to be accompanied by increasing skewness in the income distribution, since the major gainers in the sector are those who adopt yield-enhancing innovations. The policy implication is that the process of economic development will be accompanied by increasing pressure for mechanisms for urban-rural budgetary transfers, at least until the agricultural population becomes small

[17] See e.g. FAO (1971).
[18] Centro de Investigaciones Agrarias (1970), Vol. 1.

relative to the total population. These aspects of agricultural development policy — the post-import substitution and second-generational problems of the Green Revolution — have probably received too little attention in the debates on agricultural development strategies. [19]

6. Effects of policy instruments

The impacts of the selected policy instruments are summarized in tables 4, 5 and 6. Table 4 shows percentage changes, relative to the 1974 no-policy-change case, in some variables when specified policies are implemented. Table 5 shows the peso value of these changes, and table 6 is a qualitative assessment of the policy instruments in terms of the types of impacts.

With a 6.0% rate of overall GDP growth, it is evident that the agricultural employment problem is fairly intractable. [20] The most significant change is found when the interest rate is doubled. That only amounts to changing the annual employment growth rate from 2.8% to 3.1% per year over 1968—74. There is an asymmetry, however, and employment is significantly responsive in a negative direction to wage increases. A 44% wage increase by 1974 reduces the 1968—74 employment growth rate to less than 1% per year. [21] It is also evident that changes in employment and investment (or mechanization) may be either positively or negatively

[19] One early exception was Heady (1962, chapter 6), who discussed the 'double threat' posed to sector incomes by a high potential for supply expansion coupled with low income and price elasticities. Other have been Johnston and Mellor (1961), Mellor (1966, chapter 4) and Falcon (1970).

[20] This conclusion holds over all experiments with the set of policy instruments considered. The model is not structured in such a way as to allow an evaluation of policy instruments which affect the size distribution of farms and accordingly affect the scale of farm operations. The results presented in chapter IV.5 below indicate that the labor-intensity of farm operations is strongly affected by farm size. Therefore, our rather pessimistic conclusions on the employment-generating potential of agriculture should be interpreted with this *caveat* in mind.

[21] The implied elasticity of demand for labor at the mid-point of the arc is -0.31, substantially higher in absolute value than -0.19 computed from the 1968 static version of CHAC.

Table 4
Impact of policy changes on selected variables (percentage change from 1974 base solution)

	Foreign exchange premium		Higher interest rate		Higher wage rate		Water sur-charge	Fertil-izer subsidy of 30%	Supply controls			Higher interest rate (18%) and 22% higher wage
	15%	30%	18% per year	24%	increased by 22%	44%			I	II	III	
Maximand	0.9	2.1	-0.7	-1.4	-1.4	-2.8	-1.5	1.9	-0.1	-0.1	-0.1	-2.2
Farmers' profit	18.6	42.6	10.2[a]	17.3[a]	6.9	-1.7	-2.8	1.9	10.0[c]	30.0[c]	50.0[c]	8.2
Farmers' income	12.2	29.2	7.8[a]	20.3[a]	7.7	8.7	-1.9	1.9	6.3	19.3	32.2	12.6
Day laborers' income	5.8	1.9	2.9	-1.0	-9.7	2.9	-4.0	-11.5	0.9	-2.0	-1.0	-4.9
Consumers' surplus	-1.4	-3.3	-2.3	-3.9	-2.1	-2.9	-1.3	1.9	-1.5	-4.3	-7.3	-3.5
Production	0.9	1.8	-1.6	-2.9	-2.4	-3.3	-2.1	1.9	-0.3	-0.6	-0.9	-2.9
Net exports	17.9[b]	34.0	-3.0	-5.7	-2.8	-5.7	-4.3	5.0	7.3	42.7	77.1	-3.1
Employment	0.6	1.2	0.8	1.7	-6.9	-12.0	-0.2	-3.7	-0.4	-1.0	-1.1	-2.2
Long-term capital	2.9	12.1	-6.3	-16.6	6.9	13.1	-3.2	4.0	-0.3	-1.5	-1.9	-4.9
Machinery use	5.0	11.1	-5.9	-18.2	8.2	16.0	-1.1	4.5	-0.3	-1.6	-2.0	-4.5
Short-term capital	2.2	4.3	-4.1	-5.6	-3.5	-5.3	-1.5	6.0	-0.1	-0.3	-0.3	-5.4
Chemical inputs	2.3	5.9	-4.9	-4.2	-1.5	-3.7	-3.3	11.0	-0.4	+0.5	+0.3	-4.1

[a] With higher wage levels, increases in the interest rate cause farmers' profits and income to decrease.

[b] Corresponds to export growth rate of 9.3%, versus 6.8% in base case.

[c] The supply controls I, II and III were defined by raising farmers' profits to 10.0, 30.0 and 50.0% above the base solution, respectively.

Table 5
Impact of policy changes on selected variables (unit: millions of 1968 pesos except for employment, measured in thousands of man-years)

	Foreign exchange premium		Interest rate = 18%	Wage rate increased by 22%	Fertilizer subsidy of 30%	Water sur-charge	Supply controls	
	15%	30%					I	II
Sector income	+1944	+4508	+1230	+1080	+ 174	− 320	+ 978	+4939
Net exports	+ 911	+1731	− 150	− 140	+ 255	− 210	+ 372	+3924
Consumers' surplus	−1092	−2574	−3000	−1610	+1482	− 990	−1170	−5693
Employment	+ 15	+ 30	+ 20	− 169	− 91	− 4	− 10	− 27
Long-term capital requirements	+ 308	−1290	− 670	+ 730	+ 425	− 330	− 32	− 202
Budgetary effect	− 900	−2446	−	−	−1862	+1195	−	−
Real sector income [a]	+1507	+3478	+ 30	+ 436	+ 767	− 716	+ 510	+2662

[a] "Real sector income" is crudely estimated, assuming that 40% of consumption is on the part of agricultural producers.

Table 6
Qualitative impact of selected policy changes

Target	Instrument					
	Foreign exchange premium	Interest rate change	Wage change	Chemical subsidy	Water tax	Supply controls
Producers' income	++	++	++	+	−	++
Consumers' surplus	−	=	=	++	−	=
Employment	+	+	=	=	−	−
Exports	++	−	−	+	−	++
Budget	−	n.a.	n.a.	−	+	n.a.
Production	++	=	=	++	=	−

Key: ++ strongly positive
     + positive
     = strongly negative
     − negative
   n.a. not applicable
Cases chosen: Foreign exchange premium = 15%; interest rate raised to 18%; wage rate raised by 22%; supply controls of type II. (See tables 4 and 5.)

associated, depending on the policy instrument used. This is because the net employment effect is composed of both input substitution and output effects arising from any particular policy change. Moreover, there are third factors (e.g., water and chemical inputs) which have different degrees of complementarity with the use of capital and labor. For example, employment and investment changes are positively associated under a foreign exchange premium, a water surcharge, and supply controls. At least within the range of values explored, the output effect dominates the substitution effect in these cases. Employment and investment are negatively associated for changes in the interest rate and wage rate and for a subsidy on chemical inputs.

Two separate effects lie behind the response of farmers' income. With low wage levels, increases in the interest rate cause farmers' incomes to increase through the reduction of output and consequent price increases. At higher wage levels, increases in the interest rate cause a reduction in incomes, because the output-and-price effect is weaker than the cost effect of higher interest charges and the reduction in export earnings. It appears that it is not sufficient to posit two-dimensional relations between policy instruments and target variables.

Exports, as might be expected, are strongly stimulated by export subsidies. They are dampened by policy changes which increase the cost of production, such as increases in the wage and interest rates and a water surcharge. When controls on domestic market supplies are hypothesized, a dual pricing effect becomes evident. By reducing the supply on the domestic market, the controls raise the domestic prices relative to export prices, but nevertheless exports increase. This effect may be understood by reference to the marginal revenue curve. (See figure 4.) Let the export price be p_e. In the absence of supply controls, the quantity sold on the domestic market is q_d, and the quantity exported is $q_t - q_d$. Prices are equalized on the domestic and export markets. Under supply controls, the competitive market objective function is replaced, at the margin, by the monopolistic objective. For illustra-

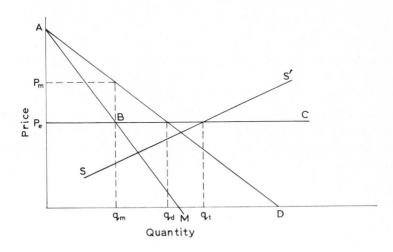

Fig. 4.

tion, it is assumed that the monopolistic objective function is adopted entirely (an extreme supply control policy). Then the effective marginal revenue curve is ABC, and the quantity sold on the domestic market is reduced to q_m. The quantity exported is correspondingly enlarged to $q_t - q_m$. At a less extreme supply control policy, the quantity marketed domestically lies between q_m and q_d.

The striking fact about supply controls is that significant increases in sector income can be attained with negligible losses in aggregate social welfare — provided that it is feasible to administer such policies. The sector income changes are achieved virtually entirely via transfers from consumers.[22] As would be expected, an optimal supply control policy results in the greatest supply reduction for the crops with the most inelastic demand.

The budgetary implications of some of these policy instruments are not negligible. (See table 5.) Here the budgetary estimates do not include administrative expenses, but only the direct outlays implied by the policy instruments. Several aspects of the budget are worth noting: (a) a foreign exchange premium (export subsidy cum tariffs) produces higher gains than a chemical input subsidy, per budgetary peso expended, in terms of additional sector employment, exports, and sector income. The chemical subsidy favors consumers. (b) It appears that appropriate levels of the water surcharge and foreign exchange premium can be set so that budgetary effects are offsetting, and yet there will be a net positive effect on exports, sector employment, and sector income. Of course, since there is a net social loss associated with distortive taxes and subsidies, consumers are penalized for these gains to producers.

In general, policy changes are non-additive in their effects on target variables. This is shown in table 4, where the rightmost column represents the combined effects of a change in the interest rate and wage rate. Policy conclusions should always be tested

---

[22] Of course, producers are also purchasers of agricultural products. With a price increase, their individual welfare does not increase *pari passu* with the increase in sector incomes. For the effects on real sector income, see the bottom line of table 5.

with a model solution focused precisely on a combined instrument.

Table 6 provides a convenient way to summarize the qualitative effects of the various policy instruments. No two are alike in terms of their impacts on producers, consumers, employment, trade, and the budget. There are always tradeoffs. The most common tradeoff is between the welfare levels of producers and consumers. However, the chemical input subsidy benefits both, at the expense of employment and the budget. Producers and consumers are penalized by the water surcharge, but the budget is benefitted. Exports and producers' income goals are complementary under four of the policy changes, but they move in opposite directions under the other two.

In Mexico, the rate of adoption of mechanized techniques is not directly subject to government control. [23] Nevertheless, it is sensitive to most of the policy instruments shown in tables 4–6. As with total long-term capital, mechanization may be positively or negatively associated with changes in employment, depending on the policy package. *A priori*, it is difficult to say whether the output or the substitution effect will dominate.

The next step in this kind of exercise is to specify the policy goals and constraints more precisely, and to experiment with different instrument packages in order to formulate a program that meets the goals reasonably well. For example, policy makers may establish a budgetary constraint, and they may set minimum acceptable levels of employment increases and consumer welfare losses. Except for the budget, these policy constraints need not be entered formally into the model. Feasible policy instruments may be altered until a satisfactory set of results is obtained. Clearly, the discussions with policy makers must yield indications of a feasible range of values for each policy instrument. By staying with this approach, one may have some confidence that the results of CHAC define an implementable program. In contrast, solutions derived from maximization of export earnings, employment, etc.,

---

[23] Bruce Johnston has pointed out to us that the rate of introduction of mechanization is influenced by government import policies in many other countries.

usually give configurations that are unattainable, given limits to producers' responses and feasible policies.

7. Concluding remarks

Inevitably, model-building is subject to the limitations of availability and reliability of data. Abstractions have to be made from the complexity of reality. A central conclusion of this study seems, however, firmly based. This is that Mexican agriculture is beginning to have to face the problem of relatively low growth rates of farm income and employment which occur in a sector constrained by the growth of domestic demand and of export demand. The possibilities of import replacement are exhausted. The other elements in the problem are the high underemployment in the sector, the facts that per capita agricultural incomes are already well below the national average for all sectors, that the income distribution within agriculture is highly skewed, and that the agricultural population continues to grow at a rapid rate.

For Mexican agricultural policy makers, the problem is no longer simply how to increase production. It is, rather, how to bring about structural changes which will lead to an expansion of domestic demand. These are the real second generation problems of the Green Revolution, and Mexico will have to confront these problems before most other developing countries.

Aside from the projections of secular trends, CHAC appears to be a useful tool for analyzing the tradeoffs implicit in sectoral policies. It gives plausible dimensions to the employment problem and to comparative advantage of individual crops in international trade. It is structured so that explicit policy instruments may be varied and their sectoral implications evaluated. The solutions reported in this chapter indicate that there are rather well-defined tradeoffs. For example, producers' incomes and consumers' welfare are almost always in conflict. In the one exception (the fertilizer subsidy case), both may be increased only at the cost of a significant decline in employment. Balance-of-payments and employment goals may or may not be in conflict, depending on the policy measure chosen. It is difficult to summarize these tradeoffs except to say that simple generalizations do not hold.

Many of the conventional policy instruments appear to be limited in their impact on employment, but clearly more should be tested. CHAC is a convenient tool for testing complex policy packages as well as individual measures. A planning model can go no further than this. Developing and implementing an innovative set of new instruments is the responsibility of policy-makers.

References

Bruno, M., 'The optimal selection of export-promoting and import-substitution projects', in: *Planning the external sector: Techniques, problems, and policies.* Report of the First Interregional Seminar on Development Planning, United Nations, 1967, pp. 88–135. (UN Publication Sales No. 67.II.B.5.)

Centro de Investigaciones Agrarias (CDIA), *Estructura agraria y desarrollo agrícola en México*, vols. I-III. México, D.F., 1970.

Falcon, W.P., 'The Green Revolution: generations of problems', *American Journal of Agricultural Economics* 52, No. 5 (December 1970).

Food and Agriculture Organization of the United Nations, *Agricultural commodity projections, 1970–1980.* Rome, 1971.

Heady, E.O., *Agricultural policy under economic development.* Ames, Iowa, Iowa State University Press, 1962.

Johnston, B.F. and J.W. Mellor, 'The role of agriculture in economic development', *American Economic Review* 51, No. 4 (September 1961).

Meiselman, D., *The term structure of interest rates.* Englewood Cliffs, N.J., Prentice-Hall 1962.

Mellor, J.W., *The economics of agricultural development.* Ithaca, N.Y., Cornell University Press, 1966.

Solís, L., *La realidad económica mexicana: retrovisión y perspectivas.* México, Siglo XXI Editores, 1970.

Thorbecke, E., and E. Stoutjesdijk, *Employment and output, a methodology applied to Peru and Guatemala.* Paris, Development Center of the OECD, 1971.

IV.4. A PROGRAMMING MODEL OF AN AGRICULTURAL DISTRICT

Luz María BASSOCO, John H. DULOY, Roger D. NORTON
and Donald L. WINKELMANN *

1. The district and the model

Except for one area, the district models included in CHAC were disaggregated only enough to allow for an analysis of policy issues at a sector-wide level. For most districts, the intention was to include sufficient detail to obtain an adequate representation of aggregate supply response and of supply response by broad ecological zones (irrigated land, dry land, and tropical). This permits broad analyses of investment choices defined spatially and by type of investment, and of comparative advantage by crop and by district. In order to keep the size of CHAC within manageable bounds, farm types within districts were not distinguished in these models. [1] One district model, however, was selected for more detailed treatment, principally in order to study the investment choices at the micro level, and how these choices are affected by different types of information flows.

The district known as El Bajío was selected for more detailed study because it produces a wide range of crops, including fruit and vegetables for the market in Mexico City, and because it contains a substantial degree of diversity of land types and of cropping patterns. [2] Of the 532,000 ha in the district, 112,500 are

---

* The authors wish to express their appreciation to Gary Kutcher for carrying out the computations reported here.

[1] Except for distinctions based on efficiency in water use.

[2] The 'district' comprises two irrigation districts, El Alto Río Lerma and La Begoña, falling within 17 municipios in the state of Guanajuato, plus surrounding non-irrigated arable lands.

irrigated by gravity-fed canals or by pumping from the rivers [3],
and another 60,000 ha are irrigated by tubewells. This is roughly
5% of the irrigated land in Mexico. Some 360,000 ha are cropped
by dryland farming. The district is a major producer of wheat,
sorghum, and corn as well as of fruit and vegetables. For short,
this district model is called BAJIO.

The basic structure of BAJIO is similar to that of the other
district models included in CHAC. In this discussion, we will concentrate on the differences which distinguish it from the other
submodels: (1) the number of farm types, (2) management skills
and (3) the range of technologies.

Table 1
Farm types and land classes in BAJIO

Farm type	Symbol	Number of farms	Average size (hectares)
Large dryland	LD	6,863	17.7
Small dryland	SD	34,569	7.0
Large irrigated	LI	3,826	23.0
Small irrigated	SI	19,861	5.0

Land class	Land subclass [a]	Total number of hectares
LD		121,476
SD		241,989
LI	Gravity, non-level	54,956
	Gravity, level	550
	Pump, non-level	32,175
	Pump, level	325
SI	Gravity water	66,807
	Pump water	32,500

[a] The amount of land in the 'level' and 'non-level' categories can be changed via
investment activities. Although there was no level land in SI farms in the base period, the
possibility of levelling SI land exists in the model.

[3] Abbreviated hereafter to 'gravity water'.

BAJIO incorporates four major farm types, based on a distinction between dryland and irrigated farming, and between 'large'
and 'small' farms (see table 1). These differences allow an approximation to an income distribution (five income classes as defined
by four groups of farm families plus landless laborers). This also
allows an analysis of the differential effects of various policy instruments and investments upon different income-earning classes.
Within each of the two broad groups of irrigated farms, the land is
further classified by source of irrigation water (gravity or well) and
by whether the land has been levelled or not. There are therefore
two classes of dryland (LD and SD) and eight classes of irrigated
land (LI and SI further sub-divided by land type and water source
as above).

In the absence of better demographic data, it was assumed that
the size of the farm family is the same for each farm class, and
that there are therefore four pools of family labor of a size proportionate to the number of farms in each of the four farm classifications. These pools are supplied in the model at a reservation
price for family labor which is lower than the wage for day labor.
While it may be likely that there are larger families on the larger
farms and particularly on irrigated farms, the model implies that
family members additional to the 'immediate' family are available
for farm work only at the same wage as day laborers. Any additional family members are treated as part of the district pool of
landless labor. One consequence of this assumption is that small
farms have a larger supply (on a per hectare basis) of relatively
cheap family labor than large farms. It is for this reason that,
although the technology sets in the model are invariant with respect to farm size, the solutions show small farms using more
labor-intensive techniques than large farms of the same type. This
result is consistent with observed behavior.

A second distinction between BAJIO and the other district
models is that an attempt was made to incorporate a measure of
management skill in the former. This was done to ensure that the
model, while allowing a choice within technology sets invariant
with respect to farm size, would reproduce distributions of yields
by crops which are similar to those observed in practice both

within and across farm types. Three levels of management skill are distinguished for crops, in ascending order of training and skills. Skills are associated with increasing yields and increasing use of complementary non-traditional inputs.

The third major distinction arises partly out of the first two. Given the number of land classes, farm types and management skills, the BAJIO model contains a wider variety of technologies for a given crop than the other district models. Four crops can be produced on dryland farms: corn, sorghum, chickpeas and beans. There are 40 cropping activities for these crops, reflecting the distinction between LD and SD, between mechanized and non-mechanized techniques, and among management skills and complementary input levels. There are 14 crops which can be grown on irrigated farms, each with cropping activities specified for LI and SI, and differing according to water source (gravity or well), to whether the land has been levelled or not, to mechanized or nonmechanized techniques, and to levels of management skill. For the 14 crops, there are 544 activities for irrigated farms and a total of 584 for the model as a whole.

2. Forms of solutions

The model of the Bajío district has been constructed in four main versions defined by whether it is in disaggregated or aggregated form and whether it is designed for solution as part of the sector model or in isolation. The solution year for all four versions is 1974.

The disaggregated versions (BAJIO), include monthly constraints on water, land and labor, corresponding in this way to the disaggregated version of the sector model, CHAC. In the aggregated version, BAJITO, corresponding to the aggregated sector model CHAQUITO, these monthly constraints were aggregated into three periods each of four months. [4] Throughout the chapter,

---

[4] BAJIO contains 381 constraints and 795 activities; BAJITO contains 164 and 684, respectively.

BAJIO and CHAC are used as generic terms for the models, unless otherwise indicated in the context.

When BAJIO is solved as part of CHAC, the cropping activities deliver to the CHAC commodity balances [5] (as is the case for all the district sub-models in the sector model), and they draw upon sector-wide factor balances for sectoral or regional resources. Product prices are endogenous to CHAC. They are exogenous to BAJIO solved in isolation. When it is solved in isolation, fixed-price product selling activities are added to it. For BAJIO, these exogenous prices were estimated in two ways: by assuming no change in base-period (1968) prices for one experiment, and by utilizing the endogenous prices from CHAC in another set of experiments. For the BAJIO-in-isolation solutions, factor supplying activities are added to replace those which were an integral part of CHAC. A district-specific pool of landless laborers is also specified. In this case, no activities representing migration outside the district are included.

These assumptions for BAJIO solved alone reflect the situation of the micro-level decision-maker. He is a price-taker, and a large part of his problem is how to estimate the price level for each crop. Also, for the local producer, as long as the wage is fixed, it is irrelevant whether there is out-migration of landless labor. When BAJIO is solved as part of CHAC, the institutional counterpart is either a sector agency which provides price forecasts to all producers or a comprehensive sector production plan.

In the solution of BAJIO alone, the fixed price assumption changes the nature of the maximand. It is no longer the sum of producers' and consumers' surpluses, but rather only the former. In other words, it represents maximization of producers' economic profits. This is not the same as maximizing producers' incomes or total incomes (including those of day laborers). The profit-maximizing objective function gives supply responses which are consistent with supply functions defined according to the usual behavioral assumptions.

---

[5] CHAC incorporates downward-sloping demand functions.

For solutions corresponding to the base period of 1968, the model does not include activities which add to the capital stock or any adjustment for increases in yields and complementary inputs associated with technical change. Such activities and adjustments are added for the 1974 solutions.

3. Investment choices

There are three sets of investment activities in BAJIO. These involve increasing the water supply or the effectiveness of its use: lining canals, installing new tubewells, and levelling land.

Plans have been developed by the Secretaría de Recursos Hidráulicos (SRH) for lining 42 km of canals which supply gravity-flow water. It is estimated that lining these 42 km will save 22,954,000 m³ of water annually. Assuming that the water saved is proportional to the number of kilometers lined, cost and water-saving coefficients can be associated with this activity. [6] Based on these assumptions, the first canal lining activity applies to 1 km of canal at a capital cost of 609,000 pesos, with a saving of 547,000 m³ of water per year. [7] A second activity, at the same cost per kilometer, is included for a further 1,335 km, but with much reduced savings of water (about 12% of the savings for the first activity). Lining canals is an investment activity of a government agency (SRH), and the costs are not directly borne by farmers. For this reason, the costs are included in the maximand but not in the rows defining incomes. Farmers are charged an institutional price for water supplied by the gravity system, and this price lies substantially below the marginal cost of the water made available by lining canals.

There are four activities in the model for installing additional tubewells – one for each of the four farm types. It is supposed

---

[6] The assumption of proportionality is obviously strong. One would expect greater water saving per kilometer the nearer the section of canal lined is to the upper reaches of the canal system, where more water passes.

[7] Since BAJIO is a static model, only one year's depreciation and interest charges enter the objective function for this activity.

that each well can pump 220,000 m^3 of water monthly, subject to a legal maximum of 1,080,000 m^3 annually. Installing wells is generally a private investment activity, and the interest on the capital costs of 200,000 pesos, plus depreciation, maintenance and pumping costs, is charged both to the maximand and the income rows. The first two of the four well-digging activities involve wells to supply dryland farms, large and small respectively. These activities, in effect, transform dryland farms into irrigated farms. It is estimated that one well supplies water to an average of 136 ha. Correspondingly, these activities are defined to transfer 136 ha from dry land to irrigated land, and similarly they transfer a proportionate number of family and farm managers. These two activities, in common with the two activities for new wells on already-irrigated land, release the constraints on the availability of monthly and annual water supplies. It should be pointed out that little is presently known about the characteristics of the aquifer. In the absence of better information, it has been assumed that lining canals have no effect upon the aquifer, and that there is an upper bound of 400 new tubewells which can be installed and operated at the intensity of 1,080,000 m^3 a year.

A third set of activities, levelling land, increases the efficiency of water use by increasing the uniformity of water application to the soil. There are four such activities in the model, applying respectively to LI and SI farms, both gravity irrigated and well irrigated. This again is a privately-financed investment. Interest and depreciation (on an assumed life of 10 years) on the capital cost of 900 pesos per hectare are charged both to the maximand and to income. In effect, these activities convert non-level land into an equal number of hectares of levelled land. The returns to the investment are realized by the fact that the cropping activities for levelled land require less water per hectare and produce higher yields.

The first and third of these sets of investment activities (canal lining and land levelling) apply only to already-irrigated land. Because irrigated farms have higher incomes than dryland farms, these activities tend to accentuate inequalities in the distribution of incomes. Well-digging on the other hand, can either add to the supply of water on already-irrigated land or it can transform dry-land farms into irrigated farms. If new wells are installed in this latter way, the effect is to reduce inequalities. This applies *a fortiori* if the wells supply water to small dryland farms, those with the lowest income of the farm types included in the model.

As in the case of CHAC, investment in all these categories is defined as the net increase in the capital stock from the 1968 base-year solution to the 1974 solutions. This comparative statics approach precludes an evaluation of the time path of investment.

The treatment of investment in machinery differs substantially from that of investment in 'water'. In CHAC (and therefore in BAJIO also), the capital costs of machinery do not appear explicitly. Instead, the model includes activities supplying machinery services, with charges in the objective function for fuel, repairs, depreciation and interest, and the salary of the machinery operator.

4. Specifying management restrictions

Farm management ability has an influence on land productivity. There are consistently observed variations in yields within any one district of relatively homogeneous soil and climate. A farmer who is familiar with his plot coaxes higher yields out of it than a hired laborer. Within the set of farmers, there are variations. Here the concern is solely with variations in management skills among farmers.

To incorporate management restrictions in a programming model, two pieces of information are required. One is the stratification of the stock of farmers by skill level. The other is identification of the production activities associated with a particular skill level, including yields and input requirements. The input requirements for each activity can be further subdivided into management and conventional inputs.

It is assumed that three levels of management can be distinguished. The lowest is that available without special training or skills and is associated with low levels of purchased inputs and yields. The second and third levels connote progressively higher levels of yields and purchased inputs. A stratification of farmers over these three levels was derived from data in a 1968 survey in the El Bajío area by the Centro de Investigaciones Agrarias. [8] Among the data reported are size of farm, tenure arrangement, and yield. Strata were based on yields. Most farmers reported yields on three to five crops, and it was almost always the case that high yields for one crop were associated with high yields for all other crops. In the few cases in which a given farmer reported yields in different strata, his assignment to a stratum depended on his yield for the most management-intensive crop. The resultant stratification is shown in table 2.

Yields obtainable with each level of management ability were derived from the same set of survey data. Associated conventional inputs were derived in the same manner as all production vectors were estimated, taking into account differential labor and other input requirements associated with yield variations. [9]

Since the production activities are normalized per hectare, the management requirements are in terms of managers of a given skill level per hectare. It is estimated that one farmer acting in a man-

Table 2
Percentage stratification of El Bajío farmers over management ability levels

Farm type	Management level [a]		
	Level I	Level II	Level III
LD	67	19	14
SD	66	23	11
LI	47	30	23
SI	74	17	9

Table 3
Management input coefficients for all cropping activities, by land class (unit: managers per hectare)

Farm type	Management level [a]		
	Level I	Level II	Level III
LD	0	0.056	0.056
SD	0	0.140	0.140
LI	0	0.044	0.044
SI	0	0.200	0.200

[a] Level I represents the most rudimentary management skills, level III the most productive.

[8] Reported in Centro de Investigaciones Agrarias (1970).
[9] The basic techniques for estimating the technology vectors are explained in chapter IV.2 above.

agerial capacity can handle up to 200 ha of corn, at one extreme, and up to 50 ha of strawberries, at the other. There is not a well-developed market for these services, and the result is that each farmer manages his own plot. [10] No class of farms as designated for BAJIO has an average farm size as great as 50 ha. Since there is one manager per farm, the management input coefficients are determined by the average farm size. For example, for large dryland farms whose average size is 17.7 ha, the coefficient of higher levels of management is 1/17.7, or 0.056 men per hectare. Table 3 sets out management input coefficients for the cropping activities of each land class. Cropping activities cultivated at management level I (the least skilled) are defined to require no special management inputs beyond ordinary agricultural labor.

5. Basic results: factor returns and utilization

In this chapter, some of the basic results of BAJIO are presented. Sensitivity analyses and the linkage with CHAC are reported in the following chapter. For comparability, all the BAJIO results in these two chapters are based on solutions for 1974.

Income levels are slightly above those computed in CHAC. For farmers, the average net income is estimated at 11,670 pesos per year [11], and for the entire labor force, the income per man-year worked is 12,080 pesos. Nearly all (97%) of the man-years worked in BAJIO are supplied by farmers. This is consistent with the relatively small size of irrigated plots in that region, in contrast to, say, the northwestern part of Mexico, where day labor is hired much more extensively.

In CHAC, for 1974, the income per man-year worked is about

---

[10] There are some exceptions in which farmers rent their land, but this statement holds as an approximation.

[11] In 1968 prices, with an interest rate of 12% and base wage rate of 13.5 pesos per day. The income figures do not change very significantly with changes in these parameters. A 22% increase in the wage rate, for example, causes only a 2% decrease in farmer's income.

Table 4
Income distribution for farm types in BAJIO
(unit: 1968 pesos)

Farm type	Income per farm	Income per hectare
LD	11,330	640
SD	5,840	834
LI	54,620	2,375
SI	16,070	3,214

9200 pesos at the same interest rate and wage structure. [12] Because of the substantial number of day laborers in CHAC, the income per person in the labor force is about 4400 pesos in 1974. These comparisons are consistent with the nature of the El Bajío area. Although there are more dryland farms than irrigated farms, the irrigation proportion is higher than in the sector as a whole. Yet the irrigated farms are not as large and prosperous as those in some other areas, notably the Northwest.

There is substantial variation in incomes according to whether a farm is dry or irrigated, large or small. The incomes per farm in the same solution are as shown in table 4. There is a ninefold difference between household income levels for large irrigated and small dryland farms. In both dry and irrigated farms, the small farms have about one-third higher incomes per hectare. This is a consequence of higher ratios of labor and management skills per unit of land.

Taking both gravity and pump water together, the annual value of water per hectare is 1370 pesos in BAJIO. [13] The difference in incomes per hectare between dryland and irrigated farms is of the order of 1,700–2,400 pesos. Superior management skills in irri-

---

[12] In BAJIO, wages account for about 16% of farmers' incomes, and in CHAC a somewhat larger share. A given wage structure is consistent with a wide range of income levels, depending on factor endowments, other factor prices, product demand conditions, etc.

[13] Including pumping costs, administrative fees for gravity water, and net returns to water. Of the 1370 pesos, 918 represent net returns, i.e., water charges cover only about a third of the value (for both gravity and pump water combined).

gated farms, associated in part with vegetable cultivation, have annual returns of 300–1000 pesos per hectare. *At 7.9 ha per manager* [14], *this is equivalent to a managerial return of 2,400–8,000 pesos per man-year.*

The returns to land also may be computed by land class from the BAJIO solution. The dual solution provides shadow prices of land by season and by the ten land classes. With proper aggregation, these may be transformed into annual shadow prices per hectare for the four farm types — that is, annual economic rents accruing to the fixed factor of farm land. Since irrigated land brings with it certain rights to gravity water and to tubewells, the rent to water endowments must be added to the land rent in the case of irrigated land. Finally, the sales value (price) of farm land may be computed by taking discounted sums of these total annual rents. The results are reported in table 5 for three different discount rates.

Informal surveys indicate that the actual sales price of farm land in El Bajío corresponds closely to table 5 for the 18% discount rate. The rate of price inflation is very small compared to the discount rate, so it would not influence the computed price significantly.

Table 5
Imputed price of farm land in BAJIO [a]
(unit: 1968 pesos per hectare)

Farm type	Annual discount rate r		
	$r = 12\%$	$r = 15\%$	$r = 18\%$
LD	3,960	3,060	2,460
SD	4,268	3,642	2,651
LI	19,250	14,875	11,958
SI	21,956	16,966	13,639

[a] The price of land is calculated as the discounted infinite stream of annual rentals accruing to the land and, in the case of irrigated land, associated water endowments. The rentals are taken from the dual solution of BAJITO for the case in which the base wage rate is 13.5 pesos/day and the cost of capital is 12%.

[14] The average size of irrigated farms in El Bajío is 7.9 ha.

Table 6
Range of labor intensities of cropping activities in BAJIO [a]
(unit: days of labor input per thousand pesos of product)

Crop	Dryland		Irrigated	
	Non-mechanized	Mechanized	Non-mechanized	Mechanized
Corn	18.9–32.8	9.3–14.1	9.5–16.6	4.6–10.3
Sorghum	18.7–36.3	8.4–12.2	8.8–16.9	5.4– 9.1
Chickpeas	18.4–25.9	18.2–25.8	16.1–17.9	15.6–17.6
Beans	27.2–29.2	15.7–20.3	18.7–24.0	13.8–17.3
Wheat			3.7– 6.8	3.5– 6.8
Barley			3.1– 5.4	2.8– 5.2
Tomatoes			7.6– 9.9	7.0– 8.9
Garlic			9.5– 9.9	5.5– 8.4
Chile			23.9–32.1	23.5–27.1
Onions			17.1–17.9	15.6–16.8
Peanuts			30.2–43.1	24.6–36.2
Lima beans			18.7–18.9	15.6–16.2
Strawberries			27.8–29.2	27.8–29.0
Alfalfa			7.2– 8.9	3.8– 4.7

[a] The indicated range represents either two or three techniques explicit in BAJIO.

One way to validate mathematical programming models is to seek meaningful dual solutions. The correspondence between the dual of BAJIO and the actual land prices in El Bajío constitutes a strong validation. It means that, at least in the aggregate, the technology set for each farm class provides an appropriate description of the process of transforming factor inputs into final output.

Another aspect of factor use is the allocation of machinery and draft animal services. Choices regarding the degree of mechanization are specified for each crop in each land class. For some crops, mechanized techniques are feasible in both the land preparation and harvesting, but nonetheless the choice of techniques exists for the plowing operation. Table 6 gives the range of variation in labor intensities introduced by the mechanization alternatives.

The degree of mechanization by farm type is given by table 7. Even though the cropping choice set is identical for large and small farms in BAJIO, the resultant patterns of mechanization are differ-

Table 7
Patterns of mechanization in BAJIO

Farm type	Thousands of hectares cultivated [a]		Mechanized share
	Mechanized	Non-mechanized	
LD	66.7	78.7	0.459
SD	0	427.3	0
LI	190.7	6.5	0.967
SI	162.9	17.2	0.904
Total	420.3	529.7	0.442

[a] Includes double cropping.

ent. Small farms concentrate on more labor-intensive techniques. [15] This is to be expected, since (per hectare) the small farms are endowed with more of the relatively cheap family labor. They also have more management skills per hectare. An additional difference in mechanization is found by comparing dryland and irrigated farms. A much higher rate of machinery use is found in the latter. This would be expected in light of the more abundant opportunities for double cropping which are provided by the presence of a year-round water supply. [16]

6. Basic results: cropping patterns

The small farms' comparative advantage in labor-intensive techniques shows up in the cropping patterns of BAJIO. In irrigated farms, where both large and small are faced with the same 14 crops from which to choose, the large ones tend to specialize in corn, barley, and alfalfa. As may be seen from table 6, these are among the least labor-intensive crops. Fruits and vegetables (strawberries, chile, tomatoes, garlic, onion, chickpeas) are grown on

[15] A similar result for Mexico was found in a study of tropical agriculture in Quintana Roo. See Bassoco and Winkelmann (1970).
[16] The greater capital-intensity of operations on large irrigated farms is consistent with the hypothesis of dualism within agriculture put forth by Trejo et al. (1970).

Table 8
Actual and optimal cropping patterns
(unit: thousands of hectares allocated to crop) [a]

Crop	1968 Estimated actual	1974, optimal BAJITO alone, at 1968 prices	1974, optimal BAJITO in CHAQUITO
Corn	252.5	294.2	388.1
Beans	13.0	210.9	137.9
Wheat	33.1	–	140.8
Sorghum	133.6	–	–
Alfalfa	4.0	12.0 [b]	–
Tomatoes	1.8	6.0 [b]	7.7
Green chile	1.0	2.0 [b]	–
Chickpeas	37.9	283.1	209.2
Barley	5.7	132.8	–
Peanuts	1.6	–	–
Onions	0.1	2.0 [b]	4.8
Strawberries	0.8	3.0 [b]	0.9
Garlic	0.4	4.0 [b]	–
Lima beans	0.9	–	–
Total	486.4	950.0	889.4

[a] Includes double cropping.

[b] The production of this crop was at an upper bound which was imposed in the fixed-price version. There were no such market limitations in the joint solution with CHAQUITO, where prices are endogenous variables.

small irrigated farms. These crops are highly labor-intensive. Here, too, a correspondence with real-world behavior is found. Large farms tend to emphasize grains, with more extensive use of machinery for land preparation and harvest, and small farms are typically truck farms.

For the entire set of farm types, table 8 provides a comparison of the optimal cropping pattern with the district's 1968 cropping pattern. These patterns are shown both for BAJITO alone and for the BAJITO solution as part of the sectoral model CHAQUITO. The difference in total area cultivated in 1968 and in the model is due to the presence of investment activities in the model which expand the cultivable area. BAJITO appears to overstate the profitability of chickpeas and beans in this district and to understate the profitability of sorghum. These comparisons should be interpreted cautiously, for actual cropping patterns are centrally controlled to some extent via allocations of credit and water. They vary rather significantly from year to year. The main point is that the model's cropping pattern appears reasonable enough to conduct experiments on investment programs and factor utilization.

The difference between the cropping patterns for BAJITO solved individually, on the one hand, and BAJITO solved as part of CHAQUITO on the other is due to two factors: (a) prices are variable in CHAQUITO but fixed in BAJITO alone, and (b) the district marketing bounds which were necessary in BAJITO because of the fixed prices, are deleted in CHAQUITO. The prices determined by CHAQUITO reflect inter-district comparative advantage in 1974. Therefore the difference between the last two columns of table 8 may be regarded as primarily a function of comparative advantage among the producing areas within Mexico. For example, wheat does not enter the solution of BAJITO alone. Under a different set of prices determined with reference to demand and to all districts' production sets, wheat is produced in BAJITO. This topic, the linkage between BAJITO and CHAQUITO, is explored further in the next chapter.

References

Bassoco, L.M., and D.L. Winkelmann, 'Programación de la producción agrícola de la parcela ejídal en tres obras de regadío en el estado de Quintana Roo'. Chapingo, México, Escuela Nacional de Agricultura, 1970.

Centro de Investigaciones Agrarias (CDIA), *Estructura agraria y desarrollo agrícola en México*, vols. I–III, México, 1970.

Trejo, S., T. Rendón and F. Urdanivia, 'La dualidad económica de la agricultura Mexicana'. Departamento de Estudios Económicos, Banco de México, 1970. (Depto. documento num. A(A70/18).)

IV.5. INVESTMENT AND EMPLOYMENT ALTERNATIVES IN THE AGRICULTURAL DISTRICT MODEL

John H. DULOY, Gary P. KUTCHER and Roger D. NORTON*

1. Introduction

This chapter reports a series of experiments on factor utilization in the model BAJITO which represents the 'project district'.[1] Labor and capital are the input factors. Capital takes two forms: that embodied in the stock of machinery, and that used for land-improving investments. Through these experiments, the model may be used to estimate the degree of flexibility in employment prospects in the district and also to estimate a schedule of returns to investment which are associated with particular wage rates. This schedule shows the amount of investment in land improvement which may be made in the district under different rates of return. It identifies the components of the schedule with various types of investment projects, and it quantifies the relationship between investment programs and employment.

With the same solutions, the location of investments by type of farm − dryland and irrigated, large and small − may be studied. The optimal investment pattern which follows from maximizing total profits for farmers in the district may imply a skewed distribution of the investment benefits over types of farms.

*The authors wish to express their appreciation to Luz María Bassoco, Apostolos Condos, Alan Manne, René Vaurs, and Donald Winkelmann for helpful comments. Malathi Parthasarathy kindly assisted with computations and tabulations.

[1] For comparability with the CHAQUITO solutions, the aggregated version, BAJITO, is used for these experiments instead of BAJIO. The model proper is described in the preceding chapter.

These experiments are directed toward employment and the returns to investment, both district-wide and by farm type. Another focus, in keeping with overall theme of this volume, is the impact on investment decisions of additional information from outside the district. That additional information is represented by the sector model. To evaluate the influence of additional information, BAJITO is solved both in isolation and as part of CHAQUITO. Since the availability of day labor in the district is more than sufficient to meet requirements in both types of solutions, the only substantive difference is the nature of the demand assumptions. In BAJITO in isolation, the product prices are fixed and hence demands are infinitely inelastic. For some garden crops, this assumption is untenable, so upper bounds ('marketing limitations') were imposed on the quantity which may be sold at that fixed price. In BAJITO as part of CHAQUITO, the demand formulation is that of CHAC[2], with downward-sloping demand curves. The marketing limitations were therefore removed. Given this difference, the major difference between BAJITO alone and BAJITO-in-CHAQUITO is rooted in the different sets of product prices. For the latter, the product prices are determined in part by specified supply conditions in other district submodels. The linkage of BAJITO with CHAQUITO conveys information to the project district about its comparative advantage in production against all other districts.

To test further the importance of prices, two versions of BAJITO-alone are defined. One incorporates base period (1967–69 average) product prices, and the other utilizes prices taken from the sector model. In all, there are three versions of the project model:

BAJITO alone with base-period fixed prices (solution type I);

BAJITO alone with fixed prices taken from CHAQUITO (solution type II);

BAJITO in CHAQUITO (solution type III).

Each version is solved several times under varying assumptions on the wage rate and the criterion rate of return to investment.

_____

[2] See above, chapter IV.1, section 8.

2. BAJITO with CHAQUITO prices

CHAQUITO includes BAJITO as one of its submodels. Therefore it may seem somewhat artificial to detach that submodel and solve it with prices obtained from the full BAJITO-in-CHAQUITO model. However, aside from the institutional analogue of micro-level decision-makers relying on sectoral price guidelines, there is formal interest in this procedure. The two solutions will differ because of the nature of the demand structure. There are demand groups in CHAQUITO, and within each group, there are limits to the degree to which the commodity mix may change. If it were optimal for the solution to lie at one of these limits in the commodity mix, an additional unit of production of one crop would require more production of at least one other crop also. Hence the shadow prices, or marginal supply prices, sometimes reflect the joint cost of additional production for one or more crops.

When these same shadow prices are entered as fixed prices in the solution of BAJITO alone, the interdependence on the demand side is removed. Therefore the prices take on quite different meanings, applying now to non-joint production. Hence the optimal cropping pattern is different from that observed in BAJITO-in-CHAQUITO.[3]

3. Investment choices

Of the various forms of investment considered in the project model, only one, canal lining, is an activity exclusively carried out by public authorities. The other forms of investment are either entirely private or are carried out by both private farmers and public agencies. Some are 'mixed' in the sense that the investment decision is made in the private sector subject to governmental

---

[3] It can be shown formally that if the system does not include such interdependence on the demand side, then the solutions are identical for BAJITO-in-CHAQUITO and BAJITO alone with prices from the former. The only exceptions are equivalent optimal solutions and cases of degeneracy.

regulation, often with construction or installation being carried out by a public agency contracting to private farmers. This multiplicity of decision makers and decision processes distinguishes the investment program in agriculture from that of, say, the energy sector. The solutions presented here are based on social rate of return criteria[4], but others can be used. The model assists in using other criteria for decisions by simulating the employment and income distributional impacts of investment programs.

In the present formulation, the outcome of investment decisions can be presented either as the quantity of investment funds demanded at various costs of capital and other resources, or as a schedule of the shadow price of capital under constrained allocations of investable funds. The former presentation was selected because it is less difficult to define meaningful *a priori* bounds on the price of investment funds than to define limits on the availability of capital. This holds for the sector as a whole and, *a fortiori*, for an individual district within the sector.

Table 1 summarizes the major results concerning the marginal efficiency of capital (MEC) in the El Bajío district.[5] The columns of this table refer to different factor price combinations. The foreign exchange premium (f) was set alternatively at zero and at 30%, the base wage rate (w) at 13.5 and 19.5 pesos per day (1968 prices), and the interest rate (r) at 12 and 24%. Only four of the resulting eight possible solutions are applicable when BAJITO is solved alone. It is possible to take account of variations in the price of foreign exchange only when considering the sector as a whole.

The types of solutions are defined by the rows of table 1. Rows 1 through 3 apply to solutions of BAJITO in isolation for 1974, using product prices set at 1968 levels (solution type I). Rows 4

[4] In the fixed price versions (solution types I and II), this is equivalent to maximizing producers' economic profits. In the variable price version (solution type III), this is equivalent to maximization of the sum of producers' and consumers' surplus.

[5] Only two points on each MEC function are available from these experiments. These two points are joined linearly to aid in interpretation of the results. In a number of other experiments where intermediate points were calculated, the resulting MEC functions were approximately linear.

Table 1

Investments in BAJITO (unit: tens of millions of 1968 pesos)

Solution type	Investment type	Factor price assumptions [a]							
		f = 0				f = 30%			
		w = 13.5		w = 19.5		w = 13.5		w = 19.5	
		r = 12%	r = 24%	r = 12%	r = 24%	r = 12%	r = 24%	r = 12%	r = 24%
BAJITO-alone, BAJITO prices (I)	Water [b]	29.6	27.3	29.6	26.4	n.a. [d]	n.a.	n.a.	n.a.
	Machinery [c]	6.1	3.4	19.7	5.6	n.a.	n.a.	n.a.	n.a.
	Total	35.7	30.7	49.3	32.0	n.a.	n.a.	n.a.	n.a.
BAJITO-alone, CHAQUITO prices (II)	Water [b]	29.6	10.3	29.6	9.9	n.a.	n.a.	n.a.	n.a.
	Machinery [c]	7.4	0	21.8	8.4	n.a.	n.a.	n.a.	n.a.
	Total	37.0	10.3	51.4	18.3	n.a.	n.a.	n.a.	n.a.
BAJITO-in-CHAQUITO (III)	Water [b]	29.6	15.1	29.6	11.0	29.6	14.3	29.6	14.5
	Machinery [c]	7.4	-0.5	11.4	1.7	2.0	-0.7	13.0	0.8
	Total	37.0	14.6	41.0	12.7	31.6	13.6	42.6	15.3

[a] f is the foreign exchange premium, w is the wage rate in 1968 pesos per day, and r is the annual rate of interest.
[b] Sum of net investment in lining canals, installing tubewells and levelling land.
[c] Defined as the change in the stock of machinery implied by changes in the level of machinery services activities from 1968 to 1974.
[d] n.a. = not applicable.

through 6 refer to solutions of BAJITO in isolation, using product prices obtained from the 1974 solution of CHAQUITO (solution type II).[6] Rows 7 through 9 refer to solutions of BAJITO as part of CHAQUITO (solution type III).

Associated with these solution types are differing assumption sets regarding the district decision maker(s). These can be specified as the following. In the case of solution type I, account is taken only of district-level information. The district is sufficiently small so that there is a negligible impact of increases of its production upon product prices. No information is available concerning the investment program or the supply response of the rest of the sector. It is therefore assumed that product prices remain constant in 1974 at the 1968 level. In the case of solution type II, information is available concerning the prices which will prevail in 1974 corresponding to the investment program and production response of the sector as a whole, given a particular set of factor prices. In solution type III, full information is available for investment decisions at the project district level. Product prices and the sectoral and district investment programs are determined simultaneously, with the effects of comparative advantage among districts at different product and factor prices influencing the determination of the investment program for the El Bajío area.

The results are summarized in figure 1. To check for labor complementarity and substitution, water-enhancing investments and machinery investments are shown separately. For each solution type, an MEC curve is shown under a base wage rate of 13.5 pesos/day. In the case of investments in new water resources, the curves for solution type I are well to the right of the others. The steepness of the type I curves suggests that the optimal level of investment is determined mostly by the physical constraints on the system: the constraints imposed by the level of the aquifer and by the area of non-levelled irrigated land. Very different results are obtained when better product price forecasts are available, as in solution type II. The MEC curves are markedly less steep. If the

---

[6] The prices were taken from the CHAQUITO solution with a base wage of 13.5 pesos, an interest rate of 12%, and a zero foreign exchange premium.

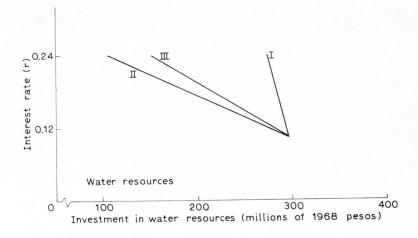

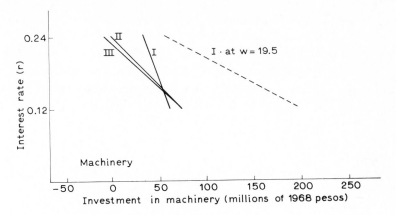

Fig. 1. MEC curves for investment in BAJITO ($w = 13.5, f = 0$).

shadow price of capital were 20% (a not unreasonable figure for Mexico) and if investment projects were evaluated at a wage rate of 13.5 pesos per day, then the investment program recommended from the type I calculations is approximately 150% greater than that appropriate to the type II solutions. In this case, a substantial overestimate [7] of the district's investment program is caused by

[7] This does not imply, of course, that the error would always be in this direction.

the failure to take account of information from competing agricultural districts.

It is not surprising that the investment program is sensitive to differences in the assumptions concerning product prices. In this instance, the effect was due both to differences in the relative prices of products and to a slight overall price increase.[8] Changes in relative prices can only be forecast by a knowledge of the supply and demand functions of the sector as a whole. It is this information which is incorporated in solution type II (at one set of factor prices) and which is lacking in solution type I. Changes in relative prices bring different output mixes into the solution. Since different crops do not have the same output/water coefficients, the changes in relative prices lead to changes in the demand for irrigation water and therefore to changes in the profitability of water-increasing investments.

The results for solution types II and III are quite similar.[9] This similarity is to be expected in a region that accounts for only 5% of the cultivated area within the sector. For both water and machinery investments, the two ways of incorporating sector-wide information give comparable results. Both cases differ substantially from solution type I.

If solution type III is taken as 'correct' for purposes of this experiment, it appears that type II is accurate enough for most investment programming when the factor price ratio ($0.24/19.5 = 0.012$) is similar to that for which the 'price forecast' was made ($0.12/13.5 = 0.0089$). It diverges from the optimal investment program when the ratio of factor prices ($0.24/13.5 = 0.018$) is substantially different than the ratio for which the price forecast was made.

For both water and machinery, the rate of return has a significant impact on the overall size of the investment program. The amount of funds which can be invested profitably in new water

[8] Based on a Fisher price index, the overall level of prices of crops which can be produced in El Bajío increased by about 5% from 1968 to 1974, according to solutions in CHAQUITO.

[9] At the higher base wage of 19.5 pesos/day, the MEC curves for investment in water resources under solution types II and III are even closer together. See table 1.

sources in El Bajío is two to three times as great at 12% as at 24%. The most profitable investments (upper part of MEC curves) are new tubewells. Land levelling occupies the lower part of the MEC curves. Canal lining does not appear to be profitable even at 12% under any of the circumstances tested. When this result was first encountered, the engineering coefficients in the canal lining activities were carefully reviewed and corroborated.[10]

The optimal amount of machinery investment is more sensitive to the rate of interest chosen. Also, the direction of error inherent in using solution type I varies with the interest rate, as shown by the crossing MEC curves in figure 1. In contrast to the case of water, investment in machinery is determined mainly by substitution between capital and labor, i.e., by relative factor prices, rather than by product prices. This may be seen by the fact that, for water, the MEC schedules for the higher wage rate are consistently below those for the lower wage, while the reverse relationship holds for the machinery curves (table 1). Where the substitution effect dominates the results, it is difficult to generalize the impact of additional product price information. One generalization can be made, however. The optimal investment in machinery is more responsive to changes in the rate of interest at the higher wage rate than at the lower. This result holds over all solutions. At the high wage rate, machinery use is more widespread (particularly on dryland farms where it has only a marginal advantage over labor and mules), and therefore its use responds to changes in the interest rate. At the lower wage rate, with a smaller stock of machinery, most of the stock is used for cultivation on irrigated farms. There it has a more clear-cut advantage over the draft animal techniques, and it is sufficiently profitable so that the level of the stock of machinery is not responsive to changes in the rate of interest. For example, at the low wage rate, the stock of machinery decreased by only 6.7% when the interest rate was increased

---

[10] Lic. Atanasio Espinosa has pointed out that if the canal lining alternatives were subdivided more finely, this probably would lead to at least one form entering the optimal solution. When the model was redefined so that canal lining was the only investment activity, it became more profitable, but still not profitable enough to yield a 12% return.

from 12 to 24%, an implied elasticity of demand for machinery stock of only -0.104 at the mid-point of the arc. At the higher wage rate the decrease is 26.3% and the elasticity of demand is -0.455.

The solutions of type III at the higher value of the foreign exchange rate did not affect these conclusions. An apparent anomaly in the results is of some interest. This illustrates the difficulties of applying *a priori* reasoning to determine the direction of changes in a model as complex as CHAQUITO. Product prices can be no lower, and in fact increase, when the premium on foreign exchange is increased from zero to 30%. Yet investment in water declines slightly when this premium increase is made (in the case of $w = 13.5$ and $r = 0.24$). The decline is from 151 million pesos to 143 million pesos. The reason for this was a switch in comparative advantage between BAJITO and another district submodel in CHAQUITO in the production of onions for export. This is a crop which happens to respond particularly well to being grown on levelled rather than on unlevelled land.

4. The distribution of investment by types of farm

So far, the discussion of investment choices in the model has been at the level of the district as a whole. There are also important choices concerning the allocation of aggregate investment among different farm types. Land can be levelled on both the large and small irrigated farms (LI or SI). Tubewells can be installed on the irrigated farms (where they add to the existing supply of irrigation water), or they can be installed on dryland farms (LD or SD). In this case, they transform dryland farming into irrigated. In all the solutions, the LI and SI activities for tubewells did not enter the optimal basis at positive intensities, so that the choice came down to that between LD and/or SD. Similarly, the model can allocate machinery services differentially among the four basic farm types.

Results drawn from solutions of BAJITO in CHAQUITO are given in table 2. Results are given for the case of a zero foreign

Table 2
Allocation of investments in BAJITO [a]

Investment type	Farm type	w = 13.5		w = 19.5	
		r = 0.12	r = 0.24	r = 0.12	r = 0.24
		Investment (unit: tens of millions of 1968 pesos)			
Tubewells	LD	6.0	8.0	–	–
	SD	2.0	–	8.0	8.0
Land levelling	LI	11.5	4.1	7.8	0.6
	SI	10.2	2.9	13.8	2.4
		Ratio of days of mule use to days of machinery use			
Machinery	LD	5.5	7.5	1.9	1.9
	SD	12.2	72.5	3.2	72.1
	LI	0.0	0.0	0.0	0.0
	SI	1.4	2.1	0.5	1.2

[a] Solutions of BAJITO in CHAQUITO for zero foreign exchange premium.

exchange premium only. The basic pattern over farm types was very similar under variations in the foreign exchange premium, regardless of whether BAJITO was solved in isolation or embedded in CHAQUITO. The optimal allocation of investment among the farm types is a function of their relative factor endowments, particularly land, labor and initial water capacity, and these are the same for all solution types.

Consider tubewells first. It is always optimal in BAJITO to allocate the limited increase in the number of wells (due to the aquifer constraint) to dryland farms. On these farms, with a zero initial endowment of irrigation water, the marginal product of water is higher than on already irrigated farms.[11] On dry land, the optimal allocation between large and small farms varies sharply with the relative prices of capital and labor. At the higher wage

---

[11] This result would probably not hold if, among other circumstances, the supply of water was severely restricted to irrigated farms and if the extension of irrigation to dry land involved a large scale gravity-fed reticulation system.

rate (19.5 pesos per day) the allocation was exclusively to small farms, at both interest rates considered. This reflects the relative abundance of family labor on small farms. At the lower wage rate (13.5 pesos per day), the allocation was more in favor of large farms. At the lowest relative price of labor (i.e., $w = 13.5$ and $r = 0.24$), the allocation was exclusively to large farms. The investment allocation dropped to three-quarters on large farms and one-quarter on small when the interest rate was varied downwards (i.e., $w = 13.5$ and $r = 0.12$). A similar, but less marked pattern, applied to land levelling on the irrigated farms. At higher labor costs, the proportion of the total investment in land levelling was always higher on small farms than on large.

For investment in machinery, the choice is not so much between higher or lower levels of machinery use but rather a choice between a machine-based or a mule-based technology. For this reason, the results in table 2 are presented as the optimal ratios of mule days to machinery days.[12] Consider, for example, the first column of results (for $w = 13.5$, $r = 0.12$). It will be seen that dryland farms use the mule-based technology much more than the irrigated farms, the ratios being 5.5 and 12.2 for LD and SD respectively, compared with 0.0 and 1.4 for LI and SI. This difference is explained mainly by the fact that the machinery technology is land saving. It enables more timely operations, and double cropping is more extensively feasible on the irrigated farms. These farms can better profit from the land-saving opportunities provided by machinery.

Machinery is also, of course, labor saving. This is reflected in two ways. First, within both classes of dry and of irrigated farms, small farms use relatively more mule days than do large farms. Taking the same solution as an example, the ratios are 12.2 for SD compared with 5.5 for LD, and 1.4 for SI compared with 0.0 for LI. This pattern holds over all the solutions. Second, the ratio of mule-use to machinery-use varies with changes in wage and interest rates, being particularly sensitive to the latter. Of particular inter-

---

[12] To assist in interpreting the results in the table, the average rate of substitution is one machine-day for 13.3 mule-days.

est is the fact that the selection of technology is virtually insensitive on SI and LI and quite sensitive on SD. Except for the small dryland farms, it is optimal to adopt a preponderately machine-based technology under a wide range of relative prices for capital and labor.

5. Employment in BAJITO

Since this monograph deals with investment analysis at different levels of decision-making, it is instructive to summarize some of the results on employment obtained the district model. The pattern of these results is similar for all solution types, so that reference is made here only to solutions of BAJITO solved in isolation

Table 3
Some results on employment from BAJITO

	Factor prices			
	$w = 13.5$		$w = 19.5$	
	$r = 0.12$	$r = 0.24$	$r = 0.12$	$r = 0.24$
Index of wage rate to interest rate	100.0	50.0	144.4	72.2
Index of production	100.0	99.1	99.4	98.3
Index of total employment	100.0	101.9	89.1	98.8
Index of employment/output ratio	100.0	102.9	89.7	100.5
Seasonal unemployment	0.15	0.16	0.06	0.13
Index of peak seasonal employment	100.0	102.6	77.0	95.9
Farmer employment rate by farm				
type (%) LD	100.0	100.0	100.0	100.0
SD	92.7	93.8	47.7	86.0
LI	100.0	100.0	100.0	100.0
SI	79.0	82.5	78.3	80.0
Seasonal unemployment of farmers				
(%) LD	12.0	15.4	6.9	8.9
SD	38.4	38.3	18.8	36.1
Index of employment of landless				
laborers	100.0	107.6	81.0	87.14
Seasonal unemployment of landless				
laborers (%)	29.7	30.2	30.3	31.2

from CHAQUITO. The main employment results are summarized in table 3.

Over the factor price combinations included in these solutions, production is virtually unresponsive to variations in the price of capital and labor.[13] Over the full range of wage and interest rate variations, the index of output varies by less than 2%, while the index of employment varies by about 11%. The conclusion is clear. Variations in the employment level are determined mainly by substitution between capital and labor rather than by the level of output.

Despite its variety of technical choices (see above, chapter IV. 4, table 6) the model does not provide a wide scope for increasing employment. This can be illustrated in a number of ways. First, the base period machinery stock was about 338 million pesos. With this and the information in table 1, it is possible to calculate the quantity $(\Delta E/\bar{E}) \div (\Delta K/\bar{K})$, where E is employment and K is capital in machinery, over the two solutions. (Two extreme values were used for the ratio of the wage to the interest rate.) This quantity may be regarded as a rough index of the elasticity of employment with respect to changes in the stock of machinery. The index is -0.37, a low elasticity of capital-labor substitution. The underemployment problem in Mexican agriculture is evidently a difficult one, and it will not be solved by the choice of techniques available for raising short-cycle crops.

Second, the demand for labor calculated from the model results is inelastic, both with respect to its own price and also with respect to the price of capital. The own-price elasticity was calculated for $r = 0.12$ and $r = 0.24$, the former corresponding to a high relative price of labor and the latter to a low. The elasticities are -0.32 and -0.09 respectively, suggesting that the already low elasticity of demand for labor declines as employment increases. The elasticity of demand for labor with respect to the rate of interest is 0.028 and 0.154, respectively, at the lower and the higher wage rates. Once again the elasticity declines as employment increases.

[13] The elasticities of output with respect to the interest rate range from -0.014 to -0.016, depending on the wage rate. The elasticities with respect to the wage rate are similarly low: -0.18 to -0.22, depending on the interest rate.

These conclusions from model solutions at the district level are consistent with the conclusions from the sectoral analysis in chapter IV. 3 above and with the DINAMICHAC linkage reported in chapter IV.6 below. To add to this picture, the index of seasonal unemployment increases monotonically with the index of employment, suggesting that employment changes are concentrated in one period of the year, rather than being spread evenly throughout the year. This last conclusion is confirmed by the fact that the index of maximal seasonal employment in table 3 moves more than proportionately with respect to the index of total employment. The index presented in table 3 undoubtedly underestimates seasonal employment, because it is based on a high level of aggregation over time, three seasons of four months each. However, there is no reason to believe that a more disaggregated treatment of time would invalidate this relationship between seasonal unemployment and total employment.

Underlying the district-wide results are substantial differences in employment patterns among types of farm. Because farmers and family labor on farms are a district resource, estimates for the total farm labor force were built up by type of farm. In this instance also, employment rates can be calculated. The employment rates presented for farm types in table 3 represent the percentage of the total available farm family labor force which receives at least four months employment on the farm.[14] The farm labor constraint on the large dry farms is binding in at least one season in all solutions, so the employment rate is constant at 100%. For irrigated farms, the treatment of farm labor is on an annual basis only. The constraint is always binding for the large farms and is always non-binding for the small.

From the farm-type results, it is apparent that unemployment of farm labor is located mainly on the small farms, both dryland and irrigated. This is true both for the average and the peak levels of employment. Despite the tendency of small farms to concentrate

---

[14] This definition is consistent with that used for the linkage of DINAMICO and CHAC. (See below, chapter IV.6.)

on labor-intensive crops (above, chapter IV.4), this is not suffi-cient to offset their greater availability of labor per hectare.

On small farms, the level of employment is more responsive to changes in factor prices. This can be seen from the results on technology choices by farm type in table 2. The machine-based technology does not have as overwhelming an advantage on these farms as on the large. The small farms switch technologies more readily in response to changes in relative factor prices.[15] These are the farms on which 83% of the district's work force is located.

Landless laborers are employed only on large irrigated farms. From the fact that employment of landless laborers is responsive to changes in the relative factor prices[16] (see table 3), it may be concluded that their employment level also is a function of capi-tal-labor substitution. This, however, is *not* the case, at least with respect to capital-labor substitution associated with varying levels of the machinery-based technology versus the mule and labor in-tensive technology. From table 3 it can be seen that the large irrigated farms use only the machinery technologies regardless of the factor price ratio. The explanation lies rather in the fact that the employment level of landless laborers is dependent upon the rate of expansion of large irrigated farms and of the availability of water upon them. This can be seen by the fact that employment of landless laborers is relatively high (table 3) when additional tubewells are installed on large dry farms, creating new large irri-gated farms (table 2). And, as discussed in the previous section, this occurs mainly when the wage rate is low and the interest rate high. Seasonal unemployment, as expected, is quite high for land-less laborers who, in fact, migrate from district to district seeking seasonal employment.

---

[15] Recall that these results come from a comparative statics model. It is not intended to suggest that such responses are instantaneous or even rapid; they are best interpreted as the outcome of a particular set of factor prices obtained over a long period.

[16] The elasticity of demand for landless laborers with respect to the wage rate is about −0.58 at both the lower and the higher interest rates. This is substantially more elastic than the demand for labor as a whole.

6. Concluding remarks

The results of BAJITO are difficult to summarize, but an attempt is hazarded. First, at the simplest level, a cropping model with investment choices under optimization and diverse farm types appears to be a workable device for formulating investment programs in a particular district. It arrays the set of investment choices against common production alternatives and resource valuations. As well as yielding an overall marginal-efficiency-of-capital schedule, it identifies each class of project with a rate of return. Given this framework, it is a simple matter to explore the implications of alternative assumptions such as different base wage rates.

Regarding the linkage with the sector models, the information contained in the latter does appear quite relevant to district-level decisions. The most relevant information consists of price forecasts. In the sector model, these are dependent in part on investment programs undertaken elsewhere in the sector. If a useful alternative price forecasting tool could be constructed which took account of the supply and demand information contained in the sector model, then it could be substituted for CHAQUITO.

The incorporation of BAJITO in CHAQUITO may also be regarded as a device for overcoming certain kinds of biases in the basic data. The BAJITO cropping pattern in the linked model reflects inter-district comparative advantage, for the input norms were estimated on a comparable basis in all districts. For BAJITO alone, an error in, say, the wheat yields may result in its exclusion from the optimal cropping pattern. Yet if this error is systematic in all districts, comparative advantage considerations may bring wheat back into the optimal solution of BAJITO in CHAQUITO. This may in fact have been the case with regard to wheat in BAJITO. (See above, chapter IV.4, table 8.)

Some elasticities of demand for factors are presented here. On the whole, they indicate much more flexibility in small farms than in large. They also indicate a relatively inflexible aggregate demand for labor. In terms of landless labor only, the demand is flexible, but it is highly seasonal. These findings are consistent with those of chapter IV.3 above. Short-cycle crops alone are not particularly promising for agricultural labor absorption.

IV.6. LINKING THE AGRICULTURAL MODEL AND THE ECONOMY-WIDE MODEL

John H. DULOY and Roger D. NORTON*

1. Introduction

In the analysis of decentralized decision-making, linkages may be defined as information flows. This volume deals with suboptimization and the relevance of different kinds of information to decision-making. There is always a cost to information gathering and processing, and so the degree of usefulness of additional information should determine whether that cost is incurred.

For this study, the levels of decision-making are taken as given. [1] The question is the extent to which information should be exchanged between the levels, and which kinds of information are most appropriate. For agriculture, this study treats three levels of decision-making: macroeconomy, sector, and investment project. This chapter discusses the sector-macroeconomy linkage. The sector-project interaction is discussed in chapter IV.5 above. This chapter deals with the question of how DINAMICO's macroeconomic results are affected by incorporation of information from CHAC.

Given the importance of agriculture in the Mexican economy, it

* The authors wish to express their appreciation to Louis Goreux and Alan Manne for helpful discussions of the issues treated in this chapter. Alan Manne's editorial assistance has made this chapter significantly more coherent and more readable than it otherwise would have been. We are grateful to Richard Inman, Gary Kutcher, and Malathi Parthasarathy for carrying out the computations and tabulations.

[1] For some determinants of the optimal degree of decentralization within an organization, see Kochen and Deutsch (1969).

is quite natural to include agriculture in a study of interdependence, both between macro-level and sectoral policies and between
project decisions and sectoral policies. However, the structural
characteristics of the sector make it difficult to design a model
which treats micro-level project choices and sectoral policies adequately and yet is compatible with a macroeconomic model. To
cite a few examples of the sector's peculiarities, supply functions
differ spatially since production is dispersed over geographically
different zones, products are numerous and their relative prices
vary over time, sometimes sharply, and input requirements and
production are markedly seasonal. It is not easy to design a model
which is appropriate to the analysis of sector policies and which
also meshes nicely with an economy-wide model.

Two distinct stances may be taken with respect to the linkage
problem. One alternative is to design a unified, perfectly compatible set of models for different levels of decision-making, and to
encourage analysts at each level to mold the statement of policy
choices to this framework. The other is to initiate separate model
building efforts, each adapted to the structure of one particular
element of the economy, and to develop essentially *ex post* linkages. While this latter approach appears cruder in the linkages, it
may compensate in its relevance to sectoral problems. Moreover, it
reflects the decentralized nature of reality – in analysis as well as
in decision-making. This has been the approach adopted with respect to the agricultural and economy-wide studies in Mexico. The
sector model, CHAC, has been designed with sector relationships
in mind. As a result, linking CHAC and DINAMICO has been in
part a process of devising *ad hoc* procedures for overcoming differences in coverage and differences in definitions.

2. Multi-level information flows

Of the various kinds of data required to construct CHAC, there are
four which may be supplied by DINAMICO: the interest rate, the
wage rate, the foreign exchange premium, and the growth rate of
aggregate income. (The latter is used to determine the magnitude

of the shift in the demand curves for agricultural products.) CHAC in turn may supply some information to be fed into DINAMICO. The two basic pieces of information are: (a) estimated changes over time in the aggregate input-mix used in agriculture, and (b) the base period rate of employment of the agricultural labor force. As might be expected, there are less formal linkages also. In the construction of the agricultural model, it was discovered that the labor estimates in DINAMICO understate the role of family labor. In agriculture, family labor cannot be ignored, so one of CHAC's contributions to the macro-economic study is an estimate of the labor force which is more appropriate to the agricultural man-power requirements. This kind of informal linkage can be as significant as more formal linkages.

The primary CHAC-DINAMICO linkage discussed here is the upward linkage, the effect of the CHAC information on the DI-NAMICO solutions, and not vice versa. The reason is straightforward. It is a simple matter to solve CHAC several times under an appropriate range of factor prices, to test the sector's response to different basic policies. *A priori*, it is not so simple to imagine alternative aggregate input-mixes for agriculture or to estimate the sectoral labor surplus. This asymmetry suggests that to a large extent sector planning can proceed independently of macro-level policy planning, and that only a few guidelines are needed: the rate of growth of GDP and the appropriate efficiency prices for capital and foreign exchange. Multi-sector models, which attempt to estimate intersectoral comparative advantage in international trade, impose heavier data requirements on the sector analysts.

For the sector-project linkage, the question is somewhat different. Since the project model is a part of the sectoral model, its influence on the sector responses is taken into account. The point to investigate is how the project decision differs with and without a sectoral model. Hence, the information flows are one way from CHAC to the project model, BAJIO. The principal pieces of information provided to BAJIO by CHAC are commodity prices which are consistent with the investment programs undertaken both in

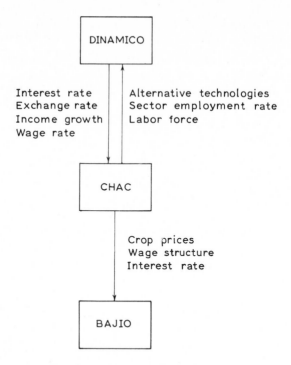

Fig. 1. Agricultural linkages.

the El Bajío area and elsewhere in the sector. CHAC also supplies information on the cost of hiring day labor, but since labor remains surplus in all solutions, this cost does not rise above the wage rate assumed for BAJIO in isolation. Also, for experiments on different exchange rates, CHAC shows the impact on the BAJIO investment program. Without the sector model, the proportion of BAJIO output going to export markets cannot be determined readily.

For the CHAC-DINAMICO linkage, the method used represents one iteration in a multi-level planning procedure. In the spirit of Kornai's man-machine planning[2], this single iteration was designed to move quite far toward convergence. Essentially, rather than

---

[2] See Kornai (1969).

adding one bit of information on sectoral choices per iteration, an entire set of sectoral choices was inserted directly in the first iteration. The sector model was solved initially under a wide range of prices on economy-wide resources, and a corresponding set of technology vectors was transmitted to DINAMICO. As long as the subsequent DINAMICO shadow prices on basic resources fall within the range already used in CHAC, there is no need for further iterations with respect to prices.

CHAC was not solved, however, under a range of assumptions on the growth rate of GDP (and hence demand). If this had been done with a sufficiently wide range of growth rates, convergence of the overall procedure might have been achieved in one iteration.[3]

Figure 1 summarizes diagrammatically the various information flows between DINAMICO, CHAC, and BAJIO.

3. Making CHAC and DINAMICO compatible

The nature of the data series available at the macro and sector levels is another factor in favor of different approaches to model design at each level. Given that the structures were designed independently, a number of transformations are required to make the solutions of CHAC suitable for inclusion in DINAMICO.

There are five major differences in coverage between the two models.[4] First, CHAC treats only short-cycle crops, whereas the corresponding sector in DINAMICO also includes tree crops, livestock, forestry, and fisheries.[5] Second, sectoral outputs are disaggregated in CHAC. It treats 33 individual agricultural crops, whereas DINAMICO treats a sectoral aggregate. Third, the two models characterize production differently in terms of types of

---

[3] Subject to the approximation implied by permitting linear interpolations between discrete alternatives on prices and growth rates.

[4] In addition, there are basic conceptual differences such as those concerning the price-elasticity of demand and the reservation price of labor.

[5] Short-cycle crops constitute about 49% of the value of production in DINAMICO's sector 1.

inputs. CHAC includes land, water and short-term credit, which are not explicit in DINAMICO. The latter includes minor inputs to agriculture (textiles, wood, metal products, etc.) which are not specified in CHAC. Fourth, in CHAC some inputs, including labor, are seasonal, whereas in DINAMICO all inputs are annual. And fifth, DINAMICO is faithful to its name in being multi-period, whereas CHAC is single-period. Although it is not dynamic, CHAC does include investment choices and technical progress. Beyond these major differences, there are other minor differences concerning the base year for pricing and so forth.

All values in DINAMICO are expressed in 1960 prices. Throughout this chapter, the convention is to use 1960 prices as the numéraire, for comparability with the other chapters treating DINAMICO.

Procedures have been devised for bridging each of these definitional gaps. They may be summarized as follows:

(a) Regarding the *differences in sectoral coverage,* CHAC is not used to delineate complete new vectors for DINAMICO's sector 1, but rather to indicate degrees of substitutability among major inputs. It is assumed that the marginal rates of factor substitution calculated in CHAC apply to all of sector 1. The base-period input-output coefficients of DINAMICO are retained and are modified over time by the ratios of input growth to output growth in CHAC. Also, it is assumed that the rate of underemployment calculated in CHAC applies to all of sector 1.

(b) Regarding *levels of output aggregation,* the CHAC outputs are aggregated by means of a production index. A Fisher quantum index for 1974 is constructed *ex post* on the basis of the prices and production levels in the 1968 and 1974 solutions of the sectoral model. The growth in this index is then applied to DINAMICO's 1968 output in sector 1.

(c) Regarding the *different types of inputs* treated in the models, the CHAC results are used to modify only the major input-output coefficients of sector 1.[6] Others are changed in ac-

---

[6] These are primarily the coefficients for unskilled agricultural labor, machinery services, chemical inputs, and investment. See table 1 for a complete list.

cordance with the rates of technological change applied elsewhere in DINAMICO. CHAC's land and water constraints do not appear in DINAMICO. Sector output constraints are therefore imposed on the vectors generated from CHAC when they are inserted in DINAMICO. These constraints represent more than land and water resource limits. They also represent the level of output chosen in a competitive market, given factor prices and sector-specific resource constraints. This is not the same as the physical productive capacity of the sector. Through appropriate policy interventions, higher sector output levels could have been achieved in CHAC with the same sectoral resource availabilities. Of course, such a solution would have shown a social welfare loss.

(d) Regarding the *seasonality of labor* in CHAC, a convention is adopted for defining persons actually employed in agriculture. Those who work at least four months of the year in agriculture are assumed to be unavailable for non-agricultural employment. Those who work less than four months a year in agriculture are assumed to be available for corresponding part- or full-time work in other sectors.

(e) Regarding the *difference in time horizons,* the 1968–74 CHAC rates of change in output and factor use norms are extrapolated to cover other DINAMICO periods.

4. The linkage

The basic procedure in the upward linkage was to aggregate each CHAC solution into a compact statement of sector technology, and then to solve DINAMICO with this as a substitute for the original DINAMICO input-output vector for agriculture. In some solutions, appropriate modifications also were made in the sectoral labor force assumptions in DINAMICO. It may be asked why an indirect linkage procedure was used. Why not a direct joining of the two models on the computer? The differences in treatment of inputs are not barriers to direct linkage, for the water and land rows could be simply adjoined to the DINAMICO matrix. Similarly, a vector which withdraws from agriculture one unit of labor each month could represent the rural-urban migration in terms of man-years.

The immediate answer is found in the fact that product demands are price-elastic in CHAC, whereas they are not in DINAMICO. This in turn is related to the basic difference in objective functions. In DINAMICO, as a measure of intertemporal utility, the maximand is a consumption stream evaluated at base year prices. In CHAC, a static price-dependent measure of social welfare is maximized: the sum of consumers' and producers' surplus at a point in time.

Hence, given factor endowments, factor prices, and overall income levels, CHAC attempts to describe the multi-market equilibrium for producers and consumers. This description is passed on to DINAMICO in the form of an aggregated vector of sectoral inputs and total output at that equilibrium point. For the linkage, CHAC was solved under 24 alternative factor price combinations, and an aggregative vector for DINAMICO is made for each of the 24 equilibrium solutions.[7] The principal effects of the input price variations are upon the coefficients for capital, labor, and foreign exchange.

These vectors refer to period 2 (1974), and they have been extrapolated backward and forward to obtain the coefficients for the other five periods in DINAMICO. Thus the linkage adds $24 \times 6 = 144$ column vectors to DINAMICO.[8]

In addition to estimates of the sector's input vector, CHAC provides a control on sector output levels. An essential element of each of these vectors is a coefficient in the sector output constraint. It states the sector's aggregate production level associated with that particular equilibrium. It is this coefficient which could not be reproduced in a direct joining of the full models. Since prices are endogenous to CHAC, it was not feasible to form a price-weighted aggregate measure of production within the solution proper. Rather, aggregate output expansion was calculated *ex*

---

[7] With 3 inputs each at 3 different price levels, there would be $3^3 = 27$ combinations. To economize on computer time, only 24 of these 27 combinations were solved.

[8] For the linkage, the original 18 vectors for agricultural production, exports and capital-labor substitution are deleted.

post as a Fisher quantum index utilizing both 1968 and 1974 endogenous prices. If r_j is the annual growth rate in the Fisher production index for case j ($j = 1, ..., 24$), then the sectoral output constraint in the augmented DINAMICO (henceforth referred to as DINAMICHAC) is written:

$$\sum_j \frac{X01t_j}{X010(1+r_j)^t} \leqslant 1, \quad \text{each } t, \tag{1}$$

where X010 is sector 1 output in the base period (1968), and

Table 1
Constraint rows in DINAMICHAC vectors [a]

Row symbol [a]	Constraint row	Changed by CHAC?	CHAC input variable (plus additional remarks)
A01t	Own input	no	
A02t	Mining production	no	
A03t	Petroleum	yes	Use of well water and machinery services
A04t	Processed food	no	
A05t	Textiles	no	
A06t	Wood, paper	no	
A07t	Chemicals	yes	Fertilizer, pesticides
A08t	Non-metallic	no	
A09t	Metals	no	
A10t	Machinery	yes	Machinery services
A11t	Construction	no	
A12t	Electricity	no	
A13t	Commerce	no	
A14t	Transportation	no	
A15t	Services	no	
B01t	Capacity	yes	Incremental capital-output ratio
DRQL1t	Skill 1 labor	no	(Insignificant in agriculture)
DRQL2t	Skill 2 labor	no	
DRQL3t	Skill 3 labor	yes	Machinery services
DRQL5t	Skill 5 labor	yes	Unskilled agricultural labor
Ft	Imported inputs	no	
ECt	Exports	yes	(Replaces row Et for agricultural exports)
CCCAGt	Sector output constraint	yes	(Non-existent in original DINAMICO; see eq. (1))

[a] See table 2 in chapter II.3 above, for constraint row identification in DINAMICO.

$X01t_j$ is the activity level in period t of the jth agricultural vector.

These sector output constraints are listed as the rows CCCAGt in table 1. The complete list of rows represented by nonzero co-efficients in each agricultural vector in DINAMICHAC is given in that table.

Table 1 shows that an export accounting row (ECt) was added to DINAMICHAC. The alternative technology vectors also describe sector export levels as part of the overall supply-demand equilibrium position in CHAC. The bounds on agricultural exports were deleted from DINAMICHAC, and the level of those exports will depend upon the particular vectors chosen in the optimal basis.

A comparison of the original DINAMICO vector with some of the alternatives generated by CHAC is given in table 2. The skill 5 labor requirements in DINAMICO appear to be consistently above those in DINAMICHAC, but these coefficients alone are misleading. DINAMICO also contains a capital-labor substitution activity for agriculture, and it is optimal to employ this activity. Taking this into account, the optimal labor-output ratio in period 2 in the basic DINAMICO solution is 0.1082, as against a coefficient of 0.1393 shown in table 2.

The representation of capital-labor substitution possibilities is actually the major difference introduced by the DINAMICHAC vectors. In the original DINAMICO formulation, agricultural capital-labor substitution was permitted in unrestricted amounts at a constant substitution rate of 15,000 pesos per man-year. In the 24 DINAMICHAC vectors, the marginal rate of capital-labor substitution ranges from 5,000 to 10,000 pesos per man-year.[9] The amount of substitution is more limited in CHAC, as shown in figure 2.

---

[9] For the effects of lowering the capital-labor substitution rate from 15,000 to 10,000 pesos per man-year, see the experiment reported in the editor's note at the end of chapter II.5 above.

Table 2

omparison of technology vectors in DINAMICO and DINAMICHAC (sign convention: inputs positive, outputs negative)

Row Symbol (t = 2)	Constraint row	DINAMICO coefficients, 1974	Illustrative DINAMICHAC coefficients, 1974 vector j [a]				
			1	7	9	15	20
A3t	Petroleum	0.0197	0.0176	0.0148	0.0167	0.0182	0.0216
A7t	Chemicals	0.0299	0.0277	0.0273	0.0297	0.0304	0.0283
A10t	Machinery	0.0116	0.0087	0.0074	0.0083	0.0090	0.0108
QRQL3t	Skill 3 labor	0.0013	0.0012	0.0011	0.0012	0.0013	0.0015
QRQL5t	Skill 5 labor	0.1393	0.1170	0.1225	0.1181	0.1071	0.1055
XCt	Exports	−0.0772 [b]	−0.0830	−0.0806	−0.1062	−0.1058	−0.0924
8O1t	Capital requirements [c]	1.0000	1.0000	0.9957	0.9970	1.0219	1.0171
Annual growth rate in sectoral output constraint, Fisher index, r_j		n.a.	4.7%	4.2%	5.0%	5.0%	4.6%
Base wage (pesos/day)			13.5	13.5	13.5	16.5	19.5
Foreign exchange premium (%)			0	0	30	30	15
Annual rate of return on capital			12	24	24	18	12

a The elements of each 1974 DINAMICHAC vector were computed as follows:

$$\left(\begin{array}{c} \text{DINAMICHAC} \\ \text{coefficient, 1974,} \\ \text{vector } j \end{array}\right) = \left(\begin{array}{c} \text{DINAMICO} \\ \text{1968 coefficient} \end{array}\right) \left[\left(\frac{\left(\begin{array}{c} \text{CHAC input} \\ \text{variable, 1974, case } j \end{array}\right)}{\left(\begin{array}{c} \text{CHAC input} \\ \text{variable, 1968} \end{array}\right)}\right) \div (1+r_j)^6\right],$$

where the CHAC inputs are as listed in the rightmost column of table 1, and where r_j is the Fisher production index used in eq. (1). DINAMICHAC vectors for the years 1971, 1977, 1980, 1983, and 1986 were extrapolated from the 1974 vectors.

b For solution of basic DINAMICO case, in which most agricultural exports were at their lower bound.

c Normalized by DINAMICO's ratio of capital to gross output in the agricultural sector. For 1968, this ratio is 2.242. See above, chapter II.2, table 7.

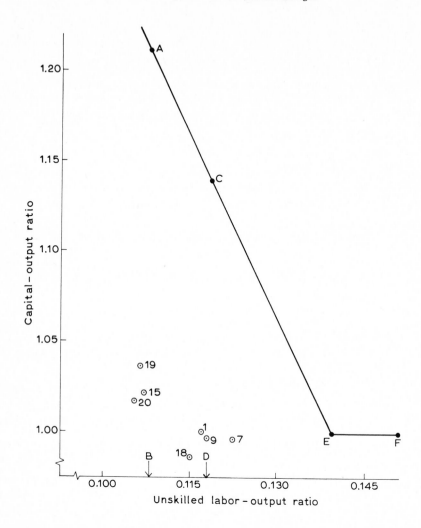

Fig. 2. Coefficients for unskilled labor and capital in agricultural vectors in DINAMICO and DINAMICHAC.

Figure 2 contains a two-dimensional projection of labor-output and capital-output *ratios* (rows DRQL5*t* and B01*t* in table 2).[10] The original DINAMICO isoquant is given by the line *ACEF.* This isoquant extends further to the left and right than is shown in this diagram. Point *E* defines the technology without capital-labor substitution. The points along segment *AE* are attainable through use of DINAMICO's single capital-labor substitution activity.

Each of the numbered points corresponds to coefficients in one of the 24 DINAMICHAC vectors. These include the five vectors of table 2 along with two others, and they encompass the extreme capital-output and labor-output ratios traced out by our 24 sets of factor price combinations. With a less restrictive − and less realistic − set of factor prices, the capital-labor tradeoff set would include points outside the range shown here.

In figure 2, the DINAMICHAC points do not form a smooth isoquant. Recall that these are only two-dimensional projections of multi-dimensional vectors. Each such vector contains other inputs that are either complementary to or substitutes for capital and labor (e.g., chemical and petroleum products). To allow for multi-dimensionality, the linkage proceeds through a set of activity vectors rather than through two-dimensional capital-labor substitution activities. In the space of all inputs and outputs, the DINAMICHAC vectors form a convex set, since the CHAC technology set is convex.

Along the DINAMICO isoquant segment *ACEF,* each point requires more capital *and* more labor than some linear combination of DINAMICHAC vectors. At low levels of labor availability, however, there are points that are feasible with the DINAMICO technology, but *not* with CHAC's. Along the extension of *ECA* to the

---

[10] The entries in row B01*t* are *average* capital-output ratios for period *t* = 2 (1974). Among the alternative DINAMICHAC vectors, these average ratios do not indicate as wide a dispersion as the corresponding marginal capital-output ratios for the period 1968−74. − Among the CHAC vectors, the incremental capital-output ratio (ICOR) ranges from 1.859 to 2.420. The range includes DINAMICO's *ex ante* ICOR of 2.242. This correspondence is one of the few instances in which it was possible to cross-validate the models prior to the linkage experiment. *Ex post*, DINAMICO's ICOR is much higher. This result can be traced directly to the high cost of the capital-labor substitution activity.

vertical axis, all the points which lie to the left of point 20 are feasible in DINAMICO but not in DINAMICHAC. Point B corresponds to DINAMICO's estimate of the agricultural labor force per unit of gross sectoral output, and point D corresponds to this ratio in DINAMICHAC. For labor availabilities less than point B, DINAMICHAC tends toward knife-edge behavior, and becomes constrained by a shortage of unskilled labor.

Points B and D are directly related to differences in estimates of the base-period agricultural labor force and rate of employment.[11] The difficulty arises from the fact that there are two census estimates of rural population. One, the *Censo de población,* virtually ignores family labor, while the other, the *Censo agrícola y ganadero,* counts more than 1.5 million family laborers in 1960. These and other differences are discussed above by Luz María Bassoco and Teresa Rendón in chapter IV.2, where they conclude that an appropriate estimate of the 1968 adult-equivalent labor force for sector 1 is 8.625 million, compared with 7.024 assumed in DINAMICO.

In agriculture, employment is quite seasonal. If total man-months of unemployment, relative to man-months of available labor, were taken as a measure of the rate of underemployment, the figure would be something like 50%. However, this measure embodies the assumption that the seasonality of agriculture can be altered without loss of efficiency. That is clearly not the case, so it is preferable to measure underemployment assuming that the degree of seasonality is alterable only at a cost. As a conservative measure, it has been assumed for the linkage experiment that the seasonality is unchanged. Furthermore, it is assumed that only those who work three months or less per year are available for urban employment, i.e., represent agricultural unemployment. The exact convention used is that agricultural unemployment (in man-years) consists of (a) one man-year for each person in the labor

---

[11] Points B and D refer to the agricultural labor force which remains *after* rural-urban migration in the model. With no rural-urban migration, both points would lie to the left of E in figure 2. This implies that the agricultural labor restrictions of the optimal solutions can be released at a cost. The cost is a reduction of the labor available for non-agricultural employment in the lowest skill category.

force who does not work at all, plus (b) 11/12 man-year for each person who works one month, plus (c) 10/12 man-year for each person who works two months, plus (d) 9/12 man-year for each persons who works three months. This measure amounts to a rate of employment of 68%, with respect to the DINAMICHAC labor force, or 81% with respect to the DINAMICO labor force.

Rather than simultaneously introduce all the information from CHAC into DINAMICO, some experiments were made with partial information flows. Four DINAMICHAC solution cases were defined. The first is the basic DINAMICO case. The others incorporate different combinations of three kinds of CHAC information: the CHAC technology vectors, the CHAC estimate of the agricultural labor force, and the CHAC estimate of the base period employment required in agriculture. Table 3 defines the four cases in terms of these variants.

Cases 2 and 3 were motivated by a desire to separate the impact of agricultural technology from that of the labor force and the degree of underemployment. Case 2 introduces only the CHAC technology, case 3 only the CHAC labor force and employment information. Case 4 combines all three inputs from CHAC.

In figure 2, point *A* represents the optimal solution of case 1, the basic DINAMICO case. Case 3, which retains the DINAMICO technology but incorporates the larger labor force of CHAC, is represented by point *C* in figure 2. In the cases involving the CHAC technology set, the optimal solutions are linear combina-

Table 3
Definitions of alternative DINAMICHAC solution cases

Solution case	Technology	Labor force	Employment–output ratio in 1968	Technology	1968 labor force (millions of workers)	1968 employment rate (%)
1.	DINAMICO	DINAMICO	DINAMICO	Constant MRS	7.024	100.0
2.	CHAC	DINAMICO	DINAMICO	Variable MRS	7.024	100.0
3.	DINAMICO	CHAC	CHAC	Constant MRS	8.625	68.0
4.	CHAC	CHAC	CHAC	Variable MRS	8.625	68.0

tions of vectors represented by the numbered points. In these cases, the labor restrictions are represented by point B (case 2) and point D (case 4).

5. Results

The basic macroeconomic results (table 4) show that the maximand and the GDP growth rate take their highest values in cases 3 and 4. Only in case 2 do they drop below the values of the basic case. While the DINAMICHAC points in figure 2 appear more efficient than the corresponding DINAMICO isoquant segments, recall that only two dimensions are shown. In case 2, the choice set is restricted to those DINAMICHAC points to the left of point A.[12] Some of those points to the left of A must be inefficient along axes other than capital and labor. In case 2, DINAMICHAC chooses to meet agricultural labor requirements by reducing the industrial labor force below its level in the original DINAMICO solution, and hence industrial output and overall growth are reduced.

However, when additional labor is introduced along with the CHAC technology (case 4), the growth rate rebounds to a level higher than in the basic case. The additional labor depresses the shadow wage sufficiently so that higher output levels are attainable along more labor intensive segments of the family of isoquants.

With a sufficient labor surplus, it makes little difference in the macroeconomic variables whether the DINAMICO or the CHAC technology is employed. (Compare cases 3 and 4.) In all cases, consumption, savings, and investment move more or less parallel to GDP. These results make it apparent that, even though the 24 technology vectors constitutes the 'formal' linkage and that revising the labor force estimate is an 'informal' linkage, the two operations are intimately related. The CHAC coefficients were computed under conditions of the CHAC labor force. Had a sig-

---

[12] Unless the rural-urban migration of the basic DINAMICO case is reduced.

Table 4
Macroeconomic results of DINAMICHAC [a]
(units: billions of 1960 pesos)

Case Variable identi- Peri-fication [b] od	Consumption 1974 2	1980 4	Savings 1974 2	1980 4	Investment 1974 2	1980 4	GDP 1974 2	1980 4	Marginal propensity to save, 1968–80 $= \dfrac{SAV^4-SAV^0}{GDP^4-GDP^0}$ (%)	Annual GDP growth, 1968–80 (%)
constant 1. 7.024 100.0%	303.59	445.84	81.88	136.82	81.88	128.18	385.47	582.66	26.3	6.92
variable 2. 7.024 100.0%	300.17	437.29	71.08	124.60	68.18	118.80	371.25	561.90	24.1	6.60
constant 3. 8.625 68.0%	309.89	461.60	84.27	143.31	84.27	134.68	394.16	604.92	26.5	7.26
variable 4. 8.625 68.0%	310.44	462.99	85.20	142.32	85.19	128.77	395.65	605.31	26.1	7.27

[a] This table is parallel to table 2 of chapter II. 2 above.
[b] See table 3 for a detailed definition of these cases.

Table 5

Trade results in DINAMICHAC, 1980 [a] (unit: billions of 1960 pesos)

| Variable / Case identification | Merchandise exports, sector i (Z_i^4) | | | | | | | | | | Exports of high-cost manufactures, at producers' prices, $\sum_{\tau=1}^{4} ZM^\tau$ | Foreign exchange earnings at market prices | | Resource gap, $RGAP^4 =$ imports $-ZA^4 - ZT^4$ |
	1	2	3	4	5	6	7	8	9	10		Merchandise exports ZA^4	Tourism ZT^4	
1 constant 7.024 100.0%	4.90	3.78	0.54	5.80	0.98	0.62	2.07	0.29	0.72	2.18	12.01	39.14	10.63	− 8.64
2 variable 7.024 100.0%	8.50	3.78	0.54	2.88	0.58	0.31	2.07	0.12	0.23	0.56	7.31	31.04	12.69	− 5.80
3 constant 8.625 68.0%	7.77	3.78	0.54	5.80	0.98	0.62	2.07	0.29	0.23	2.18	11.15	40.89	10.63	− 8.64
4 variable 8.625	12.91	3.78	0.54	5.80	0.98	0.62	2.07	0.29	0.72	2.18	2.40	37.29	17.33	−13.55

[a] This table is parallel to table 4 of chapter II. 4 above.

nificantly smaller labor force been assumed, the coefficients would have been different.

For international trade, DINAMICHAC gives a different picture than does the original DINAMICO. The choice between exports of agricultural products and exports of high-cost manufactures appears to be sensitive to the specification of the agricultural sector (table 5). In all of cases 2–4, the agricultural exports are significantly higher, and the high-cost manufactured exports lower, than in case 1. Some of the other manufactured exports also decline in cases 2 and 3. Tourism earnings are highest in case 4. This reflects a lower efficiency wage. In this case, combined merchandise and tourism exports are sufficient to significantly increase the 1980 surplus of exports over imports on current account ($RGAP^4$).

At this point, a cautionary note must be inserted on the trade results. In CHAC there is a minimum reservation wage, but in DINAMICHAC the skill 5 shadow wage falls to zero or close to zero in some cases. The shadow wages for other skills are bounded from below by the skill 5 wage plus the sum of those costs required to move up the skill ladder. The skill 5 wage is a component of the wage for each other skill.

If one believes that the reservation wage in agriculture should be substantially greater than zero, then a zero or low skill 5 wage understates the entire hierarchy of wages. More importantly, it understates the skill 5 wage by a proportionately greater amount than for the other skills. Therefore agricultural production costs are understated more than are industrial production costs. This means that the estimate of comparative advantage in world markets may be biased in favor of agriculture and against industry.

In the basic DINAMICO case, this potential bias does not enter. The costs of capital-labor substitution are sufficiently high, and the labor force sufficiently small, so as to keep the shadow wages at reasonable levels. In DINAMICHAC cases 3 and 4, however, there is a sufficient labor surplus so that the wages do drop to zero or nearly zero in several periods. While this improves the model with respect to the criticism that it had previously overstated the extent of labor shortage[13], it unfortunately introduces the trade bias. The bias is evident in cases 3 and 4.

[13] See Trejo's comments, chapter II.5 above.

Tab
Efficiency prices of la

	Case identification	Employment, 1980 RQL_s^4 (millions of persons by skill)					Efficiency wages, annual averag centered on 1980 (thousands o 1960 pesos per man-year of ski				
		1	2	3	4	5	1	2	3	4	5
1.	constant 7.024 100.0%	0.183	1.310	2.673	9.521	6.765	112.1	53.4	23.0	7.5	3.9
2.	constant 7.024 100.0%	0.173	1.264	2.611	9.113	7.493	-	-	-	-	-
3.	constant 8.625 68.0%	0.190	1.368	2.785	9.909	8.043	82.5	36.7	16.2	6.2	2.7
4.	variable 8.025 68.0%	0.185	1.377	2.778	9.789	8.389	75.2	37.9	13.4	5.0	1.8

[a] This table is similar to tables 5 and 7 of chapter II.4 above.

If case 4 is taken as the most appropriate on *a priori* grounds, the hypothesis of agricultural comparative advantage could not be tested without reformulating DINAMICHAC to incorporate a non-zero reservation wage. Clearly this question needs more work. In the meantime, the hypothesis of agricultural comparative advantage draws some support from the solutions of CHAC alone (see above, chapter IV.3).

The efficiency price of foreign exchange, relative to that of tradeable manufactures, does not behave in a simple manner (table 6). In both 1974 and 1980, it is about the same in cases 1 and 3, but higher in case 4. In the latter cases, the shadow price of foreign exchange is much below its level in cases 1 and 3, due to expanded agricultural exports, but the shadow cost of tradeable

nd foreign exchange [a]

Labor income, (billions of 1960 pesos)					Labor income, fraction of aggregate consumption	Foreign exchange efficiency price (1960 pesos of maximand per thousand 1960 pesos of item)		Efficiency price of foreign exchange relative to that of tradeable manufactures		'Own' rate of interest on foreign exchange, 1974–80, annual rate
1	2	3	4	5	(%)	1974	1980	1974	1980	
20.5	70.0	61.5	71.4	26.4	56	72.4	24.7	1.15	1.15	19.6
-	-	-	-	-	-	-	-	-	-	-
15.9	50.2	45.1	61.2	21.5	42	89.2	23.7	1.16	1.15	24.8
14.0	52.1	37.3	49.1	14.7	36	51.7	15.6	1.19	1.31	22.1

manufactures declines also, due to lower wages.[14]

Case 2, the low growth labor-limited case, exhibits peculiar behavior in the dual solution. The shadow values of foreign exchange and all labor skills are high in the terminal and post-terminal periods, and zero in all preceding periods. This indicates that the terminal conditions begin to dominate at lower growth rates. Here the linkage experiments may provide an impetus to a reformulation of the terminal conditions.

It is in the agricultural sector, of course, that the most pronounced differences between DINAMICO and DINAMICHAC are

[14] Recall that the primal results indicate a comparative advantage for agriculture only with respect to *high-cost* manufactures, and not necessarily all manufactures. In all solutions, the exports of sectors 2, 3, and 7 are at their upper bounds.

found. It appears that the linkage has improved the description of factor utilization in agriculture. The introduction of the DINAMI-CHAC technology vectors substantially reduces the sectoral investment and correspondingly increases both sectoral employment and the labor surplus. The incremental capital-output ratio for agriculture is roughly twice as high in case 1 as in cases 2—4 (table 7). Cases 2—4 look much more reasonable in light of both the CHAC results and the multi-sectoral capital flow matrix constructed for DINAMICO. They give incremental capital-output ratios ranging from 1.754 to 2.511. Case 1, basic DINAMICO, deviates from these benchmarks because it includes the capital-labor substitution activity.

Similarly, the growth rates of sectoral employment look more reasonable in cases 2—4, especially in cases 3 and 4 (table 7). For 1971—80[15], cases 2—4 show a growth rate of sector employment of 0.8% to 3.1% per year, vs. 0.1% in case 1. The apparent historical growth rate in the 1960's was around 2.0%. For the sector labor force, however, the growth rate is below the historical value in all cases except case 3 for 1971—80. It is always negative when calculated from 1968 to 1980. Historical experience may be changing, but nevertheless it appears that DINAMICO always overstates rural-urban migration[16], and DINAMICHAC tends to exaggerate the overstatement. Clearly this is an area where the basic formulation needs more attention.

In DINAMICHAC, agricultural exports behave more in accordance with recent history than in DINAMICO. (See table 7.[17]) Case 4 shows an export growth rate higher than that achieved in the decade of the 1960's. These cases are probably unduly optimistic on marketing prospects. In CHAC itself, the comparable export growth rates are lower, because wages and hence production costs are higher. Nevertheless the export prices and limitations in CHAC require closer scrutiny.

[15] For 1968—80, the employment growth rate ranges from 2.1% to 3.0% in cases 2 and 4. It is negative in case 1.

[16] Represented by the skill upgrading activity UL_4^t.

[17] The dollar value of total agricultural and agricultural processing exports expanded at a rate of 4.2% per year during 1960—70, and more rapidly during 1950—60.

Table 7
Agricultural sector variables in DINAMICHAC

Case identification	Agricultural production 1971–80 (billions of 1960 pesos)	Agricultural investment 1968–80 (billions of 1960 pesos)	Agricultural employment 1980 (millions of man-years)	Incremental sectoral capital-output ratio, 1968–80	Agricultural employment growth rate (annual) (%) 1968–80	1971–80	Agricultural labor force growth rate (annual) (%) 1968–80	1971–80	Agricultural export growth rate (%) 1968–80	1968–83
constant 1. 7.024 100.0%	248.7	133.8	6.765	4.857	−0.3	0.1	−0.3	1.1	2.0	2.0
variable 2. 7.024 100.0%	239.6	65.6	7.493	1.754	2.1	0.8	−1.0	0.8	6.8	4.6
constant 3. 8.625 68.0%	255.5	94.5	8.043	2.511	2.7	1.9	−0.6	1.6	6.0	4.2
variable 4. 8.625 68.0%	263.5	102.8	8.389	2.229	3.0	3.1	−0.3	1.0	10.6	10.2

On balance, from table 7, it appears that cases 3 and 4 are the most well-behaved. Cases 3 and 4 also appear most acceptable on the basis of the implied foreign exchange premium (table 6). It is clear, however, that when CHAC employment and labor force information are introduced, some attention must be paid to the reservation wage for skill 5.

One important way of validating the linkage is to examine the particular technology vectors in the optimal basis. In the two DINAMICHAC cases which utilize CHAC technology vectors, a total of eight of the twenty-four vectors come into use. As may be seen in table 8, when the CHAC technology is introduced without the CHAC labor force (case 2), the model concentrates on high wage rate vectors. This is a consequence of introducing a labor-intensive technology without sufficient labor, thereby creating an artificial labor scarcity. As would be expected, virtually the opposite behavior is observed in case 4, where exclusively low-wage vectors are selected in periods 1−3, low and medium wage vectors in periods 4 and 5, and medium and high wage vectors in the terminal period.

The foreign exchange premium underlying the optimal vectors moves in accordance with the efficiency price of foreign exchange which is reported in table 6. Case 4 has a high efficiency price of foreign exchange in most periods, and correspondingly it selects mainly those vectors from CHAC associated with a non-zero foreign exchange premium. Even the anomalous case 2 is consistent. It gives zero efficiency prices for foreign exchange in periods 1−5, and in most of those periods it chooses a zero-premium vector. Cases 1 and 3, of course, utilize only the DINAMICO technology.

Together, these cross-checks help to validate the linkage procedure. Exact consistency should not be expected between the DINAMICHAC solution efficiency prices and the factor prices that generated the technology vectors. This is because the CHAC and DINAMICHAC objective functions differ, and the two sets of prices are defined relative to their respective objective functions. However, if the linkage is to be meaningful, there should be a rough correspondence. Fortunately, this is the case.

Table 8
Technology vectors used in DINAMICHAC solutions

A. Vector identification:

Period	Case 2	Case 4
1	#18	#7
2	#19	#9
3	#19	#9
4	#20	#3, # 9, #15
5	#19	#1, #15
6	#19	#1, #20

B. Factor prices used to generate the vectors:

For the generation of these vectors in CHAC, the base wage ranged from 13.5 to 19.5 pesos per day; the interest rate from 12% to 24%, and the foreign exchange premium from 0 to 30%. The factor prices used in these particular vectors are as follows:

Vector	Base wage	Interest rate (%)	Foreign exchange premium (%)
1	13.5	12	0
3	13.5	12	30
7	13.5	24	0
9	13.5	24	30
15	16.5	18	30
18	16.5	24	30
19	19.5	12	0
20	19.5	12	15

6. Problems and extensions

The process of constructing and solving DINAMICHAC has been highly experimental. Although suggestive, it is not conclusive in a number of respects. Before summarizing the problems, a brief tabulation of positive outcomes is ventured:

(a) On the methodology side, Kornai's informal approach to multi-level planning appears fruitful and amenable to implementation. (See chapter V.3 below.) The alternative agricultural vectors do have particular programmatic meanings, and the choice among them is consistent with macroeconomic priorities. For example, the low-wage vectors could be associated with an employment-oriented agricultural plan. Those are the vectors selected in DI-NAMICHAC when labor surplus is a dominant condition.

(b) The inclusion of information from CHAC has overcome one of the more serious problems with DINAMICO: that of its projected labor shortage. A labor surplus emerges in DINAMICHAC, with corresponding agricultural shadow wages falling to low, even zero, levels.

(c) The CHAC information also brings into question the previous results on intersectoral comparative advantage in exports. All DINAMICHAC cases point to a comparative advantage for agriculture over high-cost manufactures, instead of vice versa. However, the wage bias pervades all cases, and so this result can only be taken as suggestive.

(d) DINAMICHAC operates with more reasonable rates of factor utilization in agriculture than does DINAMICO. The resultant incremental capital-output ratio conforms much more closely to prior expectations in DINAMICHAC, as do the growth rates of agricultural employment.

On the debit side of the ledger, a number of problems became apparent. For one thing, iterative convergence was not achieved. A measure of lack of convergence is shown in the annual GDP growth rates in table 4. In the basic DINAMICO case, the growth rate is 6.92%, whereas in case 4 of DINAMICHAC the rate is 7.27%. A subsequent iteration would entail solutions of CHAC on the basis of the higher income growth rate, in order to derive a new set of technology vectors.

A more fundamental problem is found in the inconsistent treatments of wages in CHAC and DINAMICO. Labor utilization norms which were derived on the basis of a given wage rate structure in CHAC are inserted into a model which is likely to determine different wages.

It is possible to envisage an upward transmission of the agricultural wage, from CHAC to DINAMICO. If DINAMICO were reformulated to incorporate a nonzero minimum agricultural wage,

CHAC could transmit the value of that wage associated with each technology vector. This of course would depart from the spirit of the Malinvaud and Dantzig-Wolfe procedures[18], which entail downward transmission of prices and upward transmission of quantities. In whatever manner approached, the wage question clearly is of primary importance in further work on the agriculture-macroeconomy linkage.

Another aspect of labor which is troublesome in the linkage is the excessive upgrading of skill 5 labor to skill 4 (i.e., rural-urban migration). However, this is a problem in the basic DINAMICO formulation also. It reflects the difficulty of specifying a meaningful migration relationship in a multi-sector mdel.

Low wage levels lead to an overstatement of the prospective agricultural export growth rate, especially in case 4. A reformulation of the wage structure should dampen this tendency. Nevertheless, it is likely that the costs of international marketing are understated in CHAC. It is certainly not costless to discover new markets and to negotiate upward alterations in import quotas abroad. It is evident that more attention will have to be paid to export prospects in further work with CHAC.

References

Dantzig, G.B. and P. Wolfe, 'The decomposition principle for linear programs', *Econometrica,* October 1961.

Kochen, M., and K.W. Deutsch, 'Toward a rational theory of decentralization: some implications of a mathematical approach', *The American Political Science Review* 63, no. 3 (September 1969).

Kornai, J., 'Man-machine planning', *Economics of Planning* 9, no. 3 (1969).

Malinvaud, E., 'Decentralized procedures for planning', in: *Activity analysis in the theory of growth and planning,* edited by E. Malinvaud and M.O.L. Bacharach. London, MacMillan, 1967, chapter 7.

[18] See Malinvaud (1967) and Dantzig and Wolfe (1961).

IV.7. AGRICULTURAL POLICIES AND THE ROLE
OF THE SECTORAL MODEL

Luciano BARRAZA and Leopoldo SOLÍS

1. Overview of the agricultural sector

In Mexico in 1970, 40% of the labor force was engaged in agricultural and livestock activities [1], producing 52% of exports but only 11% of gross national product.[2] These figures indicate both the importance of the sector as a source of employment and foreign exchange and the low levels of income which persist in it. The sector model CHAC embraces these diverse characteristics, and therefore it is of considerable interest in the process of attempting to frame policy options.

The contributions of the agricultural sector to Mexican economic development during the last three decades have been exceedingly important. The increases of agricultural production have satisfied the food demands of a population growing at an explosive rate, have helped minimize inflationary pressures, and have earned the foreign exchange necessary for growing levels of international trade in the presence of an inward-looking industrial sector. By means of virtually complete substitution for agricultural imports as well as expanded exports, the sector has augmented Mexico's capacity to import those goods which are indispensable for devel-

---

[1] Secretaría de Industria y Comercio (1972).
[2] Banco de México (1971).

opment. The agricultural sector also has contributed a highly elastic supply of labor to industrial enterprises.

The performance of agriculture over the past 30 years followed rather different patterns in successive periods. From 1940 to 1956, the growth of sector income exceeded that of GNP, as a response to both increases in productive capacity and stimuli in internal and external markets. From 1957 to 1970, in contrast, the sector income grew significantly slower than GNP.

Several factors arrested the momentum of the sector. The import substitution process was completed, and exports confronted increasingly restrictive quotas and the competition of new producers in the world market. On the side of domestic demand, it is likely that elasticities of demand for food products have declined as income levels have increased. [3] On the supply side, although technological advances have increased physical yields, they also have raised expenditures on purchased inputs and thus have reduced profit margins in some cases. In addition, recent agricultural investments appear to have had a lower productivity than those of earlier periods.

It is apparent that the sector's development is entering a new phase. The previous set of policies is no longer yielding an adequate rate of growth in sector income. A reformulation of policies will be required. To help illuminate the nature of the problems, we first give a brief review of past approaches to agricultural policies.

2. Objectives and policies for development of the sector

Among the specific objectives of Mexican agricultural development, the following can be identified as major ones:

(a) Satisfying domestic demand for foodstuffs.

(b) Raising incomes of producers.

(c) Earning foreign exchange by exports.

(d) Improving the income distribution.

(e) Increasing employment.

---

[3] For evidence to this effect in a cross-country sample, see Weisskoff (1971).

To attain these objectives, various instruments of agricultural policy have been utilized. In the short run they have affected agricultural product and input prices and in the long run they have altered the quantity and productivity of available resources.

Apart from the Agrarian Reform, which has been a continuing element of agricultural policy since 1916, investment in irrigation facilities and agricultural research and extension have been the major instruments of long-run policy. The irrigation program was initiated in 1926, and by 1970 it had succeeded in putting 2.9 million ha under irrigation. The program also has been oriented toward maintenance and improvement of existing irrigation works.

During this period the aims of irrigation policy have varied. From 1926 to 1934, the criterion followed for resource allocation was maximization of increases in sector income; that is, a conventional capital-productivity approach. From 1935 to 1940, the allocation of public investment was based more on the criterion of income redistribution than on factor productivity. This period saw the initiation of the large-scale projects designed to serve ejidal farmers, such as those in the Laguna region in the north-central part of the Republic. [4] After 1940, the decision criterion has included both concepts of economic efficiency and income distribution.

From the viewpoint of decision-makers, the results of the irrigation investment program have been very satisfactory in terms of both objectives. The increment in production in the irrigated zones has been striking. It has kept domestic demand satisfied and has permitted significant amounts of agricultural exports. By 1970, the irrigated areas accounted for 57% of agricultural and livestock exports. Extensive irrigation also has induced investment in complementary facilities and more use of purchased agricultural inputs, which have contributed substantially to increased yields.

The public policies on irrigation investment, combined with the behavior of private investment in agriculture, have accentuated the dualistic nature of Mexican agriculture. A commercial agriculture, associated with irrigated areas and characterized by high yields and

---

[4] Orive Alba (1971).

high incomes per hectare, coexists with a traditional agriculture in which cultivation practices conform to ancestral patterns. The former represents 16% of the cultivated area and 31% of the value of production. [5]

The dualism was even more marked before the Revolution and consequently one of the major achievements of the Revolution was the Agrarian Reform. It is the primary policy instrument aimed at income redistribution and employment increases. The program was initiated in 1916, achieved its maximal impulse between 1934 and 1940, and continues to the present day. It embodies three components: (a) the breaking up of the landholdings of the latifundia; (b) imposing a size limitation on privately-owned farms; and (c) creating a unique form of property rights called the ejido. The ejidos are constituted from land and water taken from former latifundia, and ejidal tenure is granted only to those who work the land.

This policy has modified the nature of the markets for agricultural products and factors. It has changed the pre-Reform conditions of monopolistic competition, in which producers controlled production levels by maintaining idle land, toward a system closer to perfect competition. The current market structure has permitted entry of a large number of new producers and is characterized by substantial mobility of factors of production.

In terms of the objectives for which it was designed, the Agrarian Reform has yielded significantly positive results. It achieved a substantial increase in employment, encouraging more intensive use of labor and land — both abundant resources — and by the same token brought about a rapid growth of agricultural production. There also was some movement, albeit small, toward a more equitable income distribution. Between 1916 and 1970, some 2.7 million ejidatarios received free land via the Reform. [6] A rough indication of the impact on the income distribution is given by the increasing share of agricultural output produced by ejidal farms, all of which are small-scale. Between 1930 and 1960 (the most

---

[5] Secretaría de Recursos Hidráulicos (1971).
[6] Tirado de Ruiz (1971).

recent year for which data are available), the ejidal share of output increased from 11% to 41%.

If the Agrarian Reform has by and large accomplished the goals for which it was instituted, it also has had some unforeseen effects. The creation of a multitude of small-scale agricultural holdings has resulted in a relatively inefficient ejidal subsector in which the vast majority of farmers subsist at quite marginal income levels. In addition, the Reform policy has given rise to pressures on the government budget, in view of the need to provide a continuing supply of both short-run and long-run capital to the ejidos at interest rates which the ejidatarios can afford.

The policies oriented toward augmenting production have been accompanied by regulatory actions in the product markets which took the form of establishment of guaranteed prices. The purposes of the price support policy have been three-fold: (a) to offer sufficient incentives to producers so that domestic consumption demands for certain food items can be met with domestic supplies, (b) to partially stabilize producers' incomes by eliminating most of the price fluctuations for basic crops, and (c) to enhance the real purchasing power of consumers by preventing rises in the retail prices of basic foods. Of course, goals (a) and (c) taken together imply net budgetary outlays.

The price support policy began in 1927 with intervention in the wheat market, and in the course of the following three decades it was extended to the other products of major importance in the average diet: corn, beans, rice, oilseeds, and milk. Sorghum also has been supported in order to encourage a larger supply of forage for the livestock sector. In order to effectively assure stability in consumer prices, the policy has included maintenance of regulatory reserves, through changes in external trade when necessary. On the producer side, a national system of collection and storage points has been established.

While guaranteed prices have reduced the risk to producers associated with price fluctuations, the establishment of agricultural insurance has reduced the risk associated with climatic adversities. The two policies have reinforced each other in increasing production and producers' incomes. They also have led to exports at

prices lower than the guaranteed prices, and they have biased resource allocation toward those crops protected against uncertainty. For the subsistence producer who does not participate in the
market process and for whom the major part of production is
devoted to subsistence consumption, the high guaranteed prices
simply represent larger outlays on consumption expenditures. Even
the subsistence producer buys some foodstuffs in the market, and
in village areas CONASUPO (the agricultural price policy agency)
does not offer retail subsidies.

Another important instrument of agricultural policy has been
credit policy. It operates both through public and private banks. [7]
In 1970, of the total outstanding institutional credit in the agricultural sector, 22% was held by private banks and the rest by public
banks. [8]

The private banks, which obtain their resources from deposi-
tors, channel part of them to the agricultural sector in conformity
with requirements on the amount and composition of their governmental liabilities and in accordance with selective credit controls. The latter affect the sectoral destination of their privately-
held liabilities as well as loans to the public sector. Public banks
obtain their loanable funds by contributions from the federal government, from their own assets, and via deposits from other banks.
Their lending operations to the agricultural sector constitute an
instrument for affecting the crop composition in each producing
area. In addition, in some cases the public banks' operations form
an instrument for income redistribution, as indicated by the low
rate of loan collections by the Banco Nacional de Crédito Ejidal.

The intervention of the credit policy in factor markets is reflected in the maintenance of interest rates below market levels, on the
part of both private and public banks. This is not only an agricultural policy, for it is extended to other sectors also.

Overall, the basic thrust of the credit policy has been toward
raising agricultural producers' incomes and production levels, but

---

[7] For an excellent discussion of Mexican agricultural credit policy, see Guzmán
Ferrer (1971).

[8] This figure refers to loans outstanding as of December 31, 1971. See Banco de
México (1972).

there are subsidiary aims of income redistribution and influencing
the production and spatial allocation of specific crops. This last
aim is warranted in circumstances of imperfect market information and relative price distortions — which are due in part to the
other instruments of governmental policy such as guaranteed
prices. Interventions on interest rates also assist in the encouragement of export crops, but inasmuch as the interest rate policy
encourages mechanization of farms, it tends to reduce employment levels in the sector. Agriculture clearly needs continuing inflows of capital, but some forms are more complementary to —
and less competitive with — labor. One of the standing issues of
agricultural policy is the choice of appropriate forms of capital
accumulation for the sector, in light of pressing needs for more
employment opportunities as well as for more exports and more
production in general. A general problem with credit policy is that
it does not provide sufficient longer-term institutional credit for
fixed investments. And in rainfed areas, there is also insufficient
shorter-term bank credit.

Two other factor prices are influenced by governmental policies: the wage rates for hired labor and the price of water. The
former are readjusted upward each two years, via minimum wage
laws, and the latter is subsidized. The minimum wages vary by
locality in recognition of differing labor market conditions. While
the wage legislation has positive effects on the incomes of those
who are employed, it also tends to encourage capital-labor substitution in the sector with the greatest amount of surplus labor, as
shown in chapter IV.3 of this volume.

Tax policy is not especially important in influencing sectoral
activity. There are federal income tax exemptions for ejidatarios,
for mutual agricultural credit associations [9], and for farmers with
incomes less than 2000 pesos annually. Exemptions from federal
sales taxes are made for direct sales of unprocessed agricultural
products. [10] The production and marketing of agricultural products are, however, subject to a variety of other taxes, including

[9] Ley del Impuesto sobre la Renta, Art. 50, Vc.
[10] Ley Federal del Impuesto sobre Ingresos Mercantiles, Art. 18-VII.

those at state and municipal levels. These are not always consistent with the criteria embodied in the federal tax structure.

Foreign trade policy has been oriented toward import substitution and encouragement of exports, through a variety of instruments. The most commonly used instruments are reduction of taxes for export of some products (such as strawberries, rice, beans) and using a low base price for the export tax computation for other products (such as cotton, tomatoes, and coffee). Other short-term instruments are freight rate subsidies on export crops and tieing import permits to the value of agricultural exports.

In the area of long-term policies, the investments in agricultural research and extension have been the most noteworthy in terms of raising the productivity of agricultural resources. Surprising results have come from the research with corn and wheat in order to improve the genetic quality and to determine more appropriate planting dates, fertilization levels, irrigation applications, seed densities, etc. Between 1940 and 1970 the per hectare yields of corn and wheat increased by 92% and 161%, respectively. The research and extension programs together have had a greater impact on sectoral income levels than any other set of policies. To illustrate this point, the increase in real sector income which occurred between 1930 and 1960 may be broken down into three components: 57% was due to increases in physical yields, 21% was due to changes in crop composition, and 22% was due to increases in arable land. [11] The rise in physical yields in turn is attributable to more extensive irrigation, the use of better input packages aside from water, and increased efficiency in cultivation practices.

3. Current agricultural issues

Five historical goals of agricultural policies were listed at the outset of the preceding section. One of them — meeting domestic demands for basic foodstuffs — has essentially been achieved, at least with respect to grains. [12] The growth rate of agricultural

[11] See Solís (1971).
[12] Although the rate of expansion of sector income has slowed in the past decade and a half, agricultural production has continued to expand at historical rates.

exports has decreased significantly in recent years, and balance of payments problems have become more acute, so expanded exports will remain a prime sector goal for the foreseeable future. Expanded sectoral income will also remain an urgent goal, as indicated by the foregoing discussion.

Employment problems in the sector are severe, as shown by the CHAC results (above, chapter IV.3) and the study of the Centro de Investigaciones Agrarias. [13] There are a large number of landless laborers in agriculture, in addition to the fact that most of the farmers operate at the margin of subsistence, and the sector's labor force continues to expand more rapidly than arable land. This situation has given rise to marked inequalities in the distribution of income.

At this point in history, Mexican agriculture has experienced five decades of structural transformation and rapid development, and yet it faces unresolved and pressing problems in the areas of income levels, employment and income distribution, and foreign trade. The future performance of the sector will depend in large part on a reformulation of policy measures in light of these problems and changing conditions.

It will be difficult to implement a program of income redistribution by means of redistribution of agricultural lands. The small number of hectares susceptible to redistribution imposes a limit to this program. Policies for augmenting employment are also the most appropriate for income redistribution. Measures aimed at absorbing more labor via capital labor substitution, implemented by increases in the cost of capital (or the criterion rate of return for project selection), would have a positive effect on employment. [14] Likewise, changes in patterns of internal consumption and external trade, oriented toward the more labor intensive crops and implemented by changes in relative product prices, could have favorable effects on employment and the income distribution.

In foreign trade, it is evident that the subsidies and other meas-

[13] Centro de Investigaciones Agrarias (1971).

[14] See the simulation of the employment effects of factor price changes in chapter IV.3 above.

ures for export promotion should take more account of Mexico's comparative advantage – in fruits, vegetables, cotton, some oilseeds (e.g., sesame), meat, and cattle on the hoof. The solutions of CHAC demonstrate that there is a wide range of comparative advantage among crops, and that the present export-mix could be improved substantially. Regarding imports, it is no longer obvious that total import substitution is the wisest policy. Relaxation of import permit regulations and tariffs on selected crops could benefit consumers and could also permit a redirection of sector resources to more production of crops profitable in export markets.

Aside from more rapid export growth, one of the ways to raise sector income levels is to redirect incentives policies to encourage more production of items with high domestic price and income elasticities of demand. Principally, these are livestock products and fruit and vegetables. Movement in this direction has already begun, but further steps are needed; they also would help improve the average consumption diet. The programs which help protect farmers against price fluctuations and climatic disasters should be re-examined for possibilities of incorporating such high-elasticity products. This may also imply more investment in transportation and storage facilities; in any case the implications should be spelled out. The agricultural extension program should also be reviewed for possibilities of using it to introduce new crops in certain areas.

In the irrigation program, the possibility exists of placing more emphasis on small-scale works which have a more significant impact on the income distribution, although in some instances, they may show a lower rate of return to capital. In the overall allocation of capital, there is the question of proper balance between investment in irrigation facilities and in livestock. Demand for livestock products tends to grow more rapidly than demand for crops, both internally and externally. However, cropping activities are more labor intensive, and thus more conducive to labor absorption. Expansion of livestock production does have some stimulating effects on crop production via expanded requirements for feed grains. Further investments in livestock should be accompanied by investments in exploration of more external markets and in processing plants. The same holds true for expansion of fruit and vegetable production for export.

In summary, it is evident that there are some fairly complex trade-offs in the sector, and the policies followed must constitute an integrated package for long-run and short-run instruments oriented toward well-defined objectives. At present there is a tendency for each policy instrument to be considered in isolation from the others. CHAC is extremely useful in helping to define these trade-offs and to assess the impact of different policy packages.

4. The role of the model in decision-making

In the context of decision-making, CHAC constitutes an instrument of analysis of GASA [15], a group charged with analysis of policy alternatives and reformulation of policy packages for the agricultural sector. It is composed of representatives from the various branches of the federal government which are concerned with agriculture. At the most general level, the primary role of CHAC is to define sectoral issues and trade-offs, and to test the consequences of alternative policy packages. In this sense, CHAC already has been instrumental in sharpening the understanding of sectoral issues which is presented in the preceding section. As a general equilibrium model, it embraces all the important sectoral variables and defines the limitations of the sectoral production possibility set. These limitations permit the estimation of tradeoffs which cannot be measured with partial equilibrium models.

As an example of this role, the model's solutions (above, chapter IV.3) have indicated that the recent tendency for the growth rate of sectoral income to lag behind the growth rate of sectoral production is not a passing phenomenon but rather a new phase of sector development. That this result was derived from a model based on cross-section rather than time series data only reinforces

[15] Grupo de Análisis del Sector Agropecuario.

its import. Substantial empirical evidence from CHAC is presented in chapters IV.3 and IV.4 above, which gives confidence that it constitutes a basically correct description of sector behavior.

Taken together, the CHAC results show that factor and product pricing policies can have significant effects – both positive and negative – on sector income, employment, exports, and consumers' welfare. The specific results will not be repeated in this chapter, but it is worth noting that the policy repercussions are complex and that each major instrument has a different pattern of impacts on major variables.

One set of results not reported in this volume is quite interesting from the viewpoint of sectoral policies: that interregional comparative advantage can be better captured via changes in existing spatial cropping patterns. For example, the model is probably correct in reporting that the sugar cane production in the central plateau should be shifted to tropical zones in the long run, even though yields are higher in the central plateau. Of course, this will require shifting locations of processing facilities – something which will take time – but as a long-run policy it probably is wise.

Regarding international comparative advantage, the CHAC results already have had an impact on trade patterns. It has prompted a re-examination of export policies for some crops with the result that exports of sesame and black beans were stepped up considerably. On the whole, the CHAC results suggest that it would be worthwhile to invest more funds in exploration of export markets for agricultural products.

Aside from the results concerning overall sectoral policies, the model has been shown to be a useful tool for the analysis of potential investment projects. [16] Either the entire model or submodels can be used for purposes of simulating the impacts of investment programs. Employment, income, and trade effects are simulated along with a computation of social rates of return. It is possible to group alternative forms of investment in one locality and establish a ranking among them via CHAC.

As of this writing, steps are being taken to apply the model

---

[16] See chapter IV.5 above.

further to some of these policy areas, and to extend its coverage in certain directions. The working procedure is based on continuous interaction between policy makers, agricultural specialists, and those working with the model. This permits better identification of problem areas and appropriate modifications of the model to address very particular problems. In this way, an analytic tool can become a flexible, vital part of the decision-making process, which is, after all, a continuously evolving dialogue among concerned individuals and institutions.

References

Banco de México, S.A., *Informe anual 1970*. México, 1971.

Banco de México, S.A., *Crédito agropecuario 1966–1970*. México, 1972.

Centro de Investigaciones Agrarias, *Estructura agraria y desarrollo agrícola en México*. México, 1970.

Fernández y Fernández, Ramón and Ricardo Costa, *Política agrícola*. Mexico, Fondo de Cultura Económica, 1961.

Guzmán Ferrer, Martín Luis, 'Extensión del crédito agropecuario al minifundio', in: *Bienestar campesino y desarrollo económico*, edited by I.M. de Navarrete. Mexico, Fondo de Cultura Económica, 1971.

Hertford, Reed, *Sources of change in Mexican agricultural production*. U.S. Department of Agriculture, August 1971.

Orive Alba, Adolfo, 'La irrigación como factor del bienestar campesino', in: *Bienestar campesino y desarrollo económico*, edited by I.M. de Navarrete. México, Fondo de Cultura Económica, 1971.

Secretaría de Agricultura y Ganadería, *Memoria de labores 1969–1970*. México, 1971.

Secretaría de Industria y Comercio, *IX censo de pobl#ación 1970*. México, 1972.

Secretaría de Recursos Hidráulicos, *Informe de labores 1970*. México, 1971.

Secretaría de Recursos Hidráulicos, *Estadística agrícola del ciclo 1969–70*. México, 1971.

Solís, Leopoldo, *La realidad económica Mexicana: retrovisión y perspectivas*. México, Siglo XXI Editores, 1971.

Tirado de Ruiz, R., 'El desarrollo histórico de la política agraria', in: *Bienestar campesino y desarrollo económico*, edited by I.M. de Navarrete. Mexico, Fondo de Cultura Económica, 1971.

Venezian, Eduardo y William K. Gamble, *El desarrollo de la agricultura Mexicana*. Chapingo, México, Centro de Economía Agrícola, 1968.

Weisskoff, Richard, 'Demand elasticities for a developing economy: an international comparison of consumption patterns', in: *Studies in development planning*, edited by H.B. Chenery. Cambridge, Mass., Harvard University Press, 1971.

PART V. DECOMPOSITION ALGORITHMS AND MULTI-LEVEL PLANNING

V.I. A MIXED INTEGER ALGORITHM FOR PROJECT EVALUATION

Alan S. MANNE *

1. Relation to other mixed integer algorithms

This algorithm is a specialized form of Benders' partitioning procedure for solving mixed integer programming problems. [1] It is visualized that the principal application would be for the evaluation of indivisible and interdependent investment projects. Hence we shall refer to the zero-one unknowns as 'project decision variables', to the remaining non-negative unknowns as 'continuous variables', and to the algorithm itself as IPE. Toward the end of this paper, the relation will be examined between IPE and the project evaluation criterion proposed by Little and Mirrlees (1968).

IPE (or any other variant upon Benders' partitioning procedure) is an implicit enumeration algorithm. It resembles branch-and-bound in that it proceeds by solving successive linear programming problems — at each step placing bounds upon the value of the objective function attainable with alternative combinations of the project decision variables. Both methods are similar in that there

* The author is much indebted to Richard Inman, who wrote the computer programs and performed the numerical analysis reported here. See his accompanying paper, Inman (1971). — Thanks also goes to Arthur Geoffrion, who reviewed an earlier draft of this paper, and pointed out the connection of the IPE algorithm to Benders' partitioning procedure. In addition, he noted that it would economize on computer capacity to store the list of glb's (greatest lower bounds) in implicit rather than explicit form.

[1] A general formulation of the partitioning procedure was first stated in Benders (1962). Also see Balinski (1965), pp. 271—274, Buzby (1966), Hu (1969), pp. 259—265, and Geoffrion (1970).

are only a finite number of combinations to be considered, a given combination is examined only once, and convergence is assured with only a finite number of steps.

IPE differs from branch-and-bound in that: (1) At each step, all of the zero-one variables are set at integer values. Hence, each step provides a locally optimal integer-feasible solution for an as yet untried combination of the zero-one variables. (2) Dual variables and reduced costs are generated at each step. These are employed to provide lower bounds on the value of the global minimand attainable with each of the remaining combinations of the project decision variables. Thus, each step provides both upper and lower bounds relevant to the global optimization — rather than bounds that are restricted to the particular 'branch' being explored.

Underlying Benders' partitioning procedure is the assumption that it is moderately expensive to solve an individual linear programming problem — and prohibitively expensive to solve one such problem for each of the N logically possible combinations of the zero-one variables. IPE differs from other forms of Benders' procedure in that the 'master' all-integer problem is solved through complete enumeration of the N possible combinations. From an esthetic viewpoint, enumeration is inelegant. However, since IPE takes advantage of mutual exclusivity constraints [2] between projects, this is not an obviously inefficient approach for problems where N is a moderate-sized number, say less than a million.

As yet, there is insufficient computational experience for comparing the efficiency of the proposed technique versus that of alternative mixed integer algorithms. [3] To date, there is only one reasonably certain conclusion — that with economically meaningful investment planning models, it is unnecessary to calculate explicit linear programming solutions for more than a small fraction of the logically possible total number of project combinations.

---

[2] For another mixed integer algorithm that takes advantage of mutual exclusivity constraints, see Healy (1964).

[3] Dermot Gately applied the branch-and-bound algorithm of Davis et al. (1971) to the four test problems described below in table 4. Because of differences in machine speeds and in programming techniques, this experiment did not provide fully comparable estimates of the running time required for branch-and-bound versus that for IPE.

2. The IPE lemma

Denote the continuous decision variables by x_j, and denote the kth project decision variable within set s as y_{ks}. Within each of the S mutual exclusivity sets, exactly one of the K alternative projects is to be selected. Hence:

$$\sum_{k=1}^{K} y_{ks} = 1 \qquad (s = 1, ..., S) \qquad (1)$$

$$y_{ks} = 0 \text{ or } 1 \qquad \text{(all } k \text{ and } s) \qquad (2)$$

$$x_j \geqslant 0 \qquad (j = 1, ..., J) \qquad (3)$$

Given the coefficients (a_{ij}, c_j, α_{iks} and γ_{ks}) and the right-hand side constants b_i, the mixed integer programming model consists of assigning values to the x_j and y_{ks} so as to minimize (5) subject to constraints (1)–(4):

$$\sum_{j=1}^{J} a_{ij}x_j + \sum_{s=1}^{S} \sum_{k=1}^{K} \alpha_{iks}y_{ks} = b_i \qquad (i = 1, ..., I) \qquad (4)$$

$$\min z = \sum_{j=1}^{J} c_j x_j + \sum_{s=1}^{S} \sum_{k=1}^{K} \gamma_{ks}y_{ks}. \qquad (5)$$

According to (1) and (2), the number of logically possible project combinations is [4] $(K)^S = N$. (In actual applications, it is likely that specific arguments could be employed to reduce N. E.g., a blast furnace would not be installed unless a steel mill or an iron foundry were also available at the identical location.) Now suppose that a particular combination of values has been assigned to the unknowns y_{ks}, and that these values satisfy constraints (1) and

---

[4] Here S denotes a power of K. At all other points, a raised index will denote a superscript.

(2). Let the index n be employed to identify this specific combination.

Given the combination n, the problem has been reduced to conventional linear programming format — minimization of (5) subject to constraints (3) and (4) on the continuous variables x_j, regarding the zero-one unknowns as parameters provisionally fixed at the specific values y_{ks}^n. From the simplex solution for combination n, we obtain the locally optimal values of the primal variables x_j^n and of the minimand z^n. For each of the constraints (4), there are locally optimal dual variables π_i^n, ($i = 1, ..., I$). From the dual variables, in turn we obtain the 'reduced costs', δ_{ks}^n. These quantities may be interpreted as the cost increase or decrease associated with project ks at the efficiency prices prevailing for combination n:

$$\delta_{ks}^n = \gamma_{ks} - \sum_{i=1}^{I} \alpha_{iks} \pi_i^n .$$

We shall omit the details on three special cases: (a) an unbounded solution — which would then be the global minimum, (b) the possibility that there is no feasible solution for combination n, and (c) the possibility that there remain zero-intensity artificial activities in the optimal basis — hence no dual variables for one or more of the I rows in (4). Cases (b) and (c) may be avoided by formulating the model so as to include high-cost positive and negative unit vectors for each of the I rows.

Now consider a move from combination n to some other combination m — but without explicitly solving the linear programming model for combination m. Then the key to the IPE algorithm is the following lemma:

$$z^m \geqslant z^n + \sum_{s=1}^{S} \sum_{k=1}^{K} \delta_{ks}^n (y_{ks}^m - y_{ks}^n) . \tag{6}$$

Proof of lemma: Retaining the non-negativity constraints (3) on the continuous primal unknowns x_j, rewrite (4) and (5) as the following parametric linear programming problem. The symbol θ denotes a scalar parameter, with $0 \leqslant \theta \leqslant 1$. When θ is varied from zero to unity, the simplex method will produce the local minima z^n and z^m respectively. The values y_{ks}^n and y_{ks}^m are known constants, and so the rightmost double-sum terms of (4a) and (5a) are also constants:

$$\min z = \sum_{j=1}^{J} c_j x_j + \sum_{s=1}^{S} \sum_{k=1}^{K} [\gamma_{ks}(y_{ks}^m - y_{ks}^n)]\theta + \sum_{s=1}^{S} \sum_{k=1}^{K} \gamma_{ks} y_{ks}^n \quad (5a)$$

$$\sum_{j=1}^{J} a_{ij} x_j + \sum_{s=1}^{S} \sum_{k=1}^{K} [\alpha_{iks}(y_{ks}^m - y_{ks}^n)]\theta$$

$$= b_i - \sum_{s=1}^{S} \sum_{k=1}^{K} \alpha_{iks} y_{ks}^n . \qquad (i = 1, ..., I) \qquad (4a)$$

Now interpret θ as the intensity of a new activity being introduced into the locally optimal solution for combination n, with $0 \leqslant \theta \leqslant 1$. The conventional 'reduced cost' criterion for the introduction of this new activity is

$$\sum_{s=1}^{S} \sum_{k=1}^{K} \delta_{ks}^n (y_{ks}^m - y_{ks}^n) .$$

This implies the weak inequality (6) — which was to be proved.

Remarks:

(a) Note that z^n is associated with an integer-feasible solution, and immediately provides an *upper* bound on the value of the global minimand z.

(b) The key lemma (6) establishes a *lower* bound on z^m — a bound which may be calculated solely with the linear programming results for project combination n: z^n, π_i^n, and δ_{ks}^n. If

$$\sum_{s=1}^{S} \sum_{k=1}^{K} \delta_{ks}^{n}(y_{ks}^{m} - y_{ks}^{n}) \geq 0 \,,$$

combination m may be immediately rejected, and no linear programming solution need be calculated explicitly for that combination.
The computational efficiency of IPE (or any other Benders-type
implicit enumeration algorithm) will depend upon the frequency
with which this inequality permits us to reject combinations. Note
that (6) is a criterion for rejecting project combinations — not
individual projects by themselves.

(c) The differences in project intensities $(y_{ks}^{m} - y_{ks}^{n})$ are either
$+1$, 0, or -1. Moreover, within mutual exclusivity set s, there will
be at most one positive and one negative difference.

(d) If a locally optimal solution for combination n has been
obtained through the simplex method, this immediately provides a
dual-feasible initial basic solution for combination m. (Proof: All
that has changed is a constant term in each of the rows (4a) and
(5a).) For obtaining the optimal solution with combination m, it
should be advantageous to apply the dual simplex technique, initiating the calculations from the basic solution for combination n.

3. An investment planning example: interdependence between projects in two sectors

The first example is a simplified version of a model described in
Chenery (1959). This illustrates interdependence between investment decisions in the case of steel and machinery projects. A
hypothetical Latin American country is concerned with choosing
the level of imports and exports, simultaneously selecting among
indivisible investment projects in these sectors. Costs are to be
minimized — subject to the constraint of delivering 1 MT/Y (million tons/year) of steel and 1 MT/Y of machinery to 'final demands' outside the steel and machinery sectors. It takes one ton of
steel to make one ton of machinery, but no machinery is needed
as a current account input to produce steel.

The continuous decision variables are x_1, ..., x_4, the rate of imports and exports of steel and machinery, respectively. Steel projects may be built in one of three mutually exclusive sizes: 0,2 and 4 MT/Y. Machinery projects may be built in one of three mutually exclusive sizes: 0, 1 and 2 MT/Y. Assuming that no more than one project of each type is to be built, there are three decision variables for steel projects: y_{11}, y_{21}, and y_{31}, and three for machinery: y_{12}, y_{22} and y_{32}. The number of logically possible combinations is therefore $N = (K)^S = 3^2 = 9$.

The programming tableau appears in table 1 — first the cost row, then the material balances, and then the mutual exclusivity rows. From the cost row, it can be seen that economies-of-scale are significant. E.g., in order to double the output of steel from 2 to 4 MT/Y, the annual costs would increase from \$ 320 to 520 millions/year, an increase of approximately 60%. Export earnings enter as a negative item in the cost row. Note that the costs and scales of demand have been arranged so that it is cheaper to import both steel and machinery rather than to import one item and to produce the other domestically. The global optimum, however, is achieved through a coordinated 'big push', in which both items are produced domestically, there are no imports or exports, and $y_{21} = y_{22} = 1$. With this combination of projects, the total costs are 650 \$ million/year.

Below the cost row in table 1, there are two material balance rows — for steel and machinery respectively. These correspond to equation group (4) above, with $I = 2$. Next come the two mutual exclusivity rows — one for the steel and one for the machinery sector. These correspond to equation group (1) above, with $S = 2$. It is understood that the unknowns are to satisfy the nonnegativity constraints (3) and the integer constraints (2).

Table 2 traces out the successive steps of IPE. Each column corresponds to one step — the results of the linear programming optimization for a particular combination n. Each column is divided into four parts: (a) the identification of n and the values of the dual variables π_i^n; (b) the values of the reduced costs δ_{ks}^n; (c) the locally optimal minimand z^n, together with the values of the glb (greatest lower bound) known for z^m (for all $m \neq n$); and (d)

Table 1
Detached coefficients tableau for steel and machinery example

	Continuous variables				Steel projects			Machinery projects			
	imports, steel	imports, machinery	exports, steel	exports, machinery	size: 0MT/Y	size: 2MT/Y	size: 4MT/Y	size: 0MT/Y	size: 1MT/Y	size: 2MT/Y	
Unknowns	x_1	x_2	x_3	x_4	y_{11}	y_{21}	y_{31}	y_{12}	y_{22}	y_{32}	
Costs	200	500	−50	−250		320	520		330	530	= z $ millions/year
Material balance-steel	1		−1			2	4		−1	−2	= 1 MT/Y
Material balance-machinery		1		−1					1	2	= 1 MT/Y
Mutual exclusivity-steel projects					1	1	1				= 1
Mutual exclusivity-machinery projects								1	1	1	= 1

Table 2
Successive steps of IPE for steel and machinery example

Step number		1	2	3	4	5
n	identification of combination for linear programming optimization	11	33	21	13	22
π_1^n	dual values for material balance – steel	200	50	50	200	200
π_2^n	dual values for material balance – machinery	500	250	500	250	500
δ_{11}^n	reduced costs for steel project 1	0	0	0	0	0
δ_{21}^n	reduced costs for steel project 2	−80	220	220	−80	−80
δ_{31}^n	reduced costs for steel project 3	−280	320	320	−280	−280
δ_{12}^n	reduced costs for machinery project 1	0	0	0	0	0
δ_{22}^n	reduced costs for machinery project 2	30	130	−120	280	30
δ_{32}^n	reduced costs for machinery project 3	−70	130	−370	430	−70

project combination n or m	z^n or glb, z^m (for $m \neq n$)				
11	700 [a]	700	700	700	—
12	730	—	—	—	—
13	630	630	630 [b]	880 [a]	—
21	620	620 [b]	770 [a]	—	—
22	650	650	650	650 [b]	650 [a]
23	550	650	650	800	—
31	420	620	870	—	—
32	450	750	—	—	—
33	350 [b]	750 [a]	—	—	—
global lub on z	700	700	700	700	650
global glb on z	350	620	630	650	650

[a] Denotes locally optimal minimand z^n.
[b] Denotes global glb on z.

the global lub (least upper bound) and the global glb on z.

Each of the N combinations is identified by a two-digit number — the first of which identifies the size index k of the steel project and the second the size index of the machinery project. Now suppose that the first step is taken arbitrarily, and that the project combination chosen is 11 — a zero size for both the steel and the machinery projects. Solving the continuous linear program for $n = 11$, it is observed that $z^{11} = 700$ \$ millions/year, and that the optimal dual values π_i^{11} are set by the import costs: \$ 200/ton of steel and \$ 500/ton of machinery. Using these prices to obtain the reduced costs δ_{ks}^{11}, inequality (6) provides lower bounds on costs for each of the alternative combinations m. E.g., for $m = 32$:

$$z^{32} \geqslant z^{11} + \sum_{s=1}^{2} \sum_{k=1}^{3} \delta_{ks}^{11}(y_{ks}^{32} - y_{ks}^{11})$$

$$z^{32} \geqslant z^{11} + [\delta_{11}^{11}(-1) + \delta_{21}^{11}(0) + \delta_{31}^{11}(1)] + [\delta_{12}^{11}(-1) + \delta_{22}^{11}(1) + \delta_{32}^{11}(0)]$$

$$z^{32} \geqslant 700 + [\quad 0 \quad + \quad 0 \quad -280 \quad] + [\quad 0 \quad + \quad 30 \quad + \quad 0\;]$$

$$z^{32} \geqslant 450 \;.$$

A similar calculation is employed to determine a glb for each of the eight combinations $m \neq n$, and the result is entered in the glb list of table 2. Since this first step indicates that $z^{11} = 700$, and that $z^{12} \geqslant 730$, the combination 12 may be dropped hereafter as a candidate for the global optimum. At the end of step 1, it is established that the optimal value of z must lie between the global lub of 700 and the global glb of 350. Since the lowest glb is associated with project combination 33, the second step consists of solving the continuous linear program for $n = 33$.

From table 2, it will be observed that the locally optimal solution $z^{33} = 750$, that the glb from step 1 did not provide a sharp bound, and that combination 33 may be discarded hereafter. Furthermore, with these massive scales of investment, the π_i drop substantially, and are now equal to the export prices of \$ 50/ton of steel and \$ 250/ton of machinery. Again applying the inequality (6) from the IPE lemma, the new dual values enable us to state that $z^{32} \geqslant 750$, and that combination 32 may be dropped. Furthermore, these dual values push up the glb for combinations 23 and 31.

At the end of step 2, note that the global lub remains at 700, but that the global glb has increased to 620. For step 3, we therefore set $n = 21$, solve a third linear program, see that $z^{21} = 770$, and that $z^{31} \geqslant 870$. This proves that combinations 21 and 31 may be dropped hereafter.

Two more steps – or a total of 5 linear programming solutions out of the maximum possible of 9 – are required to discard all combinations but 22, and to verify that this is a globally optimal solution with min $z = z^{22} = 650$. At this point, the dual variables again have the identical numerical values as in step 1. This provides an immediate counterexample to the conjecture that prices are sufficient to provide a signal of global optimality in the presence of indivisibilities. Both price and quantity information are utilized in the IPE optimization process. Suppose now that these five iterations of IPE are viewed as the algorithmic counterpart of a real-life administrative process. The decrease in the minimand then suggests an upper bound on what could be afforded as the cost of coordinating project decisions between the steel and the machinery sectors: $700\text{--}650 = \$ 50$ millions per year.

4. Remarks on writing a computer program for IPE

(a) If the computer's high-speed memory capacity were not a bottleneck, it would be advantageous to maintain an explicit list of the glb's – one for each of the N possible project combinations, as in table 2. Alternatively, at the cost of an increase in arithmetic operations, this list may be maintained in *implicit* form. This is done through the quantities z^n and δ_{ks}^n produced at each of the explicit simplex solutions. At each step and for each combination in turn, the glb calculation (6) is repeated – applying the quantities z^n and δ_{ks}^n obtained from previous steps. In our computer program (written for an IBM 360/67), the bounds have been stored in implicit form. This will reduce the storage capacity requirements whenever:

$$(1 + \text{number of } y_{ks} \text{ variables}) \begin{pmatrix} \text{cumulative number of} \\ \text{explicit simplex solu-} \\ \text{tions required for IPE} \end{pmatrix} < N.$$

(b) It is likely that the number of steps can be reduced through a judicious choice of starting-point(s). Clearly the initial lub can be lowered through a good guess at the least-cost combination. There is nothing in the basic logic of IPE that precludes two or more starting-points.

(c) The number of IPE iterations is influenced through a user-specified tolerance parameter $\epsilon > 0$. The algorithm is terminated whenever the global glb + $\epsilon \geqslant$ global lub. The lower the value of ϵ, the larger the number of IPE steps, but the sharper become the bounds upon the minimand. Note that the algorithm may be initiated with a high value of ϵ. After intermediate results have been examined, a lower value may be assigned to this tolerance parameter, and the calculations may be restarted.

5. An investment planning example: four locations and two time periods

Consider the problem of setting up new manufacturing capacity so as to minimize the cost of satisfying the demands for a single product at four distinct locations in two time periods. Denote the requirements (less the existing capacity) at location i, period t, by r_i^t ($i = 1, ..., 4; t = 1, 2$). The complete tableau for this dynamic model is shown in table 3. The first four rows of this tableau (FRi) refer to the requirements for first-period capacity, and the second four rows (SRi) to the requirements for second-period capacity. Let the 24 continuous variables x_{ij}^t denote the quantities shipped from location i to j in period t.

Alternative test problems have been generated by stipulating two alternative sets of requirement vectors (RHS and RHS2). The first is based upon a symmetrical geographical distribution of demands and the other upon a more realistic non-symmetrical distribution. In both cases, it is supposed that demands are growing

Table 3

Tableau for four location, two period investment planning model

Continuous variables (columns 12–43 at left are x_{ij}^1; columns 12–43 at right are x_{ij}^2; "Alternative requirements vectors" gives RHS and RHS2)

Group	Row	12	13	14	21	23	24	31	32	34	41	42	43	12	13	14	21	23	24	31	32	34	41	42	43	RHS	RHS2
First period requirements	FR1	-1	-1	-1	1			1			1															$\geq$ 5	10
	FR2	1			-1	-1	-1		1			1														$\geq$ 5	7
	FR3		1			1		-1	-1	-1			1													$\geq$ 5	3
	FR4			1			1			1	-1	-1	-1													$\geq$ 5	0
Second period requirements	SR1													-1	-1	-1	1			1			1			$\geq$ 10	15
	SR2													1			-1	-1	-1		1			1		$\geq$ 10	12
	SR3														1			1		-1	-1	-1			1	$\geq$ 10	8
	SR4															1			1			1	-1	-1	-1	$\geq$ 10	5
Mutual exclusivity	FMEX																									= 1	1
	SMEX																									= 1	1
Alternative minimand vectors	COST (100% capital cost)	0.6	0.4	0.8	0.6	1.0	0.6	0.4	1.0	0.8	0.8	0.6	0.8	0.3	0.2	0.4	0.3	0.5	0.3	0.2	0.5	0.4	0.4	0.3	0.4		
	COST1 (40% capital, cost)	0.42	0.28	0.56	0.42	0.70	0.42	0.28	0.70	0.56	0.56	0.42	0.56	0.3	0.2	0.4	0.3	0.5	0.3	0.2	0.5	0.4	0.4	0.3	0.4		

First period projects (y_k^1, $k = 1\ldots10$) and Second period projects (y_k^2, $k = 1\ldots10$)

Group	Row	1	2	3	4	5	6	7	8	9	10	1	2	3	4	5	6	7	8	9	10
First period requirements	FR1	20				10	10	10													
	FR2		20			10			10	10											
	FR3			20			10		10		10										
	FR4				20			10		10	10										
Second period requirements	SR1	20				10	10	10				20				10	10	10			
	SR2		20			10			10	10			20			10			10	10	
	SR3			20			10		10		10			20			10		10		10
	SR4				20			10		10	10				20			10		10	10
Mutual exclusivity	FMEX	1	1	1	1	1	1	1	1	1	1										
	SMEX											1	1	1	1	1	1	1	1	1	1
Alternative minimand vectors	COST (100% capital cost)	10.5	10.5	10.5	10.5	21	21	21	21	21	21	3.5	3.5	3.5	3.5	7	7	7	7	7	7
	COST1 (40% capital, cost)	8.5	8.5	8.5	8.5	17	17	17	17	17	17	3.5	3.5	3.5	3.5	7	7	7	7	7	7

over time so that

$$\sum_{i=1}^{4} r_i^1 = 20 \text{ units} \quad \text{and} \quad \sum_{i=1}^{4} r_i^2 = 40 \text{ units.}$$

Suppose that capacity may be installed in only one of three mutually exclusive sizes: 0, 10, or 20 units. In general, these indivisibilities will lead to local deficits and surpluses of capacity. Suppose, however, that the system as a whole is to have no excess capacity during either time period. The assumption of indivisibilities — coupled with that of zero excess capacity — then restricts the possibilities to ten mutually exclusive 'projects' for plant capacity initially available during the first time period. The mutual exclusivity row FMEX ensures that one and only one of these ten possibilities will be selected. E.g., the project variable y_6^1 enters into the mutual exclusivity constraints FMEX with a coefficient of 1. If the project is operated at unit intensity, this means that 10 units of capacity are to be installed at locations 1 and 3 during the first time period (rows FR1 and FR3). The construction of these plants also implies that 10 units of capacity are to be available at each of these locations during the second time period (rows SR1 and SR3).

Two alternative minimand rows are specified in table 3: COST (for which the cost of capital is taken to be 100% per period) and COST1 (with a capital cost of 40%). In both, the coefficients for each activity or project refer to the cumulative second period value of the costs. [5] The minimand coefficients for the project variables have been calculated by supposing that there is a 'setup charge' of 3.5 units each period for each plant — independent of

---

[5] E.g., for each unit shipped from location 1 to 2, the shipping costs are 0.3. For the second period shipping variable x_{12}^2, the coefficient of 0.3 therefore appears in both rows COST and COST1. For the shipping variable x_{12}^2, however, the first period cost of 0.3 cumulates to 0.6 in the second period when the cost of capital is 100% per period (row COST), but to only 0.42 when the cost of capital is 40% (row COST1).

the amount of capacity installed. [6] Once the setup charge has been paid, the other manufacturing costs are taken to be proportional to the output – regardless of the location of that output.

The numerical parameters have been chosen so that the optimal solution to this mixed integer program is not immediately obvious. The results depend upon the relative magnitudes of the transport costs, the economies-of-scale in the plant setup costs, and the cost of capital. This formulation produces four test problems – one for each of the possible combinations of the requirements vector (columns RHS and RHS2) and of the minimand vector (rows COST and COST1).

Table 4 lists the optimal values of the project variables and of the minimand for these four problems. Also shown in table 4 are the values obtained by neglecting the integer constraints on the unknowns y_k^t and solving as a conventional linear program. This provides a lower bound on the minimand for the mixed integer problem, but the bound is *not* sharp. E.g., for the vectors RHS and COST, the minimand value is 14.0 cost units for the linear programming solution versus 28.0 for the mixed integer program. Note that each of these problems has been designed so that more than one simplex solution will be required by any type of implicit enumeration algorithm – regardless of whether that algorithm is based upon branch-and-bound or upon Benders partitioning.

In evaluating an algorithm such as IPE, the principal issue is the number of steps required – the number of explicit simplex solutions to be solved before reaching a globally optimal solution. With these four problems, the number of such steps could conceivably be as large as $N = (10)^2 = 100$. In actual practice, the number has proved to be much lower, and to depend upon the particular test problem and starting-point.

Table 5 contains a frequency distribution of the number of steps required to solve each of the four investment planning

---

[6] E.g., the project decision variables y_k^2 (k = 1, 2, 3, 4) refer to setting up a single plant in period 2. The coefficients are therefore 3.5 both in rows COST and COST1. For the project decision variables y_k^1 (k = 1, 2, 3, 4), the setup is to be paid both during period 1 and 2. Hence, for row COST1 (with a 40% cost of capital), the coefficient is 1.40 (3.5) + 1.00 (3.5) ≈ 8.5.

Table 4

Optimal values, four test problems – four location, two period investment planning model

	Optimal solution to mixed integer problem				Linear programming solution, neglecting integer constraints on unknowns y_k^t			
Test problem no.	1	2	3	4	1	2	3	4
Requirements vector	RHS	RHS	RHS2	RHS2	RHS	RHS	RHS2	RHS
Minimand vector	COST	COST1	COST	COST1	COST	COST1	COST	COS
y_k^1 with $k =$ 1	1.0	1.0	1.0	1.0	0.25	0.25	0.50	0.50
2	0	0	0	0	0.25	0.25	0.35	0.35
3	0	0	0	0	0.25	0.25	0.15	0.15
4	0	0	0	0	0.25	0.25	0	0
5	0	0	0	0	0	0	0	0
6	0	0	0	0	0	0	0	0
7	0	0	0	0	0	0	0	0
8	0	0	0	0	0	0	0	0
9	0	0	0	0	0	0	0	0
10	0	0	0	0	0	0	0	0
y_k^2 with $k =$ 1	0	0	0	0	0.25	0.25	0.375	0.37
2	0	0	1.0	1.0	0.25	0.25	0.300	0.30
3	0	0	0	0	0.25	0.25	0.200	0.20
4	1.0	1.0	0	0	0.25	0.25	0.125	0.12
5	0	0	0	0	0	0	0	0
6	0	0	0	0	0	0	0	0
7	0	0	0	0	0	0	0	0
8	0	0	0	0	0	0	0	0
9	0	0	0	0	0	0	0	0
10	0	0	0	0	0	0	0	0
Value of the minimand	28.0	23.3	23.4	19.78	14.0	12.0	14.0	12.0

models – initiating IPE from each of the 100 possible starting-points. It is encouraging that the most steps are required for the two least realistic test cases – those based upon the vector RHS, with identical demands at each of the four locations. It is also encouraging that the number of steps does not appear to go up in proportion to N, the number of combinations. Earlier, a similar series of numerical experiments had been performed on five single-period plant location problems, each with $N = 35$. For those

Table 5

Frequency distribution of IPE steps, four test problems – four locations, two period investment planning model (number of combinations N = 100)

Test problem number Requirements vector Minimand vector		1 RHS COST	2 RHS COST1	3 RHS2 COST	4 RHS2 COST1
	5	0	0	2	0
	6	0	0	18	2
	7	0	0	54	62
Number of steps required for	8	0	0	26	26
optimal solution via IPE –	9	3	0	0	6
initiating algorithm from each of	10	10	0	0	3
the 100 possible starting-points	11	24	6	0	1
	12	30	34	0	·0
	13	30	59	0	0
	14	3	1	0	0
Total number of starting-points		100	100	100	100

problems, the number of IPE steps had ranged between 4 and 8. Here – with N increased by a factor of approximately 3 – the number of IPE steps ranges between 5 and 14. For results on two larger and more realistic problems (N = 648), see table 6 below.

6. Effects of external prices upon project evaluation

If there is little change in the dual variables π_i between combinations n and m – e.g., because international trade imposes narrow limits on the efficiency prices of tradable goods for a 'small' country [7] – we would expect the inequalities (6) to provide a tight bound upon z^m. Under these circumstances, in order to arrive at an optimal selection of individual projects, it is unnecessary to construct a detailed model of the domestic economy within which these projects are to operate. The efficiency prices of that economy will coincide with the exogenously determined world prices.

---

[7] Similarly, suppose that competition imposes narrow limits upon the efficiency prices within a single 'small' enterprise. Projects may then be evaluated individually at the prices that are externally fixed for that enterprise.

Little and Mirrlees (1968, chapter VII) have observed that it is then sufficient to evaluate domestic projects at the world prices.

Conversely, if external trade is limited and the individual projects are 'large', the π_i can change radically from one combination to the next. E.g., for ENERGETICOS, a process analysis of Mexico's energy sector, it is supposed that there is a 36% difference between the import price and the export price of residual fuel oil. [8] When solving by IPE, we cannot expect to reach the optimal solution in a single step. In this model — with the possibility of a 36% difference in the efficiency price of petroleum fuel from one step to the next — there may be a radical shift in the choice between electric power generating projects based upon nuclear fuel versus those based upon petroleum fuel. For electric power project decisions in Mexico, the Little-Mirrlees criterion is not a reliable guide. In order to allow for the interdependence between the efficiency price of petroleum fuel and the quantity of that item demanded by the electricity industry, multi-sector planning is needed — applying a model such as ENERGETICOS.

The IPE algorithm has been tested on one version of ENERGETICOS. This was a version in which investment projects were to be chosen so as to satisfy final demands at minimum discounted costs. The plant size, time-phasing and process choices were selected simultaneously so as to minimize the total cost of satisfying final demands. It was supposed that 27 projects were available, and that these were grouped into three mutual exclusivity sets — one set each for the steel sector (6 projects), petroleum (9 projects), and electricity (12 projects). That is, $S = 3$, and the number of logically possible combinations $N = 6 \times 9 \times 12 = 648$. The number of constraint rows $I = 272$, and the number of continuous variables $J = 350$.

Two numerical cases were solved — one corresponding to a foreign exchange premium of 60%, and the other of zero. In terms of the number of IPE steps required, the algorithm proved to be

---

[8] See above, chapter III.2, table 11. Note that the 36% difference between the import and export prices includes not only an allowance for transport and marketing costs but also a 15% preference rate for domestically produced materials.

reasonably efficient — 11 steps in the one case and 26 in the other. Even with 26 steps, this meant explicit linear programming solutions for only 4% out of the logically possible total of 648 combinations. Table 6 indicates the rate at which the gap was closed

Table 6

Computational summary — application of IPE for investment project evaluation in steel, petroleum and electricity sectors (number of combinations N = 648)

IPE step no.	60% foreign exchange premium				Zero foreign exchange premium			
	Minimand, z (billions of pesos)		Identification of project combination		Minimand, z (billions of pesos)		Identification of project combination	
	lub	glb	lub	glb	lub	glb	lub	glb
1	145.874	134.699	1,1,1	4,2,1	131.140	123.270	1,1,1	4,5,12
2	144.704	134.699	4,2,1	5,2,1	131.140	123.298	1,1,1	6,5,12
3	143.870	134.699	5,2,1	6,2,1	129.332	124.537	6,5,12	6,5,1
4	141.561	137.434	6,2,1	6,3,1	128.151	125.244	6,5,1	5,6,11
5	140.493	137.680	6,3,1	6,4,1	128.151	126.080	6,5,1	6,2,11
6	139.821	138.240	6,4,1	2,5,1	128.149	126.533	6,2,11	2,5,11
7	139.821	138.453	6,4,1	6,5,1	128.149	126.873	6,2,11	6,9,6
8	139.667	138.869	6,5,1	6,7,1	127.851	127.076	6,9,6	4,5,1
9	139.667	138.940	6,5,1	6,8,1	127.851	127.107	6,9,6	6,3,3
10	139.667	138.940	6,5,1	6,9,1	127.851	127.111	6,9,6	6,4,10
11	139.667	139.667	6,5,1	6,5,1	127.771	127.115	6,4,10	6,4,11
12					127.771	127.310	6,4,10	2,6,10
13					127.771	127.345	6,4,10	6,4,5
14					127.764	127.354	6,4,5	6,5,10
15					127.764	127.372	6,4,5	6,5,11
16					127.764	127.413	6,4,5	6,3,10
17					127.764	127.452	6,4,5	6,3,8
18					127.764	127.464	6,4,5	6,8,3
19					127.764	127.519	6,4,5	6,3,7
20					127.722	127.520	6,3,7	6,8,10
21					127.722	127.539	6,3,7	6,8,11
22					127.722	127.540	6,3,7	6,5,5
23					127.722	127.594	6,3,7	6,4,7
24					127.648	127.597	6,4,7	6,2,3
25					127.648	127.636	6,4,7	6,8,5
26					127.648	127.648	6,4,7	6,4,7

between the upper and lower bounds on the minimand. From this table, the reader can calculate the increase in the minimand that would have resulted from a numerical tolerance factor that cut off IPE computations prematurely. For further details on computational efficiency, see Inman (1971).

We will conclude on a speculative note: Does the number of IPE iterations provide a useful measure of the extent of interdependence between projects? The greater the number of such iterations, the poorer are the results that may be anticipated from single-sector project selection rules of the Little-Mirrlees type. E.g., Westphal (1971) noted that the steel and petrochemical sectors of Korea were competing for a limited total of capital available. Given that this scarce resource was to be rationed between the two sectors, the efficiency price of capital was not an exogenous datum. For steel and petrochemical project evaluation, Westphal therefore found it worthwhile to embed these choices within a multi-sector model of the Korean economy.

For Mexico, the capital rationing constraints appear to be less severe than those suggested by Westphal for Korea. The multi-sector model DINAMICO suggests that even though several of the energy sector's projects are competing claimants for scarce resources, interdependencies between projects do not arise through their effect upon the efficiency prices of capital and of foreign exchange. Within Mexico's energy sector, however, the efficiency price of petroleum fuel is *not* an exogenous datum set by the international market. The price of fuel then is a source of interdependencies between project decisions. Several iterations of information flow may be needed for project evaluation. There is two-way interdependence — no matter whether the energy sector's projects are evaluated by a planning agency or by an optimizing algorithm such as IPE.

References

Balinski, M.L., 'Integer programming: methods, uses, computation', *Management Science*, November 1965.

Benders, J.F., 'Partitioning procedures for solving mixed-variables programming problems', *Numerische Mathematik* 4, 1962.

Buzby, B.R., 'Computational experience with Benders' algorithm'. Internal memorandum, Union Carbide Corporation, 1966.

Chenery, H.B., 'Interdependence of investment decisions', in: *The allocation of economic resources*, edited by M. Abramovitz et al. Stanford, Calif., Stanford University Press, 1959.

Davis, R.E., D.A. Kendrick and M. Weitzman, 'A branch-and-bound algorithm for zero-one mixed integer programming problems', *Operations Research*, July–August 1971.

Geoffrion, A., 'Elements of large-scale mathematical programming, parts I and II', *Management Science*, July 1970.

Healy, W.C., 'Multiple choice programming', *Operations Research*, January – February 1964.

Hu, T.C., *Integer programming and network flows*. Reading, Mass., Addison-Wesley, 1969.

Inman, R., 'A user's guide to IPE'. Memorandum 71–2, Development Research Center, International Bank for Reconstruction and Development, February 1971.

Little, I.M.D., and J.A. Mirrlees, *Manual of industrial project analysis in developing countries*, Vol. II: *Social cost benefit analysis*. Paris, Development Centre of the Organization for Economic Co-operation and Development, 1968.

Westphal, L., 'An intertemporal planning model featuring economies of scale', in: *Studies in development planning*, edited by H.B. Chenery. Cambridge, Mass., Harvard University Press, 1971, chapter 4.

V.2. ON DECOMPOSING PRICE-ENDOGENOUS MODELS

Gary P. KUTCHER*

1. Decomposition and the Mexico model system

In the early 1960's, decomposition techniques were viewed by many as the most promising means of overcoming computer limitations in solving large scale mathematical programming problems. The basic premise of a decomposition algorithm is straightforward: Suppose that a computer can readily solve small problems, but not large ones. Then it may be worthwhile to break up a large block-angular problem (figure 1) into several smaller ones, solve them iteratively, and link them together in such a way that their solution is optimal for the original, indecomposed problem. Perhaps the best known decomposition algorithm is that of Dantzig and Wolfe (1961).

Economists have been quick to perceive an analogy between decomposition algorithms and the theory of multi-level organizations. (For a partial bibliography, see below, chapter V.3, table 1). The component problems (termed subprograms) may correspond to individual decision-making units, each with its own objectives and resources. The master problem may be interpreted either as a central planning bureau or as a competitive market, depending upon one's political philosophy. Thus, interest in decomposition has stemmed from two different sources: both the desire for numerical solutions to large-scale problems and also the desire to simulate actual market and multi-level planning processes involving

* The author is grateful to Clopper Almon, John H. Duloy, Louis M. Goreux, Alan S. Manne, and Roger D. Norton for helpful discussions.

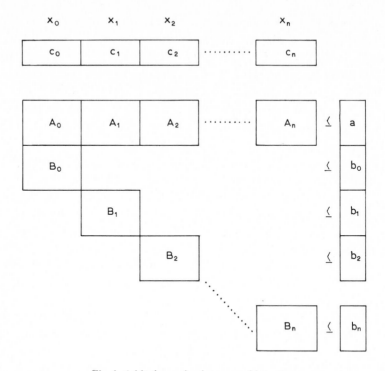

Fig. 1. A block-angular decomposable system.

price-motivated behavior, production quotas and/or resource endowments.

At the outset of the project described in this monograph, detailed consideration was given to the use of a decomposition algorithm. It was hoped that such a procedure could help in the analysis of multi-level planning techniques. (As many as five levels of
decision-making are discernible in the Mexico model system.)
Moreover, there were uncertainties concerning the adequacy of the
country's computational facilities.

As it turned out, Mexico's linear programming facilities were
capable of solving the aggregated version of the largest component
of the system, CHAC. However, experiments were conducted on
two smaller-scale model systems with a view toward the future
decomposition of CHAC and possibly the entire model system.

In this paper, several numerical experiments are reported – applying our knowledge of the economic structure to facilitate the computations. A programming model is employed to simulate a group of interrelated competitive markets for agricultural products in Mexico. The objective function is taken as the maximization of the sum of consumers' and producers' surpluses. Since the product prices are determined endogenously through supply and demand conditions, we term this a 'price-endogenous' planning model.

By organizing the block-angular structure so that the demand restrictions are incorporated in the master problem and so that the supply restrictions are decentralized into individual 'district' sub-problems, it turns out that we may accelerate the convergence of the Dantzig-Wolfe decomposition procedure.[1] Here the speed of convergence is measured, not by the actual computer execution time, but rather by the number of cycles back and forth between the master and the subprograms. The number of such cycles is critical – not only because of the time it takes to transfer information between the components of a computer program – but because of the time (and the decrease in reliability) associated with the transfer of information between the components of a multi-level planning hierarchy. See chapter V.3 below, esp. section 3.

In practice, the number of cycles has been a major impediment to the development of decomposition algorithms. It is not easy to find efficient linear programming subroutines that are 'callable' repeatedly for the purpose of a decomposition algorithm. Because of this type of difficulty with decomposition, sparse inverse methods have been developed far more intensively. By 1970, sparse inverse methods could handle up to 4,000 rows. Quite naturally, this led to a decrease of interest in decomposition. In the words of Orchard-Hays (1968, p. 240): 'Though perhaps inevitable, this is

---

[1] This experience checks with that reported by Beale et al. (1965) in their decomposition work with models of 300–500 rows. They were planning the production of oil at seven different fields to supply the requirements at three markets over a planning horizon of twelve individual years. By trial-and-error, they found that it was best to include distribution and exploration activities in the master problem, and to regard each of the seven individual producing fields as a sub-program. – Weil and Kettler (1971) developed computer programs to rearrange matrices into block-angular form, but did not report any comparison of linear programming results with the decomposed matrices.

unfortunate since decomposition is the only really promising extension to mathematical programming for large and complicated models.'

The Dantzig-Wolfe (D-W) decomposition algorithm was selected as the basis for our experiments — partly out of familiarity — and partly because its reliance on price signals seemed to offer greater promise for efficient solution of the price-endogenous agricultural models than would a quota-oriented primal decomposition algorithm. Two phases of this work are reported — first, experiments with POQUITA, a purely illustrative numerical model — and secondly, a larger and more realistic model, PACIFICO. The latter represents an aggregated form of the five Pacific Northwest irrigation submodels that appear in CHAC (Part IV). Before describing these experiments, we digress to review the D-W algorithm.

2. The rudiments of Dantzig-Wolfe decomposition

The D-W algorithm is based on the idea that a solution to the complete problem can be obtained as a convex combination of the extreme point solutions to the subprograms. (These extreme point solutions are constrained only by the resources specific to each of the subproblems.) For the submodel, the common constraints are replaced by objective function coefficients which reflect the evaluation of the common items according to a master problem. The final solution of the master (which is comprised of convex combinations of the subprogram solutions) gives the solution to the full problem. Thus, the algorithm consists of solving the subproblems, sending quantity aggregates to the master, solving the master, revising the objective function entries of the subproblems on the basis of the master's evaluation of the common constraints, solving new subproblems, etc., until an optimality test is passed. More precisely, the steps involved in cycle k of the D-W algorithm are:

(1) Solve subproblem j for non-negative activity levels x_{jk} which maximize

$$\hat{c}_{jk} x_{jk} = (c_j - \pi_{k-1} A_j) x_{jk}$$

subject to

$$B_j x_{jk} \leqslant b_j \qquad (j = 0, 1, ..., n)$$

where π_{k-1} is the vector of shadow prices on the central rows in cycle $k-1$.

(2) Aggregate to obtain the $n + 1$ extreme point vectors

$$P_{jk} = A_j x_{jk} ; \qquad c_{jk} = c_j x_{jk} .$$

(3) Solve the master problem for non-negative activity levels s_{jk} which maximize

$$\sum_j \sum_k c_{jk} s_{jk}$$

subject to

$$\sum_j \sum_k P_{jk} s_{jk} \leqslant a$$

and

$$\sum_k s_{jk} \leqslant 1.$$

(4) If none of the current P_{jk} enter the basis of the master, the previous ($k-1$th) solution of the master corresponds to the overall optimum. Otherwise, return to step 1 to begin cycle $k+1$.

For a fuller statement and proofs of equivalence and convergence, see Dantzig and Wolfe (1961), pp. 769–772. Note that this discussion has bypassed the details related to an unbounded or an infeasible solution.

The above procedure departs slightly from the original D-W formulation. Both from the viewpoint of computational simplicity and ease in economic interpretation, it is preferable to append all $n + 1$ extreme point vectors P_{jk} to the master on each cycle. The alternative would have been to calculate the reduced cost (*DJ*) of each and select only the best vector or those with positive *DJ*'s. Any vectors which do not become basic may easily be dropped from the problem on subsequent cycles if computer storage limitations so require. Thus, we prefer to use the term 'cycle' rather than 'iteration' to describe a single execution of the four successive steps of the algorithm.

3. Decomposition experiments with an illustrative model

To gain experience in the use of decomposition algorithms, we began by constructing a very simple decomposable model, PO-QUITA. Although this model consists of only 60 rows and 72 activities, it closely parallels the structure of CHAC. POQUITA has the same maximand (sum of consumers' and producers' surpluses) and includes three agricultural producing district submodels. Eight products have their prices determined endogenously, and a ninth is assumed to face a perfectly elastic export demand.

In terms of figure 1, POQUITA may be decomposed as follows: The B_j matrices, (j = 1, 2, 3) refer to the district-specific constraints. The rows of the A_j matrices include the nine commodity balances and four central resource constraints. Because of the particular importance of the submatrix of selling activities, B_0, this must be considered in more detail.

3.1. Decomposition and the structure of demand

In the basic version of POQUITA, each of the price-endogenous outputs is assumed to face a linear demand function segmented into four steps as in figure 2. Table 1 is the programming model tableau of selling activities based on the function of figure 2. Suppose that the commodity balance is included in the master, and that all segment constraints are included in subprogram zero. Then the segment constraints for all eight outputs comprise a 32 × 32 identity matrix, B_0. This structure gives rise to immediate questions as to partitioning. At one extreme (*A*), the set of selling

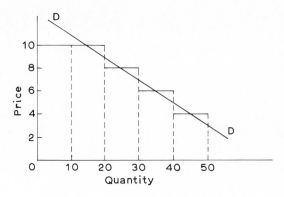

Fig. 2.

activities can be fully decomposed so that each activity comprises a single subprogram with only its single segment constraint. At the other extreme (*C*), the entire set of selling activities can be taken

Table 1
Initial demand tableau

	1	2	3	4	
OBJ	10	8	6	4	
Commodity balance	−1	−1	−1	−1	
Segment constraints	1				⩽ 20
		1			⩽ 10
			1		⩽ 10
				1	⩽ 10

Table 2
Transformed demand tableau

	1	2	3	4	
OBJ	200	280	340	380	
Commodity balance	−20	−30	−40	−50	
Convex-combination constraint	1	1	1	1	⩽ 1

Table 3
POQUITA demand set: partitioning choices

	Number of subprograms [a]	Dimensions of subprograms	Expected number of cycles for convergence
A. Fully partitioned	32	1 × 1	fewest
B. Partitioned by output	8	4 × 4	intermediate
C. Not partitioned	1	32 × 32	most

[a] Since each subprogram requires a convex-combination constraint, this also equals the number of rows in the master associated with the demand set.

as a single subprogram. In between, (*B*), the set of selling activities for each output can be considered as subprograms.

Although the choice of partitioning has obvious implications for the number of subprograms, its influence on the speed of convergence is more crucial. Consider partitioning choice A. If, say, the shadow prices π_0 are all zero, then the first set of vectors P_{j1} generated from the 32 subprograms will be equivalent to the original selling activities. Thus the master problem will have all of the demand set extreme points on the first cycle, and further solutions of these subprograms would be redundant. This is not the case, however, with the other partitioning choices. Under C, only one extreme point of the entire demand set would be generated on each cycle; many cycles may be required to generate the appropriate extreme points. Until prices have stabilized, the production proposals of the district subprograms may oscillate uselessly. With choice C, however, the master problem would be smaller than any of the others, requiring only one convex-combination constraint for the entire set of selling activities. Table 3 summarizes the trade-off among the various partitioning choices.

3.2. POQUITA decomposition solutions

Because partitioning choice C is expected to converge slowly, decomposition solutions were attempted only for A, B, and an 'expanded master' (described below). Table 4 illustrates the numerical results of these partitioning choices.

Table 4
POQUITA decomposition solution

| | | Objective function values | | |
	Cycle	Parti- tioning A	Parti- tioning B	Expanded master
	1	0.00 [a]	0.00 [a]	371.90
	2	371.90	274.48	410.50
	3	410.50	380.62	419.98
	4	419.98	423.83	431.09
	5	431.09	424.34	431.43 [b]
	6	431.43 [b]	428.58	
	7		430.84	
	8		431.43 [b]	
Number of subprograms		35	11	3
Number of subprogram solutions		50	88	15
Number of rows in master		48	24	24

[a] If the π_0 are all zero, no production takes place in the district subprograms. Hence the objective functions of these masters were both zero on the first cycle.
[b] Optimum.

The rapid convergence of choice A was quite satisfactory, but its master problem had so many rows — compared with the size of original problem — that any possible computational advantage of decomposition was negated. (Even with an extremely small computer, it is clear that decomposition would not be advantageous for a model the size of POQUITA. Recall, however, that these experiments are intended to shed light on decomposition techniques for much larger models of similar structure.)

3.3. Demand tableau transformations and the 'expanded master'

Elementary row and column operations may be performed on the demand activity tableaus (such as that of table 1) so as to obtain an equivalent structure, but with one convex-combination constraint for each item replacing the segment constraints. Table 2 is the result of these operations for the demand curve represented in figure 2 and table 1. Since this technique can significantly reduce the number of rows in a linear programming problem, it is unquestionably preferable on computational grounds. However, it does have an important ramification for decomposition: the full partitioning of choice A (where each demand activity is taken as a subproblem) is no longer possible. Maximum partitioning is now by output – equivalent to partitioning choice B. Thus the rapid convergence of choice A is not attainable under usual D-W usage when this transformation is adopted.

This led to the idea of incorporating the set of demand activities directly into the master at the outset. With the demand tableau transformations, this 'expanded master' will have no more rows than the master of partitioning choice B, but all of the demand set extreme points will be available from the start. Convergence of this problem should be identical to that of partitioning choice A except that cycle 1 will not be needed to generate the demand set extreme points. Thus cycle 1 can be based on some non-zero set of shadow prices, and not 'wasted' from the production side. A convenient means of obtaining an important set of shadow prices with which to initiate cycle 1 is to solve the expanded master before any production proposals have been generated. Although this solution will be trivial (all non-slack activity levels must be zero), the shadow prices will represent the highest possible output prices and the lowest input prices.[2]

The decomposition solution of POQUITA employing the expanded master modification and the suggested initialization is shown in the rightmost column of table 4. The advantages of this approach are evident (e.g., note the number of cycles and number of rows in the master problem). However, the significant reduction in the number of 'calls' of the linear programming computational routine is perhaps most important.

An additional feature of this approach lies in the economic interpretation of the algorithm. The expanded master can be considered as an agricultural trade agency whose task is to find a set of market-clearing prices and to induce the districts to submit

---

[2] Alternatively, these extreme π could be read directly from the input data since the output prices will correspond to those in the first demand activity for each product.

optimal plans. Because the agency has full information as to the overall demand functions, only the comparative production advantages of the individual districts need to be revealed iteratively.

We now turn to a more realistic two-level model, PACIFICO, and investigate the use of the expanded master approach when employing the demand structure used in CHAC. This introduces a further problem — demand substitution among individual agricultural products within a commodity group.

4. PACIFICO, a model of Mexico's Pacific Northwest

Although the results from the POQUITA experiments have been instructive, only so much can be learned from simple, hypothetical models. This section describes our experience in decomposing a larger and more realistic price-endogenous model.

The structure of PACIFICO largely parallels that of CHAC. It consists of modified versions of five of CHAC's district models: Río Yaqui, Río Colorado, Culmaya, El Fuerte, and the Northwest residual. The objective function is the maximization of the northwest region's consumers' and producers' surpluses, leading to equality between output prices and marginal costs. The demand structure is similar to that used in CHAC, and is comprised of regional demand and export activities. The block-angularity of PACIFICO can be ascertained from table 5 which gives a breakdown of the rows and columns.

4.1. Outputs and the demand structure

PACIFICO encompasses the production and demand of fifteen crops. (Because cotton has a joint product of seed and fiber, there are sixteen outputs in total.) The prices of all products are determined endogenously. Table 6 is a list of these outputs, their model acronyms, and base-year (1968) prices. The optimal solution prices will, in general, not be the same as these prices, but they are expected to be close.

In PACIFICO, four outputs are demanded individually using the

Table 5
PACIFICO rows and columns

Rows:

4	Region-wide accounting	
16	Region-wide commodity balances	
12	Demand set constraints	
<u>19</u>	Region-wide resource balances	
51	Total 'central' rows	
24	Río Yaqui	− specific rows
26	Culmaya	− specific rows
30	Río Colorado	− specific rows
26	El Fuerte	− specific rows
<u>30</u>	Residual	− specific rows
136	District-level rows	
187	Total rows	

Columns:

140	Selling and 'mixing' activities	
3	Export activities	
<u>7</u>	Regional factor supplying activities	
150	Region-wide activities	
34	Río Yaqui	− production and factor-supplying activities
45	Culmaya	− production and factor-supplying activities
47	Río Colorado	− production and factor-supplying activities
39	El Fuerte	− production and factor-supplying activities
<u>67</u>	Residual	− production and factor-supplying activities
232	District-level activities	
382	Total activities	

(transformed) structure described for POQUITA. Three outputs (cotton fiber (ALG), sugar cane (AZU), and tomatoes (JIT)) also have export activities which permit an unlimited quantity to be sold at Northwest average FOB prices. The remaining items in the table are sold as members of one of the four groups. In order to obtain a high degree of price accuracy, each of the demand functions was divided into fifteen segments at prices ranging between 1.5 and 0.67 of the base price.

Recall that within each demand group of CHAC, there is a

Table 6
PACIFICO outputs and demand groups

Demand group	Output	Acronym	Base price (1968 pesos/ton)
(demanded singly)	cotton fiber	ALG	4816
	sugar cane	AZU	68
	green chile	CHV	1413
	tomatoes	JIT	1200
Grains	maize	MAI	861
	wheat	TRI	800
Forages	green alfalfa	ALV	126
	dry alfalfa	ALA	354
	barley	CEG	1014
	maize	MAI	861
	sorghum	SOR	633
Oil seeds	cotton seed	SAL	831
	safflower	CAR	1544
	sesame	JON	2407
	soy beans	SOY	1600
'Fecolas'	rice	ARO	1134
	beans	FRI	1834

constant marginal rate of substitution up to certain limits within the product mix. Between these demand limits, relative prices remain constant within the group. In all cases, the mixing activities representing the extreme bundles require some positive proportion of each commodity in the group. For a two-commodity group, an indifference curve would be as shown in figure 3. Points *a* and *b* represent the two extreme bundles, and the line segment *ab* represent all permissible proportions of the two substitutable commodities.

In the framework of decomposition, this demand structure has an important consequence. Unless all of the commodities within a particular group have been produced on some previous cycle, none of the selling activities for the group can be used at a positive level. Furthermore, a particular production proposal which contains production of one output in a group which is not complete (i.e., a group in which not all outputs have been represented by some

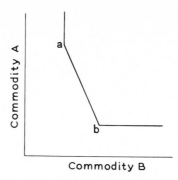

Fig. 3. Indifference curve within a two-commodity demand group.

production proposal) cannot be used at all. Thus the value of the master's objective function on early cycles may not be representative of the value of the production proposals up to that point. For example, suppose that, on the first cycle, a given district produces mostly tomatoes (a crop which may be exported) and some alfalfa. If not all of the commodities in the forages group have been produced, then this production proposal cannot be used by the master at a positive intensity.

For these reasons, a set of zero-cost 'disposal' activities were added to the decomposition version of the model. In the tomatoes-alfalfa example above, the alfalfa disposal activity permits export of tomatoes. The shadow price on alfalfa on the next cycle would, of course, be zero. [3]

4.2. Prices and production response

Since the expanded master approach reduces the task of the algorithm to inducing optimal district production plans, it is of interest to examine the generation of production subproblem extreme points.

Table 7 shows several sets of prices from master solutions and the production proposals from the Yaqui subprogram based on them. The P_{jk} vectors shown below the corresponding prices are

---

[3] Without the disposal activity, the price of alfalfa could be negative.

Table 7
Price changes and production response (Río Yaqui subprogram)

		Cycle			
		11	12	13	14
Prices [a]	ALG	4816	4816	4816	4816
(from cycle $k-1$)	SAL	804	798	798	792
	CAR	1624	1720	1739	1794
	JON	2924	2436	2375	2591
	MAI	964	958	958	989
	SOR	668	663	605	662
	SOY	1552	1540	1541	1531
	TRI	797	740	768	782
Production	WELFAR [b]	−6.303	−7.050	−7.540	−7.466
proposals [c]	ALG	6.40	−	−	−
	SAL	12.48	−	−	−
	CAR	−	−	−	78.76
	JON	−	−	−	−
	MAI	49.42	96.25	176.45	247.22
	SOR	214.55	323.67	−	68.28
	SOY	42.99	146.51	179.70	136.12
	TRI	447.75	−	−	−
EMPLOYMENT [d]		422.19	496.94	545.96	538.56
TRACTORS [e]		71.68	60.63	56.33	63.77
CHEMICALS [f]		115.20	64.58	40.71	80.82
CCCF		1.	1.	1.	1.

[a] Output prices in pesos/ton. The prices of other common items (labor, tractors, and chemicals) are not shown because they do not vary.

[b] 10^7 pesos.

[c] Production in 10^3 tons.

[d] 10^4 man-days of day labor.

[e] 10^4 tractor-days.

[f] 10^4 pesos.

incomplete and only meant to illustrate the generation of the extreme points. In these vectors, the entries in WELFAR, the maximand, are the c_{jk} defined in section 2 representing costs of the proposals. Entries in the output rows (commodity balances) are total production; these work against the demand activities in the master. Rows for tractors and chemicals are indicative of

Table 8
PACIFICO decomposition solution

Objective function (10^7 pesos)			Shadow prices (pesos/ton)					
Cycle	WELFAR	Upper bound	ALG (cotton fiber)	AZU (sugar cane)	CHV (green chili)	JIT (toma-toes)	TRI (wheat)	MAI (maize)
0	–		7,224	102	2,080	1,725	1,178	1,268
1	549.49		12,976	221	942	2,875	533	574
2	549.49		12,976	79	942	2,875	533	574
3	554.32		12,976	81	942	2,875	533	574
4	635.57		6,568	81	942	1,200	533	574
5	749.54		4,816	98	942	1,200	513	4,172
6	757.39		4,816	221	942	1,200	526	689
7	817.11	889.56	4,816	68	942	1,200	767	1,008
8	824.69	871.24	4,816	68	1,295	1,200	736	889
9	832.39	843.72	4,816	68	942	1,200	736	889
10	835.05	841.74	4,816	68	1,138	1,200	797	964
11	837.43	841.50	4,816	68	1,138	1,200	740	958
12	838.32	841.48	4,816	68	1,138	1,200	768	958
13	838.55	840.14	4,816	68	1,138	1,200	782	989
14	839.04	839.68	4,816	68	1,138	1,200	749	923
15	839.11	839.61	4,816	68	1,138	1,200	751	934
16	839.13	839.52	4,816	68	1,138	1,200	743	928
17	839.25	839.44	4,816	68	1,138	1,200	742	916
18 [a]	839.28	–	4,816	68	942	1,200	756	928
Base prices			4,816	68	1,413	1,200	800	861

[a] Optimum

variations in central resource use of the proposals. Row CCCF is the convex-combination constraint on the Yaqui subprogram in the master. This constraint summarizes the effect of district-specific resources such as land and water.

4.3. PACIFICO decomposition solution

In decomposing PACIFICO, the expanded master formulation was adopted. Each of the district models were treated as subprograms, and all of the demand, export, and factor supplying activities were

Convergence of output prices

ALV (green alfalfa)	ALA (dry alfalfa)	CEG (barley)	SOR (sorghum)	SAL (cotton seed)	CAR (safflower)	JON (sesame)	SOY (soy beans)	ARO (rice)	FRI (beans)
186	520	1,537	932	929	2,273	3,544	2,356	1,670	2,700
0	57	0	3,533	0	137,355	0	0	2,552	4,126
0	8,264	0	267	0	944	0	22,893	0	1,019,622
5,864	636	0	267	0	944	247,175	0	3,516	1,255
77	1,579	58,954	267	3,603	901	2,800	0	3,530	1,214
73	842	577	1,343	1,253	866	4,566	1,788	1,204	1,180
75	631	593	299	1,250	889	4,562	1,786	1,216	540
156	330	1,047	495	828	1,746	2,613	1,483	1,324	548
105	547	927	874	732	1,674	2,335	1,414	1,287	2,273
105	547	927	615	732	1,674	2,335	1,414	1,287	1,843
116	588	1,041	668	804	1,624	2,924	1,552	1,401	1,697
114	567	988	663	798	1,720	2,436	1,540	1,376	1,591
110	573	1,032	605	798	1,739	2,375	1,541	1,371	1,619
111	573	1,049	662	792	1,794	2,591	1,531	1,326	1,648
111	555	997	631	762	1,698	2,600	1,472	1,340	1,594
107	555	1,001	643	759	1,710	2,582	1,467	1,359	1,599
105	551	988	630	752	1,669	2,600	1,454	1,337	1,586
109	551	986	630	753	1,669	2,527	1,454	1,335	1,583
110	559	1,009	637	767	1,706	2,547	1,482	1,342	1,606
126	354	1,044	633	831	1,544	2,407	1,600	1,134	1,834

incorporated into the master at the outset. At initialization, the dimensions of the master were 56 rows (including the five convex-combination constraints on the district subprograms) and 150 activities. Recall that the dimensions of the full model were 187 rows, 382 activities. Had the demand structures been formulated as one or more subprograms, the number of rows in the master would have been reduced by at most eleven.

As with POQUITA, the algorithm was initiated by transmitting the highest output prices (shown in row 0, table 8) to the district subprograms. Also, because computer storage was not a limitation, all production proposals could be retained from previous cycles.

Table 8 shows that the algorithm required 18 cycles to attain the optimum solution of 839.28 for the objective function, WELFAR. The behavior of the objective function over the 18 cycles is interesting in that there was a rapid increase up to the seventh cycle and very slow improvement thereafter. At seven cycles, WELFAR was within 2½% of its optimal value. After the 7th cycle, prices and the objective function changed only marginally. This, together with significant shifts in production proposals despite small price changes (see table 7), indicates that the degree of comparative advantages among crops is very small between individual districts in the Northwest. Had the comparative advantages been more pronounced, they would have been exhibited in earlier cycles resulting in faster convergence. Given the eternal suspicion surrounding the numbers in models such as PACIFICO, one could argue that the solution of cycle seven is not statistically significantly better than the optimum. Since, at this point, the output prices were reasonably close to the base prices (shown in the last row of table 8), one might consider terminating the algorithm at this point. This suggests that it is worthwhile to calculate the upper bound on the maximand on each cycle. (See Dantzig, Theorem 2, p. 452.) These bounds, beginning with cycle seven, are shown beside the objective function in table 8. Note that, on cycle seven, the bound was about 13% higher than the objective function value, but by cycle eleven the difference was negligible.

The reader is invited to further examine the convergence of prices in table 8. Some of the extremely high prices in early cycles were due to the limits on substitution in demand. (The price of beans was over one million pesos on cycle two. The other member of the commodity group (rice) was in abundance from previous production proposals, but the selling activities for this group could not be used at a positive level because beans had not been produced.) Although some of these wide fluctuations in prices may not be adequately explained by economic analogy, they do perform an important algorithmic function — the generation of highly specialized production proposals. These may then be combined by the master to yield a near-optimum solution after only a few cycles.

Finally, we offer a note on the initialization of the algorithm.

Intuitively, one might think that initializing the algorithm with the base year prices (the best a priori estimates of the optimal prices) would provide a better start than 1.5 times those prices. This was attempted, with the surprising result that the objective function on the first cycle was only 189.17 as opposed to 549.49. Only seven of the fifteen crops were produced, and none of the demand groups were complete.

4.4. An extension

We have viewed the solution procedure used in decomposing PACIFICO as one of finding appropriate sets of prices to draw the required extreme points from the district production submodels. If the appropriate price vectors were known beforehand, obtaining an optimal solution would be relatively simple. In this section, a technique will be explored for obtaining many meaningful extreme points of the production submodels before commencing with the usual iterations of the algorithm.

First, let us digress to examine the computational techniques used in making these decomposition experiments, in order to point out those aspects which could have a bearing on further extensions. For the PACIFICO experiments, the district submodels were solved with a callable FORTRAN simplex subroutine. By using an advanced basis, this subroutine permitted us to obtain additional district solutions in less than one second (on a CDC 6600 computer) when minor changes were made in the objective function. However, this subroutine was not sufficiently powerful to solve the PACIFICO expanded master, and a non-callable [4] package had to be used.

This required the solution procedure to be manually interrupted after each cycle. This can be quite time-consuming if the required number of cycles is large. In addition, a high fixed cost in computer time is generally associated with using a general purpose, non-callable mathematical programming package. The result was, in the case of PACIFICO, a very high trade-off in computer time

---

[4] I.e., a routine that can only be efficiently loaded once within a given run.

between the number of complete cycles and individual district model solutions.

This suggested that it may be worthwhile to attempt to generate a series of district submodel solutions and to include these extreme points in the master directly on the first cycle. It remains to select sets of prices for generating these extreme points.

The demand functions in PACIFICO are perfectly elastic at prices above 1.5 and below 0.67 times the base price. Therefore, upper and lower bounds on any given commodity's price are immediately available. However, since there are sixteen outputs in all, there are 2^{16} price combinations — far too many for an experiment. This number was reduced in the following manner: The three exported crops can be expected to have optimal prices equal to their export prices. Thus these prices can be fixed. Furthermore, the probability that the optimal price ratios within each demand group will remain constant suggests that we can vary the extreme prices of each group together. If these simplifications are employed, the number of combinations of high and low prices is reduced to $2^5 = 32$.

An experiment was conducted in which 32 solutions were generated for each of the five district models. The 160 vectors were then appended to the original expanded master. The solution to this problem (of dimension 56 $\times$ 310) had an objective function value of 684.82, a value not otherwise attained until cycle five, according to table 8. However, two of the four demand groups could not be used because none of the 160 production proposals included production of sesame or dry alfalfa. On the next cycle, conducted in the usual manner, the extremely high shadow prices on these crops caused them to be brought in — with the objective function climbing to 822.77. This was within 2% of the overall optimum and was obtained by using the non-callable routine only twice.

5. Conclusions from the numerical experiments

The general conclusion that can be drawn from these decomposition experiments is simple. If a linear programming model is to be solved by decomposition, substantial savings may be obtained by examining the economic structure of the problem for relationships which could influence the computational procedure.

Up to this point, we are safely within the bounds of Kornai's 'a-type' interpretation (the computational aspect of decomposition), but with an important difference. Our understanding of the economic structure of the model has been employed to improve the performance of the mathematical-computational procedure. This is perhaps the *reverse* of Kornai's 'b-type' interpretation. Instead of viewing decomposition as an iterative economic planning technique, we have used our knowledge of the economy to suggest variations in the algorithm itself.

In particular, this work demonstrates that if a price-endogenous model is to be decomposed, substantial computational savings may be obtained if the price-determining submatrix is incorporated into the master. Furthermore, the number of cycles required to produce a meaningful solution can be reduced by generating several extreme point production proposals before initiating the decomposition algorithm.

From these experiments, no direct conclusions may be drawn concerning the decision to decompose or not-to-decompose. This question is highly dependent on the problem at hand, the computer, and the available simplex subroutine. Improvements in callable routines are essential to the further progress of decomposition.

References

Beale, E.M.L., P.A.B. Hughes and R.E. Small, 'Experiences in using a decomposition program', *The Computer Journal,* April 1965.

Dantzig, G.B., and P. Wolfe, 'The decomposition principle for linear programs', *Econometrica,* October 1961.

Dantzig, G.B., *Linear programming and extensions.* Princeton, N.J., Princeton University Press, 1963.

Orchard-Hays, W., *Advanced linear programming techniques.* New York, McGraw-Hill, 1968.

Weil, R.L., and P.C. Kettler, 'Rearranging matrices to block-angular form for decomposition (and other) algorithms', *Management Science,* September 1971.

V.3. THOUGHTS ON MULTI-LEVEL PLANNING SYSTEMS

János KORNAI *

Increasingly, economists have become interested in the centralization and decentralization of planning, in the linking up of models into a homogeneous model system, and in multi-level planning. The Mexican case studies provide a good opportunity for discussing these questions. This paper will not be restricted to the Mexican studies. Rather, these will be used only as illustrations in a more general analysis of multi-level planning.

Perhaps the most important study on this subject is the classical paper by Malinvaud (1967). Nevertheless, experience shows that actual planning systems, the planning models used in practice, cannot be fully described in the conceptual framework proposed by Malinvaud. This applies, e.g., to the Mexican research work. Therefore it has become important to form some new, generally valid concepts and classifications.

Section 1 reviews the theory and application of decomposition methods. Section 2 comments on the characteristics of practical multi-level planning. Section 3 deals with the evaluation of planning methods. Section 4 discusses the difficulties in the construction of multi-level planning systems. Finally, section 5 draws a few general conclusions.

* For stimulating discussions which helped to clarify the ideas presented in this paper, the author is indebted to Louis Goreux, Alan Manne, Roger Norton, and Thomas Vietorisz. He also wishes to thank Alan Manne for help in polishing the English style of this paper.

1. Decomposition methods

The decomposition algorithm was first proposed by Dantzig and Wolfe (1960, 1961). Their algorithm provides for the decomposition of a large block-angular linear programming problem into smaller, more manageable subproblems. Since the original Dantzig-Wolfe papers, a whole series of other procedures have been worked out to solve similar problems. A sample is given in table 1. This table is incomplete, although it contains 10 procedures. A more complete survey and a detailed bibliography may be found in Geoffrion (1970), which reports on some sixty decomposition methods.

1.1. Common and specific criteria

Let us first review the common characteristics of decomposition methods.

We have before us a mathematical programming problem. The set of its initial data is denoted by D. The vector of the optimal solution is denoted by P.

If a *direct method* is used instead of decomposition, we make the following transformation without a detour, in one single operation:

$$D \to P. \tag{1}$$

This happens, e.g., when a linear programming problem is solved by the simplex method.

Using a decomposition method, we get from D to P by an indirect route. First of all, the D data-set is partitioned in accordance with a *decomposition rule*. One subset is D_0, the *central* data, the other subsets are D_1, D_2, ..., D_n, the sectoral data. Starting from these data, the first iteration is carried out. The first *central computation* is based upon the central data:

$$D_0 \to [M_0^1, B_1^1, B_2^1, ..., B_n^1], \tag{2}$$

A survey of some decomposition procedures [a]

Authors	Dates of publication	Name of procedure	Information flow from the center to the sector	Information flow from the sectors to the center	Special characteristics
1	G.B. Dantzig and P. Wolfe	1960 1961	decomposition method			
2	J.F. Benders	1962	partitioning procedure			
3	J. Abadie and A.C. Williams	1963	dual decomposition method		aggregate demand for and supply of central product and resource balances	
4	J.B. Rosen	1964	primal partition programming	shadow prices of central products and resources		additional sectoral information: non-basic activities
5	E. Balas	1966	infeasibility-pricing decomposition method			
6	H. Heinemann	1970	general decomposition method			
7	J. Kornai and T. Lipták	1962, 1965	two-level planning			
8	E.V.W. Zschau	1967	primal decomposition algorithm	allocation of input quotas and output targets of central products and resources	shadow prices of central products and resources	
9	A.T. Kate	1970	direct distribution method			
10	M. Weitzman	1970	multi-level planning with production targets			additional sectoral information: modified targets

[a] The author is grateful to J. Sivák, who assisted in compiling the bibliography and this table. These decomposition methods are surveyed in two groups: according to the economic content of the information exchange between levels. Within each group, the methods are listed in the order of the date of publication.

in which M_0^1 is the *central memory content*, at the end of the 1st iteration, and B_i^1 is the *central information output* obtained from the 1st central computation and transferred for the ith sectoral computation at the end of the 1st iteration.

On the basis of the sectoral data, the first *sectoral computation* is made:

$$D_i \to [M_i^1, F_i^1] \qquad (i = 1, ..., n) , \tag{3}$$

in which M_i^1 is the *memory content of the ith sector,* at the end of the 1st iteration, and F_i^1 is the *sectoral information output* obtained from the ith sectoral computation and transferred for the central computation at the end of the 1st iteration.

The 1st iteration is followed by the 2nd, ..., sth iteration. The transformations made in the sth iteration are the following:

$$[M_0^{s-1}, F_1^{s-1}, F_2^{s-1}, ..., F_n^{s-1}] \to [M_0^s, B_1^s, B_2^s, ..., B_n^s] . \tag{4}$$

This transformation is the response function of the center.

$$[M_i^{s-1}, B_i^{s-1}] \to [M_i^s, F_i^s] \qquad (i = 1, ..., n) \tag{5}$$

This transformation is the *response function of the center.*

Both response functions are deterministic in character (leaving degenerate cases out of consideration). The information input results in an unequivocal information output.

Both response functions include a *memorizing rule*: what is to be stored in the central and in the sectoral memory from the initial data, the information inputs received before the sth iteration, and the computation results obtained before the sth iteration. In addition, they include a *rule of information release*: what message the sector should send to the center and *vice versa*.

The iterations go on, until the last, Sth iteration. In this connection a termination rule is needed to prescribe the conditions under which the center should release the special $B_i^S = B_i^*$, *terminal central information output.* This output is the instruction to carry out the terminal operations. Besides, a *solution-computing rule* must be established:

$$[M_i^S, B_i^*] \rightarrow P_i^* .$$
(6)

The $P^* = [P_1^*, ..., P_n^*]$ vector obtained as a result of transformation (6) is either identical with the optimal P solution of the ·original indecomposed problem, or else it is an acceptable approximation.

For the specification of a decomposition procedure, the following characteristics must be given:

(1) The decomposition rule of the initial set of data.

(2) The central and the sectoral response functions.

(3) Specification of the information input and output flowing between the levels.

(4) The termination rule.

(5) The solution-computing rule.

In table 1, the decomposition methods are compared with each other, according to characteristic 3 (information input-output).

1.2. Utilization and interpretation possibilities

Three possibilities for utilization and interpretation of decomposition methods are to be found in the literature and in practice.

(a) *Mathematical-computational procedure.* The original purpose of the decomposition methods was computational in character. They serve to compute the solution of large-scale mathematical programming problems.

When examining the decomposition methods from this point of view, no institutional meaning can be attributed to the concepts 'center' or 'sector'. Both the 'central' and the 'sectoral' computations are carried out on the same computer. This terminology serves only to denote the different parts of a complex algorithm and, accordingly, the blocks of the computer routine.

It is conceivable that on a computer with a given memory capacity and given operation speeds, a problem of a given structure is easier to solve with a decomposition method than with a direct method. Unfortunately there is not enough experience to decide exactly which are such cases. The question has been discussed for years, but so far – to the author's knowledge – no experimental results have been published to show which method is more efficient under which conditions. [1] To date, the rather sporadic experience suggests the following:

In case the original indecomposed extensive problem fits into the high-speed memory section of a computer, one of the direct methods will usually be quicker and simpler than any of the decomposition methods. Even for linear programming problems of 2,000 – 4,000 rows, direct methods appear to be preferable – as of this date (1971).

With an extremely large-scale problem, including many tens of thousands of rows, the use of some decomposition method seems inevitable. However, it is slow and expensive to solve problems of this size.

Between these two limits, it is open to question whether a direct or a decomposition method is more efficient. This question should be examined thoroughly. This is, however, not a problem of economic organization, but rather one of computer techniques. Therefore, it is not discussed further. At the same time, it should be noted that direct methods were employed for the linear programming computations in parts II-IV of this volume.

(b) *Descriptive theoretical model of planning.* In this case, we do not make numerical computations with a decomposition method, but use only the theoretically clarified qualitative properties of the method for the description of a few characteristics of actual planning processes and for their abstract modelling.

None of the decomposition methods is appropriate as a general model to represent all the main characteristics of planning. Their role is more limited. *Each decomposition method can stress one or another feature of a small section of the planning process.*

---

[1] Editor's note: These lines were written prior to the distribution of a report by T.M. Hogan, 'A comparison of information structures and convergence properties of several multisector economic planning procedures'. Technical Report No. 10. Berkeley, Calif., Center for Research in Management Science, University of California, May 1971.

For example, the Dantzig-Wolfe method (and also procedures 2–6 of table 1) is to be interpreted as the abstract model of a planning process, in which the main function of the planning office is to ensure supply-demand balances for the centrally controlled products and resources, and to fix the prices of those products and resources. The Kornai-Lipták method (as well as procedures 8–10 of table 1) is a model of a planning process in which the center specifies output targets and input quotas for the individual sectors. Weitzman (method 10) stresses another important feature of planning: the center starts with specifying targets that are too ambitious. After the sectors have advised on the extent of infeasibility of the plan, a feasible program is approached through step-by-step corrections.

We shall revert to this interpretation later. Here the reader's attention is called to two dangers. One danger is to draw too far-reaching economic conclusions from the *computational* qualities of the programming algorithms. Solving a linear programming problem with a direct method can be interpreted as the working of the central planning office of a centralized economy possessing complete information. On the contrary, all decomposition methods are to be considered as the model of a planning process in which part of the information is stored at the central planning office and part at the sectoral planning units. The task of planning calculations is also divided between the center and the sectors. Now it would be a grave error to draw any conclusions regarding the advantages and disadvantages of complete centralization or partial decentralization of planning from the computational experience described under (a), according to which the direct method is advantageous in many cases. From the number of the iterations and operations required by the direct simplex method or the Dantzig-Wolfe decomposition method, nothing follows as regards the theory of organization of an actual economy.

Similarly, if numerical experiments are carried out in order to compare the efficiency of the different decomposition methods, this may be useful as regards (a) computer techniques, but is of no use in (b) economic organization theory. If, say, the convergence of the Dantzig-Wolfe method is quicker than that of the Kornai-

Lipták method or of the Kate method, the only conclusion to be drawn is that the first is the more clever in computation. No conclusions may be drawn on the relative merits of a price-determining, Lange-type of socialist planning or a quantity-allocating, Gosplan-type of socialist planning. We must not forget how very far from life are the conditions on which these models are based, whereas actual planning processes must operate in a real-life and real-time environment.

Now let us turn our attention to the other danger. We must be clear in the case of a (b)-type utilization, on what is actually modelled in each algorithm. There are two possibilities. Let these be denoted by the (b1)-type and (b2)-type interpretation.

(*b1*)-*type interpretation*: The series of iterations represent the preparation of the decision, i.e. of the final plan. The center and the sectors negotiate only 'on paper'; B_i^s and F_i^s express only the exchange of information and do not affect directly the real working of the economy. It is exclusively P, the finally accepted plan, that means a decision. This controls the real processes of the economic system: production, trade, and consumption.

(*b2*)-*type interpretation*: The information outputs of each iteration, B_i^s and P_i^s affect immediately and directly the real working of the economy, and control its real processes: production, trade and consumption. It is true that such a decision is not optimal, indeed it may not be fully feasible but must be corrected in practice, yet it is a decision. The algorithm shows how these non-optimal, perhaps infeasible decisions converge to P, the feasible and optimal decision.

In the case of interpretation (b1), the algorithm is the descriptive model of the preparation of the decision, the *planning*. On the contrary, in the case of interpretation (b2), the algorithm is the model of the *everyday operation and of the everyday control of the economic system*.

Most authors use the interpretation (b1). Unfortunately, however, many of them do not make a clear distinction. Confusion is caused mainly by the fact that references to precedents in the history of the theory suggest the use of interpretation (b2). E.g., the studies of Malinvaud (1967) and Arrow-Hurwicz (1960) refer to Walras's tâtonnement processes, as well as Taylor-Lange's model of socialism. However, when describing the tâtonnement processes, it was not the coordination on paper or through negotiations of demand, supply and prices that Walras had in mind, but the real working of the everyday market in which supply, demand and price [2] adjust themselves to each other through a series of disequilibria. Similarly, following Walras, Lange also thought that it would be by observing the series of real excess supply and real excess demand, and changing the prices step by step, that the socialist planning office would succeed in establishing the desired state of the market. [3] In discussing decomposition methods, when we refer to Walras and Lange, the way is opened to the (b2)-type interpretation.

The (b1)-type interpretation — if employed with due caution — is not only allowable, but also scientifically profitable. On the contrary, the (b2)-type interpretation is misleading in this author's opinion. There are many arguments against it, but here we shall mention only one. In a real-world market, the excess supply of the tth period is added to the initial stock of the $(t+1)$th period. The excess demand of the tth period may not be added fully to the demand of the $(t+1)$th period but can increase it, or start complicated processes of substitution. In most decomposition algorithms, this problem disappears entirely. The procedure forces an equilibrium in each iteration. Or if it allows excess demand and excess supply to come about, the disequilibria of preceding iterations do not accumulate; each iteration starts with a *tabula rasa.* E.g., in Arrow-Hurwicz (1960), the excess supply that arose in the tth iteration disappears and does not add to the supply of the $(t+1)$th iteration.

Hereafter, this paper will concentrate upon the (b1)-type interpretation.

(c) *Method recommended for practical planning: the normative theoretical model of planning.* In the case of (c)-type utilization,

---

[2] See Walras (1954), pp. 170 and 520.
[3] See Lange (1938).

the responsible managers are instructed to arrange their practical planning processes according to the rules of one or another decomposition method. This means that there should be a central planning office and some sectoral planning units. Information should flow between them; the center should send the B_i^s information to the sectors, and the sectors should send the F_i^s information to the center. The planning should be iterative. In each iteration, the computations of the response functions (4) or (5) should be done on the computers of the center or of the sectors. Finally, the planning should be ended according to the termination rule and solution computing rule of the suggested decomposition method.

It happens — if only rarely — that the above-outlined view appears as a serious-minded proposal. There exist economists who claim that the planning process can be fully or almost fully computerized, and that each of its stages can be organized in accordance with the strict rules of one of the decomposition procedures. [4] The majority of authors do not go this far and leave the question partly open, on the extent to which a decomposition method should be interpreted as a normative theory for practical planning.

It is a fact that so far not one country's planning has been fully computerized. Nowhere has the planning process been organized along the lines of a decomposition algorithm. It is to be investigated, to what extent this practice is to be attributed to the theoretical ignorance and conservatism of the planners and to what extent to the lack of realism in the proposals suggesting decomposition algorithms as normative theories of planning.

The success of the (b1)-type and (c)-type interpretations is closely interdependent. Only a descriptive theory well proved empirically can serve as a starting point for theoretically well founded normative suggestions. Therefore we shall revert to discussion of the (c)-type utilization only after having examined, in the following sections, a few characteristics of actual planning processes.

[4] In the Hungarian economic literature, see, for example, Simon (1970).

2. Some characteristics of practical planning processes

Let us leave now the artificial world of studies on decomposition methods and of experimental computations carried out on computers, and let us view the actual practice of planning. It is, of course, rather difficult to talk about 'planning' in general, since this is a phenomenon which changes over time and is different in each country. Far-reaching differences of the planning systems exist not only between large groups such as the socialist, the advanced capitalist, and the developing African, Asian and Latin-American countries, but also between states within one large group. The practice of planning is essentially different in Hungary, Poland and Yugoslavia, or in France and The Netherlands, or in India and the United Arab Republic. Despite the risk of diverting attention from these differences, a few common characteristics may be noted.

2.1. Levels of the economic system

The *lower level* of the economic system and within that, of planning, is made up of the producing and trading firms and the households, i.e., the organizations in which the bulk of the real processes — production, trade, consumption — take place. These may be referred to as *real organizations*. The organizations specialized in controlling the economy and in related activities such as information gathering and processing, preparation of decisions, and planning, are on the *upper levels* of the economic system. Here belong the economic organizations of the state: the planning office, the economic ministries, the tax office and the customs office, as well as the banking system, the statistical office, the market research institutes, the associations of firms, the trade unions, etc. These may be denoted comprehensively as *control organizations*. Some of the control organizations work independently from each other on the same level. Others have relations of subordination and superordination. E.g., the central planning office is a superordinate of the planning apparatus of the special economic ministries; the central bank is a superordinate of the other banks; and the ministry of finance is a superordinate of the local financial organizations.

Several studies deal with the relations of sub- and superordination, hierarchies and quasi-hierarchies in modern economic systems. [5] Here there is no space to thoroughly investigate the question. Instead, let us have a look at figures 1 and 2. Figure 1 shows the scheme of a *perfect hierarchy*. The system has three levels: on the upper level is the C_0 center, on the middle level are the C_1, C_2 and C_3 sub-centers, and on the lower level the R_1, R_2, ..., R_6 real organizations. Each organization is subordinated to one and only one other organization. The only exception is the center, which is not subordinate to any other organization.

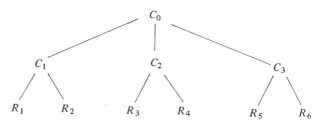

Fig. 1. Perfect hierarchy.

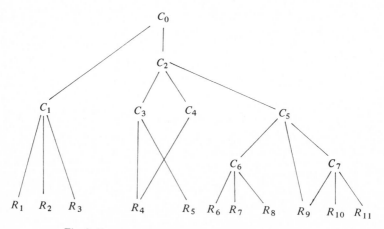

Fig. 2. Non-pure relations of sub- and superordination.

[5] See Koopmans-Montias (in press) and Kornai (1971), chapter 6.

Figure 2 is more confused. It is clear that C_0, the center, is at the top, and that the real organizations R_1, R_2, ..., R_{11} make up the lower level. Between the center and the individual real organizations, there are at some places one middle level e.g., $C_0 \rightarrow C_1 \rightarrow R_1$; at other places two intermediate levels $C_0 \rightarrow C_2 \rightarrow C_3 \rightarrow R_4$; and at still other places, three intermediate levels $C_0 \rightarrow C_2 \rightarrow C_5 \rightarrow C_7 \rightarrow R_9$. Therefore, in some spheres the system consists of three levels, in other spheres of four, and in still other fields, of five levels.

Most of the organizations are subordinated unequivocally to one other organization. There are, however, double subordinations. R_9 is controlled by C_7 but, to a certain extent, also by its superordinate organization C_5, which reaches 'over the head' of C_7. E.g., the ministry intervenes in the affairs of the factory, by-passing the trust.

A theoretical examination of the multi-level character of the economic systems cannot be carried out here. Instead, these remarks must be limited to a few practical observations:

(1) *There are no 'one-level' economic systems.* All real economies are multi-level.

(2) *There are no perfect hierarchies.* It is characteristic of all real systems to have non-pure relations of sub- and superordinations, double or multiple subordinations, chains or different lengths of sub- and superordinate relationships, existing side by side.

(3) *In almost every country in which economy-wide planning has been introduced, multi-level planning processes take place.* This has been the case from the beginning in the socialist countries, where a hierarchic division of levels has always prevailed in economic management (not only in planning but in other fields, too). In planning – beside the central planning office – the medium-level directing organizations (ministries, local organizations, boards of directors of different industrial branches), have always participated. Individual firms have also had a part in the process.

Among the advanced capitalist countries, France was the first to introduce two-level planning, and in a very emphatic form. [6] Here

---

[6] See Massé (1965) and Schollhammer (1969).

the *Commissariat du Plan* (the central planning commission) is on the upper level, and the *Commissions de Modernisation* (the sectoral commissions) are on the lower level. Later, other Western countries have also organized their planning – mainly on the French pattern – in a two- or three-level arrangement.

Planning in the developing countries shows some similar features. E.g., in working out and debating the five-year plans of India, many different organizations take part.

(4) *Two-level planning* can be realized in a relatively limited number of fields – only those where a monopoly or a few oligopolies control a whole sector, maintaining direct relations with the central planning organization, e.g., the railways, airlines and the telephone. In a typical case, one or several intermediary levels will come in between. The division of the middle level (or levels) can be effected on different principles: according to the industrial branch, or the region or the function (finance, labor). In some cases, all these principles of division are employed, and then complex and multiple relations of sub- and superordination will be established.

Accordingly, no multi-level planning system can be established as a pyramid, arranged in a perfect hierarchy. It must be understood that the multi-level form of a real planning system is not an esthetic pure form, but is full of irregularities. In some spheres, it is inevitably two-level. At the same time, in other spheres, it is of three, four or five levels. This is the case with the Mexican model system. Electric energy and oil are each produced in a single public enterprise. Therefore it is realistic here to establish two-level planning relations between the central model and the sectoral models. In agriculture, the regional points of view come to the foreground. Therefore the four following levels must be distinguished: center – agricultural sector – agricultural district – individual farm.

Theoretically, decomposition methods can be employed even in the case of more than two levels. Consider a three-level system. In each major iteration, the middle blocks would be considered as 'sectors' and effectuate the usual exchange of informations with the center. However, each major iteration would be in itself an iterative process, within which the lowest level would be a 'sector', and each middle block would be a 'center'. If we employ an algo-rithm which in a two-level model arrives at the optimum in a finite number of iterations, we can solve a three-level problem also in a finite number of major and minor iterations. Unfortunately, the word 'finite' is reassuring only for the mathematician, but not for the practical planner. The total number of iterations may be of an astronomical order. If there were no other argument, this would suffice in itself to characterize the (c)-type interpretation as ex-ceedingly naive. It is practically impossible to expect, that keeping exactly to the rules of some decomposition algorithm, an optimal solution of the planning problem will be reached through repeat-ing a thousand times, or ten thousand times, the flow of informa-tion between the different levels.

2.2. Direction of the flow of information

In the course of planning, information flows between the organiza-tions of the economic system. The direction of the flow of infor-mation is horizontal if it takes place between organizations on the same level. It is vertical, if it flows between organizations that are in sub- or superordinate relationship with each other. Finally, the direction of the information flow is undetermined if the addresser and the addressee of the information are not on the same level, but they are not in sub- or superordinate relationship with each other either.

In real planning all three directions are to be found: the hori-zontal, the vertical, and the undetermined flow of information. Naturally, real economy-wide planning is inconceivable without a vertical flow. But there is a horizontal flow, too. E.g., the indus-trial and the foreign trading ministries cooperate directly in the planning of production, exports, and imports. Or the cooperating firms exchange information between each other. An example of an information flow of undetermined direction: preliminary plan-coordination of a sectoral and a local control organization, e.g., in the case of building a major factory along a new road.

Decomposition methods very much restrict the flow of information by allowing only for vertical flow. [7] Real planning — and the practical use of mathematical planning models — is less rigid. A good example for this is the construction of the ENERGETICOS model, in the frame of the Mexican research work. The managers and specialists in three sectors — electricity, oil production and steel-making — cooperated here, both by supplying data and evaluating the results. Practically, a horizontal flow of information took place between the three sectors. This is perhaps an even more important result than the 'optimum' program obtained by the common model. In general, it will be useful to construct a multi-level system of planning models in such a way that information is exchanged not only between the different levels, but also between the coordinated cooperating organizations on the same level.

2.3. Types of information

Without pretending to completeness, we shall now enumerate five types of information, each of which has an important role in planning:

(1) *Shadow prices.* Here we think not only of the shadow prices obtained as the dual solution of a mathematical programming problem. This name describes all those prices (or price-type information) that deviate from the actual ones used in financial transactions.

In many countries, the central planning office prescribes or recommends computational discount rates for the efficiency calculations of investments, or exchange rates for social profitability calculations of foreign trade. Occasionally, this office will forecast future prices or wages. In many cases, the commercial prices of the world market or the prices of a foreign country are used instead of current domestic prices. Shadow prices usually flow (though not always) from the top downwards.

(2) *Efficiency indicators.* Both in capitalist and socialist economies, indicators are computed prior to an investment decision.

---

[7] At present one exception is known: 'reflector-programming' in which the vertical and horizontal flow of information are combined. See Simon (1970).

These show the average or marginal efficiency of the invested capital, its internal rate of return, its payout period, or other characteristics. The different indicators of 'cost-benefit' analysis also come into this category.

With these indicators, the characteristic information flow goes upwards: from the project designers or other responsible authorities toward the government, the planning office, and the financial institutions.

(3) *Real-input and real-output estimates.* There are several sub-types:

(3a) Input quotas, in case of central allocation (rationing) of resources and products. Direction of information flow: downwards.

(3b) Output target, either in the form of an obligatory production order, or else as advice. The former appears in the case of 'imperative' planning, the latter in the case of 'indicative' planning. These two forms differ only in the legal and financial consequences accompanying the information, i.e. in the tone that indicates the obligation ('must' versus 'recommended'). The contents of the information is in both cases an output target. Direction of the information: downwards.

(3c) Input-claim, or output-offer, the former on the part of the buyer, the latter on the part of the seller. The flow of information may be either vertical or horizontal. The claim goes from the buyer to the seller, or the offer goes from the seller to the buyer.

(4) *Specified action programs.* This refers to information about the organization of manufacturing new products, employing new technologies, establishing new plants. Although this information is in many cases connected with real input and output estimates, we can make a distinction. An action program does not give simply the data describing the quantity of input and output, but also the technical description and qualitative characteristics of the new product, the new technology, or the new plant. This kind of information is of great importance in medium-term and long-term planning, whether it is done in Hungary or France or Mexico.

There is no typical direction here: it may be vertical (either downwards or upwards), or horizontal (e.g., exchange of technical experience between the firms), or it may even be, according to the terminology defined earlier, undetermined. In almost every country there are special national commissions to promote technical progress. These are not direct superordinates of the producing firms, but they participate in the planning of technical progress and, in this connection, in the gathering and forwarding of action programs.

(5) *Financial indicators.* In this category belong credit demands and credit limits; also information relating to profits, taxes, customs duties and state subsidies. This type of information flows mainly vertically.

It is characteristic of real planning systems that all the enumerated types of information (or even some further types) flow simultaneously, in all directions.

Decomposition methods are based upon much more restricted forms of information flow. Usually only one type of information flows downwards, and a different type flows upwards. Is it then correct to conclude that a mathematically formalized planning algorithm is more economical of information than the heuristic practice of planning? To a certain extent, yes. Real planning processes often waste information. Some of it is forwarded, although nobody looks at it. Some is worked out, but neglected at the decision-making level, etc. Yet multiple, simultaneous flow of the different types of information cannot be considered as altogether wasteful and redundant.

In the abstract world of a decomposition algorithm, every piece of information is reliable. The initial data D give the exact description of the activities modelled, and of the expectable consequences of the plan. The computations of the response functions are infallible. At iteration s, the forwarding of the B_i^s and F_i^s information input and output is complete and unbiased. The M_0^s and M_i^s memory units store the data without error. The reality of planning practice is much less reassuring. Observations are inadequate and unreliable. There are not well defined deterministic response functions. In fact, planning calculations are often makeshift or even deliberately wrong. 'Memory' is forgetful. Information is forwarded imperfectly, or it is deliberately biased. The upper levels do not fully trust the lower levels and vice versa. As regards the horizontal flow of information, it can be biased by business secrecy, or by competition between firms, or by conflicting group interests within a bureaucracy.

All this uncertainty means that every organization taking part in planning tries to obtain a better knowledge of facts through multiple sources of information. It will therefore collect information of different types about the same phenomenon. Or, if possible, it will collect the same type of information about the same phenomenon from several parallel sources. E.g., within the frame of planning, an enterprise will try to estimate future selling possibilities and profits. It may be helped in this by information of the first type (shadow prices), second type (its own efficiency computations), third type (investigation of future input-output conditions and using information coming both from the top downwards, and horizontally, from trading partners and competitors), fourth type (qualitative and technical characteristics), and fifth type (financial indicators).

The reliability problem is present not only with the *flow* of information, but also with *storage* in memory. Here we recall the fact that — although the concrete decomposition rules differ from each other — all decomposition algorithms direct each element of the D initial set of data unequivocally to the central memory, or to the memory of one or another sector. The same datum cannot appear at two places: $D_j \cap D_k = \emptyset$ $(j, k = 0, 1, ..., n; j \neq k)$. On the other hand, actual planning is not so very strict. 'For the sake of safety', top-level organizations like to know about data which they do not actually need for their computations, but which allow them later to make a few random tests of information coming from the lower levels.

To sum up: *Redundancy* (*the multiplication of information, parallel flow, and storage at several places*) *serves to reduce uncertainty*. One piece of information (in itself unreliable) is used for the revision and correction of another (in itself also unreliable) piece of information.

Having examined this phenomenon from the angle of descriptive planning theory, we must draw a similar conclusion for normative theory. It will be useful to work out such decomposition algorithms as will ensure organically the parallel flow and mutual correction of information. [8] This, however, promises to be a difficult task theoretically. Before the formal theory is developed, the principle of the multiplication of information must be used in a heuristic way. One should never present the results of any model with too much assurance. On the one hand, many kinds of sensitivity tests must be carried out on the same model. On the other hand, the results must be compared self-critically with the computations of other models, and with the estimates produced by non-formalized practical planning.

In case the elements of a multi-level model system appear in the planning system of a country, no rigid patterns must be adopted for the direction and contents of the flow of information. E.g., it must not be decided at the start − just because it is suggested by one of the decomposition algorithms − that the shadow prices of the central computation will be conveyed for the purpose of the 'project evaluation' and that *this* will be the only downward flow of information. Similarly, it must not be decided that the sectoral plan proposals, as alternative columns, will be included in the central planning model, and this will be the only type of information that flows upwards. Both conceptions are feasible, but they are compatible with many other kinds of information flow.

At the beginning of the Mexican research work, the team could not get free of the magic circle of the decomposition algorithms (especially that of the Dantzig-Wolfe method), and would have been willing to limit the information flow between the levels to the above-mentioned two types. Later, however, it became clear that in this way the different models would be deprived of much valuable information. It is not necessary to insist in every case on strictly algorithmic transformations.

---

[8] Some economists and mathematicians dealing with decomposition methods expect that multiple flows of information will speed up convergence. In the author's opinion, this cannot be expected, and this is not the aim of the multiplication of information. In a strictly deterministic model or algorithm, this is out of place. The multiplication of information is worth introducing only into those models which formally incorporate the unreliability of both the data and the computations.

The macroeconomic model (DINAMICO) utilized more than the formal computer printouts from the agricultural sector (CHAC). The experience gathered through the construction of the CHAC model was utilized by research workers in the compilation of the labor substitution activities of DINAMICO — even if the connection between the two models was not fully formalized in this respect. The DINAMICHAC experiment represents an important step forward in the process of model linkage.

It is instructive to make a comparison of the shadow prices for the identical resource (e.g., capital in the sectors of energy production and of agriculture). From the fact that investment plans are *in reality* based upon a 10% per year cost of capital in the one sector and 15% in the other, conclusions may be drawn about the efficiency of the capital market and other institutions for central resource allocation. These inefficiencies were *not* built into the structure of the multi-sector model, DINAMICO.

Something may be learned from every decomposition method. There is a rational, practical point in each of these devices for information-forwarding. Since the descriptive theory of practical planning as well as the arsenal of decomposition algorithms will enlarge over time, we can further increase the heuristic information flow between the models of (partly formalized, partly non-formalized) multi-level model systems.

2.4. Motivation

The (b)-type, descriptive theoretical interpretation of decomposition methods starts from very strong assumptions.

First, it supposes that each sector has a well defined utility function, which it maximizes.

Second, it supposes that the center also has a well-defined utility function. This maximand is nothing else than the sum of the sectoral utility functions.

The two suppositions together imply the idea that in practical planning, there prevails strict rationality and an undisturbed harmony of global and partial interests.

The author doubts both of these suppositions. Whether examin-

ing the central or the sectoral decision-makers, experience suggests
that at the beginning of the planning process, they have not
thought over thoroughly their aims and preferences. Many times
they have several − and contradicting − ambitions and do not
beforehand consider how to coordinate them. The politician de-
ciding on national plans would like to achieve a high rate of
growth of national income and a more equitable distribution as
well as an increase of near future consumption. If he specifies his
aspiration levels numerically, they often turn out to be too ambitious. Later, in the course of the planning process, it gradually
becomes clear, what are the tradeoffs, and which aspiration must
be lowered for the sake of another.

A similar phenomenon is found at lower levels, too. Let us take,
e.g., the managers of a major state-owned firm. Several personal-
ities struggle within them, too, to serve both the national and the
firm's interests. As regards the latter, they are not unequivocal.
There may be contradictions between profitability, expansion,
reputation, security, satisfaction of the staff, and other goals. See
Kornai (1971, esp. chapters 10, 11).

*Planning is a cognitive process, in the course of which the deci-
sion-maker modifies his own interests and value judgements.* His
final opinion is formed at the time of decision-making.

It would be naive to imagine the functioning of a multi-level
model-system according to the following: Between the center and
the sectors, the iterative information exchanges are always based
upon the identical objective function. In the course of one or two
years, the decision-makers converge slowly to an optimum plan.
After this point has been reached, everybody sets out happy and
satisfied, to carry out the plan.

The real aim of a multi-level model-system is quite different
from that. It is used for search and exploration. In the model
system at all levels − in the center, at the intermediate levels and
in the firms − people use the computer to find out about their
possibilities, to make clear to themselves what are their own interests and their conflicts with other interests. They look for compro-
mises. At the same time, on the upper levels, research is carried on
to find out how partial interests may be reconciled with more
general interests.

In the future, it is likely that we will be able to simulate economic growth by the aid of computational series and sensitivity tests. These may be calculated for the elements of the model system separately at first, and then the elements may be connected either loosely or closely. It is true that in the mathematical sense, an optimization technique is used at each step. This is done, however, only to exclude inefficient programs. In the course of a planning simulation, we may use different objective functions one after the other, and alter the numerical value of the constraints and coefficients as well as the different initial assumptions of the model.

We have already brought forward several arguments against the 'naive', normative interpretation of the decomposition methods and have arrived now at a new argument. Suppose that we have surmounted all obstacles, have finished the many computations as well as the repeated information exchanges between the center and sectors, and have arrived at the closing step (6), i.e., at the *P* optimum plan. Still there would be *only one* plan in our hands with only one constellation of constraints and objective functions. This is, however, very poor information for forming final decisions. For these, variants and sensitivity tests are needed.

In the Mexican research work, there was no magic *optimum optimorum* which we could recommend, without hesitation, to the international credit-suppliers and to the Mexican government, as well as to all national energy-producing enterprises and to every agricultural producer. Instead, we carried out experiments within the model system. Different objective functions were used in the central and in the different sectoral models. In each case, it was examined how the plan reacts to the changing of the objective function. If more time and financial means had been at our disposal, it would have been worth doing more experimental computations.

3. Evaluation of planning methods

The literature on the utilization of decomposition methods in planning tends to evaluate a *real* planning process on the basis of the same criteria as for describing a *computational* process.

Accordingly,

(1) an algorithm *well-defined* in each stage is more advantageous, than a more or less heuristic method;

(2) an algorithm improving the objective function *monotonically* is more advantageous than a process in which the objective function may be reduced in some of the iterations;

(3) an algorithm reaching a solution in a *finite* number of steps is more advantageous than a process which, in a finite number of steps, only approaches a solution;

(4) a process which reaches a solution more *quickly,* through less iterations, is more advantageous than the one which converges slowly.

Doubtless, the above-mentioned criteria are important if a decomposition algorithm is judged from the point of view of an (a)-type computational utilization. They are, however, quite irrelevant in the case of a (c)-type utilization. In a real planning process, however, it is not worth stipulating the criteria specified above — and not even possible.

The abstract theory of decomposition methods starts from the fact that the following data are given: an unequivocal starting point; D, the set of data; an unequivocal criterion for recognizing the final point P, the optimum plan; and an unequivocal way in which we get from D to P. The only question is, how quick and smooth this way is.

In reality, there is no unequivocal set of data. D. Fresh information continually comes into the planning system from outside; the set of data of exogenous information $D(t_1)$, $D(t_2)$, ... is different at the times t_1, t_2, ... There are not fully developed practical planning algorithms. Operations with formalized models and strict algorithms must necessarily be combined with improvised model-constructing ideas, *ad hoc* analyses, and heuristic methods. All of this is aimed, not at determining one single P, an 'optimum' plan, but rather at a whole series of efficient, individually rational programs. These alternatives may differ essentially in their content, but they must be compared before arriving at a final decision.

It is a mistake to consider D and P as given, and the time it takes from D to P as unknown. In fact, it is exactly this time that is given. It cannot begin very early, because then there are not yet statistical data close to the action-period of the plan. It cannot end too late either, because then we would reach into the action-period, into the time of executing the plan. In the case of a five-year plan, there are at most 2–3 years at our disposal. The question is not, how the period of planning could be shortened, but how it could be most efficiently utilized.

If we take seriously the basic idea of multi-level planning (that information must be forwarded from the top level to the lower levels and vice versa), we must take into consideration the limits of patience of those individuals who take part in planning. They are ready to participate in two, or maybe three or four real 'iterations', i.e., information exchanges between the levels. Yet it would certainly be impossible to have them take part in one hundred iterations. Therefore it is not worth comparing decomposition rocess I which demands 500 iterations with process II, which demands 1500 iterations. For a practical (c)-type utilization, both are hopelessly high numbers.

In order to judge the efficiency of a practical planning process, the following must be considered:

(1) How could the planning processes be organized in a way that fresh information, arriving in the course of progress, could be adopted as smoothly as possible? The mathematical planner should not have the feeling that the new information serves purposely to vex him and to arouse the unpleasant thought, 'here we start all over again'. Processing of the data, and recalculation of partial computational results, must be done with the knowledge that the arrival of new and more exact information is part of the natural order of life.

(2) How can information exchanges between levels be made so rich in content, that only a few such exchanges are really essential?

(3) How would it be possible, within the given planning period, to explore most extensively the policy alternatives, and to present as reliably as possible the consequences of the different alternative decisions?

The Mexican research work justifies these questions. These case studies required nearly three years. During this time, alterations had to be made on the data continuously. There was no opportunity to carry out a great number of information exchanges between levels. It was possible to 'communicate' only once or twice between the levels. This is certainly too little. Much more would have been desirable, but real possibilities are in all cases very limited.

4. Some difficulties in the construction of model systems

In what follows, a few typical difficulties will be mentioned briefly. These will almost inevitably be found in the construction of multi-level model systems.

(1) *Homogeneous model-building and the researchers' individual taste.* Model-building is a special combination of science and art. When two painters paint the same landscape, their pictures will be different. Similarly, when two economists model the same planning problem, their model will be different. Each model will be characterized by the individual's conception: which objective function he 'likes', how he treats time, investment costs, terminal conditions, etc. This may be called the 'taste' of the researcher. Tastes are formed mainly by theoretical conceptions, the tradition in a special branch of literature, individual routines, and yet, undeniably, also by ideas concerning the 'esthetics' of model-building.

Differences between the tastes of model-builders do not bring about difficulties if they work in different fields, or if they compete with each other in solving similar problems. However, serious problems are encountered when we want to connect models constructed by several individuals. We must say, frankly, that such problems arose in the course of the Mexican work. Models constructed by individuals of quite different tastes ought to have been connected into a homogenous system. The difference in conceptions was caused partly by the fact that the models could not be adjusted very well to each other.

In the construction of a multi-level model-system, it is indispensable that the methodology and basic principles of the individual models should be strictly adapted to each other. In forming the common principles, all participants may help and can recommend their own ideas, but − after an agreement is reached − central guidance and control are needed to enforce the methodology. Multi-level planning means an essential decentralization of the practical planning computation − but not the decentralization of *methodology*. If researchers are allowed to construct individual models independently, each after his own ideas, the models will be incompatible, and will not fit together within a homogenous system.

(2) *Total accounting versus distinguished actions: physical versus value term indicators.* Some planning models take account of all inputs and outputs. In principle, this is the case with Leontief models, and also with programming models based on interindustry accounting data, e.g., DINAMICO. Other models dispense with the representation of *all* inputs and outputs, and are confined to the description of a few distinguished products or investment actions. In the Mexican research work, this was the case both in the energy and in the agricultural sector models. In these cases, residual inputs and outputs remain which do not appear explicitly in the sectoral models. The treatment of these residual items causes difficulty when we want to connect the two types of models − one a full-accounting, and the other representing 'distinguished actions', not full-accounting.

The following question is connected to the former, yet it is a separate problem: that of measurement. In some of these models, the levels of production, foreign trade and consumption are counted in value terms; in other models in physical terms. Full-accounting models usually count in value terms. 'Distinguished' inputs and outputs can, on the other hand, be measured also in physical terms.

Difficulties arise in any attempts to connect models using physical terms with those using value terms. The transition is not easy since the full-accounting models are not defined in terms of concrete products but usually in terms of aggregates. These aggregates are made up of many different kinds of products, and it is very difficult to define the average price of aggregates. E.g., what is the producers' cost of an 'average' barrel of petroleum products?

The above-mentioned problems are well-known among practical planners, and it arose immediately as we started to employ mathematical models in the socialist countries for the middle-range planning of production. It was an interesting experience to see exactly the same problem arise in the framework of the Mexican research work. Some of these difficulties may be overcome through *ad hoc* solutions, e.g. rules-of-thumb for aggregation. A much more thorough observation of processes measured in physical and value terms, and a careful mathematical-statistical analysis of data will be needed to enable us to deduce better-grounded formal relations between variables measured in the two different kinds of terms.

(3) *'Fineness' of disaggregation.* This is another phenomenon well known to practical planners. Every sector would like to plan its own outputs and inputs in a breakdown most suitable for it and in a degree of 'fineness', i.e. of disaggregation, which it finds most favorable from its own point of view. They expect their customers and suppliers to adapt themselves accordingly. Unfortunately, these – again considering their own interests only – demand different degrees of fineness.

The most frequent difference is the following: The supplying sector likes to plan its output in detail, because that is what makes clear its future selling position. It needs to plan its inputs only in an aggregated form.

A more simple, but less exact solution of the dilemma: forcing a compromise. The degree of fineness will be set uniformly for the supplier and the consumer, half-way between the breakdown desired by the supplier and the consumer.

The introduction of aggregating and disaggregating equations and variables into the model for connecting balance-systems of different degrees of fineness will lead to a more exact treatment of the problem. E.g., steel consumers might indicate their demands in a breakdown of only three major product groups. However, there might be 30 or 50 product balances within the steel sector. Here separate disaggregating variables are appropriate to each consuming sector. This is because it is known that the exact composition of the rolled steel demands by the building industry is quite different from that of the demands of the railways or of the machine-tool industry.

In the Mexican research work, there was little opportunity for such a detailed investigation of the aggregation problem. For this, one needs a model system that has already been well tested, and where one can rely upon earlier planning work and statistical observations.

5. Final remarks

At many points, this paper has argued against naive conceptions in connection with the introduction of multi-level model systems. We do not want to keep it a secret that the author argued even against himself (i.e., his earlier self) and, of course, against colleagues who still hold the same conception.

The author, together with his colleagues, belongs to those who, during the early 1960's, tried to contribute to the abstract theory of decomposition methods. After that, he participated in research work which gave him the opportunity to confront his theoretical conceptions with the practice of planning. He gathered such experience, first of all, in Hungary. [9] The Mexican research work supplied new insights. There were many distressing difficulties: incomprehension, conservatism, resistance, inexperience in calculation. These factors, however, do not all explain the slowness of progress. The ideas originally suggested were not mature enough. It cannot be expected, of course – as it has been made clear in the present study – that actual planning work could be *fully* transformed according to the recipes of any decomposition method known at present.

The author still believes in the principles of multi-level mathematical planning, and recommends that they be put into practice. Yet today he interprets the concept 'multi-level planning' in a

---

[9] See Kornai (1969).

broader and more flexible sense. It must not be reserved for strictly algorithmic decomposition planning processes. The same name
can justly be used to denote looser combinations of models, e.g.
the Mexican case studies. The following definition is suggested:

*Multi-level planning is operating in all cases when there are top-
level (economy-wide), middle-level (branch or regional), and perhaps lower-level models within one country, for the same period,
and an organized information flow exists between the models.*

It is, of course, not enough if we give the name 'multi-level' to
such model combinations, and then consider the matter settled.
We must try to achieve compatibility between the different
models, smooth communication, and efficient information flow.
In this respect, the Mexican research work leaves much to be
desired. The next attempts must be designed so that the individual
mathematical planning models will form a more closely knit
system.

References

Abadie, J., and A.C. Williams, 'Dual and parametric methods in decomposition', in:
    Recent advances in mathematical programming, edited by R.L. Graves and P. Wolfe.
    New York, McGraw-Hill, 1963.
Arrow, K.J., and L. Hurwicz, 'Decentralization and computation in resource allocation',
    in: *Essays in economics and econometrics.* Chapel Hill, N.C., University of North
    Carolina Press, 1960.
Balas, E., 'An infeasibility-pricing decomposition method for linear programs', *Opera-
    tions Research,* 1966.
Beale, E.M.L., 'Decomposition and partition methods for non-linear programming', in:
    Non-linear programming, edited by J. Abadie. Amsterdam, North-Holland Publ. Co.
    1967.
Benders, J.F., 'Partitioning procedures for solving mixed-variable programming prob-
    lems', *Numerische Mathematik,* 1962.
Dantzig, G.B., and P. Wolfe, 'Decomposition principle for linear programs', *Operations
    Research,* 1960.
Dantzig, G.B., and P. Wolfe, 'The decomposition algorithm for linear programs', *Econo-
    metrica,* 1961.
Geoffrion, A., 'Elements of large-scale mathematical programming', *Management
    Science, Theory,* 1970.
Heinemann, H., 'Ein allgemeines Dekompositionsverfahren für lineare Optimierungs-
    probleme', *Schmalenbachs Zeitschrift für Betriebswirtschaftliche Forschung,* 1970.

Kate, A.T., *Decomposition of linear programs by direct distribution.* Rotterdam, Netherland School of Economics, 1970. (Mimeographed.)

Koopmans, T.C., and J.M. Montias, 'On the description and comparison of economic systems', in: *Comparison of economic systems,* edited by A. Eckstein. In press.

Kornai, J., 'Multi-level programming – a first report on the model and on the experimental computation', *European Economic Review,* 1969.

Kornai, J., *Anti-equilibrium.* Amsterdam, North-Holland Publ. Co. 1971.

Kornai, J. and T. Lipták, *Kétszintü tervezés* [Two-level planning]. Budapest, Computing Center of the Hungarian Academy of Sciences, 1962. Published in English as: 'Two-level planning', *Econometrica,* 1965.

Lange, O., 'On the economic theory of socialism', in: *On the economic theory of socialism,* edited by B. Lipincott. Minneapolis, Minn., University of Minnesota, 1938.

Massé, P., 'The French plan and economic theory', *Econometrica,* April 1965.

Malinvaud, E., 'Decentralized procedures for planning', in: *Activity analysis in the theory of growth and planning,* edited by E. Malinvaud and M.O.L. Bacharach. London, Macmillan, 1967.

Rosen, J.B., 'Primal partition programming for block diagonal matrices', *Numerische Mathematik,* 1964.

Schollhammer, H., 'National economic planning and business decision-making: the French experience', *Management Review,* California, 1969.

Simon, G., 'Optimális tervezés reflektorprogramozással' [Optimal planning by reflector-programming], in: *Gazdasági fejlődés és tervezés* [Economic development and planning], edited by A. Bródy et al. Budapest, Közgazdasági és Jogi Könyvkiadó, 1970.

Walras, L., *Elements of pure economics, or the theory of social wealth.* London, George Allen, 1954.

Weitzman, M., 'Iterative multi-level planning with production targets', *Econometrica,* January 1970.

Zschau, E.V.W., *A primal decomposition algorithm for linear programming.* Graduate School of Business, Stanford University, 1967. (Mimeographed.)

SUBJECT INDEX